American Bibliography

A Preliminary Checklist
1801 to 1819

Ralph R. Shaw

and

Richard H. Shoemaker

Printers, Publishers and Booksellers Index
Geographical Index

compiled by

Frances P. Newton

The Scarecrow Press, Inc.
Metuchen, N.J., & London 1983

Library of Congress Cataloging in Publication Data

Newton, Frances P., 1929-
   American bibliography, a preliminary checklist, 1801
to 1819 : Ralph R. Shaw and Richard H. Shoemaker :
printers, publishers, and booksellers index, geographical
index.

   An Index to American bibliography, a preliminary
checklist, 1801 to 1819 / compiled by Ralph R. Shaw
and Richard H. Shoemaker. New York : Scarecrow Press,
1958-1966.
   Bibliography: p.
   1. United States--Imprints. I. Shaw, Ralph R.
(Ralph Robert), 1907-   . American bibliography
a preliminary checklist for 1801-1819. II. Title.
Z1215.N58 1983   015.73   83-3257
ISBN 0-8108-1607-5

Tables of Contents

Foreword

By Lee Ash

Finis Coronat Opus

This volume, which completes a major American bibliographical tool, represents a landmark record of American publishing in the wonderful growth years of our expanding nation.

The inspiration and drive to accomplish a careful listing "from secondary sources" of pieces published from 1801 to 1819, began with the cogent models of Charles Evans' American Bibliography, and Joseph Sabin's Dictionary of Books Relating to America, and the intention to fill in the gaps until O. A. Roorbach's Bibliotheca Americana record began.

Continuation and completion of the American Bibliography: A Preliminary Checklist, 1801 to 1819, through this twenty-third volume has been an effort of diligent application by Frances P. Newton. The addition of special lists and indexes, of which Newton's is the capstone volume, will surely satisfy the goading spirits of Ralph Shaw and Richard Shoemaker.

I regret that I never knew Dick Shoemaker well except to view his tremendous files from time to time, and be reassured that the never-ending project was ever-nearer to completion. I know, from his colleagues and students, that Dick was a shy and very modest man, an inspiration as a teacher, and a terribly hard worker who insisted that, for himself at least, the highest work standards are never sufficiently attainable and that there is always room for improvement and sensible flexible modification of rules that will justify a better product. Certainly this set of books demonstrates his nearly perfect attainment of the joint Shaw/Shoemaker goal and his dedication to Ralph Shaw's original specifications.

v

● ● ●

There is no need to memorialize Ralph Shaw formally. This was done throughout his life which was filled with successes. The library profession was effusive over every one of his innovations, all of which are recorded in numerous articles contemporary with each accomplishment, whether it was a book, a mechanical device, or a political stance; and the sum of his separate contributions to all of these landmarks is itemized in the numerous generous remarks that appeared in his obituaries and the festschrift volume edited by Norman D. Stevens (Scarecrow, 1975).

I have been asked to contribute a recollection of Ralph Shaw whom I first met as a fellow student at the Graduate Library School of the University of Chicago in 1939. Some of our other student friends, in this time of the GLS' "golden years," were Jesse Shera, Ralph Beals, Maurice Tauber, Bernard Berelson, Lowell Martin, and a number of others who have made lasting marks on the library record. And whose minds, like Ralph Shaw's and the others, would not have been stirred by Dean Louis Round Wilson, Pierce Butler, Douglas Waples, Carleton Joeckel, Leon Carnovsky, William Randall, Herman Fussler, and some of their graduate assistants?

This was, indeed, the atmosphere in which Ralph Shaw would thrive by constant oral combat with students and faculty in discussions of reading habits, library administration, and such varied problems as those posed by advanced bibliographical research, difficult translations from German, the publishing of children's books, or the description of Italian incunabula.

Part of the time that Ralph was at GLS (he was already Librarian of the Gary, Indiana, Public Library), my work assignments enabled me to see him in successful battle with city, county, and state officials, and to observe this rugged, and frequently sharp and critical man, being warmly affectionate and ever devoted and demonstrative to his first wife, Viola, who brought him to surprising levels of domesticity, and with whom he founded the Scarecrow Press.

The fire of ambition and exploitation of his sound abilities in administration charged Ralph always. He recast the operations of the Department of Agriculture Library (now the National Library of Agriculture), and brought new vision to a staff that was moved by his enthusiasm. The most memorable recollection of that time was when, at luncheon with me at the Cosmos Club, he flared at the name of Senator Joseph McCarthy and told me that he had refused to permit any of his staff except himself and his Assistant Librarian, Bella Schachtman, to be examined for security clearance in handling any "classified documents" the Library might have. He told me that there were a number of his staff members he thought were vulnerable and would not clear security surveillance. He insisted that he would "never let the government put these innocent people in a position that might jeopardize their jobs. Either Bella or I will always be available with the combination to the safe."

During the many years of responsibility that Ralph served the American Library Association, before and after his Presidency, his forthright attacks on what he saw as wrongmindedness made him many enemies and a greater number of admiring friends.

Certainly it was his broadside attacks on the Association and the work of his "Fourth Activities Committee" that turned the Association about for its entire future good, but at the same time prompted personal animosity toward him by a long-lived group of librarians, whose attacks he appeared to shrug off with casual indifference. I was witness to a terrible evening, however, when Ralph cried tearfully to Viola and me and wondered how he could recover the friendship of a man he had hot-headedly denounced in a public committee meeting. No matter how deeply embattled he was in an argument, Ralph was never indifferent to personal feelings when he was wise enough to think about them in advance.

Lest he be thought terribly humorless--since I have written of his dedicated brilliance and argumentative spirit--let me attest to Ralph's fine sense of humor, his often misinterpreted salacious remarks--always made in jest and exactly to the point--and the fun he had and gave to others in minor oral practical jokes. He celebrated April Fool's Day all day with jovial childishness, sometimes to the annoyance of his staff but always with further demonstration of his ingenuity--and no one ever suffered from his fun or was

vii

made to look ridiculous.

Hundreds, perhaps even thousands, of students have bene-
fited from Ralph Shaw's contributions as a library educator and
lecturer. His influence revised the curricula at the Rutgers library school and at the University of Hawaii, and to no less a de-
gree the lives of the faculty and students with whom he was associated, frequently at a highly personal level, at which times he was
always compassionate and concerned about special problems.

Then, in his last years, with a second devoted wife, Mary,
he finally overcame the tragedy of the cancer that had killed Viola
during cancer years parallel to his own that were so filled with
pain and eventual despair. Ralph Shaw always knew that he had
lived courageously and stood firmly for all he believed to be right.
As the years pass since his death all of us who knew him have
realized our privilege and many of us have learned to recall him
with love.

Ralph Shaw's and Richard Shoemaker's lasting bibliographical
monument will rest largely in this fine record of a major part of
American publishing history. Beyond this, though, are the printed
appraisals of their other contributions to the library profession.
Even more effusive, however, will be the recollection of their per-
sonalities by those of us who knew and loved them, albeit the pas-
sage of years will dilute these recollections and only encomia such
as this will keep their memories fresh as inspiration to those who
will follow.

• • •

Professional bookmen, collectors, scholars, and librarians
are greatly in debt to Scarecrow Press for its continuing support
of this invaluable series of books. Now, with this concluding volume to the first series, 1801 to 1819 (with the three previous volumes of Addenda, Title Index, and Corrections and Author Index,
issued in 1965 and 1966), the original basic set through 1819 is
complete.

The work continued, however, under Richard Shoemaker's di-
rection through 1829, the latter volumes with the assistance of
Gayle Cooper (who also compiled the volume for 1830). Author

and title indexes for 1820 through 1829 were compiled by M. Frances Cooper.

Subsequently, through the energy and devotion of Scott Bruntjen and Carol Rinderknecht, the years 1831 through 1834 have been published. With the cooperation of Hendrik Edelman, University Librarian at Rutgers, Bruntjen and Rinderknecht reorganized the hundreds of thousands of slips in storage on the Kilmer Campus, and prepared them for the continuation of the work.

There are now in print 121,718 descriptive entries through 1834, certainly one of the most useful bibliographical checklists for the accurate identification of American imprints. The series represents memorials not only to Ralph Shaw and Richard Shoemaker, but also stands to signal the publishers' devotion to both men, and to Ralph Shaw's intention when he established the Press.

Bethany, Connecticut
January 1983

Preface

This the twenty-third volume completes the set American Bibliography, A Preliminary Checklist, 1801 to 1819. An author index, title index, list of corrections and addenda were published previously.

This printers, publishers, and booksellers index is modeled on Bristol's Index of Printers, Publishers and Booksellers Indicated by Charles Evans in His American Bibliography. Each entry consists of a name and place, with item numbers listed underneath by date. The most complete form of each name that could be determined has been entered. The place names include city and state, with the exceptions of Baltimore, Boston, New York, and Philadelphia, where the state is omitted.

Only names actually given in the imprint are listed. Phrases such as "for the author" have been ignored. These can be located by referring to the author index. Personal names are entered in capital letters.

Corporate entries are shown in capitals and lower case type. Items printed by partners are listed under each name given in the imprint; silent partners are not included. Where identification is needed, a cross reference has been made from the partnership name to the individual names of the partners.

Newspapers and magazines are shown in capitals and lower case type underscored. They are entered by their full title as recorded in Brigham's History and Bibliography of American Newspapers, 1690-1820. Cross references have been provided for those short titles whose full titles do not begin with the city of publication.

An attempt was made to verify each name. The most helpful sources used are listed in the appended bibliography. The names were also checked in the Printer's File at the American Antiquarian Society in Worcester, Massachusetts.

Unverified names were investigated further by locating the

item in the Readex Microprint edition of <u>Early American Imprints,</u> <u>1801-1819,</u> or in the <u>National Union Catalog--Pre-1956 Imprints.</u> In many cases these items were discovered to be much later imprints or, occasionally, European imprints. These items have been omitted from Part 1 and listed in Part 3 with an explanation. Those names which could neither be verified nor disproved are included.

Another situation which called for additional checking was an item with a questionable date (for example, a printer active until 1813 has a single item in 1818). In most cases these stray items were found to be ghosts of other items in the proper time period. Many of the problems with dates seem to be the result of faulty transcription, particularly in confusing 3 and 8, 1 and 7, and 1 and 4. Also, many items with the last digit of the date uncertain were listed in the volume for 1810.

A third situation requiring investigation was geographical incongruity. In most cases this occurred when there were several names and places in the imprint and the imprint was incompletely transcribed. The item was indeed printed in the city where that printer worked, and has been indexed accordingly.

Part 2 is a geographical index by city. Under each place name are listed all personal and corporate names from Part 1, and also numbers for items with only the place given in the imprint. Names and item numbers with no place given are listed at the end of Part 2.

Part 3 lists items that were omitted with an explanation for each. This list may be considered an addition to the corrections found in volume 22 of this set.

This index was begun as a class project at Rutgers Graduate School of Library Service, with the guidance and encouragement of Robert S. Fraser. Additional assistance was received from members of the library staff at the American Antiquarian Society, Rutgers University, and Wagner College. A special word of thanks is given to my family, who patiently endured living with the thousands of index cards for "Mother's book."

Bibliography

Brigham, Clarence S. History and bibliography of American newspapers, 1690-1820. Worcester, Mass., American Antiquarian Society, 1947.

Bristol, Roger Pattrell. Index of printers, publishers, and booksellers indicated by Charles Evans in his American bibliography. Charlottesville, Bibliographical Society of the University of Virginia, 1961.

Brown, Harry Glenn. A directory of printing, publishing, bookselling and allied trades in Rhode Island to 1865. New York, New York Public Library, 1958.

_____. A directory of the book arts and book trade in Philadelphia to 1820. New York, New York Public Library, 1950.

McKay, George Leslie. A register of artists, engravers, booksellers, bookbinders, printers and publishers in New York City, 1633-1820. New York, New York Public Library, 1942.

Silver, Rollo Gabriel. The Baltimore book trade, 1800-1825. New York, New York Public Library, 1953.

_____. The Boston book trade, 1800-1825. New York, New York Public Library, 1949.

Sutton, Walter. The western book trade: Cincinnati as a nineteenth century publishing and book trade center. Columbus, Ohio State University Press, 1961.

Symbols Used in the Text

(no symbol)	printed by
bpb	printed by and published by
bsb	printed by and sold by
engr	engraved
f	printed for
pb	published by
sb	sold by
?12345	printer in doubt
12345?	date in doubt

Part 1

Printers, Publishers, and Booksellers Index

A

ABBEY, DOREPHUS (Albany, N. Y.)
1815: 34146, 34336? pb, 34753, 35707, 35850? pb
1816: 36700?, 37440, 38110, 38919

ABBEY, DOREPHUS (Oswego, N. Y.)
1817: 41712 pb

ABBEY, DOREPHUS (Watertown, N. Y.)
1817: 41157 pb

ABBEY, SETH ALDEN (Albany, N. Y.)
1815: 35850? pb
1816: 37440, 38110

ABBEY, SETH ALDEN (Oswego, N. Y.)
1817: 41712 pb

ABBEY, SETH ALDEN (Watertown, N. Y.)
1819: 46943, 48332 pb

ABBOT, --- (Haverhill, N. H.)
1810: 22124 pb

ABBOTT, JEREMIAH (Portsmouth, O.)
1818: 45395 pb

ABRAMS, ISRAEL (Wilmington, O.)

1815: 34179, 34819, 34992, 36062, 36127 pb
1816: 39800

ACOCK, WILLIAM (Philadelphia)
1819: 48654

ADAMS, ABIJAH (Boston)
1802: 1713-1714 f
1803: 3701 pb, 50374
1804: 5871 pb, 6320 pb, 7766
1805: 7907 f, 8278 pb
1806: 10276 pb, 10821, 10826, 11275, 11323
1807: 11942 pb, 12105, 13015, 13021-13022, 13029-13031, 13034 pb, 13037
1808: 14303 pb, 14328 pb, 15513, 15523, 15525, 15549, 15550 pb, 16056, 16138, 16203
1809: 17624, 18035 pb
1810: 19307 pb, 20665-20666, 20672, 20679-20680
1811: 23309, 23311, 23328-23329
1812: 24618, 25997, 26011, 26018, 26021, 26025

ADAMS, CHARLES CHAUNCEY (Poughkeepsie, N. Y.)
1810: 20189, 21292, 21393
1811: 22892, 23802 pb, 23855
1812: 24752, 26702
1813: 27804, 28885, 29877

ADAMS, DANIEL (Leominster, Mass.)
1801: 11, 147, 187, 270?,

1

?1572?
1802: 1710-1711, 3066 pb
1803: 3627, 3970, 4033, 4463,
    4800
1804: 5656-5657, 5924, 6050
    pb, 6881

ADAMS, GEORGE (Augusta,
    Ga.)
1812: 25092

ADAMS, ISAAC (Portland, Me.)
1803: 4603 pb
1805: 7924, 8079 pb, 8864 pb,
    9719, 9733
1806: 10349 pb, 10501, 11188 f
1807: 13017 pb
1809: 18441 f
1815: 35815 f

ADAMS, JOHN (Danville, Ky.)
1804: 6790 pb

ADAMS, JOHN (Philadelphia)
1802: 1994-1995, 2878, 2973
1803: 3963, 5568
1804: 5857, 6583, 7025 pb
1805: 8311, 8380, 8647, 9225,
    9722, 9752
1806: 10558, 10617, 10973,
    11363 pb
1807: 12001, 12443, 12680,
    12826, 12852, 13163, 13460
1808: 14482, 14502, 14915,
    14918, 15305, 15424, 15448,
    15823, 15991, 16053, 16121,
    16279, 16699
1809: 18393
1811: 22661

ADAMS, JOHN (Russellville,
    Ky.)
1806: 10880 pb

ADAMS, THOMAS G (New
    York)
1817: 41165 f

ADANCOURT, FRANCIS (Lan-
    singburgh, N. Y.)
1803: 3977, 4186 pb, 4954,
    5054
1804: 6088
1807: 13060

ADANCOURT, FRANCIS (Troy,
    N. Y.)
1807: 12544 pb
1810: 21274
1812: 24788 pb
1813 27867 pb, 28741, 29578,
    29873, 30022
1814: 31013, 31014 pb, 31746
1815: 33979, 34188 pb, 35765
1816: 36787, 37305 pb
1817: 40095, 40238
1818: 43678 pb, 45096, 45605
1819: 47672-47674, 49219,
    51870 pb

ADDINGTON, STEPHEN (Mount
    Pleasant, N. Y.)
1818: 46766

Advertiser (Cincinnati, O.)
1810: 19447

Adviser (Glens Falls, N. Y.)
1815: 34205

African Methodist Connection in
    the United States (Philadel-
    phia)
1817: 39949 f

AITKEN, JANE (Philadelphia)
1802: 2542, 2936 pb
1803: 3942-3943 pb, 3998,
    4026, 4489, 4815, 4829,
    4860, 4905 pb, 4907-4908,
    4946, 5595
1804: 5701, 6037, 7107-7108
1805: 8569, 9125, 9188, 9322
    pb, 9586
1806: 10391, 10626, 11049,
    11119 pb, 11151, 11205-
    11209
1807: 12541, 13366, 13372,
    13430, 14208
1808: 14486, 15032 pb, 15908,
    15916, 15993 pb, 50832
1809: 16876, 17410, 17482,
    17664, 17672-17673, 17900,
    18331, 18374, 18442
1810: 19387, 19943, 19991,
    20239, 20529-20531, 20552
    pb, 20656, 21050, 21057
    pb, 21131-21132, 21424
1811: 22211, 22497 pb, 22540,

22727, 23003, 23363, 23651
pb, 23677, 23733, 23736,
24407
1812: 24642, 25586, 26411
pb, 26441, 26444 pb, 26517,
26670, 26682
1813: 28042, 28057, 29568-
29569, 29688, 30379
1814: 31046, 32561, 51379
1815: 35695
1816: 37714, 38698
1817: 41876

AITKEN, JOHN (Philadelphia)
1801: 50206? pb
1802: 1733 pb
1805: 50610? pb
1807: 50753 pb, 50795? pb

AITKEN, ROBERT (Philadel-
phia)
1801: 564, 842 pb, 1179
1802: 1724 pb, 2904, 2927,
2936
1803: 4829, 4905
1804: 5701, 6037, 7107-7108

AITKEN, ROBERT S (Dover,
Del.)
1804: 6186 pb

AITKEN, ROBERT S (Philadelphia)
1811: 23196 f, 23974 f,
24006 f
1812: 51211 pb

AKERMAN, SAMUEL (Phila-
delphia)
1802: 2666 f
1803: 3683 pb, 3684, 4212
pb, 4358, 4910
1804: 6394, 7024, 7113, 7118

AKERS, PETER (Flemingsburg,
Ky.)
1819: 49496 pb

Albany Argus (Albany, N.Y.)
1813: 28560 pb, 29342 bsb
1816: 36748

Albany Centinel (Albany, N.Y.)
1804: 7206

Albany Register (Albany, N.Y.)
1808: 15109
1809: 16800, 17232-17233,
17628, 18230, 18234
1812: 24890, 26269, 26273,
26277-26278, 51227
1819: 48898, 48903

Albany Religious Tract Society
(Albany, N.Y.)
1815: 36578 pb

Albany Union Sunday School
Society (Albany, N.Y.)
1819: 50062 f

ALBEE, AMOS (Medfield,
Mass.)
1808: 16181 sb

ALBRECHT, ANTON (Lancast-
er, Pa.)
1809: 17604 pb, 18178 pb
1810: 20193, 20838 pb
1811: 22895 pb
1812: 25502 pb
1813: 29271 pb
1816: 38365 pb
1817: 41559 pb
1819: 48068

ALBRECHT, GEORGE (Lan-
caster, Pa.)
1807: 13174
1808: 14586, 15580-15581,
15699 pb, 16091

ALBRECHT, JOHANN (Lan-
caster, Pa.)
1801: 986, 1130-1131, 1399
1802: 2246, 2733 pb, 3133,
3500
1803: 4710 pb, 5134
1804: 6608, 6767, 6856 pb,
6863 pb, 7329, 7340
1805: 8748, 8964 pb, 9453
1806: 10947 pb
1807: 13349

ALBRECHT, PETER (Lancast-
er, Pa.)
1807: 13174
1808: 14586, 15580-15581,
15699 pb, 16091

ALBRIGHT, JACOB W (Harrisburg, Pa.)
1805: 8294 pb

ALBURTIS, JOHN (Martinsburg, Va.)
1803: 3882
1806: 10301
1809: 50912
1810: 20414, 20650 pb
1811: 22832, 23063
1812: 26049
1815: 35085 pb, 35721
1818: 45412 pb
1819: 47601, 48255

ALDERSON, THOMAS (Washington, N. C.)
1806: 11801 pb

ALDRICH, DUNBAR (Windsor, Vt.)
1818: 44013, 44166, 44981, 46637 pb
1819: 47896, 48471, 48835, 49524

ALEXANDER, JAMES (Brownsville, Pa.)
1809: 19207 pb

ALEXANDER, JAMES (Kittanning, Pa.)
1810: 22027 pb

ALEXANDER, WILLIAM (Carlisle, Pa.)
1802: 1996 pb, 3029 pb
1804: 6077
1806: 10028, 10493, 10503, 11265
1808: 15127, 15133, 15196
1809: 17197, 18649, 19027
1810: 20226
1811: 23956
1812: 24831 pb, 25532 pb, 26571
1813: 28329, 30600
1814: 30978
1816: 37221

Alexandria Expositor (Alexandria, Va.)
1804: 6169

Alexandria Gazette (Alexandria, Va.)
1814: 51362 pb

ALLCHIN, GEORGE (Philadelphia)
1813: 28459 pb

ALLEE, PRESLEY (Dover, Del.)
1804: 6071 pb, 6146 pb
1805: 8313-8317
1806: 10272-10274

ALLEN, --- (Chillicothe, O.)
1818: 46843

ALLEN, ANDREW J (Boston)
1810: 20662 f
1812: 27201? pb
1816: 39050 f
1817: 42749 pb
1818: 43414 f

ALLEN, EPHRAIM WILLIAMS (Newburyport, Mass.)
1801: 69, 283 pb, 285 pb, 1049?, 1295, 1355, 1360
1802: 2113, 3048, 3092, 3116
1803: 4683 pb, 5106
1804: 6791, 7301, 7681
1805: 8232, 9176
1806: 9911, 10751-10752, 10787, 10916, 11164, 11770-11771, 11896-11897
1807: 12068, 12385, 12741, 13089, 13245, 13311, 13613
1808: 14824 pb, 15024, 15250, 15661, 15842, 15844, 16242, 16335, 16665
1809: 16904, 18249, 18626, 18633, 18677, 19113-19114
1810: 19914, 20505, 20724, 21401
1811: 23167-23168, 23629-23631
1812: 24612, 25211 pb, 25213, 25434, 25800, 26052, 26088 f, 26380-26381, 26383, 27495
1813: 27890-27891, 28273, 29437 pb, 29824-29825 f
1817: 42194
1818: 45784

1819: 47776, 48425, 49069,
49456

ALLEN, FREDERICK P (Mid-
dlebury, Vt.)
1817: 40121, 41240, 41284?,
41429-41430, 41907, 42094,
42746?, 42779
1819: 47840

ALLEN, HORATIO GATES
(Haverhill, Mass.)
1812: 24542, 24588 pb, 24955,
25069 pb, 25501, 25519,
25701 pb, 26088, 26158 pb,
26169 pb, 26176 pb, 26216
pb, 26755 pb
1813: 27926 pb, 28012 pb,
28800 pb, 29243 pb, 29799
pb, 30492 pb, 30541 pb

ALLEN, HORATIO GATES
(Newburyport, Mass.)
1808: 15515?
1813: 27890-27891, 29824-
29825
1814: 31246, 31494, 32430-
32431, 32926, 33752, 51396-
51397

ALLEN, PAUL (Baltimore)
1814: 30737 pb
1815: 51503?

ALLEN, PHINEHAS (Pittsfield,
Mass.)
1801: 40, 95, 1382?
1802: 1844, 2329, 2364, 2516?,
3491
1803: 3649-3650
1804: 6997, 7152
1805: 8020 pb, 8125, 8191,
8772, 8863
1806: 9825, 9883, 10592,
10820
1807: 12019, 12245, 12535,
13747
1808: 15146, 15478, 16176,
16471, 50863 pb
1809: 16823 pb, 16825, 17635
1810: 19398, 20053, 20468,
20821 bf
1811: 23205, 23371, 23611,
24383, 51106

1813: 27967, 29285
1814: 31677, 31814, 32857,
33594
1815: 33827, 34150, 34194,
34347, 34527, 35089 pb,
35093, 35251, 35947, 36074
1816: 37717, 38052 pb, 38257-
38258, 38887
1817: 39967, 40187, 40927
1818: 44393-44394, 45194
1819: 48193

ALLEN, RICHARD (Philadel-
phia)
1817: 39949 f

ALLEN, RUFUS (St. Albans,
Vt.)
1808: 16122 pb

ALLEN, SOLOMON (Albany,
N. Y.)
1808: 15972 pb
1809: 17232-17233, 17628,
18230, 18415 pb

ALLEN, THOMAS (Washington,
D. C.)
1818: 46538

ALLEN, WILLIAM BROWN
(Cahawba, Ala.)
1819: 47491 pb

ALLEN, WILLIAM BROWN
(Haverhill, Mass.)
1809: 16813, 16861, 17216,
17333, 17576, 18314 pb,
18418, 50906 pb, 50937 pb
1810: 19299, 19625-19626 pb,
19913 pb
1811: 22160 pb, 22580, 22981,
23460 pb, 23504, 23672 pb
1812: 24542, 24588 pb, 24955,
25069 pb, 25501, 25519,
25701 pb, 25964, 26088,
26158 pb, 26169 pb, 26176
pb, 26216 pb, 26755 pb,
27546, 51155
1813: 27926 pb, 28012 pb,
29068 pb, 29243 pb, 29799
pb, 30492 pb, 30541 pb

ALLEN, WILLIAM BROWN
(Newburyport, Mass.)
1805: 8075
1808: 15842
1812: 25965
1813: 27890-27891, 28069,
29824-29825
1814: 30880-30881, 30894 pb,
31029 pb, 31058 pb, 31246 f,
31287, 31414 pb, 31468 pb,
32030, 32430-32431 f,
32540-32542, 32724, 32926 f,
33752 f, 51397 f
1815: 33866, 33993, 34071 pb,
34519-34523, 34874, 35264,
35371 pb, 35398 pb, 35540,
35563, 35668, 35979, 36132
1816: 36745 pb, 36967 pb,
37097, 37331, 37574, 38015,
38209, 38297, 38342 pb,
38362, 38679, 38772, 38992,
38996, 39043, 39792, 39849,
51588 pb
1817: 40503, 40613, 41208 pb,
41896 pb
1819: 49208 pb

ALLESON, ROBERT (George-
town, D.C.)
1814: 31561, 31639, 32135,
32453, 32503, 32773
1815: 33766

ALLEYNE, ABEL DUDLEY
(Dedham, Mass.)
1816: 36892 pb, 36894 pb,
36896, 37288, 37910, 38549,
38868, 38938, 39018, 51550
pb
1817: 40147, 40463, 40495,
40756, 41078, 41317, 41979,
41981, 42045-42047, 42318,
42893, 42917 pb
1818: 43249, 43661 pb, 44411,
44733 pb, 46879, 51788 pb

ALLINSON, DAVID (Burlington,
N.J.)
1802: 3548 pb, 3588 f
1803: 3845 f, 5615 f
1804: 6239 f, 6501 f
1805: 8208 f, 8509? pb, 8722
f, 8813 f, 9063 pb, 9316-

9317 pb
1806: 10600 pb, 11899 pb
1808: 14543 f, 14618 pb,
15207 f, 16722 f
1810: 21245 pb, 21929 pb
1811: 22442, 22457a pb,
22607, 22668 pb, 22694,
23429 pb, 23535, 23916,
23943 pb, 24465
1812: 24593, 24956 pb, 25085
pb, 25374 pb, 25556 pb,
26542
1813: 28239 pb, 28439 f,
28671 pb, 28672 f, 29446-
29447 pb
1815: 33771, 33828 pb,
33832 f, 33880 pb, 34575,
34836 pb, 35059 pb, 35975,
36012 pb, 36661 pb, 36663 f,
36664 pb, 51473
1816: 37156 pb, 37690 pb,
37958 pb, 38321 pb, 38329
pb, 38409 pb, 39046 pb,
39819 pb
1817: 40585, 41701 pb
1818: 44204, 44759 bf, 44776
pb
1819 48961

ALLINSON, SAMUEL (Burlington, N.J.)
1812: 26793 f

ALSOP, JOHN (Middletown,
Conn.)
1807: 13388
1808: 14948 pb

ALSOP, JOHN (New York)
1807: 13136 f, 13512 f, 13707
f
1808: 14627 pb, 14804 pb

ALSOP, RICHARD (Middletown,
Conn.)
1807: 13388
1808: 14363, 14948 pb, 50894

ALSOP, RICHARD (New York)
1807: 13136 f, 13512 f, 13707
f
1808: 14627 pb, 14804 pb,
16620

AMEN, DAVID (Botetourt
     Co., Va.)
1807:   13302

AMEN, DAVID (Fincastle, Va.)
1801:   496 pb
1805:   9108

American (Providence, R.I.)
1811:   23032, 24031
1812:   26875, 27426, 27548
1815:   34473, 34559, 36081
1819:   49483

American Academy of Arts
     and Sciences (Boston)
1818:   51761 pb

American Beacon (Norfolk, Va.)
1819:   47146

American Bible Society (New
     York)
1816:   36724 f, 36950 pb,
     51553 pb
1817:   39974 f, 40201 f, 40202
     pb, 40218 pb
1818:   43303 pb, 43304 f,
     43310 pb, 43345 f
1819:   47212-47214 f, 47228 f,
     47229 pb, 47233 f, 47341 pb

American Board of Commis-
     sioners for Foreign Mis-
     sions (Boston)
1818:   44225 f

American Citizen (New York)
1801:   1142

American Eagle (Catskill, N.Y.)
1809:   17035
1810:   19328, 19444, 19855,
     21425 pb, 21975 pb

American Friend (Marietta, O.)
1813:   27655?
1816:   38511

American Mercury (Hartford,
     Conn.)
1809:   50969

American School Class-book
     Warehouse (New York)
1819:   49108 pb, 49110 pb

American Society for the Dis-
     semination of the Doctrines
     of the New Jerusalem
     Church (Philadelphia)
1818:   45015 f

American Sunday School Union
     (Philadelphia)
1813:   29818 pb
1818:   46845 pb

American Tract Society (New
     York)
see New York Religious Tract
     Society (New York)

American Tract Society, Boston
     (Boston)
see New England Tract Society
     (Andover, Mass. and Boston)

American Yeoman (Brattle-
     borough, Vt.)
1817:   42042

AMES, HORACE (Philadelphia)
1816:   37447 pb, 38471 pb
1817:   41466 f, 42029 f, 42058
     f, 42817 f
1818:   43523 f, 44877 f, 44962
     f, 45107 pb
1819:   47510 pb, 47520 pb,
     48936 f, 48937-48938 pb,
     49018 f, 50024-50025 f,
     50171 pb

Ami des Lois (New Orleans,
     La.)
1810:   20881

ANDERSON, LEROY (Rich-
     mond, Va.)
1813:   28266 pb

ANDERSON, ROBERT P
     (Philadelphia)
1814:   32851 pb
1816:   36810, 37544, 51595 pb
1817:   40015 pb, 40115, 41047,

41336
1818: 43162-43163, 43209 pb,
44438, 44543, 46789, 46828
1819: 47048, 47076 pb, 47078,
47402 pb, 47905, 48460,
49305, 50133 pb

ANDERSON, THOMAS (Lexing-
ton, Ky.)
1804: 7373
1805: 7889, 7922, 8712

ANDERSON, THOMAS (New
Orleans, La.)
1806: 10674, 11077-11078,
11502, 11798
1807: 12910, 13296-13298,
13741, 13789, 14157, 14243
1808: 15442, 15484, 15813-
15814

ANDERSON, WILLIAM (Phila-
delphia)
1814: 32851 pb
1816: 37901 pb

Anderson & Meehan (Philadel-
phia)
see ANDERSON, ROBERT P
(Philadelphia)
MEEHAN, JOHN SILVA
(Philadelphia)

ANDREWS, EBENEZER TUR-
ELL (Albany, N.Y.)
1801: 305 sb, 1407 f
1802: 1870 sb, 2190 f, 2706
f, 2714 f

ANDREWS, EBENEZER TUR-
ELL (Baltimore)
1801: 72 pb, 305 sb, 841 f,
1430 f
1802: 1765 f, 1870 sb, 1918
f, 2190 f, 2260 sb, 2495-
2496 f, 3008 pb, 3574 f
1803: 3841 f, 3984 f, 4045
sb, 4372 pb, 4492 f

ANDREWS, EBENEZER TUR-
ELL (Boston)
1801: 29 pb, 32 pb, 156 pb,
168 pb, 293 f, 305 bsb,

620 pb, 662 pb, 670 f,
724 f, 895, 957, 959, 1154
pb, 1297, 1375, 1396, 1433
f, 1627, 1632, 50209 pb
1802: 1736, 1855 pb, 1857,
1870 bsb, 1875, 1912 pb,
1939 f, 1951 pb, 2190, 2258-
2259, 2260 bsb, 2482 f,
2698 pb, 2699, 2713 f,
3015, 3175 f, 3511, 3515
1803: 3625, 3688 pb, 3706,
3790 pb, 3812 f, 3813-3814
pb, 3839, 3980, 4045 f,
4218 pb, 4228, 4229 f,
4391-4392, 4533 f, 4811,
4815 f, 5555 pb, 5557 pb,
5561, 5585 pb, 50403 pb
1804: 5677 f, 5726 pb, 5825
pb, 5832 pb, 5845, 5849 f,
5851 pb, 5861 f, 5914, 6829
pb, 6830, 6831 f, 7059 f,
7073 pb, 7720-7721 pb,
7724-7726 pb
1805: 7826, 7851 pb, 7986 f,
7997 pb, 8039 f, 8462-8463
f, 8551 f, 8933 pb, 8972 pb,
9469 f, 50496 pb
1806: 9965 f, 10115 f, 10742a-
10743 f, 10909 f, 11296 f
1807: 11957 pb, 12038 f,
13019 pb, 13020 f, 13142 pb,
13143-13144 f, 13392 f,
13659 pb, 14181 pb
1808: 14312-14313 f, 14471
pb, 14472 f, 14485 f, 15049
f, 15655 f, 15694? f, 15951
f, 50884 f
1809: 17339 pb, 18131 f,
18391 f, 50958 f
1810: 19329 f, 19644 pb,
20148, 20661 f, 20788-
20789 f, 21048? f
1811: 22164 pb, 22168 pb,
22350 pb, 22360 f, 22766 f,
23439 f
1812: 24525 f, 24632 pb,
24793-24794 f, 24821 f,
25457-25458 f, 25998 f,
26142-26144 pb, 26435? pb
1813: 27687 pb, 27884 f,
29085 f, 29223 f, 29715 f
1814: 30647 pb, 30862 f,
30876 f, 31516 pb, 31693

pb, 32046 f, 32175-32176 f
1815: 33816 f, 34728 f,
35323 pb
1816: 36703 f, 38293 pb,
38644 pb
1817: 41363 f
1818: 44079 f, 44725 pb,
44910 f
1819: 46959-46960 pb, 47014
pb

ANDREWS, EBENEZER TUR-
ELL (Brookfield, Mass.)
1802: 1887 f

ANDREWS, JOHN (Chillicothe,
O.)
1814: 33633 pb, 33699
1815: 33967, 34338, 35864,
36593
1817: 41069, 42878, 42928
1818: 44842 pb, 45141, 45929

ANDREWS, JOHN (Warren, O.)
1819: 47711

ANDREWS, LORING (Albany,
N.Y.)
1801: 460 pb, 1024? pb,
1037, 1039-1040

ANDREWS, LORING (Charles-
ton, S.C.)
1803: 3954 f

ANDREWS, SIDNEY W (New
York)
1802: 2905
1803: 4193, 4491, 4493, 4594
1804: 5952 pb, 6137, 6239,
7642
1805: 8255, 9236, 9360

ANDREWS, WILLIAM (Boston)
1806: 10642 pb
1807: 12184 f, 12672 pb,
13528 pb, 13644 f
1808: 14978 f, 15289 f,
16704 f
1809: 16789 f, 17472 f
1810: 20324 f, 22006 pb

ANDREWS, WILLIAM (Coop-
erstown, N.Y.)
1808: 15295 f

Andrews & Cummings (Boston)
see ANDREWS, WILLIAM
(Boston)
CUMMINGS, JACOB A
(Boston)

ANDRUS, SILAS (Hartford,
Conn.)
1810: 19975 pb
1811: 23839 f
1812: 24978 f, 25143 pb,
25528 f
1813: 29640 f
1814: 31022 f, 32547 f
1815: 34872 pb, 35680 f,
35806 f, 35901 pb
1816: 38026 f, 39700 f, 51601
f
1817: 40226 f, 41216 f, 41217
pb
1818: 45551? pb, 45552-
45556 pb, 46673 f
1819: 47838 pb, 49302 pb,
50011 pb, 50012 f, 50014 pb

ANNIN, WILLIAM B (Boston)
1818: 45906 pb

Anthology Press (Boston)
1809: 17731

Anti-Monarchist (Northampton,
Mass.)
1808: 15111, 15115?
1809: 17655, 18600
1810: 19434, 21316-21317

Apollo Press (Washington,
D.C.)
1802: 1722, 2671, 2837, 2896,
3351, 3442
1814: 32380

APPEL, JOHN (New York)
1813: 28637 pb

APPLETON, JOHN SPARHAWK
(Salem, Mass.)
1801: 189 f, 571 f, 579 f,

849 f
1802: 1938 f, 1964 sb, 1969
f, 2196 sb, 3155 f
1803: 3822 f, 3914 sb, 4079 f
1804: 5947 f, 6294 pb, 6400
f, 7235 pb, 7242 pb
1805: 8109 f, 8340 f, 9304 f,
9704 f, 50536 f
1806: 11320 f
1807: 12079 pb, 12668 f,
13437 pb
1808: 14516 f, 15171 pb,
15605 f, 16686 pb
1809: 17032 pb, 17398 f,
17433 pb, 18625 pb, 19020
pb
1810: 21112 pb, 23308 f
1812: 25576 f, 26390 pb,
27491 f, 27621 pb
1813: 27943 f, 30194 pb
1814: 32172 pb, 32997 pb
1816: 39750-39751 f
1818: 46687 f, 46737-46738 f
1819: 48934 f, 51960 f

ARCHBOLD, J F (Winchester,
Va.)
1816: 39881 f

ARDEN, DANIEL D (New York)
1810: 21122 f
1813: 27679 f, 27680 pb,
28284 f, 29049 f, 29812 f
1814: 30694 pb, 30695 f,
31583 pb, 32685 f, 32753 f
1815: 34207 pb, 35546? pb,
35772 f, 35818 pb, 36556 f
1816: 36985 pb, 37482 pb,
38749 pb, 38762 pb, 39026
f, 39855 f
1817: 41479 f

ARDEN, THOMAS S (New
York)
1802: 2039 f, 2103 f, 2117
pb, 3057 f, 50288 f
1803: 3796 f, 4131 f, 4620 f,
4818 f
1804: 6019 f, 6204 f, 6702 f
1805: 8243 f, 8255 f

Argus (Portland, Me.)
see Eastern Argus (Portland,
Me.)

Argus (Richmond, Va.)
see Virginia Argus (Rich-
mond, Va.)

Argus of Western America
(Frankfort, Ky.)
1819: 51904 pb

ARION, COPELAND P J
(Madison, Ind.)
1819: 47087, 48015

ARMBRUST, JOHN (Greens-
burg, Pa.)
1817: 51691 pb

ARMOR, WILLIAM (Chambers-
burg, Pa.)
1809: 18497 pb

ARMSTRONG, ALEXANDER
(St. Clairsville, O.)
1811: 22328 pb
1813: 28342 pb
1816: 38350
1818: 43277 pb

ARMSTRONG, ALEXANDER
(Washington, Pa.)
1806: 10316
1810: 19482

ARMSTRONG, ALEXANDER
(Wheeling, Va.)
1807: 12806, 14210 pb
1809: 18485-18486

ARMSTRONG, JOHN W (Boston)
1808: 14285 f

ARMSTRONG, SAMUEL TUR-
ELL (Boston)
1804: 5972? pb
1806: 9823, 9865, 10174,
10216 pb, 10311, 10353 pb,
10355-10356, 10486, 10527-
10528, 11191-11192, 11853,
11878, 50637 pb
1807: 11931 pb, 12102, 12134
pb, 12175? pb, 12222 pb,
12459, 12714, 12716, 12930,
13011, 13109-13110 pb,
13548 f, 13575 pb, 13639,
13666, 13684, 13739 pb,

14112, 50809 pb
1808: 14327, 14356-14357,
14675, 14715, 14760-14762,
14778 pb, 14779, 14904,
15018 pb, 15255, 15394,
15631, 15657, 15904, 15948,
16303, 16345 pb, 16657,
16734, 16763
1809: 17418, 17788, 17890,
18089, 18635
1810: 19666 pb, 19927, 21402,
21527, 22093
1811: 22224, 22308, 22423 pb,
22415a pb, 22416a, 22423a
bsb, 22424a pb, 22427a f,
22568 pb, 22597?, 22839
pb, 23042-23043 pb, 23224,
23255, 23483 pb, 23615 pb,
23783 pb, 24377 pb, 24398
pb, 24490 pb, 24495 pb,
51095
1812: 24517 pb, 24590, 24597
pb, 24613 pb, 24614, 24750,
24973 pb, 25093 pb, 25110
pb, 25287-25288, 25340,
25344, 25570, 25675, 25702,
26145 pb, 26398, 26561,
26620, 26824 pb, 27597 pb,
27599-27600
1813: 27707-27708, 27731-
27732, 27754 pb, 27838 pb,
28109 pb, 28169-28170 pb,
28184 pb, 28383, 28386 pb,
28421, 28423, 28521, 28547,
28640, 28668 f, 28710, 28883,
28975 pb, 29119, 29418,
29440 pb, 29695, 29763 f,
29891, 29943, 30537, 30565,
30599 pb
1814: 30666 pb, 30668 pb,
30688, 30689 pb, 31134,
31157, 31169 pb, 31188 pb,
31215, 31339 pb, 31412,
31415 pb, 31630 f, 31756
pb, 31774, 31783 pb, 31869-
31870, 31948 pb, 32080,
32126 f, 32178-32179,
32232 pb, 32433 f, 32597-
32598 pb, 32606, 32633,
32647, 32728 pb, 32790 pb,
32807 pb, 32830, 32924,
33669, 33717-33721, 33728
pb

1815: 33840 pb, 33870, 33903
pb, 34064 pb, 34079 pb,
34124, 34129 pb, 34142-
34143, 34177 pb, 34344 pb,
34560 pb, 34609 pb, 34637,
34642 pb, 34747-34748 pb,
35326-35327 pb, 35801,
35845, 36076, 36559 pb,
36608-36609 pb, 36619 pb,
36634 pb, 36636-36638,
36640-36642, 36644
1816: 36726, 36944 pb, 37287
pb, 37315, 37384, 37401,
37511 pb, 37663 pb, 37834,
37985, 38089, 38158, 38685
pb, 39821 pb, 39854 pb,
39858 pb, 39873
1817: 39975, 39987, 40005
pb, 40196 pb, 40209-40210
pb, 40424 pb, 40541, 40754,
40830 f, 40831 pb, 41108 f,
41109 pb, 41117 pb, 41965
pb, 42051 pb, 42947 pb,
42967-42968, 42973-42974
pb
1818: 43063 pb, 43692, 43940-
43941, 45226 pb, 45609-
45610 f, 45783, 46858 f
1819: 46914 pb, 46977 f,
46980 f, 46998 f, 47338 f,
47562 f, 47862 f, 47867 pb,
47902, 47904 f, 47987 f,
48079 pb, 48208 f, 48268 f,
48291 f, 48315 f, 48372 f,
48532 f, 49019 f, 49148 f,
49341 f, 49426 f, 49484 pb,
49488, 50057 f, 50063 f,
50149 f, 50163 f, 50164?
pb, 50166 f

ARMSTRONG, SAMUEL TUR-
ELL (Charlestown, Mass.)
1809: 17175, 17280, 17396,
17447 pb, 17684-17685,
18012, 18102, 18121, 18728,
18751, 19267-19268, 50943
1810: 19547, 19805-19806,
19811, 19839? pb, 19841,
20054, 20232, 20459, 20790,
21378, 21876, 22096
1811: 22309 pb, 22566 pb,
22567, 23944 pb
1812: 26135? bsb

ARMSTRONG, SAMUEL TUR-
ELL (Portland, Me.)
1812: 26101.

ARMSTRONG, THOMAS (Phila-
delphia)
1805: 9326 f

ASHLEY, RICHARD HENRY
(Stockbridge, Mass.)
1815: 34046 pb
1816: 37902, 39786, 39795

ASHLEY, TIMOTHY (Litchfield,
Conn.)
1805: 9754 pb

ASHLEY, TIMOTHY (Spring-
field, Mass.)
1801: 796, 1397, 1673
1802: 1785, 2466, 2505-2506,
2508
1803: 4889, 4969 pb
1804: 7182 pb

Association of Fairfield County,
Connecticut
1803: 4099 f

ASTEN, ABRAHAM (New York)
1817: 41960 pb
1818: 46864 pb

ATKINSON, --- (New York)
1819: 49562

ATKINSON, JOHN (New Jersey)
1811: 22213 f

ATKINSON, SAMUEL COATE
(Philadelphia)
1818: 43064, 43276
1819: 46983-46984, 49010 pb,
49063

ATKINSON, THOMAS (Harris-
burg, Pa.)
1804: 6392, 6471, 7237, 7676

ATKINSON, THOMAS (Mead-
ville, Pa.)
1805: 8261 pb
1815: 35236 pb

ATWATER, AMBROSE (Bur-
lington, Vt.)
1810: 21910 f

Augusta Chronicle (Augusta,
Ga.)
1804: 6376
1805: 50541 pb
1806: 50681 pb
1807: 12922, 13742, 50776 pb
1808: 50853 pb
1809: 50942 pb
1810: 51008 pb

Augusta Herald (Augusta, Ga.)
1806: 9872
1812: 26749

Aurora (Philadelphia)
1801: 1143, 1299
1802: 2205, 2888
1808: 15884

Aurora Book Stores (Philadelphia)
1801: 578 pb, 945 pb

Aurora Book Stores (Washington, D.C.)
1801: 578 pb, 945 pb

AUSTIN, --- (Philadelphia)
1805: 9476 pb

AUSTIN, GALEN L (Elizabeth,
N.J.)
1812: 25357 pb, 26244
1813: 29312

AUSTIN, GALEN L (New Brunswick, N.J.)
1815: 35570

AUSTIN, GALEN L (Philadelphia)
1818: 44474
1819: 47446, 47591, 48760,
49095, 49587

AUSTIN, JOHN B (Philadelphia)
1807: 13057?
1809: 17127 pb

AUSTIN, LEMUEL (Boston)
1810: 20648 pb

AUSTIN, WILLIAM W (New
Haven, Conn.)
1810: 19495 pb, 20780 f,
21913 f

Auxilliary New York Bible and
Common Prayer Book Soci-
ety (New York)
1816: 36991, 38719-38721

Auxilliary New York Bible
Society (New York)
1816: 36951 f

AVERY, JOSEPH (Plymouth,
Mass.)
1806: 10813 f
1808: 14779 f
1812: 26864 f
1813: 27859 f
1818: 43735 pb

AVERY, SAMUEL (Boston)
1809: 17596, 18563 pb
1810: 19632, 19675 pb, 19754,
20091, 20662, 20779, 20999,
21222, 21547
1811: 22347, 22876, 23183,
23247, 23742-23744, 23834
pb, 23838 pb, 24329 pb,
24419
1812: 24687, 25009?, 25583,
27630
1818: 44395 pb, 45830 pb

AVERY, THOMAS (New London,
Conn.)
1807: 12041

B

B, H (Philadelphia)
1814: 51384

BABCOCK, ELISHA (Hartford,
Conn.)
1801: 352 f, 592, 813, 50253 f

1802: 1777, 2077 f
1803: 3698, 5041 pb
1804: 7231
1805: 7893, 9347 pb, 9442 pb
1806: 9866, 11352 pb
1807: 12007
1808: 14387, 15491, 16182 pb
1816: 37641
1818: 43703?, 43710
1819: 47704

BABCOCK, JOHN (Hartford,
Conn.)
1801: 109, 304, 308, 352 bf,
391, 443, 477-478, 541,
569, 580, 654, 672, 783,
814, 955, 1216, 1272, 1605,
50195 pb, 50203, 50213,
50253 bf
1802: 1907, 1916, 1959, 1961,
1971, 2077 bf, 2153, 2155,
2342, 2451, 2534, 2634,
2749, 2797, 2882, 3125,
3530, 3571, 50283, 50287,
50298, 50313

BABCOCK, JOHN (New Haven,
Conn.)
see also Sidney's Press (New
Haven, Conn.)
1816: 37364 pb
1818: 43727 f, 44833 f, 45706
f, 45761 f
1819: 46942 f, 46946 f, 47025
f, 47156 f, 47173 f, 47358
pb, 47503 f, 47522 f, 47568
f, 47705 f, 47723 f, 47754
pb, 48088 f, 48132 f, 48229
f, 48314 f, 48401-48403 f,
48583 f, 49146 f, 49242 pb,
49293 f, 49306 f, 49423 f,
49654 pb, 51850 pb, 51858 f

BABCOCK, S (New Haven,
Conn.)
1812: 51219 pb

BABCOCK, SIDNEY (Charles-
ton, S.C.)
1818: 45761 f
1819: 47173 f, 47723 f, 48132
sb, 48402 f

BABCOCK, WILLIAM R
(Charleston, S. C.)
1818: 45761 f
1819: 47173 f, 47723 f,
    48132 sb, 48402 f

BABSON, JOHN (Wiscasset,
    Me.)
1803: 3768?, 4127 pb, 4803
    pb
1804: 5823, 5899, 6655,
    6979?
1805: 7891, 7904, 7925, 7963,
    8497?, 8735, 8789?
1806: 9894 pb, 10029
1807: 12802?, 13748

BACHE, RICHARD (Philadel-
    phia)
1818: 44075 pb

BACKUS, --- (Edenton, N. C.)
1805: 8371 pb

BACKUS, ELEAZER FITCH
    (Albany, N. Y.)
1803: 3657 pb, 5122 pb
1804: 5736 pb, 5859 pb, 6090
    pb, 6200 pb, 6208-6209 pb,
    6222 pb, 6224 pb, 6838
    pb, 7206
1805: 50533 f
1806: 10106, 10113 f, 10402
    pb, 10651 pb, 10723, 11260,
    11752
1807: 12963 pb, 13378 f,
    13470?, 13647 pb
1808: 16097 f
1809: 17103 f, 17773 f
1811: 22735 pb, 23913 f
1812: 24999 f, 25876 f, 26399
    f
1813: 27689 pb, 28770 f
1814: 30842 f, 31370 f
1815: 34597 pb, 35023 f,
    35471 pb
1816: 36942 pb, 38443 pb
1817: 40518-40519 pb
1818: 45052 f
1819: 48832 pb

BACKUS, SIMON (Bridgeport,
    Conn.)

1808: 15507
1809: 17838 pb, 18009 pb,
    18306 pb
1810: 19834-19835, 19981,
    20263 pb
1811: 22742 pb, 24349 pb

BACON, ALLYN (Philadelphia)
1816: 51545? pb
1817: 51649? pb
1818: 44624, 51734? pb,
    51754? pb, 51815? pb,
    51849? pb

BACON, DAVID (Hartford,
    Conn.)
1816: 37415 f

BADGER, BARBER (Boston)
1816: 38006-38007 pb, 39813
    pb

BADGER, JOSEPH I (New
    Haven, Conn.)
1815: 35749 pb

BADGER, THOMAS (Boston)
1810: 21253?
1815: 34997
1817: 40088, 40290 pb, 40294,
    40506, 41172
1818: 43757 pb, 44245-44249,
    44287, 44525
1819: 47739, 47991, 48148-
    48150, 48178 pb, 49204,
    50088 pb

BAER, JOHN (Lancaster, Pa.)
1818: 44452
1819: 47206 pb, 49254 pb

BAGLEY, --- (Boston)
1818: 43531

BAILEY, DAVID (Charleston,
    S. C.)
1801: 50240 pb
1802: 50317-50318 pb
1803: 50383 pb
1806: 50744 pb

BAILEY, FRANCIS (Lancaster,
    Pa.)

1801: 1113, 1117, 1121, 1123, 1129
1802: 2042, 2087, 2863, 2869, 3115
1804: 7015 pb
1805: 9116-9118

BAILEY, FRANCIS (Octoraro, Pa.)
1801: 174
1804: 7009, 7016
1805: 9115
1806: 11120, 11127
1807: 12525

BAILEY, FRANCIS (Philadelphia)
1802: 3494
1804: 5989

BAILEY, ISAAC (Providence, R.I.)
1815: 33904 f

BAILEY, LYDIA R (Philadelphia)
1808: 14395 pb, 14639, 14845, 15291, 15306, 15987, 16292
1809: 16888 pb, 17151, 17204, 17348, 17578, 17679, 17724, 18392, 18550, 18557 pb, 18718 pb, 50920
1810: 19317-19321, 19401 pb, 20212, 20502, 21163, 21542, 50987, 50990
1811: 23434-23435, 23682, 51069
1812: 24672 pb, 24853 pb, 25026 pb, 25166 pb, 25805, 26449, 26453, 26619, 27507
1813: 27771 pb, 28076 pb, 29497, 30441
1814: 30726 pb, 31845, 31874, 32091, 32222, 32490
1815: 34901, 36039, 51462 pb, 51464, 51495, 51505, 51508
1816: 37146, 37442, 37452, 37553, 37772, 38019, 38227, 38467, 38609-38611, 38754, 38864, 38975, 39036, 39039, 39091, 39134
1817: 40349, 40557, 40723, 40791, 40957, 40992, 41049, 41057, 41121, 41146, 41306,
41485, 41786, 41983, 41991, 42160, 42168, 42189, 42238, 42240 pb, 42241, 42327 pb, 42915, 51678
1818: 43132 pb, 43136, 43234, 43649, 43737, 43865, 43909, 43948 pb, 44608, 45015, 45317, 45857, 51758 pb
1819: 47501, 47515, 48123 pb, 48159, 48270, 50173, 51853 pb

BAILEY, NOADIAH (Middletown, Conn.)
1804: 7238 pb

BAILEY, ROBERT (Lancaster, Pa.)
1802: 2865
1804: 5970, 6081, 6994
1805: 8122, 9328 pb

BAILEY, ROBERT (Philadelphia)
1802: 3494
1804: 5989
1806: 50643 pb
1807: 12022 pb, 12349, 13173, 13561

BAILHACHE, JOHN (Chillicothe, O.)
1813: 29012
1814: 32390, 32677? pb
1816: 36846, 37651, 38502 f, 39789
1817: 40106, 40864, 40865? pb, 41497, 41547
1818: 43518
1819: 47130, 48034, 48423

BAILY, GEORGE (Pittsburgh, Pa.)
1819: 48548 f

BAIRD, JOSEPH B (New Orleans, La.)
1812: 25882
1813: 28978

BAKER, JOHN (Waynesburgh, Pa.)
1815: 36514 pb

BAKER, JOHN KELSE (Bur-
lington, Vt.)
1801:   1296, 1582 pb
1802:   3049-3051

BAKER, ORAN E (Cazenovia,
N. Y.)
1808:   15955 pb
1809:   18604
1811:   22274
1812:   24724
1817:   40331

BAKER, SOLOMON (Danville,
Vt.)
1815:   33851 pb, 35949

BAKEWELL, THOMAS (New
York)
1814:   31930 f, 32424 f
1815:   34356 f
1817:   42265 f

Balance (Albany, N. Y.)
1809:   18388, 18672
1810:   20889?, 21169, 21942,
22057
1811:   24367, 24376
1812:   27436

Balance (Hudson, N. Y.)
1801:   594
1802:   1738, 3497
1805:   8619, 8622
1807:   12209, 12801 pb, 12881,
13542
1808:   15169 pb, 50849?

BALCH, --- (Boston)
1819:   47357, 47642, 48237,
48956-48957, 49314, 50168,
51869 pb, 51949 pb

BALCH, J O (Dover, N. H.)
1806:   9986, 50747 pb

BALDWIN, --- (New Haven,
Conn.)
1819:   47701 pb

BALDWIN, CHARLES N (New
York)
1816:   38452 pb, 39861 pb

1817:   39914, 41110 pb, 41165,
41639 pb, 41960 pb, 42005
pb, 42070-42071 pb, 42952
pb
1818:   44403 pb, 45065 pb,
45329, 45516 pb, 45765 pb
1819:   47118, 48211, 48306
pb, 50160 pb, 51923

BALDWIN, DAVID C (Newark,
N. J.)
1804:   7178 pb

BALDWIN, JOSIAH B (Bridgeport, Conn.)
1817:   41427 pb
1819:   48839 f

BALL, JONATHAN (Boston)
1812:   25660 pb
1814:   31722 pb

BALL, JOSIAH (Boston)
1804:   6053, 7282
1805:   8219, 8451, 8480-8481,
8668
1806:   11419
1809:   18546

Ball & Bedlington (Boston)
see BALL, JONATHAN (Bos-
ton)
BEDLINGTON, TIMOTHY
(Boston)

BALLARD, --- (Shelbyville,
Ky.)
1816:   37155

BALLARD, DAVIS C (Boston)
1819:   48329 pb

BALLS, G (Norfolk, Va.)
1817:   40588?
1819:   51865?

BALLS, THOMAS (Norfolk, Va.)
1815:   51496? pb
1817:   40903? pb

Baltimore Evening Post (Baltimore)
1809:   18257

Baltimore Patriot (Baltimore)
1813: 28680?
1817: 41351

Bangor Printing Office (Bangor, Me.)
1814: 33749? bsb
1816: 38953

BANGS, THOMAS G (Boston)
1811: 22141-22142?, 22201,
   22373, 22671, 22708, 23218,
   23988
1812: 25169, 25534, 25717,
   26008, 26029, 26126, 26350,
   26468 pb, 26567, 26678,
   26926 pb, 27612, 27619-
   27620
1813: 27690, 28350 pb, 28561,
   28793, 28847, 28908-28909,
   28911 pb, 29175, 29278,
   29813 pb, 29872, 29874,
   29967 pb, 30393 pb, 30485,
   30552, 30555
1814: 30883, 31484, 31514,
   31578-31579 pb, 31630,
   31674, 31836, 32164, 32861-
   32862, 33521, 33729 pb,
   51352-51353 pb
1815: 34125 pb, 34501, 34513?
   pb, 35072, 35413 pb, 35708,
   35860, 36119 pb
1816: 36706, 36927, 37209,
   38313, 38939 pb, 39902
1817: 40024, 40026, 40785,
   40830, 41166, 41255, 42132-
   42134, 42280-42281, 42308-
   42309, 42326, 42328, 42831,
   42836
1818: 43256, 43360, 43414,
   44680 pb
1819: 47580, 48542 pb

BANKS, DAVID (New York)
1810: 19574 f
1811: 22776 f
1812: 26290 f, 26908 f
1813: 28248 f, 29330 pb,
   30374 f
1814: 31727 f, 33499 f,
   33606 f
1815: 35458 pb, 35470 f,
   35473 pb

1816: 38444 pb, 38450 pb,
   38618 f, 38619 pb
1817: 41327 f
1818: 43390 f, 45056 f, 45074
   pb
1819: 47201, 47688 pb, 48470,
   48554, 48878, 48890, 49501,
   49977 bf

BANKS, GERARD (Fredericksburg, Va.)
1811: 23084 pb

Baptist Missionary Society of
Massachusetts (Boston)
1803: 4614 pb

BARBER, ANN (DAVENPORT)
ROUSMANIERE (Newport,
R.I.)
1802: 3000 f
1804: 5964 pb, 7193 pb
1805: 8577 f, 9257 pb
1806: 9939 pb, 10746, 11026?
   f
1807: 13301, 13321
1808: 16299 f

BARBER, JOHN (Albany, N.Y.)
1801: 60, 198, 714 pb, 1030,
   1032 pb, 1165 pb, 1697
1802: 2194, 2774, 2778-2780,
   2794, 50321 pb
1803: 3615, 3757, 4756-4758,
   4884-4885 pb
1804: 6688, 6911-6912, 6914,
   7081 pb
1805: 8218, 9014-9016, 9166
   pb
1806: 11007-11008, 11010,
   11181 pb
1807: 11956, 12693, 13228-
   13229, 13231, 13242, 13486,
   13614
1808: 14269, 15460, 15749,
   15751-15752, 15754, 15757

BARBER, JOHN (Newcastle,
Del.)
1804: 5720 pb

BARBER, JOHN H (Newport,
R.I.)
1819: 48586

BARBER, JOHN WARNER
(Hartford, Conn.)
1819:   47461 pb

BARBER, JOSEPH (New Haven,
Conn.)
1811:   23931, 23942b pb,
23960
1812:   24978, 25120 pb, 25482-
25483, 25528-25529, 26051,
26078, 26106, 51156, 51224
1813:   28479, 51336
1814:   32122
1815:   33805 pb, 35262, 35272,
36019 pb
1816:   38638, 38942

BARBER, WILLIAM (Newport,
R. I.)
1809:   18435 pb, 18903
1810:   19383, 21126
1811:   23624 f, 23697
1813:   28791 pb, 29491 pb,
29994
1815:   36068, 36112 pb
1816:   38763
1819:   48586

BARBOUR, JAMES (Huntingdon,
Pa.)
1813:   28792 pb
1814:   31776 pb
1818:   44477 pb

BARCLAY, --- (New York)
1814:   32770 pb

BARD, WILLIAM (Bardstown,
Ky.)
1811:   22257, 22258 pb, 23249
1812:   24711 pb, 24748 pb
1815:   33937-33938, 34390

BARLAS, WILLIAM (New York)
1802:   2386 f, 3581 pb, 3596-
3597 f
1804:   7053 sb
1809:   18010 f, 18587 f
1810:   19622 pb
1813:   28719 pb, 30588 f

BARNARD, JOHN (Newbury-
port, Mass.)
1802:   2113
1803:   4732 pb, 5106

BARNARD, WARREN (Whites-
town, N. Y.)
1801:   117

BARNES, JAMES (Chillicothe,
O.)
1808:   15060
1812:   25447 pb
1813:   29011
1814:   31528, 32388-32389,
32563, 32593
1815:   34740, 35528-35529

BARNES, RANDOLPH (Hart-
ford, Conn.)
1819:   47462 pb

BARNES, RANDOLPH (Pitts-
burgh, Pa.)
1818:   43506 f
1819:   47937 pb, 48786 f

BARNES, SAMUEL (Baltimore)
1807:   13203
1808:   15591, 15963 pb
1809:   ?17044, ?17500?
1810:   19414

BARNES, SAMUEL (Fell's
Point, Md.)
1816:   36797 pb

BARNES, SAMUEL (Frederick,
Md.)
1813:   27796, 29537 pb
1817:   42931

BARNES, WILLIAM E (Savan-
nah, Ga.)
1807:   13455 pb

BARNETT, MARQUIS (Bards-
town, Ky.)
1819:   47096 pb

BARNUM, CHARLES PARMER
(Poughkeepsie, N. Y.)
1815:   33961, 34603 pb
1816:   37804
1817:   41239
1819:   49430 pb

BARON, GEORGE (New York)
1804: 5805 f

BARROW, DAVID (Georgetown,
Ky.)
1816: 37261 f

BARTGIS, MATTHIAS (Fred-
erick, Md.)
1801: 334, 408 pb, 808?,
1220 pb, 1574, 1638, 50258
pb
1802: 2425 pb, 3455
1803: 4402, 5496 pb, 50396-
50397 pb
1804: 6281?, 7377, 7655,
50440
1805: 8963 pb, 9651
1806: 11754
1807: 14110 pb
1808: 15956, 16618 pb
1809: 17481, 17764 pb, 17777
pb, 18552, 19091 pb, 19192
1810: 19826, 22000
1812: 26582
1813: 28810 pb, 29152
1819: 47683, 48607 pb, 48802
f

BARTGIS, MATTHIAS E
(Gettysburg, Pa.)
1803: 4274 pb

BARTGIS, MATTHIAS E
(Rockville, Md.)
1807: 13007 pb

BARTGIS, MATTHIAS E
(Winchester, Va.)
1806: 11160 pb, 14107

BARTGIS, MATTHIAS ECHTER-
NACH (Frederick, Md.)
1810: 20197 pb
1811: 24401
1814: 32218

Bartgis's Republican Gazette
(Frederick, Md.)
1809: 18552

BARTOW, ROBERT (New York)
1816: 37351 pb

1817: 40232 f, 41446, 41447
f, 41894 f
1818: 43752 f, 45429 f, 46901
pb
1819: 46947 f, 49198 pb,
49588 f, 50185 f

BARTOW, WILLIAM AUGUSTUS
(New York)
1816: 37351 pb
1817: 40232 f, 41446, 41447
f, 41894 f
1818: 43752 f, 45429 f, 46901
pb
1819: 46947 f, 49198 pb, 49588
f, 50185 f

BARTOW, WILLIAM AUGUSTUS
(Richmond, Va.)
1819: 46947 f, 48993 pb,
49588 f

BARTRAM, ARCHIBALD
(Philadelphia)
1801: 210, 260, 333, 1114
1802: 1732 pb, 1755, 1859,
2452, 2562, 2894
1803: 4147, 4162, 4165, 5527
1804: 6034, 6171-6172, 6220,
6606, 7347, 7683
1805: 8006, 8097, 8225, 9311,
9318, 9325-9326, 9332,
9364, 9697
1806: 9954, 10016, 10044,
10049, 10176, 10222, 10474,
10514-10515, 10598, 10629,
11131, 11135 pb, 11364,
11371, 11477, 50707
1807: 12089, 12092, 12137,
12261, 12309, 12373, 12555,
12845, 12918, 13376 pb,
13479, 13503
1808: 15033, 15240

BASCOM, SAMUEL ASHLEY
(Philadelphia)
1819: 49159 f

BASON, WILLIAM P (Charleston, S. C.)
1818: 43088 pb
1819: 51874 pb

BASSETT, E (New Haven,
  Conn.)
1813: 51336 f

BASSFORD, S (Boston)
1814: 31409 pb

BATES, --- (Springfield,
  Mass.)
1808: 15396 f

BATES, ELISHA (Mount
  Pleasant, O.)
1819: 48052?

BATES, ISAAC (Ballston Spa,
  N. Y.)
1810: 20213, 21013, 21361

BATES, NATHAN (New Bed-
  ford, Mass.)
1808: 15216

BAUMAN, JOSEPH (Ephrata,
  Pa.)
1819: 47637, 47728 pb

BAUMANN, JOHANNES (Ephra-
  ta, Pa.)
1801: 558
1804: 5713 pb, 5953 pb, 6855
  pb, 6954
1805: 9046
1806: 11416 pb
1807: 12295
1808: 14952
1809: 18611

BAXTER, --- (Shippensburg,
  Pa.)
1814: 32958 pb

BAXTER, FRANCIS MARTIN
  (Georgetown, S. C.)
1808: 14335, 14562
1810: 20504, 21177
1811: 24354 pb

BAYARD, JAMES A (New York)
1805: 8304 pb
1807: 12383 pb, 12407 pb
1808: 14379 pb, 14835 f,
  15153 f
1809: 17769 f

BAYARD, JAMES A (Washing-
  ton, Pa.)
1812: 27467 pb

BAYARD, SAMUEL (New York)
1807: 12383 pb

BAZELEY, --- (Philadelphia)
1811: 22311 pb

BEACH, CHARLES ROLLIN
  (Windsor, Vt.)
1808: 15704
1809: 18573

BEACH, CYRUS (Wardsbridge,
  N. Y.)
1806: 11075 pb, 50646 pb

BEACH, LAZARUS (Bridgeport,
  Conn.)
1801: 57, 351 pb, 1319 pb
1803: 3900, 4078
1804: 5965

BEACH, LAZARUS (New York)
1802: 2792 pb, 2945
1803: 5001, 5625?
1807: 13355 pb
1812: 25900
1814: 32121 pb
1815: 35717

BEACH, NATHANIEL (Canan-
  daigua, N. Y.)
1814: 31458 pb
1815: 34681 pb

BEACH, SAMUEL B (Easton,
  Md.)
1809: 18357 pb

Beacon (Norfolk, Va.)
see American Beacon (Nor-
  folk, Va.)

BEALS, EPHRAIM C (Boston)
1807: 12522, 13696, 14123 pb
1808: 14361 pb, 14534 pb,
  14535, 14927, 16612
1809: 17055 pb

BEALS, EPHRAIM C (Exeter,
  N. H.)

1810: 19848 pb, 21458
1811: 23998 pb
1812: 25468, 26826-26827

BEARDSLEE, JAMES (Auburn, N. Y.)
1815: 34233
1816: 39724
1818: 43195, 43603, 45265, 45781

BEASLEY, JOSEPH (Edenton, N. C.)
1803: 4515
1805: 8371 pb
1806: 9902, 10068

BEASLEY, JOSEPH (Elizabeth City, N. C.)
1807: 12496 pb
1808: 14435

BECK, GIDEON (Portsmouth, N. H.)
1813: 28541, 30442 pb
1814: 30717, 30954, 31891
1815: 33913, 35267, 35684, 35948
1816: 37640, 38947
1817: 42988
1818: 43595
1819: 49516-49517

BECK, JOHN (New York)
1810: 20901 pb

BEDFORD, --- (New York)
1809: 18867

BEDLINGTON, TIMOTHY (Boston)
1812: 25660 pb
1814: 31722 pb
1816: 37004 pb
1817: 42281 f
1818: 43256 f, 44047 f
1819: 47991 f, 48237 f, 50171 pb

BEERS, ISAAC (New Haven, Conn.)
1803: 4046 f, 4624-4625 pb
1804: 7722 f
1811: 22424a pb

BELCHER, JOHN H (Boston)
1816: 36677 pb
1818: 43116

BELCHER, JOSHUA (Boston)
1804: 5972? pb
1806: 9823, 9865, 10174, 10216 pb, 10311, 10353 pb, 10355-10356, 10486, 10527-10528, 11191-11192, 11853, 11878, 50637 pb
1807: 11931 pb, 12101, 12134 pb, 12175? pb, 12222 pb, 12459, 12714, 12716, 12930, 13011, 13109-13110 pb, 13548 f, 13575 pb, 13639, 13666, 13684, 13739 pb, 14112, 50809 pb
1808: 14327, 14356-14357, 14671, 14675, 14715, 14760-14762, 14778 pb, 14779, 14904, 15018 pb, 15194, 15255, 15394, 15631, 15657, 15904, 15948, 16303, 16345 pb, 16657, 16734, 16763
1809: 16883-16884 pb, 17065 pb, 17068, 17118, 17160, 17185-17186, 17224, 17418, 17421, 17441 pb, 17468, 17595, 17683?, 17877, 17890, 17968, 18052, 18096, 18369, 18580, 18702, 18767, 18792-18793, 18896 pb, 19140, 19151, 19222
1810: 19917, 20257, 20667-20668, 20675 pb, 20729, 20748, 20749 pb, 20980 pb, 20981, 22041, 22044, 22052 pb
1811: 22162 pb, 22216, 2239(pb, 22395, 22437 pb, 2247 22662, 22969, 23122, 2322 23234, 23305, 23335, 2334 pb, 23357-23358 pb, 23401 23489, 23619 pb, 23623 pb, 23624, 23892, 24351 pb, 24437
1812: 25061, 25115, 25204, 25312, 25330 pb, 25435, 25479 pb, 25507, 25822, 25890-25891, 26041 pb, 26043-26044 pb, 26092, 26113, 26114 pb, 26156 pb, 26371 pb, 26376, 26594-

26595, 26715, 26801, 26864, 27558
1813: 27647, 27783, 27919, 28178, 28198a pb, 28236, 28438-28439, 28517 pb, 28545, 28703, 28704-28705 pb, 29075, 29104, 29188, 29435, 29660 pb, 29693, 29885, 29895 pb, 29972
1814: 30716, 30953, 31515, 31554, 31753, 31896, 32075, 32087, 32088 pb, 32374 pb, 32420, 32684, 32728 pb, 32795

BELDEN, EBENEZER (New York)
1802: 2772, 3520

BELDEN, JOHN (New York)
1815: 34378 f

BELEURGEY, CLAUDIUS (Charleston, S. C.)
1803: 5181

BELEURGEY, CLAUDIUS (New Orleans, La.)
1803: 4548, 5145 pb
1804: 5885, 6261, 7539

BELL, JARED W (New York)
1819: 48916 pb

BELL, NATHANIEL (New York)
1801: 205 sb, 289 pb, 784 f

BELL, WILLIAM DUFFIELD (Baltimore)
1814: 30801 bf, 32553, 33635a-33637

BELL, WILLIAM DUFFIELD (Hagerstown, Md.)
1815: 34323, 34789
1818: 43579, 45579, 45743 pb, 46753 pb
1819: 47566, 49318 pb

BELLAMY, EDWARD S (New York)
1819: 47168

BELLAMY, ELISHA (Boston)
1817: 42061 pb
1818: 43144, 43147, 44047
1819: 48008 pb, 49556 pb, 49649, 50050

BEMIS, JAMES DRAPER (Canandaigua, N. Y.)
1805: 7931
1808: 15922 pb
1809: 16886, 17484, 18288 pb
1810: 19471 pb
1811: 22794, 22806, 22885, 23482 pb
1812: 24540, 25673, 26462 pb, 51195 pb
1813: 28491 pb, 30450
1814: 31122, 31231 pb, 31458 pb, 31915, 32534 pb
1815: 34681 pb
1816: 36776, 37566 pb, 38526, 51603 sb
1817: 40801 pb, 40948
1818: 43257, 44001 pb, 44005 pb, 44843, 45166-45168, 51770 pb
1819: 47565, 47953 pb, 48799, 48932

BENDER, HASTINGS R (Homer, N. Y.)
1812: 25401 f

BENJAMIN, EDWIN (Towanda, Pa.)
1818: 45690 pb

BENJAMIN, JOSEPH (Ithaca, N. Y.)
1816: 37935 pb

BENNETT, ABRAHAM H (Penn Yan, N. Y.)
1818: 45232 pb

BENNETT, TITUS (Philadelphia)
1806: 10650 f, 50689 pb, 50724 pb
1807: 12103 pb, 13055 f, 13511 pb, 50784 pb
1808: 14479 pb, 15822 pb, 16280 pb, 50859 f

1809:   17795 f, 17844 pb
1810:   19317 f, 19504 f, 19505
   pb, 20835 pb
1811:   22630 f, 22743 f, 22746
   pb, 22798 f, 23123 pb,
   23267 pb, 23461 f, 24355
   pb, 24358 pb, 51061-51062
   pb
1812:   24807 f, 24808 pb,
   25872 pb, 26174 pb, 26178
   pb, 26403 pb
1813:   27651 f, 27653 f, 27876
   pb, 29245 pb, 51319 f
1814:   30849 pb, 31716 f,
   32193 pb, 32200 pb, 32664
   pb
1815:   34044 f, 34505 pb,
   34982 f, 35383 pb, 35819
   pb, 51464 f
1816:   36931-36932 pb, 38335
   pb
1817:   41319 f, 51645 pb
1818:   43281-43282 pb, 45560
   pb
1819:   47199-47200 pb, 49308
   f, 51919 pb

BENNIS, THOMAS (Philadelphia)
1806:   11847 f
1809:   19202 f

BENSON, R (Philadelphia)
1808:   15252 pb

Berean Society (Boston)
1802:   1865 f
1804:   5839 f

Berkshire Star (Stockbridge,
   Mass.)
1816:   37073, 37902

BERNHART, PETER (Harrisonburg, Va.)
1816:   38877 pb

BERRY, ELIJAH CONWAY
   (Frankfort, Ky.)
1813:   28866 pb, 28870-28871
1814:   31856-31858, 32361 pb
1815:   34297 pb, 34537, 35048-
   35050, 36098
1816:   37469, 37953 pb, 37989-
   37991, 38069

BERRY, ELIJAH CONWAY
   (Kaskaskia, Ill.)
1818:   44414-44420, 44422 pb
1819:   48321-48323

BERRY, ELIJAH CONWAY
   (Louisville, Ky.)
1803:   50354

BERRY, JOHN (Beavertown,
   Pa.)
1807:   13091 pb

BERRY, JOHN (Brownsville,
   Pa.)
1809:   17094 pb

BERRY, JOHN (St. Clairsville,
   O.)
1813:   29405
1815:   35189, 35590, 36537

BERRY, JOHN (Wellsburgh,
   Va.)
1816:   39781 pb
1817:   40515, 40677

BERTRAND, PETER (Pleasant
   Hill, Ky.)
1818:   43894

BERTRAND, PETER (Rich-
   mond, Ky.)
1815:   33934

BETTIS, WILLIAM J (Concord,
   Mass.)
1816:   38248 pb

Bible and Heart (Baltimore)
1806:   10019

Bible Office (Windsor, Vt.)
1812:   26655

Bible Society of Maine (Portland, Me.)
1809:   18358 pb
1813:   27891 f

Bible Society of Philadelphia
   (Philadelphia)
1812:   24835 f, 24863 pb

1813: 29169 pb
1816: 36968 f

Bible Warehouse (Boston)
1819: 50172

BICKLEY, HENRY (Philadel-
phia)
1813: 30431 pb

BICKLEY, JOHN (Lexington,
Ky.)
1813: 28812

BIGELOW, --- (Cambridge,
Mass.)
1807: 12724 f

BIGLOW, H (New York)
1817: 39983 pb

BIGNELL, JOHN (New York)
1807: 12900 f

BILL, GURDON (Norwich,
Conn.)
1815: 36139 f

BILL, JAMES (Catskill, N. Y.)
1813: 28666 f

BILLINGS, ELIJAH (New Bedford, Mass.)
1808: 15797 pb
1809: 17623, 18134
1810: 19801

BILLINGS, GEORGE (Boston)
1818: 44573 pb

BILLINGS, JOHN (Northamp-
ton, Mass.)
1802: 3532 f

BILLMEYER, ANDREW (York,
Pa.)
1801: 1, 1591
1802: 3483
1803: 4273
1805: 9312

BILLMEYER, DAVID (Phila-
delphia)

For all entries see BILLMEY-
ER, GEORGE (Philadelphia)
below

BILLMEYER, GEORGE (Phila-
delphia)
1814: 31105, 31425 pb, 31426-
31427, 31686 pb, 31735,
31970, 32226 pb, 32708
1815: 34075, 34101 pb, 34927-
34928 pb, 35149 pb
1816: 37198 pb, 37239 pb,
37537-37538, 37852 pb
1817: 40208 pb, 40774 pb,
41030, 41063 pb, 41207
1818: 43551, 43969, 44299 pb,
44349 pb

BILLMEYER, MICHAEL (Ger-
mantown, Pa.)
1801: 50226 pb
1802: 50276, 50300 pb
1803: 3794 pb, 4171-4172,
4360, 4485 pb, 5016 pb,
50367 pb
1804: 6465 pb, 6485 pb, 6676
1805: 8405-8406, 8602, 8629
pb, 8807, 9320 pb, 50551
pb
1806: 10373?, 10468, 10567,
11261, 11330
1807: 12131 pb, 12765 pb,
13177, 13473
1808: 14489 pb, 50856 pb
1809: 17763 pb
1810: 19519 pb, 20352 pb,
22077
1811: 22378 pb, 22785, 23165,
51101 pb
1812: 25351, 25360 pb, 25580,
25625 pb, 51208 pb
1813: 28759 pb, 28887, 29632
1819: 47219, 48248-48250 pb

BINGHAM, CALEB (Boston)
1801: 670 f, 1433 f
1802: 1855 pb, 1900 f, 1937 f,
2015 f, 2460 pb, 2500 f,
3175 f
1803: 3827 f, 3830-3831 f,
3833, 4141 f, 4533 f, 5078 f
1804: 5861 f, 5957 f, 6546 f,
6664 f

1805:   8029 f
1807:   12153 f
1808:   15388 f
1810:   19560 f, 50980 pb
1813:   27949 f
1814:   31134 f, 31774 f
1815:   34121 pb, 34124 f,
    34128 pb
1817:   40251 pb, 40785 f,
    41543 pb
1818:   43360 f, 44066 f, 45637
    pb
1819:   47357 f, 47359 f

BINNS, JOHN (Northumber-
    land, Pa.)
1802:   2977 pb
1804:   7119
1805:   9195
1806:   11214-11215

BINNS, JOHN (Philadelphia)
1807:   12428 pb
1808:   14287, 14972
1809:   17089, 17292, 18379,
    19086
1810:   19346, 19397, 20619,
    21089
1811:   22175, 22220, 23808,
    24071 pb, 24075, 51083
1812:   25104, 25254-25255,
    25715, 26415 pb, 26427 pb,
    26593
1813:   27764, 28085, 29479 pb,
    29969, 51341
1817:   40139, 40647, 41349
1818:   44448

BIOREN, JOHN (Philadelphia)
1801:   25, 238, 294, 498 pb,
    706, 822 f, 886, 1095,
    1176 pb, 1188, 1211, 1261,
    1304 pb, 1313-1314 pb,
    1408, 1592, 50252 pb
1802:   2147 pb, 2251, 2318,
    2375 f, 2483, 2850, 2852
    pb, 2921 pb, 2922, 2981,
    3033, 3185, 50323 pb
1803:   4047, 4374, 4700,
    4837 pb, 4842 bf, 4899 pb,
    5028 pb, 50335 pb, 50376
1804:   5690, 5700 pb, 5923 pb,
    6125 pb, 6452 pb, 6565,

    7002 pb, 7003, 7097 pb,
    7102, 7305 pb, 50407 pb,
    50466-50467 pb
1805:   7977 pb, 8136, 8334 pb,
    9132 pb, 9184-9185 pb,
    9272 pb, 9713, 50494 pb,
    50556, 50599 pb
1806:   9999 pb, 10286, 10650,
    11121, 11128, 11201, 11242,
    11843, 50639 pb, 50680 pb,
    50708 pb, 50719 pb
1807:   12155 pb, 12527, 13334,
    13440, 50754 pb, 50799 pb
1808:   14525-14526 pb, 14669
    pb, 14832, 15351, 15427,
    15742, 15868-15869, 15873-
    15874, 15877-15878, 15893
    pb, 16159 pb, 50822, 50850
1809:   17021, 17047-17048 pb,
    17387 pb, 17714 pb, 18184
    pb, 18332, 18453, 50907,
    50917 pb
1810:   19348 pb, 19508 pb,
    19569 pb, 20118, 20417,
    21016-21017, 21026, 50981-
    50982 pb
1811:   22213, 22405, 22406 pb,
    22662a pb, 23652, 23824 f,
    23898 pb, 51116
1812:   24878-24879 pb, 25270
    pb, 25429 pb, 25530, 25604
    pb, 26259, 26406, 26408 pb,
    26410, 26414 pb, 26634 f,
    26637-26638 f, 51164 pb
1813:   27878 pb, 27953-27954
    pb, 28692 pb, 28693, 29470,
    29484 pb, 29666?, 29803,
    29861, 29963 pb, 51274 pb
1814:   31065, 31202, 31300 pb,
    31803 pb, 31946, 32462 pb,
    32465-32466, 32471f, 32732
    pb, 32745, 33599 pb, 33663
    pb, 51363-51365 pb
1815:   34130-34131 pb, 34904,
    35244, 35825 pb, 36275 pb,
    51466 pb, 51469-51472 pb
1816:   36733 pb, 36790, 36806
    pb, 37012 pb, 37388, 37518
    pb, 37861, 38279, 38283,
    38593, 38623, 39486 pb,
    51554-51556 pb
1817:   40254-40255 pb, 40438
    f, 40759 pb, 40762 pb,

41072, 41762 pb, 41900 pb,
41901, 42311, 51646 pb
1818: 43341 pb, 43369-43370
pb, 43737 f, 44227, 44229,
44282 pb, 44483, 44689,
44799, 45234, 45260, 45919,
51734 pb, 51743 pb
1819: 47205 pb, 47363-47364
pb, 47833 pb, 47929, 49660,
51861-51862 pb

BIRCH, GEORGE L (New York)
1818: 43047, 43400, 44121,
46888
1819: 48877, 48879 pb, 48880,
49550, 49610, 49616, 51922

BIRCH, WILLIAM YOUNG
(Philadelphia)
1802: 1278-1279 f
1802: 1905 f, 3033 f
1803: 3837 f, 5592 f
1804: 6381 f
1805: 8518 f, 8521 f
1806: 11386 f
1807: 11978? pb, 12742 f,
13046 f
1808: 15037 f, 16100 f, 16128-
16129 f, 50822 f, 50850 f
1809: 18647 f, 50907 pb
1810: 19658 pb, 20113 f,
20974 f
1811: 22188 f, 22498 f, 22620
f, 23849 f, 51049 pb, 51091
pb
1812: 25165 pb, 26768 f,
51157 pb, 51197 pb
1813: 28613 pb, 51265 pb

BIRD, JAMES (Warren, R. I.)
1812: 25119 pb, 26530

BISBEE, NOAH (Newport, R. I.)
1806: 11025?

BISHOP, SAMUEL (Alexandria,
Va.)
1802: 2649 f
1803: 4328 f

BISSELL, FITCH (Warren, O.)
1816: 38510, 39790 pb

BITTERS, CHARLES (Philadelphia)
1808: 50841 pb

BLACK, DUNCAN (Fayetteville,
N. C.)
1805: 9037 pb
1809: 17494 pb
1818: 45910 pb
1819: 49650

BLACK, F (Philadelphia)
1808: 14578 pb

BLACK, JOHN (New York)
1802: 2905 pb

BLACK, WILLIAM (Dover, Del.)
1801: 396-400
1802: 2040, 2127-2129, 2216
pb, 2688
1803: 4063-4064, 50356

BLACK, WILLIAM (Wilmington,
Del.)
1803: 4188 pb, 4981
1804: 6145, 6529

BLACKBURN, GIDEON (Knox-
ville, Tenn.)
1818: 43082 f

BLACKBURN, WILLIAM (Leb-
anon, O.)
1813: 29193 pb, 29755
1814: 32157
1816: 38901?

BLACKBURN, WILLIAM (Ur-
bana, O.)
1812: 25402 pb

BLACKMAN, NATHAN (Eden-
town, Pa.)
1814: 31390 pb
1815: 36564

BLACKMAN, NATHAN (Rus-
sellville, Pa.)
1816: 36742 pb

BLACKWELL, LEWIS (Trenton,
N. J.)

1802: 2339, 2494, 2938, 3074, 3570 pb
1803: 3930, 4067, 4304 pb, 4446, 4744 pb, 4745, 4747-4748 pb, 5602 pb
1804: 6893, 6898-6899, 6901 pb

BLACKWELL, ROBERT (Kaskaskia, Ill.)
1817: 41123-41126
1818: 44414-44420, 44422 pb
1819: 48321-48323

BLAGROVE, CHARLES (Richmond, Va.)
1812: 26786

BLAGROVE, WILLIAM (Boston)
1807: 12855 pb
1808: 14535 f
1810: 21547 f

BLAKE, BILL (Bellows Falls, Vt.)
1817: 40634, 41090 pb, 41180, 41219 pb, 42783 pb
1818: 43245, 43587?, 44034, 44535 pb, 46622, 46907 pb
1819: 48392, 48448 pb, 49153 pb, 50140

BLAKE, BILL (Walpole, N.H.)
1808: 15376 pb

BLAKE, EBENEZER (Boston)
1808: 15631 f

BLAKE, GEORGE E (Philadelphia)
1804: 50418? pb
1805: 8041 pb, 8215 f, 8937 f, 9249 f, 9456-9457 pb
1806: 10030 pb
1807: 12686? pb, 50761-50762? pb
1808: 14449 f, 14451 f, 15351 f
1809: 18060? pb
1810: 19396 pb, 19575 pb, 19730? pb, 20022? pb, 21464-21465? pb, 50983-50984? pb, 51017? pb,

51039? pb
1813: 28453 pb
1814: 51442 pb
1815: 36021? pb, 51513? pb, 51522? pb
1816: 38144? pb
1817: 51650? pb
1818: 51753 pb, 51792? pb, 51821-51822? pb
1819: 51898? pb

BLAKE, LEMUEL (Boston)
1801: 1433 f
1802: 1855 pb, 2028 f, 2051 pb, 2482 f, 3175 f
1803: 3688 pb, 4300 f, 4533 f, 5585 pb
1804: 5864 pb, 6470, 6563 pb, 6578-6579 f, 7714 pb
1807: 12166 pb, 12184 f
1808: 14481 pb, 16678 pb
1809: 17249? pb, 18428 f
1810: 19704 pb, 20455 pb, 21304 f
1811: 22146 pb
1812: 24793-24794 f, 24821 f, 26781 f, 26912 pb, 27433 f
1813: 27909 pb, 28728 pb
1814: 30622-30623 pb, 31051 f, 31054 f

BLAKE, WILLIAM P (Boston)
1801: 1433 f
1802: 1855 pb, 2028 f, 2051 pb, 2482 f, 3175 f
1803: 3688 pb, 4300 f, 4533 f, 5585 pb
1804: 5864 pb, 6470, 6563 pb, 6578-6579 f, 7714 pb

BLAKESLEE, LEVI (New Berlin, N.Y.)
1819: 51933 pb

Blandford Press (Petersburg, Va.)
1801: 71, 725 pb
1802: 1764

BLAUVELT, ABRAHAM (New Brunswick, N.J.)
1801: 145, 290 pb, 314, 503, 1019 pb, 1097, 50202

1802: 2055, 2088, 2768 pb, 2969 pb, 3552, 50275, 50310 pb
1803: 4343, 4569, 4935, 50378 pb
1804: 5865 pb, 6854 pb, 7133, 50482 pb
1805: 8960 pb, 9214 pb
1806: 10107, 10153 pb, 10940 pb, 11223, 11746
1807: 12030, 13171 pb, 13432, 13447 pb, 13457
1808: 15731, 16017-16018, 16637
1809: 18463 pb
1810: 20579, 20876, 21252, 21884 pb
1811: 24369, 24426
1812: 25874, 27473
1813: 28726, 29046
1814: 31082
1816: 39726 pb

BLAUVELT, THOMAS T
(Hackensack, N.J.)
1804: 6531 pb

BLEDSOE, MOSES OWSLEY
(Frankfort, Ky.)
1809: 17863
1817: 40534 pb
1818: 44592
1819: 47074

BLEEKER, JOHN (New York)
1805: 9424 f, 9632 f
1808: 14379 pb

BLISS, --- (Utica, N.Y.)
1803: 3773 pb

BLISS, CHARLES (Springfield, Mass.)
1804: 6215
1805: 8366?

BLISS, DAVID (New York)
1806: 9918 pb, 10726 f
1817: 41093-41094 f
1818: 44357 f

BLISS, ELAM (Boston)
1806: 9956 f, 10121 f, 10562 f

1807: 11994 pb, 12446 pb, 12803 f, 12880 pb, 13556-13557 pb, 13686 pb, 13724 f, 13751 pb, 50752 pb
1808: 14388 f, 14504 pb, 14531 pb, 14607 f, 15258 pb, 15260 pb, 15386-15387 f, 15389 pb, 15548 f, 15950 pb, 15977 pb, 16142 pb, 16168 pb, 16677 pb
1809: 16996 f, 17096 pb, 17117 pb, 17251 pb, 17298 pb, 17400 pb, 17503 pb, 17606 pb, 17642 pb, 17840 pb, 17886 pb, 18487 pb
1810: 21468 pb
1812: 27592 pb

BLISS, ELAM (Charlestown, Mass.)
1809: 17199, 17251 pb, 17336, 19152

BLISS, ELAM (New York)
1819: 47934 f, 49376-49377 f

BLISS, LUTHER (Lansingburgh, N.Y.)
1804: 7109 sb
1805: 8743 pb
1806: 10368 f, 11017 pb, 11879
1807: 13217 pb, 13236 pb
1808: 14441, 15680 pb, 16339
1809: 16820 f, 16937, 18241 pb
1810: 19457, 20850, 20898 pb
1811: 22277, 23553 pb
1812: 26676
1813: 27819, 28934, 29244 pb, 29547
1814: 30788, 51451 pb
1815: 35367 pb
1816: 36855, 38384, 51603 sb
1817: 40120, 51728 pb
1819: 47673 f

BLISS, PELLATIAH (Troy, N.Y.)
1807: 12130 pb, 12152 pb, 13315 pb, 50760 pb
1808: 14518, 14522 bf
1809: 16790 pb, 16820, 17038

pb, 17039, 19241 pb
1810: 19333, 19559, 19654,
  20180 pb, 20802 pb, 21949
1811: 22147 pb, 22402 pb,
  22979 pb, 24371, 24456 pb,
  51082 pb
1812: 24553, 24884, 24902,
  24952, 26915 pb, 27455,
  27635
1813: 27948, 29224 pb
1814: 30620, 32177 pb
1815: 34127 pb, 34151, 34576,
  34963 pb, 35385 pb, 36414
1816: 37007, 38294 pb, 39119,
  51603 sb
1817: 51729 pb
1818: 44285, 44632
1819: 47198

BLOCQUERST, ANDREW J
  (Philadelphia)
1811: 22516, 22870, 23577 pb
1812: 24514 pb, 24595 pb,
  26570
1814: 32980 pb
1815: 33764, 35178 pb

BLODGETT, BENJAMIN (Bata-
  via, N.Y.)
1809: 17306 pb
1811: 23801 pb
1819: 48272 pb

BLUNT, EDMUND MARCH
  (New York)
1810: 19402, 19785 pb, 20831
  pb, 21329
1811: 22446 pb, 23485 pb,
  23622 pb
1812: 24893 pb, 25486
1813: 27969 pb
1815: 33842 pb, 34156 pb,
  35394 pb
1816: 37031 pb
1817: 40276 pb, 40278 pb,
  40296 pb
1818: 44966 f
1819: 48823 pb

BLUNT, EDMUND MARCH
  (Newburyport, Mass.)
1801: 765, 925, 969, 1603
1802: 1936-1937, 3107, 3553,

50279-50281
1803: 3766, 4041, 4350, 4484,
  4599, 4643-4644, 5530,
  5550, 5593 pb, 5599
1804: 5896 pb, 6089, 6112,
  6114, 6344, 6361 pb, 6925,
  7058, 7300, 7689, 50481 pb
1805: 8286, 8798, 9413, 9725-
  9727
1806: 9786 pb, 9813, 9833,
  10022, 10100-10101, 10248,
  10250, 10462, 10620, 11788,
  50745
1807: 12190, 13028, 13629
1808: 14359, 14380, 15658 pb,
  16260
1809: 16836 pb, 17060, 17115,
  17772, 18070

BLYTH, STEPHEN C (Salem,
  Mass.)
1807: 12623 pb

BOARDMAN, JOHN (Huntsville,
  Ala.)
1818: 43041 pb
1819: 46950-46951

BOARDMAN, NATHANIEL
  (Exeter, N.H.)
1813: 51348 pb
1814: 33619
1817: 41234 f
1818: 44549 f
1819: 47018 f, 48463 f

BOATE, THOMAS (Philadelphia)
1807: 12589 pb

BOE, H (Auburn, N.Y.)
1812: 24655

BOE, J (Auburn, N.Y.)
1812: 24655

BOGAN, BENJAMIN LEWIS
  (Alexandria, Va.)
1816: 37718
1817: 42798, 42924

BOGAN, BENJAMIN LEWIS
  (Woodstock, Va.)
1817: 42950 pb
1818: 44176

BOGERT, JAMES (Geneva,
N. Y.)
1806:   10380 pb
1809:   17607 pb
1811:   23086, 23546 pb
1812:   25505, 51195 pb
1814:   51451 pb
1815:   34771
1816:   39088, 51583 f, 51603
  sb
1817:   40333 pb, 41140 pb
1818:   43619
1819:   47234 pb, 49307, 50065
  pb

BOGERT, WILLIAM (Geneva,
N. Y.)
1815:   34771
1816:   39088, 51583 f

BOGGS, JOHN (Wilmington,
Del.)
1801:   1601 f
1803:   4280 f

BOILEAU, --- (Philadelphia)
1812:   24927 pb
1813:   29667 pb

BOLLES, FREDERICK D (Hartford, Conn.)
1817:   40069, 41664 pb, 41978,
  41992 pb, 42292 pb
1818:   43168, 43704, 43706?,
  43719, 46675, 46803
1819:   47713, 49129 pb

BOLLES, JAMES G (Boston)
1803:   5020

BOLTON, AQUILA M (Wheel-
ing, W. Va.)
1807:   12806 f

BONSAL, CALEB (Norfolk,
Va.)
1803:   3618, 3622 f, 3653 f,
  4091 f, 4387 pb, 4528 f
1804:   5824 f, 5897 pb, 6068
  pb

BONSAL, ISAAC (Baltimore)
1807:   12086 pb, 12750 f,

12857 f
1808:   15612 f

BONSAL, VINCENT (Baltimore)
1801:   103 pb, 288? pb, 313
  pb, 469 sb, 819, 880 pb,
  951, 1180 pb, 50199 pb
1802:   1922 pb, 50278 pb
1803:   3854 pb, 3966 pb, 4677
  pb, 4815 f, 4941 pb
1804:   6122 bf

BONSAL, VINCENT (Wilming-
ton, Del.)
1801:   401, 413 pb, 469 pb,
  884, 1432 pb, 1601, 50200
  pb
1802:   1792, 1923 pb, 2385 pb,
  2467 pb, 2577, 2657 pb,
  3352 pb, 3518 pb, 50331 pb
1803:   3855 pb, 3927 pb, 4065,
  4280, 4395 pb, 4429 pb,
  4904 pb, 4931-4933, 5594,
  5600, 5601 pb
1804:   5855 pb, 5961 pb, 6124
  pb, 6147, 6264 pb, 6870 pb,
  7379, 7731, 7778 pb
1805:   9473
1807:   12523 pb

Bonsal & Niles (Baltimore)
see BONSAL, VINCENT
  (Baltimore)
    NILES, HEZEKIAH (Balti-
    more)

Bonsal, Conrad & Co. (Norfolk, Va.)
see BONSAL, CALEB (Nor-
  folk, Va.)
    CONRAD, MICHAEL (Nor-
    folk, Va.)
    CONRAD, JOHN (Norfolk,
    Va.)

BONTECOU, DANIEL (Spring-
  field, Mass.)
1813:   30446 f

Book Printing Office (Boston)
1808:   16737 pb

Book Society of the Protestant
Episcopal Church in Mary-
land (Annapolis, Md.)
1816: 38521-38522 f, 38524 f
1818: 45717 f

Book Society of the Protestant
Episcopal Church in Mary-
land (Baltimore)
1811: 22538 f, 22550 f, 22706
f, 23209 f, 24051 f
1816: 38903 f

BOOKER, ARTHUR G (Rich-
mond, Va.)
1815: 35957, 51479-51480

Bookstore and Printing Office
(Boston)
1803: 4283 pb

BOOTH, BEEBE (Salem, Ind.)
1818: 44461, 44583, 45877 pb

Boston Bookstore (Boston)
1802: 2028
1810: 19470 bsb
1811: 24028 pb

Boston Chronicle (Boston)
1805: 8388
1806: 11323
1817: 42833

Boston Commercial Gazette
(Boston)
1802: 3178

Boston Daily Advertiser (Boston)
1813: 29898
1818: 45818

Boston Gazette (Boston)
1809: 18902
1812: 25928 pb, 25934 pb
1815: 33788, 36110 pb

Boston Intelligencer (Boston)
1819: 49539

Boston Patriot (Boston)
1813: 28767 pb
1814: 31438
1815: 35791

Boston Recorder (Boston)
1818: 44401

Boston Sabbath Society for the
Moral and Religious Instruction of the Poor (Boston)
1818: 43964 f
1819: 46926 pb

Boston Society for the Religious
and Moral Improvement of
Seamen (Boston)
1813: 27671 f
1815: 35692 f

Boston Weekly Magazine (Boston)
1803: 3700, 5125-5126

BOUNETHEAU, GABRIEL
MANIGAULT (Charleston,
S.C.)
1804: 5925 pb
1805: 8100 pb, 8139, 8475,
8684
1806: 10444
1807: 12194-12195, 12284,
12530 pb, 12617, 12834,
13620
1808: 14563, 15067, 15243,
16213
1809: 17983, 18395
1810: 20160, 20281, 21276
1812: 25753, 27604
1813: 28522, 51279 pb
1815: 34731

BOURNE, GEORGE (Baltimore)
1808: 14615 pb
1810: 19416

BOURNE, GEORGE (Harrison-
burg, Va.)
1813: 28029, 29050 pb, 29665
pb, 30428 pb
1814: 31150 pb, 32651 pb,
33562 pb
1815: 35968 pb

BOUVIER, JOHN (Brownsville,
Pa.)
1814: 30682 pb

BOUVIER, JOHN (Philadelphia)
1807: 12975
1808: 15331, 15891a, 50859
1809: 16837, 17177, 17401,
    17402 pb, 18062, 18607,
    18733
1810: 19466, 19504, 19731,
    19857, 19892, 19912, 19984,
    19992, 20031, 20116, 20586,
    21071, 21073, 21075-21076,
    21078, 21082 pb, 21451,
    21912, 21928
1811: 22487, 22717, 22743,
    22798, 23392, 23868, 23934,
    23939, 24324 pb
1812: 24807, 25592, 26451,
    27481
1813: 28038, 28646, 29975-
    29976
1814: 30882, 32200
1815: 36124

BOWELL, ABNER F (Fayette-
    ville, N. C.)
1813: 27703 pb
1814: 30772

BOWEN, ABEL (Boston)
1813: 29393 pb
1814: 31846
1815: 35548
1816: 37062 pb

BOWEN, DANIEL (Boston)
1802: 2172
1810: 20960
1815: 35548

BOWEN, DANIEL (Brighton,
    Mass.)
1811: 22838

BOWEN, HENRY (Boston)
1817: 41450 pb
1818: 43140-43143 pb, 43145-
    43146 pb
1819: 47053-47062 pb, 47857,
    49005, 49433 pb

BOWEN, JOSIAH (Brooklyn,
    N. Y.)
1813: 27844, 28516, 28655-
    28656, 29008-29009, 29184,

29487, 29671-29672, 29786-
    29787, 29833, 30497
1814: 31052, 31335, 31445,
    31757 pb, 31940 pb, 32156,
    32765

BOWEN, RICHARD (Winchester,
    Va.)
1807: 13117

BOWEN, THOMAS BARTHOLO-
    MEW (Charleston, S. C.)
1801: 354, 378, 750, 1071
1802: 2065, 2164, 2271
1803: 4040?, 4108, 4315
1804: 6290

BOWERS, ISAAC (Boston)
1817: 40620 pb, 41096 pb,
    41244 pb

BOWLES, LEONARD C (Boston)
1819: 47477 pb

BOWLES, LUCIUS QUINTUS
    CINCINNATUS (Montpelier,
    Vt.)
1813: 28039 f, 29069 f, 29741
    f
1814: 30625 pb, 30893 f,
    33610 f
1816: 37336 f, 39666 f, 39749
    pb
1817: 39919 f

BOWLES, SAMUEL (Hartford,
    Conn.)
1818: 43505-43506

BOWMAN, ABRAHAM (Lan-
    caster, Pa.)
1804: 7014 pb

BOWMAN, ABRAHAM (Phila-
    delphia)
1804: 6219, 7382
1816: 38073-38074, 38572
1817: 40485, 41747 pb

BOWMAN, ABRAHAM (Stras-
    burg, Pa.)
1803: 4222 pb, 4783

BOWMAN, GODFREY (Pough-
keepsie, N. Y.)
1806: 9951, 10205, 11424 pb,
50646 pb
1807: 12099 pb, 13615
1808: 14470 pb, 15682 pb,
15932

BOYCE, JOSEPH (Lynchburg,
Va.)
1819: 47147, 47154

BOYLAN, ABRAHAM H (Ra-
leigh, N. C.)
1811: ?22860, 51114 pb
1812: 25463
1813: 28572

BOYLAN, WILLIAM (Halifax,
N. C.)
1805: 8698

BOYLAN, WILLIAM (Raleigh,
N. C.)
1801: 1664 pb
1803: 4238, 4657 pb
1804: 6337, 7335
1805: 8473, 9029, 50505 pb
1806: 10027 pb, 10037,
11039, 11210
1807: 12613 pb, 50763 pb
1808: 14569, 15057-15058,
15211, 15936 pb
1809: 18514, 50919 pb
1810: 19167, 20153, 20191
1816: 37820 pb

BOYLAN, WILLIAM (Wilming-
ton, N. C.)
1802: 1986 pb

BOYLE, EGLENTONE M (New
York)
1806: 11425 pb
1811: 24003? pb

BOYLE, JOHN (Boston)
1802: 2482 f

BOYLE, P (New Jersey)
1815: 34380 f

BOYLE, T (New York)
1815: 34379 pb

BOYLSTON, RICHARD (Am-
herst, N. H.)
1809: 17188, 17713
1810: 20122, 20131, 20768,
21003
1811: 22269, 22301, 22325,
22843
1812: 24556, 24994, 26122-
26123, 27595, 27606
1813: 28005 pb, 29862
1814: 31368, 32898
1815: 34251, 35305-35306,
35308-35309, 35564, 36610
1816: 37242, 37557, 37647 pb,
37835, 38125, ?38225
1817: 40162, 40861 pb, 40862
1818: 43191, 44187, 44315-
44318, 44884, 46684
1819: 47470-47471, 48024,
48735, 48761, 49479

BRADFORD, ALDEN (Boston)
1811: 22695 f
1812: 24744 pb, 24921 pb,
24983 f, 25063 f, 25169 f,
25193 f, 25199 pb, 25853 f,
26182 f, 26185-26186 f,
26349-26350 f, 26467 f,
27609 pb, 27612 f, 27620 f,
51166 pb
1813: 27869 pb, 27976 pb,
28004 pb, 28327 pb, 28656
f, 28784 pb, 28847 f, 29205
f, 29418 f, 29487 f, 29719
pb, 29749-29750 f, 29975 f,
30515 pb, 51272 pb
1814: 31554 f, 31846 f, 32797
pb, 32798 f, 33696 pb
1815: 34618 pb, 34711 f,
34759 f, 36124 f, 36592 pb,
51489 pb
1816: 37124 pb

BRADFORD, BENJAMIN J
(Nashville, Tenn.)
1801: 1395 pb
1802: 3151 pb
1808: 14698 pb, 50834 pb
1812: 26193 pb

BRADFORD, CHARLES (Lexington, Ky.)
1808: 14453 pb, 15368, 16073

1809: 17049, 17143, 17511
  pb, 17867, 17912

BRADFORD, DANIEL (Lexing-
  ton, Ky.)
1802: 1815-1816 pb, 2262
1803: 3727 pb, 3730 pb,
  3884?, 4027, 4231-4232,
  4578, 4637 pb
1804: 5777 pb, 5882-5883,
  5977, 6213, 6330, 6423,
  6648, 6692-6693, 7112 pb,
  50475
1805: 8131, 8466-8467, 9056,
  9258
1806: 9846, 10083, 10084 pb,
  10438, 11432?, 11886
1807: 12045 pb, 12342, 12510-
  12512, 12606, 12863, 13579
1808: 14453 pb, 15051-15053,
  15368, 16073
1809: 17049, 17143, 17511
  pb, ?17542 pb, 17543,
  17867, 17912
1819: 48016

BRADFORD, FIELDING (Lex-
  ington, Ky.)
1814: 31519
1815: 34733, 35101 pb
1816: 37655, 37994, 38675,
  38895, 38954-38955
1817: 41257-41258

BRADFORD, JAMES MORGAN
  (Frankfort, Ky.)
1802: 1972, 2484
1803: 4157, 4584, 4781, 5175
  pb
1804: 6946 pb

BRADFORD, JAMES MORGAN
  (New Orleans, La.)
1804: 6968 pb
1805: 9068 f, 9069, 9072-
  9073
1806: 10674, 11077-11078,
  11502, 11798
1807: 12910, 13296-13298,
  13741, 13789, 14157, 14243
1808: 15442, 15484, 15813-
  15814

BRADFORD, JAMES MORGAN
  (St. Francisville, La.)
1811: 24039 pb
1813: 28497

BRADFORD, JOHN (Lexington,
  Ky.)
1801: 113 pb, 758
1802: 2487, 2635, 2961, 3158,
  3569, 50305
1803: 4409, 4477
1804: 6592, 50450 pb
1805: 8731
1806: 10671
1807: 12862

BRADFORD, MOSES (Wilming-
  ton, Del.)
1814: 31321 pb, 33642
1815: 34555
1816: 37420-37424, 37427

BRADFORD, SAMUEL FISHER
  (New York)
1808: 15805 f, 16245 pb
1809: 17708 pb, 17820 pb,
  18370 pb, 18448 pb, 50907
  pb
1810: 19572 f, 19607 f, 20379
  pb, 20404 f, 21254 pb,
  21376 f
1811: 22791 f
1812: 24892 f, 25224 pb, 25317
  f, 25319 pb, 25683 pb, 25726
  pb, 25839 f, 25940 pb, 26042
  pb, 26392 pb, 26670 f, 51197
  pb
1813: 27693 f, 28157 f, 28853
  pb, 28900 f, 29125 f, 29453
  f, 29455 pb, 29620 pb,
  29676 pb, 29681-29682 pb,
  29739 f, 29752 f

BRADFORD, SAMUEL FISHER
  (Philadelphia)
1801: 834 pb
1802: 2640 f, 3153 f, 50270 f
1803: 3639 f, 3987 pb, 4092
  f, 4288 pb, 4293 pb, 4319-
  4320 f, 4454 f, 4455 pb,
  4458 f, 4627-4630 f, 4663
  pb, 4815 f, 4941 pb, 5090
  f, 5140 f, 5622 pb

1804: 6580-6581 f, 7028-
7029, 7260 f
1805: 8145 pb, 8707 f, 8879
pb, 9152 pb, 50510
1806: 9974-9975, 10066 f,
10093 pb, 10096 f, 10615
pb, 10905 pb, 50653 pb,
50663 f, 50698 f
1807: 12344 pb, 12365 pb, 12
12684 pb, 13135 pb, 13138
pb, 13643 pb, 50789 f,
50790 pb
1808: 14793 f, 14794 pb,
15201 pb, 15694? f, 15806
f, 16058 pb, 16227 f,
16236 f, 16725 f, 16749 pb
1809: 17111 pb, 17128 pb,
17266 pb, 17677 pb, 17743
pb, 17899 pb, 17905 f,
17917 f, 18127 pb, 18138
pb, 18371 pb, 18425 f,
18448 pb, 19247 pb, 50907
pb
1810: 19382 pb, 19683 f,
19700 pb, 19701 f, 19825
pb, 19863 pb, 19884 pb,
19968 f, 20282 pb, 20379
pb, 20549 pb, 20559 f,
20561 f, 20698-20700 f,
20702 f, 20751 pb, 20759
pb, 20782 f, 20994 f, 21121
pb, 21208 f, 21232 f, 21319
pb, 21391 pb, 21946 pb
1811: 23846 f
1812: 24518 f, 24638 f, 24892
f, 24943 pb, 25224 pb,
25317 f, 25319 pb, 25530
f, 25683 pb, 25839 f, 25940
pb, 26042 pb, 26557 pb,
26670 f
1813: 28008 pb, 28157 f,
28333 f, 28853 pb, 28900
f, 29043 pb, 29450
29453 f, 29455 pb, 29620
pb, 29676 pb, 29681-29682
pb, 29739 f, 29752 f, 29908
f, 29960 pb, 30527 pb
1814: 30655 pb, 31174 pb,
31267 pb, 31312 f, 31733
f, 31924 f, 31945 pb,
32575-32576 pb
1815: 35575 f, 35674 pb
1819: 50171 pb

BRADFORD, THEODERICK F
(Clarksville, Tenn.)
1810: 21870 pb

BRADFORD, THEODERICK F
(Shelbyville, Tenn.)
1816: 39066 pb

BRADFORD, THOMAS (Phila-
delphia)
1801: 90, 266, 268, 298, 494,
531 pb, 532
1802: 1726 f, 1974, 1979,
1980 pb, 1981, 2017, 2233,
2266-2267, 3004, 3505
1803: 4058, 4239, 4365 pb,
4944-4945, 5026
1804: 5869, 6180, 7026-7029,
7383
1805: 8124 f, 8202, 8542 pb,
8565, 50526? pb, 50553? pb
1806: 10048 pb, 10080 pb,
10489 pb, 10624 pb, 11298
pb, 11306, 11784 f
1807: 12140 pb, 12147, 12583
pb, 13054 f, 13361 pb,
13729
1808: 15721, 15981, 16656 pb
1809: 17743 pb, 17776 f,
18277
1810: 19321 f, 19507, 19557,
20777, 21313? bsb, 21928 f
1811: 22399 pb, 23360 pb,
23735
1812: 25563 pb, 25585 pb,
26452 pb, 29570, 29571 pb
1813: 31671 pb
1814: 32562
1815: 35698
1816: 38702, 38708, 39699 pb
1817: 41787 pb, 41875, 41877-
41878 pb, 42805 f
1818: 43358 pb, 43738 pb,
44963 pb, 45406 pb, 45407,
46681 pb
1819: 47905 f, 49182, 49185,
50130 pb

BRADFORD, THOMAS GRAY-
SON (Chillicothe, O.)
1805: 9057 pb
1806: 11057, 11059-11060,
11062

BRADFORD, THOMAS GRAY-
SON (Georgetown, D. C.)
1803: 3996 pb

BRADFORD, THOMAS GRAY-
SON (Huntsville, Ala.)
1812: 25927 pb

BRADFORD, THOMAS GRAY-
SON (Nashville, Tenn.)
1808: 50834 pb
1809: 17078 pb, 18744 pb
1810: 19623 pb, 20311 pb,
20737, 21471, 21472 pb
1811: 22287, 22635, 23265,
24020 pb, 51066 pb
1812: 25076, 26075, 26854-
26856, 51167 pb
1813: 28356 pb, 29928, 29931-
29932
1814: 32216, 32922 pb, 51371
pb
1815: 34196 pb, 34742, 34816
pb, 36063, 36067 pb
1816: 37074 pb, 37625 pb,
37819 pb
1817: 40310 pb, 40787 pb,
40870, 42828
1818: 43435a pb, 44059 pb,
44101
1819: 47416, 48197 pb

BRADFORD, WILLIAM (Phila-
delphia)
1801: 90, 266, 268, 298, 494,
531 pb, 532
1802: 1726 f, 1974, 1979,
1980 pb, 1981, 2017, 2233,
2266-2267, 3004, 3505
1803: 4058, 4239, 4365 pb,
4944-4945, 5026
1804: 5869, 6180, 7026-7029,
7383
1805: 8124 f, 8202, 8542 pb,
8565, 50526? pb, 50553?
pb, 50601?, 50604?
1806: 10048 pb, 10080 pb,
10489 pb, 10624 pb, 11298
pb, 11306, 11784 f
1807: 12140 pb, 12147, 12583,
13054 f, 13361 pb, 13729
1808: 15721, 15981, 16656 pb
1809: 17743 pb, 17776 f, 18277

1810: 19321 f, 19507, 19557,
20777, 21313? bsb, 21928 f
1811: 22399 pb, 23360 pb,
23735
1812: 25563 pb, 25585 pb,
26452 pb, 29570, 29571 pb
1813: 31671 pb
1814: 32562
1815: 35698
1816: 37386 sb, 38702, 38708,
38807-38808 sb, 39699 pb
1817: 41056 sb, 41483 sb,
41555 pb, 41787 pb, 41873
sb, 41875, 41877-41878 pb,
41982 sb, 42159 sb, 42805 f
1818: 43358 pb, 43362 sb,
43738 pb, 43753 sb, 43850
sb, 44331 sb, 44337 sb,
44342 sb, 44595? sb, 44849
sb, 44963 pb, 45172 sb,
45275 sb, 45406 pb, 45407,
45505-45506 sb, 45649 sb,
45867 sb, 46681 pb
1819: 47005 sb, 47905 f,
48057 pb, 48218 pb, 48752
pb, 48984 pb, 49182, 49185,
49389 pb, 49427 sb, 50130
pb

Bradford & Inskeep (Philadelphia)
see BRADFORD, SAMUEL
FISHER (Philadelphia)
INSKEEP, JOHN (Philadel-
phia)

BRADLEE, THOMAS (Boston)
1810: 19624 pb

BRADLEY, JOHN (Philadelphia)
1809: 18522 pb

BRAEUTIGAM, DANIEL (Philadelphia)
1816: 37932 f
1818: 44352 f

BRAGG, SAMUEL (Dover,
N. H.)
1801: 861, 1335 pb, 1698
1802: 1823
1803: 3710-3711, 3795
1804: 5687

1805: 7929, 8988
1806: 9896, 11286
1807: 12715, 13169, 14126
1809: 18195
1810: 19436
1811: 22270, 23374

BRANDEBERRY, --- (Lexington, Ind.)
1816: 37344 pb, 39023

BRANDEBERRY, --- (Shippensburg, Pa.)
1814: 32958 pb

BRANDON, ARMSTRONG (Corydon, Ind.)
1816: 37926 pb
1818: 44426-44430
1819: 48334-48338

BRANDON, JESSE (Corydon, Ind.)
1818: 44426-44430
1819: 48334-48338

BRANNAN, JOHN (New York)
1806: 10239-10240 f, 10377 pb, 10429 pb, 10793 f, 10835 f
1807: 12582 pb, 12989 f, 13104 pb, 13136 f, 13425 f, 13509 f, 13512 f, 13655 pb, 13707 f, 14192 f
1808: 14627 pb, 14804 pb, 14948 pb
1810: 21087 f

BRANNAN, JOHN (Philadelphia)
1810: 21993 f
1811: 22136 pb, 23705 pb

BRANSFORD, SAMUEL (Lynchburg, Va.)
1816: 36860
1817: 40134

Brattleboro Bookstore (Brattleboro, Vt.)
1817: 41730 pb

BREGA, SOLOMON BELA (Charlestown, Mass.)
1812: 25460 pb

BRENDLE, WILLIAM (Meadville, Pa.)
1805: 8261 pb

BREWER, HENRY (Springfield, Mass.)
1801: 796, 1397, 1673
1802: 1785, 2466, 2505-2506, 2507?, 2508
1803: 4203?, 4502, 5542?
1804: 5783, 6215
1805: 8200, 8366?, 8754-8755, 8757, 8760-8761 pb, 9049?, 9230?, 9756
1806: 10684, 10696-10702, 10704?, 10714, 11889?, 11891?
1807: 12310?, 12890?, 12892, 13063, 13195
1808: 14708 pb, 15396, 15397?, 15399, 15808
1809: 17853
1810: 20524? pb
1814: 31185?

BREWSTER, M (Boston)
1816: 36714 pb, 37628 pb, 38990 pb
1819: 49024 pb

BRIGGS, JOHN (Haverhill, Mass.)
1819: 48151 f

BRIGGS, ROBERT (Arkansas Post, Ark.)
1819: 47012 pb

BRINDLE, WILLIAM (Bellefonte, Pa.)
1818: 43275 pb

BRISBAN, JAMES (New York)
1806: 10239-10240 f, 10377 pb, 10429 pb, 10793 f, 10835 f
1807: 12582 pb, 12989 f, 13104 pb, 13425 f, 13509 f, 13655 pb, 14192 f

BRITTON, ALEXANDER (Clarksburg, Va.)
1812: 25729
1813: 28709

BRITTON, FORBES (Clarks-
burg, Va.)
1812:   25729
1813:   28709

BRITTON, FORBES (Morgan-
town, Va.)
1804:   6807 pb

BRODERICK, JOHN (New York)
1815:   33776

BRODERICK, JOSEPH (New
York)
1817:   40387
1819:   47498, 49492 pb, 49552

BRODIE, ALEXANDER (New
York)
1801:   1091 f

BRONSON, ENOS (Philadelphia)
1802:   1720 f, 1846 pb, 2198
f, 2356 f, 3106 f, 3273 f
1803:   3936, 4831, 4994 pb,
4996 pb
1804:   6385 f, 7780 pb
1805:   8734, 9275, 9487 f
1806:   10408-10409, 11079,
11297, 11445 pb, 50677
1807:   12678, 14216 f
1810:   22040
1811:   22541
1812:   24605, 26777
1813:   29481
1814:   31067, 31242, 31887
1815:   34331 f, 35867
1816:   39713
1817:   42895

BRONSON, TILLOTSON (New
Haven, Conn.)
1806:   10241 f, 11834 f
1808:   16102 f

BROOKS, ELIJAH (Northamp-
ton, Mass.)
1817:   40982-40983 pb, 42900

BROOKS, ELIJAH (Salem,
N.J.)
1819:   47630, 49349 pb

BROOKS, ELIJAH (Walpole,
N.H.)
1812:   25057

BROOKS, ELIJAH (Windsor,
Vt.)
1811:   22521 pb

BROOKS, SAMUEL (Richmond,
Va.)
1806:   10609 pb

BROUGHTON, THOMAS G (Nor-
folk, Va.)
1816:   36868, 37929, 38065,
39811
1817:   40123
1819:   48942

BROWN, --- (Trenton, N.J.)
1814:   32550 f

BROWN, ANSIL (Norwich,
Conn.)
1815:   36139

BROWN, ANSIL (Windham,
Conn.)
1815:   34828

BROWN, ASAHEL (Charles-
town, Mass.)
1810:   20232 f, 20459 f, 21378
f
1817:   39907 pb

BROWN, B (Lawrenceburg,
Ind.)
1817:   40631 pb

BROWN, BENJAMIN (Pitts-
burgh, Pa.)
1811:   23663 pb

BROWN, BENJAMIN (Washing-
ton, Pa.)
1808:   16049 pb, 16054
1809:   17144

BROWN, BENJAMIN (Williamsport, Pa.)
1815:   36547 pb

BROWN, CHRISTIAN (New
York)
1802: 2103 f, 2125 pb
1803: 4292 f
1804: 6545 pb, 6882 pb
1809: 18658 pb
1810: 20757 pb
1815: 34976? pb
1818: 45477 f

BROWN, CLARK (Montpelier,
Vt.)
1806: 11765
1807: 12218 f

BROWN, DAVID (Lancaster,
Pa.)
1804: 7014 pb

BROWN, DAVID (Philadelphia)
1802: 2033
1804: 6219, 7382
1813: 28035 pb, 28038 f
1817: 40485 f

BROWN, DAVID (Strasburg,
Pa.)
1803: 4222 pb, 4783

BROWN, HORI (Brookfield,
Mass.)
1811: 23836, 24454

BROWN, HORI (Leicester,
Mass.)
1814: 31669, 31913, 32458
1815: 34004, 34707, 35337,
35399, 35589, 35664, 35682,
35882 pb
1816: 36993
1817: 40144, 42081 pb
1818: 43906, 44598
1819: 47226, 47842

BROWN, HUGH (Knoxville,
Tenn.)
1816: 38024 pb
1817: 39927, 40505, 41246,
42041
1818: 43082
1819: 47482, 47654-47655,
48662

BROWN, HUGH HALE (Provi-
dence, R. I.)
1814: 32636-32640, 32642 pb,
51372
1815: 33970, 34236, 35177,
35774-35778
1816: 38144a, 38744, 38793-
38797
1817: 41340, 41970-41974
1818: 45449, 45528, 45532 pb,
51827 pb
1819: 48387, 48573, 49278-
49279 pb, 49419

BROWN, JOHN (New York)
1801: 432 f
1802: 1920 f, 1936 f, 2162 f,
3132 pb

BROWN, JOHN (Newburgh,
N. Y.)
1808: 16163 pb

BROWN, JOHN M (Baltimore)
1814: 32204 f

BROWN, MATTHEW (Baltimore)
1801: 1201, 1676
1802: 2580
1806: 10802 f

BROWN, MATTHIAS A (Tren-
ton, N. J.)
1814: 51420 f
1815: 35450 pb

BROWN, PETER (Rutland, Vt.)
1814: 32190 pb

BROWN, SAMUEL R (Albany,
N. Y.)
1812: 24579 pb
1814: 31574 pb

BROWN, SAMUEL R (Ballston
Spa, N. Y.)
1810: 19469, 20630
1811: 24512 pb, 51089 f
1812: 25399, 26692 pb
1813: 28855 f

BROWN, SAMUEL R (Johns-
town, N. Y.)
1809: 18107 pb

BROWN, THOMAS (Boston)
1815: 36075 pb

BROWN, WILLIAM (Charles-
town, Va.)
1808: 14997 pb

BROWN, WILLIAM (Cumber-
land, Md.)
1814: 31272 pb

BROWN, WILLIAM (Hagers-
town, Md.)
1809: 17693 pb
1810: 20938
1812: 25774

BROWN, WILLIAM (Philadel-
phia)
1808: 14259, 15853, 16145,
16346
1809: 16995, 17313, 17619,
17638, 17691, 17922, 18284,
18383, 18478, 18548, 18616,
18724, 19129, 19235
1810: 19326, 19670, 19866,
20233, 20949, 21074, 21094
f, 21178, 21234 pb, 21538,
21965, 22066
1811: 22404a pb, 22460a,
22779, 22921, 23012, 23118,
23195, 23356, 23412, 23415,
23683, 23693, 23881, 24352,
24381, 24449, 24480
1812: 24576, 25191, 25474,
27370
1813: 27835, 28337, 28351,
29504 pb, 29821, 29927
1814: 30808, 31276, 31625,
32084
1815: 34117, 35637, 35643,
36045
1816: 36729, 37091, 37670,
38628, 51590
1817: 40447, 40652, 40782,
40950-40951, 41034, 41107,
41466, 42029, 42058, 42817,
42937
1818: 43069, 43247, 43523,

43608, 43686, 43688,
43777?, 43829, 43830 pb,
43981, 44236, 44369, 44397,
44400, 44556, 44877, 45345,
45561-45562, 45916, 46839-
46840
1819: 47588, 47761, 47852,
48936, 49018, 49172, 49357,
49388, 50024-50025

Brown & Bowman (Lancaster,
Philadelphia, Strasburg, Pa.)
see BROWN, DAVID
BOWMAN, ABRAHAM

Brown & Merritt (Philadelphia)
see BROWN, WILLIAM (Philadelphia)
MERRITT, SAMUEL (Phila-
delphia)

Brown & Stansbury (New York)
see BROWN, JOHN (New
York)
STANSBURY, ABRAHAM
OGIER (New York)

BROWNE, JOHN W (Cincinnati,
O.)
1804: 6649 pb
1805: 8094
1806: 10046, 10488?
1807: 12223 pb, 12745, 12969,
13571
1808: 14598
1809: 17093
1810: 19660, 19830 pb, 19994,
20074
1811: 22307, 22410a, 22656,
23770 pb
1812: 24957, 24993, 26758-
26759
1813: 28044, 29238

BROWNE, SAMUEL J (Cin-
cinnati, O.)
1812: 51231 pb
1813: 27806, 29403, 29805

BROWNEJOHN, THOMAS
(Poughkeepsie, N. Y.)
1815: 35357 pb, 35686
1816: 37378, 37559 f

BRUCE, DAVID (New York)
1806: 9978, 10054, 10059,
10239, 10793, 10835, 10893,
11815
1807: 12169, 12172, 12650,
13042, 13136
1808: 14929, 15380, 15414 pb,
15423, 15646, 16202, 16226
1809: 17014-17015, 17062,
17119, 17278, 17326-17327,
17663, 17721, 17727, 17904,
18010, 18095, 18323, 18443,
18484, 18587, 18666, 18723,
19111
1810: 19533, 20631, 21166 pb,
21300, 21344, 21398
1811: 22148, 22383, 22443a,
22458a-22459a, 22570,
22925, 23378, 23883, 23888,
23894, 24032, 24336, 24338,
24499
1812: 24587, 25282, 25317,
25678, 25876, 26057, 26081,
26131, 26351, 26399, 26533,
26587, 27576-27577, 27590
1813: 28344, 28408, 29125,
29205, 29506, 29743, 30588
1814: 30994
1815: 34058, 34068, 34237a
pb
1816: 36991, 37107 pb, 38720-
38721
1817: 40200-40201
1818: 43469 pb, 44899 pb,
45428, 45430-45431
1819: 47212, 47214 f, 47228,
47346, 47388, 49199, 49353

BRUCE, GEORGE (New York)
For all entries see BRUCE,
DAVID (New York) above.

BRUCKMAN, CARL A (Allen-
town, Pa.)
1807: 13262 pb

BRUCKMAN, CARL A (Read-
ing, Pa.)
1801: 989
1804: 6858
1805: 8968 pb

BRUCKMAN, CARL AUGUSTUS
(Reading, Pa.)
1816: 38760 pb
1818: 44367
1819: 47208-47209, 48256-
48257, 51863

BRUMLEY, ISRAEL (Norwich,
Conn.)
1813: 28176 pb

BRUNT, JONATHAN (Frank-
fort, Ky.)
1804: 5921 pb

BRYAN, CARNEY J (Newbern,
N. C.)
1806: 10164
1811: 24057 pb, 51150 pb

BRYANT, REUBEN (Greenfield,
Mass.)
1807: 13193 f

BRYCE, JOHN (Richmond, Va.)
1815: 34709 f

BRYER, --- (Charleston, S. C.)
1815: 34731

BRYNBERG, PETER (Wilming-
ton, Del.)
1801: 131, 180 pb, 330? pb,
583 pb, 589 pb, 742 pb,
809 pb, 831 pb, 1100 pb,
1277 pb, 1331 pb
1802: 1725 pb, 1888 pb, 2053
pb, 2996 pb
1803: 3805 pb, 3821, 3991 pb,
4166 pb, 4676 pb, 4928,
4986 pb
1804: 6049 pb, 6380 pb, 6573,
6865 pb, 7033 pb, 7735 pb,
50434
1805: 8003 pb, 8007 pb, 8015?
pb, 8216 pb, 8332 pb,
8502?, 8983 pb
1806: 10081, 10188 pb, 10343,
10764, 10930 pb
1807: 12325 pb, 13445, 50782
pb
1808: 14492 pb, 14740 pb,
15008 pb, 15324 pb, 15400

1809: 16908 pb, 17179, 17202,
17258 pb, 17898 pb, 18459-
18460
1810: 19529 pb, 19870 pb,
20527?, 21978 pb
1811: 22371 pb, 22579, 22613,
22699 pb, 23115 pb, 23470,
23961 pb, 24074 pb
1812: 25117 pb, 25495
1814: 32365

BUCHANAN, JOSEPH (Frank-
fort, Ky.)
1815: 35051-35052, 36337

BUCKINGHAM, AUGUSTUS (Au-
burn, N. Y.)
1819: 47531 pb

BUCKINGHAM, JOSEPH
TINKER (Boston)
1803: 4229
1804: 5677, 5849, 6831, 7059
1805: 7986, 8039, 8443, 8462-
8463, 8491 pb, 8551, 9163
pb
1806: 9953, 9965, 10115,
10183, 10289, 10742a,
10909, 11296
1807: 12452, 13019-13020,
13143-13144, 13392, 13521
1808: 14312-14313, 14472,
14485, 15049, 15655, 15951,
16036, 16103, 16166, 50884
1809: 16993, 17253, 18131,
18298, 18391, 18503, 50958
1810: 19329, 19531, 19605,
20092-20093, 20148, 20516,
20661, 20788, 21445, 21932,
51042 pb
1811: 22382, 22438, 22426a,
22490, 22585 pb, 22695-
22696, 22766, 22789, 23439,
23752, 23767, 23878 pb,
23966, 24380 pb
1812: 25391, 25457-25458,
25646, 25680, 25703, 25857
pb, 27439-27441
1813: 28083, 28540 pb, 28714,
28848, 28939, 28970 bf,
29223, 29715, 29776-29778,
29992, 30573 pb
1814: 31063, 31118, 31694,

31752 pb, 31812, 32046,
32074 pb, 32175-32176,
32552, 33528 pb, 33564 pb
1815: 33816, 34074 pb, 34170,
34174 pb, 34720 bf, 34728,
35145 pb, 35812 pb
1817: 40289, 40440, 40860 pb,
41573 pb, 41954 pb, 42811,
42959
1818: 43529, 43818, 44115,
46870 pb
1819: 47396, 47508, 47826 pb,
48267 pb, 48280, 48435,
48504, 49648 pb, 50162? pb

BUCKLEN, ISAAC (Arlington,
Vt.)
1818: 44812

BUCKLEY, BILLY (Albany,
N. Y.)
1804: 5741 pb
1805: 7894 pb

BUDD, HENRY STACY (Phila-
delphia)
1801: 210, 260, 1114
1802: 1755, 1859, 2452, 2562,
2894
1803: 4147, 4162, 4165, 5527
1804: 6034, 7347

BUEL, ALBERT D (Baltimore)
1814: 31489 pb, 32899 f

BUEL, JESSE (Albany, N. Y.)
1812: 27565
1813: 27685 pb, 29006
1814: 30635, 32286, 32864 pb,
32963
1815: 33786, 35462-35463,
35465-35467
1816: 36748, 37254 pb, 38436-
38438
1817: 41618-41622, 41630,
42179, 42918 pb
1818: 45043-45044, 45049-
45050, 45054, 46817 pb,
51809
1819: 47013, 48887, 48893-
48896, 48899-48900

BUEL, JESSE (Kingston,
  N. Y.)
1803: 3689, 50358 pb
1804: 6282 pb, 7694? pb
1805: 8422 pb
1806: 10390 pb, 50646 pb
1807: 50770 pb
1808: 14988 pb
1809: 17654
1810: 20083 pb
1811: 22803 pb
1812: 24629 pb, 25396 pb,
  26108 pb, 27379

BUEL, JESSE (Poughkeepsie,
  N. Y.)
1801: 595 pb
1802: 2680 pb, 2775 pb, 2908
  pb
1803: 4181 pb, 4876 pb,
  50358 pb
1805: 8159
1806: 9952

BUEL, JOHN (New York)
1803: 50355
1816: 36929

BUEL, SAMUEL (Burlington,
  Vt.)
1819: 47455 pb

BUELL, --- (New York)
1815: 36450 pb

BUELL, DANIEL HAND (Mari-
  etta, O.)
1813: 27655? f, 27712 pb
1815: 35794

BUELL, TIMOTHY (Marietta,
  O.)
1813: 27655? f, 27712 pb
1815: 35794

BUELL, WILLIAM SAWYER
  (Schenectady, N. Y.)
1811: 22831 pb

BUELL, WILLIAM SAWYER
  (Wilmington, Del.)
1816: 37428 pb

BULKLEY, J (Bridgeport,
  Conn.)
1810: 19635

BULL, JAMES (Northampton,
  Mass.)
1808: 16740 pb

BULL, JOHN (Waterford, Me.)
1810: 20507

BUMSTEAD, JOSEPH (Boston)
1801: 16-18 pb, 299 pb, 301
  pb, 789 pb
1802: 1855 pb, 2691 pb
1803: 3688 pb, 5585 pb
1804: 5815, 6985 pb, 7153,
  7817 pb
1806: 10058 pb, 10305 pb
1807: 11933, 13563 pb, 13600
  pb, 14246
1808: 15645 pb
1809: 17098-17100 pb
1811: 22413a pb
1813: 28032 pb

BUNCE, CHARLES W (New
  York)
1813: 29194
1814: 31568, 32243

BUNCE, GEORGE (New York)
1809: 17761, 17885, 17916,
  19141
1810: 21989
1811: 22446a, 23142, 23221,
  23370, 24359, 51118
1812: 24997
1813: 28407

BUNCE, GEORGE F (New York)
1817: 41446

BUNCE, ISAIAH (Ballston Spa,
  N. Y.)
1814: 32713 pb
1815: 35678

BUNCE, ISAIAH (Litchfield,
  Conn.)
1818: 44590 pb
1819: 48499 pb

BUNCE, JONATHAN (Cazenovia, N. Y.)
1807: 12256

BUNCE, JONATHAN (Peter-
boro, N. Y.)
1807: 12603 pb
1810: 20539
1813: 29030 pb

BUNCE, WILLIAM J (Augusta, Ga.)
1801: 66, 1322
1802: 1789, 1958 pb
1803: 3725, 3903 pb, 5545 pb
1804: 5773, 6377
1805: 7896, 8517 pb, 9415
1806: 10477 pb
1807: 12014, 12655 pb, 13065, 14195 pb
1808: 15097 pb
1809: 17615 pb, 18700
1810: 20209, 21998 pb
1811: 23788, 51092 pb
1812: 25514 pb, 26749
1813: 28625 pb
1814: 51393 pb
1815: 34781 pb, 36080, 51500
1816: 51587 pb
1817: 51667 pb
1818: 51778 pb
1819: 51894 pb

BURBANK, ABIJAH (Brattle-
boro, Vt.)
1819: 50080 f

BURBANK, CALEB (Sutton, Mass.)
1808: 14501 f

BURBANK, ELIJAH (Worces-
ter, Mass.)
1806: 11142 f
1809: 17690 f
1816: 36987 f

BURCH, ELISHA (Fredericksburg, Va.)
1804: 5798

BURCH, ISHAM (Fredericks-
burg, Va.)

1803: 5520 pb
1804: 5798

BURDAKIN, JOSEPH (Boston)
1818: 44918 pb

BURDICK, WILLIAM (Boston)
1804: 5908
1814: 31436 pb
1816: 37048 pb

BURDITT, JAMES W (Boston)
1808: 16734 f
1810: 20748 f
1811: 22162 pb, 23179 pb, 23194 f, 24351 pb
1812: 25822 f, 25824-25825 pb, 25827 f, 26092 f, 26868 pb
1814: 31894 pb
1815: 35076-35077 pb
1816: 38558 f
1817: 40526 pb, 42823 pb

BURGESS, B (Georgetown, D. C.)
1803: 3996 pb

BURKE, DAVID (Richmond, Va.)
1816: 36842, 36866

BURKE, JOHN (Richmond, Va.)
1816: 36842, 36866, 38798

BURKE, WILLIAM B (Fred-
erick, Md.)
1818: 45643 pb

BURKE, WILLIAM B (West-
minster, Md.)
1818: 46782 pb

BURKLOE, D C (New York)
1810: 21519 pb

BURKLOE, P (New York)
1810: 21519 pb

BURLING, THOMAS (Richmond, Va.)
1817: 42188 pb, 42797
1818: 46659

BURNAP, FRANCIS (Middle-
bury, Vt.)
1817: 40543, 41283, 42111 pb
1818: 43250, 43497, 43665
pb, 43696, 44224, 44370,
44391, 44835, 44912, 45269,
45274, 45550, 46643, 46645,
46747 pb
1819: 20227, 46986, 47662 pb,
47697, 48092, 48184, 48690,
49425

BURNET, ISAAC GOUVERNEUR
(Dayton, O.)
1810: 20948 pb
1815: 33785, 33965

BURNHAM, MICHAEL (New
York)
1801: 1047 pb
1802: 2363 bpb, 2788 pb

BURNSIDE, JOHN (Lancaster,
Pa.)
1804: 5667, 7017
1806: 11126, 50706
1807: 13341, 13343
1808: 15879
1809: 18339
1810: 21029, 21031

BURNSIDE, JOHN M (Easton,
Pa.)
1811: 23418 pb

BURNTON, THOMAS H (New
York)
1803: 4121 f, 4193 f, 4491
pb, 4493 f
1804: 6137 f, 7230 f
1811: 23170 pb

BURR, DAVID J (Boston)
1815: 35328 pb
1816: 38295 pb

BURR, HEZEKIAH (Hartford,
Conn.)
1818: 43190, 43505-43506,
45822, 46672
1819: 48235, 48572, 49655,
49968, 50188

BURRELL, ABRAHAM (Bing-
hamton, N.Y.)
1818: 45522 pb

BURRILL, NATHAN (Haverhill,
Mass.)
1813: 29283? pb
1814: 30983, 31850, 32799,
32836
1815: 33912, 34098 pb, 35043-
35044, 35153-35154 pb,
35453, 35614, 35954 pb,
36011, 36505 pb
1816: 36769 pb, 36889-36890,
36983 pb, 38331 pb, 38571,
38658 pb, 39731 pb, 39740
pb, 39850 pb, 39851
1817: 40227 pb, 40311, 40944,
41517, 41521 pb, 41522,
41855, 42791, 42845 pb
1818: 43339 pb, 43379 pb,
44944 pb, 45878 pb, 46718
pb
1819: 48840 pb

BURT, CHARLES (Rutland, Vt.)
1817: 41337, 42462 pb,
?42742? pb, 42777-42778,
42780
1818: 43218?, 43359 pb,
44502
1819: 46963 pb, 47141-47142,
48810 pb, 48843 pb, 49436,
49632 pb, 49983 pb

BURTON, JAMES (Augusta,
Me.)
1817: 40040 pb

BURTON, JAMES (Bangor,
Me.)
1815: 33918 pb
1818: 45684

BURTON, JAMES (Hallowell,
Me.)
1814: 30727, 30975-30976,
31634 pb, 32167, 33713
1815: 33994, 35022, 36050

BURTSELL, PETER (New
York)
1807: 13513 f

BURTUS, JAMES A (New
York)
1818: 43939 f
1819: 48812 f

BURTUS, SAMUEL A (New
York)
1812: 24824 f
1813: 28031 pb, 28033 pb
1814: 30935 pb, 31751 f,
32243 f
1815: 35835 f
1817: 40266 f, 41105 pb,
41680 pb

BUSH, JOHN WILLOUGHBY
(Lexington, Ky.)
1802: 2120 pb

BUTLER, ELIHU (New York)
1811: 22199, 22443 pb,
23436 pb

BUTLER, ELIHU (Northamp-
ton, Mass.)
1803: 5129 f
1804: 6223 f, 6499 f, 7310 f
1805: 8356 f, 8867 f, 9179 f,
9650 f, 50527 pb
1806: 9931 f, 10333 f, 10610
f, 10819 f, 11268 f, 11309 f
1807: 12410 f, 12485 pb,
12825 f, 14150 f, 14168 f
1808: 16740 pb

BUTLER, G P W (Cumberland,
Md.)
1808: 14809 pb
1809: 16838 pb

BUTLER, G P W (Huntingdon,
Pa.)
1809: 16839 pb

BUTLER, GIDEON (Clarks-
burg, Va.)
1815: 36549 pb
1816: 36873
1817: 40135
1818: 45520 pb
1819: 47155

BUTLER, JOHN BARTLETT
(Pittsburgh, Pa.)
1817: 40028 pb, 40269 pb,
40330, 41266, 41526, 42248
pb, 42818, 42876, 42987
1818: 43334a, 43344, 43458,
44161, 44179, 44228 pb,
44458, 44785 pb, 44786-
44790, 44823, 44945, 45216,
45791, 45829, 46788, 51816,
51846 pb
1819: 47817, 48548, 48666,
50059, 50067, 51929, 51934

BUTLER, JOHN WEST (Annap-
olis, Md.)
1809: 18005 pb

BUTLER, JOHN WEST (Balti-
more)
1801: 702
1802: 1765, 1806, 2005, 2454,
2495-2496, 3173
1803: 3682, 3691, 3714, 3841,
3944, 3988, 4492, 4571,
4983
1804: 5712, 5950, 5985, 5992,
6122, 6768 pb, 7202, 7795,
50414
1805: 8146, 8148-8149, 8295,
8450, 8546, 8768, 8887 pb,
9287 pb, 9491, 50495
1806: 9852, 10102, 10135,
10214, 10529, 11466
1807: 12033, 12275-12277,
12293, 12731, 13041,
13397?, 13506, 13527,
13560
1808: 14290, 14306, 14542,
14653 pb, 14711, 14714,
15021, 15042, 15140 pb,
15173, 16126 pb, 16273,
16706-16711
1809: 17133 pb, ?17990,
18782

BUTLER, JOSEPH (Staunton,
Va.)
1814: 32852 pb

BUTLER, MANN (Frankfort,
Ky.)
1818: 43895 f

BUTLER, MANN (Louisville, Ky.)
1815: 34416
1816: 36820 pb, 37597 pb, 37921, 37925
1817: 41274, 42207 pb

BUTLER, MERRILL (Boston)
1811: 23901 pb

BUTLER, SAMUEL (Baltimore)
1801: 72 pb, 305 sb, 841 f, 1430 f
1802: 1765 f, 1870 sb, 1918 f, 2190 f, 2260 sb, 2495-2496 f, 3008 pb, 3574 f
1803: 3682 f, 3841 f, 3984 f, 4045 sb, 4372 pb, 4492 f, 5177 pb, 5484 f
1804: 5712 f, 6122 f, 6197 f, 7202 f, 7376 pb, 7795 f, 50414 f, 50419 f
1805: 7873 pb, 7916 f, 8173 pb, 8175 pb, 8546 f, 9491 f, 50495 f
1806: 10189 pb, 10529 f, 10924 f, 11304 f, 11466 f
1807: 11991 f, 13722 pb

BUTLER, SIMEON (Northampton, Mass.)
1803: 5129 f
1804: 6223 f, 6499 f, 7310 f
1805: 8356 f, 8867 f, 9179 f, 9650 f, 50527 pb
1806: 9931 f, 10333 f, 10610 f, 10819 f, 11268 f, 11309 f
1807: 12410 f, 12485 pb, 12793 pb, 12825 f, 13194 pb, 14150 f, 14168 f
1810: 20015 pb, 20397 pb
1811: 22739 f
1812: 25305 f
1813: 29168 pb
1814: 30819 f, 31379 f, 33683 f
1816: 37480 f
1817: 40389 f, 40706 f, 51648 f
1818: 43383 f, 45389 f
1819: 47177 f, 47499 f, 47883 f, 49225 f

BUTLER, STEUBEN (Chester, Pa.)
1819: 49170 pb

BUTLER, STEUBEN (Wilkes-barre, Pa.)
1809: 19234
1811: 22919 pb
1813: 27672 pb
1815: 34419
1818: 46890 pb
1819: 48537

BUTLER, WILLIAM (Northampton, Mass.)
1801: 92, 94 pb, 509, 607, 759, 845, 1379
1802: 2152, 2366-2367, 2509, 2884 pb, 3126, 3563
1803: 3801-3802 pb, 4097, 4332, 4506-4507, 4854
1804: 6174-6175, 6179, 6183, 6244, 6435, 6442, 6680, 7328
1805: 8581, 9405, 9659, 9736
1806: 10521, 10586, 11178, 11476, 11870
1807: 12953-12954, 13668
1808: 14302, 14775, 15718, 15902 pb
1809: 17130, 17445, 17496, 18191, 18308, 19227
1810: 20265, 20834, 21041
1811: 22943, 23256 pb, 24418
1812: 24549, 24766, 25575, 25750, 25799, 26322
1813: 28420, 29002, 29429
1814: 30687, 31637, 32244, 33628, 33716

BUTTLES, JOEL (Columbus, O.)
1814: 30774, 33649

BUYERS, WILLIAM F (Sunbury, Pa.)
1814: 32892 pb

BUYERS, WILLIAM F (Williamsport, Pa.)
1802: 2557 pb

BUZBY, BENJAMIN C
(Philadelphia)
1807: 12411 f, 50784 pb
1808: 16143 pb, 50852 pb
1809: 18535 f, 50959 pb
1810: 20178 pb, 20215 pb,
20762 f
1811: 22365 pb
1812: 24673 pb, 27481 f
1813: 27770 pb, 27906 pb,
27915 pb, 27921 f, 27927 f,
28557 pb
1815: 51491 f
1818: 43321 f, 43333 f, 44072
pb, 44474 f, 45377 pb,
46722 f
1819: 48383-48384 f

BYBERRY, --- (Philadelphia)
1818: 45289 pb

BYRNE, JOHN (Windham,
Conn.)
1801: 1614-1615
1802: 2064, 2229, 2968
1803: 4003, 4009, 4125, 4819,
5543, 5578
1804: 6190, 6644, 7035, 7701-
7702, 7740
1805: 9714
1806: 9798, 10709, 11871
1808: 15144, 16703
1809: 17438, 19156
1810: 22004-22005
1811: 22252, 23017, 23188
1813: 30556
1814: 31369
1815: 35086, 36043 pb
1816: 37542, 37617, 38493
pb, 39040 pb
1819: 47926, 48465

BYRNE, PATRICK (Baltimore)
1812: 25785 pb

BYRNE, PATRICK (Philadel-
phia)
1801: 328, 329 f
1802: 1726 f, 1914, 2279,
2333, 2349-2352 pb, 2392,
2527 pb, 2576 pb, 2636,
2855 f, 3558 pb
1803: 3960 f, 4310-4312 pb,

4323 f, 4623 pb, 4815 f,
4914 pb, 4915 f, 4917-4918
f, 4919 pb, 4993 f, 5580
pb
1804: 5967 pb, 6411 pb, 6413
pb, 6575, 6699 f, 6995 pb,
7114, 50473 pb
1805: 7913 pb, 8563-8564 pb
1806: 10335 pb, 11108-11109
pb, 11130 pb, 11781 f
1807: 12030 f, 12384 f, 12687
pb, 12688 f, 12690 f, 13325
f, 14090 f
1808: 14687, 15154-15155 pb,
15158 pb
1809: 17665 pb, 17667-17670
pb, 18495 pb
1810: 19858 pb, 19863 pb,
20040, 20194 f, 20244 pb,
20728 pb, 21193 pb
1811: 22938 pb, 23105 pb,
23273 pb
1812: 25764 pb, 25785 sb,
26396 pb, 26571 f
1814: 30978 f

C

Cabinet (Amherst, N. H.)
see Farmer's Cabinet (Am-
herst, N. H.)

CADY, EBENEZER PEMBER-
TON (Fredericksburg, Va.)
1811: 51057
1812: 24741-24742, 25568 pb
1813: 27824
1814: 30793, 30796, 32910 pb
1815: 35558, 35892

CADY, EBENEZER PEMBER-
TON (New London, Conn.)
1805: 7971, 8281?, 8282,
8976 pb, 9242 pb, 9349 pb,
9761-9762
1806: 9955, 10092, 10201 pb,
10245-10246, 10379 pb,
10623, 10956 pb, 11353 pb,
11487 pb, 11916, 50665,
50728 pb

1807:   12318, 12339 pb, 12955,
13185 pb, 13582 pb, 14190,
14247
1808:   14818, 15327

CADY, HEMAN (Plattsburgh,
N. Y.)
1812:   26115 f, 26133 f

CAIN, JOHN (New York)
1819:   49552 f

CALDWELL, J R (Brattleboro,
Vt.)
1818:   46761

CALDWELL, JAMES (Warren-
ton, Va.)
1817:   41724 pb

CALDWELL, SAMUEL B T
(Leesburg, Va.)
1817:   40902 pb, 42040 pb

CALLENDER, CHARLES (Bos-
ton)
1813:   28464 pb, 28910 pb,
29423 pb
1814:   30701 pb, 31034 pb,
31484 f, 31812 f, 31895 f,
32233 pb, 33670 f, 33671
pb, 51390 pb
1815:   36009 pb, 36599 pb
1818:   44192 pb, 46833 pb
1819:   47495 pb

CALLENDER, JAMES (Balti-
more)
1808:   15499 f

CAMAK, JAMES (Milledge-
ville, Ga.)
1819:   48072-48073

CAMERON, J A (Mount Pleasant, N. Y.)
1818:   46768 pb

CAMMEYER, WILLIAM (Phila-
delphia)
1819:   48654

CAMP, GEORGE (Sackets Harbor, N. Y.)
1817:   40093, 42027 pb
1818:   43194, 44164, 45185
1819:   47113

CAMP, GEORGE (Utica, N. Y.)
1813:   27861, 27871a, 29001,
29864, 30391
1814:   30633, 31045 pb, 31177
pb, 31367 pb, 31466, 31820,
32136 pb, 32407, 33524
1815:   33902, 34786 pb, 34863-
34865, 34875, 35276, 36125
1816:   37803, 37896, 38259
pb, 38528 pb

CAMP, TALCOTT (Utica, N. Y.)
1815:   34786 pb
1816:   38259 pb

CAMPBELL, JAMES (Balti-
more)
1815:   34380 f

CAMPBELL, JOHN WILSON
(Petersburg, Va.)
1816:   51638 pb
1817:   51725 pb

CAMPBELL, JOHN WILSON
(Philadelphia)
1813:   28070 pb
1814:   31074 pb
1815:   34292 f
1816:   37183 f

CAMPBELL, JOSEPH (Morgan-
town, Va.)
1804:   6807 pb
1805:   ?8941
1806:   10295, 10552-10553,
10712
1807:   12061, 12907?

CAMPBELL, ROBERT (Phila-
delphia)
1801:   1261 f

CAMPBELL, SAMUEL (New
York)
1801:   169 f, 581 f, 867 f,
949 f, 956 f, 50227 pb

1802: 1915 f, 2574 f, 50302
pb, 50308 f
1803: 3788 f, 4815 f, 4924 f,
4941 pb
1804: 7813 pb, 50411 f
1805: 7999 f
1806: 10895 f
1807: 12132 f, 12908 pb,
50758 f
1808: 14508 pb, 15380 f,
16004 pb, 16007 pb
1809: 17663 f, 17794 f,
17904 f, 18450 pb
1811: 22535 pb, 24336 f
1812: 25190, 25706 pb
1816: 37900 pb, 38934 f
1818: 43331 pb, 44405 pb,
44562 f, 44932 pb, 46721
pb
1819: 48473 f, 48808 pb

CAMPBELL, WILLIAM (Union-
town, Pa.)
1811: 22808 pb

CAMRON, JAMES B (Hamilton,
O.)
1817: 41425 pb
1819: 48142 pb

CAMRON, WESLEY (Hamilton,
O.)
1817: 41425 pb

CAMRON, WILLIAM (Madison,
Ind.)
1814: 31794

CAMRON, WILLIAM A (Leban-
on, O.)
1817: 40514
1818: 43575

CANFIELD, PHILEMON (Elizabeth, N.J.)
1814: 31635, 31861, 51452?
pb
1815: 34849

CANFIELD, RUSSELL (Eliza-
beth, N.J.)
1814: 31635, 31861, 51452? pb
1815: 34849

CANFIELD, RUSSELL (Mount
Pleasant, N.Y.)
1801: 1348, 50201 pb

CAREW, J W (Brooklyn, N.Y.)
1802: 3117? f
1810: 21530? f

CAREY, MATTHEW (Philadel-
phia)
1801: 22 pb, 171 f, 250 f,
275 pb, 278-279 pb, 280 f,
338 f, 386 f, 404 f, 458 f,
552-553, 636 f, 730-731 f,
823 f, 933 f, 1108 pb,
50248 f
1802: 1709, 1726-1727 f,
1876 f, 1878 pb, 1884 f,
1987 pb, 1995 f, 2002 f,
2055 f, 2170 f, 2376 f,
2561a, 2655 f, 2682 sb,
2686 pb, 3024 f, 3029 pb,
3154 f
1803: 3638 pb, 3799-3800 pb,
3826 f, 3835 pb, 3888 pb,
3928, 4115 pb, 4352 pb,
4446 f, 4783 f, 4815 f,
4842 f, 4910 f, 4941 pb,
5172 pb, 5318-5320 f,
5321 pb, 5527 f, 50341 pb
1804: 5729 pb, 5848 pb, 5857
f, 5981 f, 5982 pb, 5989,
6658 f, 6815 pb, 7027-7029,
7118 f, 7511-7512 pb, 7513,
50428 pb
1805: 7988-7989 pb, 7991-
7993 pb, 8001 pb, 8004,
8009 pb, 8025 f, 8026 pb,
8134 pb, 8136 f, 8147 pb,
8158 f, 8542 pb, 50501
1806: 9940 pb, 9967 pb, 9973,
9976 pb, 10002 pb, 10033 pb,
10086 pb, 10089 pb, 10137
pb, 10371 f, 10401 f, 10405-
10406 pb, 10492, 10493 f,
10503 f, 11463-11464 pb,
11784 pb, 50648 pb, 50675 f
1807: 11926 pb, 11947-11948
pb, 12128 pb, 12157 pb,
12268 pb, 12289 f, 12297,
12455 f, 12732 pb, 12778
pb, 12823 pb, 12851 f,
12931 pb, 13147 f, 13700 f,

38617 pb, 38680 f, 38694
pb, 38753, 38828 f, 38837
pb, 38864 f, 38892 f, 39055
pb, 39057 pb, 39060 pb,
39639 pb, 39658 f, 39771
pb, 39772-39773, 39807 pb,
39897 pb, 51603 sb
1817: 39915 pb, 40143 pb,
40205 pb, 40325 pb, 40354
pb, 40378 f, 40395-40398
pb, 40400-40402 pb, 40490
pb, 40558 pb, 40585 f, 40655
pb, 40664 pb, 40720 pb,
40723 f, 40757 pb, 40761 f,
40788 pb, 40907 pb, 40954-
40955 pb, 41009 pb, 41035
pb, 41039 pb, 41068 pb,
41071 pb, 41081 f, 41164
pb, 41170 pb, 41213 pb,
41227 f, 41498 pb, 41673
pb, 41707 pb, 41890 pb,
41919 pb, 41945 pb, 42021
pb, 42024 pb, 42057 pb,
42125 f, 42218 pb, 42283
pb, 42773 f, 42863-42864
pb, 42865
1818: 43004-43005 pb, 43244
pb, 43306-43307, 43325-
43326 pb, 43373 pb, 43490
pb, 43533, 43534-43535 pb,
43741 pb, 43813 pb, 43890
pb, 43909 f, 43950 pb,
43978, 44526 f, 44577-
44578 pb, 44581, 44660 pb,
44689 f, 44759-44760 f,
44799 f, 44882 pb, 45016
pb, 45104 f, 45105 pb,
45199 f, 45222 pb, 45290
pb, 45464 f, 45468 pb,
45470, 45595 pb, 45600
pb, 45665-45668 pb, 45764
pb, 45775 pb, 46696 pb,
46754 pb, 46755-46757
1819: 47043 pb, 47216 pb,
47366 pb, 47458 f, 47490
pb, 47512-47513 pb, 47515
f, 47567 pb, 47790 pb,
48161 pb, 48167 pb, 48174
pb, 48199 f, 48310 f, 48395
f, 48484 pb, 48645 pb,
48661 f, 48756 f, 49014 pb,
49032 pb, 49094 pb, 49095
f, 49234, 50086

CAREY, PATRICK (Knoxville,
Tenn.)
1819: 48440 pb

CAREY, PATRICK (Rogers-
ville, Tenn.)
1815: 34385, 35805 pb
1816: 38140
1817: 41409

CAREY, THOMAS (Haverhill,
Mass.)
1817: 40261 f

CAREY, THOMAS (Salem,
Mass.)
1818: 43095 pb, 43386 f,
46902 f
1819: 47371? pb

CARGILE, A (Philadelphia)
1814: 31730 pb

CARITAT, HENRY (New York)
1801: 257 f, 825 f, 859 f
1802: 2497 pb, 2611 pb
1803: 3707 pb, 4373 f, 4591
pb
1805: 8853 pb
1811: 23861? f

CARLISLE, DAVID (Boston)
1801: 670, 724, 1267, 1374,
1433
1802: 1900, 2015, 2500, 2713,
3175
1803: 3827, 3830-3831, 3857,
4045, 4142-4143, 4153, 4300,
4450, 4464, 4488, 4500,
4533, 5067, 5078, 5096,
5156, 5583
1804: 5658, 5860-5861, 6319,
6664, 7127, 7144, 7710
1805: 7902, 8029, 8034, 8036,
8057, 8152-8153, 8437-8438,
8696, 8744, 8928, 9044,
9282, 9469, 9494, 9663 pb,
9683, 9706
1806: 9996 pb, 10067, 10105,
10237-10238, 10253-10254
pb, 10344, 10748, 10756,
11067, 11090, 11321, 11381,
11489, 11772 pb, 11830

1807: 12153, 12526, 12683,
12738, 12923, 13524, 13573-
13574, 13724, 14130 pb
1808: 14372, 14520, 15388,
16218-16219

CARLISLE, DAVID (New York)
1809: 18117 pb
1814: 32151

CARLISLE, DAVID (Troy, N.Y.)
1810: 21949

CARLISLE, DAVID (Walpole,
N.H.)
1801: 97, 461, 574-575, 1143,
1346, 1352, 50205 pb

CARLISLE, THOMAS (Walpole,
N.H.)
1801: 97, 574-575, 1143,
1346, 50205 pb

Carlisle Herald (Carlisle, Pa.)
1816: 51566 pb
1817: 51656 pb

CARLTON, WILLIAM (Salem,
Mass.)
1801: 393?, 1288, 1290?,
1344
1802: 2541, 3038?, 3040 pb,
3104, 3395?
1803: 3704, 3755, 4962?,
5014, 5158
1804: 5837, 6548, 6736, 7224,
7316
1805: 8697, 9504

CARMONT, JOHN (Savannah,
Ga.)
1807: 12551 pb

CARNAGHAN, GEORGE (Balti-
more)
1811: 23069 f

CARNEY, DAVID L (Cincin-
nati, O.)
1807: 13734 pb
1809: 18283 pb, 19215 pb

CARNEY, JOHN (Blakely,
N.C.)
1819: 47378 pb

CARNEY, JOHN (Fayetteville,
N.C.)
1818: 46892
1819: 48739, 49210

CARNEY, JOHN (Newbern,
N.C.)
1806: 10164, 10315

Carolina Observer (Fayetteville, N.C.)
1819: 48739

CAROTHERS, MOSES (Hills-
borough, O.)
1818: 44319 pb

CAROTHERS, WILLIAM (Ber-
wick, Pa.)
1818: 43290 pb

CARPENTER, FREDERIC
(Palmer, Mass.)
1810: 19725? f

CARPENTER, ISAIAH H
(Barnard, Vt.)
1812: 25162, 25380, 25384,
25572, 26302, 26342?,
26573?, 27520, 27521?,
27522
1813: 27899, 27951, 28094,
28231
1814: 31582, 31763

CARPENTER, ISAIAH H
(Woodstock, Vt.)
1805: 9039 pb

CARPENTER, JOSEPH (Cin-
cinnati, O.)
1801: 1491, 1569, 1590 pb
1802: 2820
1803: 4791?
1805: 9054, 9443
1811: 23285 pb, 23593 pb,
24467 pb
1812: 26516? pb, 27578,
51232 pb

1813: 28674?, 29838 pb
1814: 31155, 31687, 32831?

CARPENTER, JOSEPH (Lancaster, O.)
1807: 13282 pb

CARPENTER, STEPHEN CULLEN (Charleston, S.C.)
1805: 8918 pb

CARPENTER, WILLIAM ALLISON (Buffalo, N.Y.)
1818: 45853 pb

CARPENTER, WILLIAM ALLISON (Fredonia, N.Y.)
1817: 40457 pb

CARR, BENJAMIN (Philadelphia)
1803: 50357? pb
1804: 50438? pb, 50451? pb
1805: 8142 pb, 50506? pb, 50569? pb
1808: 50848? pb, 50868? pb, 50893? pb
1809: 50921 pb

CARR, JOSEPH (Baltimore)
1802: 50319? pb, 50325? pb
1805: 50509? pb, 50514? pb, 50590? pb, 50626? pb
1806: 50691? pb, 50727? pb
1807: 50796? pb
1810: 20222? pb, 50988? pb, ?51011? pb, 51021? pb
1811: 51070 pb
1813: 28081 pb
1815: 51531? pb, 51541? pb
1816: 51558? pb, 51641? pb
1818: 51744? pb, 51748? pb, 51751-51752? pb, 51789-51790? pb, 51830? pb

CARR, MARY (Philadelphia)
1815: 34360 pb

CARR, ROBERT (Baltimore)
1802: 1759
1808: 14630

CARR, ROBERT (New York)
1803: 5088

1806: 10240
1808: 15805

CARR, ROBERT (Philadelphia)
1801: 7, 144, 166, 386, 708, 836, 1141, 1156, 1265, 1307
1802: 1884, 1906, 1989-1990, 1991 pb, 2569, 2579, 2594, 2640, 3033, 3161, 50270
1803: 3837, 4024-4025, 4457-4458, 4627-4628, 5592, 50368
1804: 5850, 5856, 6381, 6578, 6580, 7346
1805: 8435, 8518, 8521, 8707, 8879, 9235, 9459, 9679
1806: 10088, 10899, 11386, 50663 pb
1807: 12289, 13046, 13364, 14165
1808: 14702, 14793, 15329 pb, 15806, 16236-16237
1809: 18371, 18425
1810: 19551, 19607-19608
1811: 22634, 23193?
1812: 25833?, 25912, 26117
1813: 27738, 28333, 28665, 29450, 29505, 29732, 29908

CARR, WILLIAM (Philadelphia)
1810: 19551, 19607-19608
1811: 22634, 23193?
1812: 25833?, 25912, 26117
1813: 27738, 28333, 28665, 29450, 29505, 29732, 29908

Carr & Schetky (Philadelphia)
see CARR, BENJAMIN (Philadelphia)
 SCHETKY, GEORGE (Philadelphia)

CARSON, JOHN (Philadelphia)
1818: 43726 f, 45589 pb
1819: 48809 pb

CARTER, JAMES B (Georgetown, D.C.)
1810: 20187
1811: 23785, 23968 pb
1813: 28097, 29920 pb
1814: 32608 pb
1816: 37685

CARTER, JOHN (Lynchburg,
  Va.)
1801: 687?
1803: 3747

CARTER, JOHN (Providence,
  R. I.)
1801: 241, 256, 614, 914,
  996, 1204, 1207, 1243
1802: 1863, 1940, 2744
1803: 3891-3892, 4098 pb,
  4259, 4646-4647, 4721-4722,
  4939, 4972 pb
1804: 5919, 6173, 6877 pb
1805: 8383, 8396, 8978
1806: 9938, 10958 pb, 11230,
  11259, 11278-11282, 11285
1807: 12357, 13186 pb, 13488,
  13491-13494
1808: 14596, 15711, 16022,
  16065, 16069
1809: 17291, 18187 pb, 18466-
  18467, 18796
1810: 20847
1811: 23503 pb, 51068 pb
1812: 25850, 26210 pb, 26612-
  26615
1813: 29280 pb, 29654a-
  29657, 30514?

CARTER, JOHN MICHEL
  (Baltimore)
1817: 42250 f

CARTER, JOHN MICHEL
  (Georgetown, D. C.)
1811: 23785, 23968 pb
1813: 29920 pb
1814: 32645, 32909 pb
1818: 45841 pb

CARTER, JOHN MICHEL
  (Petersburg, Va.)
1818: 45842-45844 pb

Carthage Press (Carthage,
  Tenn.)
1809: 16936

CARTWRIGHT, HENRY L
  (Hopkinsville, Ky.)
1813: 30517 pb

CARVER, JAMES (Philadelphia)
1818: 43378 pb

CATION, JAMES (Albany, N. Y.)
1810: 21466 f

CATTELL, DAVID (Browns-
  ville, Pa.)
1817: 42961 pb

Centinel (Boston)
see Columbian Centinel (Boston)

Centinel (Burlington, Vt.)
see Vermont Centinel (Burlington, Vt.)

CHAIN, HUGH (Alexandria,
  La.)
1817: 41294 pb

CHALK, JOHN (Philadelphia)
1802: 50319 pb

CHAMBERLAIN, ROYALL T
  (Auburn, N. Y.)
1813: 28095 pb

CHAMBERLAIN, ROYALL T
  (Union Springs, N. Y.)
1812: 25040 pb

CHAMBERLAIN, WILLIAM
  (Boston)
1819: 47785 pb

CHAMBERS, --- (New York)
1817: 41652 pb
1819: 49332

CHAMBERS, DAVID (Zanesville,
  O.)
1811: 23588 pb, 23589
1812: 25047, 26338
1813: 29399-29401
1815: 33777
1816: 38504-38505

CHANDLER, JEHU (Annapolis,
  Md.)
1811: 22153, 23158
1812: 25951 pb, 25954-25955,

25958-25960
1813: 29062-29063, 29065-
       29066
1814: 32016, 32017 pb
1816: 38147-38150
1817: 41355
1818: 44390, 44704, 45132
1819: ?47542, 48596

CHANEY, JACOB (Ports-
   mouth, O.)
1818: 45395 pb

CHANNING, HENRY (Boston)
1814: 31114-31115 pb, 31118 f

CHAPIN, HENRY (Canandaigua,
   N. Y.)
1803: 4218 pb, 4718 pb

CHAPLIN, JOSEPH (Rowley,
   Mass.)
1816: 39849 f

CHAPMAN, BENJAMIN (Phila-
   delphia)
1811: 22444a f
1812: 25923 pb
1813: 29618 f, 29619 pb
1814: 31040 f
1815: 34696 pb, 35171 f,
       35743 pb

CHAPMAN, EDMUND (Bethel,
   Mass.)
1810: 20657 f

CHARLES, WILLIAM (New
   York)
1807: 12934 pb, 12994 pb
1808: 14650, 15970 pb
1810: 20578 pb

CHARLES, WILLIAM (Phila-
   delphia)
1808: 14717 pb, 14773 pb,
       15174 pb, 16334 pb
1809: 17170 pb, 17315 pb,
       17391 pb, 17757 pb, 18468,
       50933 pb
1810: 19582 f, 19993 f,
       20825 pb, 21162 pb, 21164
       pb, 21505 pb, 21963 pb,

50993 pb
1811: 22660 pb, 23006 f,
       23018 f, 23240 f, 51098 f
1812: 26492 pb, 51182 f
1813: 30394 pb
1814: 31352 f, 31421 pb, 32104
       pb, 32477 pb, 51360? pb,
       51399 f
1815: 33795?, 34462, 34904
       f, 35005 pb, 35733-35734
       pb, 36106?, 51526-51527 pb
1816: 37505 pb, 37708 pb,
       37742 pb, 37747-37749 pb,
       38538 pb, 39053 pb, 39652
       pb
1817: 39944 pb, 39961 pb,
       40044 pb, 40611, 40746 pb,
       40748 pb, 40971 pb, 41129
       pb, 41300 pb, 41539-41541
       pb, 42217 pb, 42252 f,
       42768 pb
1818: 44958 pb, 51764 pb
1819: 47044-47045 pb, 47894
       pb, 48819 pb, 51891 pb

CHARLESS, JOSEPH (Lexing-
   ton, Ky.)
1803: 3728 pb, 3952 pb, 4137,
       4427 pb, 4433 pb, 4906,
       4980, 5034
1804: 5714 pb, 5716, 5776 pb,
       5888, 6227, 6428 pb, 6532,
       6694, 7397, 50413, 50415
       pb, 50452 pb
1805: 8024 pb, 8165, 8344,
       8379, 8598, 8663, 8719,
       9052, 9293, 9433-9434
1806: 10116, 10717, 11836 pb
1807: 11979 pb, 12864 pb

CHARLESS, JOSEPH (Louis-
   ville, Ky.)
1807: 12942 pb

CHARLESS, JOSEPH (Philadelphia)
1801: 171, 329, 338, 364
1802: 2349, 2997 pb, 3064,
       3190 pb, 3522

CHARLESS, JOSEPH (St. Louis,
   Mo.)
1808: 15451, 15624 pb

1809: 16954
1810: 20593
1813: 29180
1814: 32148
1815: 35293
1816: 38271
1817: 40450 pb, 41459
1818: 44874, 51755 pb
1819: 48716

Charleston Courier (Charleston, S. C.)
1805: 8138
1806: 10843, 11388
1807: 12467
1813: 28065
1818: 43763

Charleston Gazette (Charleston, S. C.)
1814: 31672

CHARLTON, --- (Richmond, Va.)
1815: 33984

CHARLTON, JOHN K M (Washington, Ga.)
1815: 34749 pb
1816: 38464 pb

CHARLTON, SEYMOUR P (Norfolk, Va.)
1816: 36858, 37588
1818: 43084, 43227
1819: 47146, 47152

CHARTER, NATHANIEL (Walpole, N. H.)
1805: 8028, 8264, 8292, 9113
1806: 10001, 10207, 11237, 11253, 50700 pb
1807: 11964, 12081, 12454, 12592, 12874

CHASE, EBEN R (Deering, N. H.)
1818: 43875

CHASE, EBENEZER (Andover, N. H.)
1819: 47659

CHASE, SEPHEN (Portland, Me.)
1805: 7841

CHATTERTON, PETER (Elizabeth, N. J.)
1818: 46615 pb
1819: 49112, 49960 pb, 50184

CHAUNCEY, ELIHU (Philadelphia)
1802: 1846 pb
1803: 3936, 4831, 4994 pb, 4996 pb
1804: 6385 f, 7780 pb

CHEETHAM, JAMES (New York)
1801: 642, 815
1802: 2018, 2019 f, 2020 pb, 2021-2022, 2024
1803: 3956 pb, 3957-3958, 4022, 4753, 5494, 6006 f
1805: 9010-9011 pb, 9013
1806: 10123, 10844, 10872 pb, 10994-10997, 11000-11001
1807: 11936, 13051
1808: 14680 pb

CHEEVER, NATHANIEL (Hallowell, Me.)
1807: 12869
1808: 14273 pb, 14574, 15264, 15641, 15898, 15927, 16156
1809: 17243, 17279, 17491, 17579, 17835, 17873, 18136, 18620, 19287 pb
1810: 19343 pb, 20220-20221, 21535, 22030
1811: 22260, 22452, 22509 pb, 22914-22915, 23716, 23717 pb, 23897, 24037, 24361
1812: 24712, 24775, 24917, 25159, 25526, 26164 bf
1813: 27792, 27794-27795, 27847-27848, 28001-28003, 28126 pb, 29235, 29442
1814: 30754-30756, 31008, 31275, 31594 pb, 31867 pb, 32109
1815: 33940-33942, 34182, 34500, 34711, 35365 pb, 35711, 35747

1816:   36825-36826a, 38234
   pb, 38325 pb, 38541, 39087
1817:   40083-40084, 40345 pb,
   40741, 40918, 41332 pb,
   41520 pb
1818:   44942 pb

CHEVEE, JAMES B (New York)
1817:   41612

CHICKERING, JABEZ (Dedham,
   Mass.)
1815:   34639-34640

CHILD, ASA (Johnstown, N. Y.)
1807:   12985 pb
1811:   24472
1815:   35227
1816:   39887
1819:   47034

CHILD, LEMUEL (Boston)
1809:   18619?
1810:   20965

CHILD, S P (Baltimore)
1813:   27755 pb, 28410, 28720,
   29056, 29241

CHILD, WILLIAM (Ballston
   Spa, N. Y.)
1801:   1237 pb
1805:   7969
1808:   15296 pb
1810:   19308 pb, 20641 pb

CHILD, WILLIAM (Johnstown,
   N. Y.)
1805:   8919 pb
1806:   ?10890
1807:   12985 pb

CHILES, SAMUEL (Fredericksburg, Va.)
1803:   5520 pb

CHILSON, ASAPH (Newport,
   R. I.)
1804:   6477 f, 6560 pb

CHIPMAN, SAMUEL (Middle-
   bury, Vt.)
1810:   19928 f, 21449 f
1811:   22978 pb

CHIPMAN, SAMUEL (Ver-
   gennes, Vt.)
1801:   1577

CHITTENDON, GEORGE (Hud-
   son, N. Y.)
1801:   98 pb
1802:   1738, 1770, 1871, 3045,
   3046 f
1803:   4202

Christian Disciple Society
   (Boston)
1819:   50035 f

Christian Messenger (Middlebury, Vt.)
1818:   44912, 45274, 45550,
   45823-45825
1819:   49425

Chronicle (Philadelphia)
see   Columbian Chronicle
   (Philadelphia)

Chronicle (Warren, O.)
see   Western Reserve Chronicle (Warren, O.)

CHURCH, DANIEL (Arlington,
   Vt.)
1816:   36734 pb

CHURCHILL, GEORGE (Albany,
   N. Y.)
1814:   30610, 30829 bf
1815:   34146, 34336? pb,
   34753, 35707
1816:   36700?, 38919

CHURCHILL, SYLVESTER
   (Windsor, Vt.)
1809:   16895, 17357 f, 17771,
   18752, 19265
1810:   19570, 20438, 20707,
   20795, 20868, 20870, 20880,
   21113, 21203-21204, 21520
   pb, 22074

CIST, CHARLES (CARL)
   (Philadelphia)
1801:   59 pb
1802:   1761 pb
1803:   3678 pb, 4385

1804: 5705 pb
1805: 7865 pb, 8010, 8495-
8496, 8544, 8600, 9050,
9111
1806: 9839 pb, 11429

CIST, CHARLES (CARL)
(Washington, D. C.)
1801: 1093, 1608

CIST, MARY (Philadelphia)
1806: 11914

CLAP, EBENEZER (North-
ampton, Mass.)
1805: 8501
1807: 12255, 12410, 12643
1808: 14277, 14426

CLAP, WILLIAM TILESTON
(Boston)
1801: 50251 f
1805: 9509 pb
1807: 12304 pb, 12591 f,
13295 f
1810: 20636 f

CLAPP, HENRY (Nantucket,
Mass.)
1816: 37286 f

CLAPP, JOSHUA B (New Lon-
don, Conn.)
1818: 43169, 45518 pb
1819: 48397 pb, 49065, 50114

CLAPP, WILLIAM W (Boston)
1810: 22046?
1812: 25280, 26590 pb
1813: 27993 pb
1814: 31964
1815: 34229
1819: 49096, 49539

CLAPP, WILLIAM WARLAND
(Buckstown, Me.)
1805: 8503 pb, 8682 pb,
9087
1806: 10072, 11390
1807: 12049, 13062 pb
1808: 14424, 14541, 15016
1809: 16956, 17240, 18153 pb
1810: 19432 pb, 19486, 20723

CLAPP, WILLIAM WARLAND
(Northampton, Mass.)
1815: 34698 pb, 34852, 35041
pb, 36581, 36584 pb
1816: 37598, 37789, 38668,
39853

CLARK, --- (Albany, N. Y.)
1814: 30656 f

CLARK, --- (Baltimore)
1804: 6197, 6585, 50453
1805: 8362 pb, 8546
1806: 10187, ?10191, 10496,
10796, ?10840, 10852,
10991, 11304, 50726 pb

CLARK, AARON (Albany,
N. Y.)
1818: 43625 f

CLARK, ALANSON (Greenfield,
Mass.)
1818: 44037-44038 f, 44232 f,
44320 pb, 45316 pb
1819: 49383 f

CLARK, DANIEL (Manlius,
N. Y.)
1817: 40976, 41209
1818: 45173 pb

CLARK, DARIUS (Bennington,
Vt.)
1813: 29869
1814: 31431, 31455 pb, 31555,
32118?
1815: 34629, 34679, 35263,
35270, 35624-35625
1816: 38532 pb, 38966, 39073,
39663
1817: 41380 pb, 41503, 42181
1819: 48187, 50186

CLARK, EPAPHRAS (Middle-
town, Conn.)
1811: 23882 pb
1814: 31591 pb
1815: 35869 f, 36014-36015 f
1816: 38344 f, 38890 pb
1817: 42074 pb
1818: 43898, 44273, 44467,
44652

1819: 47081, 47176 pb, 47479, 47978, 48657 pb, 48874 pb, 49286, 49379 pb, 49432

CLARK, GEORGE (Charles-town, Mass.)
1819: 49340 pb, 49341 f

CLARK, ISRAEL W (Albany, N. Y.)
1817: 40595
1818: 43576, 43645, 44141, 45029, 45773
1819: 48364, 48897, 50115

CLARK, ISRAEL W (Cherry Valley, N. Y.)
1812: 26365 pb

CLARK, ISRAEL W (Coopers-town, N. Y.)
1814: 33592 pb
1817: 41091

CLARK, ISRAEL W (Hartwick, N. Y.)
1813: 27913 pb
1814: 30885, 31145, 33609

CLARK, JOHN C (Philadelphia)
1817: 40651
1818: 43751, 43755-43756, 43759, 44526, 44761, 44802-44803, 44962, 45183, 45212, 45820
1819: 47590, 47606, 47891, 48230, 48437, 48491, 49098, 49411, 49535, 49991, 50156, 51872

CLARK, JONATHAN (Zanes-ville, O.)
1815: 36588
1816: 36786, 38508, 39838

CLARK, JUSTIN (Montrose, Pa.)
1816: 39037 pb
1818: 44878 pb

CLARK, LOT (Norwich, N. Y.)
1814: 33559 pb

CLARK, M (Philadelphia)
1818: 45935

CLARK, SAMUEL W (Hudson, N. Y.)
1815: 35329
1817: 42340
1818: 45872

CLARK, THOMAS (Portland, Me.)
1801: 1446 f
1803: 4579 f, 5068 pb, 5070 pb
1804: 6701 f, 50481 f
1805: 9273 pb
1806: 11188 f

CLARK, ZENA (Potsdam, N. Y.)
1816: 38691 pb

Clark & Raser (Philadelphia)
see CLARK, JOHN C (Phila-delphia)
    RASER, MATTHIAS (Phila-delphia)

CLARKE, DAVID (Louisville, Ga.)
1812: 24603 pb

CLARKE, JAMES (Louisville, Ga.)
1816: 36721 pb

CLARKE, JOHN (Philadelphia)
1813: 28756 f

CLARKE, THOMAS (Boston)
1801: 315 engr

Classic Press (Philadelphia)
1804: 5971, 6500, 6675, 7227, 7246, 7657
1805: 8435, 9086
1806: 10754

CLAYTON, EDWARD B (New Brunswick, N. J.)
1814: 30973 f

CLAYTON, EDWARD B (New
York)
1816: 37033, 37799
1817: 40318 pb, 40407, 40676,
40818, 41327, 41495, 41891,
42197, 42881-42885
1818: 43512, 43516, 43651-
43652, 43654, 43867? pb,
44168, 44579, 44880, 45182,
45231, 45319, 45421, 45573,
45575, 45635, 45654-45657,
45663, 45683, 45787, 45860,
46648
1819: 46929, 47449-47450,
47651-47652, 48137, 48738,
48891 pb, 49315, 49380,
49449, 49589

CLAYTON, HENRY (New York)
1815: 34058, 34181, 34269,
34306, 34805, 35030, 35783,
35788
1816: 37632, 38962, 39010

CLEIM, CHRISTIAN (Baltimore)
1808: 15700
1809: 16834, 16902, 18179
1810: 19491, 20536, 20833,
20839, 21366
1811: 23493 pb

CLEIM, CHRISTIAN (Ephrata,
Pa.)
1804: 5713 pb, 5953 pb, 6855
pb, 6954

CLINE, JOHN (Philadelphia)
1807: 12403
1809: 17079
1810: 19627 pb, 19630, 19771
pb
1811: 22454
1812: 25798 f

CLINE, WILLIAM (Columbia,
S. C.)
1817: 42174, 42176, 51652
pb

CLINGAN, JOSEPH (Williamsport, Pa.)
1818: 46652 pb

CLOUGH, --- (Gilmanton,
N. H.)
1804: 6390, 50458 pb

CLOUGH, JOHN (New York)
1803: 3759, 3788, 3793, 4705
1804: 5805, 7394, 7773,
50446-50447 pb
1805: 8749 pb
1806: 9983

COALE, --- (Wilmington, Del.)
1817: 40843 pb

COALE, EDWARD JOHNSON
(Baltimore)
1809: 17641 f, 17645-17646 f,
17888 pb, 18360 f, 18782 f
1810: 19349 f, 19487 f, 19571
f, 20034 pb, 20402 f, 20758
f, 21309 f, 21375 f, 21943
pb
1811: 22155 f, 22183 f, 22407
f, 22450 pb, 22558 pb,
22642 f, 24366? pb, 24372 f
1812: 25506 pb, 25932 pb,
26107 f, 26345 f, 26346 pb,
26743 f
1813: 27714 f, 28658 f, 28701
f, 28906 pb, 28958 pb, 29197
f, 29457 f, 29674 f, 30480 f
1814: 30899 f, 31070 f, 31569
f, 31898 pb, 32546 f, 32899
f, 33734 f
1815: 33846 f, 34189 f, 34936
f, 35046 f, 35633 f, 35718
f, 36059 f, 36420 pb, 36483
pb
1816: 36732 pb, 37059 f,
37071 f, 38122 pb
1817: 40155 pb, 40960 pb,
40961 f, 41064 f, 41516 pb,
41870 f, 42307 f
1818: 43067 f, 43650 f, 43838
f, 43980 pb, 44155 pb, 44208
f, 44261 f, 44267 f, 44450
f, 45397 pb
1819: 46990 pb, 48165? pb

COALE, WILLIAM (Frankford,
Pa.)
1810: 20135 pb
1811: 22889 pb, 23287-23288

COALE, WILLIAM (Havre-
de-Grace, Md.)
1818:   43405 pb

COALE, WILLIAM (Newtown,
Pa.)
1802:   1957 pb
1804:   5660, 5662
1805:   8428 pb, 9279 pb, 9351

COALE, WILLIAM (Philadel-
phia)
1813:   30440 pb

Coale & Maxwell (Baltimore)
see COALE, EDWARD JOHN-
̅̅̅̅SON (Baltimore)
    MAXWELL, NATHANIEL
    G (Baltimore)

Coale & Thomas (Baltimore)
see COALE, EDWARD JOHN-
̅̅̅̅SON (Baltimore)
    THOMAS, MOSES (Baltimore)

COBBETT, HENRY (New
York)
1817:   41495 f

COCHRAN, ANN (Philadelphia)
1811:   22628
1812:   25419, 25670, 51173 pb
1813:   28645 pb, 28946, 29482
    pb, 29495, 29628, 29728
1814:   32629? pb

COCHRAN, JAMES (Windsor,
Vt.)
1810:   19827 pb
1811:   22590 pb
1812:   24829 pb

COCHRAN, JESSE (Windsor,
Vt.)
1811:   22349 pb, 22381 pb
1812:   24988 pb
1814:   30790, 30854, 31142,
    31309 pb, 31702 pb, 31962,
    32182 pb, 32229 pb, 32473
    pb, 32880, 32923, 33573,
    33704 pb, 33710
1815:   33981, 33990, 34049,
    34335, 34547 pb, 34606,

34636, 35119, 35304, 35409
    pb, 35417 pb, 35419 pb,
    35616, 35654 pb, 35748,
    36130, 36600 pb, 36602
1816:   36971 pb, 37240, 37966,
    38377 pb, 38536, 39664,
    39666 f
1817:   40459, 41572 pb, 41746
    pb
1818:   45718

COCHRAN, ROBERT (Philadelphia)
1801:   636, 677, 730, 1083,
    1309
1802:   1727, 1742, 1876, 1999,
    2651, 2666, 2889, 3528
1803:   3640, 3872, 4051, 4087
    pb, 4855
1804:   7041
1805:   50516 pb
1806:   11331, 11370
1807:   12312 pb, 12405 pb,
    12455
1808:   14608, 15129, 15410,
    15801, 16701
1809:   17241 pb, 17477 pb,
    18352 pb
1810:   19792, 21056
1811:   22434, 22555 pb, 24076

CODY, ISAAC (Schenectady,
N. Y.)
1814:   33741 f

COFFEEN, HENRY (Watertown,
N. Y.)
1810:   19345 pb, 19438
1812:   26597 pb

COHEN, H (Richmond, Va.)
1817:   40507 f

COLBY, ZEBULON (Hamilton,
O.)
1814:   32119 pb
1815:   35271
1816:   38615 pb

COLCORD, JOHN P (Portland,
Me.)
1811:   23072, 23942i-23942k

COLE, BENJAMIN (Brattle-
borough, Vt.)
1805: 8580 f
1806: 10449 f, 10713 f
1809: 17122 f
1814: 32769 pb

COLE, BENJAMIN (Canan-
daigua, N.Y.)
1814: 31915 f

COLE, EDWARD (Lewistown,
Pa.)
1804: 7811

COLE, JOHN (Baltimore)
1802: 2481, 2531, 2549, 2975
pb
1803: 3981 pb
1804: 6047, 6055 pb, 6352,
7132, 7743-7744, 50419
1805: 7916, 8206 pb, 8349,
8465, 8485, 8488, 9212-
9213, 9742
1806: 10173 f, 10452 pb,
10802, 11222
1812: 25311 f, 26732 f
1813: 28281 f, 28659 f, 28720
f, 29236 f, 29275 f, 29781 f
1814: 30989 f, 31062 f, 31590
f, 31800 f, 32538 f
1815: 34842 f, 35342 f, 35633
f, 35781 f
1816: 37082 f, 38686 pb,
38806 f

COLE, JOHN ORTON (Albany,
N.Y.)
1819: 47646 pb, 49138 pb

COLE, MATTHEW M (Scho-
harie, N.Y.)
1818: 45135 pb
1819: 48489

COLE, SAMUEL (Baltimore)
1803: 3716, 3981 pb, 4265,
4471, 4934, 5597
1804: 5767 pb
1806: 10173 f, 10189 pb
1807: 12086 pb, 12750 f,
12857 f
1808: 15612 f, 50870 f

Cole & I. Bonsal (Baltimore)
see COLE, SAMUEL (Balti-
more)
BONSAL, ISAAC (Baltimore)

Cole & Hewes (Baltimore)
see COLE, JOHN (Baltimore)
HEWES, JOHN (Baltimore)

COLEMAN, WESLEY (Cincin-
nati, O.)
1815: 34917 f
1816: 37620 f

COLERICK, JOHN (Washington,
Pa.)
1801: 244
1802: 3536
1803: 4086, 5574
1804: 50487 f
1805: 50631 f
1806: 10318

COLES, ANN (Philadelphia)
1813: 29482 pb, 29704, 51346
1814: 30740, 30784, 32399,
32871, 51432 pb
1815: 34821, 35609

COLES, BENJAMIN (Philadelphia)
1816: 37104 pb

COLES, DENNIS (Newburgh,
N.Y.)
1801: 520
1802: 50328 pb
1803: 4955 pb
1804: 6673, 7645, 7786
1805: 8423 pb
1806: 11263 pb

COLLETT, ISAAC (Staunton,
Va.)
1811: 22172
1812: 25221, 25393?, 26134?,
26836?, 27408, 27414
1813: 28000
1818: 45776

COLLETT, ISAAC (Winchester,
Va.)
1807: 12847
1808: 16125

COLLIER, --- (Savannah, Ga.)
1806: 9890

COLLIER, THOMAS (Benning-
ton, Vt.)
1801: 83, 1160 pb, 1665
1802: 1782, 2407 pb, 2581,
2809, 3142, 3271 pb, 3598

COLLIER, THOMAS (Litch-
field, Conn.)
1801: 591, 871, 1144
1802: 2696 pb
1804: 6786
1805: 8231
1807: 12739
1808: 15036

COLLIER, THOMAS (Troy,
N. Y.)
1802: 2438, 3180 pb
1803: 3752 pb, 3778 pb, 4253
pb

COLLIER, WILLIAM (Boston)
1815: 51512 pb

Collier & Stockwell (Benning-
ton, Vt.)
see COLLIER, THOMAS
(Bennington, Vt.)
STOCKWELL, WILLIAM
(Bennington, Vt.)

COLLINS, BENJAMIN SAY
(New York)
1816: 36964, 37099, 38341
1817: 40194, 40213, 40227,
41513, 41824-41825, 41895,
42845
1818: 43294-43295, 43299,
43301 bf, 43309, 43313,
43319, 43322, 43329 f,
43343 pb, 43798, 44604 f,
44937, 44939, 44944, 44953-
44954, 46670, 46678, 46679
pb, 46683 pb, 46718, 51742
1819: 47222, 47224, 47227,
47230, 47372 f, 48405 f,
48788, 48803, 48815, 50015
pb, 50064

COLLINS, ISAAC (New York)
1801: 5, 226, 227 pb, 431,
489, 544-545, 695, 816,
974 pb, 1028 pb, 1174 pb,
1186
1802: 1978, 2039 f, 2282,
2284, 2287, 2292, 2445,
2464, 2571, 2612, 2709 pb,
2715 pb, 2716, 2717 pb,
2719, 2789, 2791, 2964,
3002, 3059
1803: 3666 pb, 3931 pb, 4195,
4252, 4632, 4633 pb, 4664
pb, 4692 pb, 4701-4702 pb,
4759 pb, 5590
1804: 5846 pb, 6140, 6293,
6614 pb, 6922, 6977 pb,
7197, 7248 pb, 50409
1805: 7980, 8224, 8363, 8550,
8881, 8943 pb, 8949 pb,
8952, 9019, 9376, 9502-
9503, 9763-9768, 50575 pb
1806: 9966 pb, 10334 pb,
10928 pb, 10933 pb, 11043,
11081 pb, 11289
1807: 12125 pb, 12992 pb

COLLINS, JOSEPH BUDD (New
York)
1816: 36964, 37099, 38341
1817: 40194, 40213, 40227,
41513, 41824-41825, 41895,
42845
1818: 43294-43295, 43299,
43301, 43309, 43313, 43319,
43322, 43798, 44937, 44939,
44944, 44953-44954, 46670,
46678, 46718, 51742
1819: 47222, 47224, 47227,
47230, 48788, 48803, 48815,
50064

COLLINS, JOSEPH S (Chillicothe, O.)
1806: 11057-11058, 11061
1807: 13278, 13280
1809: 16931, 18278-18279,
18280-18281 f, 18282
1810: 20627, 20945 pb, 21455
1811: 23591, 24038 pb
1812: 26339-26340

COLLINS, LEWIS (Washington,
Ky.)
1819: 47089

COLLINS, THOMAS (Burling-
ton, N. J.)
1818: 46678 pb

COLLINS, THOMAS (New York)
1807: 12080 pb, 12885 pb,
13114, 13155-13156 pb,
13158 pb, 13160-13162 pb,
13303, 13380
1808: 14448 pb, 14460 pb,
14729-14730, 14880, 15213-
15214 pb, 15474, 15675 pb,
15684-15685 pb, 16094
1809: 16983 pb, 17125 pb,
17474, 17701 pb, 18111 pb,
18145-18146 pb, 18155 pb,
18157 pb, 18584 pb, 50950
pb
1810: 19352 pb, 19500 pb,
19724, 19789 pb, 20167,
20399 pb, 20581 pb, 20799?
pb, 20804-20805 pb, 20813
pb, 20823 pb, 21290 f
1811: 22298 pb, 22814, 23037
pb, 23451 pb, 23453-23454
pb, 23465-23466 pb, 23468
pb, 23471 pb, 23474 pb,
23555 pb, 23958, 24029 pb
1812: 24746 pb, 24799-24800
pb, 24824 f, 25054, 25109,
25392 pb, 26159-26160 pb,
26162 pb, 26166 pb, 26170
pb, 26913 f
1813: 27851 pb, 28440 pb,
28605 pb, 28889 pb, 29757,
29808 pb, 29940 pb, 30583
pb
1814: 30673, 30864-30865 pb,
31462, 32130 pb, 32191-
32192 pb, 32194 pb, 32199
pb, 32206 pb, 32208 pb,
32414 pb, 32591 pb
1815: 33992 pb, 34230 pb,
34949 pb, 35346 pb, 35352
pb, 35355 pb, 35368 pb,
35381-35382 pb, 35474 pb,
35653 pb, 36078 pb
1816: 36925 pb, 36928 pb,
36952 pb, 37075 pb, 37100

pb, 37576, 37638, 38317
pb, 38322 pb, 38326-38327
pb, 38332 pb, 38341 pb,
38453 f, 38557 pb, 38624 pb
1817: 40137 pb, 40174 pb,
40195 f, 40204 pb, 40521-
40522, 40853, 41046 pb,
41512-41514 pb, 41523,
41528 pb, 41532 pb, 41534
pb, 41640, 41812-41813,
42273 pb
1818: 43051, 44322 pb, 44436
pb, 44516 pb, 44937 pb,
44939 pb, 44953-44955 pb,
45070, 45205 pb, 45320 pb,
45396 pb, 45709 pb, 45753,
46731 pb
1819: 47162 pb, 47215 pb,
48115 pb, 48404 f, 48428
pb, 48788, 48795 pb, 48803
pb, 48815 pb, 49531

COLLINS, WILLIAM (Philadelphia)
1818: 43247 f, 43410 pb,
45596 pb
1819: 47852 f, 47879 pb,
49017 f

Collins & Co. (New York)
see COLLINS, THOMAS (New
͞York)

Collins & Hannay (New York)
see COLLINS, BENJAMIN SAY
͞(New York)
HANNAY, SAMUEL (New
York)

Collins & Perkins (New York)
see COLLINS, THOMAS (New
͞York)
PERKINS, BENJAMIN D
(New York)

Collins, Perkins & Co. (New
York)
see COLLINS, ISAAC (New
͞York)
PERKINS, BENJAMIN D
(New York)

COLMAN, --- (Baltimore)
1817: 40259 pb

COLTON, RODERICK MER-
RICK (Greenfield, Mass.)
1815: 34054-34055

Columbian Associated Library
(New York)
1805: 9236 f

Columbian Bookstore (Troy,
N. Y.)
1815: 35428 pb

Columbian Centinel (Boston)
1803: 3860 bsb
1815: 34797 pb, 36115 pb

Columbian Chronicle (Philadelphia)
1817: 39930

Columbian Minerva (Dedham,
Mass.)
1804: 5819 pb

Columbian Phenix (Providence,
R. I.)
1810: 20643, 22031

Columbian Post-Boy (Warren,
R. I.)
1812: 26530, 51250

Columbian Printing Office
(New York)
1805: 7958 pb, 7981

Columbian Register (New
Haven, Conn.)
1818: 43705? bsb

Columbus Gazette (Columbus,
O.)
1817: 41201
1818: 45140, 45144-45145,
45148
1819: 48969, 48971, 49211?

COLVIN, JOHN B (Baltimore)
1802: 2135 pb

COLVIN, JOHN B (Frederick,
Md.)
1802: 2976 pb, 3383 pb

1803: 3834, 4487
1804: 6054
1805: 8221 pb

COLVIN, JOHN B (Washington,
D. C.)
1808: 14744 pb, 15630 pb

COMBES, NATHANIEL L
(Bridgeton, N. J.)
1816: 37486 pb

Common Prayer Book Society
of Pennsylvania (Philadelphia)
1818: 45431 f

Company of Flying Stationers
(New York)
1807: 11998 f
1811: 22207 f, 22208? f
1816: 36761 f
1817: 40016 f

COMSTOCK, JAMES (Ballston
Spa, N. Y.)
1810: 20213, 21013, 21361
1811: 23007, 24471
1812: 26805
1814: 30771, 31299, 31771,
32551
1815: 34115, 34584, 34586,
35358
1816: 39870
1817: 40240, 41342, 42310,
51693
1818: 43202, 45267 pb, 45881
1819: 49390, 49435

COMSTOCK, SETH (New Haven,
Conn.)
1804: 6017

CONANT, AUGUSTUS F (Bur-
lington, Vt.)
1814: 32371 pb

CONANT, DANIEL (Boston)
1805: 9371 pb
1806: 11375 pb

CONANT, JONATHAN (Albany,
N. Y.)
1807: 13254 pb

CONDIE, THOMAS (Philadelphia)
1806: 10536 pb

Connecticut Academy of Arts and Sciences (New Haven, Conn.)
1815: 34427 pb
1819: 47978 f

Connecticut Herald (New Haven, Conn.)
1804: 7369, 7739
1816: 37478, 38757, 38958
1817: 40511

Connecticut Journal (New Haven, Conn.)
1816: 37017, 37335
1817: 41254, 42814, 42981, 42983

Connecticut Mirror (Hartford, Conn.)
1815: 51481 pb

Connecticut Religious Tract Society (New Haven, Conn.)
1801: 464? f
1809: 17102, 17382 f

CONNER, JAMES (New York)
1819: 48245

CONOVER, PETER (Newark, N.J.)
1817: 40914, 40966 pb, 41460 pb, 41657 pb

CONOVER, PETER (Paterson, N.J.)
1815: 34019 pb

CONRAD, ---. (New York)
1803: 4634 f

CONRAD, ANDREW (Philadelphia)
For all entries see CONRAD, CORNELIUS (Philadelphia) below.

CONRAD, CORNELIUS (Philadelphia)
1805: 50608 pb
1806: 9837 pb
1807: 12083 f, 12819 f, 13394 pb
1808: 15012 pb, 15302 pb, 15678 pb, 15882 pb, 16337 pb
1809: 16845-16846 pb, 16943 pb, 17089 f, 17163 pb, 18593 pb, 18770 pb, 19086 f
1810: 19567 pb, 19584 pb, 20065 pb, 20806 pb, 21089 f, 21233 pb, 21241 f, 21330 pb
1811: 22327 pb, 22389 pb, 22425 pb, 22781 pb
1812: 26644 pb

CONRAD, EPHRAIM (New York)
1810: 19903
1811: 23819
1812: 25294
1813: 28593, 29642 pb, 29876
1814: 31477, 31747, 33754
1815: 35485 pb
1816: 37194
1817: 40189, 40806, 40908
1818: 44875, 45028 pb, 45039, 45071, 45631
1819: 46931, 47875, 48130, 48219 pb, 48696, 48915, 49035, 49448, 49477, 49544 pb, 49546 pb, 49975

CONRAD, JOHN (Baltimore)
1801: 104? pb, 161 pb, 237 f, 238 pb, 479 f, 963 pb, 1132 pb, 1188 f, 1263 f, 1274 pb, 1592 f
1802: 1759 f, 1845 pb, 2124 f, 2483 f, 2528 pb, 2543 f, 2632 pb, 2637 pb, 2981 f, 3006 f, 3064 f, 3075 f, 3084 f, 3573 f, 3575 f, 50323 f
1803: 3618, 3622 f, 3653 f, 3674 pb, 3880-3881 pb, 3883 f, 4019 f, 4376 pb, 4387 pb, 4527-4528 f, 5600 f
1804: 5703 pb, 5824 f, 5897 pb, 6068 pb, 6122 f, 6577 pb

1805: 8448 pb, 50608 pb
1806: 50720 pb
1807: 12293 f
1808: 16337 pb

CONRAD, JOHN (Charleston,
S. C.)
1815: 34794 pb

CONRAD, JOHN (Norfolk, Va.)
1803: 3618, 3622 f, 3653 f,
4091 f, 4387 pb, 4528 f,
5600 f
1804: 5824 f, 5897 pb, 6068
pb

CONRAD, JOHN (Petersburg,
Va.)
1803: 3618, 3622 f, 3653 f,
4091 f, 4387 pb, 4528 f,
5600 f
1804: 5824 f, 5897 pb, 6068
pb, 50479 pb
1805: 9672 pb
1806: 11777 pb, 50741 pb
1807: 12246 f, 14137 pb
1808: 16313 f, 16646 pb
1809: 50972 pb

CONRAD, JOHN (Philadelphia)
1801: 52 pb, 160 f, 161 pb,
237 f, 238 pb, 243 pb,
294 f, 479 f, 499 pb, 588
f, 963 pb, 1108 pb, 1132
pb, 1188 f, 1263 f, 1274
pb, 1592 f
1802: 1726 f, 1843 f, 1845
pb, 2124 f, 2483 f, 2528
pb, 2542-2543 f, 2632 pb,
2981 f, 3006 f, 3064 f,
3075 f, 3084 f, 3573 f,
3575 f, 50270 f, 50323 f
1803: 3618, 3622 f, 3639 f,
3653 f, 3804 pb, 3849 f,
3874 pb, 3880-3881 pb,
3883 f, 3948 f, 4091 f,
4288 pb, 4293 pb, 4319 f,
4365 pb, 4376 pb, 4387 pb,
4454 f, 4458 f, 4527-4528
f, 4531 pb, 4621 f, 4783
f, 4801 f, 4815 f, 4941 pb,
5004 pb, 5552 f, 5600 f
1804: 5727 pb, 5824 f, 5897

pb, 6068 pb, 6072 pb, 6396-
6397 f, 6398 pb, 6399 f,
6402 f, 7028-7029, 7047 pb,
7061 pb, 7260 f, 7492 f,
7675 f
1805: 8447-8448 pb, 8707 f,
9185 f, 9289-9290 f, 50599
f
1806: 9926 f, 9929 pb, 11201
f, 50720 pb
1807: 13148 f, 50790 pb
1813: 27719 pb, 30538 f
1814: 30672 pb, 33531 pb
1815: 34160 pb, 34538-34539
pb, 34794 pb, 35062 pb,
35069 f, 36153 pb
1816: 36783 f, 37340 f, 38034
pb, 38035 f, 38500 pb, 38620
f, 38655 f

CONRAD, JOHN (Washington,
D. C.)
1801: 161, 237-238, 294, 479
f, 963, 1132, 1188 f, 1263
f, 1274 pb, 1592 f
1802: 1845 pb, 2124 f, 2483
f, 2528, 2543 f, 2632, 2981
f, 3006 f, 3064 f, 3075 f,
3084 f, 3573 f, 3575 f
1803: 3618, 3622 f, 3653 f,
3881 pb, 3883 f, 4091 f,
4376 pb, 4387 pb, 4527-4528
f, 5600 f
1804: 5824 f, 5897 pb, 6647
pb

CONRAD, MICHAEL (Baltimore)
1801: 104? pb, 161 pb, 237 f,
238 pb, 479 f, 963 pb, 1132
pb, 1188 f, 1263 f, 1274 pb,
1592 f
1802: 1759 f, 1845 pb, 2124 f,
2483 f, 2528 pb, 2543 f,
2632 pb, 2637 pb, 2981 f,
3006 f, 3064 f, 3075 f, 3084
f, 3573 f, 3575 f, 50323 f
1803: 3618, 3622 f, 3653 f,
3674 pb, 3880-3881 pb, 3883
f, 4091 f, 4376 pb, 4387 pb,
4527-4528 f, 4815 f
1804: 5703 pb, 5824 f, 5897
pb, 6068 pb, 6122 f, 6577 pb
1805: 8448 pb, 50608 pb

1806: 50720 pb
1808: 16337 pb

CONRAD, MICHAEL (Norfolk, Va.)
1803: 3618, 3622 f, 3653 f, 4091 f, 4387 pb, 4528 f, 5600 f
1804: 5824 f, 5897 pb, 6068 pb

CONRAD, MICHAEL (Petersburg, Va.)
1803: 3618, 3622 f, 3653 f, 4091 f, 4387 pb, 4528 f, 5600 f
1804: 5824 f, 5897 pb, 6068 pb, 50479 pb
1805: 9672 pb
1806: 11777 pb, 50741 pb
1807: 12246 f, 14137 pb
1808: 16313 f, 16646 pb
1809: 50972 pb

CONRAD, MICHAEL (Washington, D. C.)
1803: 3618, 3622 f, 3653 f, 3881 pb, 3883 f, 4091 f, 4376 pb, 4387 pb, 4527-4528 f, 5600 f
1804: 5824 f, 5897 pb, 6647 pb

CONRAD, SOLOMON WHITE (Philadelphia)
1801: 4, 165, 883, 926-927, 1269, 1641, 1658, 50267
1802: 1708, 1935, 2231, 2459, 2656, 2659, 2862, 3098
1803: 3770, 3877, 4510, 4648, 4649 pb, 4651, 4679, 4833-4834, 5570, 5598
1804: 5698-5699, 5911-5912, 6030, 6036, 6228, 6291 pb, 6292, 6309, 6431, 6433 pb, 6594, 6775, 7251, 7263, 50436
1805: 7850, 7861, 7951 pb, 8196, 8223 pb, 8486, 8487 pb, 8737-8738 pb, 9096, 9138, 9157, 9335 bsb, 9503 f, 9755 pb, 50537 pb, 50538

1806: 9815, 9834, 9869 pb, 10151-10152, 10233 pb, 10456-10457, 10483 pb, 10678? pb, 10942, 11101, 11104, 11136, 11163 pb, 11288 pb, 11377 pb, 11460 pb, 11811 pb, 50678, 50719 f
1807: 11951 f, 12113 pb, 12127 pb, 12324, 12494 pb, 12495, 12632, 12659 pb, 12823 pb, 12870, 13128 pb, 13328 pb, 13384-13385 pb, 13417 pb, 13554-13555, 13635, 13641
1808: 14259 f, 14307 pb, 14665 pb, 14747 pb, 15072 f, 15075 pb, 15122 pb, 15374 pb, 15947 pb, 15974 pb, 16145 f, 16723 pb
1809: 16788 pb, 16995 f, 17001 pb, 17431 pb, 17619 f, 18383 f, 18616 f, 18622 pb, 19235 f
1810: 19293 pb, 19326 f, 19509 pb, 19822 pb, 19862 pb, 20169 pb, 20497? pb, 21090 pb, 21348 f, 21965 f
1811: 22221 f, 22426 pb, 22547 f, 22588 pb, 22683 f, 22687 pb, 22712 pb, 23683 f, 23684 pb, 23690 f, 23881 f, 24348 f, 24352 f, 24356 pb
1812: 24576 f, 24896 pb, 25127 pb, 25789 f, 25790 pb, 26397 pb, 26465? f, 27405 f
1813: 27648 pb, 28351 f, 30482 f
1814: 30616 f, 30728 f, 30847 f, 32484 pb, 32733 pb
1815: 33808 pb, 34449 pb, 34951 pb, 35055 f, 35820 f, 36429 pb, 51528 pb
1816: 36690 pb, 38674 pb, 51590 f
1817: 39951 pb, 41278 f, 41500 pb, 41801 f
1818: 43026 pb, 44920 f, 45183 f, 45315 f, 45375 pb, 45561-45562 f, 46669 pb
1819: 46941 pb, 48427? pb, 50007 f

Constitutionalist (Exeter, N. H.)
1812: 25468, 26826-26827
1814: 33619

CONVERSE, SHERMAN (New
   Haven, Conn.)
1817: 42814
1819: 47186, 47354, 47525,
   47709, 47768, 47860, 48180,
   48481, 49641, 49970, 50182
   pb

COOK, --- (Richmond, Va.)
1805: 50623 pb

COOK, DANIEL POPE (Kaskaskia, Ill.)
1817: 41123-41126

COOK, JOHN (Albany, N.Y.)
1814: 32879 f

COOK, JOHN (Baltimore)
1805: 7915 pb

COOK, JOHN (Petersburg, Va.)
1807: 14138 pb

COOK, JOHN F (Baltimore)
1814: 30801, 32553, 33635a-
   33637

COOK, JOHN L (Baltimore)
1809: 18471
1810: 20286, 21944, 21956
1811: 22962-22963

COOKE, EDWARD B (Cin-
   cinnati, O.)
1818: 44437 pb
1819: 47620

COOKE, INCREASE (Hartford,
   Conn.)
1801: 950 f, 955 f

COOKE, INCREASE (New
   Haven, Conn.)
1802: 2031 f
1803: 3784 f, 4182 f, 4327 f,
   4733 f, 4893 f, 4921 f
1804: 6256 f, 6383-6384 f,
   6443 f, 7722 f

1805: 8398 f, 8527 f, 8681 sb,
   9283 pb, 9696 f
1806: 9812 f, 10061 f, 10249
   f, 10308 f, 10773 f, 10904
   f, 11217 f, 11467 f, 11833
   f, 50657 f, 50671 f, 50734
   sb
1807: 11949 f, 12701 f, 12710
   f, 12909 f, 13477 f, 13704
   pb, 14109 f, 14199 f, 50768
   f, 50777 f
1808: 15027 pb, 15593 f,
   16695 pb, 50858 f, 50886 f
1809: 17102 f, 17273 f, 17307
   f, 17386 f, 17514 f, 17520-
   17521 pb, 17760 f, 17814 f,
   17979 f, 18078-18079 f,
   18223 f, 18446 f, 18655 f,
   18787 f, 19137 f, 50916 pb,
   50968 sb
1810: 19832 pb, 19869 f, 20049
   f, 20250 pb, 20705 f, 20731
   pb, 21223 f, 21416 f, 21437
   f, 22033 f, 22073 f, 51014 f
1811: 22614 f, 22625 f, 23382
   pb, 23718 f, 23837 pb
1812: 25041 f, 25158 f, 25160
   f, 25219 f, 25350 f, 25426 f,
   25584 f, 25709 f, 25942 f,
   25946 f, 26038 f, 26073 pb,
   26181 f, 26192 f, 26348 f,
   26737 f, 26741 f, 26779 f,
   27471 f, 27551 f, 51158
   f, 51160-51161 f, 51189
   f
1813: 28223 f, 28857 f, 28936
   f, 28985 f, 29047 f, 29123 f,
   29162 f, 29692 pb, 29788 f,
   29883 f, 51271 f, 51295 f,
   51308 f, 51324 f
1814: 31223 f, 31585, 31819 f,
   31821-31822 f, 32008-32009
   f

COOKE, OLIVER DUDLEY
   (Hartford, Conn.)
1801: 950 f, 955 f
1802: 1971 f, 2030 f, 2750 pb,
   3125 f
1803: 4103 f, 4336 f, 4382 f,
   4459 f, 4486 f, 4593 f, 5056
   f
1804: 5694 f, 5984 f, 6311 f,

6444 f, 6813 f, 7277 f,
7732 f
1805: 8449 pb, 8501 f
1806: 11195 f, 11832 f
1807: 12642 pb, 12831 f,
13116 f, 13568 f, 14190 f
1808: 15023 f
1809: 17102 f, 18381 f, 18382
pb, 19137 f, 50968 sb
1810: 19828 f, 20174 f, 20255
f, 20346 f, 20444 f, 21448 f
1811: 22886 f, 23430 pb,
23729 pb, 23942d f
1812: 25739 f
1813: 27912 pb, 28521 f
1814: 31149 f, 31223 f, 31235
pb, 31556 f, 31584 f, 31643
f, 32020-32021 f, 32826 f,
32883-32885 f, 33616 pb,
33743 pb
1815: 34255 f, 34341 pb,
34857-34857a f, 35196-35197
f, 36512 pb, 36562 f, 36655
f
1816: 37680 f, 38616 pb,
38665 pb, 51577 pb
1817: 40359 f, 41704 pb,
42019 pb, 42115 f
1818: 43311 f, 43318 pb,
43504-43507 f, 43728 f,
44054 pb, 45308 pb, 45716
pb, 45724 f
1819: 47478 pb, 47480 f,
49064 pb, 51850 pb

COOLEDGE, DANIEL (Bolton,
Mass.)
1807: 13497 pb

COOLEDGE, DANIEL (Con-
cord, N.H.)
1809: 17056 f, 17272 pb
1810: 19384 f, 19831 pb,
20452 f
1811: 22351 f, 22592-22593
pb, 23077 f, 23706 pb
1812: 24897 f, 25132-25133
pb, 26814 pb
1813: 28495 pb, 28966 pb,
29282 f
1814: 30878 f
1815: 35438 pb
1818: 43020 f, 44513 pb

COOLEDGE, DANIEL (Walpole,
N.H.)
1805: 8264 f, 9113 f, 9266 f
1806: 10231? pb, 11395 pb

COOLEY, SAMUEL (Spring-
field, Mass.)
1802: 2466 f

COOPER, --- (Philadelphia)
1812: 24926 pb

COOPER, EZEKIEL (New York)
1804: 5683 f, 6038 f, 6163 sb,
6307-6308 f, 6773-6774 f,
7207 f, 7344 f, 7742 f,
7761 sb
1805: 7818 pb, 7981 f, 8417
f, 8441 f, 8765 f, 8898a
pb, 8900 pb, 8901 f, 9715-
9716 f
1806: 9937 f, 10172 f, 10688
f, 10864 f, 11294 f, 11848-
11850 f
1807: 13074 f, 13076 f
1808: 14678 f, 15292 f, 15591
f, 16104 f

COOPER, EZEKIEL (Philadelphia)
1801: 4 f, 165 f, 324 f, 883 f,
926-927 f, 1269 f, 1320 pb,
1641-1642 f, 1658 f, 50267
f
1802: 1708 f, 1742 f, 1771 pb,
1935 f, 1960 f, 2231 f, 2656
f, 2658-2659 f, 2692 pb
1803: 3770 f, 3872 f, 4467-
4468 pb, 4510 f, 4648 f,
4649 pb, 4651 f, 5570 f
1804: 6309 f, 6775 f, 7198 f

COOPER, WILLIAM (George-
town, D.C.)
1808: 15804
1809: 17426-17427, 19155
1810: 20027-20030
1811: 23173
1812: 25740 bf, 25741 pb
1813: 30494

COOPER, WILLIAM (Washing-
ton, D.C.)
1808: 14355, 15147, 16359,

16406
1809: 18410 pb
1810: 20357, 21969
1811: 24446, 51090
1812: 25318 pb, 25816 pb,
25817 bf, 26347 pb, 26841
pb, 27127 pb
1813: 28618, 29239 pb, 30494
f
1814: 33333, 33334 pb
1816: 38281 pb

COPELAND, JARED WARNER
(Middlebury, Vt.)
1817: 41284?
1818: 43216, 43251-43254,
44215, 46607
1819: 47451, 47840, 48488,
49980, 50116, 50159

CORNISH, ORLANDO B
(Philadelphia)
1819: 48541 pb

CORNMAN, ADAM (Philadel-
phia)
1813: 28241, 30381
1814: 31257
1815: 51477

Corporation of the City of
New York (New York)
1807: 14224 f

CORSE, JOHN (Alexandria,
Va.)
1811: 22171 pb
1813: 28158
1814: 31069
1815: 35943
1818: 44763

CORSS, RICHARD L (Catskill,
N.Y.)
1813: 28666 pb

CORSS, RICHARD L (Hudson,
N.Y.)
1816: 38758, 38866
1817: 40271
1818: 45630 pb
1819: 49011 pb

Cortland Repository (Homer,
(N.Y.)
1819: 48124

CORWIN, MOSES B (Urbana,
O.)
1812: 25402 pb

CORWINE, JOAB H (Maysville,
Ky.)
1814: 31386 pb
1815: 51507 pb

CORWINE, JOAB H (Washing-
ton, Ky.)
1808: 14887 pb

CORWINE, RICHARD (Mays-
ville, Ky.)
1814: 31386 pb
1815: 51507 pb

CORWINE, RICHARD (Washington, Ky.)
1808: 14887 pb

CORY, BENJAMIN (Herkimer,
N.Y.)
1801: 648 pb
1806: 11116 pb

COTTEN, GODWIN BROWN
(New Orleans, La.)
1815: 35137

COTTING, SAMUEL (Worcester,
Mass.)
1806: 10032

COTTOM, PETER (Alexandria,
Va.)
1801: 33, 1589, 1643, 1690
1802: 1860, 2348, 2649, 3026
1803: 4328, 4622, 4690, 5536
pb, 5572, 50397 f
1804: 5688 pb, 6281? f, 6871,
7115 pb, 7390
1805: 8296, 8529, 8538 f,
9490 pb, 9671 pb, 9717,
50532, 50555 pb
1806: 9913, 10387 pb, 10491,
10857, 11776, 50635 pb,
50739 pb, 50746 pb

1807: 14141, 14235, 50775
pb, 50817 pb
1808: 14322 pb, 14445, 15679,
15683 pb, 16663 pb, 50895
pb
1809: 17539, 18154 pb, 18404
1810: 19463, 20108, 20143,
21921, 21967, 51003 pb
1811: 22169, 22294, 22923,
51046 pb, 51147 pb
1812: 25028, 25533, 26154,
27583
1813: 28352 pb

COTTOM, PETER (Richmond,
Va.)
1810: 19800? f
1813: 51289 pb
1814: 30681 pb, 51380 pb
1815: 51479-51480 f
1816: 38847 f, 38848 pb,
39080, 51564-51565 pb
1817: 39993 f, 42285? pb,
51655 pb
1818: 51759-51760 pb
1819: 47736 pb, 51873 pb

COTTOM, RICHARD (Peters-
burg, Va.)
1810: 20143 f, 21921 f
1814: 31247 pb

COTTON, EDWARD (Boston)
1805: 8057 f, 9493 pb, 9494
f
1806: 10584 f, 11913 sb,
50652 pb
1809: 17067 f
1810: 19598 f
1811: 23778 pb
1812: 25814 f, 26869 pb
1813: 27994 pb
1814: 31762 f, 33664 f
1816: 37047 f
1818: 43417 f

COUPEE, FRANCIS (Salisbury,
N. C.)
1801: 598 pb, 827, 50239 pb
1802: 2928
1806: 11885 pb
1807: 11986
1808: 50843 pb

1811: 22629 pb, 22666, 22722
pb
1812: 24728, 25095
1813: 28661 pb, 28998

Courier (Ballston Spa, N. Y.)
see Saratoga Courier (Ballston Spa, N. Y.)

COURTNEY, JOHN (Richmond,
Va.)
1801: 124, 129
1802: 1833, 1835-1836, 2090,
50329-50330 pb
1803: 3742-3743, 3745, 50400
pb
1804: 5796, 5800, 7667, 50430
pb
1805: 8257

COVEL, ZENAS (Kingston,
N. Y.)
1813: 27998 pb

COVERLY, NATHANIEL (Bos-
ton)
1803: 4021 pb, 4806 pb, 5487
pb, 5549 pb
1804: 7325
1805: 8183?, 9232
1807: 13570
1808: 14841?
1810: 19938?, 20085? pb,
20280?, 20511-20512? pb,
20518? pb, 21261, 21386?,
21497?, 21536?, 21939?,
22103?, 22121? pb
1811: 22141-22142? f, 22192,
22304 pb, 22341 pb, 22519
pb, 23011 pb, 23016,
23223?, 23904, 51137 pb
1812: 24686 pb, 24768 pb,
24898, 24934 pb, 24942,
24981?, 25228 pb, 25279 pb,
25597, 25615 pb, 25765,
26204?, 26213 f, 26220?,
26529?, 26822, 26878,
26924, 27468, 27470, 27544
pb
1813: 27741 pb, 28016, 28019-
28021, 28088?, 28387? pb,
28698?, 28950?, 28954,
29057, 29264, 29286 pb,

29319, 29452 pb, ?29492,
29527, 29532, 29533 pb,
29702?, 29957, 29966,
30436 pb, 30469-30471,
30553, 51277 pb, 51280,
51310, 51317
1814: 30817-30818?, 30944,
30955, 30992, 30999, 31042,
31073, 31073a? pb, 31083,
31138, 31239, 31250 pb,
31398, 31760, 31928,
32004?, 32210, 32217 pb,
32447 pb, 32449, 32832 pb,
32972, 33748, 51430
1815: 33844, 34008 pb, 34056,
34153, 35064 pb, 35411,
35537, 35572 pb, 35583-
35584, 36423 pb, 36516,
36518-36519
1816: 36893, 36895, 37629
pb, 38037, 38307, 38361?,
38470 pb, 38563 pb, 39020,
39742, 39783
1817: 40501
1818: 43653 pb, 44006-44007,
44214, 44262?, 44289 pb,
44374 pb, 44815-44819,
44969 pb, 44976 pb, 45106
pb, 45229 pb, 45679 pb,
45696 pb, 46668 pb
1819: 47798 f, 48201 pb,
48365 pb, 48681 pb, 49072
pb, 49510 pb, 49541 pb,
50122

COVERLY, NATHANIEL (Salem,
Mass.)
1801: 208 pb, 1057, 1431
1802: 2230, 2468?, 2795-
2796, 2993, 3603
1805: 7864

COWAN, JAMES (Easton, Md.)
1802: 2946-2947

COWDERY, BENJAMIN
FRANKLIN (Hamilton, N.Y.)
1819: 48143 pb

COWPER, JOHN (Norfolk, Va.)
1804: 5890, 6929 pb
1805: 8265

COX, --- (Shelbyville, Ky.)
1816: 37155

COX, HORATIO J (Trenton,
N.J.)
1817: 41590-41592
1818: 45005-45007

COX, ISAAC (Corydon, Ind.)
1816: 37927 pb
1817: 41135-41137

COX, ISAAC (Jeffersonville,
Ind.)
1818: 44432 pb

COX, LEVI (Wooster, O.)
1817: 41690 pb

COX, WALTER (New York)
1817: 40786 pb

COXSHAW, AARON (Detroit,
Mich.)
1810: 19877?, 20644?, 20843,
21138-21140? pb
1811: 22178, 23133 pb, 24009
pb

CRAIG, JOHN D (Baltimore)
1806: 9851, 10141, 10972,
11293 pb

CRAIG, ROBERT H (Baltimore)
1812: 25181 f

CRAMER, ZADOK (Natchez,
Miss.)
1811: 22637 pb
1813: 28983

CRAMER, ZADOK (New Or-
leans, La.)
1813: 28984 pb

CRAMER, ZADOK (Pittsburgh,
Pa.)
1801: 1158 f, 1404 pb
1802: 2096 f, 2902 f
1803: 4873 f, 50372 f, 50385
f
1804: 6094 bpb, 6095 pb, 7064-
7066 pb, 50468 pb

1805: 8260 pb, 9156, 50521 pb
1806: 9842-9843, 10224-10226 pb, 10914 pb, 11789 pb, 50661-50662 pb
1807: 12220, 12367 pb, 12646, 14151 pb, 50816
1808: 14381, 14796 bf, 14797-14798 pb, 16672-16673 pb, 16720 pb, 16746 pb
1809: 17203, 17320 pb, 18399 pb, 50930 bf
1810: 19652 pb, 19886-19890 pb, 19902 pb, 51033 pb
1811: 22409a pb, 22636 pb, 22637, 22639 pb, 22734, 22998, 23880 pb, 51077 pb
1812: 25182 pb, 25263, 25540 pb, 25864 pb, 25949 pb, 26172 pb, 27421 pb, 51183 pb, 51188 f
1813: 28232, 28244 pb, 28313, 28349 pb, 28554, 28647, 28945, 28947 pb, 29253 pb, 29548, 30605 pb, 51291-51292 pb
1814: 30710, 30979 pb, 31260 f, 31261-31263 pb, 31923 f, 33629-33630, 51376 pb, 51414 pb, 51433 f
1815: 34470-34472 pb, 35347 f, 36421 f, 36472 f
1816: 36970 f, 37355-37356 f, 38039 f, 38067 f, 39137 pb, 51567 f, 51605 f, 51607 pb
1817: 40589 f, 40591-40592 pb, 42807 pb, 42818 f, 51657 pb
1818: 43309 pb, 43766-43769 pb, 43915 pb, 43917 pb, 43977, 44572 pb, 46617 pb
1819: 47746-47748 pb, 48782 pb, 51875 pb, 51917 pb

CRANDAL, EDWARD BURDICK (Cherry Valley, N. Y.)
1812: 26365 pb

CRANDAL, EDWARD BURDICK (Hartwick, N. Y.)
1813: 27913 pb
1814: 30885, 31145, 33609

CRANE, BENJAMIN (New York)
1812: 24824 f
1818: 43328 f
1819: 48295 pb

CRANE, J (Schenectady, N. Y.)
1814: 33741 f

CRANE, JOHN AUSTIN (Camden, N. J.)
1819: 48087 pb

CRANE, JOHN AUSTIN (Newark, N. J.)
1806: 10314
1807: 13602 pb
1808: 16169 pb, 16170
1809: 17141, 18011
1811: 22453, 22749
1812: 27571
1813: 28458 pb

CRANE, JOHN AUSTIN (Woodbury, N. J.)
1817: 40924 pb

CRANE, NOAH (Lebanon, O.)
1809: 16929

CRARY, WILLIAM (Boston)
1804: 7652?
1806: 10795?
1807: 12993

CRAWFORD, J R (Winchester, Va.)
1813: 28355 pb

CRAWFORD, JOHN R (Martinsburg, Va.)
1811: 23063 f

CRAWFORD, THOMAS (Louisville, Ky.)
1811: 24423 pb

CREAGH, WILLIAM H (New York)
1818: 45042
1819: 49565 pb

CREERY, JOHN (Baltimore)
1816: 39905 f

CRIDER, --- (Salisbury, N. C.)
1811: 22629 pb, 22722 pb
1812: 24728, 25095
1813: 28661 pb, 28998

CRISSY, JAMES (Hackensack,
N. J.)
1804: 6531 pb

CRISSY, JAMES (New Bruns-
wick, N. J.)
1811: 23484 pb

CRISSY, JAMES (New York)
1810: 20026 pb, 20201 pb,
20957 pb, 20978 pb, 21122
1811: 22900 pb, 23604 pb,
23886 pb, 23890 pb, 51086
pb

CROCKER, BENJAMIN (Boston)
1819: 51895 pb

CROCKER, C (Boston)
1817: 40454, 41449

CROCKER, URIEL (Boston)
1819: 46926, 46932, 46977,
46979-46980, 46998, 47338,
47359, 47399, 47562, 47862,
47903-47904, 47987, 48208,
48268, 48291, 48315, 48372,
48532, 49019, 49148, 49426,
50057, 50063, 50149, 50163,
50166

CROFT, FRANCIS (Philadel-
phia)
1818: 43247 f, 43410 pb,
45596 pb
1819: 47852 f, 47879 pb,
49017 f

CROOKER, RICHARD (New
York)
1802: 2019, 2615, 2787?,
2994, 3509, 50308
1803: 3851, 5075
1811: 22435

CROOKSHANKS, AARON (Mays-
ville, Ky.)
1818: 44478

CROSBY, JOHN (Montpelier,
Vt.)
1813: 28841 f, 29767-29768 f

CROSBY, OLIVER (Dover,
N. H.)
1812: 24791 f, 25187

CROSBY, WILLIAM (Auburn,
N. Y.)
1816: 36771 pb, 38905
1817: 40041, 42147
1819: 47792

CROSBY, WILLIAM (Boston)
1814: 31810, 33688

CROSBY, WILLIAM (Geneva,
N. Y.)
1816: 37693 pb

CROSS, CALEB (Newburyport,
Mass.)
1803: 4642 pb, 5174
1804: 6178, 6810, 7078 pb

CROSSFIELD, JEHIEL (Wash-
ington, D. C.)
1814: 31184, 31504, 33223
1815: 34668 pb

CROSWELL, HARRY (Albany,
N. Y.)
1808: 16615 pb
1809: 16890 pb
1812: ?27436, 27437 f

CROSWELL, HARRY (Catskill,
N. Y.)
1802: 50286 pb

CROSWELL, HARRY (Hudson,
N. Y.)
1801: 98 pb
1802: 1738, 1770, 1871, 3045,
3046 bf, 3497
1803: 4202
1805: 8005, 8619, 8622
1806: 9963-9964

1808: 15169 pb
1809: 18665

CROSWELL, MACKAY (Catskill, N. Y.)
1801: 1377
1802: 50286 pb
1804: 5994 pb, 6358, 7096, 50420 pb
1805: 8267 pb
1807: 50767 pb
1809: 50932 pb
1811: 22276, 22336, 22619
1812: 24726, 51184 pb, 51252 pb
1813: 28250 pb
1815: 51483 pb
1817: 41726 pb
1818: 44002 pb, 45704, 51771
1819: 47954-47955, 47957

CROW, JOHN (Charlestown, S. C.)
1802: 2043, 2161, 2667 pb
1803: 3934 pb, 4244

CROWELL, TIMOTHY BLOOMFIELD (Goshen, N. Y.)
1813: 29854
1815: 33884
1819: 47985-47986

CROWELL, TIMOTHY BLOOMFIELD (Newburgh, N. Y.)
1812: 25837

CRUGER, DANIEL (Owego, N. Y.)
1801: 49 pb
1802: 3567?

CRUKSHANK, J (Philadelphia)
1805: 9170
1806: 11185
1807: 13418
1808: 15973, 15975
1809: 18417
1810: 51035 pb
1811: 51129 pb
1812: 51239 pb
1813: 29543 pb
1814: 51434 pb

CRUKSHANK, JAMES (Philadelphia)
1801: 54 pb, 231 pb, 418 pb, 644 pb, 993 pb, 999 pb, 1085 pb, 1108 pb, 1167-1168 pb, 1345 pb, 1434 pb, 1594 pb, 50245 pb
1802: 1726 f, 2389 pb, 2747 pb, 2858 pb, 2912 pb, 50322 pb
1803: 4278 pb, 4451-4452 pb, 4880 pb, 4886 pb, 5132 pb, 50387 pb
1804: 6382 pb, 7028-7029, 7085 pb
1805: 9169 pb
1806: 9838 pb, 10016 f, 11114 pb, 11184-11185 pb
1807: 13416 pb

CRUKSHANK, JOSEPH (Philadelphia)
1801: 54 pb, 231 pb, 418 pb, 644 pb, 993 pb, 1085 pb, 1108 pb, 1167-1168 pb, 1345 pb, 1434 pb, 1594 pb, 50245 pb
1802: 1726 f, 2389 pb, 2747 pb, 2858 pb, 2912 pb, 50322 pb
1803: 3781 pb, 4278 pb, 4451-4452 pb, 4880 pb, 4886 pb, 5132 pb, 6044, 50387 pb
1804: 6382 pb, 6432, 7085-7086 pb
1805: 8210, 8389, 8525, 9436
1806: 10016 f, 11780-11781, 10579, 11155 pb
1807: 12813, 13690
1808: 14346 pb, 15102, 15404 pb, 15862 pb, 16230, 50876 pb
1809: 16851, 17959 pb, 18385, 50960 pb
1810: 19356 pb, 21045 pb, 21111 pb, 21382
1811: 23715 pb
1812: 51238 pb
1813: 27718 pb, 51331 pb
1814: 32533 pb
1815: 51528 pb
1817: 41320 pb

CRUMBIE, ROBERT (New
York)
1806: 10815-10816
1808: 15398 pb

CRUMBIE, ROBERT (Peeks-
kill, N. Y.)
1808: 16713 pb
1809: 18709, 19223 pb

CRUTCHER, GEORGE (Clarks-
ville, Tenn.)
1814: 32612 pb

CRUTCHER, GEORGE B
(Russellville, Ky.)
1817: 40076, 40114

CUMMINGS, JACOB ABBOTT
(Boston)
1805: 8732 f, 8734 f, 9332 f
1806: 10676 f
1807: 12672 pb, 13644 f
1808: 14978 f, 15289 f, 16704
f
1810: 19752 pb, 22006 pb
1811: 22659 pb
1812: 24572 f, 24584 f
1813: 27681-27682 pb, 27701 pb,
27837 pb, 27941 pb, 28100
pb, 28104 pb, 28129 pb,
28256 pb, 28287 pb, 28379
f, 28381 f, 28402-28403 pb,
28406 pb, 28465 pb, 28690
pb, 28970 f, 29573 f, 29734
pb, 29797 pb, 28269 f,
29773 f, 29914 pb, 30477
f, 30570 pb, 51296 f
1814: 30627 f, 30873 f, 30914
f, 31063 f, 31116 pb, 31273
pb, 31977 f, 32141 pb,
32420 f, 32445 pb, 32609
pb, 33522 pb, 33596 f, 33727
pb
1815: 33991 pb, 34061 pb,
34159 pb, 34330 f, 34482-
34483 pb, 34524 pb, 34558
pb, 34811, 35250 pb, 36424
pb, 36623 pb, 36627 pb,
36647 pb
1816: 37062 pb, 37266 f,
37745 pb, 38519 f, 38631

pb, 39695 f
1817: 39921 pb, 40247 pb,
40314 pb, 40342 pb, 40353 f,
40597-40600 pb, 40900 pb,
40977 pb, 41272 pb, 42242
pb, 42762
1818: 43122-43123 pb, 43430,
43782-43785 pb, 43805 pb,
43906 sb, 43914 pb, 44270
pb, 44295 pb, 45565 pb,
45864 f, 46704 pb
1819: 47037 pb, 47543 f,
47759-47760 pb, 47769-
47770 pb, 47775 f, 47816
pb, 48047 pb, 48100 pb,
48506 pb, 49321 pb, 49385
pb, 50167 pb

CUMMINGS, THOMAS W (New
York)
1819: 49497 pb

CUMMINS, EBENEZER HAR-
LOW (Philadelphia)
1816: 37535 pb

CUMPSTON, THOMAS
1815: 34484 pb

CUNNINGHAM, HENRY H
(Windsor, Vt.)
1808: 14635 f, 15728 pb

CUNNINGHAM, JOHN (Glens
Falls, N. Y.)
1813: 30445 pb

CUNNINGHAM, JOHN (Windsor,
Vt.)
1808: 14305
1809: 17053, 17058-17059,
17357, 50926
1810: 19467
1812: 25315

CUNNINGHAM, JOHN H (Philadelphia)
1817: 39949, 40484, 40823
1818: 43557, 43630, 43660,
45510
1819: 47024 pb, 49296, 49309,
49555

CURTIS, A (Auburn, N. Y.)
1817: 40328? pb

CURTIS, DAVID (Providence,
R. I.)
1818: 46785 f

CURTIS, ROBERT I (Erie, Pa.)
1813: 29384 pb
1816: 37695 pb, 51597 pb,
51625 pb

CURTIS, ROBERT I (Mayville,
N. Y.)
1819: 47573 pb

CURTIS, SAMUEL (Amherst,
N. H.)
1804: 6106 f
1806: 10244 f

CUSACK, --- (Philadelphia)
1819: 48546, 49116 pb

CUSACK, MICHAEL B (Ben-
nington, Vt.)
1815: 35008

CUSHING, CALEB (Concord,
Mass.)
1819: 46967, 50100

CUSHING, HENRY (Providence,
R. I.)
1803: 4978 f
1805: 9700 pb
1810: 21214 f

CUSHING, JOHN (Baltimore)
1818: 44466? pb

CUSHING, JOHN DEAN
(Salem, Mass.)
1819: 47170-47171, 47524,
47900-47901, 47913, 47989,
48934, 51960

CUSHING, JOSEPH (Amherst,
N. H.)
1802: 2213 pb
1803: 3609, 3774-3775, 3967,
4037, 4155, 4368
1804: 5649 pb, 5828, 6015,

6061, 6106, 6269, 6624 pb,
6981, 7129, 7154, 7278
1805: 7952, 7954, 8151, 8186
pb, 8187, 8189, 8276?,
8391, 8426, 8611-8612,
8924-8925, 9194, 9366
1806: 9858, 10070, 10111,
10244, 10584, 10906, 10967,
11804
1807: 12197, 12199, 12379,
12387, 12832 pb, 12964,
13115, 13605, 14222
1808: 14619-14620, 14789,
14812, 14936, 15723, 15840,
16204
1809: 16882, 17187, 17331,
17744, 17923 pb, 17924,
18130, 19125

CUSHING, JOSEPH (Baltimore)
1811: 23114? pb, 23884 pb,
23885 f, 23888-23889 f
1812: 25716 f, 26184 f, 26579
f, 26704-26707 f, 26709 f
1813: 27904 pb, 28185 f,
29171-29172 f, 29745 f,
29747 f, 30402-30403 f
1814: 30895 f, 31041 pb,
31076 pb, 31080 f, 31596 f,
31844 f, 31892 f, 31916 f,
32605 f
1815: 34217 pb, 34257 f,
34260 f, 34796 pb, 35746 f,
35877-35878 pb
1816: 36978 f, 37021-37022 f,
37070 pb, 37705-37706 pb,
37722-37724 f, 37727 pb,
37961 f, 38774? f, 39660 f,
39711 pb, 51633 pb
1817: 39947 pb, 40303-40305
pb, 41038 f, 41517 f, 41553
pb, 41865 f, 42018 f, 42165
f, 42774 pb, 42830 pb, 42980
f, 51654 f
1818: 43433 f, 43612 pb,
43993 pb, 44156 pb, 44194
pb, 44466 pb, 44853 f, 44856
pb, 44983 pb, 45469 f, 45883
pb
1819: 47016 f, 47917 f, 47943
pb, 48366 f, 49260 f, 49619
pb, 51899 f, 51955 pb

CUSHING, JOSHUA (Boston)
1807: 13897
1808: 14516, 14621 pb, 14632-
14634, 14725, 14935, 15171
pb, 15339, 16261, 16302,
16394?
1809: 17441 pb, 17629 pb,
18040, 18894-18895?, 18896
pb, 19228, 19275

CUSHING, JOSHUA (Gallipolis,
O.)
1819: 47129, 48062 pb

CUSHING, JOSHUA (Salem,
Mass.)
1801: 37, 189, 191, 508, 571,
579, 652, 849, 858, 893,
1081, 1107, 1284, 1354
1802: 1879, 1945, 1962-
1963?, 1964, 1969, 2188,
2196, 2470
1803: 3703, 3765, 3822,
3914, 4016, 4079, 4158,
4285, 4401, 5076, 5538,
5616-5617
1804: 5639, 5944-5945, 5947,
6052, 6245, 6305, 6400,
6451, 6472, 6492 pb, 6506,
6524, 6735, 6770?, 6951,
7057, 7226, 7798, 7800
1805: 7870, 7982-7983, 8065-
8066, 8109, 8171, 8303,
8340, 8637, 8792, 9025,
9093-9095, 9107, 9295,
9302-9304, 9386-9388,
9407, 9412, 9704, 50536
1806: 9796, 9844, 9961,
10370, 10414, 10532, 10601,
10829-10830 pb, 11216,
11428 f
1807: 12300, 12464, 12755,
12804, 12837, 12988, 13166,
13682, 14145
1808: 15605
1809: 17398
1812: 25293, 25338-25339,
25576, 26305, 26684, 26687,
27418, 27491, 27616-27617
1813: 27943, 28089 pb, 28263,
28357-28358, 29071, 29373,
29388, 29459, 30575
1814: 31119, 31290
1815: 33860

CUSHING, MILTON FOSTER
(Danbury, Conn.)
1808: 16098

CUSHING, MILTON FOSTER
(Somers, N. Y.)
1809: 18654 pb
1810: 20558
1811: 22193 pb, 22430a

CUSHING, THOMAS CROADE
(Salem, Mass.)
1801: 189 f, 382, 384, 511,
571 f, 579 f, 849 f, 1081 f,
1293
1802: 1869, 1938 f, 1964 sb,
1969 f, 2004, 2196 sb, 2317,
2532, 3044, 3155 f
1803: 3822 f, 3914 sb, 4079 f,
4596-4598
1804: 5947 f, 6294 pb, 6400
f, 7036, 7235 pb, 7242 pb
1805: 8109 f, 8340 f, 9304 f,
9704 f, 50536 f
1806: 10398, 11245, 11320 f,
11423 pb
1807: 12079 pb, 12317, 12668
f, 13437 pb
1808: 14516 f, 14961, 15171
pb, 15605 f, 16686 pb, 16765
1809: 17032 pb, 17398 f, 17433
pb, 17464, 18625 pb, 18648,
18650, 19020 pb
1810: 19480, 19583, 20051,
20076 pb, 20861 pb, 20862,
21004, 21112 pb, 21266,
21540 pb
1811: 22387, 22394, 23308 bf,
23864, 23989, 24491
1812: 24866 pb, 24872, 25355,
25576 f, 26304, 26390 pb,
26400, 26686, 26725, 27491
f, 27621 pb
1813: 27943 f, 30194 pb
1814: 30802, 30929 pb, 32172
pb, 32568, 32997 pb, 51436
pb
1815: 34310, 34320, 34502,
34635, 35311, 35839, 36462-
36463, 36470, 36520 pb
1816: 36666, 38338 pb, 38707,
39750-39751 f
1817: 39908-39909, 40689,
41343-41344, 41530 pb,

41955
1818: 43391 pb, 43436 pb,
    43537, 43958, 44528, 44753,
    45327, 45623, 45628, 46687
    bf, 46737 bf, 46738 f,
    46874, 46882-46883
1819: 47377, 47912, 48637,
    48663, 48934 f, 49106,
    49226, 51960 f

Cushing & Appleton (Salem,
    Mass.)
see CUSHING, THOMAS
    CROADE (Salem, Mass.)
    APPLETON, JOHN SPAR-
    HAWK (Salem, Mass.)

CUTLER, JAMES (Boston)
1801: 218, 239, 436, 466
    pb, 766, 992, 1080, 1227-
    1229, 1358, 1367
1802: 1706, 1715-1717, 1926,
    2490, 3576, 3606
1803: 3859, 3864, 4261,
    4263, 4322, 4595, 4600,
    4820-4821, 5124
1804: 6116, 6409, 6621
1805: 7831, 8390, 8557,
    8591, 8791, 8872, 8873 pb,
    9466
1806: 9882, 10218, 10348,
    10421, 11235, 11474 pb
1807: 12575 pb, 12880 pb,
    13145, 13740 pb
1808: 14457, 14827, 15084,
    15389 pb, 15831, 15938,
    15939? pb, 16075, 16085-
    16086, 16115, 16345 pb,
    16396?, 16777 pb
1809: 16824 pb, 16833 pb,
    17066, 17338, 17493 pb,
    17547, 17858, 17874, 17886
    pb, 17933, 18029-18030,
    18049-18050, 18051 pb,
    18054, 18307, 18316, 18472?,
    18667, 18772, 18898, 18902
1810: 19602, 19604, 19957,
    20513, 20600, 20674, 20681
    pb, 20683, 20697, 21217,
    21220
1811: 22647 pb, 23181 f,
    23182, 23245, 23711, 24410
    pb, 24510

1812: 24753 pb, 25346, 25444
    pb, 25894-25898, 25980,
    26004 pb, 26005, 26022-
    26024, 26026-26027
1813: 27697, 28198a pb, 28428,
    28706 pb, 29081 pb, 29086-
    29087, 29092, 29094, 29096-
    29098, 29106 pb, 30192 pb
1814: 30700, 31329 pb, 31523,
    31649 pb, 31967 pb, 32047-
    32049, 32062-32064, 32066,
    32961 pb, 51408
1815: 33789, 34000 pb, 34172
    pb, 34411 pb, 34706, 35029,
    35204-35205, 35212-35214
1816: 37489, 37645, 38016,
    38156, 38164, 38165 pb,
    38166, 38177-38179, 38182,
    38416 pb, 39114 pb
1817: 40666, 41268 pb, 41364,
    41367, 41369-41370, 41956
    pb, 42150 pb
1818: 44014, 44726-44727,
    44730, 44742, 44744, 44752
    pb, 44895, 45835
1819: 48742

CUTLER, JONATHAN (Provi-
    dence, R. I.)
1810: 19906 f

                    D

DACQUENY, AMBROISE
    (Charleston, S. C.)
1801: 533

DACQUENY, JOHN (New Or-
    leans, La.)
1810: 19798-19799, 20962,
    21179 pb
1811: 23606

DACQUENY, JOHN A
    (Charleston, S. C.)
1802: 50312
1804: 6338-6339

Daily Advertiser (Boston)
1814:   31964
1817: 42813

DALY, GEORGE (Lancaster,
Pa.)
1813: 29044 f

DANFORTH, ALLEN (Taunton,
Mass.)
1814: 30904
1815: 35587
1816: 37866
1817: 40006, 40320
1819: 47031

DANFORTH, J (Taunton,
Mass.)
1812: 26087, 27490 pb

DANIEL, ROBERT T (Raleigh,
N. C.)
1806: 10037 f

DANIELS, IRA (Springfield,
Mass.)
1818: 44238 pb
1819: 47556

DARLING, --- (New York)
1803: 4193 f, 4491 pb, 4493
f
1811: 23170 pb

DARLING, CARLOS C (Mont-
pelier, Vt.)
1807: 12432

DAUBY, AUGUSTINE G
(Rochester, N. Y.)
1816: 38829 pb
1817: 40559

DAVENPORT, T M (Abbe-
ville, N. C.)
1818: 51750 pb

DAVENPORT, THOMAS M
(Cambridge, S. C.)
1813: 28285

DAVENPORT, THOMAS M
(Edgefield, S. C.)
1811: 22202 pb

DAVENPORT, THOMAS M
(Tuscaloosa, Ala.)
1819: 47080 pb, 49652 pb

DAVIES, BENJAMIN (Philadelphia)
1801: 55 pb
1802: 1758 f, 2045, 2336-2337
pb, 2340 pb

DAVIS, AUGUSTINE (Richmond,
Va.)
1801: 1429
1805: 7947, 9665 f
1806: 11244
1807: 12073
1809: 19122 pb
1812: 24702, 26336
1815: 33984

DAVIS, CORNELIUS (Auburn,
N. Y.)
1818: 45781 f

DAVIS, CORNELIUS (New
York)
1801: 450 f, 455-456 f, 544-
545 f, 1631 f
1802: 1967 pb, 2282 f, 2284
f, 2287 f, 2292 f, 2612 f
1804: 5834 pb, 7214 f
1809: 17450 f, 18287? f
1810: 20308 pb
1811: 23844 pb
1812: 25307, 26667 pb

DAVIS, CORNELIUS (Utica,
N. Y.)
1813: 30391 f

DAVIS, GEORGE (Richmond,
Va.)
1810: 20319, 51009

DAVIS, JOHN (Philadelphia)
1805: 8716 bsb, 50558 pb

DAVIS, MATTHEW LIVINGSTON
(New York)
1801: 169, 434, 722
1802: 2883

DAVIS, MOSES (Hanover, N. H.)
1801: 263, 385, 550, 1629
1802: 2323 pb, 2563, 2848,
2920
1803: 3875, 3908, 4532
1804: 5963, 6118-6119, 6280,

6950, 7736, 7755
1805: 8071, 8715, 8820, 8986
1806: 10071, 10073, 10336,
10434, 11097-11098, 11426,
11779
1807: 12239, 13533, 13591,
50764
1808: 15026

DAVIS, PARIS (Baltimore)
1819: 48304 f

DAVIS, SAMUEL H (Albany,
N. Y.)
1814: 30676 f

DAVIS, SAMUEL H (Alex-
andria, Va.)
1819: 47102, 47676 pb

DAVIS, THOMAS (Philadelphia)
1816: 37842, 38208
1817: 40152, 41525, 41529,
42073, 42252 pb
1818: 43075 pb, 43457 f,
43478, 43482 pb, 43547 pb,
44653, 44661 pb, 44670 pb,
44775 pb, 45357 pb
1819: 47132, 48093 pb, 48095
pb, 48169 pb, 48373 pb,
48375 pb, 48536 pb, 49140
pb, 50053 pb, 51911 pb,
51930 pb

DAVIS, WILLIAM A (New
York)
1801: 169, 434, 722
1802: 2035, 2693, 2883, 3005
pb
1803: 3818, 4923-4924
1804: 6019, 6702, 7099-7100
1805: 8011, 8434, 9203, 9315
1806: 10565, 11219, 11911
1807: 12139
1809: 17971, 18175
1810: 20469
1811: 23861
1812: 24667-24668
1813: 28284

DAVIS, WILLIAM A (Washington, D. C.)
1815: 36258?, 36272, 36282,

36289, 36291, 36304-36305,
36309-36310, 36315, 36320-
36323, 36330, 36334, 36340,
36368
1816: 37087, 39180, 39360-
39362, 39364-39365, 39481,
39484-39485, 39490-39492,
39495, 39497, 39499-39512,
39514, 39516-39542, 39544-
39545, 39547-39566, 39578-
39579, 39587, 39630-39634
1817: 42357, 42460, 42466-
42468, 42598-42599, 42604-
42626, 42628-42635, 42638-
42640, 42642-42643, 42645,
42659-42664, 42683, 42747,
42835
1818: 43486, 45479 pb
1819: 46981, 47046, 47418-
47419, 47836, 48821 pb,
49422, 49899d, 50049

DAVISON, GIDEON MINER
(Rutland, Vt.)
1813: 27725, 27820, 27930 pb,
28249?, 28311, 30405, 30408,
30559
1814: 30789, 30890, 31673,
31678-31679, 31683, 31854,
31914, 32014?, 32854 pb,
32962 pb, 33611
1815: 35188, 36580 pb
1816: 37076, 38054, 38535,
39662, 39666 f
1817: 41337, 42462 pb, 42742?
pb, 42777-42778, 42780
1818: 43359 pb, 44502

DAVISON, GIDEON MINER
(Saratoga Springs, N. Y.)
1819: 49360 pb

DAVISON, RICHARD (Warren-
ton, N. C.)
1802: 2808 pb
1803: 3873 pb

DAVISSON, --- (Trenton, N. J.)
1816: 38413 pb

DAVISSON, ANANIAS (Harrisonburg, Va.)
1813: 28029, 29050 pb, 29665

pb, 30428 pb
1814: 31150 pb, 32651 pb,
 33562 pb
1816: 37404 pb
1818: 45777 pb

DAWSON, RUSSEL (Lynchburg,
 Va.)
1816: 36872, 37495 pb
1818: 43221

DAY, AMBROSE (Louisville,
 Ga.)
1801: 563, 565-566
1802: 2307, 2310
1803: 4269-4270
1804: 6372
1805: 8512
1806: 10475-10476
1807: 12653
1809: 17613

DAY, AMBROSE (Sparta, Ga.)
1803: 4183 pb

DAY, CALVIN (Portland, Me.)
1803: 4126 pb
1804: 5998

DAY, DAVID MERRICK (Buf-
 falo, N. Y.)
1815: 35495 pb
1819: 47115

DAY, MAHLON (New York)
1812: 26294 pb
1815: 34768 pb, 35477 pb,
 35489 pb
1816: 38432
1817: 41637 pb
1818: 43789 pb, 45511, 46124
 pb
1819: 47856 pb, 48983, 51939

DAY, MATTHIAS (Trenton,
 N. J.)
1801: 1436 pb

DEAN, THOMAS (Boston)
1802: 1934 pb, 2102, 2589
1803: 3700, 3858, 4208, 4472,
 5009, 5125-5126
1804: 5892, 6367, 6522, 6747,

6970, 7210, 7296 pb
1805: 7890, 8053-8054 pb,
 8059 pb, 8072, 8665, 8721,
 9498, 9778
1806: 9827

DEAN, WILLIAM E (New York)
1815: 35844
1819: 47771 pb

DEANE, JOSEPH C (Stanford,
 N. Y.)
1803: 4511 f

DEARBORN, NATHANIEL
 (New York)
1811: 23959 pb

DEARBORN, NATHANIEL
 (Newport, R. I.)
1808: 15064

DEARE, LEWIS (Elizabeth,
 N. J.)
1812: 26244 f
1813: 29312 f

DEARE, LEWIS (New Bruns-
 wick, N. J.)
1810: 21369-21370
1811: 23239, 23298, 23413,
 23414 pb, 23586, 23759,
 24332-24333, 24389
1812: 24839-24841, 24968,
 24970, 24975, 25080, 25467,
 25552, 25853-25854, 25968,
 26197, 26525, 27447-27448,
 27478-27479
1813: 27842 pb, 27846 pb,
 27952 pb, 27959 pb, 28708,
 29028, 29318, 29590, 29706,
 29916, 30455, 30495, 51333
1814: 30973, 30991, 32550,
 32580 pb, 32617 pb
1815: 34185, 34280, 34809,
 35195 pb, 35286, 35570,
 35723, 35958 pb, 36088 pb,
 36480, 51530 pb
1816: 37813, 37858, 38084,
 38354 pb, 38732, 38767,
 38854, 38957 pb, 38977-
 38978 pb, 39707
1817: 40241, 41693 bf
1818: 43380 pb

DEARE, LEWIS (New York)
1803: 4193, 4491, 4493, 4594
1804: 5952 pb, 6137, 6239, 7642
1805: 8255, 9236, 9360
1806: 11768

DEARTH, GOLDEN (Bristol, R. I.)
1808: 14272, 15167, 15316, 15708

DEARTH, GOLDEN (Warren, R. I.)
1809: 17087 pb

Dedham Gazette (Dedham, Mass.)
1813: 28424-28425
1814: 30813-30814, 31480, 32061, 32428, 32660, 33737
1815: 34638-34640, 35200, 35211, 35516-35517, 35559, 35846-35847, 36338, 36635
1816: 36897, 38211, 38547-38548, 38869, 39804

DEFFEBACH, LEWIS (Doylestown, Pa.)
1816: 37470 pb

DeFOREST, DeLAUZIN (New Haven, Conn.)
1812: 24845 pb, 25306 f, 25309 f, 25762 f, 26078 f, 26737 f, 27502 f
1813: 28479 f
1814: 31302 f, 31307 pb, 31694 f, 32008 f
1815: 34542 f, 36047 f, 51485 f

DeGELONE, F (New York)
1819: 51937 pb

DEGRAND, PETER PAUL FRANCIS (Boston)
1819: 47400 pb

DeJEANE, JOSEPH (New York)
1816: 37037 pb

DeKRAFFT, --- (Washington, D. C.)
1809: 17363?

DeKRAFFT, EDWARD (Washington, D. C.)
1816: 37554, 38823, 39146, 39567
1817: 41080 pb, 41224, 42358-42359, 42469, 42602-42603, 42627, 42636-42637, 42641, 42644, 42651, 42653-42658, 42667, 42675, 42678, 42687, 42717, 42730, 42829
1818: 44196, 44720, 45128, 45276, 45924, 45927, 45941, 46126-46128, 46132, 46310-46394, 46397, 46399, 46401-46420, 46422-46442, 46444-46445, 46451-46452, 46454-46455, 46459, 46467-46468, 46483, 46501, 46513, 46557, 46561, 46565, 46572-46574, 46576, 46578-46581, 46585, 46593-46594 pb, 46598-46599, 46604-46605, 46609-46611
1819: 47679, 47981, 48540, 49666, 49671, 49673, 49749, 49751, 49804-49812, 49814-49829, 49831-49832, 49834, 49837-49844, 49846, 49848-49856, 49858-49861, 49866-49867, 49869, 49871, 49873-49874, 49878-49884, 49886-49894, 49896, 49899, 49900-49901, 49939-49940, 49948, 49950-49951, 49953-49954

DELAMAR, PETER (Philadelphia)
1802: 2130? pb

DELAPLAINE, JOSEPH (Philadelphia)
1810: 20005 pb, 20216 f, 20484 f, 20565-20566 f
1812: 24929 pb, 25345 pb
1813: 29776-29778 f

Delaware Gazette (Delaware, O.)
1819: 47125

DELL, --- (Baltimore)
1818: 44648 pb

DEMAREE, SAMUEL R (Danville, Ky.)
1805: 8130, 8679 pb

DEMING, HALSEY (Louisville, Ky.)
1817: 41197 pb

DEMING, JOHN (Hancock, Mass.)
1816: 38921

DEMING, L (Boston)
1810: 20198? pb
1812: 25700? pb, 25810? pb

Democrat (Northampton, Mass.)
1802: 1822
1812: 24718

Democratic Press (Philadelphia)
1808: 14882
1809: 17463
1817: 40253, 41349
1818: 43684, 44448

DENHAM, PETER (Philadelphia)
1807: 12088

DENHAM, PETER (Southwark, Pa.)
1807: 12285

DENIO, JOHN (Greenfield, Mass.)
1802: 1831, 2225, 2511, 2995
1803: 3741, 4317, 5133
1804: 5782, 6235, 6321-6322, 6732, 7288-7289, 7334
1805: 7974, 8442, 8736, 8821, 8833, 8892, 9022, 9042
1806: 11086, 11434, 11877
1807: 12064, 13193 bf, 13683
1808: 14670, 15162, 15830
1809: 17906, 17925, 19131
1810: 20533, 22060
1811: 22348, 22739, 22819, 23058, 24010-24011

1812: 24530, 24589, 24818, 25002, 25305, 26842, 27444 pb
1813: 27663, 27762, 28236 pb, 28328, 28679, 28785 pb, 29458, 29646 pb, 29648
1814: 30718, 30720, 31248 pb, 31379, 31976, 32401, 33682, 33684
1815: 34459, 34919, 35364, 35425 pb, 35534, 36010, 36479 pb, 36574
1816: 38383
1817: 40393, 41001 pb, 41118 pb, 41565, 42906
1818: 43215, 44028 pb, 44037-44038, 44232, 44687-44688 pb, 45157, 45811-45812, 46808 pb
1819: 47139, 47457, 48926, 49521 pb, 49523 pb, 49543, 50146

DENIO, JOHN (Randolph, Vt.)
1801: 844, 1078, 1333

DENISON, HENRY (Milledgeville, Ga.)
1819: 48075 pb

DENNIS, JOSEPH (Norwalk, Conn.)
1802: 2448 pb

DENNISTON, DAVID (New York)
1801: 134, 642, 751, 815
1802: 2018, 2019 f, 2021-2022, 2024
1803: 3956 pb, 3958

DENNY, GEORGE (Chillicothe, O.)
1808: 16271 pb
1809: 18280-18281
1810: 19661 pb, 20947
1811: 22916 pb, 23590
1813: 29396-29397
1814: 30835, 30926
1815: 35058, 35526-35527, 35792 bf
1816: 38502

DENTON, GABRIEL (Goshen,
N. Y.)
1805: 9065 pb
1809: 18294 pb

Depository (Baltimore)
1815: 36558 pb

DERRICK, PHILIP (West
Chester, Pa.)
1816: 36803 pb

DESHLER, GEORGE W
(Easton, Pa.)
1815: 35989 pb
1818: 43990 pb
1819: 51887 pb

DeSILVER, ROBERT (Phila-
delphia)
1808: 15690 pb
1811: 51116 f
1812: 25042 pb, 25203 pb
1813: 29475 pb, 29803 f,
30526 pb, 51314 pb
1814: 30675 pb, 32025-32026
pb
1815: 34587 pb, 36481 f,
51458 pb
1817: 40361 f, 40379 f, 41147
pb
1818: 43127 pb, 43725 f,
44805 pb, 51765 pb
1819: 47494 f, 48213 pb,
49475 pb, 51878 pb

DeSILVER, THOMAS (Philadelphia)
1810: 20794 pb, 21033 pb,
21116 pb
1811: 51116 f
1812: 25042 pb, 25203 pb,
25969 pb
1813: 28318 pb, 29475 pb,
29803 f, 51263 pb, 51314
pb
1814: 30675 pb
1815: 51458 pb, 51477 f
1816: 36727 pb, 36969, 37011
pb, 38199 f, 38229?, 39079
pb, 39081-39082 pb, 39115
pb, 51546 pb
1817: 39971 pb, 40759 pb,

42284 pb
1818: 43751 f, 43755-43756 f,
43759 f, 45861 pb
1819: 47040 pb, 47494 f,
49476 pb, 51878 pb

DESNOUES, JOSEPH (New
York)
1808: 14820 pb
1810: 20335
1811: 22447, 24023
1812: 26076
1813: 27973
1814: 31905, 31925 pb
1815: 34158 pb, 34793, 34902,
35298 pb, 35736
1816: 37720, 37771, 37893
1817: 41242, 41916, 42234
1818: 43939, 44563, 45477
1819: 48806 pb, 49073 pb

DEVALCOURT, T (Baton
Rouge, La.)
1819: 47174 pb

Diamond Press (Baltimore)
1813: 27661
1814: 33643

DICEY, --- (Northampton,
Mass.)
1802: 3542

DICKINS, ASBURY (Philadelphia)
1801: 219 f, 236 f, 700 f,
829 pb, 1558 pb

DICKINSON, --- (Murfrees-
borough, N. C.)
1812: 25685 pb
1813: 27805

DICKINSON, ABEL (Philadelphia)
1804: 6658
1805: 8134, 9020, 50513
1806: 10262, 10323, 10362,
11022, 11823
1807: 12989-12990, 13744,
14234, 50789
1808: 14264, 15177, 15221,
15428, 15614, 16194, 16277,

16608, 16700
1809: 16990 pb, 17020 pb,
17080, 17358, 17393 pb,
17592, 17759 pb, 17795,
18150, 18452 pb, 18457 pb,
18556, 19231
1810: 19527 pb, 20173, 21875
1811: 23461, 23921, 24006,
51126 pb
1812: 24761, 24828, 25068,
25450, 26121, 26300, 26426
pb, 26439, 26698
1813: 28040, 28186, 28345,
28463, 28756, 28829, 29669,
29993, 30437
1814: 30823

DICKINSON, ABEL (Whitehall,
Pa.)
1807: 12173, 12228, 12705,
13607
1808: 14691

DICKINSON, DAVID (Philadelphia)
1815: 34402 bf, 34403, 34474,
34678 pb, 35687, 51491
1816: 37468, 38411 f, 39658
1817: 40192, 40528, 40649,
41288, 42003 pb, 42849
1818: 43726, 43740 pb,
44133, 44480 pb, 44898,
44900, 44902, 45011 pb,
45371 pb, 46702 pb, 51818
pb
1819: 47405, 48067 pb, 48426,
49193? pb, 49558 pb, 50046
pb

DICKINSON, KETURAH (Philadelphia)
1814: 30987, 31023, 31030,
31264, 31430, 32107 pb,
32352, 32727, 33546, 33598,
33733, 51402
1815: 34246-34247, 34256,
34380, 34396, 34592, 34724,
34862, 35034, 35331, 35694,
35696-35697, 35699, 35737,
35739, 35820-35822, 36589
1816: 37352
1819: 51867 pb

DICKINSON, RODOLPHUS
(Greenfield, Mass.)
1814: 33683
1816: 39826

DICKMAN, THOMAS (Green-
field, Mass.)
1802: 2238, 3560? pb

DICKMAN, THOMAS (Spring-
field, Mass.)
1806: 10520 pb
1808: 16733
1809: 17082, 17710, 17894
1810: 19840, 19964, 19974,
20523, 21205 pb
1811: 22143, 23186-23187,
23625
1812: 24663, 25004, 25593 pb,
25826 pb, 25829, 26803,
27453
1813: 30458
1814: 30820 f, 30951, 31448,
31897, 32215, 33575
1815: 35020, 35388, 36055
1816: 38033, 38546, 38850 pb
1817: 40089, 40567, 42023,
42043
1818: 44524, 45201

DICKMAN, THOMAS (Worces-
ter, Mass.)
1809: 17892-17893

DICKSON, JAMES (Lewistown,
Pa.)
1811: 23137 pb

DICKSON, JOHN (Petersburg,
Va.)
1804: 5951, 50429 pb
1805: 9102
1806: 9916
1807: 12075, 12246
1808: 14446, 50900 f
1810: 19464
1811: 23297, 24345a, 51144 f

DICKSON, ROBERT (Lancaster,
Pa.)
1801: 1115, 1120, 50208 pb
1802: 2871, 2876

DICKSON, WILLIAM (Lancaster, Pa.)
1801: 1115, 1120, 50208 pb
1802: 2871, 2876
1803: 4084 pb
1804: 6164 pb, 7020
1805: 8327
1806: 10294 pb
1807: 13272, 13338-13339, 13345 pb
1808: 15202 pb
1809: 18335, 18344-18345, 18351
1810: 20447 pb
1811: 22793, 23656
1812: 24635 pb
1813: 28832 pb
1817: 40245, 40821, 41756 pb
1818: 45691 pb
1819: 48935

DIETRICK, JACOB D (Hagerstown, Md.)
1803: 5485 pb
1804: 6860-6861 pb, 6862 f
1805: 8064 f, 8300 pb, ?8552 pb, 8966 f
1806: 9849, 9969 pb, 9977 pb, 10949, 10952 pb, 11050 pb
1808: 15705 f
1810: ?21443 pb

DIETRICK, JACOB D (Staunton, Va.)
1807: 13636 pb
1811: 23498

DIETRICK, JACOB D (Winchester, Va.)
1805: 8967 f

DILLARD, --- (Winchester, Ky.)
1819: 47094

DILLWORTH, SAMUEL (Norfolk, Va.)
1816: 37952

DILLWORTH, SAMUEL (Petersburg, Va.)
1815: 34516 pb

DILLWORTH, SAMUEL (Vincennes, Ind.)
1817: 40074, 41138 pb

DINGEE, JOHN (Brownsville, Pa.)
1817: 42961 pb

DINMORE, RICHARD (Alexandria, Va.)
1802: 1739 pb

DINMORE, RICHARD (Georgetown, D.C.)
1808: 15804
1809: 17426-17427, 19155

DINMORE, RICHARD (Washington, D.C.)
1802: 2148
1807: 13718, 14162 pb
1808: 14335, 15147, 16359, 16406
1809: 18410
1810: 20357

Directors of the Principal Bank (Raleigh, N.C.)
1811: 23571 f

DISMUKES, ALEXANDER H (Blakely, N.C.)
1819: 47378 pb

DISMUKES, ALEXANDER H (Fayetteville, N.C.)
1818: 46892
1819: 48739, 49210

DIX, JOSEPH (Barnard, Vt.)
1812: 25162 f, 25380 f, 25384 f, 25572 f, 26302 f, 26342?, 26456 pb, 26573? f, 27520 f, 27521? f, 27522 f
1813: 27899 f, 27951 f, 28094 f, 28231 f
1814: 31582 f, 31763 f

DIX, JOSEPH (Bennington, Vt.)
1815: 35008 f

DIXON, JOHN (Richmond, Va.)
1801: 534?, 536 pb

1802: 1833, 1835-1836,
2090, 2273, 2275?, 2276,
50329-50330 pb
1803: 3743, 3745, 4246-4247,
4795, 50400 pb
1804: 6340-6341, 6468
1805: 8477

DIZABEAU, JOHN B (Baltimore)
1804: 5991 pb

DOBBIN, CATHERINE BOSE
(Baltimore)
1815: 33917 pb
1816: 36680

DOBBIN, GEORGE (Baltimore)
1802: 2100, 2939, 3144
1803: 4233, 50363
1804: 6331, 6334, 7407
1805: 8184
1806: ?10008, 10020, 10187 f,
10190 pb, 10236, 10291,
10931 pb, 11053 pb, 11884
pb
1807: 12035, 12188 pb, 12329
pb, 12439, 12998, 13481,
13514, 13595
1808: 14412?, 14748-14749 pb,
15373, 15503, 15612, 15668,
15803, 16178, 50870
1809: 16793, 16900, 17167-
17168, 17180, 17198 pb,
17545, 17697, 17726, 17882,
18100, 18126 pb, 18140,
18360, 18651
1810: 19400, 19415, 19589,
19739, 19795-19796, 19819,
20285, 20424, 20742-20743,
21277
1811: 22454a, 22559, 23278,
23708, 23791 pb
1812: 25108, 25311, 25953,
26495, 26823
1813: 27694 pb, 28281, 28879,
29059 pb
1814: 31193, 32692

DOBBIN, THOMAS (Baltimore)
1802: 2100, 2939, 3144
1803: 4233, 50363
1804: 6331, 6334, 7407
1815: 33782a? pb

Dobbin & Murphy (Baltimore)
see DOBBIN, CATHERINE
BOSE (Baltimore)
MURPHY, THOMAS (Baltimore)

DOBELBOWER, LEWIS (Philadelphia)
1810: 21374, 21991

DOBSON, THOMAS (Philadelphia)
1801: 68 pb, 210 f, 260 f,
1211 f
1802: 1755 f, 1859 f, 2149 pb,
2562 f, 3177, 3188 pb
1803: 3816 pb, 4147 f, 4161,
4162 f, 5164 pb
1804: 5747 pb, 6034 f, 6171 f,
6172 pb, 6606 f, 7347 f
1805: 8006 f, 8097 f, 8225 f,
8370, 9311 f, 9318 f, 9697
f, 50606? f
1806: 9944 pb, 9954 f, 10044
f, 10049 f, 10176 f, 10222 f,
10514-10515 f, 10598 f,
11371 f, 11398 pb, 11477 f
1807: 12092 f, 12137 f, 12442
pb, 12555 f, 12845 f, 13049
pb, 13503 f
1808: 14791 f, 14816 f, 15240
f, 15401 f, 16113 f, 16114
pb
1809: 17101 f, 17423 f, 18803
f
1810: 19883 f, 20796 f, 20943
f, 21064 f, 21246? pb, 21874
pb, 22114 f
1811: 22137-22138 f, 22305 pb,
22632 f, 22786 pb, 23130,
24475 f
1812: 25587 pb, 26716 pb,
27566 f
1813: 28093 pb, 28400 f,
29663 f, 29903 f
1814: 30738 pb, 30857 pb,
31255 f, 31327 pb
1815: 34442 f, 34814 pb, 35340
f, 36040 pb
1816: 37369 pb, 37370 f, 37575
f, 37590 f, 37938 pb, 38238 f
1817: 39985 f, 40405 f, 40488
pb, 40583 f, 40727, 41415 f,

41426 pb, 42140 pb, 42274
pb, 42938 pb
1818: 43065 f, 43520 pb,
43558 pb, 43634 f, 43760 f,
43866 pb, 43910 pb, 44292
f, 44526 f, 45184 f, 45342
f, 45363 f, 45540 f, 45646
f, 45692 f, 46825 f, 46842 f
1819: 47529 pb, 47824

DOCKSTADER, JACOB (Caze-
novia, N. Y.)
1807: 12256

DOCKSTADER, JACOB (Peter-
boro, N. Y.)
1807: 12603 pb

Doctrinal Tract Society (New
Haven, Conn.)
1818: 45887 pb

DODD, HENRY (Salem, N. Y.)
1801: 881
1803: 4023?
1804: 6429, 6615, 6638 pb,
6641 pb, 6945 pb, 7137-
7139
1805: 7946, 8337, 8578,
9218-9220
1806: 9910, 10169, 10812,
11085 pb, 11228-11229,
11459
1807: 12067, 12456, 12476,
12691, 12886
1808: 14299?, 15239, 16021
1809: 18116 pb
1810: 21157-21158, 21447
1811: 23763-23765, 24370,
24413
1812: 26551-26552, 27452 pb,
27529
1813: 29598, 29600-29603,
29606, 30507, 30512
1814: 30972, 31173 pb, 32585
1815: 35314, 35729, 35730-
35731 pb
1816: 38741-38742
1817: 41464, 41467-41468,
41886
1818: 45418, 45882
1819: 47583 pb, 50048

DODGE, C (Albany, N. Y.)
1811: 22306 f, 23364 f
1812: 25613 f, 25635 f, 26059
f

DODGE, C (New York)
1817: 40751

DODGE, STEPHEN (New York)
1810: 20712 f, 22131 f
1811: 22326 f, 23365 pb, 23366
1813: 27872 f, 29843 f
1814: 30866 f, 30933 pb,
32729 pb, 32742 pb, 51361
pb
1815: 34020? pb, 36474 f
1816: 36965 f, 37374 pb, 37754
f, 38401 f, 38601 f, 38993 f,
38994 pb, 39798 pb
1817: 42193 f
1818: 51799 pb
1819: 48118a pb, 49416 pb

DOLE, SAMUEL (Newburyport,
Mass.)
1802: 3557 f
1807: 13268 f
1808: 15163 f, 15786 f

DONALDSON, ARTHUR (Phila-
delphia)
1815: 34478 f

DONALDSON, ROBERT (New
York)
1818: 44060 pb

DONOVAN, DANIEL (Philadelphia)
1806: 10729 pb

DOOLITTLE, AMOS (New
Haven, Conn.)
1805: 8701 pb
1813: 29045 pb

DORCHESTER, ELIASAPH
(Rome, N. Y.)
1818: 45171 pb

DORCHESTER, ELIASAPH
(Utica, N. Y.)
1814: 32302?

1815: 34628?
1816: 36839 pb, 39882
1817: 42761 pb

DORNIN, BERNARD (Baltimore)
1809: 17166 pb, 17167-17168
    f, 17180 f, 17726 f, 18140
    f, 18642 pb
1810: 19400 f, 19738 pb,
    19739 f, 19740-19741 pb,
    20285 f, 20424 f, 20742-
    20743 f
1811: 22454a f, 22489 pb,
    22728 pb, 23708 f
1812: 25036 pb, 26662 f,
    26780 pb
1813: 28090 pb, 28098 f
1815: 35182 f
1816: 37633 pb

DORNIN, BERNARD (New
    York)
1804: 5967 pb, 6403 f, 7274
    f, 50473 pb
1805: 8436 f, 50510 f
1806: 10383 f, 10693 pb,
    11303 f
1807: 12534 f, 12664 f,
    12970 pb, 13543 f, 14148
    pb
1808: 14550 f, 14568 f, 14982
    pb, 15020 pb, 16308 pb

DORNIN, BERNARD (Philadel-
    phia)
1817: 40149 pb, 41264 pb,
    42189 f
1818: 43136 f, 43291 pb,
    45857 f
1819: 48274 pb, 48325 pb

DOUBLEDAY, ULYSSES
    FREEMAN (Albany, N. Y.)
1814: 30945 pb, 32604 pb,
    32763 pb
1815: 34154 pb

DOUBLEDAY, ULYSSES
    FREEMAN (Ballston Spa,
    N. Y.)
1815: 35852 pb
1816: 37414

1817: 42319
1818: 44664, 45634 pb
1819: 47140, 47717, 49613

DOUGHTERY, DANIEL (Phila-
    delphia)
1815: 34307 f

DOUGHTY, ISAAC T (Pough-
    keepsie, N. Y.)
1819: 48309 pb

DOUGLAS, FRANCIS (Portland,
    Me.)
1809: 16950?
1810: 19376, 21351
1811: 23691
1812: 24713
1813: 29703
1814: 32137
1815: 34296, 35280, 35830
1816: 37775, 38111, 38678 pb,
    39856 pb
1817: 40092, 40536, 41331,
    42028, 42096, 42821
1818: 44365, 45270, 46608
1819: 47564, 47948 pb, 48559,
    48562-48567, 48571 pb, 49511

DOUGLAS, GEORGE (Baltimore)
1802: 2707, 2836, 3559 pb
1803: 4060 pb, 4260 pb, 4490
    pb, 4804 pb, 4809 pb
1804: 5826 pb, 6317 pb
1805: 8454 pb, 9741 pb
1806: 9980, 10927 pb

DOUGLAS, GEORGE (New York)
1812: 27525 pb

DOUGLAS, GEORGE (Peters-
    burg, Va.)
1801: 626 pb, 774 pb, 1588 pb
1802: 1764 pb, 3478 pb

DOUGLASS, --- (Morristown,
    N. J.)
1805: 7987, 8739 pb

DOW, --- (Newtown, Pa.)
1802: 1957 pb

DOW, LORENZO (New York)
1808: 15323 pb

DOWNING, JORDAN (Lexing-
ton, Ky.)
1814: 30941
1815: 34450 pb, 35375, 35744
pb

DOWNING, JORDAN (Philadelphia)
1813: 28282, 29483 pb, 29509,
51319, 51327 pb

DRAKE, JACOB (Delaware, O.)
1818: 43836 pb

DREW, WILLIAM C (Cincin-
nati, O.)
1816: 37965 f

DRISCOL, DENNIS (Philadelphia)
1801: 1390 pb

DUANE, WILLIAM (Philadel-
phia)
1801: 133 pb, 135, 356, 495
pb, 578, 945, 1299, 50256
pb
1802: 2134, 2205, 2360,
2829?, 2864, 2888, 3037,
3268
1803: 3617, 3675, 3709, 4112-
4113, 4133, 4323, 4783 f,
4835, 4856, 5127, 5193
1804: 6195, 7006, 7590
1805: 8215, 8346-8347,
8399, 8418, 8937, 9089,
9128 pb, 9136 pb, 9137,
9249, 9307 f, 9308, 9394-
9396
1806: 10203, 10779 pb, 11123
pb, 11462, 50696 pb
1807: 12468-12469, 12470-
12471 f, 13667 f, 13936 f
1808: 14278 pb, ?14570 pb,
?14860 pb, 15039 pb, 15043
pb, ?15833, 16372, 16590
1809: 17217 pb, 17408, 17492
pb, 17534 pb, 17648 pb
1810: 20000 pb, 20629 pb,
?20940

1811: 22689, 22726, 23228,
23685 pb
1813: 28368, 29765 pb
1814: ?31359
1815: 34566? pb

DUANE, WILLIAM (Washing-
ton, D. C.)
1801: 1451, 1477
1802: 1722, 1766, 2202, 2300,
2318 f, 2671, 2837, 2896,
3194-3195, 3197-3203, 3208,
3212, 3217-3233, 3235,
3237-3250, 3252, 3254-3259,
3264-3265, 3275-3278, 3287-
3289, 3293, 3300, 3303,
3309-3310, 3314, 3323,
3328, 3350-3351, 3355,
3358-3361, 3364, 3375-3376,
3378, 3387, 3392, 3396-
3397, 3414, 3434, 3438,
3441-3442
1803: 4110-4111, 5197, 5201-
5203, 5208, 5214-5215,
5218-5222, 5224-5229, 5231,
5235-5238, 5241-5245, 5247-
5248, 5251-5254, 5257-5258,
5261, 5263, 5265-5272,
5274, 5277, 5285-5286,
5288, 5291, 5296, 5324-
5326, 5328-5329, 5337-
5344, 5349-5351, 5354,
5356-5360, 5369, 5373-
5374, 5390, 5393, 5396,
5400-5401, 5405, 5407,
5409, 5413, 5418, 5420-
5421, 5423-5425, 5428,
5438-5439, 5442, 5446,
5448, 5451, 5454, 5457,
5466-5467, 5473, 5475,
5477, 5479, 5521, 5614
1804: 5680, 6760, 7510, 7515,
7524-7528, 7532, 7544,
7546-7547, 7551, 7582,
7585-7586, 7635-7636
1805: 8172, 8419, 8538, 8832
pb, 9512-9513, 9515, 9518,
9533, 9535, 9538, 9541,
9548-9551, 9554-9555,
9557-9558, 9568-9569,
9578, 9581, 9585, 9592,
9594-9596, 9598, 9600,
9603-9604, 9607-9608,

9629, 9631, 9637, 9639-
9641, 9676
1806: 9805, 10896, 11492,
11506, 11548-11549, 11553,
11556, 11560, 11586, 11619,
11630, 11636, 11654, 11703,
11733
1807: 12430, 13094, 13792-
13794, 13898-13899, 13910,
13916, 13935, 13990, 14036

DUANE, WILLIAM JOHN
(Philadelphia)
1815: 36275 pb
1816: 39486 pb

DUBOIS, WILLIAM (New York)
1806: 10661? pb
1817: 41231 pb, 51666? pb,
51698? pb, 51703? pb
1818: 44916? pb

DUFFY, WILLIAM (George-
town, D. C.)
1816: 51559
1817: 40153 pb, 40207, 40215,
40420, 41099, 41341, 41827,
42810 pb
1818: 43356, 45749

DUFIEF, NICOLAS GOUIN
(Philadelphia)
1801: 734 pb
1817: 42001 sb

DUHY, CHARLES W (Bristol,
R. I.)
1807: 13152 pb

DUKE, JOHN C (Charleston,
S. C.)
1817: 40675

DUNCAN, MATTHEW (Kaskas-
kia, Ill.)
1814: 31786-31787, 31788 pb
1815: 34989
1816: 37911

DUNCAN, MATTHEW (Russell-
ville, Ky.)
1808: 14994 pb
1810: 21136
1813: 28802

DUNHAM, J (Trenton, N. J.)
1816: 37057 f

DUNHAM, JOHN MOSELEY
(Boston)
1802: 2166, 2248, 2978 pb
1803: 4266 pb, 4807 pb, 4909,
5587
1806: 11876 f
1807: 12594 pb, 13183? f,
13184 f, 13435 f, 13436 pb,
14221 f
1808: 15996 f
1810: 20845 f

DUNHAM, JOSIAH (Windsor,
Vt.)
1810: 21957 pb
1812: 25466

DUNHAM, NATHANIEL (Milton,
Vt.)
1816: 38330 f

DUNHAM, NOAH (Milton, Vt.)
1816: 38330 f

DUNHAM, WILLIAM W (Provi-
dence, R. I.)
1802: 2955 bf
1808: 14336 pb
1809: 16858 pb, 16859, 18509?,
18511 pb
1810: 19656, 19684, 20727,
21186, 21484 pb
1811: 23032, 24031, 51067

DUNKIN, L L (Charlestown,
Ind.)
1818: 44431 pb

DUNN, ISAAC (Laurenceburg,
Ind.)
1819: 48339 pb

DUNN, JAMES C (Georgetown,
D. C.)
1816: 38240 pb
1817: 41550 pb

DUNN, JAMES C (Washington,
D. C.)
1819: 49584 pb

DUNNAVANT, MARVEL W
(Halifax, N. C.)
1818: 44220 pb

DUNNAVANT, MARVEL W
(Petersburg, Va.)
1815: 34516 pb
1816: 37122, 37836, 38785 pb
1817: 39994 pb, 40128

DUNNAVANT, WILLIAM W
(Halifax, N. C.)
1818: 44220 pb

DUNNELL, REMARK (Wor-
cester, Mass.)
1814: 33020 f

DUNNING, JOHN BOTSFORD
(Middletown, Conn.)
1801: 164, 409, 1662, 1679
1802: 2076, 2181-2182, 2427-
2428, 2971, 3047
1803: 3836, 4421, 4727, 5006,
50401
1804: 5752, 6241, 7141, 7785
1805: 8385, 8667, 9760
1808: 16305

DUNNING, JULIUS L (New
York)
1809: 18901 f
1810: 20313 pb, 20765 f,
21661 pb
1813: 28606 f, 28740 pb,
30193 pb
1814: 30711 pb

DUNNING, TERTIUS (Middle-
town, Conn.)
1801: 164, 409, 1662, 1679
1802: 2076, 2181-2182, 2427-
2428, 2971, 3047
1803: 3836, 4421, 4727, 5006,
50401
1804: 5752, 6241, 7141, 7785
1805: 8385, 8667, 9760
1808: 16305
1809: 17946, 18141 pb, 19177
1810: 20412
1811: 23156, 23505, 23942f
1812: 25241, 25745, 26592,
27486, 27513

1813: 28875, 30498
1815: 35869, 36014-36015
1816: 38904, 38946
1817: 40023, 40556, 40767,
40826
1818: 44840, 45671

DUNOTT, MILLER (Wilming-
ton, Del.)
1814: 31332 pb

DURAND, --- (New York)
1816: 38201 pb

DURELL, HENRY (New York)
1817: 42099 pb

DURELL, WILLIAM (New York)
1801: 170 f, 173 pb, 242 f,
430 f, 729, 949, 1327 f,
1381 pb, 1691, 50232
1802: 1854 f, 2103 f
1803: 3793 f, 3819 f, 3887,
4925 f, 5625? f
1807: 13420 pb
1808: 15259 f, 15261 pb,
15978-15980 f
1809: 17639 pb, 17642, 17643-
17644 f, 17647 pb, 17841-
17842 pb, 18422 f, 18670 pb
1811: 22148 pb, 23119-23120
pb
1812: 25677-25678 f, 26496 f,
26730 pb, 26838 f, 26839 pb
1813: 28503 pb, 29865 pb,
29866 f, 29904 pb
1815: 34699 pb, 36041 pb
1816: 37602-37605 pb

DuVAL, PHILIP (Richmond,
Va.)
1813: 28266 pb
1816: 38738, 38798, 39674-
39679 pb
1817: 40124-41025, 41225,
41903, 51724
1818: 43223, 45445

DuVAL, PHILIP (Staunton, Va.)
1814: 32852 pb

DUYCKINCK, BENJAMIN T
(Augusta, Ga.)

1812: 25092
1818: 51777 pb

DUYCKINCK, EVERT (New York)
1801: 204 f, 273 f, 423 f, 1634 f, 50232 f
1802: 1740 f, 1867 f, 2039 f, 2103 f, 2109 f, 2136 f, 2165 f, 2861 f, 2883 f, 3036 f, 3457 pb, 3512 f
1803: 3825 pb, 3851 f, 4122 f, 4196 f, 4277 f, 4572 f, 5188 pb, 5498 f, 5524 f
1804: 5853 pb, 6257 f, 6345 f, 6685 f, 6842 f, 7158 f, 7723 f, 7734 f, 50411 f
1805: 8000 pb, 8104 f, 8121 pb, 8182 f, 8269 f, 8357 pb, 8404 pb, 8609 f, 9285 f, 9298 f, 9357 pb, 50582 pb
1806: 9871 pb, 9972 pb, 9978 f, 9993 pb, 10155 pb, 10156, 10234 f, 10367 pb, 10482 f, 10706 pb, 11028 pb, 11468 f, 11757 pb, 11815 f, 11880 f, 50668-50669 f, 50697 f
1807: 12108 pb, 12111-12112 f, 12163 pb, 12286 f, 12593 f, 12675 pb, 12978 pb, 13290 f, 13362 pb, 13501 f, 13650-13651 pb, 13754 f
1808: 14902 f, 15131 pb, 15588 f, 15677 pb, 15953 f, 16093 f, 16240 f, 50840 pb
1809: 17007 pb, 17011 pb, 17014 f, 17018 f, 17037 pb, 17300 pb, 17304 pb, 17436 pb, 17761 f, 17885 f, 17916 f, 17973 f, 18158 pb, 18175 f, 18291 pb, 18449 f, 18636 pb, 18637 f, 19026 pb, 19085 pb, 19141 f, 19162 pb
1810: 19525 pb, 19555 pb, 19779 pb, 19966 pb, 20014 pb, 20059 f, 20230 pb, 20469 f, 20814 pb, 21044 pb, 21107 f, 21989 f
1811: 22362 pb, 22398 pb, 22417 f, 22435 f, 22446a f,

22533 f, 22544 pb, 22792 f, 22908 pb, 23142 f, 23279 pb, 23370 f, 23862 f, 24338 f, 24359 f, 51118 f
1812: 24526 f, 24824 f, 24882 pb, 24950 f, 24992 f, 24997 f, 25171 f, 25334 pb, 25947 f, 26651 pb, 26712 f, 27475 pb, 51202 pb
1813: 27649 pb, 27676 pb, 27721 f, 27886 pb, 27914 f, 28030 f, 28107 pb, 28378 pb, 28407 f, 28555 f, 28948 f, 29055 pb, 29135 f, 29138 f, 29194 f, 29215 pb, 29441 f, 29643, 29701 f, 29946 f, 30486 f, 30594 f, 51261 f, 51281 f
1814: 30618 f, 30715 f, 30888 f, 31154 f, 31233 f, 31303 pb, 31417 pb, 31548 pb, 31568 f, 31580 pb, 31751 f, 32410 f, 32418 f, 32422 f, 32460 f, 32474 pb, 32682 f, 32697 f, 32897 f
1815: 33877 f, 33881 pb, 34038 pb, 34069 f, 34077 pb, 34123 pb, 34253 f, 34272 f, 34451 pb, 34550-34551 f, 34607 f, 34973 pb, 35369 f, 35935 f, 36047 f, 36117 f, 36528 pb, 51529 f
1816: 36966 pb, 36984 f, 37010 f, 37019 f, 37342 pb, 37417 f, 37474 pb, 37481 pb, 37734 f, 37900 pb, 38385, 38599-38600 f, 38641 pb, 38669 pb, 39103 f, 39655 f, 51603 sb
1817: 40250 f, 40263 pb, 40264 f, 40565 pb, 41260 pb, 41263 pb, 41335 f, 41679 pb, 41774 f, 41775 pb, 41857 pb, 41863 f, 42090 f
1818: 43006 pb, 43289 pb, 43320 pb, 43408 pb, 43424 f, 43450 f, 43582 pb, 43819 f, 43893 f, 44304 f, 44605 f, 45174 f, 45577 pb, 45592 pb, 46714 f, 51746 pb
1819: 47899 pb, 48406 f, 48667 f, 48805 pb, 49066 pb, 49068 f, 49157 f, 49168

f, 50068 f, 50150 pb, 50191
f, 51884 pb

DWIER, HENRY (Hartford,
    Conn.)
1801:   1276?

DWIGHT, TIMOTHY (New
    Haven, Conn.)
1818:   43898 f

DYCKMAN, JACOB (New
    York)
1810:   20901 pb

DYER, OLIVER (Windham,
    Conn.)
1803:   4094

                E

Eagle (Castine, Me.)
1810:   19653, 20276, 22039

Eagle (Catskill, N. Y.)
see   American Eagle (Catskill,
    N. Y.)

Eagle (Maysville, Ky.)
1814:   51403 pb

EAKEN, --- (Philadelphia)
1803:   3692, 3922, 4107, 4619,
    4668, 4870, 4952, 5529,
    5631

EARLE, EDWARD (Philadelphia)
1807:   12281 pb
1808:   14321 pb, 14591 f, 15834
    f, 16050 f, 16079 pb, 16080
    f, 16096 f, 16101 pb, 16158
    f, 16246 f, 16658 f
1809:   16966 f, 17041 pb,
    17346 f, 17462 f, 17470 f,
    17632 f, 18434 f, 18483 f,
    18517 pb, 18528 pb, 18581
    f, 18586 pb, 18640 pb,
    19211 f
1810:   19478 f, 19688 f, 19709
    pb, 19711 f, 19861 pb,

20301 f, 20393 f, 21145 f,
    21301 f, 21303 pb, 21334 f,
    21936 pb
1811:   22196 f, 22312 f, 22324
    f
1812:   25278 pb, 25754 pb,
    25777 f, 27545 f
1813:   29212 f, 29219 f, 29910
    f
1814:   30828 f, 31059 pb,
    31699 f, 31947 f, 32161 f,
    32165 f
1815:   34014 f, 34047 f, 34276-
    34277 f, 34485 pb, 34486 f,
    34491 pb, 34495 pb, 34905
    f, 35026 pb, 35317 pb,
    35565 f, 35856 f, 35918 pb,
    35983 f, 35997 f, 36589 f
1816:   36884 pb, 37347 f,
    37392 pb, 38085 f, 38734-
    38735 f, 38998 f, 39860 f
1817:   40458 f, 40687 f, 41016
    f, 41100 pb, 41187 f, 41964
    f, 42232 f, 42923 f
1818:   43577, 43811 pb, 44397
    f, 44399 pb, 44475 f, 44904-
    44905 f, 45311-45312 f,
    45868 f, 45869 pb
1819:   47517 f, 47588-47589 f,
    49388 f, 49474 pb

EARLY, ALEXANDER (Rogers-
    ville, Tenn.)
1815:   34385

EASTBURN, JAMES (New
    York)
1812:   24769 f, 24983 f, 25098
    pb, 25353 pb, 25754 pb,
    26351 f, 26391 pb, 26802
    pb, 27406 f, 27576-27577 f
1813:   28046 pb, 28047 f, 28127
    pb, 28230 pb, 28243 f,
    28253 f, 28334 f, 28408 f,
    28442 f, 28609 pb, 28655-
    28656 f, 28660 pb, 29008-
    29009 f, 29033 f, 29163 f,
    29184 f, 29205 f, 29212 f,
    29219 f, 29221 f, 29487 f,
    29506 f, 29671-29672 f,
    29696 pb, 29777 pb, 29785
    pb, 29786-29787 f, 29790
    pb, 29798 pb, 29833 f,

29863 pb, 30497 f
1814: 30702 pb, 30878 pb,
    30916 pb, 30993 pb, 30994
    f, 31052 f, 31056 pb, 31135
    pb, 31338 pb, 31391 pb,
    31408 f, 31445 f, 31547 f,
    31569 f, 31587 pb, 31632-
    31633 pb, 31642 pb, 31665
    pb, 31737 f, 31926 f, 31995
    f, 32156 f, 32628 pb, 32725
    pb, 32765-32766 f, 32827
    pb, 32839 pb, 32869 pb,
    32966 f
1815: 34120 pb, 34357 f,
    34397-34399 pb, 34488 f,
    34539-34540 pb, 35010-
    35011 pb, 35168-35169 f,
    35317 pb, 35829 f, 35873 f,
    35983 f
1816: 37343 pb, 37879 f,
    37974 pb, 38130 f, 38748
    f, 38832 f
1817: 39921 pb, 40170 f,
    40581 f, 40730 pb, 40765
    f, 41067 f, 41150 f, 41261
    f, 41262 pb, 41323 pb,
    41487 f, 41678 pb, 41706
    pb, 41717 pb, 41718 f,
    41720 pb, 41722 f, 41738
    f, 41832 f, 41860 f, 42037
    pb, 42050 f, 42069 f, 42076
    f, 42079 f
1818: 43006 pb, 43066 pb,
    43239-43240 f, 43445 f,
    43512 f, 43516 f, 43746
    pb, 43792 pb, 43801 pb,
    43864 f, 43911 pb, 44023
    f, 44221 pb, 44481 f, 44486
    pb, 44542 pb, 44564 pb,
    44579 f, 44880 f, 45182 f,
    45319 f, 45354 f, 45583 pb,
    45635 f, 45647 pb, 45652-
    45653 pb, 45654-45657 f,
    45658 pb, 45659 f, 45663 f,
    45664 pb, 45669 pb, 45683
    f, 45787 f, 45800 f, 45865
    pb, 46648 f, 46706 f
1819: 47734 f, 47918 f,
    48226 pb, 48738 f, 49381 f

EASTBURN, ROBERT (New
    Brunswick, N. J.)
1807: 12897 f, 13326 pb,

    13327 f
1808: 14738-14739 pb, 16683
    f, 50840-50841 pb
1809: 16994 pb

EASTBURN, ROBERT (New
    York)
1809: 16999 pb

Eastern Argus (Portland, Me.)
1804: 5779, 5998
1805: 8654, 9264, 9455
1808: 14349
1809: 16950?
1810: 19472 pb
1812: 25230 pb
1815: 36111 pb
1817: 40092, 42821
1819: 49511

EASTIN, THOMAS (Alexandria,
    La.)
1813: 29626 pb

EASTIN, THOMAS (Columbia,
    Tenn.)
1810: 22025 pb

EASTIN, THOMAS (Nashville,
    Tenn.)
1805: 8673 pb
1807: ?12958-12959
1809: 18502 pb
1810: 20826 pb
1812: 25497, 26521

EASTIN, THOMAS (St. Stephens,
    Ala.)
1815: 34839 pb
1818: 43036-43040

EASTIN, THOMAS (Washington,
    Miss.)
1813: 29959
1814: 32946 pb

EASTON, B G (Hartford, Conn.)
1811: 22320 pb

EASTON, J (Salisbury, N. C.)
1810: 20422

EASTWICK, S (Philadelphia)
1817: ?40273 pb, 40313 pb
1818: 43438 pb

EATON, EBENEZER (Danville,
    Vt.)
1807: 12235, 12967, 13261 pb
1808: 14593, 15344
1809: 17848
1810: 19437, 19455-19456,
    19693, 20537, 21895
1811: 22827, 22878, 24340
1812: 27387, 27389
1814: 30764, 30786, 31093,
    31767, 32856, 32896, 33532
1815: 33851 pb, 33948, 34552
    pb, 35260, 35949
1816: 37290, 38232, 39650?
1817: 40118, 41661, 41967
1818: 44847, 45472
1819: 48376, 48697

EATON, EBENEZER (Scipio,
    N. Y.)
1801: 1646 pb

EATON, THEOPHILUS (Oxford,
    N. Y.)
1808: 15326, 15995 pb

EBNER, HEINRICH (Allentown,
    Pa.)
1818: 44134 pb, 44811 pb
1819: 48443, 49374

EBNER, HEINRICH (Northamp-
    ton, Pa.)
1815: 34565
1816: 38712 pb

Echo (Lynchburg, Va.)
1816: 36872

Economical School (New York)
1810: 20515, 20564
1811: 22139 pb, 22447, 23217,
    23851, 24023, 51045
1812: 25811, 26603

EDDY, HENRY (Shawneetown,
    Ill.)
1818: 44421 pb
1819: 48324 pb

EDDY, ISAAC (Weathersfield,
    Vt.)
1813: 28139 pb
1814: 31378, 32231, 32238,
    32454, 33516
1815: 34051 pb, 34458, 34615
    pb, 35138, 35266, 35891 pb,
    36597
1816: 36711, 38820

EDES, BENJAMIN (Augusta,
    Me.)
1806: 10649
1807: 12661

EDES, BENJAMIN (Baltimore)
1809: 16901, 17641, 17645-
    17646, 17913, 18328
1810: 19349, 19487, 19714,
    19794, 19905, 20050 pb,
    20219, 20670, 20996, 21167,
    21168 pb, 21309, 21964
1811: 22183, 22234, 22452a,
    22485, 22642, 22664, 22913,
    23776, 23899, 24036, 24372
1812: 24697 pb, 24972, 25181,
    25198, 25220 pb, 25760,
    26333, 26732, 26743, 26771,
    27636
1813: 27714, 28196, 28658-
    28659, 28701, 29236, 29781,
    30481
1814: 30989, 31050 pb, 31060
    pb, 31061-31062, 31308,
    31522, 31590, 32001, 32382,
    32538
1815: 33821, 33846, 33865 pb,
    34060 pb, 34108, 34617 pb,
    34735, 34842, 34860 pb,
    34950, 35175, 35230 pb,
    35342, 35633, 35746, 35781,
    35793 pb
1816: 36731, 36992 pb, 37021-
    37022, 37088, 37877, 38639,
    38680, 38790, 38965, 39846
1817: 40760, 40858 pb, 41870,
    42307
1818: 43153, 43838, 45469,
    45801
1819: 47550-47551, 48202,
    48304, 48824

EDES, BENJAMIN (Boston)
1801:   252 pb
1802:   2510, 2567 pb

EDES, BENJAMIN (Newbury-
port, Mass.)
1807:   13247 pb

EDES, PETER (Augusta, Me.)
1801:   1384 pb
1802:   1921, 3492
1803:   4139, 4281
1804:   6304 pb, 6357, 6386-
6388, 6656, 7196 pb, 7244
1805:   7835, 8498?, 9041,
9043, 9186, 9685
1806:   10588 pb, 10772 pb,
10863, 11068
1807:   12380, 13310, 13359,
13653
1808:   15119, 15572, 15923
1809:   16816, 17452 pb,
18691, 18778 pb
1810:   20326 pb
1811:   22203, 23116
1812:   25524, 27550 pb
1813:   28473, 29986
1814:   31349, 33574

EDES, PETER (Baltimore)
1818:   43151

EDES, PETER (Bangor, Me.)
1815:   33919 pb
1816:   39802-39803

EDES, PETER (Hallowell, Me.)
1801:   1604
1802:   3143
1811:   23478
1812:   26164
1813:   27962, 29985, 30496

EDES, RICHARD WALKER
(Baltimore)
1818:   34151

EDES, RICHARD WALKER
(Savannah, Ga.)
1819:   51907 pb

Edes & Leakin (Baltimore)
see EDES, BENJAMIN

(Baltimore)
LEAKIN, THOMAS I (Balti-
more)

EDMANDS, THOMAS (Boston)
1805:   8378, 8770
1806:   10339, 11895 pb
1807:   12082, 12207 pb, 12234
pb, 12263 pb, 12332 pb,
12713, 13646, 13671 pb,
13676 pb, 14236 pb
1808:   14350, 14497 pb, 14524
pb, 14554, 14692, 14877 pb,
15206, 15271, 15562 pb,
15571 pb, 15651-15652,
15971 f, 16293, 16652 pb,
16674 pb, 16675? pb, 16745
pb, 16766, 50838 pb
1809:   16802 pb, 16868 pb,
16892, 16907, 17042 pb,
17230 f, 17324 f, 17443,
17449, 17580 pb, 17740 pb,
17754 pb, 18014 pb, 18108
pb, 18120 pb, 18122-18123
pb, 18159 pb, 18269, 18271-
18272, 18428, 18518, 18734
pb, 19270-19271 pb, 19274,
19288, 50923 pb
1810:   19530 pb, 19538, 19564
pb, 19599, 19667-19669? pb,
19671 pb, 19678 pb, 19723,
19772 pb, 19786 f, 19787
pb, 19926 pb, 19982 pb,
20042 pb, 20089 pb, 20175
pb, 20259? pb, 20310 pb,
20781 pb, 20916 pb, 20920,
20934, 20998 pb, 21108 f,
21143? pb, 21218, 21236 pb,
21514 pb, 22083 pb, 22097
pb
1811:   22149 pb, 22229 pb,
22248 pb, 22468 pb, 22551
f, 22663 pb, 22691 pb, 22693
f, 22697, 22714 pb, 22763
pb, 22961, 23008 pb, 23040-
23041 pb, 23106 pb, 23145 pb,
23575, 23617 pb, 23635 pb,
23731 pb, 23817, 23955,
23978 pb, 23980, 24047,
24048 pb, 24053, 24348a pb,
24432, 24433 pb, 24476,
51094 pb
1812:   24570 pb, 24615 pb,

24681-24684 pb, 24716,
24776, 24931 pb, 24977 pb,
24986 pb, 25018-25019 pb,
25096 f, 25126 pb, 25210,
25222 pb, 25423 pb, 25471,
25472 pb, 25532 pb, 25545-
25547, 25616 pb, 25642 pb,
25710 pb, 25751 pb, 25948
pb, 25962 pb, 25966 pb,
26130 pb, 26136?, 26185-
26186, 26303, 26493 f,
26575, 26717 pb, 26742 pb,
26894 pb, 26902, 27472,
27626 pb, 27638 pb
1813: 27797?, 27859, 27862,
27870, 27873, 27910 pb,
27923 pb, 27949-27950,
28096 pb, 28162 f, 28166
pb, 28324 pb, 28390 pb,
28455 pb, 28476-28477,
28592 pb, 29134 pb, 29369-
29370 pb, 29377 pb, 29511,
29560, 29639, 29658 pb,
29664? pb, 29925, 29926
pb, 30484 pb, 30489 pb,
51339-51340 pb
1814: 30758-30761, 30810,
30822 pb, 30963 pb, 31179
sb, 31467, 31537 pb, 31810
f, 32197 pb, 32373, 32522
pb, 32648, 32737 pb, 32919,
32952
1815: 33793, 33944, 34005,
34062 f, 34095 pb, 34152
pb, 34169, 34274 pb, 34337
pb, 34366 sb, 34671 pb,
34754 pb, 34820, 34986 pb,
35242 pb, 35361 pb, 35378
pb, 35511, 35514, 35656
pb, 36136, 36503 pb, 36552
1816: 36672, 36791 pb, 36828,
36857, 36943 f, 36979 pb,
37162 pb, 37226 pb, 37268
pb, 37619, 38346 pb, 38489,
39064 pb, 39728 pb
1817: 39926 pb, 39943 f,
39972 pb, 40048 pb, 40050,
40086, 40171, 40181 pb,
40195 f, 40211 f, 40288,
40360 pb, 41119 pb, 41171
bpb, 41172 f, 41482 pb,
41484, 41518 pb, 41675,
41966 pb, 42000

1818: 43008 pb, 43138-43139,
43188, 43273, 43419, 43422,
43477 pb, 43640-43641 f,
43657 pb, 43960, 44108 pb,
44184 pb, 44487 pb, 44501,
45703 pb, 45838 pb, 45848
pb, 45923?
1819: 46920 pb, 47049 pb,
47103, 47169 pb, 47195 pb,
47210 f, 47337 pb, 47395
pb, 47500 pb, 47563 pb,
47642 f, 47643 pb, 47972
pb, 48077, 48131 pb, 48320,
48345 pb, 48367 pb, 48400
pb, 48424, 48494, 48497,
48557 pb, 48702-48703 pb,
48746 pb, 48764 pb, 48798
pb, 48959 pb, 49131-49136
pb, 49143-49144 pb, 49188
pb, 49230 pb, 49241 pb,
49341 f, 49382 pb, 49386-
49387 pb, 49460 pb, 50139
pb, 50172 pb, 50179-50180

EDRINGTON, JOHN PRICE
(Bardstown, Ky.)
1815: 33937-33938, 34390
1816: 36823 pb
1817: 40080-40081
1818: 43180 pb

EDWARDS, J (Philadelphia)
1811: 23083

EDWARDS, JAMES L (Boston)
1812: 26696 pb

EDWARDS, JAMES L (Peters-
burg, Va.)
1807: 14140 pb
1808: 16313

EDWARDS, WILLIAM (Boston)
1808: 16684 pb

EDWARDS, WILLIAM (Portland,
Me.)
1806: 11105 f, 11340-11341 f,
11822 f

EELLS, NATHANIEL (New London, Conn.)
1805: 7971, 8281?, 8282,

8976 pb, 9242 pb, 9349 pb,
9761-9762
1806: 9955, 10092, 10201 pb,
10245, 10623, 10956 pb,
11353 pb, 11916, 50728 pb
1807: 12318, 14247

EHRENFRIED, JOSEPH (Allentown, Pa.)
1812: 25470 pb
1813: 28347 pb
1814: 31347 pb

EHRENFRIED, JOSEPH (Lan-
caster, Pa.)
1808: 16648 pb
1810: 19490, 19692 pb, 20358
pb, 20425, 20509, 20713
1811: 22953-22954 pb, 23679
1812: 24756, 26583 pb, 26846
1813: 27645 pb, 29634 pb
1814: 30982
1815: 33896, 34894
1816: 38021
1817: 42801
1818: 45486, 46624 pb
1819: 47026? pb

EICHBAUM, WILLIAM (Natchez,
Miss.)
1813: 28983

EICHBAUM, WILLIAM (Pitts-
burgh, Pa.)
1810: 19652 pb, 19887 pb,
19889-19890 pb, 19902 pb,
51033 pb
1811: 22409a pb, 22636 pb,
22638-22639 pb, 22734,
22998, 23880 pb, 51077 pb
1812: 25182 pb, 25263, 25540
pb, 25864 pb, 25949 pb,
26172 pb, 27421 pb, 51183
pb, 51188 f
1813: 28232, 28244 pb, 28313,
28349 pb, 28554, 28647,
28945, 28947 pb, 29253
pb, 29548, 30605 pb, 51291-
51292 pb
1814: 30710, 30979 pb, 31260
f, 31263 pb, 31923 f,
33629-33630, 51376 pb,
51414 pb, 51433 f

1815: 34470 pb, 34472 pb,
35347 f, 36421 f, 36472 f
1816: 36970 f, 37355-37356 f,
38039 f, 38067 f, 39137 pb,
51567 f, 51605 f, 51607 pb
1817: 40589-40590 f
1818: 43367 pb, 43679, 44074
pb, 44933 pb, 44951 pb,
51774 pb
1819: 47578 pb, 48007 pb,
48786, 49512 pb, 49559,
51879 pb, 51892 pb

ELDER, JACOB (Harrisburg,
Pa.)
1805: 8294 pb
1806: 9811, 10256
1807: 13616
1814: 31437 pb
1815: 35594
1816: 38576

ELDREDGE, NATHANIEL T
(New York)
1814: 32346 pb

ELFORD, JAMES (Charleston,
S.C.)
1818: 45786 pb

ELIAS, --- (Richmond, Va.)
1819: 49459

ELIOT, JOHN (Boston)
1809: 17174, 18512, 18521,
18602
1810: 19594?, 19753, 19755-
19756, 19897 pb, 19898,
20033 pb, 20043, 20056,
20317, 20481, 20636, 21119,
21249, 21270, 21346 pb,
21487, 21507, 21889
1811: 22134 pb, 22433, 22693,
22788 pb, 22797, 22858,
22973, 23180, 23344, 23768,
23816 pb, 23875-23876,
23927, 23938, 24027, 24438
1812: 24528, 24538, 24862,
24912-24913, 24979, 25006
pb, 25105 pb, 25114, 25196,
25711, 25744, 25771-25772,
25727, 25849, 26035, 26354,
26681, 26694, 26799, 26828-

26829, 27355, 27427, 27432-
27433, 27543, 27614
1813: 27671, 27938, 28060,
28101, 28171 pb, 28861,
28907, 28912, 29108, 29110,
29113, 29386-29387, 29443,
29615, 29899
1814: 30627, 30806, 30907,
30957, 31026, 31097 pb,
31098, 31117, 31298 pb,
31377, 31608 pb, 31741,
31871-31872, 31977, 32076,
32437-32438, 32496, 32809,
32888, 32931 pb, 33723
1815: 33784, 33855, 34113,
34159 pb, 34171, 34264 pb,
34464, 34477, 34498, 34716,
34861, 35167, 35218 pb,
35538, 35692, 35769 pb,
35912, 36052-36053 pb
1816: 36675, 36756-36757,
36999, 37053, 37140 pb,
37299, 37362, 37578, 37583,
37618, 37682, 37798, 37978,
38188-38189, 38558, 38565,
38856, 38865 pb, 38969,
39019
1817: 40237, 40292, 40308,
40408, 40417, 40630, 41004,
41296-41297, 41375, 41432,
41728, 41968, 42044, 42067,
42237, 42336, 42969 pb,
42970, 42975
1818: 43350, 43659, 43672-
43673, 44268, 44657, 45203,
45336, 45383, 45419, 46821

ELLIOT, JONATHAN (New
York)
1810: 21873 pb
1811: 22754 pb, 23558 pb

ELLIOT, JONATHAN (Wash-
ington, D. C.)
1813: 29539, 30187, 30483
1814: 31068, 31517, 31653,
32662, 32757?, 32927-
32928, 33224-33225, 33504,
33506, 33571-33572
1815: 34433, 34892, 36158,
36250, 36491 pb
1816: 37491, 37551, 38038,
39584

1817: 39977-39978, 40461,
40478 pb, 40529, 41405,
42601 pb, 42748 pb, 42786,
42843, 51722-51723
1818: 45901, 46460

ELLIOT, NATHAN (Catskill,
N. Y.)
1807: 11975 pb, 12296, 13520,
13559
1808: 14391, 14930 pb, 15431,
16109
1809: 17142, 17815, 18426-
18427, 18687
1810: 19328, 19855, 20021,
22065 pb
1811: 22747 pb, 22753 pb
1813: 29716 pb
1814: 31754 f
1816: 38866 f
1818: 45705 f, 51771 f
1819: 47955 f

ELLIOT, WILLIAM (New
Brunswick, N. J.)
1806: 10644
1807: 12489-12490 pb, 12897,
13327, 13726 pb
1808: 14308, 14738-14739 pb,
15694?, 16286, 16683, 50840-
50841 pb
1809: 16994 pb, 17006 pb,
18166 pb
1810: 20830?
1811: 23484 pb

ELLIOT, WILLIAM (New York)
1803: 4289? f, 4448 pb
1804: 6551? pb, 7792? pb
1809: 16999 pb, 17428 pb,
17794, 18276 pb, 18432
1810: 20026 pb, 20177, 20201
pb, 20957-20958 pb, 20978
pb, 21122, 21314 pb
1811: 22900 pb, 23604 pb,
23886 pb, 23890 pb, 51086
pb
1812: 25328 pb, 25559

ELLIOT, WILLIAM (Washing-
ton, D. C.)
1814: 33591 pb

ELLIOT, WILLIAM (White
House, N. J.)
1810: 21189? pb, 51006? pb

ELLIOTT, HUGH (Philadelphia)
1818: 44255? pb

ELLIOTT, JOHN M (New
York)
1819: 47168

ELLIOTT, SAMUEL J (Charleston, S. C.)
1807: 13758 pb

ELLIOTT, WILLIAM P
(Lewistown, Pa.)
1811: 23137 pb

ELY, --- (Chillicothe, O.)
1818: 46843

ELY, ALEXANDER (Suffield,
Conn.)
1801: 50257?

ELY, GEORGE (Williams-
burg, O.)
1814: 33648 pb

Emerald (Boston)
1806: 9823, 11878
1808: 14968, 16161

EMERSON, CALEB (Marietta,
O.)
1810: 22029 pb

ENGLEDOW, ROBERT (Wythe
Court House, Va.)
1809: 18499 pb

ENGLES, SILAS (Baltimore)
1806: 9851, 10141, 10972,
11293 pb

ENGLES, SILAS (Philadelphia)
1804: 5930 pb, 6379
1805: 8076 bf, 9191
1806: 10932a

ENGLES, SILAS (Pittsburgh,
Pa.)

1811: 23727, 23793, 23806,
51102
1812: 24611, 24844, 24958,
25442, 25549, 25641, 26558,
27482, 27569, 51210
1813: 27980, 28372, 28663,
28769, 29136
1814: 32516, 32564
1815: 33969, 34078, 34452,
35396, 35649, 36536
1816: 36676 pb, 37730, 38649-
38650, 38852
1817: 41736, 51700
1818: 45793 pb

ENGLISH, DAVID (Georgetown,
D. C.)
1801: 99, 1686

Enquirer (Richmond, Va.)
1805: 7949, 8540, 9665
1809: 18254, 18643, 19259
1814: 32397, 33708

Episcopal Prayer Book and
Tract Society for the Eastern
Diocese (Boston)
1815: 34012 f
1816: 37521 f

Epitome of the Times (Norfolk,
Va.)
1801: 462

EPPS, W (Troytown, N. Y.)
1810: 19760?

ERBEN, PETER (New York)
1807: 50804? pb

ERMANTINGER, JOHN STERLY
(New York)
1815: 35750 pb

ERRETT, HENRY (New York)
1811: 22773 f

ESCAVAILLE, JOSEPH (Baltimore)
1803: 3718 pb

ESLER, --- (Philadelphia)
1815: 34554

ESSEX, WILLIAM (Lexington,
Ky.)
1814: 30670 f, 32971 pb
1815: 51492 f

Essex Patriot (Haverhill,
Mass.)
1818: 44965

Essex Register (Salem, Mass.)
1801: 726 pb
1805: 9588
1813: 28643 pb
1815: 34791 pb

ETHERIDGE, SAMUEL (Boston)
1806: 9956 f, 10121 f, 10562
f, 11385
1807: 11994 pb, 12446 pb,
12803 f, 12880 pb, 13556-
13557 pb, 13686 pb, 13724
f, 13751 pb, 50752 pb
1808: 14388 f, 14504 pb,
14531 pb, 14607 bf, 15258
pb, 15260 pb, 15386-15387
f, 15389 pb, 15548 f, 15950
pb, 15977 pb, 16142 pb,
16168 pb, 16677 pb
1809: 16996 f, 17096 pb,
17117 pb, 17251 pb, 17298
pb, 17400 pb, 17503 pb,
17606 pb, 17642 pb, 17840
pb, 17886 pb, 18487 pb

ETHERIDGE, SAMUEL
(Charlestown, Mass.)
1801: 24, 64, 91, 138, 255
pb, 297, 383, 600 pb, 618,
?619, 623, 1373 pb, 1380,
1426, 1647, 1655, 50223-
50224 pb, 50266
1802: 1719, 2003, 2116 pb,
2150 pb, 2174, 2239, 2393
pb, 2700 pb, 2745 pb,
2853, 2903 pb, 3055?, 3065
pb, 3166? pb, 3481 pb,
3550 pb
1803: 3789 pb, 3797 pb, 3886
pb, 3946, 4179 pb, 4361
pb, 4379, 4607 pb, 4618,
4670, 4684 pb, 4685, 4686
pb, 4696, 5571, 50342 pb
1804: 5695, 5862 pb, 6126

pb, 6216, 6352, 6414, 6547,
6625 pb, 6749, 6825 pb,
6828 pb, 6972 pb, 7267 pb,
7304, 7317
1805: 8156 pb, 8248 pb, 8905
pb, 8934, 8953, 9079 pb,
9092, 9223, 9243 pb, 9277
pb, 50632 pb
1806: 9924, 9956, 10415 pb,
10817, 11080 pb, 11913 pb
1807: 11963 pb, 12347 pb,
12350, 13566
1808: 15487, 16142 pb, 16155
1809: 17199, 17251 pb, 17336,
19152
1810: 20457-20458 pb, 20792
pb, 20913 pb
1811: 22332, 23443 pb
1812: 24815-24816, 25014 pb,
25367, 25517, 25999, 26146,
26559-26560 pb
1813: 27831, 28641 pb, 29635
pb, 29748, 29751 pb, 51342
pb
1814: 32782-32783, 32973
1815: 34812 pb, 34859 pb
1816: 37982, 38194
1817: 40014, 42824
1818: 43959, 44582, 45488 pb,
45603
1819: 47695, 47917, 50041

EUSCHEDE, JOHN (Harlem,
N. Y.)
1817: 41316 pb

EVANS, BRITTON (Philadelphia)
1812: 26795 pb

EVANS, JOHN (New York)
1808: 14970 pb
1819: 47175 pb

EVANS, JOHN JOSEPH
(Charleston, S. C.)
1803: 3758, 4128
1804: 6978, 7804 pb

EVANS, JOHN JOSEPH (Savannah, Ga.)
1807: 13043, 13485 pb, 14214
1809: 19022
1810: 22038

Evening Gazette (Boston)
1815: 34659 pb
1816: 38781

EVENS, WILLIAM (Natchez,
  Miss.)
1818: 44092, 44828, 44872
  pb
1819: 47108, 48682, 48714-
  48715

EVERETT, DAVID (Marietta,
  O.)
1813: 27655? f, 27712 pb

EVERETT, OLIVER (Boston)
1809: 16794 pb, 16795, 16797
  pb, 16847 pb, 17069 pb

Everett & Munroe (Boston)
see EVERETT, OLIVER
  (Boston)
  MUNROE, ISAAC (Boston)

EVERITT, JOHN F (Savannah,
  Ga.)
1807: 13043, 13485 pb, 14214
1809: 19022

EWER, CHARLES (Boston)
1817: 41449 f, 41450 pb,
  41569 f, 42280 f
1818: 43806 f, 44027 f, 44548
  f, 44861 pb, 45226 pb
1819: 47740 pb, 48587 f,
  48709-48710 f, 49166 f,
  50073 f, 50171 pb

EWER, CHARLES (Portsmouth,
  N. H.)
1816: 38362 pb

EWING, PUTNAM (Hopkins-
  ville, Ky.)
1819: 48420 pb

EWING, PUTNAM (Russell-
  ville, Ky.)
1814: 33632 pb
1818: 43174

F

FAGAN, AUGUSTINE (Philadelphia)
1811: 22427, 22733, 22924 pb,
  23121, 23197-23198, 23824
1812: 25787, 26634-26635,
  26638-26639, 26913
1813: 27683, 28041, 28460,
  28472 pb, 28548, 28583,
  28898, 29128, 29254, 29324,
  29436, 29576
1814: 31112 pb, 32956
1815: 34044, 34307, 35055,
  36481, 36632, 51484
1819: 48383-48384

FAIRBAIRN, WILLIAM (Philadelphia)
1804: 5959 pb

FAIRCHILD, JOHN F (Norwich,
  N. Y.)
1808: 15800 pb
1810: 20568
1811: 22517 pb

FAIRCHILD, JOHN F (Sher-
  burne, N. Y.)
1806: 11066 pb

FAIRCHILD, PLATT B (Ogdensburgh, N. Y.)
1815: 35837 pb

FAIRLAMB, SAMUEL (Marietta,
  O.)
1806: 10511, 11292
1807: 12702
1808: 16207
1809: 16930, 18523, 18545
1814: 30631, 32760

FAIRMAN, D (Boston)
1810: 22109 engr

FAIRMAN, G (Albany, N. Y.)
1802: 2140 engr

FAIRMAN, GIDEON (Newbury-
  port, Mass.)
1808: 15393 pb

FALCONER, WILLIAM (New
York)
1802: 2039 f, 2103 f, 2136 f
1803: 3759 f
1804: 5805 f, 7270 pb
1806: 10895 f
1811: 22380 f, 22535 pb,
 24336 f

1812: 25706 pb

FANSHAW, DANIEL (New York)
1815: 34058, 34181, 34269,
 34306, 34805, 35030, 35252,
 35783, 35788
1816: 37120 pb, 37260, 37350,
 37632, 37956, 38153, 38368
 pb, 38401, 38962, 39010,
 39901
1817: 40232, 41095, 41128,
 41894, 42153, 42282, 42296,
 42991, 51671
1818: 43061, 43345, 43580,
 43873, 44567, 44651, 45060,
 45376, 45570, 45727, 46628,
 46666, 46905
1819: 46974-46975, 47214,
 47228, 50008 pb

Fanshaw & Clayton (New York)
see FANSHAW, DANIEL
 (New York)
 CLAYTON, HENRY (New
 York)

FARMER, JOHN (Concord,
N. H.)
1813: 28483 f

Farmer (Lebanon, O.)
1818: 43770, 44665

Farmer's Cabinet (Amherst,
N. H.)
1805: 8426
1811: 22269
1812: 24994

Farmer's Herald (Stockbridge,
Mass.)
1809: 19203-19205, 19260
1810: 20124

Farmers Repository (Charlestown, Va.)
1811: 22420a

FARNHAM, JOHN HAY (Frank-
fort, Ky.)
1818: 44592

FARNHAM, ROBERT (Boston)
1810: 21253?
1817: 40088, 40290 pb, 40294,
 40506, 41172

Farnham & Badger (Boston)
see FARNHAM, ROBERT
 (Boston)
 BADGER, THOMAS (Boston)

FARNSWORTH, HAVILA (New-
port, R. I.)
1801: 1243
1804: 7190

FARNSWORTH, OLIVER (Cin-
cinnati, O.)
1819: 47616 f

FARNSWORTH, OLIVER (New-
port, R. I.)
1801: 142, 554-555, 596 pb,
 641 sb, 967, 997 pb, 1050
 pb, 1239-1241, 1243-1244,
 50247
1802: 2813, 2988, 2990 pb,
 50269 pb
1803: 4796 pb, 4974, 4977,
 50344, 50352-50353
1804: 6477, 6637, 6961 pb,
 7149 pb, 7190-7191, 7194
 pb, 7763
1805: 7878 pb, 8073, 9256-
 9257 pb
1807: 50807 pb
1809: 19253

FARNSWORTH, OLIVER (Wind-
sor, Vt.)
1809: 17201, 17357 f, 17377,
 17771, 17792, 18752, 19109
 pb, 19265
1810: 19570, 20438, 20707,
 20795, 20868, 20870, 20880,

21113, 21203-21204, 21520
pb, 22074
1812: 24575
1815: 34198 pb, 34199

FARNSWORTH, OLIVER (Wood-
stock, Vt.)
1818: 45714

FARQUAR, WILLIAM (Louis-
ville, Ky.)
1812: 25887 pb
1814: 31939

FARRAND, DANIEL W (Al-
bany, N. Y.)
1810: 19327 pb
1812: 25304 pb, 26576 f

FARRAND, DANIEL W (Phila-
delphia)
1814: 31507 pb

FARRAND, JOSEPH (New
York)
1818: 45064, 45413
1819: 47734, 48472 pb, 48539,
49563 pb, 49566

FARRAND, WILLIAM POWELL
(Boston)
1808: 14356-14357 f, 14590
pb, 14904 f, 15151 pb, 15255
f, 15834 f, 15904 f, 16157
pb, 16179 pb, 16237 f,
16657 f
1809: 17206 pb, 17683 f,
17704 pb, 17788 f, 18089
f, 18189 pb, 18558 pb,
18635 f, 18656 pb, 18728
f, 19204 f
1810: 19484 pb, 19927 f,
20056 f, 20103 pb, 20257
f, 20917 f, 21283 pb, 21402
f, 21527 f, 21795, 21935
pb, 22104? f
1812: 26135? sb

FARRAND, WILLIAM POWELL
(Philadelphia)
1804: 7750 f
1805: 8122 f, 8430 pb, 50530
pb

1807: 12545 pb, 12718 pb,
12965 f, 13364 f, 13365 pb,
13507-13508 pb, 13567 f,
13660 f, 13706 f, 14165 f,
50790 pb
1808: 14353 pb, 14369 pb,
14624 pb, 15384 pb, 15570
pb, 15766 pb
1809: 16969 pb, 17207 pb,
17775 f, 18346 pb, 18368 f
1810: 19397 f, 19484 pb,
19697 f, 20088 f, 20647 f,
21032 f, 21865 f
1811: 22187 pb, 22220 f,
22223 pb, 22412a f, 22548
f, 23044 f, 23650 f, 23662
pb, 23914 pb, 23997 f
1812: 24582 pb, 27383-27384
f, 27574 f
1813: 27768 pb

Farrand & Nicholas (Philadel-
phia)
see FARRAND, WILLIAM
‾‾‾POWELL (Philadelphia)
NICHOLAS, CHARLES J
(Philadelphia)

Farrand, Hopkins & Co.
(Philadelphia)
see FARRAND, WILLIAM
‾‾‾POWELL (Philadelphia)
HOPKINS, BENJAMIN B
(Philadelphia)

Farrand, Hopkins, Zantzinger
& Co. (Philadelphia)
see FARRAND, WILLIAM
‾‾‾POWELL (Philadelphia)
HOPKINS, BENJAMIN B
(Philadelphia)
ZANTZINGER, THOMAS
(Philadelphia)

FAUST, DANIEL (Columbia,
S. C.)
1801: 1343
1802: 3100, 4573 pb
1803: 5082
1804: 7293-7294
1805: 9401-9402, 9734
1806: 11399
1807: 13619a, 13621, 13623

1808: 16220-16222
1809: 18659
1810: 19950, 21388, 21882 pb
1811: 23603 pb, 23962
1812: 26471, 26782-26784
1813: 29013-29014, 29829-
29830
1814: 32820-32821, 32823
1815: 35982
1816: 38982
1817: 41386, 42171-42173,
42175
1818: 43675, 45767 pb
1819: 48203, 48652, 48672,
49461, 49463, 49465

FAUST, JACOB JOHN
(Columbia, S. C.)
1801: 1343
1802: 3100, 4573 pb
1803: 5082
1804: 7293-7294
1805: 9401-9402, 9734
1806: 11399
1807: 13619a, 13621, 13623
1808: 16220-16222
1809: 18959
1810: 19950, 21388, 21882
pb
1811: 23603 pb, 23962
1812: 26471, 26782-26784
1813: 29013-29014, 29829-
29830
1814: 32820-32821, 32823
1815: 35982
1816: 38982
1817: 41386, 42171-42173,
42175
1818: 45767 pb

FAY, GALEN HOUGH (Haver-
hill, Mass.)
1801: 1169
1802: 1705, 2522, 3054, 3503
1803: 3648, 4888, 5490 pb
1805: 9306

FAY, T C (Philadelphia)
1818: 45470

FAY, THOMAS CHITTENDEN
(New York)
1813: 28152 pb, 28153-28154,

28305, 28569, 29409
1815: 35497 f

FAY, THOMAS CHITTENDEN
(Onondaga, N. Y.)
1811: 23260 pb

FAY, WILLIAM (Rutland, Vt.)
1801: 638, 1308, 1425?
1805: 8597
1806: 10539
1807: 12564, 12619, 12735
1808: 14442?
1809: 16938, 18296, 18315,
18638, 19087, 19104 pb
1810: 19773, 20482, 20635,
20853?
1811: 22291, 22646, 23853?,
23942a?, 24339, 24341 pb,
24345
1812: 24685 pb, 24740 pb,
25566, 27388
1813: 27725, 27820, 27930
pb, 28249?, 28311, 30405
bf, 30408, 30559
1814: 30789, 30890, 31673,
31678-31679, 31683, 31854,
31914, 32014?, 32854 pb,
32962 pb, 33611
1815: 35188, 36580 pb
1816: 37076, 38054, 38535,
39662, 39666 f
1817: 41337, 42462 pb, 42742?
pb, 42777-42778, 42780
1818: 43218?, 43359 pb, 44502
1819: 46963 pb, 47141-47142,
48810 pb, 48843 pb, 49436,
49632 pb, 49983 pb

Federal Gazette (Baltimore)
1818: 43440
1819: 47422

Federal Republican (Baltimore)
1808: 15942?
1809: 18135, 18471, 19220

FEE, ROBERT (Brownsville,
Pa.)
1818: 46776 pb

FEE, ROBERT (Washington,
Pa.)
1817: 42874 pb

FELCH, CHEEVER (Walpole,
N. H.)
1808: 14374, 15278, 16190
1809: 16939, 17114, 18437
1810: 19334 pb, 19458, 19702
pb, 21286

FELL, FREDERICK S (Savan-
nah, Ga.)
1813: 29924

FELTHOUSEN, JACOB D
(Mount Holly, N. J.)
1816: 37089, 39092

FELTHOUSEN, JACOB D (Philadelphia)
1815: 51514 pb

Female Society in Salem for
Promoting Religious Knowledge (Salem, N. Y.)
1805: 9219 f

Female Tract Association of
Friends (Philadelphia)
1819: 49247 f

Female Union Society for the
Promotion of Sabbath
Schools (New York)
1816: 37907 f, 37946 pb,
39122 f
1818: 46781 f

FENNO, JOHN WARD (New
York)
1801: 327 f, 572 f

FENTON, DANIEL (Mill-Hill,
N. J.)
1810: 19866 f
1811: 22713 f, 24390 pb,
24400 f

FENTON, DANIEL (Trenton,
N. J.)
1806: 10031 f
1809: 17271 f, 17516 f, 17598
f, 17692 f, 18421 f, 18547 f
1810: 19629-19630 f, 22112 f
1811: 23537 f, 23586 f,
24386 f, 24389 f

1812: 24839 f, 25950 pb,
26761, 26920 pb
1813: 28880 pb, 28933 f,
29318 pb
1815: 33847 pb, 34144 pb,
34180 pb, 35944 pb
1816: 37057 f, 38885 pb
1817: 40206 pb, 41693 f,
42127 pb, 42145-42146 f
1818: 44974 pb
1819: 48685 pb, 49331 pb

FENTON, ELISHA (Trenton,
N. J.)
1817: 40206 pb, 41693 f,
42127 pb, 42145-42146 f
1818: 44974 pb
1819: 48685 pb, 49331 pb

FERGUSON, BARTIMEUS
(Burlington, Vt.)
1814: 32371 pb

FERGUSON, BARTIMEUS
(Middlebury, Vt.)
1813: 28192 pb
1814: 30787, 31323 pb, 32779,
33533, 33539 pb, 33614 pb,
33738
1815: 34946

FERGUSON, JAMES (Cincinnati,
O.)
1818: 43994 f

FERGUSON, ROBERT (Pitts-
burgh, Pa.)
1814: 31260, 51415 pb, 51433
1815: 34244, 35124, 35243,
35347, 36421, 36469, 36472
1816: 36970, 37355-37356,
38039, 38067, 38251, 38786,
51567, 51605
1817: 40589-40590, 41751

FERO, HENRY (Albany, N. Y.)
1815: 34896 f
1816: 37703 f

FERO, HENRY (Brooklyn,
N. Y.)
1816: 36936 f

FERO, HENRY (Troy, N.Y.)
1812: 24902 f

FERRELL, JAMES (Natchez, Miss.)
1802: 2675

FESSENDEN, WILLIAM (Brattleboro, Vt.)
1803: 4966 pb, 5569
1804: 6298
1805: 8954, 9748
1806: 10040, 10094, 10541, 10743
1807: 12429 pb, 12563 pb, 12848 pb, 12891, 13419 pb
1808: 14398 f, 14868, 15152, 16254 pb
1809: 17122, 17666, 17945, 19172
1810: 20540, 20655 pb, 21286 f, 21419-21420 pb
1811: 22333 pb, 22396, 22624, 22738, 23578, 23673-23674
1812: 24626 pb, 24738, 25326-25327, 25697 pb, 25793, 25908
1813: 27840, 28043 pb, 28325, 28417, 28512 pb, 28546-28546a, 28611 pb, 28843 pb, 28850, 28888, 28897 pb, 29017, 29434, 29556 f, 29691 pb, 29878 pb, 30503
1814: 31207 pb, 31234 pb, 31510 pb, 31570 pb, 31593, 31598 pb, 31607 pb, 31704 pb, 31728-31729 pb, 31766 pb, 31823 f, 32095 pb, 32213 pb, 32535 pb, 32543 f, 32610, 32772 pb, 33626 pb
1815: 36524 pb

FESSENDEN, WILLIAM (Vergennes, Vt.)
1801: 1577

FESSENDEN, WILLIAM (Walpole, N.H.)
1808: 15208 pb

FIELD, MATHEW (New York)
1817: 41223 pb

FIELD, THOMAS (Petersburg, Va.)
1801: 271 sb, 710?
1803: 3915
1804: 5801

FILLEBROWN, THOMAS (Concord, N.H.)
1817: 40685

FILLMORE, LAVIUS (Middlebury, Vt.)
1812: 27400 pb
1813: 27947 f, 30414 f, 30416 f
1814: 31978 f, 33540 f, 33543 pb
1815: 34122 f, 35421? pb, 36436 f, 36439 pb

FINCH, E E (Boston)
1814: 31810 f

FINDLAY, JONATHAN S (Cincinnati, O.)
1801: 1491, 1569, 1590 pb
1802: 2820

FINDLAY, JONATHAN SMITH (Washington, Ky.)
1803: 5567 pb

FINLEY, ANTHONY (Philadelphia)
1809: 17929 f, 18559 f
1810: 20471 pb, 20587 pb, 20615 f
1811: 22456a pb, 22541 f, 22621 pb, 22853 pb, 22995 f, 23039 pb, 23895 pb, 23984 f
1812: 24745 pb, 24797 f, 25170 pb, 25854 f, 26182 f, 26189 pb, 26349-26350 f, 26528 f, 26766 f
1813: 28123 pb, 28124 f, 28359 pb, 28411 f, 29976 f
1814: 31140-31141 f, 32798 f
1815: 34028 pb, 36124 f
1816: 36921 pb, 36923 pb, 37778 f
1817: 40175 f, 40432 pb, 40911 f, 41314 pb, 42129 f, 42229 f

1818: 43109 f, 43274 pb,
    43279 pb, 44471 f, 44559
    f, 44649 pb, 44773 pb,
    45460 f, 45599 pb
1819: 47898 f, 47974 f, 48011
    pb, 48380 f, 48751 f, 49336
    pb, 49357 f

FINLEY, JAMES (West Union,
    O.)
1816: 38667 pb
1817: 41499

Finley & Hopkins (Philadelphia)
see FINLEY, ANTHONY
    (Philadelphia)
    HOPKINS, WILLIAM H
    (Philadelphia)

FINNELL, NIMROD L
    (Winchester, Ky.)
1815: 33936? pb, 35053 pb
1816: 37222

FISH, FRANCIS G (Burlington,
    Vt.)
1814: 31037 pb
1815: 33879, 35702
1816: 38330

FISH, JOSHUA (Albany, N. Y.)
1817: 41200 f

FISHBACK, JAMES (Lexing-
    ton, Ky.)
1814: 33650 pb

FISHER, HENRY M (Baltimore)
1811: 23069

FISHER, REDWOOD (Philadel-
    phia)
1813: 28508 pb
1814: 31276 f

FISHER, SAMUEL ROWLAND
    (Philadelphia)
1811: 23197 f, 23410 pb
1812: 25106 pb, 25600 pb,
    26914 pb

FITCH, JOHN (Middlebury, Vt.)
1801: 928 pb, 50262 pb

1802: 1783, 2919, 3464 pb
1803: 3754 pb, 4422, 5503,
    5623
1804: 6776, 7269, 7661, 7662
    pb
1805: 8242, 8476, 8829, 9451,
    9657 pb
1806: 9809, 10063, 11866

FITZGERALD, JOHN (Clarks-
    ville, Tenn.)
1819: 47636 pb

FITZGERALD, JOHN (Mobile,
    Ala.)
1819: 47682 pb

FITZ RANDOLPH, DAVID (New
    Brunswick, N. J.)
1811: 22612 pb, 22852 pb
1814: 32785
1815: 34210
1816: 36837
1817: 40838
1818: 43029

FITZ RANDOLPH, JAMES (New
    Brunswick, N. J.)
1811: 22612 pb, 22852 pb
1814: 32785
1815: 34210

FITZWHYLSON, WILLIAM H
    (Philadelphia)
1815: 36589 f

FITZWHYLSON, WILLIAM H
    (Richmond, Va.)
1807: 50815 pb

FLAGG, AZARIAH CUTTING
    (Plattsburgh, N. Y.)
1812: 25909, 26115, 26133,
    26437-26438, 27580
1813: 30508
1817: 42939
1818: 43021, 44280
1819: 49127

FLAGG, HENRY COLLINS
    (New Haven, Conn.)
1817: 40511, 41771, 41930
1818: 43463, 43465, 43526 pb,

44384, 45435, 45475 pb
1819: 47019 pb, 47504, 47700
pb, 47753-47754 pb, 47796,
48360, 49242 pb

FLAGG, TIMOTHY (Andover,
Mass.)
1812: 27596
1813: 27730 pb, 27735, 28234,
28379, 28381, 28833, 28972
pb, 29461, 29566, 29573,
29685, 29784, 29896, 30571,
51296
1814: 30637, 30640, 30816,
30834, 30860, 30873, 31075,
31121, 31245, 31293, 31342,
31413 pb, 31476, 31485,
31618, 31782, 31791, 32126-
32127, 32154, 32162, 32246,
32360, 32405, 32476, 32498,
32559 pb, 32565, 32627 pb,
32649, 32749, 32887, 32902,
32934-32939, 33583, 33596,
33600, 33602-33603 pb,
33615, 33679
1815: 33852, 33867, 34021
pb, 34043, 34273 pb, 34330,
34465, 34479, 34583, 34590,
34702, 34799, 34818, 34841,
34855, 34953 pb, 35096 pb,
35224, 35279 pb, 35287,
35318, 35585, 35627, 35666
pb, 35675-35677, 35689,
35701 pb, 35764, 35786,
35904 pb, 36030, 36089,
36095, 36476, 36493, 36615-
36618, 36639, 36643
1816: 36688 pb, 36904,
36912, 37132 pb, 37161 pb,
37345 pb, 37383, 37443,
37460, 37479, 37494, 37499
pb, 37737 pb, 37880, 37882,
37915, 38290 pb, 38390,
38682 pb, 38809, 38935,
39047, 39090, 39142, 39693-
39695, 39738, 39750, 39874,
51593
1817: 40000-40001, 40156 pb,
40161 pb, 40603, 40614-
40615, 40733 pb, 40834 pb,
40882 pb, 40964, 41087,
41148, 41271, 41444 pb,
41660, 41808, 41829 pb,

41984, 42109, 42139, 42803,
42820, 42940 pb, 42957,
51670
1818: 43071, 43083, 43266,
43278, 43562, 43564, 43754,
43776, 43803, 44044, 44225-
44226, 44325 pb, 44381 pb,
44424, 44440 pb, 44442,
44756, 45158, 45162 pb,
45164 pb, 45202, 45225,
45382 pb, 45404, 45416 pb,
45541, 45702, 45713 pb,
45814, 45871 pb, 45885,
46710, 46730 pb, 46738,
46867, 46875 pb
1819: 46993, 46999-47000,
47184, 47362, 47719, 47733,
47827 pb, 47882, 47999 pb,
48221, 48281, 48492, 48750
pb, 48844 pb, 48928, 49007,
49163-49165 pb, 49166,
49527-49530 pb, 50056,
50135 pb, 50143, 50144 pb,
50152

FLEET, JOHN (Boston)
1801: 85 pb, 962
1802: 1779 pb, 3502
1803: 3870, 4561 pb
1804: 5735
1805: 8806 pb

FLEET, THOMAS (Boston)
1801: 85 pb, 962, 1383
1802: 1779 pb, 3502
1803: 3870, 4434, 4561 pb
1804: 5735, 6540 pb, 6880 pb,
7765
1805: 8483, 8806 pb, 9281 pb
1806: 10945 pb, 11376
1807: 12758 pb, 13441 pb
1808: 14557, 15743

FLEMING, DAVID (Warren, O.)
1812: 26923 pb

FLEMING, THOMAS (Charles-
ton, S. C.)
1819: 51874 pb

FLEMMING, DAVID (Mercer,
Pa.)
1811: 24425

FLETCHER, JAMES F
(Boston)
1807: 13108 pb

FLETCHER, JOHN (Boston)
1807: 12574

FLETCHER, JOHN R (Cin-
cinnati, O.)
1817: 40499 pb, 40500 f

FLETCHER, JOSHUA (Lan-
caster, Mass.)
1806: 10525 f

FLETCHER, JOSHUA (Phila-
delphia)
1810: 19357 f, 19850 pb

FLETCHER, N H (Kennebunk,
Me.)
1805: 9449 pb

FLOYD, BENJAMIN (Ports-
mouth, N. H.)
1810: 19406 f

FOLEY, THOMAS (Ebensburg,
Pa.)
1819: 48096, 48981 pb

FOLLETT, ORAN (Batavia,
N. Y.)
1819: 49480 pb

FOLSOM, BENJAMIN (East-
port, Me.)
1818: 43905 pb
1819: 47099

FOLSOM, BENJAMIN (Walpole,
N. H.)
1812: 25261 pb

FOLWELL, RICHARD (Phila-
delphia)
1801: 248 pb, 264, 337,
419 pb, 679, 1456, 1484
pb, 1487-1490 pb, 1677
1803: 5022, 5318-5320
1805: 9411 pb
1810: 21673 pb
1813: 28459 pb

FONTAINE, JEAN BAPTISTE
LeSEUR (New Orleans, La.)
1803: 4537
1804: 6766
1805: 9071

FOOTE, THOMAS S (Williamsburg, O.)
1813: 29536 pb

FORBES, GEORGE (Albany,
N. Y.)
1812: 25913 f
1813: 29006 f

FORBES, JOHN (New York)
1812: 24769, 25052
1813: 27679, 28243, 28442,
28838, 29812, 29831
1814: 30695, 31408, 31547,
31727, 31737, 32685
1815: 34691?, 35282 pb,
35772, 36556
1816: 36722, 36905, 37418,
37464, 37600 pb, 38911,
39026, 39034, 39078 bf
1817: 40272, 40624 pb, 41093-
41094, 41251, 41721, 41858
pb, 42022

FORCE, PETER (Washington,
D. C.)
1815: 36258?
1818: 43486, 45479 pb, 46631
1819: 46981, 47046, 47418-
47419, 47836, 48821 pb,
49422, 49899d, 50049

FORD, JOHN W (Lebanon,
Tenn.)
1818: 44550 pb

FORDYCE, J (Baltimore)
1816: 37302 pb

FORDYCE, JOHN (Philadelphia)
1813: 28186 f, 29200 pb,
51276 pb

FORMAN, AARON (New York)
1802: 1915, 3057
1803: 4071 pb, 5524
1804: 6685, 6991, 7813

1805: 8970, 9145-9146,
9319, 50583 f
1806: 10298 pb, 10895, 11071
f, 11379, 11389 pb
1807: 12798, 12799 pb, 12900,
13294 f, 13610 pb, 50812
pb
1808: 14909 pb, 15285 pb,
15899 pb, 16208 pb, 16655
pb, 16659 pb, 50875 pb,
50887 pb
1809: 16975, 17397, 17637
pb, 17791 pb, 18390 pb,
18419 pb, 18645-18646 pb,
50956 pb, 50964, 50965 pb
1810: 19539 pb, 20391 pb,
20419-20420, 21085 pb,
21371-21373 pb, 50999 pb
1811: 22702 pb, 23071 pb,
23455 pb, 23951 pb, 51104
pb, 51139-51141 pb
1812: 24824 f, 25705 pb,
25766 pb, 25788 pb, 26464
pb, 26598 pb, 26764-26765
pb, 27419 pb, 51176 pb,
51247 pb
1813: 27887 pb, 28795 pb,
29514 pb, 29809-29811 pb,
51335 pb
1814: 30674 pb, 31107 pb,
31201, 31779 pb, 32153
pb, 32357 pb, 32805-32806
pb, 51439 pb
1815: 34981 pb, 35961, 51534-
51535 pb
1816: 37899 pb, 38632 pb,
38634 pb, 38959, 51626-
51627 pb
1817: 41815 pb

FORMAN, GEORGE (New
York)
1803: 3819, 4770, 4925
1804: 7214
1805: 8086, 8599, 8998
1806: 9877, 50729
1807: 12458, 13471, 13544
1809: 16885 pb, 16974,
16977, 17359 pb, 17360,
17450, 17733 pb, 18287?,
18533, 19269
1811: 23366, 23918 pb
1812: 25551 pb, 26578

1813: 28990, 29049, 29331
1814: 30950 pb, 32618-32619
pb
1815: 35754 pb, 36442
1816: 38214
1817: 39989, 41632
1818: 44286 pb, 45483
1819: 48664 pb, 48904

FORREST, JAMES (Northum-
berland, Pa.)
1817: 41770 pb

FORSTER, JOSEPH (Philadelphia)
1805: 9109 pb

FOSTER, --- (Otsego, N.Y.)
1818: 51819 pb

FOSTER, DAVID C (Ports-
mouth, N.H.)
1813: 28541, 30442 pb
1814: 30717, 30954, 31891
1815: 33913, 35267, 35684,
35948
1816: 37640, 38947
1817: 42988
1818: 43595
1819: 49516-49517

FOSTER, JAMES (Circleville,
O.)
1817: 41694 pb

FOSTER, JOHN WELCH (Portsmouth, N.H.)
1819: 47960 f, 51877 pb

FOSTER, JONATHAN (Winchester, Va.)
1810: 21195 pb
1811: 22295, 22478, 22549,
22610
1812: 24743
1813: 27822
1814: 30794, 31471, 32448 pb,
33646, 33657
1815: 33986, 34362?
1816: 36864, 37998, 39075-
39076, 39881
1817: 40127, 40399 pb, 40470
pb, 40920, 41151, 42271-

42272
1818: 43225, 44062 pb,
  45858, 46881 pb
1819: 48348, 48659, 49586

FOSTER, ROBERT (Ports-
mouth, N. H.)
1818: 44063 f

FOSTER, THEODORE A
(Providence, R. I.)
1802: 2955 f

FOSTER, WILLIAM (Pitts-
burgh, Pa.)
1808: 14991, 16317 pb

FOWLER, GEORGE (Philadel-
phia)
1810: 20133 f

FOXALL, HENRY (Georgetown)
1807: 13506 f

FRAILEY, LEONARD (Balti-
more)
1805: 8546 f
1806: 11411 pb
1808: 14934?, 15105

FRANCIS, DAVID (Boston)
1802: 1750, 1794, 1849 pb,
  1865, 1933, 1965, 2242,
  2324, 2326-2328, 2482,
  2518, 2630, 3063, 3146,
  3453 pb
1803: 3971, 4145, 4341, 4388,
  4672 pb, 4689, 4799, 5039,
  5050, 5147
1804: 5839, 5895 pb, 5956,
  6027, 6185, 6866, 6971,
  7201, 7254, 7400, 50477
1805: 8099 pb, 8381, 9271
  pb, 50619
1806: 9800, 9816 pb, 9829,
  9865, 11400, 11491, 11872
1807: 12006 pb, 12023 pb,
  12106, 12179-12180, 12502,
  13469, 13498, 13572 pb,
  13625, 13680
1808: 14315-14316, 14386
  pb, 14476 pb, 14938 pb,
  15087-15088, 15110, 15198

pb, 15290 pb, 15297 pb,
15352, 15395 pb, 15402,
15433 pb, 15456 pb, 15479,
15508 pb, 15863, 15984,
16023 pb, 16078, 16177,
16225, 16227, 16252 pb,
16365, 16375, 16654 pb,
50889
1809: 16787, 16877 pb, 16991
  pb, 17067, 17104-17105 pb,
  17192 pb, 17312 pb, 17422
  pb, 17430 pb, 17526, 17599,
  17600 pb, 17675, 17818,
  17861 pb, 17889 pb, 18026
  pb, 18032 pb, 18056, 18268
  pb, 18359 pb, 18725? pb,
  19133 pb, 19290 pb
1810: 19390 pb, 19598, 19600,
  19615, 20062 pb, 20136,
  20181-20183, 20266, 20279
  pb, 20299 pb, 20437, 20597
  pb, 20601-20602 pb, 20686-
  20687, 20755, 20763-20764,
  20778 pb, 20968, 21011,
  21012 pb, 21040 pb, 21088
  pb, 21144 pb, 21288? pb,
  21331, 21358 pb, 21397,
  21429? pb, 21511?, 21970?,
  21980 pb
1811: 22212 pb, 22419a pb,
  22442a pb, 22510 pb, 22511?
  pb, 22887 pb, 22888, 22944 pb,
  22946, 23079 pb, 23427-23428
  pb, 23613, 23778 pb, 24055 pb
1812: 24967, 24995 pb, 25193,
  25276 pb, 25341 pb, 25372-
  25373 pb, 25490-25493, 25510
  pb, 25535, 25650-25651,
  25703 f, 25835 pb, 25904
  pb, 25911 pb, 26182, 26502
  pb, 26585-26586, 26869 pb,
  27146
1813: 27829, 27977 pb, 27987,
  27991-27992 pb, 28140,
  28322, 28369 pb, 28444,
  28448 pb, 28450 pb, 28599
  pb, 28691 pb, 28846 pb,
  28961? pb, 28994 pb, 29165,
  29561 pb, 29579 pb, 29637-
  29638, 29650, 29948, 29988
  pb, 30435 pb
1814: 30684?, 30848, 30968,
  31057, 31439, 31442-31443

pb, 31588-31589 pb, 31851
pb, 31895, 31988, 32022
pb, 32236-32237 pb, 32510
pb, 32719 pb, 32798, 33670,
51405 pb
1815: 33995, 34053 pb, 34063
pb, 34663, 34895, 34967-
34968, 35057 pb, 35078 pb,
35140 pb, 35166, 35232,
35415 pb, 35760-35761,
35859
1816: 37049, 37220 pb, 37248,
37579, 37683, 37760, 38081
pb, 38105, 38107, 38197,
38309 pb, 38374 pb, 38530,
38534, 38775, 38776 pb
1817: 40037 pb, 40244, 40353,
40362-40363 pb, 40373 pb,
40502, 40620 pb, 40629
pb, 40845, 40888, 41096
pb, 41244 pb, 41299, 41321,
41371 pb
1818: 43014, 43355, 43365-
43366 pb, 43509 pb, 43525,
43821 pb, 43924 pb, 43980
pb, 44032 pb, 44066, 44079,
44324 pb, 44379 pb, 44628
pb, 44924 pb, 45364 f,
45534 pb, 45582 pb, 45897
pb
1819: 48371, 48522-48523
pb, 49289, 49482, 49490
pb, 49635 pb

FRANCIS, JOHN WAKEFIELD
(New York)
1810: 20901 pb

FRANCIS, SIMEON (New Lon-
don, Conn.)
1818: 43169, 45518 pb
1819: 48397 pb, 49065, 50114

FRANK, JACOB (Baltimore)
1802: 2062 f

FRANK, JACOB (New York)
1806: 11134
1807: 13454 pb
1808: 14304, 14858, 16282
1809: 17376 pb, 17819, 18243
pb, 18779 pb

FRANK, LEWIS P (Philadelphia)
1814: 31244 pb

Frankfort Argus (Frankfort,
Ky.)
see Argus of Western America
(Frankfort, Ky.)

FRANKLIN, --- (Newbern,
N.C.)
1803: 4779 pb
1804: 6143 pb, 6148 pb, 6639
pb

FRANKLIN, EDWARD (Phila-
delphia)
1818: 43398 f

FRANKLIN, SAMUEL (Phila-
delphia)
1819: 48546, 49116 pb

Franklin Company (New York)
1808: 15156 pb
1811: 22459 pb, 22939 pb,
23436 pb

Franklin Herald (Greenfield,
Mass.)
1815: 36010

Franklin Juvenile Book-Store
(New York)
1819: 48779 pb

Franklin Press (Baltimore)
1815: 34435
1816: 37833

Franklin Press (Richmond,
Va.)
1809: 19121
1819: 47145, 47420, 48145?,
48990, 49282-49283 pb,
49284, 49291 pb, 49421,
49438

Franklin Press (Washington,
D.C.)
1802: 1753 pb, 2148, 3205

Franklin Press (Wilmington,
Del.)

1801: 402
1802: 2741

FRANKS, LEWES P (Towanda,
  Pa.)
1816: 39716 pb

FRARY, JONATHAN (Albany,
  N.Y.)
1808: 16615 pb
1809: 16890 pb
1811: 22928 pb

FRARY, JONATHAN (Hudson,
  N.Y.)
1808: 15169 pb
1809: 18665

FRARY, TIMOTHY (Green-
  field, Mass.)
1811: 22182 f, 23125 f
1816: 39670

FRASER, DONALD (New York)
1810: 19516 pb

Frederick-Town Herald (Frederick, Md.)
1804: 7771
1810: 20462

Fredonian (Chillicothe, O.)
1813: 28573, 29012
1814: 32390, 32677?
1815: 34900, 35161

FREEMAN, JOHN (Dover, Del.)
1804: 6186 pb

FREEMAN, JOHN (Newcastle,
  Del.)
1805: 9021 pb

FREEMAN, JOHN (Philadelphia)
1810: 20060

Freeman's Friend (Portland,
  Me.)
1809: 17805? pb, 18623 pb

Freemason's Magazine (Philadelphia)
1811: 22868-22869

FREER, ANTHONY (Kingston,
  N.Y.)
1818: 45061 pb

FREER, SAMUEL S (Kingston,
  N.Y.)
1801: 643
1802: 3488, 50301 pb
1803: 5189 pb
1807: 12539 pb
1808: 14989 pb
1809: 50939 pb
1810: 20084 pb
1813: 28487 pb, 28597
1814: 31454 pb
1815: 34676 pb
1818: 45061 pb

FRENCH, BRONSON (Pough-
  keepsie, N.Y.)
1809: 17483 pb

FRENCH, EBENEZER (Balti-
  more)
1812: 24699 pb
1813: 28160, 28680?, 28721,
  29889
1814: 31351, 31645
1816: 37186
1818: 43543

FRENCH, EBENEZER (Boston)
1806: 10689 pb
1807: 12017
1809: 17753
1810: 21219 pb
1811: 22672, 23314, 23333,
  23349, 24024

FRENEAU, PETER (Charleston,
  S.C.)
1803: 3856
1804: 5693 pb
1805: 8630
1808: 14683
1809: 17571-17572

FRICK, HENRY (Milton, Pa.)
1816: 38260 pb
1818: 43457

FRICK, JACOB (Philadelphia)
1816: 36728 pb

1817: 40031
1819: 47015, 49183

FROST, JOHN H A (Boston)
1818: 19373?, 43296, 43314,
    43417, 43453, 43991, 43997,
    45200, 45219, 45271, 45746,
    45789, 46695
1819: 47220-47221, 47437,
    47945, 48825, 50030 pb,
    50031, 50078, 50183

FRY, WILLIAM (Philadelphia)
1802: 3172 f
1803: 4783 f, 5074 pb, 50333
    f
1805: 8124, 8306, 8409
1807: 11961 pb, 12083, 12091,
    12257-12258, 12272 pb,
    12384, 12688, 12690, 12742,
    12757, 12819, 13325, 13567,
    13578, 13660, 13706, 14090
1808: 14253, 14591, 14649,
    14816, 15015, 15038, 15153,
    15266, 15333, 15670, 15834,
    16050, 16080, 16096, 16100,
    16113, 16158, 16206, 16658,
    16689
1809: 16784, 16963, 16966,
    17026, 17028, 17043, 17101,
    17161, 17228, 17346, 17462,
    17470, 17632, 17775-17776,
    18368, 18380, 18434, 18483,
    18559, 18581, 19211
1810: 19296, 19363, 19478,
    19543-19544, 19688, 19697,
    19701, 19711-19712, 19715,
    19718-19719, 19800, 19883,
    20024, 20088, 20130, 20393,
    20443, 20456, 20503, 20615,
    20647, 20796, 20943, 21032,
    21145, 21301, 21334, 21865,
    22117
1811: 22137-22138, 22196,
    22312, 22386, 22506, 22548,
    22632, 22711, 22828, 22995,
    23044, 23130, 23177, 23614,
    23650, 23846, 23984, 23997,
    24337, 24342a, 24474-24475
1812: 24520, 24797, 24864,
    24877, 25010, 25777, 25839,
    26048, 26345, 26528, 26704-
    26707, 26709, 26767, 27383-

27384, 27545, 27566, 27574
1813: 28061-28062, 28124,
    28400, 28411, 28768, 28965,
    29374, 29593-29594, 29663,
    29739-29740, 29745, 29747,
    29750, 29903, 29910, 30402-
    30404, 30439, 30522, 30528,
    30558
1814: 30650, 30728, 30828,
    31049, 31255-31256, 31400,
    31465, 31651 pb, 31699,
    31947, 32546, 32600, 33734
1815: 33923-33924, 34014,
    34028 pb, 34267, 34276-
    34277, 34292, 34410, 34442,
    34486, 34807, 34939, 35054,
    35340, 35496 pb, 35542,
    35565, 35603, 35952, 35983,
    36565
1816: 36807 pb, 37000, 37036,
    37152, 37183, 37190, 37196,
    37216, 37370, 37575, 37590,
    38023, 38042, 38199, 38206,
    38238, 38614, 38892, 38974,
    38983, 39660, 39860, 51618
    pb
1817: 39985, 40062 pb, 40175-
    40176, 40405, 40458, 40469,
    40583, 40691, 40911, 41070,
    41391, 41415, 41709, 41782-
    41783, 41871, 42014, 42154,
    42229, 42904 pb, 42914,
    42923, 42926
1818: 43109, 43232, 43352,
    43573, 43633-43634, 43667
    pb, 43725, 43760, 44205,
    44292, 44464, 44475, 44559,
    44957, 45103, 45184, 45243,
    45285, 45293, 45301 pb,
    45342, 45363, 45431, 45460,
    45463, 45540, 45646, 45692,
    46784, 46794, 46825, 46842,
    46911
1819: 46985, 47021, 47038,
    47351, 47680, 47684, 47824,
    47898, 47974, 48182, 48318
    pb, 48350, 48550, 48656,
    48661, 48751, 49075 pb,
    49076, 49159, 49212, 49845,
    49946

FRYER, GEORGE (Baltimore)
1801: 1389

1802:   2062, 2207 pb
1803:   4469
1804:   6197, 6585, 6691,
        50453
1805:   8362 pb, 8546
1806:   10187, ?10191, 10496,
        10796, ?10840, 10852,
        10991, 11304, 50726 pb
1807:   12018, 12327, 13050,
        ?13081, 13204?
1808:   14882, ?15092 pb,
        15498

FULLEN, JAMES (Philadelphia)
1814:   31244 pb

FURMAN, JOHN K (New York)
1801:   420, 517, 722 f, 1022-
        1023
1810:   20574

G

GADDIS, RICE (Wilmington,
   O.)
1815:   34179, 34819, 34992-
        34993, 36062, 36127 pb
1816:   39800
1817:   42068
1819:   47473

GAINE, HUGH (New York)
1801:   169 f

GAINES, HERBERT P (Glas-
   gow, Ky.)
1818:   44200 pb

GAINES, XENOPHON J
   (Lexington, Ky.)
1818:   43549 pb

GALBRAITH, JOHN (Butler,
   Pa.)
1818:   43508 pb

GALES, JOSEPH (Raleigh,
   N. C.)
1801:   639 pb, 1059-1060?,
        1061-1062, 1076

1802:   2472, 2802-2807
1803:   4258, 4773?, 4774-4776,
        4777?, 4778
1804:   6364, 6365 pb, ?6934?,
        6935-6939
1805:   8500, 9030-9035
1806:   10463, 11036-11038,
        11200
1807:   12641, 12844, 13066,
        13257-23160
1808:   14279 pb, 15083, 15777-
        15783
1809:   17597, 18260, 18262-
        18264
1810:   20925?, 20926-20927,
        ?20929?, 20930
1811:   22882, 23457, 23571-
        23573
1812:   24565 pb, 25077-25078
        pb, 25487, 26312? pb
1813:   28064, 28077 pb, 28595
1814:   31092, 31553 pb, 31680
        pb
1816:   37677, 38478 pb, 38485,
        38692 pb
1817:   40101, 40606, 40884,
        41672, 42251 pb
1818:   43351?, 43656, 44119,
        44314, 45114 pb
1819:   46944, 48060, 48198,
        48370 pb, 48769, 48982

GALES, JOSEPH (Washington,
   D. C.)
1810:   21669, 21674?
1813:   28268 pb, 30196
1814:   32155 pb, 33228 pb
1815:   34354, 36159, 36276,
        36365
1816:   39487-39489
1817:   39924 pb, 40604
1819:   47716 pb, 49002, 49674,
        49744, 49746-49747, 49813,
        49830, 49833, 49835-49836,
        49847, 49862-49865, 49868,
        49870, 49872, 49875-49877,
        49885, 49895, 49899c, 49947,
        49958

GALLAHER, ANDREW N
   (Mifflintown, Pa.)
1817:   41434 pb

GALLAUDET, CHARLES (New
York)
1815: 34374 f

GALLAUDET, PETER WAL-
LACE (New York)
1818: 43403 f, 44114 pb,
44121 f, 44123 f, 44446 f,
44452 f, 44567 f, 45079 f,
45611 pb, 45727 f, 46713 f,
46888 f, 51741 pb
1819: 49393 f

GAMBLE, R (Baltimore)
1812: 25614, 26662
1813: 28098, 28185, 29457

GANGWEHR, GEORGE (Car-
lisle, Pa.)
1817: 40404 pb

GANNETT, DEBORAH (Dedham,
Mass.)
1802: 3141 f

GARDENIER, BARENT (New
York)
1814: 33577
1815: 34460 pb

GARDINER, --- (New York)
1815: 36450 pb

GARDINER, JAMES B
(Franklinton, O.)
1812: 25459 pb

GARDINER, JAMES B (Mari-
etta, O.)
1807: 12328 pb
1809: 17303 pb

GARDINER, SUSANNAH (Philadelphia)
1819: 48065 f

GARDNER, --- (Norwich,
Conn.)
1804: 6875 pb

GARDNER, SAMUEL (Ports-
mouth, N. H.)
1805: 7879, 8411, 8490,

8990, 8992, 8994
1806: 10963-10966, 11112
1807: 13196-13197, 13703
1808: 15334, 15726, 15994
1809: 17657

GARDNER, SIMON (Boston)
1818: 44091 pb, 44714, 44724,
44728, 44731, 44743
1819: 47871, 48623-48624,
48626-48627, 49630

GARNETT, JOHN (New Bruns-
wick, N. J.)
1808: 14308 f

GARROW, --- (Newbern, N. C.)
1803: 4779 pb
1804: 6143 pb, 6148 pb, 6639
pb

GASSNER, O (Philadelphia)
1806: 11918 f

Gazette (Chillicothe, O.)
see Scioto Gazette (Chillicothe,
O.)

Gazette (Portland, Me.)
1802: 2645
1803: 5584
1806: 11380?
1807: 12586, 12951
1808: 14900, 15050, 15843
1809: 18783
1810: 19613
1811: 22817, 23726 pb
1812: 24944
1813: 28904 pb, 29187
1815: 34798 pb, 35301
1819: 49516-49517

Gazette (Portsmouth, N. H.)
see New Hampshire Gazette
(Portsmouth, N. H.)

Gazette of the United States
(Philadelphia)
1803: 3936, 4831, 5091

Gazetteer (Lexington, Ky.)
see Independent Gazetteer
(Lexington, Ky.)

GAZLAY, WARD M (New-
burgh, N. Y.)
1806: 11175 pb
1807: 12058
1811: 22676
1812: 24727
1813: 29837, 30372?
1816: 39004
1818: 43382 pb
1819: 49470 pb

GEIB, ADAM (New York)
1812: 25523? pb
1817: 51699? pb
1818: 44308? pb, 51813? pb,
51823? pb

GEIB, JOHN (New York)
1817: 51699? pb
1818: 44308? pb, 51813? pb,
51823? pb

GEIB, WILLIAM (New York)
1817: 51699? pb
1818: 44308? pb, 51813? pb,
51823? pb

GEMMILL, WILLIAM (York,
Pa.)
1819: 51948

General Committee of Re-
publicans (New Haven,
Conn.)
1804: 5881 f, 6576 f

General Protestant Episcopal
Sunday School Union (New
York)
1818: 44345? pb

Genesee Missionary Society
(Manlius, N. Y.)
1817: 41209 f

Geneva Gazette (Geneva,
N. Y.)
1819: 47626

Genius of Liberty (Leesburg,
Va.)
1817: 40046

GEORGE, --- (Philadelphia)
1814: 33511 pb

GEORGE, DANIEL (Portland,
Me.)
1802: 1818

Georgetown Gazette (Georgetown, S. C.)
1816: 37887

Georgia Advertiser (Augusta,
Ga.)
1819: 47625

GERARD, WILLIAM (Frankfort,
Ky.)
1808: 14373 pb, 15436
1809: 17863, 18716
1810: 20366, 20486, 20488-
20489
1811: 22255 pb, 23147, 23151-
23154
1812: 25779-25782
1813: 28866 pb, 28870-28871
1814: 31856-31858, 32361 pb
1815: 34297 pb, 34537, 35048-
35050, 36098
1816: 37395 pb, 37469, 37953
pb, 37989-37991, 38069
1817: 41188-41191, 42131

GETTYS, THOMAS R (Bedford,
Pa.)
1813: 29980 pb

GETZ, GEORGE (Reading, Pa.)
1816: 36934 pb

GEYER, JOHN (Philadelphia)
1801: 1576
1802: 2694, 2729, 3456
1803: 5497
1804: 7656
1805: 8810, 9652
1806: 11755
1807: 12948, 14111
1808: 15917, 16619
1809: 19092
1810: 21909
1811: 24335

GIBBS, HENRY WILLIAM
(Easton, Md.)
1810: 20138 f

GIBSON, JAMES BROWN
(Salem, N.Y.)
1819: 50044

GIDEON, ---
1814: 32368?

GIDEON, JACOB (Washington,
D.C.)
1818: 43080 pb, 44017 pb,
44309, 46700, 46708 pb
1819: 47997, 49280, 49949,
49952, 50042, 50047

GILBERT, JOHN F (Frank-
ford, Pa.)
1810: 21399 pb
1811: 22889 pb, 23287-23288
1812: 25686 pb
1814: 31716

GILBERT, SAMUEL (Boston)
1802: 1934 pb, 2102, 2589
1803: 3700, 3858, 4208,
4472, 5009, 5125-5126
1804: 5892, 6367, 6522,
6747, 6970, 7210, 7296 pb
1805: 7890, 8053-8054 pb,
8059 pb, 8072, 8665, 8721,
9498, 9778
1806: 9827

GILFERT, GEORGE (New
York)
1801: 50220?
1802: 50294? pb, 50309? pb,
50311? pb
1804: 50460? pb
1805: 8312, 50570? pb
1806: 9958?, 50684? pb

GILKISON, JOHN C (Clinton,
O.)
1813: 29406 pb

GILKISON, JOHN C (Mansfield,
O.)
1818: 45159 pb

GILKISON, JOHN C (St.
Clairsville, O.)
1809: 17804 pb

GILLELAND, JAMES C (Pittsburgh, Pa.)
1811: 23372 pb

GILLESPIE, JOHN (Philadelphia)
1819: 49221 pb

GILLESPY, EDWARD (New
York)
1813: 28122 pb, 28638 pb,
29717 pb, 29970
1815: 34333 pb

GILLET, JACOB (New York)
1815: 34358 f, 35960 f, 36005
pb

GILLEY, WILLIAM B (New
York)
1814: 30653 f, 31099 f, 31991
pb, 33606 f
1815: 34856 f, 34920 pb,
34930 f, 35932 pb, 51465 f
1816: 36718 pb, 37102 pb,
37506 f, 37608 f, 37855 f,
38001 pb, 38053 pb, 38130
f, 38870 f, 38986 f
1817: 40230-40231 pb, 40875
pb, 41066 f, 41095 f, 41862
f, 41895 pb, 42148 pb,
42279 pb, 42282 f
1818: 43332 pb, 43382 pb,
43449 pb, 43916 f, 44025 f,
44143 pb, 44202 f, 44494
pb, 44887 f, 45385 f, 45836
f, 45860 f, 45905 pb, 46719
pb, 46780 f, 46853-46855 pb,
46856 f
1819: 46919 f, 47345 pb,
47373 f, 47450 f, 47878,
47895 f, 48220 f, 48253 pb,
48254 f, 48422 f, 48757 f,
49161 f, 49162 pb, 49201 f,
49202 pb, 49249 pb, 49380
f, 49589 f, 49979 pb, 49989
f

GILLMOR, WILLIAM (Harris-
burg, Pa.)
1810: 20264 pb
1811: 22813 pb, 23835 pb
1812: 24996, 26703 pb
1813: 28137 pb, 30000
1814: 32767
1816: 38040 pb, 38139

GILMAN, JOHN (Newburyport,
Mass.)
1805: 7976, 8090, 8508, 8896
pb, 9172 pb, 9177-9178,
50500? pb
1806: 10075, 10100 f, 10381,
11189-11190
1807: 12118 pb, 12165, 12362
pb, 12556, 13090, 13589
1808: 14276 pb, 14604, 14722,
15283, 15574, 15603-15604,
15613 pb, 15856
1809: 16814, 16947, 17213-
17214, 17621 pb, 17941,
18093, 18362, 18678, 19158?,
19167, 50929 pb, 50944
1810: 19324, 19588, 19680,
20094 pb, 20411, 20577
pb, 20912, 20969 pb, 21092
pb, 21541?, 21974
1811: 22144, 22949 pb, 23560,
23610 pb
1812: 24679, 25520-25521,
26120?, 26648, 27450 pb,
27451
1813: 27696, 27826, 28099,
28412 pb, 28498, 28724,
28761 pb, 28901-28903,
29207, 29213, 29964? pb
1814: 30612, 31717, 32247,
32450-32451, 32567, 32951,
51396 f
1815: 35122 pb, 35757,
35939? pb
1816: 37905 pb
1817: 40385? pb
1818: 43522 pb, 43802,
45210, 45782 pb
1819: 47385, 47773-47774,
48195, 49413, 49611

GILMAN, SAMUEL KINSMAN
(Hallowell, Me.)
1818: 43184-43185, 43604

pb, 44173 pb, 46691
1819: 47097, 47100, 48090 pb,
48792 pb, 49155 pb, 49473

GILMAN, WHITTINGHAM
(Newburyport, Mass.)
For all entries see GILMAN,
JOHN (Newburyport, Mass.)

GIMBREDE, THOMAS (New
York)
1813: 44339 pb

GIRD, HENRY (New York)
1803: 3652

Gleaner (Wilkes-Barre, Pa.)
1812: 25692

GLEASON, JOSEPH (Fairhaven,
Mass.)
1812: 24936 pb

GLEASON, JOSEPH (New Bed-
ford, Mass.)
1811: 23499 pb

GLEASON, PETER BUEL
(Hartford, Conn.)
1803: 3879, 4103, 4336, 4364,
4382, 4459, 4486, 4593,
4726 bf, 5053, 5056, 5186,
5582, 50361-50362
1804: 5665, 5668, 5694, 5804,
5879, 5984, 6189, 6311,
6444, 6813, 6874 pb, 7092,
7262, 7277
1805: 7854 pb, 8083?, 8143,
8157, 8228?, 8230?, 8287,
8606, 8796 pb, 8877, 8885,
8948, 9180, 9330 pb, 9358
pb, 9693
1806: 9826 pb, 9971, 10039,
10091, 10095 pb, 10171,
10312 pb, 10351-10352,
10384, 10412, 10419, 10551,
10559, 10585, 10594, 10710,
10849, 10873, 11195, 11202,
11227 pb, 11232, 11249,
11301, 11346, 11470 pb,
11488 f, 50685
1807: 11960, 11968 pb, 12151
pb, 12212, 12233, 12278,

12341, 12445, 12447 pb,
12585, 12624, 12685, 12698,
13098, 13116, 13130, 13157
pb, 13164 pb, 13425, 13568,
13588 pb, 13756, 14121,
14156, 14197
1808: 14331 pb, 14672, 14759,
14769 pb, 15023, 15407 pb,
15620-15621, 15897, 15928,
16263, 16721, 16736
1809: 16828 pb, 16909, 17277,
17286, 18103, 18381, 18583
pb
1810: 19338 pb, 19558 pb,
19828, 19837, 19853, 20238,
20323, 20346, 20444, 20498,
20752, 20822, 21118, 21433-
21434, 21448, 22061
1811: 22177 pb, 22407a,
22596, 22601, 22615, 22720,
22994, 23015, 23027, 23053,
23259, 23404, 23430 pb,
23459 pb, 23467 pb, 23632,
23722, 23766 pb, 23810,
23823, 23839, 23841, 23942d,
24050, 24072, 24430, 24440,
51096 pb
1812: 24592 pb, 24666, 24938
pb, 25135-25137, 25148,
25161, 25331 pb, 25404,
25554, 25739, 25786, 26093,
26208 pb, 26328, 26630,
26711 pb, 26820
1813: 27698 pb, 27863 pb,
28205, 28208, 28652, 28733,
29178, 29237 pb, 29240 pb,
29242, 29557, 29894, 29965,
51304 pb
1814: 30659 pb, 30826-30827,
30923 pb, 31120, 31211-
31212, 31237, 31387, 31643,
31907, 31975, 32111 pb,
32142, 32205 pb, 32381,
32439, 32652, 32722, 33580
pb, 51406
1815: 33829 pb, 34420, 34634,
34848, 35162 pb, 35176,
35184 pb, 35278, 35289,
35515 f, 35566 pb, 35567,
35680, 35795 pb, 36027 pb,
36028, 36628-36630
1816: 36715 pb, 36902, 37313,
37415, 37623, 37816 pb,

38094-38095, 38263, 39024
pb, 39025, 39067, 39136,
39830
1817: 39910, 39933, 39969,
40359, 40540, 41453, 41993,
42072 pb
1818: 43054 pb, 43311, 43504,
43565 pb, 43689, 43690 pb,
43707, 44240, 44272, 44865,
44938, 45384, 45810 pb
1819: 46969 pb, 47627 pb,
47694 pb, 47788, 47995,
48181 pb, 48512, 48713,
49491

GLEIM, CHRISTIAN (Harris-
burg, Pa.)
1811: 22316, 23068 pb
1814: 32469-32470, 32716
1815: 35068, 35599
1816: 38579, 38581, 38589
1817: 41748, 41754, 41760
1818: 45239-45240, 45248-
45249, 51817 pb
1819: 49039, 49044

GLENDINNING, WILLIAM
(Raleigh, N. C.)
1805: 7960 pb, 8695 pb

GLOVER, E (Columbus, O.)
1816: 39775

GLOVER, J (Oxford, N. Y.)
1803: 4218 pb, 4718 pb

GODDARD, WILLIAM GILES
(Providence, R. I.)
1814: 30909, 31015-31016,
31206, 31376, 32587, 32932
1815: 34473, 34559, 35524,
36081
1816: 38196, 39839
1817: 40341, 41908, 42943
1818: 44206, 51763 pb
1819: 48302, 49483

Goddard & Mann (Providence,
R. I.)
see GODDARD, WILLIAM
GILES (Providence, R. I.)
MANN, WILLIAM METCALF
(Providence, R. I.)

GOEB, FREDERICK (Chambersburg, Pa.)
1808: 15894 pb

GOEB, FRIEDRICH (Schellsburg, Pa.)
1814: 51440 pb
1815: 51536 pb
1816: 51630 pb
1817: 51714 pb
1818: 51831 pb
1819: 51943 pb

GOEB, FRIEDRICH (Somerset, Pa.)
1811: 51080 pb
1812: 27527 pb, 51188 pb
1813: 27883 pb
1814: 30871 pb

GOLDSMITH, ALVAH BRADLEY (New Haven, Conn.)
1816: 36692 f, 36916 f, 38245 f
1817: 40148 f, 40443 f, 42116 f, 51689 f
1818: 43670 pb, 44389? pb, 44834 f, 45586 pb, 45780 pb, 45902 pb
1819: 47983 pb, 49640 pb, 50001 f

GOMEZ, BENJAMIN (New York)
1801: 172

GOODALE, EZEKIEL (Hallowell, Me.)
1804: 6386 f, 50425 f
1805: 9685 f
1806: 10485 pb
1807: 12869 f
1808: 15641 f
1809: 17243 f, 17491 f, 17579 f, 17873 f, 18136 f, 18492 pb, 18620 f
1810: 21516 pb
1811: 23116 f, 23716 f
1812: 25159 f, 25524 f, 26164 f
1813: 27828 pb, 27962 f, 28126 pb, 29235 f, 29985-29986 f, 30496 f

1814: 30727, 30975-30976, 31594 pb, 31634 pb, 32167, 32723 pb, 33713 bf
1815: 33875, 33994, 34183, 34573 pb, 34755, 35022 bf, 35345 pb, 35716, 35898, 35923, 36050, 36550-36551
1816: 37008, 37060-37061, 37225 pb, 37277, 38014 pb, 38325 pb, 39703
1817: 40085, 40297-40299, 40329 pb, 40357, 40919, 40978 pb, 41549, 42195, 42941
1818: 43012, 43186, 43396-43397, 43426-43428, 43854 bf, 44673 pb, 44675, 45785, 46698 pb, 51829
1819: 47010, 47410-47412, 47656, 48080, 48090 pb, 48138 pb, 48490, 48569 pb, 48778 pb, 48792 pb, 49006 pb, 49486 pb, 49554, 49592-49594, 50009, 51897 pb

GOODENOW, STERLING (Bennington, Vt.)
1807: 14184

GOODENOW, STERLING (Troy, N.Y.)
1805: 8427 pb, 50533
1806: 10077, 10078 pb, 10960 pb, 11094
1807: 12788 pb, 12960 pb, 14226 pb
1808: 14622 pb, 15274 pb, 15277 pb, 16136 pb, 16193 pb, 16348 pb

GOODMAN, DUKE (New York)
1819: 49117 pb and sb

GOODMAN, GEORGE F (Philadelphia)
1812: 25202, 27533 pb
1818: 44905
1819: 50120

GOODRICH, ANDREW THOMPSON (New York)
1812: 25194 pb, 25306 f, 26349-26350 f

1813: 29222 f, 29624 f
1814: 33659 f
1815: 35890 pb, 36016 f
1816: 36751 f, 37777 pb,
    38053 pb
1817: 40365 pb, 40936 pb
1818: 43510 f, 43511 pb,
    43980 pb, 44011 pb, 44022
    f, 44183, 44359 f, 44891 f,
    45335 pb, 45379 f, 45686 pb
1819: 47168 f, 47449 f, 48163
    pb, 48740 f

GOODRICH, SAMUEL GRIS-
WOLD (Hartford, Conn.)
1816: 36949 pb, 36962a f,
    36964 pb, 37204 f
1817: 40570 f, 41866 pb
1818: 43299 pb, 43317 pb,
    43425 pb, 43565 pb, 43729
    f, 43922 f, 44122 f, 44182
    pb, 44241 pb, 45156 pb,
    45822 f, 46709 pb, 46793
    f, 46851 f
1819: 47180 f, 47479 f,
    47481 f, 48094 f, 48099
    pb, 48235 f, 48572 f, 48784
    pb, 49491 f, 49655 f, 49968
    f, 50188 f

GOODRICH, SOLOMON PORTER
(Utica, N.Y.)
1803: 4218 pb, 4718 pb

GOODRIDGE, SEWALL (Sutton,
    Mass.)
1807: 12051, 13088
1808: 14501, 15126, 15209,
    16680
1809: 17157, 17690, 17699,
    18092, 18313, 19258
1810: 19365 pb, 19435, 19548-
    19549, 19777 pb, 20367,
    20657, 22091 pb
1811: 22265, 22319 pb, 22482,
    22512, 22640, 22737

GOODRIDGE, SEWALL (Wor-
    cester, Mass.)
1802: 1721 pb, 2965, 3551
1803: 3923, 4286, 4526, 5007
1804: 5903, 6824, 7654, 7757
1805: 8788
1807: 12052

GOODWIN, GEORGE (Hartford,
    Conn.)
1801: 93, 151, 339, 341-343,
    345, ?346, ?348, 349, 424?,
    427, 449, 936-937, 1209,
    1270, 1372, 1440 pb, 1621,
    1630?, 1633, 1639 pb, 1681,
    50197, 50210
1802: 1793, 1852, 2063, 2066,
    2069-2070, ?2072-2073,
    2078, 2114, 2169, 2232,
    2672, 2998, 3017, 3070,
    3124, 3513?, 3517, 3519
    pb, 3534, 3577
1803: 3776, 3815 f, 3919,
    4001, 4005-4008, 4010,
    4012, 4029, 4039, 4043,
    4124 f, 4140, 4189, 4412,
    4534, 4563-4564, 4655,
    4726 f, 4892 f, 4940, 5002,
    5033, 5120, 5558, 5559?,
    50349?, 50375
1804: 5829, 5913, 5999, 6059,
    6062-6063, 6065, 6109,
    6210, 6242-6243, 6325,
    6568, 6779-6780, 6792-
    6793, 7146, 7287, 7321,
    7728, 7732
1805: 7961, 7968, 8023 pb,
    8046 pb, 8229, 8234-8240,
    8250, 8266, 8283-8284,
    8288, 8358 pb, 8361, 8635,
    8640, 8911, 9224, 9500,
    9680
1806: 9949, 10012, 10198-
    10200, 10399, 10418, 10420
    pb, 10469, 10757, 10881,
    11337 pb, 11366, 11407,
    11422, 11488, 11831 f,
    11832
1807: 12090, 12097, 12320,
    12334, 12336-12338, 12486
    pb, 12831, 12956, 13357,
    13363, 13426 pb, 13657,
    14167, 14186, 14198
1808: 14468, 14499 f, 14679,
    14764-14767, 14903 f,
    15157, 15611, 15896, 16108,
    16264, 16705
1809: 16979, 16998 pb, 17046,
    17107, 17282 pb, 17284,
    17437, 17897, 17986, 18273,
    18698, 19173, 19177 f,
    19178, 19208, 19237

1810: 19423, 19494 pb,
19513, 19845, 20045, 20190,
20241 pb, 20242, 20256,
20608, 20639, 22122
1811: 22228, 22321 pb, 22352,
22377, 22599 pb, 22604,
22757, 22937, 23505 f,
23975, 23996, 24405 pb
1812: 24543, 24785, 24822,
24832, 25144-25146 pb,
25150, 25335, 25561, 25607
pb, 26215, 26431 pb, 26432,
27499-27501, 27509-27510
1813: 27864, 27885, 27911,
28211 pb, 28215, 28217 pb,
28635, 28927, 29149, 30453,
30504
1814: 30837, 30863, 30877,
30892, 31217 pb, 31220,
31381, 31775, 32632, 33627
1815: 34024 pb, 34067, 34213,
34324 pb, 34423-34424 pb,
34428, 34804, 35909 pb,
36525, 36527
1816: 36830, 36915 pb, 36922,
36963 pb, 37317-37318 pb,
37320 pb, 37328, 37503,
37507-37508, 37615, 37616
pb, 37663 pb, 38819 pb,
39808 pb
1817: 40165, 40216, 40225
pb, 40226, 40474 f, 40544-
40545 pb, 40549, 40627,
40753, 41011, 41235, 41315
pb, 41773, 42221, 42302 pb,
42857, 42897
1818: 43242, 43261 pb, 43269,
43316, 43507, 43555, 43674,
43691, 43699-43700 pb,
43711, 43774, 43931 pb,
43935, 43936 pb, 44122-
44123, 45724, 46857
1819: 47002 pb, 47187 pb,
47339 pb, 47610, 47863 pb,
47892, 47906 pb, 47933 pb,
47947 pb, 47963, 49016,
49525 pb, 49643, 50102

GOODWIN, HENRY (Hartford,
Conn.)
1815: 33823, 34271, 34381,
34426 pb, 34800?, 34893?,
34912-34914, 34934, 35336?,

35740-35741, 35782, 35937
pb, 36498, 36662 pb
1818: 43932? pb

GOODWIN, OLIVER (Litchfield,
Conn.)
1808: 14720, 14758, 15136,
15219, 15242 pb, 15245,
15434, 15666, 50844 pb,
50847, 50854, 50891

GOOLD, G (Portland, Me.)
1805: 8545 pb, 50592 pb

GORDON, --- (Harrodsburg,
Ky.)
1814: 31927 pb

GORE, HENRY (Frankfort,
Ky.)
1810: 19425 pb, ?19918, 19919
1812: 25945

GOSS, MARK (Montpelier, Vt.)
1810: 20137
1811: 22432a, 22508, 22523,
23787 pb, 24365 pb, 24503
1812: 26165, 26514 pb, 27434
pb, 27622, 27629
1813: 28039, 28841, 29052,
29767-29768, 29782, 29978-
29979, 30406, 30409, 30413
1814: 30785, 30811, 30825,
30893, 31144, 31483, 31974,
32158, 32355, 33536, 33541,
33610, 33726, 33735
1815: 33976, 34541, 35617,
36437, 36653
1816: 36774, 37336, 37751,
38237, 38472, 39665, 39749
1817: 40712 pb

GOSS, SAMUEL (Montpelier,
Vt.)
1807: 12065, 12638, 12883
1808: 14840, 15820, 16624
1809: 17530
1810: 19694, 20329

GOSS, SAMUEL (Peacham, Vt.)
1801: 1688
1802: 3179, 3589-3590
1803: 4565

1804: 7228, 7799
1805: 7928, 8446, 9653
1806: 9908, 10018, 10053,
    11900
1807: 14163 pb
1809: 17131, 19266
1810: 20228

GOSS, SYLVESTER T (Boston)
1818: 43108, 43157, 44493
    pb, 44770, 44925, 45190?
    pb, 46799
1819: 46923 pb, 46961, 47006
    pb, 47547, 47553-47554,
    47653, 47666, 47977?,
    48477-48479, 48587, 48709-
    48710, 48987, 48998, 49220
    pb, 49361, 49487, 50108,
    50177

GOSS, SYLVESTER T (Haver-
    hill, N. H.)
1819: 48858 pb

GOULD, ABRAHAM JONES
    (Andover, Mass.)
1812: 27596
1813: 27730 pb, 27735, 28234,
    28379, 28381, 28833, 28972
    pb, 29461, 29566, 29573,
    29685, 29784, 29896, 30571,
    51296
1814: 30637, 30640, 30816,
    30834, 30860, 30873, 31075,
    31121, 31245, 31293, 31342,
    31413 pb, 31476, 31485,
    31618, 31782, 31791, 32126-
    32127, 32154, 32162, 32246,
    32360, 32405, 32476, 32498,
    32559 pb, 32565, 32627 pb,
    32649, 32749, 32887, 32902,
    32934-32939, 33583, 33596,
    33600, 33602-33603 pb,
    33615, 33679
1815: 33852, 33867, 34021
    pb, 34043, 34273 pb, 34330,
    34465, 34479, 34583, 34590,
    34702, 34799, 34818, 34841,
    34855, 34953 pb, 35096 pb,
    35224, 35279 pb, 35287,
    35318, 35585, 35627, 35666
    pb, 35675-35677, 35689,
    35701 pb, 35764, 35786,

35904 pb, 36030, 36089,
    36095, 36476, 36493, 36615-
    36618, 36639, 36643
1816: 36688 pb, 36904, 36912,
    37132 pb, 37161 pb, 37345
    pb, 37383, 37443, 37460,
    37479, 37494, 37499 pb,
    37737 pb, 37880, 37882,
    37915, 38290 pb, 38390,
    38682 pb, 38809, 38935,
    39047, 39090, 39142, 39693-
    39695, 39738, 39750, 39874,
    51593
1817: 40000-40001, 40156 pb,
    40603, 40614-40615, 40733
    pb, 40834 pb, 40882 pb,
    40964, 41087, 41148, 41271,
    41444 pb, 41660, 41808,
    41829 pb, 41984, 42109,
    42139, 42803, 42820, 42940
    pb, 42957, 51670
1818: 43071, 43083, 43266,
    43278, 43562, 43564, 43754,
    43776, 43803, 44044, 44225-
    44226, 44325 pb, 44381 pb,
    44424, 44440 pb, 44442,
    44756, 45158, 45162 pb,
    45164 pb, 45202, 45225,
    45382 pb, 45404, 45416 pb,
    45541, 45702, 45713 pb,
    45814, 45871 pb, 45885,
    46710, 46730 pb, 46738,
    46867, 46875 pb
1819: 46993, 46999-47000,
    47184, 47362, 47719, 47733,
    47827 pb, 47882, 47999 pb,
    48221, 48281, 48492, 48750
    pb, 48844 pb, 48928, 49007,
    49163-49165 pb, 49166,
    49527-49530 pb, 50056,
    50135 pb, 50143, 50144 pb,
    50152

GOULD, ELIAS BALDWIN
    (New York)
1811: 24035
1817: 40765, 40956, 41067,
    42192, 42288
1818: 44020

GOULD, ELIAS BALDWIN
    (Newark, N. J.)
1807: 13105 pb

1808:   14787, 14801
1809:   17591, 17680, 18784 pb

GOULD, FRANCIS (Haverhill,
  Mass.)
1804:   6461 pb
1805:   8188, 8720, 8923, 8929
1806:   10337
1807:   12250, 13044

GOULD, JOHN KEEP (Canan-
  daigua, N. Y.)
1803:   5576
1804:   7697
1805:   7931

GOULD, STEPHEN (New York)
1803:   5491
1804:   6002, 6084 pb, 6910,
  7063
1805:   8539, 8703
1806:   10655, 10707, 11003,
  11015-11016, 11054, 11408
1807:   11950, 12013 pb, 12695
  pb, 13368, 13738
1808:   14549 pb, 14655, 14910
  pb, 15762 pb, 16360
1809:   16967 pb, 19278
1810:   19369 bf, 19574 f,
  20195
1811:   22776 f
1812:   24609?, 25100, 25250,
  25550, 25638, 25639-25640
  pb, 25803, 26266 pb, 26290
  f, 26908 bf, 27356, 27377
1813:   27841, 28248 f, 28606,
  28617, 28814, 29016, 29153,
  29330 pb, 29802, 30374 f,
  30523
1814:   30653-30654, 31727 f,
  32566 pb, 32768, 32895,
  33499 bf, 33525, 33606 bf,
  33662, 51395
1815:   35458 pb, 35470 f,
  35473 pb, 35588, 36474,
  36500 pb
1816:   36930, 38444 pb,
  38450 pb, 38618 f, 38619
  pb
1817:   41327 f, 42322 pb
1818:   44366 f, 45074 pb
1819:   47688 pb, 49977 f

GOULD, STEPHEN (Newark,
  N. J.)
1801:   721, 1017 pb
1802:   2712 pb
1803:   4576

GOULD, WILLIAM (Albany,
  N. Y.)
1811:   22776
1813:   28248 f
1816:   38618 f, 38619 pb
1817:   41327 f
1818:   43390 f, 45053 pb, 45056
  f
1819:   47688 pb, 48884 pb,
  49977 f

GOULD, WILLIAM (New York)
1810:   19574 f
1811:   22776 f
1812:   26290 f, 26908 f
1813:   28248 f, 29330 pb,
  30374 f
1814:   31727 f, 33499 f, 33606
  f
1815:   35458 pb, 35470 f,
  35473 pb
1816:   38618 f, 38619 pb
1817:   41327 f

Gould & Banks (New York)
see GOULD, STEPHEN (New
    York)
    BANKS, DAVID (New York)

Gould & Van Pelt (New York)
see GOULD, STEPHEN (New
    York)
    VAN PELT, PETER (New
    York)

Gould & Van Winkle (New York)
see GOULD, STEPHEN (New
    York)
    VAN WINKLE, CORNELIUS
    S (New York)

Gould, Banks & Gould (New
  York)
see GOULD, STEPHEN (New
    York)
    BANKS, DAVID (New York)
    GOULD, WILLIAM (New
    York)

GOULDING, LEVI (Worcester, Mass.)
1808: 14392, 14536, 14967, 15585
1809: 16796

GRAFF, MICHAEL (Ephrata, Pa.)
1801: 1300 pb

GRAHAM, ALEXANDER (Easton, Md.)
1817: 40719 pb
1818: 43353
1819: 51936

GRAHAM, JAMES (Lynchburg, Va.)
1805: 8811 pb

GRAHAM, WILLIAM S (Greenburg, Pa.)
1811: 24427 pb
1812: 25567 pb

GRAM, J (New York)
1813: 29643

GRANT, --- (Brooklyn, N.Y.)
1810: 21530?

GRANT, JOHN (Middletown)
1808: 15983 f

GRANT, JOSHUA D (Shelbyville, Ky.)
1818: 43177
1819: 47093

GRANTLAND, FLEMING (Lynchburg, Va.)
1809: 17947 pb

GRANTLAND, FLEMING (Milledgeville, Ga.)
1811: 22903, 22934
1812: 25511-25513
1813: 28619-28624
1814: 31575-31577
1815: 34589, 34778-34780
1816: 37699-37701, 39722
1817: 40904-40906
1818: 44147-44148, 44150-44151

GRANTLAND, SEATON (Milledgeville, Ga.)
1809: 17616 pb
1810: 20204-20206, 20208
1811: 22903-22904, 22934
1812: 25511-22513
1813: 28619-28624
1814: 31575-31577
1815: 34589, 34778-34780
1816: 37699-37701, 39722
1817: 40904-40906
1818: 44147-44148, 44150-44151
1819: 47639 pb

GRANTLAND, SEATON (Richmond, Va.)
1805: 50623 pb
1806: 10632, 11031a, 11367, 12528 pb, 50742-50743 pb
1807: 13045
1808: 15575, 16340 pb, 16641, 16647 pb, 16751, 50829 pb, 50900 pb
1809: 18527

GRANTLAND, THOMAS B (Huntsville, Ala.)
1816: 36696 pb
1817: 51644? pb

GRATER, GEORGE WILSON (Baltimore)
1818: 44967

GRATTAN, WILLIAM (New York)
1818: 45055-45056
1819: 47201, 48470, 48554, 48878, 48890, 49501, 49977

GRAUPNER, GOTTLIEB (Boston)
1802: 50297? pb
1805: 8553 pb, 50544 pb
1807: 50794? pb
1809: 50908 pb
1810: 20236? pb, 20478 pb, 20985? pb
1811: 51099? pb
1812: 24641 pb
1813: 29185? pb
1815: 35854 pb, 51523? pb
1819: 47828 pb, 48108 pb

GRAVES, BARTHOLOMEW
(Philadelphia)
1803: 4073, 4129, 4638, 4815
1804: 5647 pb, 5740, 6092,
       6299, 6401, 6500, 6784,
       7219
1805: 8227 pb, 9140 pb, 9141,
       9159 pb, 9307, 9447 pb
1806: 9850, 10771, 10898,
       11170-11171 pb, 11472 bf,
       11847
1807: 12364, 12451, 12851,
       13667, 13699
1808: 14799 pb, 15007 pb,
       15480 pb, 16546 pb
1809: 17917, 19202
1810: 19706, 20133 bf, 20194,
       20216, 21411
1811: 23638
1812: 24637-24638, 25155 pb

GRAVES, HORACE (Deer-
   field, Mass.)
1815: 34574
1816: 36940-36941

GRAVES, HORACE (Green-
   field, Mass.)
1814: 30859, 33683

GRAVES, HORACE (Northamp-
   ton, Mass.)
1805: 8501
1807: 12204, 12255, 12410,
       12643, 12796
1808: 14277, 14426

GRAY, EDWARD (Suffield,
   Conn.)
1801: 426, 593, 655, 812,
       1276, 1598 pb
1802: 1748 pb, 2226, 2357,
       3149
1803: 3651 pb, 4394, 4581,
       4730, 4792 pb, 5629,
       50366
1804: 6479, 6626, 7684
1805: 7857, 8759, 9381 pb
1806: 10571

GRAY, GEORGE LEWIS
   (Baltimore)
1803: 4251, 5017 pb

GRAY, GEORGE LEWIS (Nor-
   folk, Va.)
1804: 5890, 6929 pb
1805: 8265

GRAY, HARRISON (Portsmouth,
   N. H.)
1818: 43094 f

GRAY, JOHN (Alexandria, Va.)
1801: 1589 f
1802: 2332 pb
1803: 4715 f, 5116 f, 5526 f
1804: 7375 pb
1805: 50555 f
1806: 50635 pb

GRAY, JOHN (New York)
1813: 29897
1815: 35998
1817: 42202
1818: 43103, 45429
1819: 46947, 49494, 49588

GRAY, JOHN C (Danbury,
   Conn.)
1804: 6883 pb
1805: 7967 pb, 8980 pb
1807: 13077 pb
1808: 15017, 15982
1809: 17287 pb, 17829-17830,
       50913 pb
1810: 50977 pb
1812: 25226 pb

GRAY, JOHN C (New Haven,
   Conn.)
1816: 39013 pb
1817: 39931, 40166 pb, 40511,
       40626 pb, 41771, 41900c,
       41930-41931, 42200 pb,
       42219 pb
1818: 43463, 43465, 43526 pb,
       44384, 45435, 45475 pb
1819: 47019 pb, 47504, 47700
       pb, 47753-47754 pb, 47796,
       48360, 49242 pb

GRAY, PHILIP J (Woodbury,
   N. J.)
1819: 47675 pb

GRAY, ROBERT (Alexandria, Va.)
1801: 1589 f
1802: 2332 pb
1803: 4715 f, 5116 f, 5526 f
1804: 7375 pb
1806: 10408 f, 10971 f, 11443 f
1807: 14139 pb
1808: 50867 pb, 50898 pb
1811: 22582 f, 51145 f
1814: 32228 f

GRAY, ROBERT (Newburgh, N.Y.)
1818: 44193 f

GRAY, ROBERT (Philadelphia)
1805: 8144 pb

GRAY, WILLIAM FAIRFAX (Fredericksburg, Va.)
1811: 51146 f
1812: 51257 pb
1815: 35558 f, 36451 pb
1816: 36862-36863, 36870-36871, 38060 pb, 38466 pb, 39686 pb
1817: ?40890 pb, 41928 pb
1819: 47149, 47153, 50070-50071 pb

GRAY, WILLIAM W (Lynchburg, Va.)
1809: 17343
1810: 20609
1816: 36872, 37495 pb

GRAY, WILLIAM W (Richmond, Va.)
1817: 40507, 42188 pb
1818: 45544, 46686
1819: 47145, 47420, 48990, 49281, 49284, 49421, 49438

GRAYSON, JOHN (Washington, Pa.)
1817: 42832 pb
1819: 47607

GREEN, CHARLES D (Georgetown, D.C.)
1801: 99, 1686

GREEN, CHARLES D (New Brunswick, N.J.)
1812: 25467 f
1813: 29318 f

GREEN, FREDERICK (Annapolis, Md.)
1801: 624, 875?, 876, 878-879?, 1693
1802: 2596? pb, 2597 pb, 2599, 2600-2601 pb, 2602, 2603?
1803: 4333, 4587-4589
1804: 6718? pb, 6719-6720 pb, 6722-6729, 7805
1805: 8839, 8841-8852, 9047, 9296 pb
1806: 10801, 10803-10806, 10808, 10810-10811
1807: ?13000?, ?13001, 13002-13003, 13005-13006
1808: 14975, 15502, 15504-15506
1809: 17992-18003, 18490, 19281
1810: 20652-20654, 22115
1811: 23294?

GREEN, JACOB (Albany, N.Y.)
1810: 19327 pb
1812: 25304 pb, 26576 f
1813: 27945 f, 28007 f
1815: 34487 pb, 34492 pb, 34493-34494 f

GREEN, JAMES (Natchez, Miss.)
1801: 582

GREEN, JOHN (Lancaster, O.)
1807: 13282 pb

GREEN, JOHN W (New London, Conn.)
1802: 2684 f

GREEN, JONAS (Annapolis, Md.)
1811: 23292, 23295?
1812: 24779, 25801
1813: 27779 pb, 29060, 29061 pb, 29064 pb
1815: 34457, 35192, 35996-35997

1816: 37732 pb, 37984, 38521-
38522, 38524-38525, 38730,
38903
1817: 39938, 40316, 41353-
41354, 41357-41358, 41696,
41698, 41900d-41900e
1818: 44705, 44708-44709,
45437, 45717
1819: 47004, 48599, 48600
pb, 48604-48605, 48722,
48962?, 49206, 49345

GREEN, PETER N (Haverhill,
Mass.)
1817: 40261 bf, 40769 pb
1818: 44965, 45763, 46900
pb, 46902
1819: 48151, 48407 pb, 48408,
49169 pb

GREEN, SAMUEL (New Lon-
don, Conn.)
1801: 44, 344, 377 pb, 585
pb, 764, 846, 947? pb,
995 pb, 1137, 1266, 1298
pb
1802: 2111 pb, 2237, 2354
pb, 2546, 2559, 2684, 2743,
3011, 3069
1803: 3796, 4314 pb, 4719
pb, 5043 pb
1804: 5827, 6108, 6421 pb,
6841, 6876 pb, 7257a pb
1805: 8281-8282 f
1806: 10246 f
1807: 12382? pb
1808: 14416-14417, 14770,
14818 f, 15170, 15710 pb,
16152?
1809: 16910-16911, 17289,
18186 pb, 18598 pb
1810: 19838, 19847, 20616,
20846 pb, 21336 pb
1811: 22251, 22318, 22605
pb, 22655 pb, 22886, 23502
pb, 23597, 23942e, 24257
pb, 51138 pb
1812: 25152 pb, 25206 pb,
26209 pb, 26632-26633,
51244 pb
1813: 28216 pb, 29279 pb,
51294, 51334 pb
1814: 30836, 31222 pb,

31279 f, 31280-31281 pb,
31556, 31613 pb, 32235 pb,
51438 pb
1815: 34022 pb, 34430 pb,
34507 pb, 34508 f, 35414,
51533 pb
1816: 36778 pb, 37326 pb,
37379 pb, 37398 pb, 37680,
37812, 38375 pb, 39133,
51624 pb
1817: 40474, 40554 pb, 41059,
41570 pb, 42006, 51713 pb
1818: 43717 pb, 43775, 43795
pb, 43812 pb, 44146 pb,
44198 pb, 44931, 44978 pb,
45797
1819: 47710 pb, 47765 pb,
48014 pb, 48162, 48396 pb,
48833 pb, 51941 pb

GREEN, THOMAS (Boston)
1819: 48008 pb, 49649

GREEN, THOMAS (Bowling
Green, Ky.)
1819: 49467 pb

GREEN, THOMAS (Charlestown,
Mass.)
1819: 48085 pb

GREEN, THOMAS (New Haven,
Conn.)
1801: 81 pb, 150, 347, 487,
1008 pb, 50254 pb
1802: 1778, 1784, 1947, 2067-
2068, 2071, 3599-3600
1803: 3699, 4011, 5042 pb,
5627 pb, 5628
1804: 5737, 6064, 6569,
7806 pb, 7807, 7809 pb
1805: 7892, 8241, 9348 pb,
9776-9777
1806: 9864
1807: 12008, 50811 pb
1808: 16769
1811: ?51130
1813: ?51285
1815: ?34425
1817: 42982

GREEN, THOMAS CLARKE
(New London, Conn.)
1801: 234 f

GREEN, TIMOTHY (Fred-
ericksburg, Va.)
1804:   5797
1805:   7948
1806:   9914
1807:   12071-12072
1808:   14443
1809:   16940
1810:   19459
1811:   51057, 51142
1812:   24741-24742, 25568 pb
1813:   27824
1814:   30793, 30796, 32910 pb
1815:   35558, 35892
1818:   43224, 43228, 44128

GREEN, WILLIAM (New York)
1805:   8984

GREENLEAF, DANIEL (Bur-
lington, Vt.)
1806:   10136

GREENLEAF, DANIEL (Wor-
cester, Mass.)
1801:   76, 340, 681, 50230
1802:   2009, 2097-2098, 2359,
2814, 2857, 3058, 3078-
3079, 3506-3507
1803:   4059, 4351

GREENLEAF, JOSEPH (Boston)
1807:   12020 f, 13675 f
1808:   15647 f
1809:   17839 pb
1810:   21338 f
1811:   23892 f
1813:   28940 pb

GREENLEAF, OLIVER C
(Boston)
1801:   9 f, 188 pb, 425 f,
620 pb, 670 f, 1262 f,
1267 f, 1433 f
1802:   1711 f, 2003 f, 2051
pb, 2482 f, 3175 f
1803:   4340 f, 4533 f
1804:   5861 f, 6450 pb, 7212
pb
1807:   13529 pb
1808:   14497 pb
1809:   17138 pb, 17253 f,
18330 f, 18503 f

1810:   21487 f
1812:   26912 pb
1813:   28047 f

GREENOUGH, WILLIAM (Bos-
ton)
1806:   10133, 10504, 10612,
10833, 10911 pb, 11796
1807:   12107 pb, 12184, 12668,
12947, 13108 pb, 13295,
13644, 13714
1808:   14978, 15289, 15386-
15387, 15403, 15548, 15553-
15555, 15925-15926, 15996,
16031 pb, 16042, 16060,
16267-16268, 16704, 16779
1809:   16962 pb, 16996-16997,
17660-17661, 18402
1810:   19294, 19512, 21302 pb,
21304, 21482, 22054 pb
1811:   22351, 22360, 23184,
23678, 23792, 24378-24379,
24479
1812:   24821, 25048, 25998,
26781
1813:   27884
1814:   30862, 34062
1816:   36943
1817:   40195, 40211
1819:   47210

GREENOUGH, WILLIAM
(Charlestown, Mass.)
1802:   2210
1804:   5666

GREENOUGH, WILLIAM (Hav-
erhill, Mass.)
1814:   30983, 32799, 32836
1815:   36509 pb

GREER, CHARLES (Harrisburg,
Pa.)
1817:   41764

GREER, WILLIAM (Columbia,
Pa.)
1814:   31818
1819:   47669 pb, 49636

GREER, WILLIAM (Harrisburg,
Pa.)
1813:   29472-29473

1815: 35591
1816: 37830, 38578
1817: 41330, 41750 pb
1818: 43683 pb

GREER, WILLIAM (Lancaster,
  Pa.)
1804: 7018 pb
1805: 9124, 50591 pb
1806: 10691 pb, 11124
1807: 12797 pb, 13333, 13618
  pb
1808: 15121
1809: 19130
1810: 20345, 21023, 21027,
  21248
1811: 23108, 23655, 23660
1812: 25634, 26412, 26422,
  26427a pb

GREER, WILLIAM (Philadelphia)
1812: 26636-26637
1813: 30505
1815: 35622, 35631, 35817,
  35967
1816: 37948
1817: 40622, 40809, 42152,
  42802
1818: 44167, 45593, 45744,
  45771
1819: 47975, 49443

GRIDLEY, TIMOTHY (Exeter,
  N. H.)
1811: 23501 f, 23519 f
1812: 26233 pb
1813: 28922 f

GRIEVES, THOMAS (Hagers-
  town, Md.)
1814: 30630

GRIFFIN, C (Hallowell, Me.)
1818: 43093 pb

GRIFFIN, DANIEL (New York)
1815: 34380 f

GRIFFIN, THOMAS (New York)
1812: 24586 f, 24814 f,
  25081-25084 f, 25086 f,
  25088 f, 25282 f, 25943 f
1813: 28772 f, 29016 f,

29051 f, 30564 pb, 44339 pb
1814: 32186 f, 32342 pb,
  32423 f, 32895 f, 33700 pb

GRIFFIN, WILLIAM (Newburyport, Mass.)
1808: 16250 pb

GRIFFITH, HUGH M (New
  York)
1801: 1098 f
1802: 2388 pb, 2739 f, 3023?
  pb

GRIGG, JACOB (Norfolk, Va.)
1814: 30791?

GRIGG, JOHN (Philadelphia)
1818: 44255? pb

GRIGGS, ANTHONY (Philadelphia)
1811: 23461, 23921, 51126 pb
1812: 24761, 25450, 26426 pb,
  26698
1813: 28756, 29993, 30437
1814: 30987, 31023, 31030,
  31264, 31430, 32107 pb,
  32352, 32727, 33546, 33598,
  33733, 51402
1815: 34246-34247, 34256,
  34380, 34396, 34592, 34724,
  34862, 35034, 35331, 35694,
  35696-35697, 35699, 35737,
  35739, 35820-35822, 36589
1816: 37352
1817: 40346-40347, 40378,
  41081, 41319, 41800 pb,
  42805
1818: 43321, 43388, 44175,
  44855, 44947, 45104, 45318,
  46750
1819: 48704, 48759, 49062 pb,
  49308, 50010, 51867 pb

GRIGGS, J C (New Brunswick,
  N. J.)
1819: 49062 pb

GRIGGS, JOSEPH (Philadelphia)
1818: 43321, 43388, 44175,
  44855, 44947, 45104, 45318,
  46750

1819: 48704, 48759, 49062
pb, 49308, 50010, 51867 pb

Griggs & Dickinson (Philadelphia, 1811-1813)
see GRIGGS, ANTHONY
(Philadelphia)
DICKINSON, ABEL (Philadelphia)

Griggs & Dickinson (Philadelphia, 1813-1817)
see GRIGGS, ANTHONY
(Philadelphia)
DICKINSON, KETURAH
(Philadelphia)

Griggs & Dickinson (Philadelphia, 1818-1823)
see GRIGGS, ANTHONY
(Philadelphia)
GRIGGS, JOSEPH (Philadelphia)
DICKINSON, KETURAH
(Philadelphia)

GRIMES, JAMES (Randolph, Vt.)
1801: 1078 f

GRIMES, JOHN A (Paris, Ky.)
1808: 16715 pb

GRIMES, JOHN A (Richmond, Ky.)
1810: 19429 pb
1811: 23248 pb
1812: 24976
1814: 30749

GRIMLER, BENJAMIN (Lancaster, Pa.)
1802: 3018
1804: 7011, 7682 pb
1805: 9122-9123, 9127, 9130, 9240
1806: 10057 pb
1807: 12497, 13347-13348?, 13350
1808: 15165 pb, 15590, 15875, 15885, 15887, 50877
1809: 17688 pb, 18334, 18336, 18337 pb, 18343, 18347,

18349, 18534, 18715
1810: 21024, 21030, 21034?, 21035, 21285
1811: 22527, 23654, 23659, 23872 pb
1812: 26413
1817: 41763
1818: 43971 pb, 44540

GRIMLER, HENRY (Lancaster, Pa.)
1802: 3007, 3018
1804: 7682 pb
1805: 9240
1806: 10057 pb
1807: 12497, 13350
1808: 15590, 15885, 15887
1810: 21285
1811: 22527, 23872 pb

GRISWOLD, EZRA (Columbus, O.)
1814: 30774, 33649
1815: 33966
1816: 37471, 38004, 38512 pb
1818: 43011 pb, 43589, 44095, 45441
1819: 48030? pb

GRISWOLD, JACOB (New Haven, Conn.)
1802: 2396 f
1803: 4013 pb

GRISWOLD, JOHN (New York)
1807: 12326 pb

GRISWOLD, ZECHARIAH
(New Haven, Conn.)
1804: 6017

GROESBEEK, JOHN C G
(Schoharie, N.Y.)
1809: 16840 pb

GROFF, JOSEPH (Philadelphia)
1801: 25 f, 1141 f
1802: 1726 f, 2855, 3594 f

GROFF, JOSEPH (Washington, D.C.)
1801: 202, 1486, 1609, 1684
1802: 1791, 2450, ?3422

GROFF, R (Philadelphia)
1802: 3573
1803: 3949

GROSS, --- (Frederick, Md.)
1815: 35645 pb

GROTJAN, PETER A (Philadelphia)
1812: 25573-25574 pb
1814: 31203-31204, 33235 pb

GROVES, --- (Augusta, Ga.)
1816: 37702 pb

GRUBER, JOHN (Hagerstown, Md.)
1801: 415, 988 pb
1802: 2737 pb
1803: 4494, 4496, 4712 pb
1805: 7895, 8064, 8407 pb, 8966
1806: 10950 pb, 50699 pb
1807: 12850, 13176 pb, 13550
1808: 15341 pb, 15643 pb, 15701, 16649 pb
1809: 18180, 20354
1810: 20840
1811: 23494 pb, 24444-24445
1812: 26202 pb, 27416 pb
1813: 29272
1814: 31862, 32225 pb, 33558, 51413 pb
1815: 34434 pb, 34838, 35035, 36013 pb, 36455 pb, 36535 pb
1816: 39691 pb
1817: 41923, 42799 pb
1818: 44297, 46665 pb
1819: 48444 pb, 48527 pb, 49251 pb, 49252, 49663, 50004 pb

GUERIN, BERTRAND (Lexington, Ky.)
1810: 20429 pb

GUIRR, --- (Philadelphia)
1814: 33511 pb

GUTHRIE, WILLIAM (New York)
1817: 42323 pb

GWIN, --- (Nashville, Tenn.)
1812: 26521

GWIN, JOHN (Russellville, Ky.)
1813: 27790, 29835 pb

GWYNN, WILLIAM (Baltimore)
1812: 26337 pb
1815: 33782 pb
1818: 43440
1819: 47422

H

HAAS, JACOB (Lynchburg, Va.)
1811: 22297, 23361 pb, 51088
1812: 25292
1813: 27823
1816: 36859-36860, 36867, 36869
1817: 40134
1818: 43221

HADLOCK, JAMES (Hartford, Conn.)
1814: 30956 pb
1815: 34165 f

HAGEN, PETER ALBRECHT VON (Boston)
1802: 50309? pb
1810: 21924? pb

HAGERTY, JOHN (Baltimore)
1807: 13481 f, 13514 f, 13595 f
1808: 14290 f, 14306 f, 14714 f, 15021 f, 16273 f, 16706-16707 f, 16709-16711 f
1810: 19523 f
1811: 22357-22358 f
1812: 24820 f
1813: 29054
1814: 31910 pb, 32018 pb
1815: 35991, 36532-36533

Halcyon Press (New York)
1811: 51073
1812: 26554

HALE, DAVID (Boston)
1811:   22342 pb
1814:   30902 pb, 33681 f
1815:   36006 sb
1816:   37236 pb

HALE, HORATIO G (Hartford,
   Conn.)
1810:   22125 pb
1812:   24798, 25427, 25637,
   25657-25658, 26148, 27536
   pb, 27541, 27634, 51192,
   51207
1813:   27702, 28114, 28227,
   28712 pb, 28754, 28976,
   28988 pb, 29770 pb, 29801,
   30175, 30452, 30477-30478
1814:   30662, 30853, 31132
   pb, 31133, 31404, 31602,
   31629, 31698, 31719-31721,
   31994 pb, 32020-32021,
   32513, 32710, 32734,
   32929 pb, 33580 pb, 33742
1815:   36020 f
1816:   37680 f, 38616 pb,
   38665 pb, 51577 pb
1817:   40359 f, 41704 pb,
   42019 pb, 42115 f
1818:   43311 f, 43504-43507
   f, 43728 f, 44054 pb,
   45716 pb, 45724 f
1819:   47478 pb, 47480 f

HALE, MERVIN (Elizabeth,
   N. J.)
1814:   31635 f
1815:   34849-34850 f
1818:   44650 f
1819:   48538-48539 f

HALE, NATHAN (Boston)
1817:   42813

HALE, SALMA (Walpole, N. H.)
1805:   8028, 8264, 8292, 9113
1806:   10001, 10207, 11237,
   11253, 50700
1807:   11964, 12069, 12081,
   12454, 12592, 12791, 12873-
   12875, 12889

HALE, SAMUEL H (Lebanon,
   Ohio)

1811:   23202, 23380
1812:   25425

HALL, ALLMAND (Wilmington,
   N. C.)
1802:   50316 pb
1804:   6436

HALL, DAVID (Philadelphia)
1818:   43064, 43276
1819:   46983-46984, 49010 pb,
   49063

HALL, E (Cincinnati, Ohio)
1812:   24993 f

HALL, GEORGE WASHINGTON
   (Portland, Me.)
1810:   19371 f, 20377 f,
   20606-20607 pb

HALL, H (New York)
1816:   37037 pb

HALL, HARRISON (Philadelphia)
1816:   38279 f, 38283 f
1817:   40648 f, 40975 f, 41162
   f, 41391 f, 41953 f
1818:   43820 f, 44233 f,
   44483 f, 45458 f, 45932 pb
1819:   48378 pb, 48736 pb

HALL, JASON (Boston)
1818:   44770, 44925

HALL, JOHN H (Newton, N. J.)
1813:   29902 pb

HALL, SALMON (Newbern,
   N. C.)
1804:   6867 pb
1805:   8951 pb
1807:   13141 pb, 50819 pb
1808:   16762, 50902 pb
1809:   18247 pb
1811:   24057 pb, 51150 pb

HALL, SALMON (Wilmington,
   N. C.)
1809:   18788 pb

HALL, SAMUEL (Boston)
1801:   157 pb, 179 pb, 222 pb,

664, 749, 872 pb, 909,
958 pb, 1387 pb, 1433 f,
1618 pb
1802: 2191 pb, 2482 f, 3067
pb, 3146 f, 3147 pb, 3171,
3175 f, 3269 pb, 50280 f
1803: 3749 pb, 3971 f, 4176
pb, 4194 pb, 5050 f, 5147 f
1804: 5956 f, 6023-6025 f,
6027-6029 f, 6277 pb, 6478
pb, 6748 pb, 7331 f, 50477
f
1805: 9362 pb, 9460 pb,
50619 f
1808: 15256 pb, 15653, 50889
f

HALL, SAMUEL (Castine, Me.)
1809: 17419 pb
1810: 19653, 20276, 22039
1811: 24056 pb
1812: 24533, 24714, 25186,
26677

HALL, SAMUEL (Dedham,
Mass.)
1813: 28288 pb, 28424-28425

HALL, SERGEANT (Baltimore)
1813: 28053, 28235, 28278,
28443, 28500, 29034, 29053
pb, 29192
1814: 31160, 31619, 31892,
33593

HALL, SERGEANT (St. Louis,
Mo.)
1817: 40755 pb, 41404
1818: 44158

HALL, WILLIAM (Philadelphia)
1807: 50806 pb
1808: 50881 pb
1809: 17159, 17221, 18114,
18414 pb
1810: 21109 pb, 21379
1811: 23713 pb
1812: 26494 pb
1813: 51329 pb
1818: 45370?

Hall & Atkinson (Philadelphia)
see HALL, DAVID

(Philadelphia)
ATKINSON, SAMUEL COATE
(Philadelphia)

Hall & Goss (Boston)
see HALL, JASON (Boston)
GOSS, SYLVESTER T
(Boston)

Hall & Hiller (Boston)
see HALL, SAMUEL (Boston)
HILLER, JOSEPH (Boston)

Hall & Pierie (Philadelphia)
see HALL, WILLIAM (Phila-
delphia)
PIERIE, GEORGE W
(Philadelphia)

Hallowell Bookstore (Hallowell,
Me.)
1811: 23478 f

HALSEY, JACOB BENTON
(Newark, N.J.)
1801: 361

HALSEY, SILAS (Trenton,
N.J.)
1806: 10989, 11658
1807: 13205, 13207-13209

HALY, J (New York)
1819: 47386 pb, 47484 f,
47486 pb, 48352-48354 f,
49026-49027 f, 49263 f

HAMILTON, ADAM R (Goshen,
Mass.)
1819: 50106

HAMILTON, ALEXANDER
(Bellefonte, Pa.)
1814: 30677 pb

HAMILTON, ALEXANDER
(Harrisburg, Pa.)
1812: 24600 pb

HAMILTON, HUGH (Harris-
burg, Pa.)
1816: 38139

HAMILTON, HUGH (Lancaster,
Pa.)
1808: 16315 pb
1809: 17434
1810: 21020 pb

HAMILTON, JOSEPH (George-
town, S. C.)
1806: 9831

HAMILTON, W (Philadelphia)
1810: 21872?

HAMILTON, WILLIAM (Lan-
caster, Pa.)
1801: 350, 1118-1119, 1125-
1126
1802: 2870, 2875, 3496 pb,
4840, 4844, 4848
1803: 50381, 50398
1805: 9353
1806: 10448, 10664 pb, 11125
1807: 13340, 13770
1808: 15870, 16146 pb, 16634,
16648 pb
1810: 19490, 19781, 20426,
21018-21021 pb, 21180,
22018 pb
1811: 23479, 23653?
1812: 24830 pb, 26150 pb,
26151, 26424, 26700 pb
1813: 29232
1815: 33895, 35070, 35808
1818: 44919

HAMLEN, BENJAMIN L
(Hartford, Conn.)
1816: 37595 pb, 51601
1817: 41216, 41832
1818: 43922, 44276 pb,
45095 pb, 46793

Hamlen & Newton (Hartford,
Conn.)
see HAMLEN, BENJAMIN
‾‾‾L (Hartford, Conn.)
NEWTON, ABNER (Hart-
ford, Conn.)

HAMMOND, CHARLES (St.
Clairsville, O.)
1813: 29405 f

HAMMOND, ELISHA (Brook-
field, Mass.)
1819: 47687 f

Hampshire Gazette (Northampton, Mass.)
1815: 36581

Hampshire Missionary Society
(Northampton, Mass.)
1804: 6174 f

Hampshire Register (Northampton, Mass.)
1817: 42900

HANBURG, ABRAHAM D (New
York)
1803: 4631 f

HANCOCK, WILLIAM (Phila-
delphia)
1803: 4358, 4910

HANKE, GEORGE (Lebanon,
Pa.)
1819: 48464 pb

HANNA, ANDREW (Baltimore)
1801: 101, 321, 365 pb, 389,
588, 1190, 1268, 1616 pb
1802: 1734, 1803, 1809, 2048
pb, 2212, 2223, 2254, 2499
pb, 2520, 2529 pb, 2906-
2907 pb, 3062 pb, 3128
1803: 3713, 3715, 4004 pb,
4032 pb, 4163 pb, 4180 pb,
4296 pb, 4337, 4339, 4400
pb, 4430 pb, 4514 pb, 4681
pb, 4761 pb, 4879 pb, 4881
pb, 4970 pb, 4983 f, 5032
pb, 5480, 50348 pb
1804: 5761-5762, 5764-5765,
5807 pb, 5950 f, 6085 pb,
6193, 6225, 6283-6284,
6691 f, 6717, 6839 pb, 6845?
pb, 6872 pb, 7076 pb, 7239
pb, 7252
1805: 7914, 8271 pb, 8310,
8424 pb, 8585, 8674 pb,
8916, 8917 pb, 8936 pb,
8946, 8975 pb, 9162 pb,
9198 pb, 9206 pb, 9356,

50523 pb, 50609 pb
1806: 9806, 9836 pb, 9840
pb, 9886, 10019, 10359
pb, 10388, 10403, 10522,
10606 pb, 10627-10628,
10853 pb, 10854, 10879,
10924-10925, 11212, 11336
pb, ?11795, 50672 pb
1807: 12031? pb, 12032,
12034, ?12224, 12354 pb,
12537, 12580 pb, 12581,
12657 pb, 12681 pb, 12817
bf, 13058 bsb, 13096 pb,
13522 pb, 13713
1808: 14352 pb, 14408, 14410,
14503, 14506 pb, 14785 pb,
14870, 14986, 15142, 15304,
15379, 15672 pb, 15992 pb,
16005 pb, 16597, 50890 pb
1809: 16896, 16897 pb, 17314
pb, 17341 pb, 17349 pb,
17478 pb, 17851 pb, 17902,
18220 pb, 18582, 19292 pb,
50934
1810: 19410, 19412, 19462,
19750 pb, 19751, 19875
pb, 20081 pb, 20327 pb,
20499, ?20651 pb, 20769,
21117 pb
1811: 22232, 22236? pb,
22439a-22440a pb, 22770
pb, 22800, 23738, 23896
pb, 51053 pb
1812: 24693, 24855 pb,
25188, 25233, 25417 pb,
26344 pb, 26457 pb

HANNA, DAVID (Philadelphia)
1816: 38944 pb
1818: 43758 pb, 44402 pb,
44489 pb

HANNAY, SAMUEL (New
York)
1818: 43301 f, 43329 f,
43343 pb, 44604 f, 46679
pb, 46683 pb
1819: 47372 f, 48405 f,
50015 pb

HANNON, TIPPO S (Augusta,
Ga.)
1819: 48074 pb

HANNON, TIPPO S (Tarboro,
N. C.)
1814: 32530 pb

HANSON, ALEXANDER CONTEE
(Baltimore)
1809: 18471 f

HANSON, ALEXANDER CONTEE
(Georgetown, D. C.)
1812: 25412 pb
1814: 31284 pb

HAPGOOD, GEORGE NEGUS
(Warren, O.)
1819: 47711

HARBY, ISAAC (Charleston,
S. C.)
1814: 32824 pb
1815: 36561
1816: 38029

HARDCASTLE, JOHN (New
York)
1804: 5818, 6004-6005, 6007,
6082, 6167, 6297, 7074
1805: 8302, 8318, 8444, 8471
pb, 8583, 9017 pb, 50578?
1806: 10158, 10162, 10202,
10433, 10464, 10510, 10523,
10679, 10762, 11446
1807: 12374, 12601, 12744,
12816
1808: 14252, 15864
1809: 17392, 17732, 18227,
18674 pb
1810: 20400 pb, 21105 pb
1811: 22964 pb
1812: 26139, 26881 pb
1813: 28418, 28687, 28921,
29037 pb, 29326, 29332 pb,
29339 pb
1815: 33781, 34739 pb, 35454
pb, 35835
1816: 37794
1817: 40375
1818: 51783 f
1819: 48155 f

HARDCASTLE, THOMAS (New
York)
1809: 19147

Hardcastle & Pelsue (New
York)
see HARDCASTLE, JOHN
(New York)
PELSUE, WILLIAM L
(New York)

Hardcastle & Van Pelt (New
York)
see HARDCASTLE, JOHN
(New York)
VAN PELT, PETER (New
York)

HARDING, JESPER (Philadelphia)
1818: 45297, 45539
1819: 49454

HARDT, --- (Frederick, Md.)
1815: 35645 pb

HARDT, PETER (York, Pa.)
1819: 49395 pb, 51905

HARDY, NATHANIEL KIM-
BALL (Concord, N.H.)
1812: 26063 pb

HARGROVE, WILLIAM (New
York)
1814: 30858

HARMER, JOSEPH (Baltimore)
1807: 13627

HARMER, JOSEPH (New
York)
1811: 22337 pb, 23089 pb,
24487 pb
1813: 28700 pb

HARMER, JOSEPH (Winchester,
Va.)
1804: 5799, 6534 pb

HARMON, ZEBULON (Balti-
more)
1816: 36880 pb, 37302 pb,
39894 f

HARNEY, JOHN M (Savannah,
Ga.)
1818: 44152 pb

HARPER, --- (Shepherdstown,
Va.)
1817: 41280
1818: 44769
1819: 49171 pb

HARPER, GEORGE KENTON
(Chambersburg, Pa.)
1807: 13523 pb, 14196 pb
1809: 17870
1810: 20818
1811: 23080
1812: 25381
1813: 29023, 29627 pb
1815: 35109

HARPER, GEORGE KENTON
(Gettysburg, Pa.)
1805: 8040 f

HARPER, JAMES (New York)
1817: 40433, 40435, 41318,
41335, 41797, 41860, 42090
1818: 43049, 43258, 43301,
43582, 43631, 43819, 43864,
44537, 44562, 44604-44606,
45854
1819: 47347, 47372-47373,
47539, 48473, 48509, 49199,
50033, 50068

HARPER, JOHN (New York)
1817: 40433, 40435, 41318,
41335, 41797, 41860, 42090
1818: 43049, 43258, 43301,
43582, 43631, 43819, 43864,
44537, 44562, 44604-44606,
45854
1819: 47347, 47372-47373,
47539, 48473, 48509, 49199,
50033, 50068

HARPER, ROBERT (Gettysburg,
Pa.)
1803: 4482
1805: 8040 bf
1807: 12876
1811: 22609
1812: 24529

HARPER, ROBERT G (Gettys-
burg, Pa.)
1817: 41312 pb

HARRINGTON, D (Baltimore)
1814: 32001 f
1815: 35175 f

HARRIS, ELI (Athens, Ga.)
1808: 15099 pb

HARRIS, ELI (M'Minnville,
Tenn.)
1816: 38302 pb

HARRIS, ELI (Nacogdoches,
Tex.)
1819: 49579 pb

HARRIS, ELI (Richmond, Ky.)
1809: 17634 pb
1810: 21243

HARRIS, J (Bangor, Me.)
1818: 45684

HARRIS, JOHN (Cadiz, O.)
1816: 37147 pb

HARRIS, SAMUEL (Baltimore)
1818: 45503 sb

HARRIS, THEOPHILUS (Philadelphia)
1819: 48389-48390 f

HARRIS, WILLIAM C (York,
Pa.)
1815: 36660 pb

HARRISON, --- (Philadelphia)
1812: 24927 pb
1813: 29667 pb

HARRISON, CHARLES (New
York)
1809: 18290 pb

HARRISON, MATTHEW
(Lansingburgh, N.Y.)
1803: 4999 pb
1804: 7109 sb

HARRISON, SAMUEL (Phila-
delphia)
1806: 10154
1808: 15998

1817: 41401 pb
1818: 44792 pb, 44796 pb,
45425
1819: 48669 pb

HARRISON, WILLIAM (Phila-
delphia)
1806: 10783 pb

HARRISSON, JOHN (New York)
1802: 3108
1803: 5148 pb, 50343?
1804: 6612 pb

HARROD, JOHN J (Baltimore)
1814: 31489 pb, 32899 f
1815: 34991? pb
1816: 37082 f, 38965 f
1818: 44172 pb, 45747 pb
1819: 47356 f, 47722 f, 48172
pb, 48456 f

HARROW, JAMES D (Fred-
ericksburg, Va.)
1818: 43224, 43228, 44128

HART, EDSON (Elizabeth,
N.J.)
1819: 47185 f, 47767 f, 47859
f, 48179 f

HART, HENRY (New York)
1810: 21478 sb

HART, WILLIAM (Hartford,
Conn.)
1814: 31022
1815: 35806
1816: 36962a
1818: 43300

HART, WILLIAM (Middletown,
Conn.)
1814: 31344 pb, 31511, 32019
pb, 32784 pb

HART, WILLIAM (New York)
1807: 13042 f

Hartford Evangelical Tract Society (Hartford, Conn.)
1816: 37118 f, 37516 pb,
37549 pb, 38288 f, 38672

pb, 38810 pb, 39008 pb
1817: 39913 pb, 39928 pb,
   40145 f, 40993 f
1818: 43361 pb, 44454 pb,
   45542 f, 45710 pb, 46847
   pb

HARTMAN, JOSEPH (Lebanon,
   Pa.)
1815: 34045 pb, 34453 pb
1816: 39651 pb
1818: 44350, 46912 pb
1819: 48086, 49578

HARVEY, JOSEPH H (Raleigh,
   N.C.)
1814: 31526
1819: 48948

HASTINGS, CHARLES (Utica,
   N.Y.)
1818: 45707 f

HASTINGS, JONATHAN (Boston)
1808: 14388 f, 14504 pb,
   14531 pb, 14607 f, 15258
   pb, 15260 pb, 15950 pb,
   15977 pb, 16142 pb, 16168
   pb, 16677 pb
1809: 16996 f, 17061 pb,
   17096 pb, 17117 pb, 17251
   pb, 17298 pb, 17400 pb,
   17503 pb, 17606 pb, 17642
   pb, 17840 pb, 17886 pb,
   18487 pb, 18669 pb

HASTINGS, JONATHAN
   (Charlestown, Mass.)
1809: 17199, 17251 pb,
   17336, 19152

HASTINGS, WILLIAM (Newburyport, Mass.)
1816: 36986
1818: 43340, 43804, 43807,
   43942, 44911, 45187

HASWELL, ANTHONY (Bennington, Vt.)
1801: 200, 810, 1184, 1580,
   1651, 1661
1802: 1917, 2384, 2417,

2887, 3103, 3110?, 3458,
   3461 pb, 3462
1803: 4148, 5104, 5143, 5500,
   5502, 5522
1804: 5759, 5794, 6080, 6159,
   6300, 6459? pb, 6771, 7037
   pb
1805: 8095, 8319, 8570, 9309,
   9654, 9656
1806: 9921 pb, 10392-10393,
   10535, 10790, ?11076,
   11758, 11762?, 11874
1807: 12294 pb, 12316, 12543
   pb, 12730 pb, 13466, 13710,
   14108, 14115-14116, 14175
1808: 14599, 14928, 14993,
   15128, 15203, 15320?,
   15413, 15582 pb, 15976,
   16621 pb, 16755
1809: 17378, 17444, 17486,
   17984, 18524, 18686, 19095-
   19096
1810: 19673, 19876, 20087 pb,
   20090, 20296, 20307, 20542,
   21368, 22075, 51004 pb
1814: 31908? pb
1815: 34884, ?34885?, 34886

HASWELL, ANTHONY (Middlebury, Vt.)
1802: 1783 f
1806: 10862

HASWELL, ANTHONY JOHNSON
   (Bennington, Vt.)
1818: 43610 pb

HASWELL, WILLIAM (Bennington, Vt.)
1811: 22231, 22772, 22804,
   22826, 23449, 23942
1812: 24568-24569?, 25398
1813: 28488, 28490 pb
1818: 46636
1819: 49982? pb

Haswell & Smead (Bennington,
   Vt.)
see HASWELL, ANTHONY
   (Bennington, Vt.)
   SMEAD, BENJAMIN (Bennington, Vt.)

HATHAWAY, JAMES G (Auburn, N. Y.)
1814: 31108 pb
1815: 34232, 34233 f

HATHAWAY, JAMES G
(Fayette, N. Y.)
1817: 42091 pb

HAWKINS, DAVID (Providence, R. I.)
1806: 9822, 10358, 11284
1807: 12094
1808: 14336 pb
1809: 16858 pb, 16859, 18509?, 18511 pb
1810: 19656, 19684, 20727, 21186, 21484 pb
1811: 23032, 24031, 51067
1812: 24670, 26616, 26874-26875, 27426, 27548
1813: 29151, 29944
1814: 32586 pb

HAWLEY, EDWARD M
(Newark, N. J.)
1802: 2144 pb

HAY, PETER (Bridgeton, N. J.)
1815: 36490 pb
1817: 41598-41599

HAYES, JOHN (Baltimore)
1801: 108 pb

HAYES, MICHAEL (Ovid, N. Y.)
1817: 41716 pb

HAYS, A C (Columbia, Tenn.)
1819: 47668 pb

HAZARD, THOMAS (Boston)
1816: 37630? pb

HAZEN, DAVID (Boston)
1818: 43235 pb

HAZZARD, --- (Philadelphia)
1818: 43389 pb

HEARD, JOSIAH (Zanesville, O.)
1816: 39903

HEARD, PHINEHAS (New York)
1801: 786 pb
1802: 1854, 1915, 3057
1803: 4071, 4289, 5524

Heard & Forman (New York)
see HEARD, PHINEHAS (New York)
FORMAN, AARON (New York)

HEARTT, DENNIS (Philadelphia)
1804: 6658
1805: 8134, 50513
1806: 11022
1810: 21067 pb
1811: 22412a, 23128-23129, 23196, 51133
1812: 24705?, 24732, 24760, 24963, 24989, 25022, 25365, 26574, 26750, 27591
1813: 27801 pb, 27809, 27881, 28419, 28518-28520, 28559, 30417
1814: 30741, 32419
1815: 34813
1816: 36847, 37055 pb
1817: 40438
1818: 45125, 45638, 46790-46792, 51848 pb

HEATON, DAVID (Providence, R. I.)
1801: 641 sb, 913 f, 1441 f
1802: 2641 f
1803: 3619?, 4990, 5533
1804: 5646 pb, 6069, 6138?, 6139, 6248?, 6494, 6706 pb, 6843 pb, 7161 pb, 7192, 7343, 7708, 7779, 50416
1805: 8392?, 8616?, 9154, 9233, 9251, 9730-9731
1806: 9822 f, 11258
1807: 11981, 11996-11997, 12503, 13468 pb, 13691
1808: 14477 pb, 14940, 16002, 16341
1809: 17755 pb

1810: 19906
1811: 22765

HEATON, NATHANIEL (Providence, R. I.)
1802: 1954 pb
1803: 3968, 3999, 4645, 4978

HEATON, NATHANIEL
(Wrentham, Mass.)
1801: 302, 447, 451-452,
640-641 pb, 864, 913, 930,
1213, 1406, 1441, 50211
1802: 1797, 2041, 2186-2187,
2189, 2390 pb, 2420, 2641,
2748, 2925, 3093, 3157,
50284?
1803: 4159-4160, 4198, 4481,
4901, 4903
1805: 8753?
1812: 51230?

Heaton & Williams (Providence, R. I.)
see HEATON, DAVID (Providence, R. I.)
    WILLIAMS, BENOMI
    (Providence, R. I.)

HECKERT, DANIEL (York, Pa.)
1808: 14973 pb

HEDGE, LEMUEL (Windsor, Vt.)
1816: 37115 pb, 37157 pb,
37230 f, 37371 pb, 37761
pb, 38388 pb, 38677 pb,
39045 pb

HEISKELL, FREDERICK
STEIDINGER (Knoxville, Tenn.)
1816: 38024 pb
1817: 39927, 40505, 41246,
42041
1818: 43082
1819: 47482, 47654-47655,
48662

HEISKELL, JOHN (Winchester, Va.)
1812: 24554, 26040, 26116

pb, 26488?
1813: 27769?
1814: 30906, 31243
1815: 33910?, 34263, 34897
1817: 42819 pb
1818: 44124, 44777, 46655
1819: 47150

HEISKELL, WILLIAM (Winchester, Va.)
1809: 19142
1810: 21888

HELLINGS, JOHN (Chillicothe, O.)
1815: 35792 f

HELLINGS, JOHN (Philadelphia)
1809: 17592 f, 18556 f
1810: 20005 pb, 20216 f,
20565-20566 f
1811: 23196 f, 23974 f, 24006
f
1812: 51211 pb

Hellings & Aitken (Philadelphia)
see HELLINGS, JOHN (Philadelphia)
    AITKEN, ROBERT S (Philadelphia)

HELMBOLD, GEORGE (Lancaster, Pa.)
1802: 2867, 2870 f
1803: 3631 bf, 4838-4839,
4841, 4843 pb, 4845, 4849 bf
1804: 7012

HELMBOLD, GEORGE (Philadelphia)
1801: 335 f, 1576
1802: 3456
1803: 5497
1804: 6194
1806: 11234 bpb
1817: 41130 pb

HELY, JAMES (Louisville, Ga.)
1801: 563, 565-566
1802: 2307, 2310
1803: 4269-4270
1804: 6372

HELY, JAMES (Savannah, Ga.)
1804:   7297 pb

HENDERSON, THOMAS
(Georgetown, Ky.)
1814:   32139 pb
1815:   35157, 51456 pb

HENDERSON, THOMAS
(Raleigh, N.C.)
1808:   16249 pb
1809:   17586 pb, 18541, 18543,
19144
1810:   20318 pb
1811:   22280, 23214, 24461,
51100 pb
1812:   24730, 25403, 25627
pb, 26314, ?26315?,
26317? pb, 26319-26320,
27528
1813:   28731 pb, 29233,
29380? pb, 29381a? pb,
29382
1814:   31011, 31689, 32366
1815:   33964?, 34891, 35503?,
?35504?, 35505, 35506 pb
1816:   37825 pb, 38480-
38481? pb, 38482, 38483?
pb
1817:   40102, 41667?, 41669-
41670, 51673 pb
1818:   44927? pb, 45116?
pb, 45117, 51784 pb, 51793
pb
1819:   48207 pb, 48944? pb,
48945-48946, 51926

HENDRICKS, WILLIAM
(Madison, Ind.)
1813:   30518 pb
1814:   31794

HENKEL, AMBROSE (New-
market, Va.)
1806:   10346 pb, 10375
1807:   12519, 12577, 12635
pb, 14105, 14142 pb
1808:   14954 pb, 14965,
15091, 15411 pb
1809:   17736 pb, 17943 pb,
18489
1810:   20321-20322, 20718a-
20719

1811:   22135 pb, 22524 pb,
22893 pb, 22907, 22988-
22992, 23250 pb, 23497,
23645
1812:   1273, 25359 pb, 25628
pb, 25630 pb, 25631, 25852
pb, 25917, 26199
1813:   28451 pb, 28732 pb,
29562 pb, 29612, 29629 pb,
30390 pb
1814:   31429, 31842? pb,
31971, 32375, 32686
1815:   35036?
1816:   37826

HENKEL, ANDREW N (New-
market, Va.)
1809:   17209

HENKEL, SOLOMON (New-
market, Va.)
1809:   17209 f, 17210 pb
1814:   31428 pb
1815:   34655-34656a pb, 36099,
36456 pb
1816:   37519, 37531, 37827-
37829, 38737
1817:   40775, 41031-41033
1818:   43967-43968
1819:   48209

HENRY, ISAAC N (St. Louis,
Mo.)
1818:   44157, 45612 pb

HENRY, ROBERT NORRIS
(Philadelphia)
1818:   43545, 44397 f
1819:   48513 f, 49365 pb

HENRY, SAMUEL (New York)
1814:   31692 f

Herald (Greenfield, Mass.)
see Franklin Herald (Greenfield, Mass.)

Herald (Natchez, Miss.)
see Mississippi Herald
(Natchez, Miss.)

Herald (New Haven, Conn.)
see Connecticut Herald (New
Haven, Conn.)

Herald (Poughkeepsie, N.Y.)
see Republican Herald
(Poughkeepsie, N.Y.)

Herald (Stockbridge, Mass.)
see Farmer's Herald (Stockbridge, Mass.)

Herald of Gospel Liberty
(Philadelphia)
1811: 22935, 24025
1812: 26871

Herald of Gospel Liberty
(Portland, Me.)
1810: 21355, 21357 pb
1811: 23072, 23172 pb,
23200 pb, 23942i-23942j,
23942k f

HERBERT, STEWART (Hagers-
town, Md.)
1814: 30630

HERMAN, JOHN (Lancaster,
O.)
1816: 37533
1817: 40886 pb
1818: 44973 pb
1819: 47921-47922, 48828 pb

HERSCHBERGER, JOHN
(Chambersburg, Pa.)
1809: 18177 pb
1810: 20361, 20534, 20837,
21036, 22055, 51013 pb
1811: 23492
1812: 26201, 26796 pb
1813: 29270 pb, 29855 pb
1815: 35148, 35297 pb

HERSCHBERGER, JOHN
(Harrisburg, Pa.)
1808: 50823 pb

HEWES, JOHN (Baltimore)
1804: 6047, 6055 pb, 6352,
7132, 7743-7744, 50419
1805: 7916, 8206 pb, 8349,
8360 pb, 8465, 8485, 8488,
9212-9213, 9742
1806: 10439, 10450-10453,
10800, 10802, 11222

1807: 12627, 12628 pb, 12630
1808: 15071?, 15073?
1809: 17582 pb, ?17583 pb,
17584
1810: 20165 pb, 20166

HEWITT, JAMES (New York)
1801: 1695? pb, 50225? pb
1802: 50285? pb, 50295? pb,
50299?
1803: 50346-50347? pb
1804: 50461? pb
1805: 50546 pb, 50560? pb
1807: 50771? pb, 50780? pb,
50781 pb, 50820? pb
1811: 51079 pb

HEWS, ABRAHAM (Boston)
1818: 43108, 43157, 44493
pb, 45190? pb, 46799
1819: 46923 pb, 46961, 47547,
47553-47554, 47653, 47666,
48998, 49220 pb, 50108,
50177

HICKCOX, ASA W (Wooster,
O.)
1817: 41690 pb

HICKMAN, NATHANIEL (Philadelphia)
1818: 43389 pb, 44067 pb

HIGGINS, WILLIAM (New York)
1817: 40422 f

HIGHTOWER, PLEASANT R
(Milledgeville, Ga.)
1816: 38253 pb

HILL, BENJAMIN (Portsmouth,
N.H.)
1804: 6886, 6888, 6890, 7000
1805: 7959, 8660 pb, 8989,
8991, 8993

HILL, CYRUS (Montpelier, Vt.)
1817: 41605

HILL, GEORGE (Baltimore)
1803: 3691 f
1805: 8146 f
1808: ?15172 pb, ?15390 pb
1811: 22485 f, 23725 f

HILL, ISAAC (Concord, N. H.)
1808: 14467
1809: 16978, 17694, 18199
    pb
1810: 19685-19686, 20856-
    20858, 21251, 21343
1811: 22317, 22408a, 22955,
    22975, 22984, 23033, 23510-
    23512, 23514, 23732, 23852
1812: 24920, 25234, 25385
    pb, 25437, 25581, 26138
    pb, 26141, 26224-26225,
    26227-26228, 26369, 26671,
    26816, 27579, 27611
1813: 27925, 27964, 28922,
    29282, 29290, 29293, 29296,
    29298, 29890, 30491
1814: 30875-30876, 31161,
    31950-31951, 32524, 32528,
    32881
1815: 34201, 34514, 35134,
    35261, 35439 pb, 35550-
    35551, 35945
1816: 37175 pb, 38059,
    38233, 38235 pb, 38236,
    38392-38393, 38400 pb,
    38853, 39127
1817: 40268, 40270, 41413,
    41576-41579, 41585 pb,
    41854 pb, 42080 pb, 42741,
    42901
1818: 43052, 43193, 43790,
    43899, 44936 pb, 44991-
    44992, 44995, 44998 pb,
    45109, 45697, 46903
1819: 47110-47111, 47864,
    47966, 48273, 48679, 48762,
    48777 pb, 48837, 48851-
    48852, 48856, 48862 pb,
    49013, 49233 pb

HILL, JOHN (Savannah, Ga.)
1806: 9890, 10478 pb

HILL, THOMAS HOWARD
    (Baltimore)
1814: 30737 pb
1815: 51503?

HILL, WALTER RUSSELL
    (Concord, N. H.)
1811: 22317, 22408a, 22955,
    22975, 23033, 23510-23511,

23514, 23732, 23852
1812: 24920, 25234, 25385
    pb, 25437, 25581, 26138
    pb, 26141, 26224-26225,
    26227-26228, 26369, 26671,
    26816, 27579, 27611
1813: 27925, 27964, 28922,
    29282, 29290, 29293, 29296,
    29298, 29890, 30491
1814: 30875-30876, 31161,
    31950-31951, 32524, 32528,
    32881
1815: 34201, 34514, 35134,
    35261, 35550-35551, 35945

HILLER, JOSEPH (Boston)
1803: 3971 f, 4176 pb, 4194
    pb, 5050 f, 5147 f
1804: 5956 f, 6023-6025 f,
    6027-6029 f, 6277 pb, 6478
    pb, 6748 pb, 7331 f, 50477 f
1805: 9363 pb, 50619 f
1808: 50889 f

HILLHOUSE, DAVID P (Colum-
    bia, S. C.)
1816: 37181 pb, 38203

HILLHOUSE, DAVID P (Wash-
    ington, Ga.)
1801: 943 pb
1809: 17614

HILLHOUSE, SARAH (Washing-
    ton, Ga.)
1805: 8515

HILLIARD, WILLIAM (Boston)
1810: 19752 pb
1811: 22659 pb
1812: 24572 f, 24584 f
1813: 27681-27682 pb, 27701
    pb, 27837 pb, 27941 pb,
    28100 pb, 28104 pb, 28129
    pb, 28256 pb, 28269 f,
    28287 pb, 28379 f, 28381 f,
    28402-28403 pb, 28406 pb,
    28465 pb, 28690 pb, 28790
    f, 29573 f, 29734 pb, 29773
    f, 29797 pb, 29914 pb, 30477
    f, 30570 pb, 51296 f
1814: 30627 f, 30873 f,
    30914 f, 31063 f, 31116 pb,

31273 pb, 31977 f, 32141
pb, 32420 f, 32445 pb,
32609 pb, 33522 pb, 33596
f, 33727 pb
1815: 33991 pb, 34061 pb,
34159 pb, 34330 f, 34482-
34483 pb, 34524 pb, 34558
pb, 35250 pb, 36424 pb,
36623 pb, 36627 pb, 36647
pb
1816: 37062 pb, 37266 f,
37745 pb, 38519 f, 38631
pb, 39695 f
1817: 39921 pb, 40247 pb,
40314 pb, 40342 pb, 40353
f, 40597-40600 pb, 40900
pb, 40977 pb, 41272 pb,
42242 pb, 42762
1818: 43122-43123 pb, 43430,
43782-43785 pb, 43805 pb,
43906 sb, 43914 pb, 44270
pb, 44295 pb, 45565 pb,
45864 f, 46704 pb
1819: 47037 pb, 47543 f,
47759-47760 pb, 47769-
47770 pb, 47775 f, 47816
pb, 48047 pb, 48100 pb,
48506 pb, 49321 pb, 49385
pb, 50167 pb

HILLIARD, WILLIAM (Cam-
bridge, Mass.)
1801: 465, 483, 612, 629
pb, 632, 665-666, 1056
pb, 50237 pb
1802: 1763, 1911, 1913,
2240, 2379-2380, 2560 pb,
2830, 2897, 2899, 3140,
3499
1803: 3838 pb, 4220, 4346-
4347, 4504-4505, 4509,
5138-5139, 5547, 5579,
5605
1804: 5926, 6111, 6312,
6454, 6456-6457, 6490-
6491, 6564 pb, 6587,
6622, 6998, 7323, 7707,
7781 pb
1805: 8455, 8590, 8592-
8593, 8631 pb, 8632, 8756,
8758 pb, 8773, 8793 pb,
9155 pb, 9192, 9467, 9690,
9746, 50630?

1806: 10306, 10431, 10506,
10546, 10550, 10580, 10587,
10834, 11046, 11089, 11165-
11166, 11312 pb, 11440,
11818, 50712
1807: 12247, 12264 pb, 12520,
12721-12722, 12724, 12726,
12728, 12810 pb, 13072 pb,
13434 pb, 13670-13672 pb,
13727
1808: 14822, 15030, 15692-
15693, 16025, 16687, 16750
1809: 16826 pb, 16831 pb,
16891, 16951, 16984, 17004,
17009, 17512, 17518 pb,
17706, 17717-17719, 17766,
17985, 18317, 18578, 19209,
19250, 19291
1810: 19304, 19502, 19911,
20293, 20368 f, 20369,
20582 pb, 20966-20967 f,
21055, 21202, 21940, 21959-
21960
1811: 22176, 22421-22422,
22417a-22418a, 22481 bf,
22493 pb, 22617, 22658,
22659 pb, 22840, 23031,
23038, 23138 pb, 23246,
23644, 23687, 23692
1812: 24572, 24584, 25089,
25212, 25369-25371 pb,
25504 pb, 25609, 25620,
25910, 25944 bf, 26360-
26361, 26479 pb, 26515,
26569, 27461, 27492 bf,
51205
1813: 27681-27682 pb, 27701
pb, 27837 pb, 27941 pb,
28104 pb, 28255, 28256 pb,
28269 bf, 28465 pb, 28690
pb, 28715 pb, 28765-28766,
28860, 29390 pb, 29555,
29773
1814: 30914, 31115 pb, 31273
pb, 31289, 31399 pb, 31440
pb, 31492, 31660, 31662,
31744, 32128, 32480, 33727
pb
1815: 33762-33763, 34118,
34219, 34315, 34321 pb,
34382, 34482 pb, 34524 pb,
34684 pb, 34881, 34964 pb,
35335, 35933, 36008, 36477,

36513, 36594, 36624, 36627
pb, 51501 pb
1816: 36996 pb, 37062 pb,
37206, 37266, 37746 pb,
37807, 37809-37810, 37823,
38087 pb, 38180, 38190,
38519, 38631 pb, 39872,
39885, 51584
1817: 39998 pb, 40314 pb,
40322, 40586, 40597 pb,
40842, 40878, 41186, 41470,
41847, 41990, 42762 pb,
42822, 42908 pb, 51672 pb
1818: 43784 pb, 43805 pb,
43962, 44113, 44270, 44295-
44296, 44363, 44533, 44534
pb, 45160, 45230, 45864,
46704
1819: 47543, 47769-47770,
47775, 48189, 48264, 48468,
48638-48639 pb, 48642,
48691, 48994, 49297, 49447,
50036-50037, 50145 pb

HINCKLEY, --- (Burlington,
Vt.)
1814: 31037 pb

HINDS, JUSTIN (Hanover, N. H.)
1811: 22543 pb, 22618 f,
23508-23509 f
1815: 34359 f, 34441 f
1819: 48794 pb

HINDS, JUSTIN (Montpelier,
Vt.)
1812: 26118 f

HINDS, JUSTIN (Walpole, N. H.)
1807: 12101 f
1808: 14956 f

HINES, JOHN B (Columbia,
S. C.)
1817: 42174, 42176, 51652 pb

HINES, JOHN B (Milledge-
ville, Ga.)
1817: 41942 pb
1819: 48072-48073

HINKLE, JACOB (Lancaster,
O.)
1806: 11857 pb

HIRST, THOMAS (Philadelphia)
1813: 51346 f

HITT, DANIEL (New York)
1808: 15385 pb, 15589 f,
15592 f
1809: 17515 pb, 18071 f, 18173
f
1810: 19756 f, 20112 f, 20123
pb, 20730 pb, 22016-22017 f
1811: 22173 f, 22363 f, 22557
f, 22648 f, 23375-23377 f,
23827 f, 23911 f
1812: 24810 pb, 25107 f,
25379 f, 25382 f, 25496 pb,
25565 pb, 25594 pb, 25596
pb, 25699 pb, 25841 pb,
25961 pb, 26068 f, 26069
pb, 26070 f, 27519 f, 27523
pb
1813: 27644 pb, 27692 pb,
27743 pb, 27756 f, 27844 f,
28174 f, 28252 f, 28516 f,
29154 f, 29155 pb, 29156-
29158 f, 29267 pb, 29679 f,
29680 pb, 29689 f, 29769 f
1814: 30850 f, 31472 f, 31789
pb, 31802 f, 32114 f, 32115
pb, 32116-32117 f, 32667 f,
32744 f, 33644 f, 33645 pb,
33680 f
1815: 34084 f, 34087 f, 34386-
34387 f, 35268-35269 f,
35535 f, 35802-35803 f,
35895 f, 36036-36037 f,
36539 f, 51463 f
1817: 40203 f, 40217 pb
1818: 43302 pb

Hive (Northampton, Mass.)
1801: 394
1804: 6045, 6136, 6407, 6434,
6927, 7775-7776

HOADLEY, ABRAM (New
Haven, Conn.)
1815: 36121 f

HOBBY, WILLIAM J (Augusta,
Ga.)
1804: 5773, 6377
1805: 7896, 8517 pb, 9415
1806: 10477 pb
1807: 12014, 12655 pb, 13065,

14195 pb
1808: 15097 pb
1809: 17615 pb, 18700
1810: 20209, 21998 pb
1811: 23788, 51092 pb
1812: 25514 pb, 26749
1813: 28625 pb
1814: 51393 pb
1815: 34781 pb, 36080, 51500
1816: 51587 pb

HODGE, ABRAHAM (Halifax,
   N. C.)
1801: 249 pb, 660 pb
1803: 3917, 4386
1804: 6487
1806: 10545 pb

HODGE, ABRAHAM (Raleigh,
   N. C.)
1801: 1664 pb
1803: 4238

HODGE, JOHN (Athens, Ga.)
1814: 30713 pb

HODGMAN, STEPHEN (Rut-
   land, Vt.)
1802: 1802, 3463 pb
1804: 7754

HOFF, JOHN (Charleston,
   S. C.)
1804: 5810 pb
1805: 50552 pb
1806: 9814 pb, 10120 pb,
   10331, 10570, 11351 pb,
   11457 pb, 11867, 50686 pb
1807: 12077 pb, 12225-12227
   pb, 12599 pb, 12769 pb,
   13409, 13717, 14215
1808: 15046, 15251, 15350
   pb, 15895, 15965, 16013
1809: 16865, 17390, 17559,
   17566, 17686-17687, 17964
   pb, 17982, 18319-18320,
   18465
1810: 19542, 20126 pb,
   20223, 20237, 20356 pb,
   20359, 20362, 20364-
   20365, 20613, 20810 pb,
   20878 pb, 21228
1811: 22514, 22830, 22841,

22880, 23025, 23284, 23584,
   23739, 23747, 23779
1812: 24860, 25051, 25157,
   25214, 25465, 25668, 26046,
   27535
1813: 27673, 27811-27812,
   27936, 28221 pb, 28415,
   28549, 28762, 51270 pb
1814: 30970, 30988 pb, 31125-
   31126, 31490 pb, 31503,
   31736 pb, 32007, 32558,
   33234
1815: 34110, 34929 pb, 35024,
   35092, 35556 pb, 35727
1816: 37160, 37214, 37500,
   37626, 38051 pb, 38544-
   38545, 38736, 38987 pb,
   51585, 51594 pb, 51628
1817: 40749, 41902 pb, 51690
   pb
1818: 43348, 43646, 43734,
   43926, 44053 pb, 44056,
   45443, 45918, 51757, 51786
   pb
1819: 48001, 48251, 49009,
   49213, 49499, 49538, 50101
   pb

HOFF, JOHN (Philadelphia)
1802: 2220, 3073
1803: 4877 pb
1804: 5810 pb, 5934 pb, 5937
   pb, 6603, 7072 pb, 7788

HOGAN, ANDREW (Philadelphia)
1814: 30725 pb
1815: 34478

HOGAN, DAVID (Philadelphia)
1801: 353 pb, 404, 603, 1095,
   1150, 1166 pb, 1230
1802: 2001, 2251 f, 2477 pb,
   2891, 2911 pb
1803: 5005 pb, 50377 pb,
   50386 pb
1804: 5731, 6075 pb, 6497 pb,
   7084 pb, 7123 pb
1805: 9168 pb, 9682 pb, 9692,
   9703 pb, 50489 pb
1806: 10816 f, 11157, 11183
   pb, 11307 pb, 11881-11882
   pb
1807: 12647 pb, 13414 pb,

14153 pb, 14182 pb
1808: 14382, 14783 f, 16027
    pb, 50882 pb
1809: 16875 pb, 17831 pb,
    18378 pb, 18494 pb, 19168
    pb
1810: 19378 f, 20773 f,
    21077 pb, 21110 pb, 21235
    pb, 21374 f, 21461 f, 21985
    f, 21991 f
1811: 22434 f, 22433a pb,
    23222 f, 23476-23477 f,
    23714 pb, 24384 pb
1812: 24757 pb, 25003 pb,
    25262 f, 25735 f, 25736
    pb, 26147 f, 26262 pb,
    26536, 26698 f, 51170 pb,
    51237 pb
1813: 28797 pb, 51330 pb
1814: 30804 pb, 32532 pb,
    33598 f, 33623 pb, 33652
    pb, 33654 pb
1815: 33999 pb, 34827 pb,
    36585 pb
1816: 38319 pb, 38417 pb,
    39753 pb, 39836-39837 f
1817: 40002 f, 40346 f,
    40649 f, 41515 pb, 41804
    pb, 41851 pb, 42001 sb,
    42921 pb
1818: 43262-43263 pb,
    43949 pb, 43953, 44456
    pb, 44701 pb, 44713 pb,
    44772 pb, 45021 pb
1819: 47445 pb, 48549 pb,
    49100 pb, 51935 pb

HOIT, WILLIAM (Boston)
1811: 22427a

HOLBROOK, JOHN (Brattle-
borough, Vt.)
1815: 34254 pb, 34340 pb,
    34393 pb, 34697 pb, 34782
    pb, 35343 pb
1816: 36854, 36945-36946,
    36958a pb, 37099 pb, 37457
    pb, 37599, 37656, 39059,
    39666 f, 39756 pb, 39777
    pb, 39825
1817: 40198 pb, 40872, 41399
    pb, 42848, 42853-42854 pb
1818: 43297 pb, 44102,

45186? pb, 45386 pb, 46741
    pb
1819: 47211, 47222-47223 pb,
    48610 pb, 48791 pb, 48838
    pb, 49154 pb, 49378 pb,
    49417 pb, 49542, 50080,
    50081 pb

HOLCOMB, MICHAEL (Car-
lisle, Pa.)
1818: 43539 pb

HOLDEN, OCTAVIUS A (To-
wanda, Pa.)
1816: 38262 pb

HOLEMAN, JACOB HARROD
(Frankfort, Ky.)
1819: 48417

HOLEMAN, WILLIAM B
(Frankfort, Ky.)
1819: 48417

HOLLAND, ANTHONY HENRY
(Buckstown, Me.)
1807: 12049
1808: 15016
1811: 22262, 23230 pb, 23276
    pb
1812: 25525, 25527

HOLLIDAY, BENJAMIN (Franklin, Mo.)
1819: 48719 pb

HOLMES, N B (New York)
1819: 48211 f

Holston Intelligencer (Abingdon,
Va.)
1807: 13697

HOLT, CHARLES (Hudson,
N.Y.)
1802: 2517
1803: 4399 pb
1804: 7315 pb
1805: 8268, 8633 pb, 8800
1806: 10747, 10919

HOLT, CHARLES (New London,
Conn.)

1801: 811 f
1802: 1856 pb, 2075

HOLT, CHARLES (New York)
1809: 17257 pb
1810: 21278

HOLT, DAVID (Herkimer,
  N. Y.)
1805: 8429 pb
1809: 17121 pb

HOMAN, JOHANN GEORGE
  (Reading, Pa.)
1819: 51863 f

HOMANS, BENJAMIN (Boston)
1804: 6216 pb, 7082 f, 50472
  f
1805: 7830 f, 8368 f, 8696 f,
  8744 f, 8904 f

HOMANS, JOHN (Boston)
1804: 6216 pb, 7082 f, 50472
  f
1805: 7830 f, 8368 f, 8696 f,
  8744 f, 8904 f

HOOD, JOHN BANN (Camden,
  S. C.)
1803: 3925 pb
1804: 7204

HOOD, JOHN BANN (Fort Stoddert, Miss.)
1811: 23407 pb

HOOD, JOHN BANN (Hunts-
  ville, Miss.)
1816: 37897 pb

HOOD, JOHN BANN (Knoxville,
  Tenn.)
1805: 8826, 9461-9464
1806: 11436-11437
1807: 13677?
1808: 16714 pb
1809: 17711, 18737-18738,
  18740, 18742

HOOD, JOHN BANN (Pulaski,
  Tenn.)
1818: 43167

HOOD, JOHN BANN (Rogers-
  ville, Tenn.)
1814: 33651 pb
1815: 33864

HOOKER, WILLIAM (New York)
1818: 44966 f
1819: 47382 f, 48823 pb,
  48888 f

HOOKER, WILLIAM (Newbury-
  port, Mass.)
1808: 15393

HOOKER, WILLIAM GRISWOLD
  (Middlebury, Vt.)
1809: 16812 pb
1810: 19492? f, 19586 sb,
  21049 f
1817: 41887 sb

HOOPER, J (Charlestown,
  Mass.)
1807: 12833 pb

HOOPER, JOSHUA (Boston)
1814: 30851, 31084, 31459,
  31543 pb, 31546, 32112 pb,
  32900
1815: 33898, 33905, 33911,
  34285, 34377, 34788, 34942,
  35094, 35133, 35833, 36271
1816: 36804, 37285 pb, 38032,
  38556, 38696, 38855, 39705,
  39719-39720
1818: 45204

HOPE, THOMAS (Philadelphia)
1804: 6495 pb
1812: 27358 pb

HOPKINS, BENJAMIN BRON-
  SON (Philadelphia)
1807: 11987 pb, 12091 f,
  12262 pb, 12281 pb, 12474
  pb, 12678 f, 12965 f, 13578
  f, 50790 pb, 50810 pb
1808: 14321 pb, 14591 f,
  15015 f, 15834 f, 16041 pb,
  16050 f, 16079 pb, 16080 f,
  16096 f, 16101 pb, 16158 f,
  16206 f, 16246 f, 16658 f
1809: 16966 f, 17041 pb,

17346 f, 17462 f, 17470 f,
17632 f, 18434 f, 18483 f,
18517 pb, 18528 pb, 18581
f, 18586 pb, 18640 pb,
19211 f
1810: 19556 pb, 19688 f,
19709 pb, 20392 pb, 20393
f, 20939 pb, 21936 pb,
22117 f
1811: 22401 pb, 22412a f,
22548 f, 23044 f, 23650 f,
23832 pb, 23895 pb, 24347a
pb, 24466 pb
1812: 27383-27384 f, 27574 f
1815: 34807 f

HOPKINS, BENJAMIN BRON-
SON (Pittsburgh, Pa.)
1810: 19556 pb
1811: 51102 f
1812: 24844 f, 24965 pb,
25424 pb, 25442 f, 26558 f,
27482 f, 27569 f, 51210 f
1813: 28769 f

HOPKINS, ELLIOTT (Sharon,
Conn.)
1801: 1303

HOPKINS, GEORGE FOLLET
(New York)
1801: 170, 203 pb, 242, 281,
319, 326 pb, 432 bf, 645
pb, 825, 859, 1671, 1685
1802: 1842-1843, 1992 pb,
2039 bf, 2162, 2218 pb,
2462 pb, 2568 pb, 3163 pb,
3578 pb
1803: 3842 bsb, 4076-4077,
4201 pb, 4631, 4634, 4695
pb, 4698, 5498 bf
1804: 6041, 6074, 6731 bsb,
7205 bf
1805: 7885 pb, 7886-7888,
8243, 8304 pb, 8641, 8812
pb, 8880, 8956 pb, 9012,
9448
1806: 9817, 9863, 10043,
10142 pb, 10516, 10770,
10814 pb, 10855, 10907,
11084, 11138, 11262, 11409,
11632, 11840, 50698
1807: 12004, 12407 pb, 13086,

13227, 13239, 13461 bf,
13475
1808: 14379 pb, 14550, 14835
f, 14839 pb, 15153 f, 15293
pb, 15610
1809: 17769 f
1813: 29968 pb
1815: 35338 pb, 35472
1816: 36724, 36765, 37406,
37601 pb, 37796, 38618,
39005

HOPKINS, JOHN (Baltimore)
1819: 46965 f

HOPKINS, WILLIAM HECTOR
(Philadelphia)
1809: 17929 f, 18559 f
1810: 20587 pb

Hopkins & Earle (Philadelphia)
see HOPKINS, BENJAMIN
       BRONSON (Philadelphia)
       EARLE, EDWARD (Phila-
       delphia)

HOPKINSON, J (Philadelphia)
1818: 43577

Hornet (Frederick, Md.)
1809: 18552

HOSFORD, ELIJAH (Albany,
N.Y.)
For all entries see HOS-
FORD, ELISHA (Albany,
N.Y.) below

HOSFORD, ELISHA (Albany,
N.Y.)
1806: 10145 pb, 10269 pb,
10366, 11863, 11893 pb
1807: 13080, 13378
1808: 14696, 14718 pb, 14844,
15342, 15477, 15558, 15691
pb, 15900, 16028, 16175,
16259, 16309 pb, 16347,
16754, 16760
1809: 17010 bf, 17103, 17242
pb, 17461 pb, 17653, 17773,
17857, 17915, 18058, 18200,
18265, 19160, 19216, 19251,
19257 pb, 50935

1810: 19780, 19793, 19941,
20382, 20706, 20808 pb,
20867, 21165, 21521, 22072,
22127
1811: 22306, 23140 pb, 23352,
23364, 23398, 23524, 23913,
24062, 51074, 51081
1812: 24838, 24971, 24974,
24980, 25613, 25635, 25645
pb, 25684, 25888 pb, 25913,
26037, 26056, 26058-26059,
26212, 26576, 26577 pb,
27437
1813: 28007, 28051 pb, 28770,
28856, 28989, 29120, 29309,
29607, 29630, 29729, 29973,
29984, 30548, 30563, 51282
1814: 30842, 30870 pb, 30980,
31187, 31310, 31370, 31718,
31758, 32083, 32303, 32471i-
32472, 32879, 33709, 33740
1815: 34052, 34091-34093,
34476, 34712 pb, 34801,
35159-35160 pb, 35350,
35353 pb, 35900, 35908,
35985 pb, 36501 pb
1816: 36977, 37246, 37280
pb, 37282, 37416, 37844,
37873, 38044, 38195, 38402,
38487, 38920 pb, 39118,
39762, 39845, 51552 pb,
51562
1817: 40168 pb, 40339 pb,
40607 pb, 40696 pb, 40844,
41487, 41722, 41884, 42016,
42037, 42079, 42216 pb,
42224
1818: 43272 pb, 43327, 43502,
43622, 43780 pb, 43826,
44481, 44492, 44666, 44783,
44813, 45001, 45121, 45660,
45800, 45866, 45898, 46715,
46746 pb, 46841
1819: 47189 pb, 47487, 47718,
47757 pb, 47850 pb, 48495
pb, 48665, 48772 pb, 48790,
48796 pb, 48842 pb, 48952,
49469, 49507, 49614 bsb,
49623, 50054 pb, 51851,
51857 pb

HOSKINS, HENRY (Wiscasset,
Me.)

1801: 772, 1315
1803: 4802

HOSKINS, TIMOTHY (Caldwell,
N. Y.)
1818: 44538 pb

HOSKINS, TIMOTHY (Salem,
N. Y.)
1817: 41472

HOSMER, CHARLES (Hartford,
Conn.)
1809: 17288 pb
1810: 19677, 20127, 20255,
22036
1811: 22767, 23789
1812: 24798, 25427, 25637,
25657-25658, 26148, 27536
pb, 27541, 27634, 51192,
51207
1813: 27702, 28114, 28227,
28712 pb, 28754, 28976,
28988 pb, 29770 pb, 29801,
30175, 30452, 30477-30478
1814: 30662, 30853, 31132
pb, 31133, 31404, 31602,
31629, 31698, 31719-31721,
31994 pb, 32020-32021,
32513, 32710, 32734, 32929
pb, 33580 pb, 33742
1815: 33946, 34165, 34646 pb,
34857-34857a, 34871, 34906,
34938, 35515, 35759, 35894,
36562, 36656
1816: 37710 pb, 38648

HOSMER, CHARLES (Litch-
field, Conn.)
1808: 14720, 14758, 15136,
15219, 15242 pb, 15245,
15434, 15666, 50844 pb,
50847, 50854, 50891

HOUGH, GEORGE (Concord,
N. H.)
1801: 36, 258, 1007, 1403,
1680
1802: 1966, 2047, 2382 pb,
2383, 2758-2760, 3584,
3592
1803: 4324, 4735-4738, 4991,
5611, 5618

1804:   6016, 6275, 6690 pb,
    6885, 6887, 6889, 7098,
    7794, 7801
1805:   8074, 9088, 9305, 9417,
    9759, 9772
1806:   10209, 10582, 10761 pb,
    10762, 10784, 10875, 11295
    pb, 11305, 11327, 11827,
    11860, 11875
1807:   12392 pb, 12532, 13661,
    14180, 14238
1808:   14454, 15181, 15195,
    15349, 15468-15469, 15724-
    15725, 15788
1809:   17056, 17124, 17272 pb,
    17712, 17876, 17987, 18192-
    18194, 18198, 18539
1810:   19384, 19831 pb, 20452
    bf, 20617, 20735, 22088-
    22089, 22094-22095
1811:   22415, 22593 pb, 22970-
    22971, 23077, 23368, 23522,
    23706 pb, 23746, 24492,
    24497-24498
1812:   24897, 24987, 25132
    pb, 25139, 25571, 25603,
    25871 pb, 25916, 26236-
    26237, 26353, 26646, 26825
    pb, 27459-27460 pb, 27608
    pb, 27615 pb
1813:   27695, 27970, 28141,
    28483, 28654, 28662, 29015,
    29291-29292, 29294-29295,
    29297, 29299-29300, 29302-
    29304, 29431, 29545 pb,
    29552, 29690, 29792, 29796,
    29958 pb, 30434, 30577,
    30579
1814:   31038, 31165 pb, 31306
    pb, 31563, 31654-31656,
    31675, 31875 pb, 32248-
    32250, 32252, 32436, 32665,
    32789, 32945, 33583 f,
    33730-33731, 51418
1815:   34082, 34499, 34531,
    34909, 35163, 35307, 35430,
    35435-35436, 36613, 36645,
    51478, 51538
1816:   37127, 37555-37556,
    38126, 38397-38399, 38555,
    39003, 39852, 51609
1817:   40091?, 40456, 41005,
    41492, 41583-41584, 42135,

    42266, 42985 pb, 51694
1818:   43020, 43454-43455,
    43618, 44557, 44997, 45405,
    51756, 51804-51805
1819:   47608, 47691 pb, 47696,
    47789, 48039, 48857, 48859-
    48861, 49012, 49312

HOUGHTON, PETER (Brattle-
    boro, Vt.)
1808:   15298 pb

HOUGHTON, THEOPHILUS
    LILLY (Goshen, N.Y.)
1818:   45402 pb

HOUGHTON, THEOPHILUS
    LILLY (Haverhill, N.H.)
1808:   14781 pb, 16180
1809:   18707-18708
1810:   19316 pb

HOUGHTON, THEOPHILUS
    LILLY (Newburgh, N.Y.)
1818:   45177 pb

HOUSE, ELEAZER G (Boston)
1807:   12214
1808:   14777, 14968, 14987,
    15103, 15381, 15473, 15971,
    16161, 16638 pb, 16692
1809:   17097, 17137 pb, 17230,
    17329, 17480, 17700, 17807,
    17883, 18330, 18634
1810:   19640, 19786, 19871?,
    19879, 20082, 20106, 20774,
    20979, 21108, 21365, 21937
1811:   22551, 22576, 22802,
    22847, 23431, 24404, 51072
1812:   25096, 25394-25395,
    25508, 25814, 26487, 26493,
    26756, 27422, 27498 pb,
    51172
1813:   28162, 28486, 28633-
    28634, 28913, 28987, 29535
1814:   30707, 30924 pb, 31048
    pb, 31078-31079, 31453,
    31525, 31571 pb, 31885,
    32825 pb, 32845, 32921,
    32966, 33523, 33624
1815:   34772 pb, 34962 pb,
    35079 pb, 35513, 36160,
    36415-36416 pb

1816: 37411-37412 pb
1817: 39999, 40635
1818: 43828, 46811
1819: 47799-47800 pb, 47809,
   48022, 48038, 48040, 48109
   pb, 48633

HOUSTON, --- (New York)
1812: 25552 f, 25967 pb

HOUSTON, --- (Trenton, N.J.)
1816: 38413 pb

HOW, JAMES C (Philadelphia)
1818: 43853 f

HOWARD, JACOB (Jones-
   borough, Tenn.)
1819: 47868 pb, 48577 pb

HOWARD, RALPH (Windsor,
   Vt.)
1812: 26655

HOWARD, W (Philadelphia)
1813: 51316

HOWE, HEZEKIAH (New Haven,
   Conn.)
1811: 22424a pb
1812: 24845 pb, 25306 f,
   25309 f, 25762 f, 26078 f,
   26737 f, 27502 f
1813: 28479 f
1814: 31171 pb, 31302 f,
   31307 pb, 31694 f, 32008 f
1815: 34542 f, 36047 f, 51485
   f
1816: 36691? f, 37152 f
1817: 40335 pb, 41933 f,
   41977 f
1818: 43066 pb
1819: 47602 pb, 47796 f,
   48845, 49286 f, 49970 f

HOWE, JOHN (Ballston Spa,
   N.Y.)
1812: 26663 pb
1813: 28855

HOWE, JOHN (Enfield, Mass.)
1819: 50103

HOWE, JOHN (Greenwich,
   Mass.)
1803: 4405 pb, ?4590?
1804: 6511, 7716
1805: 8308, 8655, 8683? pb,
   9400
1806: 10330 pb, 10518, 10597
   pb, 11139 pb, 11868
1807: 12449, 12640, 12740,
   12785 pb
1808: 14546, 15273 pb
1809: 17781 pb, 18407
1810: 19931-19933
1812: 25655 pb

HOWE, JONATHAN (Charles-
   town, Mass.)
1806: 10910
1807: 12171, 12448, 12637,
   13597
1809: 17371 pb, 18682
1810: 19405 pb
1813: 27775 pb
1814: 32975
1815: 36135
1818: 45909

HOWE, S (Enfield, Mass.)
1805: 8561

HOWE, SOLOMON (Greenwich,
   Mass.)
1807: 12516 pb

HOWLAND, BENJAMIN RUS-
   SELL (Providence, R.I.)
1814: 30942 f, 32644 pb,
   32693 f
1816: 37743 pb

HOWORTH, GEORGE (Phila-
   delphia)
1818: 44653 f
1819: 48169 pb

HOYT, WILLIAM (Concord,
   N.H.)
1806: 10195 pb
1807: 13750 pb
1808: 14343 pb

HRABOWSKI, RICHARD
   (Charleston, S.C.)
1809: 17390 f

HUBBARD, JABEZ (Durham)
1805:   8268 f

HUBBARD, JOHN F (Norwich,
    N. Y.)
1816:   38490 pb
1818:   43055
1819:   48125

HUBBARD, RUSSELL (Norwich,
    Conn.)
1808:   14311, 14881, 15719,
    16099 pb, 16105, 16262
1809:   16987-16988, 17502,
    18697
1810:   19664, 19836, 20144,
    20852, 21226, 21544, 21926
1811:   23203, 23257-23258,
    23830 pb, 23919, 23946 pb,
    24416
1812:   24707, 25845, 26054,
    26218, 26329
1813:   27786, 29268, 29867,
    29892-29893
1814:   31213, 31831, 32379,
    32675 pb, 32699, 33757 pb
1815:   33926, 34888
1816:   36773, 36812, 37314,
    37319 pb, 37903, 38386
1817:   40068, 40621, 41676
1818:   43796-43797 bf, 43998
    pb, 44612
1819:   47766 pb

HUBBARD, THOMAS (Norwich,
    Conn.)
1801:   975
1802:   2180, 2679, 3016
1803:   4014 pb, 5187
1804:   6665

HUDSON, BARZILLAI (Hart-
    ford, Conn.)
1801:   93, 151, 339, 341-343,
    345, ?346, ?348, 349,
    424?, 427, 449, 936-937,
    1209, 1270, 1372, 1440
    pb, 1621, 1630?, 1633,
    1639 pb, 1681, 50197,
    50210
1802:   1793, 1852, 2063,
    2066, 2069-2070, ?2072-
    2073, 2078, 2114, 2169,

2232, 2672, 2998, 3017,
    3070, 3124, 3513?, 3517,
    3519 pb, 3534, 3577
1803:   3776, 3815 f, 3919,
    4001, 4005-4008, 4010,
    4012, 4029, 4039, 4043,
    4124 f, 4140, 4189, 4412,
    4534, 4563-4564, 4655,
    4726 f, 4892 f, 4940, 5002,
    5033, 5120, 5558, 5559?,
    50349?, 50375
1804:   5829, 5913, 5999,
    6059, 6062-6063, 6065,
    6109, 6210, 6242-6243,
    6325, 6568, 6779-6780,
    6792-6793, 7146, 7287,
    7321, 7728, 7732
1805:   7961, 7968, 8023 pb,
    8046 pb, 8229, 8234-8240,
    8250, 8266, 8283-8284,
    8288, 8358 pb, 8361, 8635,
    8640, 8911, 9224, 9500,
    9680
1806:   9949, 10012, 10198-
    10200, 10399, 10418, 10420
    pb, 10469, 10757, 10881,
    11337 pb, 11366, 11407,
    11422, 11488, 11831 f,
    11832
1807:   12090, 12097, 12320,
    12334, 12336-12338, 12486
    pb, 12831, 12956, 13357,
    13363, 13426 pb, 13657,
    14167, 14186, 14198
1808:   14468, 14499 f, 14679,
    14764-14767, 14903 f,
    15157, 15611, 15896, 16108,
    16264, 16705
1809:   16979, 16998 pb, 17046,
    17107, 17282 pb, 17284,
    17437, 17897, 17986, 18273,
    18698, 19173, 19177 f,
    19178, 19208, 19237
1810:   19423, 19494 pb, 19513,
    19845, 20045, 20190, 20241
    pb, 20242, 20256, 20608,
    20639, 22122
1811:   22228, 22321 pb, 22352,
    22377, 22599 pb, 22604,
    22757, 22937, 23505 f,
    23975, 23996, 24405 pb
1812:   24543, 24785, 24822,
    24832, 25144-25146 pb,

25150, 25335, 25561, 25607
pb, 26215, 26431 pb, 26432,
27499-27501, 27509-27510
1813: 27864, 27885, 27911,
28211 pb, 28215, 28217 pb,
28635, 28927, 29149, 30453,
30504
1814: 30837, 30863, 30877,
30892, 31217 pb, 31220,
31381, 31775, 32632, 33627
1815: 34024 pb, 34067, 34213,
34324 pb, 34423-34424 pb,
34428, 34804, 35909 pb,
36525, 36527
1816: 36948, 37118, 37317-
37318 pb, 37323, 37445,
?37454, ?37501, 37517,
?37550, 37744 pb, 38288-
38289, ?39009, 39757 pb
1817: 39928, 39986, 40145,
40199, 40384, 40486, 40544-
40545 pb, 40553, 40885,
40993, 42110 pb, ?42850,
42855 pb
1818: 43062 pb, 43298, 43639,
43699-43700 pb, 43714-
43715, 43728, 43930, 45720
pb, 46742, 46760
1819: 46992, 47699, 47706-
47708, 47795, 47994, 50082

HUDSON, EDWARD (Philadel-
phia)
1804: 6411 pb, 6413 pb

HUDSON, ELI (New Haven,
Conn.)
1810: 20041 pb, 20120, 20584,
21526, 51027
1812: 26918
1813: 27860, 28206, 28213,
29996
1814: 31218-31219, 33745-
33746
1815: 34605, 34806, 34882,
36024
1816: 37017

HUDSON, HENRY (Philadelphia)
1815: 33879 pb, 34965?
1816: 36760 pb

HUDSON, THOMAS (Boston)
1819: 48836

HUESTIS, SAMUEL (New York)
1819: 47496 f, 48451 pb

HUGHES, JAMES (Louisville,
Ky.)
1816: 36820 pb, 37597 pb
1817: 41274, 42207 pb

HUGHES, JAMES (Port Gibson,
Miss.)
1818: 45381 pb

HUGHS, JOSEPH S (Delaware,
O.)
1818: 43836 pb

HUKILL, --- (Winchester,
Ky.)
1819: 47094

HULL, HENRY (Hudson, N.Y.)
1806: 9963 f

HULL, HENRY (Stanford,
N.Y.)
1802: 3001
1803: 4083 f, 4334 pb, 4431 f,
4562 f
1805: 8067 f, 8492 f, 8554 f

HULL, JAMES (Fredonia, N.Y.)
1818: 43197

HULL, JOHN FRANKLIN (Hud-
son, N.Y.)
1806: 9963 f

HULL, JOHN FRANKLIN (Stanford, N.Y.)
1802: 3001 f
1803: 4083 f, 4334 pb, 4431
f, 4562 f
1805: 8067 f, 8492 f, 8554 f

HULL, SAMUEL P (Geneva,
N.Y.)
1818: 43628, 44388, 45102

HUMBER, EDWARD (Perryopo-
lis, Pa.)
1817: 40533 pb

HUMPHREYS, ASHETON Y
(Philadelphia)

1810: 19372 pb, 20355 pb,
21255 pb, 21490 pb
1811: 22456 pb, 22645 pb,
22653 pb, 22918 pb, 23762,
24434 pb
1812: 24625 pb, 25386 pb,
26548, 26740 pb, 26883 pb

HUMPHREYS, DANIEL (Phila-
delphia)
1803: 4836
1805: 8033 pb, 8140
1806: 10602
1808: 14480

HUMPHREYS, JAMES (Phila-
delphia)
1801: 206, 370 pb, 584 pb,
682 pb
1802: 1720, 1726 f, 2025 pb,
2095 pb, 2118, 2297 pb,
2353 bsb, 2394 pb, 2849
pb, 2931, 3095, 3106 f,
3152 pb, 3153-3155, 3495,
3593 pb, 3594
1803: 3684 f, 3686 pb, 4284
pb, 4308 pb, 4413 pb, 4425,
4470 pb, 4671 pb, 4863 pb,
5192
1804: 6412 pb, 6561 pb, 6808
pb, 7790 pb
1805: 8069 pb, 8375 pb, 8408,
8576, 8589, 8610 pb, 8717
pb, 8766, 9438 bsb
1806: 10064 pb, 10327 pb,
10341-10342 pb, 10786 pb
1807: 12639 pb, 12689, 13275
pb, 13317, 13700
1808: 14746 pb, 14774 pb,
14811 pb, 15224 pb
1809: 17155, 17260 pb, 17709,
17774 pb, 17907 pb, 17980
pb, 18753
1810: 20172 pb, 20271 pb

HUMPHREYS, JAMES Y
(Philadelphia)
1810: 19372 pb, 20355 pb,
21255 pb, 21490 pb
1811: 22456 pb, 22645 pb,
22653 pb, 22918 pb, 23762,
24434 pb
1812: 24625 pb, 25386 pb,

26548, 26740 pb, 26883 pb
1813: 29806

HUNN, ANTHONY (Harrodsburg,
Ky.)
1816: 38358 pb

HUNT, --- (Boston)
1806: 10911 pb
1807: 12107 pb, 12668, 13108
pb, 13295, 13714

HUNT, GEORGE (Greenfield,
Mass.)
1818: 44037-44038 f, 44232 f,
44320 pb, 45316 pb
1819: 49383 f

HUNT, GILBERT J (New York)
1803: 4448 pb
1804: 6551? pb, 7792? pb
1808: 14403
1819: 48298 pb

HUNT, JOHN (Wilmington, O.)
1817: 42068 f

HUNT, JOHN (Xenia, O.)
1814: 32395 pb

HUNT, WILLIAM (Easton,
Mass.)
1802: 2061 f

HUNT, WILLIAM GIBBES (Lexington, Ky.)
1819: 47212, 50096 pb

HUNTER, JAMES A (Baltimore)
1810: 19633 pb

HUNTER, JOHN (Philadelphia)
1812: 26751 pb

HUNTER, WILLIAM (Frankfort,
Ky.)
1801: 754-757
1802: 1817 pb, 2449, 2485-
2486, 50304
1803: 4474-4476
1804: 6589-6591, 7374
1805: 8726-8729
1806: 10663, 10665 pb, 10667-

10668, 10739-10740, 11465
1807: 12043 pb, 12861 pb
1808: 15360-15361, 15364-
15365
1809: 17864-17866

HUNTINGTON, DAVID (New
York)
1813: 28854 pb, 29204 pb,
29742 f, 30595 pb, 30603 f
1814: 30642 f, 30932 pb,
31110 pb, 31170 f, 31251 f,
31254 f, 33606 f, 33760 f
1815: 33876 pb, 34181 f, 34268
f, 34306 f, 34691? f, 35030
f, 35252 f, 35679, 35807 f
1816: 37229 f, 37349 f,
38660 f, 38960 pb, 38961-
38962 f, 39010 f

HUNTINGTON, JOSEPH DEN-
NISON (Middlebury, Vt.)
1801: 928 pb, 50262 pb
1802: 1783, 2919, 3464 pb
1803: 3754 pb, 4422, 5503,
5623
1804: 6776, 7269, 7661,
7662 pb
1805: 8242, 8476, 8829,
9451, 9657 pb
1806: 9809, 10063, 10076
pb, 10139, 10197, 10445,
10862, 10868, 11764 pb,
11766 pb, 11866
1807: 12252, 12306, 12340,
12358, 12598, 13078, 13131,
14119-14120
1808: 14813, 15078, 16064,
16625, 16629 pb
1809: 17594, 18083, 18713,
19099, 19103 pb, 19107-
19108 pb
1810: 19586, 19928, 21449,
21900-21901, 21906 pb,
21996-21997, 22110 pb
1811: 23369

HUNTINGTON, JOSEPH DEN-
NISON (New London, Conn.)
1801: 811

HUNTINGTON, M (Newbern,
N.C.)
1815: 33963?

HUNTINGTON, MINOR (Mur-
freesborough, N.C.)
1812: 25685 pb
1813: 27805

HUNTINGTON, R (Windham,
Conn.)
1808: 15144 f

HURTEL, JOHN F (Philadel-
phia)
1817: 40738, 41951, 42038,
51702
1818: 44209-44210 pb, 45591
pb

HURTIN, JOHN G (Goshen,
N.Y.)
1801: 358
1805: 9065 pb

HUSS, JOHN (Marietta, Pa.)
1813: 29048 pb

HUSSEY, P (Mt. Pleasant, O.)
1818: 44658 pb

HUTCHENS, JOHN (Providence,
R.I.)
1815: 34116 pb
1816: 37024-37025, 37359
bpb, 37514, 37743 pb, 37865,
38743, 38926 pb, 39831-
39833
1817: 40009, 40340, 40725,
41026, 41677, 42277-42278
1818: 43243, 43544, 44360,
44387, 45213, 45448, 45450,
45453-45454, 45543, 45676,
45698, 46785-46786, 46871-
46872
1819: 47677 pb, 48300, 48589
pb, 49167, 49217-49218,
49405 pb, 50085 pb, 51915

HUTCHINSON, EBENEZER
(Hartford, Vt.)
1818: 44981 f
1819: 48578, 48835 f

HUTCHINSON, SYLVESTER
(Trenton, N.J.)
1815: 34180 pb
1816: 37057 f

HUTCHINSON, W (Hartford, Vt.)
1818: 44981 f

HUTTER, CHARLES LEWIS (Allentown, Pa.)
1817: 41238 pb
1819: 47923, 51918 pb

HUTTER, CHRISTIAN JACOB (Allentown, Pa.)
1810: 21545 pb

HUTTER, CHRISTIAN JACOB (Easton, Pa.)
1806: 11041 pb
1808: 14462-14463, 15891 pb
1809: 16970-16971, 17575, 19083 pb, 19198 pb
1810: 19489, 21038 pb, 21174, 21922 pb
1812: 24782 pb, 26580 pb
1813: 27856
1815: 35606
1816: 39138 pb
1817: 40718 pb
1818: 45119 pb
1819: 48949 pb, 49373

HUTTER, CHRISTIAN JACOB (Lancaster, Pa.)
1801: 985 pb, 50246 pb
1802: 2732 pb, 2877, 3007 f
1803: 4709
1806: 9942

HUTTON, J G (Washington, D.C.)
1819: 51956 pb

HYDE, HENRY (Portland, Me.)
1816: 37779 f
1818: 43384 f, 44335 f

HYDE, JONATHAN LYMAN (Portland, Me.)
1812: 24803 f, 24944 f, 26101 f
1813: 29703 f

HYDE, WILLIAM (Portland, Me.)
1816: 37779 f

1818: 43384 f, 44335 f
1819: 48133 f, 49967

Hyde, Lord & Co. (Portland, Me.)
see HYDE, JONATHAN LYMAN (Portland, Me.)
LORD, ERASTUS A (Portland, Me.)

HYER, WALTER W (New York)
1807: 12352
1809: 17310 pb

I

IDE, SIMEON (Brattleboro, Vt.)
1817: 39995 pb, 40117, 40267 pb, 40633, 40848? pb, 41019, 42010, 42042, 42313 pb

IDE, SIMEON (New Ipswich, N.H.)
1815: 34083 pb, 34140-34141, 35065, 35577-35578, 36601
1816: 37634 pb, 38564, 39814
1817: 40849 pb

IDE, SIMEON (Windsor, Vt.)
1818: 44013, 44166, 44981, 46637 pb
1819: 47896, 48471, 48835, 49524

Impartial Compiler (Shelbyville, Ky.)
1819: 48037

Impartial Observer (Richmond, Va.)
1807: 11973

Imprenta Espanola (New York)
1812: 27381

Independent Gazetteer (Lexington, Ky.)
1805: 8712

Independent Republican (Chillicothe, O.)
1810: 20946

Index (Newburgh, N. Y.)
see Political Index (Newburgh,
N. Y.)

Indiana Gazette (Corydon, Ind.)
1817: 40073

INGERSOLL, JONATHAN
(Ithaca, N. Y.)
1815: 35897 pb

Inquisitor (Cincinnati, O.)
1819: 47615

INSKEEP, ABRAHAM H (New
York)
1808: 15805 f, 16245 pb
1809: 17708 pb, 17820 pb,
18370 pb, 18448 pb, 50907
pb
1810: 19572 f, 19607 f, 20379
pb, 20404 f, 21254 pb,
21376 f
1811: 22791 f
1812: 24892 f, 25224 pb, 25317
f, 25319 pb, 25683 pb,
25726 pb, 25839 f, 25940
pb, 26042 pb, 26392 pb,
26670 f, 51197 pb
1813: 27693 f, 28157 f, 28853
pb, 28900 f, 29125 f, 29453
f, 29455 pb, 29620 pb,
29676 pb, 29681-29682 pb,
29739 f, 29752 f
1814: 30655 pb, 31592 f,
31924 f, 31945 pb, 32575
pb
1815: 35575 f

INSKEEP, JOHN (Philadelphia)
1807: 12365 pb
1808: 14793 f, 14794 pb,
15201 pb, 15806 f, 16058
pb, 16236 f, 16725 f, 16749
pb
1809: 17111 pb, 17128 pb,
17266 pb, 17677 pb, 17743
pb, 17899 pb, 17905 f,
17917 f, 18127 pb, 18138

pb, 18371 pb, 18425 f,
18448 pb, 19247 pb, 50907
pb
1810: 19382 pb, 19683 f,
19700 pb, 19701 f, 19825
pb, 19863 pb, 19884 pb,
19968 f, 20282 pb, 20379
pb, 20549 pb, 20559 f,
20561 f, 20698-20700 f,
20702 f, 20751 pb, 20759
pb, 20782 f, 20994 f, 21121
pb, 21208 f, 21232 f, 21319
pb, 21391 pb, 21946 pb
1811: 23846 f
1812: 24518 f, 24638 f, 24892
f, 24943 pb, 25224 pb,
25317 f, 25319 pb, 25530 f,
25683 pb, 25839 f, 25940
pb, 26042 pb, 26557 pb,
26670 f
1813: 28008 pb, 28157 f,
28333 f, 28853 pb, 28900 f,
29043 pb, 29450 f, 29453 f,
29455 pb, 29620 pb, 29676
pb, 29681-29682 pb, 29739 f,
29752 f, 29908 f, 29960 pb,
30527 pb
1814: 30655 pb, 31174 pb,
31267 pb, 31312 f, 31733 f,
31924 f, 31945 pb, 32575-
32576 pb
1815: 35575 f, 35674 pb

Intelligencer (Columbus, O.)
see Western Intelligencer
(Columbus, O.)

Intelligencer (Hamilton, O.)
see Miami Intelligencer (Hamilton, O.)

Intelligencer (Haverhill, Mass.)
see Merrimack Intelligencer
(Haverhill, Mass.)

Investigator (Charleston, S. C.)
1812: 25274

IREDALE, WILLIAM H (Glas-
gow, Ky.)
1814: 32444 pb

IRVINE, BAPTIS (Baltimore)
1807: 14213 pb

ISLER, PETER (Bairdstown, Ky.)
1807: 12265 pb
1809: 50975 pb

ISLER, PETER (Natchez, Miss.)
1812: 26094-26095, 26097-26098, 26099 pb
1813: 29179, 30002
1814: 30763, 32143-32145
1815: 35290
1816: 36681, 38264-38269
1817: 41455
1819: 48331 pb, 49431 pb

ISLER, PETER (Winchester, Va.)
1804: 5799, 6534 pb

ISRAEL, JOHN (Pittsburgh, Pa.)
1801: 1158, 1232
1802: 2902
1803: 4136, 4873, 50372 pb, 50385
1804: 7067-7068

ISRAEL, JOHN (Washington, Pa.)
1802: 2753, 2962

ISRAEL, JOSEPH (Marietta, O.)
1809: 17303 pb
1811: 22314
1812: 26727

ISRAEL, JOSEPH (Zanesville, O.)
1812: 27642 pb
1813: 28877
1814: 31277, 32673 pb

J

JACKSON, --- (New York)
1806: 10613 pb

JACKSON, WILLIAM (Philadelphia)
1804: 7077 pb

JAMES, ALBERT A (Glasgow, Ky.)
1819: 48419 pb

JAMES, JOSEPH (Baltimore)
1809: 18363 f
1810: 19794 f, 21291 pb
1819: 49375 pb

JANNEY, GEORGE F (Baltimore)
1816: 37666 f
1818: 43150 pb

JANSEN, --- (New York)
1819: 48190

JANSEN, BENJAMIN G (New York)
1817: 41612
1818: 43500, 44594

JANSEN, GEORGE (New York)
1801: 723 pb
1804: 50463 f
1805: 50574 pb
1806: 10296 pb
1807: 13433 pb
1808: 15438 pb

JANSEN, LEWIS B (New York)
1809: 17756

JANSEN, THOMAS B (New York)
1801: 709 f, 723 pb
1802: 1757 f, 2039 f, 2146 f, 2405, 2515 pb, 2664 pb, 3010 pb
1803: 3798 pb, 4085 pb, 4197 f, 4951 pb, 5079 pb, 5163 f, 5508 pb
1804: 7791 pb, 50446 f
1805: 8824 pb, 8970 f, 9475 pb, 9495 f, 50491 f, 50498 f
1806: 10538 pb, 50656 f
1808: 15438 pb
1809: 17756
1814: 51355 pb, 51374 pb
1817: 41612 f

JEFFERIS, SAMUEL (Baltimore)
1807: 13113 f

1809: 18125 pb, 18773 f
1810: 21938 pb
1811: 22452a f
1812: 25676 pb, 26495 f, 26911 pb
1813: 28054 pb, 30441 f
1814: 30844 f
1819: 50032 pb

JENKINSON, JOHN (Cincinnati, O.)
1815: 35061 f

JENKS, ELEZER ALLEY (Portland, Me.)
1801: 114, 287 f, 445, 673, 738, 932, 1446, 1654
1802: 1762 f, 2469 pb, 2645, 2833 pb
1803: 4370, 4895 pb, 5535, 5584
1804: 6475, 6496 pb, 6666, 6701, 6781, 7093, 7396
1805: 8543, 9506

JENKS, WILLIAM (Portland, Me.)
1803: 4579
1805: 7924, 8079 pb, 9182 pb, 9719, 9733
1806: 10349 pb, 10501

JEWETT, JOSEPH (Baltimore)
1816: 38774? f
1817: 40304, 41865 f, 42830 pb, 42980 f
1818: 43433 f, 43612 pb, 43993 pb, 44194 pb, 44853 f, 44856 pb, 44983 pb, 45883 pb
1819: 47016 f, 47917 f, 47943 pb, 48366 f, 49260 f, 49619 pb, 51899 f, 51955 pb

JOCELYN, NATHANIEL (New Haven, Conn.)
1816: 37436 f
1819: 47348-47349 pb, 47983 pb, 50001 f

JOCELYN, SIMEON (New Haven, Conn.)
1804: 6820 f

JOCELYN, SIMEON SMITH (New Haven, Conn.)
1819: 47348-47349 pb, 47983 pb, 50001 f

JOHNS, THOMAS (Chambersburg, Pa.)
1812: 25381 f

JOHNSON, --- (New Orleans, La.)
1808: 15392 pb

JOHNSON, BENJAMIN (Philadelphia)
1801: 745 pb, 747 pb, 748, 761, 768, 817, 971, 972 pb, 973, 1178, 1408 f, 1435, 1659
1802: 1883 pb, 2099 pb, 2126 pb, 2211 pb, 2372 pb, 2410 pb, 2476 pb, 2650 pb, 2678 f, 2710 pb, 2922 f, 3012, 3105 pb, 3185 f, 3554
1803: 4070 pb, 4455 pb, 4460 pb, 4461 f, 4694 pb, 4703 pb, 50376 f
1804: 5661 pb, 5663 pb, 5670-5671 bpb, 5690 f, 5723 bpb, 5850 f, 5856 f, 5960 bpb, 6278 pb, 6395 pb, 6410 bpb, 6420 bpb, 6439 pb, 6565 f, 6782-6784 f, 6848-6849 pb, 7028-7029, 7054 pb, 7089 pb, 7090 f, 7091 bf, 7346 f, 7712-7713 pb, 50431 f, 50465 f
1805: 7833 pb, 7979 pb, 8018 pb, 8211 pb, 8262-8263 pb, 8596 bf, 8706 pb, 8944 pb, 9020 f, 9783 pb, 9784 bf
1806: 9870 f, 9917, 10085 pb, 10134 pb, 10220-10221 bf, 10263 pb, 10537, 10637 f, 10646 pb, 10929 pb, 11022 f, 11052 pb, 11103 pb, 11418 pb, 11899 pb, 50689 pb
1807: 12792?, 12842 pb, 12939, 12975 f, 13121-13127, 13129 pb, 13165 pb, 13318 pb, 13674 f, 13744 f, 14169 pb, 50784 pb

1808: 15033 f, 15664 f,
15681 pb, 15970 pb
1809: 17244 pb, 17305, 17701
pb, 17846, 18142 pb, 18150
f, 18324 pb, 18605 pb,
50946 pb
1810: 19466 f
1812: 25756 pb, 25873 pb,
26132 pb, 26173 pb, 26451
f, 26733 pb
1813: 27669 pb, 27917 pb,
27956 pb, 28245-28246 pb,
28290 pb, 28646 f, 28753
pb, 28845 pb, 28878 pb,
29208-29209 pb, 29217-
29218 pb, 29465 pb
1814: 31640 pb, 32163 pb
1815: 34474 f, 35376 pb
1816: 37352 f
1817: 40192 f, 41218 pb,
41288 f, 41480 pb
1818: 44254 pb, 44636 f,
44898 f, 44900 f, 44901 pb,
44902 f, 44903 pb, 44907
pb, 45712 pb
1819: 47446 f, 47793 pb,
48759-48760 f, 49587 f,
50010 f

JOHNSON, DANIEL (Portland,
Me.)
1804: 6185 f
1805: 8837 f, 8897 f, 9269 f,
?9645 pb
1806: 10065 f, 10114 f,
11167 f
1807: 11980 f, 12298 pb,
13009 f, 13053 f

JOHNSON, ENOCH (New York)
1818: 44132 pb

JOHNSON, ENOCH (Philadelphia)
1814: 30985 pb
1815: 34203 pb

JOHNSON, JACOB (Lexington,
Ky.)
1810: 20464 pb, 20492 pb

JOHNSON, JACOB (Philadelphia)
1801: 745 pb, 747 pb, 748,
761, 768, 817, 971, 972 pb,
973, 1178, 1408 f, 1435,
1659
1802: 1726 f, 1924 pb, 2211
pb, 2227 pb, 2399 pb, 2406
f, 2410 pb, 2476 pb, 2537
pb, 2650 pb, 2678 f, 2710
pb, 2878 f, 2922 f, 2930 pb,
3105 pb, 3185 f, 3556 pb,
3605 pb
1803: 4050 pb, 4073 f, 4129
f, 4165 f, 4213 pb, 4374 f,
4460 pb, 4461 f, 4462 pb,
4518 pb, 4679 f, 4688 f,
4703 pb, 4870 f, 4922 f,
4987 pb, 5146 pb, 5160 pb,
50350 pb, 50369 pb, 50376
f, 50392 pb
1804: 5670-5671 pb, 5723 pb,
5808 pb, 5809 f, 5854 pb,
5891 pb, 6120 pb, 6165 f,
6218 pb, 6219-6220 f, 6278
pb, 6288 f, 6316 pb, 6401
f, 6410 pb, 6420 pb, 6659
pb, 6782-6784 f, 6849 pb,
6989, 7028-7029, 7089 pb,
7090-7091 f, 7113 pb, 7203
pb, 7330 pb, 7382 f, 7387-
7388 pb, 7683 pb, 7730 pb,
50417 f, 50421 pb, 50426 pb,
50431 f, 50465 f, 50484 pb
1805: 7833 pb, 8262-8263 pb,
8298-8300 pb, 8372-8373 pb,
8397 pb, 8596 f, 8705-8706
pb, 8808 f, 8944 pb, 9325
f, 9385 pb, 9480 pb, 9679 f,
9707 pb, 9732 pb, 9783 pb,
9784 f
1806: 10007 pb, 10038 pb,
10220-10221 f, 10247 pb,
10474 f, 10505 pb, 10607
pb, 10629 f, 10647 pb, 10742
pb, 10929 pb, 11132 pb,
11302 pb, 11392 pb, 11480
pb, 11823 f, 50651 f, 50689
pb
1807: 12127 pb, 12173 f,
12196 pb, 12361 f, 12453
pb, 12505 pb, 12759 pb,
13163 f, 13354 pb, 13383
pb, 13407 pb, 13427 pb,
13340 f, 13504 pb, 13561 f,
13685 pb, 14170 pb, 50784
pb

1808: 14362 pb, 14482 f,
14502 f, 14532 f, 14571 pb,
14686 pb, 14712 pb, 14828
pb, 14845 f, 14915 f, 14918
f, 15009 pb, 15033 f, 15041
pb, 15130 pb, 15133 f, 15177
f, 15291 f, 15305-15306 f,
15312 pb, 15332 pb, 15343
pb, 15353 pb, 15424 f,
15439, 15440 pb, 15614 f,
15798 pb, 15811 pb, 15823
f, 15852 pb, 15987 f, 15991
f, 16121 f, 16153-16154 pb,
16194 f, 16279 f, 16281 pb,
16292 f, 16312 f, 16656
pb, 50860 pb
1809: 16832 pb, 17000 pb,
17204 f, 17274 pb, 17313 f,
17348 f, 17399 pb, 17424 f,
17531 f, 17532 pb, 17533 f,
17638 f, 17679 f, 17691 f,
17720 pb, 17734, 17832 pb,
17843 pb, 17845 pb, 17875
pb, 17918 f, 18137 pb,
18150 f, 18156 pb, 18182
pb, 18284 f, 18327 f,
18392-18393 f, 18542 pb,
18550 f, 18649 f, 18733 f,
18794 f, 19127 pb, 19174
pb, 50905 pb, 50925 pb
1810: 19318 f, 19342 pb, 19521
pb, 19551 f, 19581? pb,
19736 f, 19861 pb, 19892 f,
19894 pb, 19912 f, 19984 f,
19992 f, 19995 pb, 20031 f,
20192 f, 20212 f, 20229 pb,
20233 f, 20463 pb, 20494 f,
20586 f, 20605 f, 20807 pb,
20815-20816 pb, 20820 pb,
20949 f, 21071 f, 21072 pb,
21073-21076 f, 21078 f,
21080 pb, 21163 f, 21184
f, 21395 pb, 21513 pb,
21542 f, 21546? pb, 21887?
pb, 21912 f, 21982 pb,
22069 f, 22082 pb, 22129
pb, 22130? pb, 50990 f
1811: 22221 f, 22427 f,
22522 pb, 22594 f, 22717 f,
22744 pb, 22782 pb, 22799
pb, 22849 f, 22909 pb,
22921 f, 23012 f, 23094
pb, 23108 f, 23121 f, 23124

pb, 23198 f, 23226 pb,
23229 f, 23392 f, 23422 f,
23434-23435 f, 23456 pb,
23461 f, 23643 pb, 23677 f,
23682 f, 23693 f, 23694 pb,
23868 f, 23873 pb, 23934 f,
23939 f, 23956 f, 23992 f,
24033 pb, 24353 pb, 24364
pb, 24394 pb, 24428 f
1812: 24576 f, 24852 f, 24883
pb, 24939 pb, 25106 pb,
25216-25217 pb, 25416 pb,
25419 f, 25450 f, 25600 pb,
25755 pb, 26083 pb, 26177
pb, 26179 pb, 26458 pb,
26635-26636 f, 26639 f,
27413 pb
1813: 27683 f, 27897 pb,
28041 f, 28245-28246 pb,
28282 f, 28337 f, 28462 pb,
28548 f, 28583 f, 28842 pb,
28845a pb, 29254 f, 29255
pb, 29324 f, 29436 f, 29509
f, 29518-29519 pb, 29576 f,
29819 pb, 30437 f, 30505 f
1814: 31276 f, 31566 pb,
31818 f, 31827 f, 31829 pb,
32222 f, 32227 pb, 32399 f,
32419 f, 32490 f, 32906 pb,
33546 f, 33560 pb, 51402 f
1815: 34117 f, 34190 pb,
34506 pb, 34534, 34833-34834
pb, 35006 pb, 35622 f,
35631 f, 35643 f, 35817 f,
35821 f, 35868 pb, 35967 f,
36468 pb, 51484 f, 51505 f
1816: 37338 pb, 37399 pb,
38603 pb, 38622 pb, 39758
pb, 39893 pb

JOHNSON, JACOB (Richmond,
Va.)
1805: 50625 pb
1806: 50651 f, 50689 pb
1807: 12173 f, 50785-50786 pb
1808: 50861 pb
1809: 50945 pb
1810: 20320 pb, 51016 pb
1811: 51109 pb
1812: 51168 pb, 51212 pb
1813: 51312 pb, 51345 pb
1815: 51506 pb

JOHNSON, JOHN (Hallowell,
Me.)
1807: 13009 f

JOHNSON, JOHN B (Cazenovia,
N. Y.)
1819: 47117

JOHNSON, JOHN BURGESS
(Hamilton, N. Y.)
1817: 41017, 41173 bpb,
41328 pb, 41471

JOHNSON, JOHN BURGESS
(Morris Flats, N. Y.)
1818: 44278 pb, 44886? pb,
46775? pb, 51739
1819: 49222

JOHNSON, JOHN BURGESS
(Morrisville, N. Y.)
1818: 44669 pb

JOHNSON, JOHN BURGESS
(Norwich, N. Y.)
1810: 22028
1815: 33956

JOHNSON, JOHN BURGESS
(Oxford, N. Y.)
1809: 17194 pb
1812: 25708

JOHNSON, JOSEPH (Portland,
Me.)
1812: 26567 f

JOHNSON, PAUL R (New York)
1801: 327, 456, 610 pb,
1329, 1409
1802: 2525 pb, 2967 pb
1808: 15189 pb

JOHNSON, PETER A (Morris-
town, N. J.)
1810: 19973 f, 20300 f
1811: 23411 pb, 23413 f
1812: 24841 f
1813: 27958 pb, 29028 f
1814: 30931 pb, 31549 f,
31690 f, 31987 f
1815: 33882 f, 34582 f,
35173 pb, 35700 f

1817: 41464 f
1818: 43459 pb, 44301 f

JOHNSON, RICHARD (Philadelphia)
1816: 38612 pb

JOHNSON, ROBERT (Philadelphia)
1801: 691
1802: 2540 pb, 2678
1803: 4024-4025 f, 4291 f,
4461 f
1804: 5670-5671 pb, 5723 pb,
5960 pb, 6410 pb, 6420 pb,
6784 f, 7089 pb, 7090-7091
f, 50431 f, 50465 f
1805: 7832-7833 pb, 8107 f,
8262-8263 pb, 8596 f, 8607
pb, 8706 pb, 8808 f, 9278,
9783 pb, 9784 f
1806: 10003 pb, 10220-10221 f,
10262 pb, 10302-10303 pb,
10481 pb, 11299 pb, 11906
pb, 50689 pb
1807: 50784 pb
1809: 16845-16846 pb
1811: 23921 f

JOHNSON, ROBERT (Worcester,
Mass.)
1801: 981 pb

JOHNSON, WILLIAM H (New
Orleans, La.)
1808: 15619 pb

Johnson & Warner (Lexington,
Ky.) (Philadelphia) (Richmond, Va.)
see JOHNSON, JACOB
‾‾‾‾WARNER, BENJAMIN

JOHNSTON, --- (Philadelphia)
1812: 24926-24927 pb
1813: 28013 pb, 29667 pb

JOHNSTON, P W (Camden,
S. C.)
1816: 37154

JOHNSTON, P W (Charleston,
S. C.)
1815: 34057

JOHNSTON, RICHARD (New York)
1810: 50979 f
1812: 26934 pb
1814: 32994 pb

JOHNSTON, ROBERT (Frankfort, Ky.)
1810: 20490
1811: 22465
1814: 31291
1815: 35051-35052, 36337
1816: 37993

JOHNSTON, SAMUEL REED (Pittsburgh, Pa.)
1818: 43367 pb, 43679, 44074 pb, 44933 pb, 44951 pb, 51774 pb
1819: 47578 pb, 48007 pb, 48786, 49559, 51879 pb, 51892 pb

JOLINE, JOHN K (Freehold, N.J.)
1814: 32834 pb

JOLINE, JOHN K (Mount Holly, N.J.)
1815: 35990 pb

JONES, --- (Philadelphia)
1802: 1944? pb
1810: 21059, 21321
1819: 49364 f

JONES, CALVIN (Raleigh, N.C.)
1808: 16249 pb

JONES, E (Baltimore)
1814: 31128 pb

JONES, HANNUM (Freehold, N.J.)
1819: 48724 pb

JONES, HANNUM (Paterson, N.J.)
1817: 40186 pb

JONES, HORATIO (Stockbridge, Mass.)
1801: 743, 1172

JONES, JOSEPH (Wilmington, Del.)
1804: 6850 pb
1805: 8893 pb, 8930, 8932, 9210-9211
1806: 10437 pb, 10508, 10640, 11173
1807: 12161, 12866
1808: 14879
1809: 17370 pb, 50936

JONES, JOSIAH (Providence, R.I.)
1807: 13534
1808: 14742 pb, 15062, 15861, 16066-16067, 16070-16071
1809: 17800, 18504-18508 pb
1810: 19655 pb, 20396, 21093, 21210-21214, 22031
1811: 22824, 23698, 23813-23815
1812: 24734, 24954 pb, 25432, 26611, 27586
1814: 32588, 32589 pb, 32693, 32866
1817: 39962
1818: 43912-43913, 45688
1819: 47581, 47873 pb

JONES, LOUIS (New York)
1803: 4750

JONES, MERIWETHER (Norfolk, Va.)
1802: 2058 f

JONES, MERIWETHER (Richmond, Va.)
1801: 123, 271 sb, 1584-1585
1802: 3470-3471, ?3473?, 3474, 5511, 5513
1804: 7667 f, 7668, 7670, 7672

JONES, MITHRA (Philadelphia)
1808: 15180 pb, 15220 pb, 16087 pb
1809: 18221 pb, 19189 pb

JONES, WALTER (Milledgeville, Ga.)
1816: 38253 pb
1819: 48075 pb

Jones & Wheeler (Providence,
R. I.)
see JONES, JOSIAH (Provi-
dence, R. I.)
WHEELER, BENNETT H
(Providence, R. I.)

JORDAN, AUGUSTUS C (Nor-
folk, Va.)
1801: 130, 1325
1802: 3472
1803: 3668-3670
1804: 5990, 6295, 50448 pb
1805: 7950, 50557 pb
1806: 10859, 11032 pb, 11887
1807: 50787 pb
1808: 14465, 15117

Journal (Ballston Spa, N. Y.)
see Saratoga Journal (Ballston Spa, N. Y.)

Journal (New Haven, Conn.)
see Connecticut Journal (New
Haven, Conn.)

Journal (Windsor, Vt.)
see Vermont Journal (Windsor, Vt.)

JOYNER, NATHANIEL (Pough-
keepsie, N. Y.)
1801: 595 pb

JUDAH, NAPHTALI (New York)
1802: 3514 f, 3581 pb
1803: 4389 f

JUNGMANN, GOTTLOB (Read-
ing, Pa.)
1801: 989
1802: 2736
1803: 3786 pb, 4714
1804: 6858
1805: 7983, 8968 pb
1806: 9873, 10951
1807: 13180 pb, 50791 pb
1808: 16038?
1816: 38999

JUNGMANN, JOHN E (Read-
ing, Pa.)
1816: 38999

JUNGMANN, JOHN G (Reading,
Pa.)
1814: 32131-32132

JUNGMANN, JOHN G (Sunbury,
Pa.)
1812: 26326 pb
1818: 44488 pb, 45111 pb

JUSTICE, JOSEPH (Elizabeth,
N. J.)
1819: 48538

JUSTICE, JOSEPH (Trenton,
N. J.)
1817: 41590-41592
1818: 45005-45007
1819: 48865-48868

JUSTICE, JOSEPH P (Phila-
delphia)
1816: 38561, 39671 pb
1817: 42792 pb
1818: 45464, 46621 pb

Juvenile Library (New York)
1819: 47368 pb

K

KAMMERER, JOSEPH R (Philadelphia)
1805: 8124, 8306, 8409
1807: 11961 pb, 12083, 12091,
12257-12258, 12272 pb,
12384, 12688, 12690, 12742,
12757, 12819, 13325, 13567,
13578, 13660, 13706, 14090
1808: 14253, 14591, 14816,
15015, 15038, 15153, 15266,
15333, 15670, 15834, 16050,
16080, 16096, 16100, 16113,
16124 pb, 16158, 16206,
16246, 16658, 16689
1809: 16784, 16963, 16966,
17026, 17028, 17043, 17101,
17228, 17346, 17462, 17470,
17632, 17775-17776, 18368,
18380, 18434, 18483, 18559,
18581, 19211

1810: 19296, 19363, 19478, 19543-19544, 19688, 19697, 19701, 19711-19712, 19715, 19718-19719, 19883, 20024, 20088, 20130, 20393, 20443, 20456, 20503, 20615, 20647, 20796, 20943, 21032, 21145, 21301, 21334, 21865, 22117
1811: 22137-22138, 22196, 22386, 22506, 22548, 22632, 22711, 22828, 22995, 23044, 23130, 23177, 23614, 23650, 23846, 23984, 23997, 24337, 24474-24475
1812: 24520, 24864, 24877, 25777, 25839, 26345, 26528, 26704, 26767, 27383-27384, 27545, 27566, 27574

KAPPEL, MICHAEL J (Catskill, N.Y.)
1813: 28092 pb
1814: 31403 pb, 31754

KAPPEL, MICHAEL J (Savannah, Ga.)
1817: 40072, 42056 pb

KAY, ROBERT (Lexington, Ky.)
1803: 3728 pb

KEAN, JOHN E (Augusta, Ga.)
1818: 51777 pb

KEATINGE, G S (Frederick, Md.)
1814: 32214

KEATINGE, GEORGE (Baltimore)
1801: 407 pb, 712 pb, 733 pb, 746 pb, 852 pb, ?1388 pb, 1607 pb
1802: 2479-2480 pb
1803: 3983 f, 4469 f
1804: 6047 f, 6585 f, 7083 pb, 7385 pb, 7743 f, 50449 pb
1805: 8173 pb, 8175 pb, 8718 pb, 8840 pb
1806: 10459 pb, 10657-10658 pb, 10799 pb, 11411 pb, 50699 pb

1807: 12853 pb, 13288 pb, 13735 pb
1808: 14926 pb, 15499 f, ?15501 pb, 15848, 16090 pb

KEATINGE, GEORGE (Westminster, Md.)
1817: 42880 pb

KEATINGE, HENRY SEMPLE (Baltimore)
1803: 3791 pb
1806: 10656
1807: 12898 pb, 13191 pb
1808: 15257 pb, 15347
1809: 17501, 18006
1810: 19910

KEELER, DAVID (Louisville, Ky.)
1815: 34416 f

KEEMLE, CHARLES (Norfolk, Va.)
1816: 37952

KEEMLE, CHARLES (Vincennes, Ind.)
1817: 41138 pb

KEEN, WILLIAM C (Hamilton, O.)
1814: 31849 pb, 32119 pb, 32391
1815: 35271

KEEN, WILLIAM C (Vevay, Ind.)
1816: 37928 pb, 39069

KEENON, JOHN G (Cynthiana, Ky.)
1817: 40965 pb

KELLEY, --- (New York)
1818: 43047, 43400, 44121, 46888

KELLEY, --- (Philadelphia)
1805: 9476 pb

KELLEY, JOHN C (Somerville, N.J.)
1815: 35452 pb

KELLEY, SAMUEL (Philadelphia)
1805: 50594
1806: 50711

KELLOGG, LEONARD (Auburn, N. Y.)
1815: 34233

KELLOGG, LEONARD (Manlius, N. Y.)
1808: 15215a pb
1809: 17977 pb
1816: 37913, 38022, 38773, 39868
1817: 40976, 41209

KENDALL, AMOS (Frankfort, Ky.)
1816: 37395 pb
1817: 41188-41191, 42131
1818: 43895, 44084, 44506, 44508-44509
1819: 47982 pb, 48413, 48415-48416, 49631

KENDALL, CHARLES (Windsor, Vt.)
1813: 28515

KENDALL, JESSE (Lancaster, Pa.)
1811: 23660
1813: 29044

KENDALL, JOHN (Xenia, O.)
1818: 45476 pb

KENNARD, TIMOTHY (Boston)
1809: 18286 pb
1810: 20734

KENNEDY, ANDREW (Northumberland, Pa.)
1802: 2932-2933
1803: 4912-4913, 4915-4918
1804: 6014 pb, 7121
1805: 8659
1818: 45280 pb

KENNEDY, ANDREW (Rockville, Md.)
1819: 49313 pb

KENNEDY, JAMES (Alexandria, Va.)
1814: 32196 f, 33612 pb
1817: 40337 pb

KENNEDY, JAMES (Baltimore)
1812: 25621
1817: 40054, 40961, 41795
1818: 43124 pb, 43650, 44208, 45447

KENSETT, THOMAS (Cheshire, Conn.)
1814: 32710 f

KENSETT, THOMAS (New Haven, Conn.)
1814: 30952 pb
1816: 38141 pb

KENSETT, THOMAS (Newburgh, N. Y.)
1817: 41629 pb

Kentucky Advertiser (Winchester, Ky.)
1819: 47094

Kentucky Auxiliary Bible Society (Lexington, Ky.)
1819: 47212 f

Kentucky Gazette (Lexington, Ky.)
1804: 6592 sb
1809: 50952
1810: 19426
1812: 25461
1814: 31518
1815: 34733
1816: 37994
1817: 41194
1818: 45473

Kentucky Reporter (Lexington, Ky.)
1818: 46877
1819: 48418

Kentucky Tract Society (Paris, Ky.)
1816: 37996 pb, 38056 f

KER, SAMUEL (Savannah, Ga.)
1817: 41490 pb

KESSLER, CARL AUGUST (Reading, Pa.)
1807: 13335 pb, 13465

KID, ROBERT (Baltimore)
1808: 14630 f, 16059 pb, 16238 f, 16272 pb

Kid & Thomas (Baltimore)
see KID, ROBERT (Baltimore)
    THOMAS, MOSES (Baltimore)

KILBOURN, JOHN (Columbus, O.)
1815: 34404 pb
1816: 38004 f
1817: 41201 f
1818: 44515 pb
1819: 48423 f

KIMBER, EMMOR (Philadelphia)
1803: 3997 pb
1804: 6030, 6291 pb, 6292, 6431, 6433 pb, 6594 f, 6603 pb
1805: 7850, 7861, 7951 pb, 8196, 8223 pb, 8486, 8487 pb, 8737-8738 pb, 9096, 9138, 9157, 9335 bsb, 9503 f, 9755 pb, 50537 pb, 50538
1806: 9815, 9834, 9869 pb, 10151-10152, 10233 pb, 10456-10457, 10483 pb, 10678? pb, 10942, 11101, 11104, 11136, 11163 pb, 11288 pb, 11377 pb, 11460 pb, 11811 pb, 50678, 50719 f
1807: 11951 f, 12113 pb, 12127 pb, 12324, 12494 pb, 12495, 12632, 12659 pb, 12823 pb, 12870, 13128 pb, 13328 pb, 13384-13385 pb, 13417 pb, 13554-13555, 13635, 13641
1808: 14259 f, 14307 pb, 14665 pb, 14747 pb, 15072 f, 15075 pb, 15122 pb, 15374 pb, 15947 pb, 15974 pb, 16145 f, 16723 pb
1809: 16788 pb, 16995 f, 17001 pb, 17431 pb, 17619 f, 18383 f, 18616 f, 18622 pb, 19235 f
1810: 19293 pb, 19326 f, 19509 pb, 19822 pb, 19862 pb, 20169 pb, 20497? pb, 21090 pb, 21348 f, 21965 f
1811: 22221 f, 22426 pb, 22547 f, 22588 pb, 22683 f, 22687 pb, 22712 pb, 23683 f, 23684 pb, 23690 f, 23881 f, 24348 f, 24352 f, 24356 pb
1812: 24576 f, 24896 pb, 25127 pb, 25789 f, 25790 pb, 26397 pb, 26465? f, 27405 f
1813: 28351 f, 30482 f
1814: 30616 f, 30728 f, 30847 f, 32484 pb, 32733 pb
1815: 34410 f, 34505 pb, 34952 pb, 35054-35055 f, 35820 f, 35952 f, 36133 f, 51495 f
1816: ?38370
1819: 48427? pb

KIMBER, THOMAS (Philadelphia)
1811: 23356 f
1812: 25791 pb, 26668-26669 f
1813: 30580 f
1814: 31624 pb, 31625 f, 32084 f, 32495 pb, 51431 pb
1815: 35953 pb
1816: 37308 pb, 37366 pb, 37769 pb, 37999, 38628 f, 38925 pb, 39866 pb, 51600 pb
1817: 40017 pb, 40650 f, 41278 f
1818: 43409 f, 43682 pb, 46743? pb
1819: 47680 f, 48426 f

Kimber & Conrad (Philadelphia)
see KIMBER, EMMOR (Philadelphia)
    CONRAD, SOLOMON W (Philadelphia)

Kimber & Richardson (Philadelphia)
see KIMBER, THOMAS
‾‾(Philadelphia)
RICHARDSON, JOHN (Philadelphia)

Kimber & Sharpless (Philadelphia)
see KIMBER, THOMAS
‾‾(Philadelphia)
SHARPLESS, BLAKEY
(Philadelphia)

KIMMEL, ALLEN W (Shawneetown, Ill.)
1818:   44421 pb
1819:   48324 pb

KING, CHARLES (New York)
1819:   46970 pb

KING, JOSIAH (Burlington, Vt.)
1805:   7945, 8087

KINGSLAND, JOSEPH (New York)
1816:   37033, 37799
1817:   40318 pb, 40407, 40676,
    40818, 41327, 41495, 41891,
    42197, 42881-42885
1818:   43512, 43516, 43651-
    43652, 43654, 43867? pb,
    44168, 44579, 44880, 45182,
    45231, 45319, 45421, 45573,
    45575, 45635, 45654-45657,
    45663, 45683, 45787, 45860,
    46648
1819:   46929, 47449-47450,
    47651-47652, 48137, 48738,
    48891 pb, 49315, 49380,
    49449, 49589

KINGSLEY, ELIJAH (Stockbridge, Mass.)
1810:   19665 pb
1812:   26382 f, 26720 f
1813:   29214 pb
1814:   31668 f, 31824 f, 32748
    f, 33661 f

KINGSTON, JOHN (Baltimore)
1808:   14290 f, 14306 f,

14714 f, 14977 f, 15021 f,
    16273 f, 16707-16711 f
1809:   17872 f
1810:   19639 f, 19905 f, 20075
    f, 20499 f, 20833 f, 20996 f
1811:   22829 f, 22917 f, 23161-
    23163 f, 23828 pb, 23833 f,
    23866 f
1812:   25218 f, 26129 f, 26386
    f
1813:   28119 f, 28410 f, 28803
    pb, 28881 f, 29589 f
1814:   31488 pb, 32668 pb
1816:   38012 f
1817:   41205 pb
1819:   47846 f

KINNERSLEY, T (New York)
1813:   27888? pb
1818:   45426? pb
1819:   48543 pb

KIPP, JOHN C (Ogdensburg,
    N. Y.)
1810:   20944 pb
1811:   23587 pb

KIPP, L (Ogdensburg, N. Y.)
1811:   23587 pb

KIRK, THOMAS (Brooklyn,
    N. Y.)
1801:   184, 627, 1196, 50221
    pb
1802:   2184, 3516
1803:   4620-4621, 5159, 5603
1805:   7998-7999, 8088 pb,
    8387
1806:   10720
1807:   12119, 12132, 12160 pb,
    12162 pb, 12219, 12437 pb,
    13192, 13519, 14172
1808:   14869 pb, 15674, 16089,
    16141 pb, 50903
1809:   17236-17237, 17730,
    17930 pb, 18731
1810:   20254, 20312, 21859
1811:   22375, 22698 pb, 22701
    pb, 22723, 22967, 23096,
    23238, 23506, 24391
1812:   24814, 24885, 24945-
    24950, 25163, 26760, 26851
    pb
1813:   28138 pb

KIRK, THOMAS (New York)
1803: 3887
1804: 6307-6308, 6773-6774,
      7056, 7789
1805: 8089, 8330, 8333 pb,
      8584 pb, 9286 pb
1806: 10383, 11303
1807: 12534, 12664, 12709,
      13512-13513, 13543
1808: 14678
1809: 17880
1812: 25353 pb, 25754 pb,
      27406
1813: 28046 pb, 28047 f,
      28127 pb, 28230 pb, 28408
      f, 28442 f, 28609 pb, 28655-
      28656 f, 28660 pb, 29008-
      29009 f, 29163 f, 29184 f,
      29205 f, 29212 f, 29219 f,
      29487 f, 29671-29672 f,
      29696 pb, 29777 pb, 29785
      pb, 29786-29787 f, 29790
      pb, 29833 f, 30497 f
1814: 30702 pb, 30878 pb,
      30916 pb, 30993 pb, 30994
      f, 31052 f, 31056 pb, 31135
      pb, 31338 pb, 31391 pb,
      31408 f, 31445 f, 31547 f,
      31569 f, 31587 pb, 31632-
      31633 pb, 31642 pb, 31665
      pb, 31737 f, 31926 f,
      31995 f, 32156 f, 32628 pb,
      32725 pb, 32765-32766 f,
      32827 pb, 32839 pb, 32869
      pb, 32966 f
1815: 34120 pb, 34357 f,
      34397-34399 pb, 34488 f,
      34539 pb, 35010-35011 pb,
      35168-35169 f, 35317 pb,
      35819 f, 35873 f
1816: 37135? pb, 37497 f,
      37879 f, 38832 f
1817: 40184 f, 40364 pb,
      40372 f, 40431 pb, 40433 f,
      40434 pb, 40435 f, 40436-
      40437 pb, 40508 pb, 40512
      f, 40513 pb, 40616 pb,
      40729 pb, 40901 f, 40945
      f, 41103-41104 pb, 41210
      pb, 41465 f, 41473 pb,
      41796-41797 f, 42052 pb,
      42059 f, 42929 pb
1818: 43452 f, 43466 pb,

43513 pb, 43514, 43563 pb,
      43566-43567 f, 43793 pb,
      43809 pb, 43846 f, 43921 f,
      44518 f, 44765 f, 44892-
      44893 pb, 45130 f, 45227 f,
      45466 f, 45660 f, 45845 pb,
      51833 pb
1819: 46919 f, 47052 f, 47539
      f, 47786 pb, 47939 pb,
      48103-48105 f, 48430 pb,
      48725 f, 48741 f, 48941 pb,
      49612 pb

Kirk and Mercein (New York)
see KIRK, THOMAS (New
    York)
    MERCEIN, THOMAS R (New
    York)

KITE, BENJAMIN (Philadelphia)
1807: 11988 pb, 12001 f,
      12257 f, 12283 pb, 12360,
      12443 f, 12680 f, 12757 f,
      12826 f, 13132 pb, 13460 f,
      13607 f, 50774 pb, 50784 pb
1808: 14286 pb, 14530 pb,
      14612 pb, 14811 pb, 14873-
      14874 pb, 15038 f, 15100
      pb, 15135 pb, 15221 f,
      15331 f, 15670 f, 16053 f,
      16106-16107 pb, 16689 f,
      16773 pb
1809: 16788 pb, 17177 f,
      17316 f, 17742 pb, 18094 f,
      18714 pb
1810: 19731 f, 19783 pb,
      19857 f, 19991 f, 20116 f,
      20383 pb, 20502 f, 21062
      pb, 21083 f, 21178 f, 21240
      pb, 21424 f, 21538 f, 50992
      pb
1811: 22487 f, 23002 pb,
      23164 pb, 23363 f, 23423 pb,
      23676 sb, 23920 pb, 24065
      pb, 24357 pb, 24407 f,
      24480 f
1812: 25797 pb, 26833 pb,
      27370 f
1813: 27916 pb, 28036 pb,
      28048 pb, 28787 f, 28818
      pb, 28886 pb
1814: 31873 pb, 31874 f,
      32481 pb, 32727 f, 33518 f

1815: 33819 pb, 34016 f, 35146 pb, 36045 f, 51508 f
1816: 36876 pb, 37233 pb, 37338 pb, 37773 pb, 37885 pb, 38019 f, 38849 f, 39129 pb, 39763 f, 39774 pb, 39861a pb
1817: 39968 f, 40763, 41552 pb, 41697 f, 41743 f, 41948 f, 42227 f, 42291 f, 42886 f, 42905 pb, 42955 f, 51678 f
1818: 43086 f, 43237 f, 43621 f, 43985 f, 44219 pb, 44521 pb, 44547 f, 45134 f, 45165 pb, 45325 f, 45598 pb, 45650 f, 45808 f, 45828 f, 45907 f, 45908 pb, 46748 f, 46834 f, 46865 f, 51834 pb
1819: 46968 f, 47605 f, 50007 f, 51906 pb, 51945 pb

KITE, THOMAS (Philadelphia)
For all entries see KITE, BENJAMIN (Philadelphia) above

KLERT, --- (Philadelphia)
1804: 6628

KLINE, GEORGE (Carlisle, Pa.)
1803: 3616, 4138
1804: 7688 pb
1805: 9190
1806: 10417, 10554, 11266, 11898
1807: 12475
1808: 16660
1810: 20214, 21295 pb, 21297

KLIPSTINE, --- (Winchester, Va.)
1819: 50000 pb

KNAP, LISCOMB (Henrietta, N.Y.)
1819: 49962 pb

KNEASS, WILLIAM (Philadelphia)
1810: 20506? pb

KNEELAND, ABNER (Walpole, N.H.)
1811: 23566 pb

KNOWLES, JAMES DAVIS (Providence, R.I.)
1819: 48302

KOCH, JOHANN F (Hagerstown, Md.)
1815: 36458 pb
1816: 39144 pb

KOLB, GEORGE (Frederick, Md.)
1818: 44130-44131 pb
1819: 47755 pb, 48588, 48801 bf, 48802, 49481 pb, 49633

KOLLOCK, ISAAC ARNETT (Elizabeth, N.J.)
1808: 16187 f
1809: 17954, 18444
1814: 30891 pb, 33608 pb
1816: 38123 pb, 38124, 38701, 38845, 39855
1817: 42095 pb

KOLLOCK, ISAAC ARNETT (New Brunswick, N.J.)
1810: 21197 pb

KOLLOCK, ISAAC ARNETT (Newark, N.J.)
1807: 13105 pb

KOLLOCK, ISAAC ARNETT (Salem, N.J.)
1817: 42873 pb
1818: 51738

KOLLOCK, SHEPARD (Elizabeth, N.J.)
1801: 601 pb, 1564 pb
1802: 3452 pb, 3527?
1803: 4116, 4325, 50399 pb
1804: 6896, 7639 pb
1805: 9291, 9644 pb
1806: 11745 pb
1807: 12500, 12567, 13206, 14100 pb
1808: 15734, 16187, 16231, 16606 pb
1809: 18213, 19078

1810: 20872, 21135, 21403,
  21869 pb
1811: 22339 pb, 22587? pb,
  22790 pb, 22932?, 22977?
  pb, 23526-23527, 23730?
  pb, 23734, 23740 pb, 23741,
  24323 pb
1812: 26242-26243, 26518,
  26520 pb, 27366 pb
1813: 27939 pb, 29313, 29572,
  30382 pb
1814: 32256-32257, 33513 pb
1815: 35443-35444, 35525,
  35811 pb, 36418
1816: 38405, 39649 pb
1817: 41588-41589, 41879 pb,
  42754 pb
1818: 44568, 45003

KOLLOCK, SIMON (Elizabeth,
  N. J.)
1808: 16187 f

KOLLOCK, SIMON (Wilming-
  ton, Del.)
1806: 10081 f

KORTZ, JOHN (Hudson, N. Y.)
1816: 37675 pb

KRIDER, JAMES (Salisbury,
  N. C.)
1819: 47721

KRUPP, ABRAHAM (Mathetchy,
  Pa.)
1814: 31148 pb

L

LADD, RUSSEL (Philadelphia)
1812: 26221 pb

LAFOURCADE, PETER M
  (Philadelphia)
1810: 20267
1811: 22366 pb
1816: 39131
1817: 40783
1818: 43982

LAINE, WILLIAM FREDERIC
  (Hallowell, Me.)
1819: 47376 f, 49118 pb

LAKE, DANIEL (Trenton,
  N. J.)
1813: 27723-27724 f, 27784,
  27845 pb, 29322 f, 29804 f,
  51323 pb
1814: 32207 pb, 32550 f

LAKIN, JAMES (Philadelphia)
1815: 34983 pb

LAMB, JOHN F (Lynchburg,
  Va.)
1812: 25292
1813: 27823
1816: 36859, 36867, 36869

LAMBDIN, J H (Pittsburgh,
  Pa.)
1817: 40028 pb, 40269 pb,
  40330, 41266, 41526, 42248
  pb, 42818, 42876, 42987
1818: 43334a bf, 43344 bf,
  43458, 44161 bf, 44179 bf,
  44181 pb, 44458, 44785,
  44786-44790 bf, 44823,
  44945 bf, 45215 f, 45216 bf,
  45791 bf, 45829 bf, 46788
  bf, 51816 bf, 51820 pb,
  51846 pb
1819: 47414, 47817 bf, 48548,
  48666 bf, 49021 f, 49022 pb,
  50059, 50067 bf, 51928 pb,
  51929 bf, 51934

LAMBERT, I (New York)
1818: 51825 pb

LAMBERTE, THEODORE (New
  Orleans, La.)
1808: 14912 pb, 50836 pb
1811: 51047 pb

LAMSON, E T (New York)
1812: 27613 pb

LANG, JOHN (New York)
1801: 21, 1685 f
1805: 8641 f

LANGDON, JOHN (New York)
1805: 9319 f

LANGDON, RICHARD C
(Natchez, Miss.)
1818: 44866, 44868, 45490
1819: 48084

LANGE, DANIEL P (Hanover,
Pa.)
1805: 8582 pb
1808: 14464, 14509, 16265
1810: 21187
1814: 32882

LANGLEY, --- (Rochester,
N. Y.)
1810: 19760? f

LANIER, JAMES (Danville,
Va.)
1819: 49301 pb

LAPPON, JOHN JAY (Delhi,
N. Y.)
1819: 47814 pb

LARGIN, GEORGE (New
York)
1809: 18867
1810: 21114?, 21332
1811: 22581 pb, 23054, 23908,
23994, 24058
1812: 24620, 24961, 24964,
24983, 25012, 25484,
25693
1813: 29137, 29206, 29221,
29759, 29921
1814: 30937, 31917, 32976
1815: 35960, 36262
1816: 37028?, 37527 pb,
37909, 39084 pb, 39366
1817: 40032
1818: 44043 pb, 45678
1819: 49392

Largin & Thompson (New
York)
see LARGIN, GEORGE
(New York)
THOMPSON, THOMAS (New
York)

LARKIN, EBENEZER (Boston)
1801: 24 f, 1380 f, 1433 f,
1626 pb, 50198 pb
1802: 1711 f, 2102 f, 2160 f,
2239 f, 2482 f, 2503 pb,
3175 f
1803: 3641 pb, 3688 pb, 4030
sb, 4696 f, 4894 f, 5585 pb
1804: 6098 f
1805: 9687 f
1806: 10133 f, 10504 f
1808: 15403 f, 15554 f, 16060
f
1809: 17661 f, 18402 f
1813: 27910 pb

LARKIN, JOSEPH (Boston)
1805: 8953 f
1806: 10133 f, 10504 f
1808: 14944 pb, 15403 f,
15554 f
1809: 17476 pb
1810: 21338 f, 22046 f
1813: 28940 pb, 51318? f

LARKIN, SAMUEL (Boston)
1801: 24 f, 1380 f, 1626 pb,
50198 pb
1802: 1711 f, 2160 f, 2239 f,
2503 pb

LAW, WILLIAM (Cheshire,
Conn.)
1801: 800? pb

LAWRENCE, DANIEL (Phila-
delphia)
1806: 10328 pb

LAWRENCE, DANIEL (Stan-
ford, N. Y.)
1802: 2478, 2983, 3001, 3181
bsb
1803: 3623 pb, 4083, 4334 pb,
4431, 4444 pb, 4511, 4562,
4971
1804: 6073?, 6104 pb, 6535
pb, 6601 pb, 7184
1805: 8067, 8297 pb, 8323,
8492-8493, 8554, 8690 bsb,
9263 bsb, 9324, 9709
1810: 19385 pb, 20272, 20387
pb

LAZELL, JOHN A (Buffalo,
N. Y.)
1819: 51903 f, 51927 f

LEAKIN, THOMAS I (Balti-
more)
1809: 16901, 17641, 17645-
17646, 17913, 18328

LEARNED, MOSES (Wilbraham,
Mass.)
1808: 15586, 15983

LEAVENWORTH, DAVID
(Albany, N. Y.)
1801: 45, 929, 1407
1802: 1737, 1747 pb, 1811,
1864, 2234, 2706, 2714,
2785, 3272, 50271 pb
1803: 4045 sb, 4887

LEAVENWORTH, HIRAM
(Waterloo, N. Y.)
1818: 43128 pb, 43129, 44863

LEAVITT, DUDLEY (Exeter,
N. H.)
1807: 12899 pb
1811: 23201 pb, 23500 pb

LEAVITT, DUDLEY (Gilman-
ton, N. H.)
1801: 50228 pb
1802: 50303 pb
1804: 6390, 50458 pb
1805: 8909, 50492 pb

LE BRETON, A (Philadelphia)
1807: 12559 pb

LE BRETON, EDWARD A
(New York)
1817: 41149 f

LECLERC, HILAIRE (New
Orleans, La.)
1809: 16856 pb

Ledger (Norfolk, Va.)
see Norfolk Gazette and
Publick Ledger (Norfolk,
Va.)

Ledger (Portsmouth, N. H.)
see Republican Ledger (Portsmouth, N. H.)

LEE, --- (Schenectady, N. Y.)
1814: 33741 f

LEE, CHARLES (Philadelphia)
1803: 4092, 4319, 4454, 4629,
5090, 5140, 5596
1804: 6396

LEE, JESSE (Baltimore)
1804: 6225 f

LEE, RICHARD (Kennebunk,
Me.)
1804: 6417 f

LEE, RICHARD (New York)
1805: 9360 f

LEE, RICHARD (Springfield,
Vt.)
1814: 32794 f

Lee's Patent and Family Medi-
cine Store (New York)
1816: 38047? pb
1817: 40779 pb, 41236 pb

LEFEVER, JACOB (Gettysburg,
Pa.)
1818: 45521 pb

LEIBERT, PETER (German-
town, Pa.)
1801: 307

LEIBERT, PETER (Philadel-
phia)
1813: 28131 f

LEIGH, JOSEPH (Portsmouth,
N. H.)
1805: 8995 pb, 9450 f

LEONARD, --- (Boston)
1810: 19603 pb

LEONARD, STEPHEN BANKS
(Owego, N. Y.)
1814: 32416 pb

LE PELLETIER, --- (Balti-
more)
1810: 20472 pb

LEPPER, WILHELM DANIEL
(Hanover, Pa.)
1801: 1575
1802: 1790
1806: 10846, 11427

LEPPER, WILLIAM DANIEL
(New Lisbon, O.)
1808: 15795
1810: 19446
1811: 22282
1812: 24733 pb
1813: 27808
1814: 30776
1819: 47127, 48173

LESTER, HUBBARD (Phila-
delphia)
1809: 18775 pb

LETSON, WILLIAM (New
Brunswick, N.J.)
1816: 38767 f
1819: 47441 pb

LEVENWORTH, SETH M
(Madison, Ind.)
1813: 30518 pb

LEVESQUE, FRANCIS (New
York)
1814: 32696 pb

LEVIS, ISAAC (Philadelphia)
1810: 19573 f, 20035 pb,
20405 f, 21062 pb, 21377 f
1811: 22873 pb, 23676 sb

LEVIS, WILLIAM (Philadelphia)
1814: 32786 pb

LEVY, BENJAMIN (New York)
1810: 21954 pb

LEWIS, BENJAMIN FRANK-
LIN (Newburgh, N.Y.)
1813: 29250 pb
1816: 38254 f
1817: 40170, 40352 pb,

41256 f, 41629 pb
1818: 44004 pb, 44193, 51779
pb, 51802 pb
1819: 46916, 47958 pb, 48091
pb, 48194 pb, 49267

LEWIS, ELDAD (Lenox, Mass.)
1808: 14780, 15246, 16667 pb
1809: 17469

LEWIS, ELDAD (Newburgh,
N.Y.)
1811: 23559 pb
1812: 25031, 25837 bf
1816: 51603 sb
1817: 41116 f

LEWIS, FREEMAN (Pittsburgh,
Pa.)
1814: 31923 f

LEWIS, GEORGE (Ovid, N.Y.)
1815: 35896 pb

LEWIS, GEORGE (Waterloo,
N.Y.)
1817: 42839 pb

LEWIS, H C (Washington,
D.C.)
1814: 32380 f

LEWIS, HENRY C (Philadel-
phia)
1810: 21453 pb
1818: 44536 pb, 44574 pb,
46620 pb

LEWIS, JAMES (York, Pa.)
1815: 36146 pb
1819: 51948

LEWIS, JOHN T (Pendleton,
S.C.)
1812: 26749 f

LEWIS, JUNIUS S (Catskill,
N.Y.)
1818: 44949 pb, 45343 f,
46732 pb
1819: 47954 f

LEWIS, URIAH C (Newburgh,
N.Y.)

1812: 25837
1816: 38254
1817: 41116
1818: 45343
1819: 47932, 49231 pb, 49803

Lexicon Press (Burlington, N. J.)
1811: 22694
1812: 26793
1813: 28672
1815: 35059 pb, 36663
1816: 38321 pb

Lexington Advertiser (Lexington, Ky.)
1819: 48016

Liberty Hall (Cincinnati, O.)
1807: 13679
1810: 21384
1811: 23770
1812: 26759

Libraires Associes (Boston)
1811: 22372

LILLY, JAMES M (Paris, Ky.)
1818: 44439 pb

LILLY, ROBERT (Boston)
1814: 30685, 31055 pb, 31338 pb, 31391 pb, 31769 pb, 32670 pb, 32868-32869 pb
1815: 33822 pb, 33909, 33925 pb, 34239 pb, 34250 pb, 34308 pb, 34312-34314 pb, 34316-34319 pb, 34348-34349 pb, 34463 pb, 34540 pb, 34619 pb, 34621-34622 pb, 34649, 34758 pb, 34868-34869 pb, 34936, 34937 pb, 35143 pb, 35229 pb, 35250 pb, 35316 pb, 35501 pb, 35703-35704 pb, 35853 pb, 35874 pb, 35879 pb, 35994 pb, 36059, 36060 pb, 36072, 36404 pb, 36422, 36424 pb
1816: 36707 pb, 36782 pb, 36909 pb, 36926 pb, 37103 pb, 37125 pb, 37207-37208 pb, 37243 pb, 37291 pb, 37301 pb, 37348 pb, 37367 pb, 37485 pb, 37496 pb, 37528 f, 37738, 37777 pb, 37822, 37854 pb, 37857 pb, 37858 f, 37874 f, 37894 pb, 37976-37977 pb, 38008 pb, 38017 f, 38106 pb, 38167 pb, 38202 pb, 38291 f, 38530 f, 38552 f, 38566 pb, 38617 pb, 38791 pb, 38826 pb, 38828 f, 38837 pb, 38864 f, 38883 pb, 38892 f, 38985 pb, 39054-39055 pb, 39057 pb, 39060-39061 pb, 39109 pb, 39654, 39658 f, 39780 pb, 39843, 39867 pb, 39872 f, 39889 pb, 51570-51576 pb
1817: 39925 pb, 40248, 40354 pb, 40441 pb, 40602 pb, 40726 pb, 40899 pb, 40941, 40973 pb, 40980 pb, 41015, 41168 pb, 41481 pb, 41822-41823 pb, 41841 pb, 42053 pb, 42128 pb, 42222 pb, 42226, 42247 pb, 42262-42263, 42960 pb
1818: 43233 pb, 43372 pb, 43439, 43530 pb, 43560 pb, 43814 pb, 43918 pb, 43979, 44061 pb, 44125, 44218, 44223, 44291 pb, 44293, 44447 pb, 44625-44626, 44838 pb, 45122 pb, ?45347?, 45590 pb, 45799 pb, 45852, 46682 pb, 46693
1819: 47485 pb, 47502 pb, 47555, 47596-47597, 47633 pb, 47741 pb, 47802 pb, 47876-47877 pb, 47880 pb, 47907, 48069 pb, 48112 pb, 48129 pb, 48139 pb, 48287, 48431 pb, 48433-48434 pb, 48636, 48747-48749 pb, 48955, 49128 pb, 49160 pb, 49270, 49299, 49533, 49945 pb, 49971 pb, 50035 pb, 51855 pb, 51880-518881 pb

LINCOLN, DANIEL WALDO (Boston)
1808: 15339

LINCOLN, ENSIGN (Boston)
1801: 9, 500, 790, 847,
　　1088, 1262, 1447
1802: 1796, 1829, 1903 pb,
　　2092, 2094, 2689 pb, 2851
　　pb, 2881, 3080, 3109,
　　3489, 3501 pb
1803: 3712, 3739, 3862,
　　3868-3869, 3909 pb, 3910-
　　3912, 4049, 4100-4102, 4299,
　　4309 pb, 4330 pb, 4355 bf,
　　4509, 4530 pb, 4536 pb,
　　4615, 4678 pb, 4769 pb,
　　4992, 5586 pb, 5630 pb
1804: 5751, 5756, 5790,
　　5803, 5876, 5938 pb, 5940
　　pb, 5942-5943 pb, 5948 pb,
　　5957, 6023-6025, 6029,
　　6078 pb, 6234, 6462 pb,
　　6546, 6629 pb, 6684, 7124
　　pb, 7308, 7320, 7331, 7695,
　　7759
1805: 7866, 7901, 8111-8114
　　pb, 8207, 8376 pb, 8378,
　　8566, 8672, 8764, 8770,
　　9158, 9686, 9728, 50502?
　　pb
1806: 9853, 9997 pb, 10204
　　pb, ?10260?, 10338-10339,
　　10347, 10502, 10517?, 10526,
　　10630, 10733, 10878, 11338
　　pb, 11895 pb, 11910
1807: 12082, 12114-12115,
　　12207 pb, 12234 pb, 12240-
　　12242?, 12243, 12263 pb,
　　12332 pb, 12346 pb, 12493,
　　12713, 12803, 13480, 13645
　　pb, 13646, 13670-13672 pb,
　　13676 pb, 14218 pb, 14236
　　pb
1808: 14350, 14394, 14497
　　pb, 14524 pb, 14554, 14692,
　　14877 pb, 14914 pb, 15206,
　　15271, 15562 pb, 15571 pb,
　　15651-15652, 15971 f,
　　16293, 16652 pb, 16674 pb,
　　16675? pb, 16745 pb,
　　16766, 50838 pb
1809: 16802 pb, 16868 pb,
　　16892, 16907, 17042 pb,
　　17230 f, 17324 f, 17443,
　　17449, 17580 pb, 17740 pb,
　　17754 pb, 18014 pb, 18108

pb, 18120 pb, 18122-18123
pb, 18159 pb, 18269, 18271-
18272, 18428, 18518, 18734
pb, 19270-19271 pb, 19274,
19288, 50923 pb
1810: 19530 pb, 19538, 19564
　　pb, 19599, 19667-19669? pb,
　　19671 pb, 19678 pb, 19679?
　　pb, 19723, 19772 pb, 19786
　　f, 19787 pb, 19926 pb,
　　19982 pb, 20042 pb, 20089
　　pb, 20175 pb, 20259? pb,
　　20310 pb, 20781 pb, 20916
　　pb, 20920, 20934, 20998
　　pb, 21108 f, 21143? pb,
　　21218, 21236 pb, 21514 pb,
　　22083 pb, 22097 pb
1811: 22149 pb, 22229 pb,
　　22248 pb, 22468 pb, 22551
　　f, 22663 pb, 22691 pb,
　　22693 f, 22697, 22714 pb,
　　22763 pb, 22961, 23008 pb,
　　23040-23041 pb, 23106 pb,
　　23145 pb, 23575, 23617 pb,
　　23635 pb, 23731 pb, 23817,
　　23955, 23978 pb, 23980,
　　24047, 24048 pb, 24053,
　　24348a pb, 24432, 24433 pb,
　　24476, 51094 pb
1812: 24570 pb, 24615 pb,
　　24681-24684 pb, 24716,
　　24776, 24931 pb, 24977 pb,
　　24986 pb, 25018-25019 pb,
　　25096 f, 25126 pb, 25210,
　　25222 pb, 25423 pb, 25471,
　　25472 pb, 25532 pb, 25545-
　　25547, 25616 pb, 25642 pb,
　　25710 pb, 25751 pb, 25948
　　pb, 25962 pb, 25966 pb,
　　26130 pb, 26136?, 26185-
　　26186, 26303, 26493 f,
　　26575, 26717 pb, 26742 pb,
　　26894, 26902, 27472, 27626
　　pb, 27638 pb
1813: 27797?, 27859, 27862,
　　27870, 27873, 27910 pb,
　　27923 pb, 27949-27950,
　　28096 pb, 28162 f, 28166 pb,
　　28324 pb, 28390 pb, 28455
　　pb, 28476-28477, 28592 pb,
　　29134 pb, 29369-29370 pb,
　　29377 pb, 29511, 29560,
　　29639, 29658 pb, 29664? pb,

29925, 29926 pb, 30484 pb,
30489 pb, 51339-51340 pb
1814: 30758-30761, 30810,
30822 pb, 30963 pb, 31179
sb, 31467, 31537 pb, 31810
f, 32197 pb, 32373, 32522
pb, 32648, 32737 pb, 32919,
32952
1815: 33793, 33944, 34005,
34062 f, 34095 pb, 34152 pb,
34169, 34274 pb, 34337 pb,
34366 sb, 34671 pb, 34754
pb, 34820, 34986 pb, 35242
pb, 35361 pb, 35378 pb,
35511, 35514, 35656 pb,
36136, 36503 pb, 36552
1816: 36672 pb, 36791 pb,
36828, 36857, 36943 f,
36979 pb, 37162 p, 37226
pb, 37268 pb, 37619, 38346
pb, 38489, 39064 pb, 39728
pb
1817: 39926 pb, 39943 f,
39972 pb, 40048 pb, 40050,
40086, 40171, 40181 pb,
40195 f, 40211 f, 40288,
40360 pb, 41119 pb, 41171
bpb, 41172 f, 41482 pb,
41484, 41518 pb, 41675,
41966 pb, 42000
1818: 43008 pb, 43138-43139,
43188, 43273, 43419, 43422,
43477 pb, 43640-43641 f,
43657 pb, 43960, 44108 pb,
44184 pb, 44487 pb, 44501,
45703 pb, 45838 pb, 45848
pb, 45923?
1819: 46920 pb, 47049 pb,
47103, 47169 pb, 47195 pb,
47210 f, 47337 pb, 47395
pb, 47500 pb, 47563 pb,
47642 f, 47643 pb, 47972
pb, 48077, 48131 pb, 48320,
48345 pb, 48367 pb, 48400
pb, 48424, 48494, 48497,
48557 pb, 48702-48703 pb,
48746 pb, 48764 pb, 48798
pb, 48959 pb, 49131-49136
pb, 49143-49144 pb, 49188
pb, 49230 pb, 49241 pb,
49341 f, 49382 pb, 49386-
49387 pb, 49460 pb, 50139
pb, 50172 pb, 50179-50180

LINCOLN, EZRA (Boston)
1816: 20789, 39751
1817: 41108, 41154, 41363,
41883, 42235 pb
1818: 44910, 45610, 46736
1819: 47969, 48279

LINCOLN, LEMUEL (Hartford,
Conn.)
1803: 3879, 4103, 4336, 4364,
4382, 4459, 4486, 4593,
4726 bf, 5053, 5056, 5186,
5582, 50361-50362
1804: 5665, 5668, 5694, 5804,
5879, 5984, 6189, 6311,
6444, 6813, 6874 pb, 7092,
7262, 7277
1805: 7854 pb, 8083?, 8143,
8157, 8228?, 8230?, 8287,
8606, 8796 pb, 8877, 8885,
8948, 9180, 9330 pb, 9358
pb, 9693
1806: 9826 pb, 9971, 10039,
10091, 10095 pb, 10171,
10312 pb, 10351-10352,
10384, 10412, 10419, 10551,
10559, 10585, 10594, 10710,
10849, 10873, 11195, 11202,
11227 pb, 11232, 11249,
11301, 11346, 11470 pb,
11488 f, 50685
1807: 11960, 11968 pb, 12151
pb, 12212, 12233, 12278,
12341, 12445, 12447 pb,
12585, 12624, 12685, 12698,
13098, 13116, 13130, 13157
pb, 13164 pb, 13425, 13568,
13588 pb, 13756, 14121,
14156, 14197
1808: 14331 pb, 14672, 14759,
14769 pb, 15023, 15407 pb,
15620-15621, 15897, 15928,
16263, 16721, 16736
1809: 17277, 17286, 18103,
18381, 18583 pb

LINCOLN, SIMEON (Hartford,
Conn.)
1814: 31022
1815: 35806
1816: 36962a
1818: 43300, 44275, 46851
1819: 47180, 47480, 48036,
48061, 48094, 48176

LINCOLN, SIMEON (Middle-
town, Conn.)
1814: 31344 pb, 31511, 32019
pb, 32784 pb

Lincoln & Edmands (Boston)
see LINCOLN, ENSIGN
(Boston)
EDMANDS, THOMAS (Boston)

Lincoln & Gleason (Hartford,
Conn.)
see LINCOLN, LEMUEL
(Hartford, Conn.)
GLEASON, PETER BUEL
(Hartford, Conn.)

LINDSAY, GEORGE (Albany,
N.Y.)
1815: 34801 f
1816: 36977 f
1817: 42841 pb

LINDSAY, GEORGE (New
York)
1809: 18537
1810: 21962 pb
1811: 24045-24046 f, 24511 f
1812: 24959-24960 pb, 24961 f
1813: 28507 pb, 29759 f,
29921 f
1815: 35887 pb
1818: 45678 f
1819: 49392 pb

LINDSEY, BENJAMIN (New
Bedford, Mass.)
1807: 13182 pb
1808: 14478, 14886
1809: 18423, 19249
1810: 20268
1812: 26103
1813: 30542
1814: 31652
1815: 34831, 34945, 35407
1816: 37079
1817: 41932
1818: 43658, 44547, 45233,
46787
1819: 47167, 50128

LINDSLEY, ELEAZER (Wash-
ington, D.C.)
1814: 33698

LINES, HENRY (New Haven,
Conn.)
1815: 35262 f

LINGAN, JOSEPH A (Charlestown, Ind.)
1818: 44431 pb

LINGAN, JOSEPH A (Winchester, Va.)
1806: 11160 pb, 14107
1809: 17372 pb, 18480

LINN, J S (Delaware, O.)
1819: 49320

LIPPINCOTT, JOSEPH (Philadelphia)
1806: 50701 pb
1808: 15738 pb
1809: 18219 pb
1810: 19634 pb

LIPPITT, J FRANCIS (Providence, R.I.)
1815: 34624 pb

LISA, JOAQUIN DE (New Or-
leans, La.)
1809: 18067 pb

LITCH, SAMUEL (Jaffrey,
N.H.)
1807: 13069 f

Litchfield Journal (Litchfield,
Conn.)
1818: 45478

Literary Exchange (New York)
1811: 22778, 24347

LITTELL, ELIAKIM (Phila-
delphia)
1816: 37241 pb
1818: 43545, 44397 f
1819: 48513 f, 49365 pb

LITTLE, --- (Philadelphia)
1804: 7198

LITTLE, EDWARD (Exeter,
N.H.)

1814: 32536 f, 32791 f
1817: 41816 pb

LITTLE, EDWARD (Newbury-
port, Mass.)
1808: 14360 pb
1809: 17115 f, 17293 f, 17331
f, 18046 f, 19169 f
1810: 19295 f, 20678 f,
21086 pb, 21458 f
1811: 22445 pb, 22682 f,
23263 f, 23324 f, 23325 pb,
23326 f, 23396 f, 23440 f,
23724 f, 24403 f, 24443 f
1812: 24893 pb, 25965 f,
26171 pb, 26463 pb, 27404 f
1813: 28272 pb, 28916 pb,
30420 f
1814: 31288 f, 31764 pb,
32432 f, 32504 pb, 33568 f
1815: 35638 f, 36444 f
1816: 38334 f, 39669 f,
39702 f

LITTLE, EDWARD (Portland,
Me.)
1816: 38078 f

LITTLE, RUFUS (Philadelphia)
1816: 37509 f
1819: 50075 pb

LITTLE, WILLIAM (Brooklyn,
N. Y.)
1806: 10172, 10745 pb, 11793
1807: 12215 pb, 14091

LITTLE, WILLIAM (New York)
1806: 9937, 10688, 10864,
11294, 11850
1807: 13074-13075, 13701

LLOYD, --- (Lancaster, Pa.)
1803: 3631 f, 4849 f

LLOYD, JOHN (Chambers-
burg, Pa.)
1811: 23080 f

LLOYD, JOSEPH (Philadelphia)
1809: 18354 pb

LLOYD, THOMAS (Philadelphia)
1806: 11472 f

LOCKERMAN, MATTHEW R
(Wilmington, Del.)
1806: 11115 pb, 11173 f
1807: 11990 pb, 12161 f
1808: 14879 f
1809: 17202 f
1811: 22613 f, 23470 f, 51075
pb
1812: 25116 pb, 26190 f,
26701 f
1816: 38077 f

LOCKWOOD, FREDERICK (New
York)
1818: 43047 f, 43400 f,
44537 f, 44950
1819: 47227 f, 47370 pb,
47374 pb, 48210 f, 48509 f,
48807 pb

LOCKWOOD, LAMBERT
(Bridgeport, Conn.)
1810: 19834-19835, 19981,
20263 pb
1811: 22742 pb, 24349 pb
1812: 25963 pb
1814: 31307 pb, 31341 pb,
32198 pb
1815: 34455 pb, 35352 pb,
35362 pb, 35379 pb
1816: 36947 pb
1817: 40212-40213 pb

LOCKWOOD, LAMBERT (New
York)
1818: 43047 f, 43400 f, 44537
f, 44950
1819: 47227 f, 47370 pb,
47374 pb, 48210 f, 48509 f,
48807 pb

LODGE, JAMES (Cincinnati,
O.)
1817: 42875 pb
1818: 43161, 43943, 46769
pb, 51845 pb
1819: 47616, 49551

LODGE, JAMES (Dayton, O.)
1815: 33785, 33965

LODGE, JOHN (Corydon, Ind.)
1816: 37926 pb

LODGE, JOHN (Madison, Ind.)
1819: 47087, 48015

LODGE, JONATHAN (Danville,
Pa.)
1815: 34664 pb

LOGAN, ANDREW (Beaver,
Pa.)
1813: 27854 pb, 28247 pb
1817: 40158 pb

LOGAN, ANDREW (Cleveland,
O.)
1818: 43637-43638 pb

LOGAN, JAMES (Beaver, Pa.)
1813: 28247 pb
1818: 46771 pb

LONG, GEORGE (New York)
1806: 10297, 11187, 11328,
50656, 50668 pb
1807: 12111-12112, 12286,
12331, 12509, 12673, 12704,
12777, 12779, 12859, 13118,
13159 pb, 13549, 14147 pb,
50758-50759
1808: 14610-14611, 14625,
15588, 15768-15769, 15953,
15978, 16093, 16188 pb,
16240
1809: 16955, 17018, 17644,
17762, 17972-17973, 18118,
18449, 18451, 18637, 19224
1810: 20618, 21107, 21339,
21891, 50979
1811: 22364, 22675, 22773,
22792, 23104, 23771, 23862,
23965
1812: 24526, 24824, 24843,
25924 pb, 27480
1813: 27721, 27886, 27914,
28120, 29135, 29138, 29216
pb, 29946, 30486, 30594,
51261, 51281
1814: 30618, 30619 pb, 30886,
30887 pb, 30888, 31154,
31233, 31751, 32410, 32474
pb, 32682, 32843-32844
1815: 34048 pb, 34069, 34272,
34414 pb, 34549 pb, 34550-
34551, 34607, 36047,

51465, 51526
1816: 36935 pb, 36973 pb,
36974, 36984, 37063, 37153
pb, 37734, 37850, 37856 pb,
37944 pb, 38333 pb, 38599,
39655, 39732 pb, 51563 pb
1817: 40264-40266, 41112 pb,
41163 pb, 41261, 41479,
41774, 41885
1818: 43328-43330, 43825 pb,
44012 pb, 44258-44259 pb,
44404, 44472 pb, 44580 pb,
44630 pb, 45059 pb, 46706,
46707 pb, 46714, 46720
1819: 47730 pb, 47804 pb,
47918, 47961 pb, 48157 pb,
48308 pb, 48382 pb, 48667,
48905 pb, 49068, 49156 pb,
49157, 49158 pb, 49381,
50191, 51859 pb, 51882 pb,
51883-51884, 51901 pb

LONG, ISAAC (Hopkinton,
N.H.)
1819: 47225 pb

Long Island Star (Brooklyn,
N.Y.)
1809: 16946

LONGCOPE, SAMUEL (Easton,
Pa.)
1801: 148
1802: 2406
1803: 4069 pb

LONGLIVE, TIMOTHY (Boston)
1812: 26925

LONGSTRETH, THOMAS
MIFFLIN (Philadelphia)
1812: 27367 pb
1813: 27652 pb, 27654 pb,
30383 pb
1814: 51446 pb
1817: 51719 pb

LONGWORTH, DAVID (New
York)
1801: 48 pb, 53 pb, 504 pb,
529 pb, 806-807 pb, 1602
pb, 50194 pb
1802: 1866 pb, 2049 pb, 2550-

2551 pb, 2654 pb, 2704,
3003 f, 3013 pb, 3068 pb,
3112 pb, 3607 f, 50307 pb
1803: 3654 pb, 3848 pb,
3978 pb, 4093 pb, 4117-4118
pb, 4119 f, 4390 f, 4473 pb,
4535 pb, 4673 pb, 4751 pb,
5045 pb, 5101 pb, 5525 pb
1804: 5689 pb, 5870 pb, 6008
pb, 6048 pb, 6100 pb,
6102 pb, 6162 pb, 6168 pb,
6202 pb, 6254 bsb, 6482
pb, 6588, 6616 f, 6654 pb,
6667 pb, 6816 pb, 6959 pb,
7070 pb, 7255 pb, 7378 pb,
50410 pb
1805: 7868 pb, 7882 pb,
8016 pb, 8201 pb, 8293 pb,
8324 pb, 8623 pb, 8702
pb, 8724-8725 pb, 8782 pb,
8797 pb, 8935 pb, 9058
pb, 9084 pb, 9248, 9250
pb, 9280 pb, 9321 pb,
9344-9345 pb, 9486 pb,
50518 pb
1806: 9803 pb, 9828 pb,
9989-9990 pb, 10109 pb,
10165 pb, 10179-10182 pb,
10184-10186 pb, 10212 pb,
10219 pb, 10285 pb, 10286
f, 10287-10288 pb, 10290
pb, 10292-10293 pb, 10350
pb, 10360 pb, 10416 pb,
10471 pb, 10490 pb, 10563-
10564 pb, 10572 pb, 10574-
10575 pb, 10583 pb, 10596
pb, 10894 pb, 11064 pb,
11107 pb, 11169 pb, 11276-
11277 pb, 11358 pb, 11902
pb, 11908 pb, 50694 pb
1807: 12095 pb, 12359 pb,
12436 pb, 12438 pb, 12477-
12481 pb, 12674 pb, 12768
pb, 12770 pb, 12777 f,
12779 f, 12820? pb, 12821
pb, 12839 pb, 12859 f,
12882 pb, 12924 pb, 12937
pb, 13118 f, 13149 pb,
13300, 13360 pb, 13562
pb, 13574 f, 13583-13586
pb, 13715 pb, 13716? pb,
14250 pb, 50783 pb
1808: 14332-14334 pb, 14376

pb, 14450 pb, 14510 pb,
14584-14585 f, 14637 pb,
14682 pb, 14695 pb, 14733-
14736 pb, 14750 pb, 14808
pb, 14866-14867 pb, 14885
pb, 14969 f, 15034 pb,
15247 pb, 15253 pb, 15310
pb, 15355-15358 pb, 15382-
15383 pb, 15426 pb, 15427
f, 15476 pb, 15638-15639
pb, 15775 pb, 15796 pb,
15821 pb, 16061-16062 pb,
16147 pb, 16184-16185 pb,
16192 pb, 16226 f, 16244
pb, 50828 pb, 50864 pb
1809: 16869 pb, 16889 pb,
17081 pb, 17092 pb, 17145-
17146 pb, 17238 pb, 17254-
17255 pb, 17328 pb, 17382
pb, 17388 pb, 17456-17457
pb, 17471 pb, 17519 pb,
17603 pb, 17727 f, 17770
pb, 17796 pb, 17798 pb,
17806 pb, 17808 pb, 17859
pb, 17881 pb, 17903 pb,
17910 pb, 17919 pb, 17952
pb, 17966 pb, 18310 pb,
18408 pb, 18473-18474 pb,
18601 pb, 19124 pb, 50948
pb
1810: 19402 f, 19641 pb,
19682 pb, 19785 pb, 19807-
19808 pb, 19867 pb, 19880
pb, 19962 pb, 19967 pb,
20007 pb, 20057 pb, 20348
pb, 20371 pb, 20374 pb,
20421 pb, 20450 pb, 20514
pb, 20560 pb, 20626 pb,
20701 pb, 20964 pb, 20972
pb, 20981 f, 21104 pb,
21120 pb, 21207 pb, 21287
pb, 21329 f, 21504 pb,
50998 pb, 51020 pb
1811: 22411a f, 22496, 22507,
22573 pb, 22575 pb, 22657
pb, 22692 pb, 22703-22704
pb, 22725 pb, 22732 pb,
22736 pb, 23020 pb, 23030
pb, 23036 pb, 23131 pb,
23215 pb, 23269-23270 pb,
23353 pb, 23391 pb, 23442
pb, 23594 pb, 23707 pb,
23712 pb, 23922 pb, 23924-

23926 pb, 23964 pb, 23965
f, 51113 pb
1812: 24604 pb, 24674-24677
pb, 24749 pb, 24781 pb,
24868-24869 pb, 25025 pb,
25043 pb, 25091 pb, 25268
pb, 25271-25272 pb, 25295
pb, 25301-25302 pb, 25347-
25349 pb, 25653 pb, 25679
pb, 25681 pb, 25776 pb,
25804 pb, 25813 pb, 25840
pb, 25844 pb, 25856 pb,
25858 pb, 25877 pb, 25920
pb, 26125 pb, 26155 pb,
26306 pb, 26486 pb, 26608
pb, 26656 pb, 26852 pb,
26873 pb, 27368 pb, 27373
pb
1813: 27877 pb, 28066 pb,
28177 pb, 28222 pb, 28331-
28332 pb, 28373 pb, 28437
pb, 28524-28539 pb, 28600
pb, 28782 pb, 28806 pb,
28828 pb, 28864-28865 pb,
28895 pb, 28937 pb, 28973
pb, 29228-29229 pb, 29408
pb, 29426 pb, 29516 pb,
29541 pb, 29652 pb, 29762
pb, 29954 pb, 30384 f,
30429 pb
1814: 31373 pb, 31375 pb,
31420 pb, 31495-31498 pb,
31742 pb, 31750 pb, 31806-
31807 pb, 31835 pb, 31876-
31877 pb, 31949 pb, 32110
f, 32180-32181 pb, 32526
pb, 32634 pb, 32672 f,
33753 pb, 33761 pb
1815: 33778 pb, 33831 pb,
34216 pb, 34266 pb, 34363
f, 34371 f, 34395 pb,
34489 pb, 34572 pb, 34602
pb, 34665 pb, 34746 pb,
34770 pb, 34947 pb, 34990
pb, 35099 pb, 35111 pb,
35130-35131 pb, 35299 pb,
35518 pb, 35659 pb, 35736
f, 36096 pb
1816: 36768 pb, 36879 pb,
36938 pb, 37033 f, 37130
pb, 37284 pb, 37298 pb,
37316 pb, 37363 pb, 37382
pb, 37476 pb, 37767 pb,

37799 f, 37893 f, 37947 f,
37960 pb, 37987-37988 pb,
38091-38092 pb, 38198,
38282 pb, 38299 pb, 38451
pb, 38663-38663a pb, 38670
pb, 38923 pb, 39056 pb,
39068 pb, 39857 pb
1817: 40020 pb, 40045 pb,
40138 pb, 40242-40243 pb,
40295 pb, 40351 pb, 40367-
40368 pb, 40394 pb, 40407
f, 40426 pb, 40523-40525
pb, 40659 pb, 40665 pb,
40667 pb, 40699 pb, 40711
pb, 40802 pb, 40827 pb,
40863, 40981 pb, 41182 pb,
41185 pb, 41214 pb, 41381
pb, 41383 pb, 41469 pb,
41494 pb, 41504-41506 pb,
41636 pb, 41714 pb, 41891
f, 41916 f, 41975 pb, 42100
pb, 42107 pb, 42305 pb,
42837 pb, 42881-42885 f,
42954 pb, 51682-51683 pb
1818: 43058, 43354 pb, 43669
pb, 43778-43779 pb, 43851-
43852 pb, 43858 pb, 43862
pb, 44094, 44343 pb, 44527
pb, 44576 pb, 44850 pb,
44928 pb, 45062 pb, 45149
pb, 45193 pb, 45360-45362
pb, 45526 pb, 45572 pb,
45585 pb, 45700 pb, 45745
pb
1819: 46925 pb, 47182 pb,
47576 pb, 47830 pb, 48242-
48243 pb, 48262 pb, 48293
pb, 48296 pb, 48328 pb,
48388 pb, 48493 pb, 48766
pb, 48940 pb, 48979 pb,
49029 pb, 49966 pb

LONGWORTH, THOMAS (New
York)
1811: 22496, 22507, 22703-
22704 pb, 22725 pb, 22732
pb, 23030 pb, 23036 pb,
23215 pb, 23270 pb, 23391
pb, 23924-23925 pb, 23964
pb
1812: 24676-24677 pb, 24749
pb, 24781 pb, 25025 pb,
25091 pb, 25271-25272 pb,

25348-25349 pb, 25653 pb,
25679 pb, 25681 pb, 25776
pb, 25856 pb, 26125 pb,
26155 pb, 26486 pb, 26656
pb
1813: 28437 pb
1815: 34489 pb
1816: 37663 pb
1818: 44563 f, 44610 pb
1819: 48025-48026 f, 48027
    pb, 48265 pb, 48442 pb,
    49409 pb

LOOKER, JAMES H (Cincinnati,
    O.)
1812: 51231 pb
1813: 27806, 29403, 29805
1814: 30919, 31358, 31923,
    32394
1815: 34342, 34595, 35530,
    35573, 35956
1816: 37244, 37620, 38554,
    38717
1818: 43488, 43883-43884
    pb, 43994
1819: 47126, 47447, 47779-
    47781, 47946, 48500 pb,
    48553, 48684, 48953?

LOOKER, JOHN MILTON
    (Salem, N. Y.)
1803: 5540 pb
1805: 8456

LOOKER, JOHN MILTON
    (Waterford, N. Y.)
1802: 3498

LOOMIS, GEORGE JEPSON
    (Albany, N. Y.)
1814: 32189 pb
1815: 34406 pb, 34493-34494,
    35295 pb
1816: 37078, 37780, 38343
    pb, 39818, 39828
1817: 39958, 40338, 41200
1818: 43043, 43599, 43677
    pb, 44941 pb, 44952 pb,
    44982 pb, 51826
1819: 46956, 47190 pb, 47417,
    48814 pb, 48816, 50060 pb,
    50062

LOOMIS, LEONARD (Bethany,
    Pa.)
1818: 46734 pb

LOOMIS, SIMEON LORENZO
    (Hartford, Conn.)
1816: 36962a f
1818: 43300 bf, 46673
1819: 47462 pb, 50012

LOOMIS, SIMEON LORENZO
    (Middletown, Conn.)
1814: 30744, 31225 pb, 31473-
    31474, 32269 pb, 32547,
    32549
1815: 35017, 35665, 35796,
    36020

LOPEZ, MATTHIAS (New York)
1818: 46864 pb

LOPEZ, MATTHIAS (West
    Farms, N. Y.)
1813: 30516 pb

LORD, ERASTUS A (Portland,
    Me.)
1812: 24803 f, 24944 f, 26101
    f
1813: 29703 f

LORD, JOHN HAINES (Oswego,
    N. Y.)
1819: 48996 pb

LORD, JOHN HAINES (Water-
    town, N. Y.)
1817: 41157 pb
1818: 43593, 44459, 44460 pb,
    44768

LORD, MELVIN (Boston)
1814: 31885 f
1816: 37092 f
1818: 19373? f, 43034 pb,
    43453 f, 43991 f, 43997 f,
    44755 pb, 45219 f, 45789 f
1819: 47220-47221 f, 47427
    pb, 47437 f, 47945 f, 48641
    pb, 48825 f, 50031 f, 50069
    f, 50079 pb, 50183 f, 51877
    pb

Lorenzo Press (Philadelphia)
1804:	6385
1807:	14229
1808:	14456
1811:	22541
1812:	24605

LORING, BENJAMIN (Boston)
1817:	42044 f

LORING, JAMES (Boston)
1801:	12 pb, 14, 30, 100,
	115, 139, 157 pb, 193-195,
	212 pb, 425, 473 pb, 546
	pb, 549, 597 pb, 671 pb,
	894 pb, 911, 920 pb, 953,
	954 pb, 1086 pb, 1280, 1353,
	1357 pb, 1400, 1433 f,
	1606, 50255
1802:	1756, 1799, 1837 pb,
	1840, 1898, 1901-1902,
	2006, 2092 f, 2094 f, 2105
	pb, 2151 pb, 2185 pb, 2257,
	2281 pb, 2283 pb, 2285-
	2286 pb, 2288-2291 pb,
	2293, 2294 pb, 2374, 2482
	f, 2539, 2585 pb, 2631 pb,
	2641 f, 2665? pb, 2690 pb,
	2708, 2711, 2718 pb, 2752?
	pb, 2851 pb, 2854, 2913
	pb, 3094, 3118, 3175 f,
	3591
1803:	3629, 3680 pb, 3708
	pb, 3719, 3753 pb, 3756,
	3806 pb, 3809 pb, 3812 bf,
	3813-3814 pb, 3824, 3829,
	3865, 3918 pb, 3945, 3955,
	4135? pb, 4141, 4214, 4254-
	4257 pb, 4298, 4340, 4355
	bf, 4440-4441, 4442 pb,
	4616 pb, 4658-4659, 4725?,
	4780, 4894, 5064 pb, 5066,
	5107, 5110, 5548 pb
1804:	5664, 5754, 5755 pb,
	5757, 5861 f, 5873-5875,
	6011 pb, 6079, 6093, 6214,
	6252 pb, 6353-6355, 6408,
	6446-6449, 6493, 6566 pb,
	6619-6620, 6695, 6750 pb,
	6765, 6840 pb, 6844, 6975-
	6976 pb, 7249 pb, 7256,
	7280 pb, 7283 pb, 7285?,
	7395, 7703-7704, 50425

1805:	7871 pb, 7908 pb, 7942,
	7953 pb, 8022 pb, 8031 pb,
	8106, 8155 pb, 8494 pb,
	8528 pb, 8548, 8587-8588,
	8837, 8861 pb, 8866, 8874
	pb, 8884, 8890 pb, 8895 pb,
	8922 pb, 8979? pb, 9175 pb,
	9369-9370 pb, 9426-9430,
	9435 pb, 9684 pb, 9687,
	9699
1806:	9824, 9876, 9881 pb,
	9906, 9981 pb, 9992 pb,
	10014, 10017 pb, 10055-
	10056 pb, 10178 pb, 10426
	pb, 10461 pb, 10512, 10557
	pb, 10781, 10832 pb, 10838
	pb, 10842, 10860 pb, 10918
	pb, 11320, 11484, 11803 pb,
	11814 pb, 50649 pb
1807:	12024 pb, 12062, 12136,
	12145-12146, 12150 pb,
	12236 pb, 12251, 12280,
	12308, 12762, 12981, 13020
	f, 13035 pb, 13064 pb,
	13067 pb, 13079 pb, 13314,
	13413 pb, 13464, 14171?
1808:	14261 pb, 14319, 14402
	pb, 14438, 14476a pb, 14481
	pb, 14498, 14521, 14548,
	14552-14553 pb, 14559 pb,
	14613 pb, 14676 pb, 14684
	pb, 14726, 14810 pb, 14876
	pb, 14878 pb, 14942 pb,
	15178 pb, 15190, 15276,
	15317 pb, 15557 pb, 15600
	pb, 15644 pb, 15673 pb,
	16150 pb, 16256, 16311 pb,
	16679 pb
1809:	16789, 16933, 16934?,
	17036, 17249? pb, 17589 pb,
	17778, 17837, 18013 pb,
	18057 pb, 18405 pb, 18560,
	19254
1810:	19404 pb, 19451, 19560,
	19562 pb, 19563, 19704 pb,
	19768 pb, 19904 pb, 20039,
	20140 pb, 20370, 20430,
	20695 pb, 20798 pb,
	20803 pb, 20848?, 21006
	pb, 21048?, 21176, 21354
	pb, 22013-22014, 51034 pb
1811:	22284, 22308 f, 22397,
	22429 pb, 22440, 22850? pb,

23348 pb, 23388, 23450
pb, 23681, 24489
1812: 24525, 24806, 24846 pb,
24875 pb, 24876, 24911,
25453 pb, 25454, 26036 pb,
26067 pb, 26161, 26568 pb,
26664-26665, 26714 pb,
27476, 27555 pb
1813: 27750 pb, 27774, 27810,
27873, 27946, 28056 pb,
28179 pb, 29116-29117 pb,
29234 pb, 29508, 29641,
29795?, 30446
1814: 30730-30731, 30812 pb,
30921-30922, 30967 pb,
32078 pb, 32241 pb, 32398
pb, 32444 pb, 33667 pb,
33701
1815: 33862 pb, 34175, 34299,
34726, 35222-35223 pb,
35424?
1816: 36703, 36791 pb, 36848,
37047, 37456, 37792, 37942,
38191 pb, 38193 pb, 38315
pb, 38323, 38379?, 51619
pb
1817: 39972 pb, 40109-40110,
40579 pb, 40679 pb, 40683
pb, 40977 pb, 40985 pb,
41376-41377 pb, 41507-
41508 pb, 41511, 41691 pb
1818: 43165, 43211?, 43494,
43871 pb, 44231 pb, 44243
pb, 44755 pb, 44929 pb,
44935 pb, 45153 pb, 46831
pb, 46846
1819: 46962, 47050 pb, 47135,
47194 pb, 47442, 48608 pb,
48641 pb, 48775 pb, 48787
pb, 48980 pb, 49099 pb,
49227 pb, 49343 pb, 50139
pb

LORING, JOSIAH (Boston)
1805: 9699 f

LORING, THOMAS (Wilming-
ton, N. C.)
1816: 37164a pb

LORING, THOMAS (Wiscasset,
Me.)
1808: 14573, 14814

LORRAIN, THOMAS W (Colum-
bia, S. C.)
1815: 36058 pb

LORRAIN, THOMAS W (New
Orleans, La.)
1818: 45018 pb

LORRAIN, THOMAS W (Petersburg, Va.)
1817: 39994 pb, 40128

LOTHIAN, ROBERT (Boston)
1807: 12522 f, 13696 f

LOTHROP, JASON (Meredith,
N. H.)
1814: 51370 pb
1815: 34909 f

LOTHROP, REUEL (Meredith,
N. H.)
1815: 34776

LOUDON, ARCHIBALD (Car-
lisle, Pa.)
1804: 5638 pb, 5898, 6230
1805: 8049-8051 pb, 8070,
8272 pb, 8617, 9229 pb,
9346, 9393, 9452
1806: 11344, 11448, 50651,
50664 pb, 50667 pb
1807: 12174, 12734, 12940 pb,
13148
1808: 14532, 15412, 15449-
15450
1809: 16880, 17311, 17350
1810: 21188 pb
1811: 23737 pb
1812: 25164
1813: 28591, 29941
1816: 36764, 37119
1817: 40029

LOUDON, SAMUEL C (New
York)
1801: 420, 517, 722 f, 1023
1805: 8008 pb, 8089 f, 8550 f

Louisiana Courier (New Orleans, La.)
1809: 18301

LOVEGROVE, --- (Baltimore)
1818: 44648 pb

LOVEGROVE, JAMES (Baltimore)
1816: 37666 f

LOW, ESTHER (New York)
1810: 20428 pb, 21533 pb, 21966
1814: 31692
1816: 37105 pb

LOW, JOHN (New York)
1801: 1106? f
1802: 2739
1804: 6233 pb, 7053 sb
1805: 7863 pb, 8971 pb
1807: 12351 pb, 12945 pb
1808: 14258, 15455
1810: 19816
1811: 23777 pb
1812: 26652 pb, 26729
1813: 28396, 29678 pb
1814: 30606 pb, 31388 pb, 31513, 32427 pb, 32602 pb, 32863
1815: 34050 pb, 34137 pb, 34570 pb, 35520-35521 pb
1816: 37750, 38498 pb, 39840
1817: 41682 pb, 42930 pb
1819: 50134 pb

LOW, SOLOMON G (Boston)
1818: 45818

LOW, THOMAS POOLE (New York)
1815: 35922
1816: 37592 pb, 38351
1817: 41609
1818: 45022 pb, 45024

LOWELL, DANIEL (Danville, Vt.)
1818: 45109 f

LOWELL, SAMUEL (Plattsburgh, N. Y.)
1809: 16844 pb
1810: 19696, 19791 pb, 20988
1811: 23709 pb
1812: 26323 pb

LOWERY, M L (Philadelphia)
1807: 12305

LOWRY, WILLIAM (Steubenville, O.)
1806: 11856 pb

LUCAS, ALEXANDER (Raleigh, N. C.)
1811: ?22860, 51114 pb
1812: 25463
1813: 28572, 29852
1814: 31166, 31527, 31972, 51429 pb
1815: 34761, 35310, 35507, 36003
1816: 37649, 38836

LUCAS, FIELDING (Baltimore)
1805: 50608 pb
1808: 16337 pb, 16752 pb
1809: 17650? pb
1810: 19983? pb
1811: 22559 f, 22745 f, 23278 f, 23952 pb, 24474 f
1812: 24850 f, 25008 f, 25267 f, 25676 pb, 25768? pb, 25775 pb, 26157 f, 26184 f, 26345 f, 26346 pb, 26495 f, 51206 pb
1813: 27903 pb, 28185 f, 28446 pb, 28502 pb, 28523 pb, 28720 f, 28955 pb, 29171-29172 f, 29241 f, 30558 f
1814: 30895 f, 30899 f, 30939 f, 31041 pb, 31076 pb, 31080 f, 31186? pb, 31478 pb, 31596 f, 31834 f, 31844 f, 31916 f, 32397 f, 32408 f, 32512 f, 32700 f, 32743 pb, 32818 f, 33530 f, 33708 f
1815: 33853 pb, 33885 f, 34257 f, 34260 f, 34796 pb, 35015 pb, 35351 f, 35719 f
1816: 37027 f, 37126 f, 37483? pb, 37705-37706 pb, 37711 f, 37722-37724 f, 37727 pb, 37729? f, 37961-37962 f, 38068? pb, 38109? pb, 38529 f, 39128 f
1817: 39946 f, 39984 pb, 40229 f, 40658 f, 40709 f, 41037 pb, 41155 f, 41249 f,

41334 f, 41516 pb, 41564
pb, 41892 f, 42936 f
1818: 43554 pb, 43961 pb,
44156 pb, 44172 pb, 44820
f, 44854 f, 44857 f, 45151
f, 45152 pb, 45747 pb,
46635 pb, 46676 pb, 46701
pb, 46837-46838
1819: 47423 pb, 47490 pb,
47735 f, 47745 pb, 47772 f,
47917 f, 48097 pb, 48102?
pb, 48266 f, 48385 f, 48606
pb, 48644 f, 48700 pb,
48986 f, 49175 pb, 49196
pb, 49333 f

LUDGATE, A C (New York)
1804: 6636 pb

Luminary (Richmond, Ky.)
1818: 43183

LUND, HANS (Boston)
1813: 28191 pb

LUND, HANS (Charlestown,
Mass.)
1812: 27431

LYFORD, WILLIAM GILMAN
(Staunton, Va.)
1805: 8132 pb
1808: 15077, 16251 pb
1809: 18498 pb

LYLE, ABRAHAM I (Paris,
Ky.)
1817: 41881

LYLE, JOEL R (Paris, Ky.)
1810: 21363-21364
1812: 26754
1813: 28276

LYLE, JOHN (Paris, Ky.)
1814: 30898 pb, 31816 pb,
33605 pb
1815: 34010 pb, 34585 pb,
35574 pb
1816: 36975 pb, 38056,
38115 pb, 38218 pb, 38811
pb, 39733 pb
1817: 40969 pb, 41329
1818: 46820

LYLE, JOHN N (Georgetown,
Ky.)
1816: 37261, 37698 pb, 37995
1817: 40075, 41196
1818: 43178
1819: 47030

LYLE, JOHN R (Paris, Ky.)
1817: 41881

LYMAN, ASA (Portland, Me.)
1810: 19371 f, 20377 f,
20606-20607 pb
1811: 22750 f, 22982 f, 23199
pb, 23254 f, 23598 f, 24406
f, 24477 f
1812: 24628 pb, 25138 pb,
25712 f, 26478 f

LYMAN, LUKE CLARK (Middletown, Conn.)
1811: 23882 pb
1815: 35869 f, 36014-36015 f
1816: 38344 f, 38890 pb
1817: 42074 pb
1818: 43898, 44273, 44467,
44652
1819: 47081, 47176 pb, 47479,
47978, 48657 pb, 48874 pb,
49286, 49379 pb, 49432

LYMAN, M (Boston)
1810: 21333 pb

LYNCH, JOHN (Richmond, Va.)
1809: 17054, 19123 pb
1810: 20319, 21322, 51009

Lynchburg Press (Lynchburg,
Va.)
1809: 17343

Lynchburg Star (Lynchburg,
Va.)
1807: 12076 pb, 50803 pb

LYON, JAMES (Alexandria,
Va.)
1802: 1739 pb

LYON, JAMES (Mobile, Ala.)
1813: 29185 pb

LYON, JAMES (New Orleans,
La.)
1803:   5190 pb
1804:   6671

LYON, JAMES (Savannah, Ga.)
1802:   2313 pb
1803:   4271, 5402
1804:   5774   .

LYON, JAMES (Washington,
D. C.)
1802:   2148

LYON, M (Washington, D. C.)
1810:   20610 pb

LYON, OLIVER (Troy, N. Y.)
1804:   5793, 50435 pb
1805:   7936, 8460 pb, 8767 pb
1806:   9909, 10432 pb
1807:   12066, 12135, 12597
pb, 12679, 14173
1808:   15045, 15138, 16035
1809:   17535 pb, 17981

LYON, ZEBULON (Troy, N. Y.)
1801:   516 pb, 50215 pb
1802:   1832, 2250 pb, 2299,
2345, 2513
1803:   4225 pb, 4295, 5071,
50334
1804:   6078, 6406

M

Mc---, A (Trenton, N. J.)
1811:   23065 f

MACALASTER, ALEXANDER
(Fayetteville, N. C.)
1815:   35611 pb

MACANULTY, BARNARD
BRIAN (Boston)
1805:   9368 pb

MACANULTY, BARNARD
BRIAN (Salem, Mass.)
1801:   1368 pb

1802:   1756 f
1804:   7317 f, 7318 pb
1805:   9435 pb

M'ARDLE, JOHN P (Clinton,
O.)
1814:   32796
1815:   35965-35966

M'ARDLE, JOHN P (Mount
Vernon, O.)
1816:   38513 pb
1817:   40105, 40429

M'BRIDE, JAMES (Hamilton,
O.)
1814:   32391 f

M'CAHAN, JAMES (Indiana,
Pa.)
1814:   30663 pb

M'CAHAN, JOHN (Huntingdon,
Pa.)
1801:   686 pb
1810:   20415

M'CALL, ROGER (Exeter,
N. H.)
1812:   26328 f

M'CALL, T (Lexington, Ky.)
1814:   30941, 31979 pb

M'CARRELL, JOHN (Shippens-
burgh, Pa.)
1806:   10417 f

McCARTEE, WILLIAM J
(Schenectady, N. Y.)
1807:   13267 pb
1810:   20937 f
1813:   29729 f

M'CARTY, WILLIAM (New
York)
1809:   17309 pb, 17969
1810:   19761 pb, 19920, 20406
pb, 21515 pb

M'CARTY, WILLIAM (Phila-
delphia)
1811:   23067 pb

1812:   25719 f
1813:   27722 f, 28946 f, 29704
        f
1814:   32629? pb
1815:   34862 f, 35681 f
1816:   37842 bf, 37843 pb,
        38208, 39877-39878 pb,
        51579 pb
1817:   40152, 40910 sb, 41058
        pb, 41525, 41529, 42073,
        42252 pb
1818:   43075 pb, 43457 f,
        43478, 43482 pb, 43547 pb,
        44653, 44661 pb, 44670 pb,
        44775 pb, 45357 pb
1819:   47132, 48093 pb, 48095
        pb, 48169 pb, 48373 pb,
        48375 pb, 48536 pb, 49139-
        49140 pb, 50053 pb, 51911
        pb, 51930 pb

M'Carty & Davis (Philadelphia)
see M'CARTY, WILLIAM
     (Philadelphia)
     DAVIS, THOMAS (Philadel-
     phia)

M'CLANE, JOHN (Lexington,
   Ky.)
1815:   33906 pb

M'CLANE, WILLIAM (Lexing-
   ton, Ky.)
1815:   33906 pb

M'CLANE, WILLIAM (Phila-
   delphia)
1813:   28520 f

M'CLEAN, JOHN (Lebanon, O.)
1807:   12696, 14206 pb
1808:   16776

M'CLEAN, NATHANIEL
   (Lebanon, O.)
1809:   16929
1810:   21156
1811:   23202, 23380
1812:   25425
1813:   29193 pb, 29755

M'CLEAN, NATHANIEL
   (Xenia, O.)
1814:   32395 pb

M'CLEAN, WILLIAM (Lebanon,
   O.)
1814:   32157

M'CLELLAN, ROBERT (York,
   Pa.)
1805:   8275

McCLURE, DAVID (Philadel-
   phia)
1815:   51509 pb

M'CLURE, WILLIAM (Dayton,
   O.)
1808:   14834 pb

M'CONNELL, MATTHEW
   (Philadelphia)
1813:   28675 pb, 29467 pb,
        51343 f

M'CORKLE, WILLIAM (Greensburg, Pa.)
1801:   50193 pb
1803:   5626

M'CORKLE, WILLIAM (Phila-
   delphia)
1804:   6329 pb, 7045 pb
1805:   8246
1806:   50710

MacCOUN, DAVID (Lexington,
   Ky.)
1808:   16717 f
1809:   50952 f
1810:   20269 f
1811:   22471 f, 22950 f
1812:   27503 f

MacCOUN, JAMES (Lexington,
   Ky.)
1808:   16717 f
1809:   50952 f
1810:   20269 f
1811:   22471 f, 22950 f
1812:   27503 f

M'CREA, SAMUEL (Baltimore)
1802:   1754 pb

M'CULLOCH, EBENEZER
   (Philadelphia)
1807:   14160 pb, 14228 pb,

14242 pb
1808: 50901 pb
1811: 51084 pb

M'CULLOCH, JOHN (Philadelphia)
1801: 254 pb, 312 pb, 854
pb, 1321 pb, 1689 pb
1802: 1726 f, 1892 pb, 2561
pb, 2926 pb, 50282 pb,
50320 pb
1803: 3906 pb, 3965 pb, 4205
pb, 4566 pb, 5044 pb, 5093
pb, 5619 pb
1804: 6022 pb, 6687 pb, 7106
pb
1805: 8194 pb, 8401, 8816
pb, 9743, 9774 pb
1806: 10792 pb, 11314 pb,
50695 pb
1807: 12962 f, 13377 pb,
50866 pb
1809: 19277 pb, 50949 pb
1810: 51043 pb
1811: 23264 pb
1813: 29010 pb

M'CULLOCH, WILLIAM (Philadelphia)
1807: 12962, 13564 pb
1808: 14673 pb, 14999 pb,
16312, 16698
1809: 17424, 17517 pb, 17531,
17533, 17918, 18164 pb,
18327, 18614 pb, 18794,
19164, 50940
1810: 19582, 19757 pb, 19993,
20328, 20330-20332, 20494,
20773, 21007, 22069, 51005
pb
1811: 22338, 22807 pb, 22849,
23006, 23018, 23222, 23240,
23271, 23476-23477, 24501
pb, 51098, 51149 pb
1812: 25352, 26642 pb,
51182, 51215 pb
1813: 27715 pb, 28254, 28944
pb, 29010 pb, 30472 pb,
51347 pb
1814: 30708-30709 pb, 31352,
31493 pb, 33733 f, 51399,
51407 pb, 51450 pb
1815: 33997, 35156 pb, 36083

M'CULLOUGH, RANDALL
(Corydon, Ind.)
1819: 48335, 48337

M'CURDY, JAMES (Natchez,
Miss.)
1814: 30763, 32143-32145,
32715
1815: 35390, 35391 pb, 35392,
35855 pb

M'DERMUT, ROBERT (New
York)
1804: 50447 f
1806: 9983 f, 11911 f
1809: 17208 pb
1810: 19966 pb, 20013 f,
21891 f
1811: 22375, 24391 f
1813: 27679 f, 27680 pb,
28284 f, 29049 f, 29812 f,
51262 pb
1814: 30694 pb, 30695 f,
31583 pb, 32685 f, 32753 f
1815: 34207 pb, 35546? pb,
35772 f, 35818 pb, 36556 f
1816: 36985 pb, 37482 pb,
38749 pb, 38762 pb, 39026
f, 39855 f
1817: 42022 f
1818: 43050 pb

M'DONALD, DONALD (New
York)
1815: 35960 f, 36005 pb

M'DONNELL, ALEXANDER
(Athens, Ga.)
1808: 15099 pb
1814: 30713 pb

M'DOWELL, CHARLES (Bed-
ford, Pa.)
1805: 7965 pb
1811: 23807
1816: 38813 pb
1818: 45019 pb

M'DOWELL, CHARLES (Lan-
caster, Pa.)
1803: 4380 pb
1804: 7018 pb
1805: 9124, 50591 pb

MacDUFFEE, DANIEL (Goshen,
  N. Y.)
1816: 37919 pb
1817: 41393 pb

MacDUFFEE, DANIEL (Pough-
  keepsie, N. Y.)
1811: 23802 pb

M'DUFFEE, DONALD (New
  York)
1819: 48472 pb, 48539, 49563
  pb, 49566

M'FARLAND, JOHN (Cham-
  bersburg, Pa.)
1815: 34562 pb

M'FARLAND, JOHN (Harris-
  burg, Pa.)
1818: 43683 pb

M'FARLAND, JOHN (Shippensburg, Pa.)
1817: 42186 pb

M'FARLANE, MONTEITH (New
  York)
1801: 1091
1806: 10297, 11187, 11328,
  50656, 50668 pb
1807: 12111-12112, 12286,
  12331, 12509, 12673, 12704,
  12777, 12779, 12859, 13118,
  13159 pb, 13549, 14147 pb,
  50758-50759
1808: 14610-14611, 14625,
  15588, 15768-15769, 15953,
  15978, 16093, 16188 pb,
  16240
1809: 16955, 17018, 17644,
  17762, 17972-17973, 18118,
  18449, 18451, 19224

M'FARLAND, JOHN (Carlisle,
  Pa.)
1817: 42185 pb
1818: 44298

M'FETRICH, SAMUEL H
  (Philadelphia)
1804: 5897, 7198
1805: 8021 pb

M'GILLDA, --- (New York)
1812: 25550 f

M'GIRR, WILLIAM (Browns-
  ville, Pa.)
1817: 42961 pb

M'GLASHAN, DANIEL (Albany,
  N. Y.)
1814: 30610, 30829 bf

McGLASSIN, GEORGE (Win-
  chester, Va.)
1819: 48224 pb

M'GRANAGHAN, WILLIAM
  (Clarksburg, Va.)
1819: 48333 pb

M'GRANAGHAN, WILLIAM
  (Morgantown, Va.)
1815: 35300 pb

M'HENRY, JAMES (Baltimore)
1807: 13560 f

M'ILHENNY, WILLIAM (Bos-
  ton)
1810: 19572 f, 21254 pb

M'INTYRE, ARCHIBALD C
  (Darien, Ga.)
1818: 43810 pb

M'INTYRE, PATRICK (Leesburg,
  Va.)
1808: 16666 pb
1809: 18097

MACK, EBENEZER (Ithaca,
  N. Y.)
1817: 39982 pb

MACK, STEPHEN (Owego,
  N. Y.)
1803: 3662 pb
1804: 7309 pb
1805: 9481
1809: 18312 pb

M'KAY, --- (Washington, D. C.)
1809: 17363?

McKEAN, W (New York)
1816: 36749 pb

M'KEEHAN, DAVID (Natchez,
    Miss.)
1811: 23480 pb
1812: 26565

M'KEEHAN, DAVID (Pittsburgh,
    Pa.)
1807: 12646 f

M'KEEN, THOMAS H (Clarks-
    ville, Tenn.)
1819: 49621 pb

M'KENZIE, JOHN (Philadel-
    phia)
1810: 19357, 20559, 20702,
    21208, 21232
1811: 22368, 22434a, 22492,
    22594, 23229, 24428

MACKEY, JOHN (Charleston,
    S. C.)
1812: 25274, 25722 pb
1813: 28819 pb, 29124

M'KNIGHT, JAMES (Mount
    Holly, N. J.)
1816: 37089, 39092

M'KNIGHT, JAMES (Philadel-
    phia)
1815: 51514 pb

M'KOWN, JOHN (Boston)
1814: 31035

M'KOWN, JOHN (Charlestown,
    Mass.)
1815: 35226, 35706

M'KOWN, JOHN (Portland,
    Me.)
1805: 8897, 9181, 9269
1806: 10024 pb, 10114, 10937-
    10938, 10992, 11105,
    11167, 11340, 11822
1807: 11980, 12048, 12192-
    12193, 12835, 13009, 13032,
    13053, 13068 pb, 13070-
    13071, 13151, 13443 pb

1808: 14255, 14265-14267,
    14423, 14428, 14592, 14996
    pb, 15587, 15854-15855
1809: 16866?, 16916-16917,
    16923, 16949, 17834, 18441
1810: 19371, 19375, 19430,
    19611-19612, 20376-20377,
    20485, 22098 pb
1811: 22261, 22409, 22448-
    22449 pb, 22461, 22740,
    22750, 22982, 23026, 23254,
    23397 pb, 23598, 24063,
    24406, 24477
1812: 26089-26090

M'LARAN, WILLIAM (St.
    Francisville, La.)
1819: 48519 pb

M'LAUGHLIN, J (Washington,
    D. C.)
1818: 43491 pb

McLAUGHLIN, NATHANIEL
    (Petersburg, Va.)
1807: 14138 pb

McLAUGHLIN, WILLIAM F
    (Petersburg, Va.)
1807: 13482 pb

McLAUGHLIN, WILLIAM F
    (Philadelphia)
1801: 636, 677, 730, 1083,
    1309
1802: 2104, 2264, 2548, 2666,
    3019, 3159
1803: 3763, 3960, 4213, 4801,
    4877-4878 pb, 4993
1804: 5719, 5809, 6101, 6399,
    6699, 6782-6783, 7072 pb
1805: 7955 pb, 7985 pb, 8436,
    9159 pb
1806: 10401, 11170-11171 pb,
    11816 pb, 50675
1807: 13402 pb
1810: 20070 pb

M'LEAN
see also M'CLEAN

McLEAN, CHARLES D (Nash-
    ville, Tenn.)

1816: 36850
1817: 40113, 42902
1818: 43213
1819: 47689

MACLEAN, DAVID (Greens-
  burg, Pa.)
1811: 22942 pb

M'LEAN, NORMAN (Savannah,
  Ga.)
1807: 13455 pb

McLEAN, WILLIAM (Utica,
  N. Y.)
1802: 2519

McMAHON, THOMAS F (Phila-
  delphia)
1817: 42001 sb
1819: 48550 f

McMANAMAN, CHARLES D
  (Williamsburg, O.)
1818: 43643 pb

M'MILLAN, ALEXANDER
  (Augusta, Ga.)
1803: 4268
1804: 7200
1805: 9310

M'MILLAN, ALEXANDER
  (Milledgeville, Ga.)
1807: 12652

M'MULLIN, JOHN (Lexington,
  Va.)
1801: 1264 pb

M'MURTRY, --- (Harrods-
  burg, Ky.)
1814: 31927 pb

M'QUEEN, ALEXANDER
  (Pittsburgh, Pa.)
1815: 36469 f

M'RAE, ALEXANDER G
  (Clarksburg, Va.)
1815: 36549 pb
1816: 36873

M'WILLIAMS, JOHN (Washington, N. C.)
1815: 33848 pb

MADDOX, JOHN (Richmond,
  Va.)
1819: 49292 pb

MADOX, D T (Lexington, Ind.)
1816: 37344 pb, 39023

MAFFET, SAMUEL (Wilkes-
  barre, Pa.)
1810: 21444 pb
1819: 47131, 47134, 48537,
  49058

MAGAURAN, --- (Baltimore)
1812: 25621
1817: 40961
1818: 43124 pb, 43650, 44208,
  45447

MAGAW, WILLIAM (Philadel-
  phia)
1810: 21461 f

MAGEE, ALEXANDER (Car-
  lisle, Pa.)
1815: 34446 pb

MAGEE, JAMES (Hagerstown,
  Md.)
1803: 4680 pb

MAGILL, SAMUEL (Baltimore)
1807: 12463, 12999
1808: 14411, 14648, 14959,
  14977, 15499, 15962 pb
1809: 17872, 18401 pb
1810: 19491, 19997, 20536,
  20833, 20839, 21310 pb,
  21366

MAGILL, SAMUEL (Cumber-
  land, Md.)
1813: 27691 pb

MAGRUDER, WILLIAM (Cum-
  berland, Md.)
1815: 33825 pb

MAIDEN, T (New York)
1816: 38250 pb

MALLORY, DANIEL (Boston)
1808: 14356-14357 f, 14590
pb, 14904 f, 15151 pb,
15255 f, 15834 f, 15904 f,
16157 pb, 16179 pb, 16237
f, 16657 f
1809: 17206 pb, 17683 f,
17704 pb, 17788 f, 18089
f, 18189 pb, 18558 pb,
18635 f, 18656 pb, 18728 f,
19204 f
1810: 19484 pb, 19927 f,
19963 pb, 20054 f, 20056 f,
20103 pb, 20110 pb, 20200
pb, 20257 f, 20461 pb,
20624 pb, 20917 f, 21283
pb, 21402 f, 21527 f, 21795,
21930-21931 pb, 21935 pb,
22093 f, 22104? f
1811: 22155 f, 22696 f, 22789
f, 22978 pb, 23781-23782
pb, 24333 f, 24498 f
1812: 26135? sb

MALLORY, DANIEL (George-
town, D. C.)
1813: 28608-28609 pb, 28768
f, 51321 pb
1814: 31308 f, 32133-32134
pb, 32165 f, 32875 pb,
32925 pb, 51443 pb
1815: 35799 pb, 51498 pb
1816: 37869 pb

MALLORY, SAMUEL (Bridge-
port, Conn.)
1803: 4653
1804: 5965, 6993 pb
1805: 8080 pb, 9066
1806: 50751

MALLORY, SAMUEL (New
York)
1802: 2792 pb, 2945

MALTBY, ABIEL H (New
Haven, Conn.)
1816: 36692 f, 36916 f,
38245 f
1817: 40148 f, 40443 f,

42116 f, 51689 f
1818: 43670 pb, 44389? pb,
44834 f, 45586 pb, 45780 pb,
45902 pb
1819: 47188 pb, 47467 pb,
48081 pb, 48688. pb, 48785
pb, 48846 pb, 49458 pb,
49640 pb, 49969, 50001,
50058 pb, 50104

MALTBY, B (Waterloo, N. Y.)
1818: 43128 pb

MANN, --- (Boston)
1818: 45760 pb

MANN, CAMILL M (Baltimore)
1813: 29262 pb

MANN, CHARLES (Frederick,
Md.)
1817: 42931 f

MANN, DANIEL (Dedham,
Mass.)
1818: 44463, 44930 pb, 44999

MANN, HERMAN (Boston)
1816: 38927
1817: 40284, 40343

MANN, HERMAN (Dedham,
Mass.)
1801: 621, 865, 1341, 1402
1802: 2208 pb, 2301, 2584 pb,
2605, 2607-2609 pb, 3141
bsb, 3156 pb
1803: 3901, 3992 pb, 4206,
4498, 4900
1804: 6129, 6249, 6640, 7155
pb, 7341 pb
1805: 7845, 8101, 8393-8395,
8523 pb, 8699, 9026 pb,
9187, 50493 pb
1806: 10267, 10635, 11204,
11251, 11350 pb
1807: 12591, 12824, 13401,
13579a pb, 13681, 14245
1808: 15837-15838, 15859,
16076, 16139, 16181, 16304
1809: 16982, 17409, 18274,
18520, 18585, 18597 pb,
18746

1810: 20448 pb, 20708,
20983, 21224, 21335, 21432,
21489
1811: 22376, 22436a, 22670,
22673 pb, 23113, 23579 pb,
23626-23627, 23928, 23937,
24393
1812: 24560, ?25246?, 25273,
26308, 26309 pb, 26375,
26377, 26821, 26865-26866
1815: 34145, 35344 pb, 35913
1816: 37410, 37513, 38138
pb, 38475, 39673
1817: 40284, 40343, 40672 pb
1818: 43094, 43386, 44409,
44679 pb, 45524, 46694
1819: 47658 pb, 47777-47778,
47965, 47984, 48319, 48737,
49358

MANN, HERMAN B (Providence,
R. I.)
1813: 28025, 28161, 28509,
29433, 29540, 29722-29724,
29905 pb, 29952, 29982
1814: 30942, 32590, 51411
1815: 33904, 36582

MANN, JACOB (Morristown,
N. J.)
1805: 7987, 8193, 8739 pb
1806: 10104, 10125 pb, 10148
pb, 10307 pb
1807: 12303 pb, 12644
1808: 14697, 15836 pb, 16739
1809: 17218, 17833
1810: 19782 pb
1811: 22536
1812: 25072 pb
1813: 28145-28146 pb, 29875
1814: 31158 pb, 31549, 31690,
31987
1815: 34353 pb, 34582, 35700
1816: 37249 pb
1817: 40476 pb
1818: 43623, 44301, 45008-
45010, 45890, 46898
1819: 47621 pb

MANN, JACOB (Trenton, N. J.)
1801: 1012, 1015, 1330?,
1436 pb

MANN, JOHN (Dover, N. H.)
1812: 24791-24792
1813: 28764
1814: 31139, 32251
1815: 34215, 34261, 35431,
35667?
1816: 36962
1817: 40146, 40692, 41077
1818: 45807 pb

MANN, WILLIAM HAYNES
(Dedham, Mass.)
1816: 37513
1817: 40284, 40343, 40672 pb
1818: 43094, 43386, 44409,
44679 pb, 45524, 46694
1819: 47658 pb, 47777-47778,
47965, 47984, 48319, 48737,
49358

MANN, WILLIAM METCALF
(Providence, R. I.)
1814: 30909, 31015-31016,
31206, 31376, 32587, 32932
1815: 34473, 34559, 35524,
36081
1816: 38196, 39839

MANNING, --- (New York)
1810: 22131

MANNING, JAMES (Bethany,
Pa.)
1818: 46734 pb

MANNING, THOMAS S (Phila-
delphia)
1801: 1674
1803: 4320, 4688
1804: 5884, 6278, 50423
1805: 9342 pb, 50564 pb
1806: 10716, 10731, 11441
1807: 13134 pb, 13139-13140
pb, 13375
1809: 18594-18595 pb
1810: 20783?, 21230-21231 pb
1811: 22966
1813: 28198, 29674
1814: 31089, 31529
1815: 34517 pb, 34741, 35234
1816: 37653-37654, 37778
1817: 40412, 40866-40867,
41282 pb

1818: 44098
1819: 48035, 49080

MANNING, WILLIAM (Boston)
1801: 12 pb, 14, 30, 100,
115, 139, 157 pb, 193-195,
212 pb, 425, 473 pb, 546
pb, 549, 597 pb, 671 pb,
894 pb, 911, 920 pb, 953,
954 pb, 1086 pb, 1280,
1353, 1357 pb, 1400, 1433
f, 1606, 50255
1802: 1756, 1799, 1837 pb,
1840, 1898, 1901-1902, 2006,
2092 f, 2094 f, 2105 pb,
2151 pb, 2185 pb, 2257,
2281 pb, 2283 pb, 2285-
2286 pb, 2288-2291 pb,
2293, 2294 pb, 2374, 2482
f, 2539, 2585 pb, 2631 pb,
2641 f, 2665? pb, 2690 pb,
2708, 2711, 2718 pb, 2752?
pb, 2851 pb, 2854, 2913
pb, 3094, 3118, 3175 f,
3591
1803: 3629, 3680 pb, 3708
pb, 3719, 3753 pb, 3756,
3806 pb, 3809 pb, 3812 bf,
3813-3814 pb, 3824, 3829,
3865, 3918 pb, 3945, 3955,
4135? pb, 4141, 4214,
4254-4257 pb, 4298, 4340,
4355 bf, 4440-4441, 4442
pb, 4616 pb, 4658-4659,
4725?, 4780, 4894, 5064
pb, 5066, 5107, 5110,
5548 pb
1804: 5664, 5754, 5755 pb,
5757, 5861 f, 5873-5875,
6011 pb, 6079, 6093, 6214,
6252 pb, 6353-6355, 6408,
6446-6449, 6493, 6566 pb,
6619-6620, 6695, 6750 pb,
6765, 6840 pb, 6844, 6975-
6976 pb, 7249 pb, 7256,
7280 pb, 7283 pb, 7285?,
7395, 7703-7704, 50425
1805: 7871 pb, 7908 pb,
7942, 7953 pb, 8022 pb,
8031 pb, 8106, 8155 pb,
8494 pb, 8528 pb, 8548,
8587-8588, 8837, 8861 pb,
8866, 8874 pb, 8884, 8890

pb, 8895 pb, 8922 pb, 9175
pb, 9369-9370 pb, 9426-
9430, 9435 pb, 9684 pb,
9687, 9699
1806: 9824, 9876, 9881 pb,
9906, 9981 pb, 9992 pb,
10014, 10017 pb, 10055-
10056 pb, 10178 pb, 10426
pb, 10461 pb, 10512, 10557
pb, 10781, 10832 pb, 10838
pb, 10842, 10860 pb, 10918
pb, 11320, 11484, 11803 pb,
11814 pb, 50649 pb
1807: 12024 pb, 12062, 12136,
12145-12146, 12150 pb,
12236 pb, 12251, 12280,
12308, 12762, 12981, 13020
f, 13035 pb, 13061 pb,
13064 pb, 13067 pb, 13079
pb, 13314, 13413 pb, 13464,
14171?
1808: 14261 pb, 14319, 14402
pb, 14438, 14476a pb, 14481
pb, 14498, 14521, 14548,
14552-14553 pb, 14559 pb,
14613 pb, 14676 pb, 14684
pb, 14726, 14810 pb, 14876
pb, 14878 pb, 14942 pb,
15178 pb, 15190, 15276,
15317 pb, 15557 pb, 15600
pb, 15644 pb, 15673 pb,
16150 pb, 16256, 16311 pb,
16679 pb
1809: 16789, 16933, 16934?,
17036, 17249? pb, 17589 pb,
17778, 17837, 18013 pb,
18057 pb, 18405 pb, 18560,
19254
1810: 19404 pb, 19451, 19560,
19562 pb, 19563, 19704 pb,
19768 pb, 19904 pb, 20039,
20140 pb, 20370, 20430,
20695 pb, 20798 pb, 20803
pb, 21006 pb, 21048?, 21176,
21354 pb, 22013-22014,
51034 pb
1811: 22284, 22308 f, 22397,
22429 pb, 22440, 22850?
pb, 23348 pb, 23388, 23450
pb, 23681, 24489
1812: 24525, 24806, 24846 pb,
24875 pb, 24876, 24911,
25453 pb, 25454, 26036 pb,

26067 pb, 26161, 26568 pb,
26664-26665, 26714 pb,
27476, 27555 pb
1813: 27750 pb, 27774, 27810,
27873, 27946, 28056 pb,
28179 pb, 29116-29117 pb,
29234 pb, 29508, 29614,
29795?, 30446
1814: 30730-30731, 30812 pb,
30921-30922, 30967 pb,
32078 pb, 32241 pb, 32398
pb, 32445 pb, 33667 pb,
33701
1815: 33862 pb, 34175, 34299,
34726, 35223 pb
1816: 37936 pb
1817: 40683 pb

MANNING, WILLIAM (Wor-
cester, Mass.)
1814: 30665, 31808, 32920
1815: 33837, 34037, 34708,
35004, 35553
1816: 36693, 36799-36801,
37128, 37197, 37403, 37534,
37715-37716, 37735-37736,
37937 bf, 38705, 38746
1817: 40055-40057, 40087,
40573 pb, 40829, 40925-
40926, 40937, 41153 pb,
41233 pb, 41819, 41849-
41850, 42177?, 42264,
42267-42268, 42270, 42840,
42944
1818: 43155-43156, 43189,
43246, 43635, 43791, 43843,
43974, 44445 pb, 44678,
45369, 45802 pb, 46703,
46822, 46848-46849
1819: 46964, 46972, 47068-
47070, 47104, 47107, 47465-
47466, 47507, 47635 pb,
47763-47764, 47915, 48359,
48439, 48466, 48498, 48575,
48999, 49030, 49147 pb,
49149-49150, 49452, 49534
pb, 50131, 50141, 50147,
50170, 51876

MANSON, THOMAS PESCUD
(Richmond, Va.)
1809: 50953 pb
1810: 19460
1811: 22245?

MANSUR, ELIJAH (Amherst,
N.H.)
1819: 47762, 50089

MARCH, ANGIER (Newbury-
port, Mass.)
1801: 284, 1640
1802: 1985, 2112, 2195, 2377
f, 2414, 2504 pb, 2587 pb,
2762 pb, 3503 f, 3557
1803: 3985 pb, 4275, 4318 pb,
4453 pb, 4457 f, 4662 pb,
5031 pb, 5089 pb, 5141 pb,
5173 pb, 5621 pb
1804: 6178 f, 6426 f, 6810 f,
7058 f, 7259 pb, 7300 f,
7749 pb
1805: 8090 f, 8169 pb, 8508
f, 9080 pb, 9176-9178 f
1806: 11189-11190 f, 11873 f,
50715 pb

MARCH, JOHN (Georgetown,
D.C.)
1805: 50532 f
1807: 13285 f
1809: 17974

MARCHANT, PETER TIMOTHY
(Charleston, S.C.)
1807: 12063, 12467, 12616 pb
1808: 14659 pb, 15328 pb

MARKS, SAMUEL (New York)
1813: 29412 pb
1814: 30648, 32002-32003,
32149
1815: 34268, 34409, 34567
1816: 39895
1817: 40994, 41864 pb, 42946
1818: 43085, 44022-44025,
44600-44601
1819: 48156, 48441, 48812,
49441

MAROT, WILLIAM (Philadel-
phia)
1818: 44653 f
1819: 48461 f

MARSCHALK, ANDREW
(Natchez, Miss.)
1801: 938
1802: 2083 pb, 2674, 2677 pb

1804: 5692, 6686 pb, 6794, 6796
1805: 9649
1806: 10326, 10885
1807: 13617?
1808: 15622, 15687 pb, 16742-16743
1815: 35292, 36489 pb
1816: 38270 pb, 38703
1817: 40090 pb, 41454, 41458 pb
1818: 44092, 44828, 44867 pb, 44869-44870, 44872 pb, 44873 pb
1819: 47108, 48682, 48714-48715

MARSCHALK, ANDREW (Washington, Miss.)
1813: 29959, 30473 pb
1814: 32011, 32146 pb, 32946 pb, 51410 pb

MARSH, GUY C (New Haven, Conn.)
1818: 44160 pb

MARSH, LUTHER (Elizabethtown, N.Y.)
1812: 26604 pb

MARSH, WILLIAM S (Hartford, Conn.)
1814: 31238 f, 31815 f
1815: 35827 f
1816: 37920 pb, 38112 pb, 38656 pb
1818: 43053 pb, 43498 pb, 43702 pb, 43847 pb, 44647 pb, 51796 pb
1819: 49034 pb

MARSHALL, HUMPHREY (Frankfort, Ky.)
1810: 19354 pb

MARSHALL, WILLIAM (Philadelphia)
1801: 604
1802: 2590 pb
1804: 7123 pb

MARSHALL, WILLIAM (Richmond, Va.)
1804: 6627 f

MARSTON, BENJAMIN (Boston)
1816: 36713 pb, 37627 pb

MARTIN, ALEXANDER (Baltimore)
1801: 527
1803: 5484
1804: 7371, 7538 pb, 7640-7641

MARTIN, DAVID (Frederick, Md.)
1819: 48588 f, 49633 f

MARTIN, FRANCOIS XAVIER (Newbern, N.C.)
1801: 873 pb, 1246
1802: 2173? pb, 2199 pb, 2801 pb, 2917 pb
1803: 3826, 4130? pb, 4586 pb, 4979? pb
1804: 6714 pb, 6940-6941 pb

MARTIN, GEORGE A (Petersburg, Va.)
1816: 38230 pb

MARTIN, JAMES (Baltimore)
1818: 44284 f

MARTIN, JAMES (Philadelphia)
1809: 17724 f
1813: 29372 f

MARTIN, WILLIAM W (Winchester, Ky.)
1814: 31859 pb, 33702 pb

MARVIN, THEOPHILUS ROGERS (Norwich, Conn.)
1817: 40068, 40621, 41676
1818: 43796-43797, 44612
1819: 47766 pb

MASON, JAMES M (Cincinnati, O.)
1816: 36844, 37307, 37965, 39788
1817: 40103 pb, 40104, 40499

pb, 40500, 42875 pb, 42962 pb
1818: 43206, 43552, 45310, 46769, 46869 pb
1819: 47361, 47614 pb, 47617, 47619, 49223

MASON, JOSEPH (Warren, R. I.)
1812: 25119 pb, 26530, 26562-26563

MASON, THOMAS (New York)
1816: 37337 f, 37831 pb, 37912 f, 38241 f, 38243 f, 38839 f
1817: 40151 f, 40185 f, 40358 f, 41318 f, 41419-41422 f, 42236 f, 42869 pb
1818: 43049 f, 43078 f, 43258 f, 43631 f, 43887 f, 44048 f, 44546 f, 44825 f, 44827 pb, 44829 pb, 44830-44831 f, 44883 pb, 45161 f, 45854 f, 46762-46764 f, 46805 f
1819: 47629 f, 47845 f, 47993 f, 48357 f, 48683 f, 48686a f, 49582 f

Massachusetts Historical Society (Boston)
1801: 27, 222, 833, 872, 958
1804: 6488-6489 pb
1809: 17430
1819: 47782 pb

Massachusetts Missionary Society (Boston)
1803: 4615 pb

Massachusetts Society for Promoting Christian Knowledge (Boston)
1811: 22224 f

Massachusetts Spy (Worcester, Mass.)
1809: 18020, 18900, 19229
1810: 19309

Mast Burnard Co. (New York)
1815: 36442 f

MASTIN, JEREMIAH (Newbern, N. C.)
1806: 10164 f

MATCHETT, EDWARD (Baltimore)
1809: 17879, 18170-18172
1810: 19639, 20588

MATCHETT, RICHARD J (Baltimore)
1807: 13532
1811: 23940
1812: 26739
1816: 37082, 39894
1817: 41946, 41962
1818: 44267
1819: 47067, 47356, 47722, 48552, 49000, 49333, 50192

MATHEWS, JOHN R (Lancaster, Pa.)
1805: 8245 pb, 9120 pb
1806: 11129
1807: 13330-13331, 13649

MATLACK, EMMOR (Philadelphia)
1819: 47405 f, 48461 f

MAULOUIN, A P A (New York)
1804: 6804 pb

MAUND, THOMAS MARTIN (Baltimore)
1815: 34107 pb, 34654? pb
1816: 36958 pb, 38020, 38328 pb, 38339 pb, 38875-38876 pb, 39690
1817: 39996, 40160, 40234-40235, 40307, 40418 pb, 40896 pb, 40909, 40917 pb, 41143, 42060 pb, 42063 pb, 42118 pb, 42347, 42863 pb, 51668-51669 pb, 51710-51712 pb
1818: 43666, 43965 pb, 43970, 44136 pb, 44162 pb, 44302 pb, 44484, 45312, 45644 pb, 45711, 45778, 46664, 46778
1819: 46995, 47920, 48128, 48225 pb, 48526 pb, 48758 pb, 48989, 49240, 49369 pb, 49395 pb, 50003, 50097

MAURO, PHILIP (Baltimore)
1813:   28467, 28650 pb, 28817
        pb, 29197, 30461 pb, 30549
1814:   30844, 30895, 31397
        pb, 31569, 31883 pb, 32800

MAURY, EVARIST (St. Louis,
   Mo.)
1818:   44157

MAVERICK, PETER (New
   York)
1804:   6704 pb
1816:   38201 pb

MAVERICK, PETER (Newark,
   N. J.)
1811:   22741 engr

MAVERICK, PETER (Wash-
   ington, D. C.)
1818:   46130 engr

MAXWELL, --- (Shepherds-
   town, Va.)
1817:   41280

MAXWELL, HUGH (Bellefonte,
   Pa.)
1816:   37918 pb

MAXWELL, HUGH (Lancaster,
   Pa.)
1817:   41766 pb

MAXWELL, HUGH (Mifflin-
   burg, Pa.)
1815:   33797 pb

MAXWELL, HUGH (Philadel-
   phia)
1801:   219, 236-237, 240,
        292, 557, 661, 700, 731,
        1170 pb, 1231, 1263, 1274,
        1278-1279, 1668
1802:   1845, 2157, 2168,
        2305, 2338, 2371, 2458,
        2543, 2831, 2842, 3006,
        3022, 3033, 3075, 3086,
        3106, 3172, 3575
1803:   3639, 3653, 3844 pb,
        3874, 3883, 4290-4291,
        4398, 4415, 4527-4528,

4630, 5027, 5073-5074 pb,
5528, 50333
1804:   5640, 5641 pb, 5708 pb,
        5816 pb, 5869 f, 5884 f,
        5976, 5979 pb, 6424, 6503,
        6523 pb, 6553, 6579, 6581,
        6675, 6778, 6817 pb, 6987,
        7004, 7028-7029, 7049,
        7052, 7143, 7246, 7657,
        7750
1805:   7819, 8043 pb, 8116 pb,
        8119, 8127 pb, 8652, 8657
        pb, 8732, 9327 pb, 9342 pb
1806:   9850 f, 10676, 10898 f,
        11250 pb
1807:   12800 pb, 13134 pb,
        13609 pb
1808:   15867

MAXWELL, JAMES (Philadel-
   phia)
1807:   11921-11922, 13351 pb,
        13640
1808:   14254, 15313, 16140,
        16644
1809:   16785, 17029
1810:   19683, 19968, 20158,
        20561, 20698-20700, 20994,
        21241, 21281? pb, 21993
1811:   22463, 22552, 22867,
        22871, 22896, 23661, 23784,
        23981
1812:   24518-24519, 24623,
        24892, 25130, 25719, 25731-
        25732, 26085, 26261, 26388,
        26745, 26909
1813:   28115, 28499, 28574,
        28578, 28900, 29170, 29198,
        29212, 29219, 29620 pb,
        29622 pb, 29687 pb, 29749,
        29752
1814:   30611 pb, 30638, 31017,
        31053, 31274, 31393, 31469,
        31733, 31924, 32161, 32165,
        32471g, 32814, 32838, 33656
1815:   34002 pb, 34783, 34935,
        35069, 35253, 35319, 35726,
        35745, 35856
1816:   36783, 37136-37137,
        37143, 37219, 37340, 37368,
        37679, 37859-37860, 38035,
        38280, 38620, 38655, 38734-
        38735, 38998, 39810

1817: 39950, 40379, 40648,
    40687, 40933 pb, 40975,
    41162, 41187, 41237, 41345,
    41476, 41489, 41742, 41861,
    41953, 42078, 42129, 42232,
    42816
1818: 43442, 43467, 43515,
    43820, 43842, 44233, 44368,
    44473, 44766, 44888, 44904,
    45217, 45458, 45485, 45661,
    46618
1819: 46939, 47484, 47486,
    47488, 47494, 48350, 48352-
    48354, 48381 pb, 49015,
    49026-49027, 49317, 49557

MAXWELL, NATHANIEL G
    (Baltimore)
1815: 33846 f, 34189 f, 34936
    f, 35046 f, 35633 f, 35718
    f, 36059 f, 36420 pb
1816: 36732 pb, 37059 f,
    37071 f, 38122 pb
1817: 40960 pb, 41064 f,
    41516 pb, 42307 f
1818: 44967 f, 45367 pb,
    45723 f, 46635 pb
1819: 47343 f, 48266 f,
    48394 pb, 48655 pb, 48756
    f, 48824 f, 48991 f

MAXWELL, ROBERT R
    (Baltimore)
1802: 2409

MAXWELL, THOMAS (Wash-
    ington, Ga.)
1805: 8771 f

MAY, DANIEL (Hagerstown,
    Md.)
1814: 31862, 32225 pb, 33558
1815: 34434 pb, 34838, 35035,
    36013 pb, 36455 pb, 36535
    pb
1816: 39691 pb
1817: 41923, 42799 pb
1818: 44297, 46665 pb
1819: 48444 pb, 48527 pb,
    49251 pb, 49252, 49663,
    50004 pb

MAY, J J (Hagerstown, Md.)
1801: 728

MAYER, BENJAMIN (Harris-
    burg, Pa.)
1801: 58, 153, 924
1802: 1882
1803: 5142 pb
1804: 6392, 6471, 7237, 7676
1806: 11915
1808: 15886, 50823 pb
1809: 17165

MAYER, SALOMON (York, Pa.)
1801: 1135
1803: 3895

MAYO, FREDERICK A (Rich-
    mond, Va.)
1815: 51457 pb
1818: 51840 f

MAYO, GEORGE (Philadelphia)
1816: 38208 f
1818: 44774 pb
1819: 48654 f

MEAD, JOEL K (Washington,
    D. C.)
1816: 38359 pb

MECUM, --- (Philadelphia)
1803: 3692, 3922, 4107, 4619,
    4668, 4870, 4952, 5529,
    5631

MEEHAN, JOHN SILVA (Bur-
    lington, N. J.)
1813: 27699?, 28672
1815: 33832

MEEHAN, JOHN SILVA (Phila-
    delphia)
1816: 36810, 37544, 51595 pb
1817: 40015 pb, 40115, 41047,
    41336
1818: 43162-43163, 43209 pb,
    44438, 44543, 46789, 46828
1819: 47048, 47076 pb, 47078,
    47402 pb, 47905, 48460,
    49305, 50133 pb

MEEKER, ISAAC (Newark,
    N. J.)
1808: 15288 pb
1813: 27841 f
1814: 51395 f

MEETEER, SAMUEL (Balti-
more)
1818:   44177 f

MEETEER, WILLIAM (Balti-
more)
1818:   44177 f

MEGAREY, HENRY I (New
York)
1819:   47346 pb, 49199 f

MEGRAW, --- (Philadelphia)
1812:   24927 pb
1813:   29667 pb

MEIN, JOHN (New York)
1814:   31587 pb

MELCHER, JOHN (Ports-
mouth, N. H.)
1801:   143, 1001-1006, 1249
pb, 1250
1804:   5678, 7307
1805:   8507 pb

MELISH, JOHN (Philadelphia)
1813:   28314-28315 pb, 28316,
29142 pb
1814:   32100 f, 32603 f
1815:   33891 pb, 35246 f,
35247 pb, 35249 f
1816:   37388 f, 37389, 38219
pb, 38220 f, 38221 pb
1817:   41401 pb
1818:   44791-44792 pb, 44794-
44796 pb, 44797 f, 45425
1819:   48668-48669 pb, 51954
pb

MELSHEIMER, CHARLES
THEODORE (Frederick, Md.)
1810:   20162 pb
1811:   22233, 23367, 23379
pb
1813:   27857 pb, 29524 pb,
29730 pb

MELSHEIMER, CHARLES
THEODORE (York, Pa.)
1815:   36146 pb
1817:   40773

MENNESSIER, FRANCIS (Cin-
cinnati, O.)
1810:   19315 pb

MENTZ, GEORGE W (Phila-
delphia)
1807:   12766-12767 f
1810:   19520 pb, 19734, 20353
f
1811:   22418 pb, 22419-22420 f
1812:   24984 f, 25618 pb,
26797 pb, 26843 pb, 27631
pb
1813:   27907 pb, 28022 pb,
28760 f, 29425 pb, 29856,
29912 f
1815:   34252 pb, 35739 f
1816:   36988 pb, 37853 f,
38415 pb
1817:   40824, 41303, 41524 pb,
41604 pb, 41935 f
1818:   43478 f, 44351 f, 45020
pb, 51806 pb
1819:   48374 pb, 51921 pb

MERCEIN, THOMAS R (New
York)
1815:   34374, 34578, 35115,
35317, 35679 f, 35938, 36412
1816:   36720 pb, 36953 pb,
37135? pb, 37271 pb, 37497
f, 37506, 37608, 37785,
38053 pb, 38292 pb, 38870,
38986
1817:   40183, 41084 bf, 40372
bf, 40431 pb, 40433 f,
40434 pb, 40435 f, 40436-
40437 pb, 40508 pb, 40512
f, 40513 pb, 40616 pb,
40729 pb, 40901 bf, 40945
bf, 41103-41104 pb, 41210
pb, 41419, 41465 bf, 41473
pb, 41625, 41628, 41683,
41796 bf, 41797 f, 41989
pb, 42052 pb, 42059 bf,
42929 pb
1818:   43452 f, 43466 pb,
43513 pb, 43514, 43563 pb,
43566-43567 f, 43793 pb,
43809 pb, 43846 f, 43921 f,
44518 f, 44765 f, 44892-
44893 pb, 45130 f, 45227 f,
45466 f, 45660 f, 45845 pb,

51833 pb
1819: 46919 f, 47052 f,
47539 f, 47786 pb, 47939
pb, 48103-48105 f, 48430
pb, 48725 f, 48741 f, 48941
pb, 49612 pb

MERCEIN, WILLIAM A (New
York)
1815: 34374, 34578, 35115,
35317, 35679 f, 35938,
36412
1816: 36720 pb, 36953 pb,
37271 pb, 37506, 37608,
37624, 37785, 38053 pb,
38292 pb, 38870, 38986
1817: 40183-40184, 40372,
40901, 40945, 41419, 41465,
41625, 41628, 41683, 41796,
41989 pb, 42059
1818: 43091, 43120, 43452,
43503, 43566-43568, 43592,
43615 pb, 43846, 43921,
44518, 44667, 44765, 45027,
45073, 45130, 45466, 46603
pb
1819: 46919, 47035, 47052,
47539, 47660, 47737, 48066,
48103-48105, 48741, 49020,
49344, 51946 pb

Mercury (Hartford, Conn.)
see American Mercury (Hartford, Conn.)

MERKLEIN, H (Chambers-
burg, Pa.)
1815: 34837 pb

MERRELL, ANDREW (Utica,
N.Y.)
1818: 45707 f

MERRELL, IRA (Utica, N.Y.)
1803: 4641, 4826, 5509-5510
pb
1804: 5691 pb, 6822, 6832,
50454 pb
1805: 7853, 7858 pb, 7935,
8889 pb
1806: 10719, 11751
1807: 12737, 13358
1808: 15934, 15949, 16676 pb

1811: 22275, 22553, 22622?
pb, 22690?, 23001, 23211-
23212?, 23563, 24073? pb
1812: 24664, 24680, 24795-
24796, 24922-24924, 25310,
25654, 26331
1813: 27767, 27861, 27871-
27871a, 28164, 28382,
28696, 29001, 29864, 30391
1814: 30633, 31045 pb, 31177
pb, 31367 pb, 31466, 31820,
32136 pb, 32407, 33524
1815: 33902, 34786 pb, 34863-
34865, 34875, 35276, 36125,
38259 pb

MERRIAM, EBENEZER (Brook-
field, Mass.)
1801: 1139
1802: 1821, 1887, 1893, 1894-
1895 pb, 2956 pb, 3058 f,
3486 pb, 3487, 3493
1803: 4204 pb, 4568, 4592 pb,
4816, 5115
1804: 5852, 6177, 6181, 6251,
7034 pb, 7088, 7314, 7693,
7715 pb
1805: 7867, 8038 pb, 8386 pb,
8420, 8862, 9085, 9437,
9505
1806: 9970, 11142
1807: 12133, 12376, 12571,
13016, 13693
1808: 14490, 14941, 15640,
50888 pb
1809: 18367 pb, 18692
1810: 19302, 19524, 19978,
19980, 20746, 21427
1811: 22361, 22414, 22569,
22825, 23419, 23836, 23847
1812: 24847 pb, 25433, 25445-
25446, 26770, 26812, 27442-
27443, 27477, 27514-27515,
51163
1813: 27656, 29490 pb, 29563-
29565, 29817
1814: 30874, 31043, 32687-
32688, 33520, 51351?
1815: 34065-34066, 34081,
34094 pb, 34717, 35545,
35963, 36465
1816: 36960, 36980-36981,
36987, 37609 pb, 37815,

38151, 38873 pb, 38889,
38930, 38964 pb, 39729
1817: 40150, 40344, 40569,
40840-40841, 41493,
42225
1818: 43336, 43484, 43872,
44640, 44698, 45602, 45740-
45742, 46716, 46818-46819,
46899, 51832 pb
1819: 47587, 47687, 48119,
48368, 49071

MERRIFIELD, PRESTON (Montpelier, Vt.)
1812: 26119 f

MERRIFIELD, PRESTON (Wal-
pole, N. H.)
1807: 12592 f

MERRIFIELD, PRESTON
(Windsor, Vt.)
1808: 14305 f, 15490 f,
15704 f
1809: 17053 f, 17059 f,
17268 pb, 17705 pb, 17771
f, 18105 f, 18573 f, 50926 f
1810: 19467 f, 19767, 19827
pb, 20339?, 20638?, 20649
f
1811: 22246 f, 22381 pb,
22431a f, 22590 pb, 22842 f
1812: 24829 pb, 25129 pb,
26659 f, 26674 f, 27585 f
1813: 28840 f
1815: 34458 f, 35814 f

Merrifield & Cochran (Wind-
sor, Vt.)
see MERRIFIELD, PRESTON
⎯⎯(Windsor, Vt.)
COCHRAN, JAMES (Windsor,
Vt.)

Merrimack Bible Society
(Newburyport, Mass.)
1813: 27891 f

Merrimack Intelligencer (Haverhill, Mass.)
1814: 30983

MERRITT, SAMUEL (Philadelphia)
1808: 14259, 15853, 16145,
16346
1809: 16995, 17313, 17619,
17638, 17691, 17922, 18284,
18383, 18478, 18548, 18616,
18724, 19129, 19235
1810: 19670, 19866, 20233,
20949, 21074, 21178, 21538,
21965, 22066
1811: 22547, 22683, 22779,
22941, 23412, 23690
1812: 25789, 26455, 26465?,
26668-26669
1813: 27834, 28261, 29609,
30482, 30580
1814: 30616, 30847, 31032,
31140-31141, 31350, 32754-
32755
1815: 33841, 34601, 35630,
36105, 36133
1816: 37085, 37762, 38049,
38751
1817: 39979, 41768-41769,
42101, 42769
1818: 43089 pb, 44433

MERSHON, JOHN (Trenton,
N. J.)
1801: 309, 1011, 1013-1014,
1016, 1018 pb
1802: 1741, 2355, 2764, 2766-
2767
1803: 4178, 4749 pb
1804: 6900 pb, 6903, 7125 pb,
50488
1805: 9002, 9005 pb
1806: 10985, 10990 pb
1807: 13210 pb

MESIER, PETER A (New York)
1802: 2039 f, 3005 pb
1803: 5498 f
1804: 5853 pb, 6381 f, 6483
pb, 7030 pb, 7389 f
1805: 8000 pb, 8012 pb, 9203
f, 9744 f, 50507 pb
1806: 9972 pb, 10206 pb,
10565 f, 11219 f, 50660 f
1807: 12979 pb, 13500 pb
1809: 17007 pb, 17762 f
1810: 21308 pb, 51029 pb

1811:   22362 pb, 24338 f
1812:   25488 pb
1814:   31751 f
1816:   37849 pb, 37879 f

Messenger (Canandaigua, N. Y.)
see Ontario Messenger (Canandaigua, N. Y.)

Messenger (Middlebury, Vt.)
see Christian Messenger (Middlebury, Vt.)

METCALF, ELIAB WIGHT
  (Cambridge, Mass.)
1808:   15692-15693, 16025,
  16750
1809:   16831 pb, 16891, 16951,
  16984, 17004, 17512, 17518
  pb, 17706, 17717-17719,
  17766, 17985, 18317, 18578,
  19209, 19250, 19291
1810:   19304, 19502, 19911,
  20293, 20368-20369, 20582
  pb, 20966-20967, 21055,
  21202, 21940, 21959-21960
1811:   22176, 22421-22422,
  22417a-22418a, 22481,
  22493 pb, 22617, 22658,
  22840, 23031, 23038, 23138
  pb, 23246, 23644, 23687,
  23692
1812:   24572, 24584, 25089,
  25212, 25369-25371 pb,
  25609, 25620, 25910, 25944,
  26360-26361, 26479 pb,
  26515, 26569, 27461, 27492,
  51205
1813:   27681-27682 pb, 27701
  pb, 27837 pb, 27941 pb,
  28104 pb, 28255, 28256
  pb, 28269, 28465 pb, 28690
  pb, 28715 pb, 28765-28766,
  28860, 29390 pb, 29555,
  29773
1814:   30914, 31115 pb, 31273
  pb, 31289, 31399 pb, 31440
  pb, 31492, 31660, 31662,
  31744, 32128, 32480, 33727
  pb
1815:   33762-33763, 34118,
  34219, 34315, 34321 pb,
  34382, 34482 pb, 34524 pb,

  34684 pb, 34881, 34964 pb,
  35335, 35933, 36008, 36477,
  36513, 36594, 36624, 36627
  pb, 51501 pb
1816:   36996 pb, 37062 pb,
  37206, 37266, 37746 pb,
  37807, 37809-37810, 37823,
  38087 pb, 38180, 38190,
  38519, 38631 pb, 39872,
  39885, 51584
1817:   39998 pb, 40314 pb,
  40322, 40586, 40597 pb,
  40842, 40878, 41186, 41470,
  41847, 41990, 42762 pb,
  42822, 42908 pb, 51672 pb
1818:   43784 pb, 43805 pb,
  43962, 44113, 44270, 44295-
  44296, 44363, 44533, 44534
  pb, 45160, 45230, 45864,
  46704, 51749 pb
1819:   47543, 47769-47770,
  47775, 48189, 48264, 48468,
  48638-48639 pb, 48642,
  48691, 48994, 49297, 49447,
  50036-50037, 50145 pb

METCALF, JOHN (Northamp-
  ton, Mass.)
1816:   37480
1817:   40389, 40706, 51648
1818:   43383, 45389
1819:   47177, 47499, 47883,
  49225

METCALF, JOHN (Wendell,
  Mass.)
1814:   30819-30821
1816:   38932 pb

Methodist Connection in the
  United States (New York)
1805:   7818 f
1806:   11849-11850 f
1809:   17515 f, 18173 f
1810:   22016-22017 f
1811:   23827 f
1812:   24810 f, 25107 f, 25379
  f, 27519 f
1813:   27644 f, 27692 f, 27743
  f, 29267 f
1814:   30850 f, 31789 f, 32115-
  32117 f, 33644 f, 33680 f
1815:   34084 f, 34087 f, 35268-

35269 f, 36036-36037 f,
36539 f

Methodist Connection in the
United States (Windsor, Vt.)
1818:   45718 f

Methodist Episcopal Church
(New York)
1804:   5812 f, 6163 f, 7209 f,
7344 f, 7761 f
1816:   37337 f, 37912 f
1817:   40151 f, 40358 f, 41421
f, 42236 f
1818:   43049 f, 43078 f, 43258
f, 43631 f, 43887 f, 44048
f, 44546 f, 44825 f, 44830
f, 44883 f, 45854 f, 46762-
46764 f, 46805 f
1819:   47993 f, 49582 f

METTEZ, THEOPHILUS
(Detroit, Mich.)
1812:   24811, 24819, 25024,
25439, 26071
1816:   38244

METZ, GEORGE (Wilmington,
Del.)
1815:   34191 pb

MEYER, JACOB (Philadelphia)
1803:   50379? pb
1810:   19736, 20192, 20605,
20842 pb, 21059, 21184,
21321
1811:   22221, 22905-22906,
23289 pb, 23422, 23496
pb, 23805 pb, 23992
1812:   24852, 25623, 25906
pb, 51220 pb
1813:   28433, 29251 f, 30500 f
1814:   31104 f
1816:   37056 pb
1818:   44639

Miami Intelligencer (Hamilton,
O.)
1815:   33833

Middle Street Bookstore (Newburyport, Mass.)
1807:   13589

1809:   18356 bsb
1810:   20519 bsb

MIDDLEBROOK, ELIJAH (New
Haven, Conn.)
1813:   29162
1814:   32122 f

Middlesex Bookstore (Charlestown, Mass.)
1815:   35226 f, 35706 f

MILL, JOHN (Charleston, S.C.)
1819:   48508 f, 49464 pb

MILLEN, JOHN (Darien, Ga.)
1818:   43810 pb

MILLER, --- (Sangerfield,
N.Y.)
1816:   37438, 39121

MILLER, ARCHIBALD ED-
WARD (Charleston, S.C.)
1816:   38654 pb
1817:   40452, 40610, 40869,
40881, 41437 pb, 41840 pb,
42106, 42231 pb
1818:   43585, 43800 pb, 44100
pb, 44165, 44310, 44361,
45341, 45346 pb, 46733? pb
1819:   47001, 47072, 47421,
47692, 47742-47744, 47834,
48042, 48154, 48508, 48964,
49215, 49406, 49418, 49451,
49495, 49520, 49644-49645?

MILLER, DAVID CADE (Ball-
ston Spa, N.Y.)
1804:   7232 pb
1806:   9901
1807:   12660
1808:   14375, 16168a
1810:   19469, 20630

MILLER, DAVID CADE (Bata-
via, N.Y.)
1819:   48272 pb

MILLER, DAVID CADE (Johnstown, N.Y.)
1809:   18107 pb

MILLER, GAVIN (Staunton,
Va.)
1812:   24858 pb

MILLER, GEORGE (New York)
1804:   7687 pb

MILLER, H (New York)
1804:   7687 pb

MILLER, ISAAC (Mobile, Ala.)
1819:   47682 pb

MILLER, JAMES M (Auburn,
N. Y.)
1819:   47523 pb

MILLER, JAMES M (Ballston
Spa, N. Y.)
1811:   51089 pb

MILLER, JAMES M (Detroit,
Mich.)
1809:   16782, 16903, 17205,
18072, 18074, 18075? pb,
18077 pb
1810:   19749

MILLER, JAMES M (Norwich,
N. Y.)
1812:   25124 pb
1813:   29922 pb

MILLER, JOHN (Pendleton,
S. C.)
1807:   13087 pb
1811:   22286
1813:   27815

MILLER, JOHN (Providence,
R. I.)
1814:   30909, 31015-31016,
31206, 31376, 32587, 32932
1815:   34116 pb
1816:   37024-37025, 37188,
37359 pb, 37514, 37743 pb,
37865, 38743, 38926 pb,
39831-39833
1817:   40009, 40340, 40725,
41026, 41677, 42277-42278
1818:   43243, 43544, 44360,
44387, 45213, 45448, 45450,
45453-45454, 45543, 45676,
45698, 46785-46786, 46871-
46872
1819:   47677 pb, 48300, 48589
pb, 49167, 49217-49218,
49405 pb, 50085 pb, 51915

MILLER, JOHN (Steubenville,
O.)
1806:   11856 pb

MILLER, SAMUEL (Carthage,
Tenn.)
1808:   16716 pb

MILLER, SAMUEL (Fort Stoddert, Miss.)
1811:   23407 pb

MILLER, SAMUEL (Knoxville,
Tenn.)
1808:   16296-16297

MILLER, SOLOMON (New Ber-
lin, Pa.)
1817:   40771-40772
1818:   43885, 44070, 44522-
44523 pb
1819:   47218 pb

MILLER, TOBIAS HAM (Portsmouth, N. H.)
1818:   44434

MILLER, WILLIAM A (Wilm-
ington, Del.)
1818:   43987

Miller, Goddard & Mann
(Providence, R. I.)
see MILLER, JOHN (Provi-
dence, R. I.)
GODDARD, WILLIAM GILES
(Providence, R. I.)
MANN, WILLIAM METCALF
(Providence, R. I.)

MILLESS, WILLIAM (Balti-
more)
1816:   37483?
1817:   40709
1818:   44177, 44311 pb, 45279

MILLIGAN, JOSEPH (George-
town, D. C.)
1808: 15804 f
1809: 17426-17427 f, 17974 f,
19155 f
1810: 20027-20030 f
1811: 23173 f, 51085 pb
1812: 25740 f, 25741 pb, 25816
pb, 25817 f, 26175 pb, 26347
pb, 27127 pb
1813: 28441 pb, 29238 pb,
30494 f
1814: 32645 f, 33334 pb,
51392 pb
1815: 34892 f
1817: 40653 pb
1818: 44127 f, 44283 pb, 46884
pb
1819: 49280 pb

MILLS, EPHRAIM (Burlington,
Vt.)
1818: 43214, 43698, 45368,
46640, 46646 pb
1819: 48755, 49985, 51888 pb,
51947 pb

MILLS, SAMUEL (Burlington,
Vt.)
1806: 10136
1807: 12375, 13545-13546,
14118
1808: 14440, 14763, 14922,
15068, 15409, 16191 pb,
16344
1809: 17745, 18544, 18568,
19101, 19239, 19242, 19256
1810: 19561, 19936, 20055,
20389, 21051, 21899, 21902,
21910
1811: 22290 pb, 22504-22505,
22560 pb, 23464 pb, 23473
pb, 23618, 23867, 24343,
24346, 24412
1812: 26690, 27376, 27393
pb, 27398, 27402
1813: 29004, 29718, 30373,
30415, 30540
1814: 30856, 31012, 33542
1815: 34883, 35363 pb, 35427,
36428 pb
1816: 36853, 36914, 38316,
38893 pb, 39666 bf, 51551 pb

1817: 40119, 41018, 41519 pb,
41531 pb, 42784 bf, 51721
pb
1818: 44984?

MILLS, THOMAS (Burlington,
Vt.)
1818: 43214, 43698, 45368,
46640, 46646 pb
1819: 48755, 49985, 51888 pb,
51947 pb

MILTENBERGER, ANTHONY
FELIX WYBERT (Baltimore)
1810: 20543, 20758, 21953 pb
1811: 22745 bf, 22926 pb,
23866, 23952 pb, 24463 bf,
51148 pb
1812: 24608, 24985 pb, 25000
pb, 25218, 25431, 25952 pb,
26183 pb, 26837 pb, 26868
pb, 26921 pb
1813: 27827 pb, 28119, 28550
pb, 28648-28649 pb, 28739
pb, 28804, 28881, 29589
1814: 31703 pb
1816: 38012

MINER, ANDREW (Windsor,
Vt.)
1805: 8834

MINER, ASHER (Doylestown,
Pa.)
1804: 6192, 7022 pb
1805: 8025
1806: 10376, 10876 pb
1808: 14545
1813: 28610, 29173 pb, 51264
pb
1814: 31209, 31893, 32138 pb,
51354 pb
1815: 35284, 35285 pb, 35608
pb
1816: 37547, 38261 pb, 51617
pb
1817: 40761, 41448 pb
1818: 44859 pb, 45261 pb
1819: 47366, 48310, 48706,
49061

MINER, ASHER (Newtown, Pa.)
1817: 42208 pb
1818: 45199

MINER, ASHER (Wilkesbarre,
Pa.)
1801: 250, 843 pb
1802: 2655, 3082 pb
1803: 3705

MINER, CHARLES (West
Chester, Pa.)
1818: 46653 pb
1819: 50092 pb

MINER, CHARLES (Wilkes-
barre, Pa.)
1802: 2655, 3082 pb
1803: 3705
1808: 14576, 15463
1811: 22919 pb
1812: 25140?, 25692

Minerva (Raleigh, N. C.)
1812: 25463, 26311 pb
1813: 28571-28572, 29852
1814: 31166, 31526-31527,
31972
1815: 35310, 35507
1816: 38836, 51614

Minerva Press (Utica, N. Y.)
1811: 22247

MING, ALEXANDER (New
York)
1801: 551, 689 pb, 1223
1802: 1977 pb, 2193, 2298
pb, 2436 pb, 3524 pb
1803: 4424 pb, 50364 pb
1804: 5975 bpb, 6363, 6526
pb
1805: 8013 pb, 8670 pb, 8907,
9424, 9632
1806: 9984, 10603 pb, 10877
pb, 11218
1807: 12798 f, 13093
1808: 14694, 15284 pb, 15615
1809: 17790 pb, 18098, 50927
pb
1810: 20418 pb, 20747, 21659,
50994 pb
1811: 23070 pb, 23399-23400
pb
1812: 25704 pb, 26091 pb,
26496
1813: 28794 pb, 29174 pb

1814: 31777 pb, 31778, 51409
pb
1815: 34509 pb, 34980, 51511
pb
1816: 37898 pb
1817: 41111 pb, 42158, 42861
pb
1818: 44860 pb
1819: 48707 pb

MINIS, --- (Pittsburgh, Pa.)
1818: 45791 f

MINNS, THOMAS (Boston)
1801: 106, 211, ?887, 888,
889-890 pb, 899-900, 902
pb, 911
1802: 1798, 1801, 2547, 2616-
2617, 2626-2627, 2629 pb,
3139
1803: 3655 pb, 4151, 4601-
4602, 4608-4612, 4617, 4724
pb, 4943, 50373 pb
1804: 6586 pb, 6705 pb, 6737-
6739, 6741-6745, 6751-6753,
7793
1805: 7855, 8098 pb, 8855-
8857, 8868-8871, 8876,
9340
1806: 10822, 10825, 10828 pb,
10833, 11356 pb

MINOR, --- (Richmond, Va.)
1809: 50953 pb
1810: 19460

MINTZ, DAVID B (Newbern,
N. C.)
1806: 10164 f, 10315 f

MIRTAN, CADI (New Orleans,
La.)
1813: 28924

MISSILDINE, ROBERT (Charleston, S. C.)
1819: 49538 f

Mississippi Herald (Natchez,
Miss.)
1802: 2914 pb

Missouri Gazette (St. Louis,
    Mo.)
1816: 38108

MITCHELL, --- (New Orleans,
    La.)
1811: 24068 pb

MITCHELL, ANDREW C (Phila-
    delphia)
1814: 30667 pb

MITCHELL, EDWARD (New
    York)
1805: 7999 f
1806: 10895 f
1807: 12132 f, 12908 pb,
    50758 f
1808: 14508 pb, 15380 f,
    16004 pb, 16007 pb
1809: 18050 pb

MITCHELL, ISAAC (Albany,
    N. Y.)
1806: 10113, 11272 pb

MITCHELL, ISAAC (Kingston,
    N. Y.)
1803: 50358 pb
1804: 6282 pb, 7694? pb

MITCHELL, ISAAC (Pough-
    keepsie, N. Y.)
1802: 2680 pb, 2775 pb,
    2908 pb
1803: 4181 pb, 4876 pb,
    50358 pb
1805: 8159
1812: 26324 pb

MITCHELL, JAMES (New Or-
    leans, La.)
1812: 26358

MITCHELL, JOHN S (Savan-
    nah, Ga.)
1812: 24601 pb

MITCHELL, SAMUEL AU-
    GUSTUS (Philadelphia)
1816: 37447 pb, 38471 pb
1817: 41466 f, 42029 f,
    42058 f, 42817 f

1818: 43523 f, 44877 f, 44962
    f, 45107 pb
1819: 47510 pb, 47520 pb,
    48936 f, 48937-48938 pb,
    49018 f, 50024-50025 f,
    50171 pb

MITCHELL, WILLIAM (Rus-
    sellville, Ky.)
1806: 10880 pb

Mobile Gazette (Mobile, Ala.)
1819: 48721

MOCKRICHUFSKY, P N (Rich-
    mond, Va.)
1811: 23064

MOCKRICHUFSKY, W (Rich-
    mond, Va.)
1811: 23064

MOFFETT, DARIUS (Natchez,
    Miss.)
1801: 701 pb

MOFFITT, ROBERT (Troy,
    N. Y.)
1801: 516 pb, 683, 1312, 1410,
    50215 pb
1802: 1832, 2250 pb, 2299,
    2345, 2513
1803: 4225 pb, 4295, 5071,
    50334
1804: 5793, 6087, 6406,
    50435 pb
1805: 7936, 8460 pb, 8767 pb
1806: 9909, 10432 pb
1807: 12135

Moffitt & Lyon (Troy, N. Y.)
see (1801-1804) MOFFITT,
    ROBERT (Troy, N. Y.)
    LYON, ZEBULON (Troy,
    N. Y.)
    (1804-1807) MOFFITT,
    ROBERT (Troy, N. Y.)
    LYON, OLIVER (Troy,
    N. Y.)

Moniteur de la Louisiana (New
    Orleans, La.)
1803: 4537

1804: 6766
1805: 9071

Monitor (Columbus, O.)
see Ohio Monitor (Columbus,
O.)

Monitor (Washington, Ga.)
1804: 6086, 7195

MONTAGU, MATTHEW (Phila-
delphia)
1809: 18106 pb

Montpelier Bookstore (Montpelier, Vt.)
1811: 22194, 22820

MOORE, J (Hudson, N. Y.)
1807: 12943 f

MOORE, JACOB BAILEY
(Concord, N. H.)
1819: 47110-47111, 47966,
48273, 48679, 48762, 48777
pb, 48837, 48851-48852,
48856, 48862 pb, 49013,
49233 pb

MOORE, JOHN C (Trenton,
N. J.)
1812: 26259 f, 51209 pb
1813: 27723-27724 f, 27784,
27845 pb, 28664 f, 29322 f,
29804 f, 51323 pb
1814: 32207 pb, 32550 f

MOORE, ROBERT (Hudson,
N. Y.)
1807: 12943 f

MOORE, ROBERT (New York)
1804: 7105 pb
1807: 12943 f
1810: 21966 f
1812: 26180 pb
1816: 39725 f

MOORE, SAMUEL (Easton,
Pa.)
1815: 35989 pb

MOORE, SOUTHWICK H (Man-
lius, N. Y.)
1816: 38991 pb

MOORE, THOMAS P (Danville,
Ky.)
1814: 31701

MOORE, WILLIAM (Carthage,
Tenn.)
1808: 14647 pb
1810: 19453, 21362 pb
1811: ?23935

MOORE, WILLIAM (Knoxville,
Tenn.)
1808: 16295-16297 f

MORFORD, EDMUND (Charles-
ton, S. C.)
1806: 11333 pb
1807: 12987 pb, 12990 f,
13642 pb
1808: 14659 pb
1809: 18588 pb
1810: 19885, 20844 pb, 21154
1811: 22463 f, 23695, 51128
1812: 24539 pb, 25178, 25919
1817: 40609 pb

MORFORD, EDMUND (Phila-
delphia)
1810: 21993 f
1811: 22136 pb, 23705 pb

MORGAN, AUGUSTUS (Binghamton, N. Y.)
1813: 29538 pb

MORGAN, CHAUNCEY (Bing-
hamton, N. Y.)
1812: 24941 pb

MORGAN, CHAUNCEY (Oxford,
N. Y.)
1813: 29428 pb
1817: 40172

MORGAN, EPHRAIM (Cincin-
nati, O.)
1809: 18283 pb
1814: 31688
1815: 34447, 34917?, 35061,

35395 pb, 35987, 36544
1817: 40810 pb, 42875 pb
1818: 43161, 43943, 46769
pb, 51845 pb
1819: 47616, 49551, 50016 pb

MORGAN, JOHN (Philadelphia)
1802: 2044 pb, 2236 pb,
2336-2337 pb, 2340 pb,
2569 f, 2842 f
1803: 4217 f, 4466 f
1805: 9342 pb
1809: 18594-18595 pb

MORISON, --- (Baton Rouge,
La.)
1819: 47174 pb

Morning Chronicle (New York)
1803: 3614

MORRIS, DAVID (Williamsburg,
O.)
1814: 33648 pb

MORRIS, JOHN (Erie, Pa.)
1819: 47910 pb

Morris County and Westchester
Associated Presbyteries
(Goshen, N. Y.)
1801: 163 pb

MORRISON, SAMUEL AYERS
(Keene, N. H.)
1818: 43319 pb

MORSE, EVANDER (Onondaga,
N. Y.)
1816: 37687 pb

MORSE, JEDIDIAH (Charles-
town, Mass.)
1803: 3946 f

MORSE, SAMUEL (New Haven,
Conn.)
1801: 1376 pb

MORSE, SAMUEL (Savannah,
Ga.)
1802: 2313 pb
1803: 4271, 5402
1804: 5774

MORSE, WILLIAM WALKER
(New Haven, Conn.)
1801: 199, 380, 543, 602 pb,
763, 828 pb, 866, 869,
1105, 1439, 1443-1444,
50249
1802: 1925, 1968, 2081,
2110?, 2154, 2170, 2396,
2558, 2565, 2586, 2638 pb,
2751 pb, 2828, 3021, 3031,
3052, 3081, 3184, 3480,
3521, 3555, 3561, 50274,
50306 pb
1803: 4525 pb, 4625, 4953 pb

MORSE, WILLIAM WALKER
(Philadelphia)
1804: 7260

MORTON, ABNER (St. Albans,
Vt.)
1809: 17184 pb
1810: 20139 pb

MORTON, ALEXANDER C
(New York)
1810: 21994 pb

MORTON, JOHN P (Louisville,
Ky.)
1807: 14204 pb

MOSS, EDWARD G (Newbern,
N. C.)
1805: 8472 pb

MOTT, --- (New York)
1818: 43126, 43590, 46692

MOTT, GABRIEL F (Blakeley,
Ala.)
1818: 43392 pb

MOWER, NAHUM (Windsor,
Vt.)
1801: 446, 856 pb, 1009, 1669
pb
1802: 2177-2178, 2588, 3182
1803: 4245, 4828
1804: 5927, 6598, 6891 pb
1805: 8445, 8763, 8834, 8938,
9183 pb, 9374, 9705 pb
1806: 10413, 10913, 11362,
11760

MOWRY, CHARLES (Downington, Pa.)
1808: 16294 pb
1809: 16848 pb
1816: 39776
1818: 44213, 44504

MOWRY, JOHN (New Orleans, La.)
1804: 6672 pb
1805: 9068
1806: 10675
1808: 14955 pb
1811: 22985

MUCK, P (Charleston, S.C.)
1810: 20771 pb

MUNDAY, WILLIAM (Baltimore)
1807: 12033 f
1812: 24696 f

MUNGER, GEORGE (New Haven, Conn.)
1816: 37436 f

MUNROE, ALVAN (Baltimore)
1818: 43154 pb

MUNROE, EDMUND (Boston)
1802: 1750, 1794, 1849 pb, 1865, 1933, 1965, 2242, 2324, 2326-2328, 2482, 2518, 2630, 3063, 3146, 3453 pb
1803: 3971, 4145, 4341, 4388, 4672 pb, 4689, 4799, 5039, 5050, 5147
1804: 5839, 5895 pb, 5956, 6027, 6185, 6866, 6971, 7201, 7254, 7400, 50477
1805: 8099 pb, 8381, 9271 pb, 50619
1806: 9800, 9816 pb, 9829, 9865, 11400, 11491, 11872
1807: 12006 pb, 12023 pb, 12106, 12179-12180, 12502, 13469, 13498, 13572 pb, 13625, 13680
1808: 14315-14316, 14386 pb, 14476 pb, 14938 pb, 15087-15088, 15110, 15198 pb, 15290 pb, 15297 pb, 15352,

15395 pb, 15402, 15433 pb, 15456 pb, 15479, 15508 pb, 15863, 15984, 16023 pb, 16078, 16177, 16225, 16227, 16252 pb, 16365, 16375, 16654 pb, 50889
1809: 16787, 16877 pb, 16991 pb, 17067, 17104-17106 pb, 17192 pb, 17312 pb, 17422 pb, 17430 pb, 17526, 17599, 17600 pb, 17675, 17818, 17861 pb, 17889 pb, 18026 pb, 18032 pb, 18056, 18268 pb, 18359 pb, 18725? pb, 19133 pb, 19290 pb
1810: 19390 pb, 19598, 19600, 19615, 20062 pb, 20136, 20181-20183, 20266, 20279 pb, 20299 pb, 20437, 20597 pb, 20601-20602 pb, 20686-20687, 20755, 20763-20764, 20778 pb, 20968, 21011, 21012 pb, 21040 pb, 21088 pb, 21144 pb, 21288? pb, 21331, 21358 pb, 21397, 21429? pb, 21511?, 21970?, 21980 pb
1811: 22212 pb, 22419a pb, 22442a pb, 22510 pb, 22511? pb, 22887 pb, 22888, 22944 pb, 22946, 23079 pb, 23427-23428 pb, 23613, 23778 pb, 24055 pb
1812: 24967, 24995 pb, 25193, 25276 pb, 25341 pb, 25372-25373 pb, 25490-25493, 25510 pb, 25535, 25650-25651, 25703 f, 25835 pb, 25904 pb, 25911 pb, 26182, 26502 pb, 26585-26586, 26869 pb, 27146
1813: 27829, 27977 pb, 27987, 27991-27992 pb, 28140, 28322, 28369 pb, 28444, 28448 pb, 28450 pb, 28599 pb, 28691 pb, 28846 pb, 28961? pb, 28994 pb, 29165, 29561 pb, 29579 pb, 29637-29638, 29650, 29948, 29988 pb, 30435 pb
1814: 30684?, 30848, 30968, 31057, 31439, 31442-31443 pb, 31588-31589 pb, 31851

pb, 31895, 31988, 32022
pb, 32236-32237 pb, 32510
pb, 32798, 33670, 51405 pb
1815: 33995, 34053 pb, 34063
pb, 34663, 34967-34968,
35057 pb, 35078 pb, 35140
pb, 35166, 35232, 35415 pb,
35760-35761, 35859
1816: 37049, 37220 pb, 37248,
37579, 37683, 37760, 38081
pb, 38105, 38107, 38197,
38309 pb, 38374 pb, 38530,
38534, 38775, 38776 pb
1817: 40037 pb, 40244, 40353,
40362-40363 pb, 40373 pb,
40502, 40620 pb, 40629
pb, 40845, 40888, 41096 pb,
41244 pb, 41299, 41321,
41371 pb
1818: 43014, 43355, 43365-
43366 pb, 43509 pb, 43525,
43821 pb, 43924 pb, 43980
pb, 44032 pb, 44066, 44079,
44324 pb, 44379 pb, 44628
pb, 44924 pb, 45364 f,
45534 pb, 45582 pb, 45897
pb
1819: 48371, 48522-48523 pb,
49289, 49482, 49490 pb,
49635 pb

MUNROE, ISAAC (Baltimore)
1814: 31645
1816: 37186
1818: 43543

MUNROE, ISAAC (Boston)
1806: 10487, 10562, 10824 pb,
11186? pb, 11428
1807: 12020, 12176 pb, 12211
pb, 12666, 12938, 13575
pb, 13599, 13675, 13708 pb
1808: 14270-14271 pb, 14515
pb, 14558 pb, 14792, 15200,
15204?, 15516 pb, 15561
pb, 15647, 15660 pb, 15772,
16671 pb
1809: 16794 pb, 16795, 16797
pb, 16847 pb, 17031 pb,
17069 pb, 17173
1810: 20571, 20572 pb, 22045
1811: 22672, 23314, 23319,
23332 pb, 23333, 23349,

24042
1812: 24873 pb
1813: 28684 pb, 29820 pb

Munroe & Francis (Boston)
see MUNROE, EDMUND (Bos-
ton)
FRANCIS, DAVID (Boston)

Munroe & French (Boston)
see MUNROE, ISAAC (Boston)
FRENCH, EBENEZER
(Boston)

Munroe, Francis & Parker
(Boston)
see MUNROE, EDMUND (Bos-
ton)
FRANCIS, DAVID (Boston)
PARKER, SAMUEL H (Bos-
ton)

MUNSON, JOHN (New Haven,
Conn.)
1802: 1784

MUNSON, JOHN (Stonington,
Conn.)
1807: 11984 pb

MUNSON, P H (Hudson, N. Y.)
1808: 50849? f

MURDEN, JOSEPH T (New
York)
1817: 41510
1818: 43199, 43390, 44366,
44926, 45206, 46780, 51824

MURDEN, JOSEPH T (Perth
Amboy, N. J.)
1819: 48474 pb, 48871 pb

MURDOCK, E (New York)
1816: 38301 pb

MURPHY, JOHN S (New York)
1819: 48770 f

MURPHY, THOMAS (Baltimore)
1804: 6593, 7075?, 7094 pb
1805: 8118, 8184, 9060
1806: ?10008, 10020, 10173?,

10187 f, 10190 pb, 10236,
10291, 10931 pb, 11053 pb,
11884 pb
1807: 12035, 12188 pb, 12329
pb, 12439, 12998, 13481,
13514, 13595
1808: 14412?, 14748-14749
pb, 15373, 15503, 15612,
15668, 15803, 16178, 50870
1809: 16793, 16900, 17167-
17168, 17180, 17196 pb,
17545, 17697, 17726, 17882,
18100, 18126 pb, 18140,
18360, 18651
1810: 19400, 19415, 19586,
19739, 19796, 19819, 20285,
20424, 20742-20743, 21277
1811: 22454a, 22559, 23278,
23708, 23791 pb
1812: 25108, 25311, 25953,
26495, 26823
1813: 27694 pb, 28281, 28879,
29059 pb
1814: 31193, 31838 pb, 32692
1815: 33917 pb
1816: 36680, 37483?
1817: 40709
1818: 44177, 44311 pb, 45279
1819: 46965, 47016

MURPHY, WILLIAM (Newtown,
N. Y.)
1815: 36056 pb
1818: 46634 pb

MURPHY, WILLIAM (Williamsport, Pa.)
1814: 31973 pb

MURPHY, WILLIAM G (Phila-
delphia)
1815: 34234 pb

MURRAY, JOHN (New York)
1802: 2719 f

MURRAY, JOHN L (Hamilton,
O.)
1819: 48142 pb

Museum Press (Philadelphia)
1806: 50705 pb

MUSSEY, CHARLES (Portland,
Me.)
1817: 42269 pb

MYER, WILLIAM (New Bruns-
wick, N. J.)
1815: 34185, 34280, 35195 pb,
35723, 35958 pb, 36088 pb,
51530 pb
1816: 37813, 37858, 38084,
38354 pb, 38732, 38767,
38854, 38957 pb, 38977-
38978 pb, 39707
1817: 40241, 40483, 40814 pb,
41562, 41601, 41693 bf,
41900g
1818: 44974 pb, 45438
1819: 47517, 47752, 48505,
49207

N

NANCREDE, PAUL JOSEPH
GUERARD de (Boston)
1801: 1283 pb, 1374 f, 1433 f
1802: 1919 pb, 2593 pb, 2722
pb, 3175 f, 50289 f
1803: 3857 f, 4488 f, 4533 f,
5018 pb
1804: 6319 f, 7127 f, 7144 f

NASHEE, GEORGE (Chillicothe,
O.)
1808: 16271 pb
1809: 18280-18281
1810: 19661 pb, 20947
1811: 22916 pb, 23590
1813: 29396-29397
1814: 30835, 30926
1815: 35058, 35526-35527,
35792 bf
1816: 38502, 38503? pb
1817: 41686-41687
1818: 43607 pb
1819: 47584 pb, 48970 pb

National Intelligencer (Washington, D. C.)
1811: 24139 pb
1813: 28159 pb
1819: 49748

National Register (Washington,
  D. C.)
1817: 40306

National Standard (Middlebury,
  Vt.)
1818: 44215

NEAL, ABNER (Baltimore)
1804: 7744 f
1806: 9852 f, 11466 f
1807: 11991 f, 12731 f
1810: 19997 f, 21366 f
1811: 22724 pb
1812: 24972 f, 26732 f, 27636
  f
1813: 28281 f, 28659 f, 28720
  f, 29236 f, 29275 f, 29781 f
1814: 30989 f, 31062 f,
  31590 f, 31800 f, 32538 f
1815: 34842 f, 35342 f,
  35633 f, 35781 f
1816: 37082 f, 38686 pb,
  38806 f, 38951 pb
1818: 43284 pb, 43629 f,
  44049-44050 f
1819: 47342 pb, 49067 f

NEAL, CHRISTIANA (PALMER)
  (Philadelphia)
1814: 31422 pb

Neal, Wills & Cole (Baltimore)
see NEAL, ABNER (Baltimore)
  WILLS, FRANCIS M (Baltimore)
  COLE, JOHN (Baltimore)

NEELY, --- (Philadelphia)
1802: 1944? pb

NEGRIN, JOHN J (Charleston,
  S. C.)
1803: 50393 pb
1805: 8974? pb
1806: 10098, 10943 pb, 50687
  pb
1807: 12618 pb, 12620, 13172,
  13287 pb

NEGRIN, JOHN J (New York)
1808: 15807 pb

NEGRIN, JOHN J (Philadelphia)
1810: 20563 pb

NEILSON, OLIVER H (Balti-
  more)
1814: 31646 pb

NELSON, JOHN DIXON
  (Charleston, S. C.)
1801: 984

NELSON, JOSEPH (Poughkeepsie, N. Y.)
1809: 19185
1810: 21293
1811: 23101 pb

NELSON, REUBEN W (Corydon,
  Ind.)
1816: 37927 pb
1817: 41135-41137

NELSON, REUBEN W (Jeffer-
  sonville, Ind.)
1818: 44432 pb

NELSON, RICHARD (Pough-
  keepsie, N. Y.)
1815: 33961, 34603 pb
1816: 37804
1817: 41239

NELSON, THOMAS (Poughkeepsie, N. Y.)
1806: 9952 f, 50646 pb
1807: 12399, 13606, 14124

NEVERSINK, THOMAS (Phila-
  delphia)
1809: 17577 pb

New England Palladium (Boston)
1815: 36110 pb

New England Repertory (Newburyport, Mass.)
1803: 4817, 4982
1804: 7787

New England Tract Society
  (Andover, Mass. and Boston)
1814: 31245 f, 31252 pb,
  31342 f, 31485 f, 31486 pb,

32154 f, 32162 f, 32649 f,
32815 pb, 32878 pb, 33732
pb
1815: 33852, 34465 f, 34583
    f, 34818 f, 35096 f, 35536
    pb, 35701 f, 35786 f, 36048
    pb, 36089 f, 36493 f
1816: 36904 f, 37455 pb, 37880
    f, 37915 f, 38559 f, 38673
    pb, 38693 pb, 38809 f, 38935
    f, 39047 f, 39090 f, 39142
    f, 39738 f, 51593 f
1817: 41271 f, 41984 f, 51670
    f
1818: 43278 f, 43722-43723
    pb, 43754 f, 44424 f, 44442
    f, 45202 f, 45404 f, 45541
    f, 45885 f
1819: 47559 pb, 47882 f,
    48492 f, 48928 f, 50056 f

New Hampshire Bible Society
    (Concord, N. H.)
1813: 27891 f

New Hampshire Gazette (Ports-
    mouth, N. H.)
1803: 4891
1804: 7284
1808: 16331?
1809: 16893?, 16952, 18795,
    19286
1810: 19406
1812: 24689, 24758, 25074
1813: 28011
1818: 43595, 44063

New Hampshire Missionary
    Society (Concord, N. H.)
1807: 13478 pb

New Hampshire Patriot (Con-
    cord, N. H.)
1811: 22408a
1812: 26231 pb

New Hampshire Sentinel
    (Keene, N. H.)
1816: 39698

New Hampshire Tract Society
    (Concord, N. H.)
1813: 29552 f

New Printing Office (Portland,
    Me.)
1806: 9893

New York Bible and Common
    Prayer Book Society (New
    York)
1818: 45428

New York Bible Society (New
    York)
1813: 28017 pb
1815: 34103 f
1816: 36951 f

New York Courier (New York)
1815: 33874

New York Evening Post (New
    York)
1802: 2363 bpb

New York Gazette (New York)
1801: 21
1815: 34729 pb, 35478 pb

New York Herald (New York)
1807: 14166

New York Religious Tract Soci-
    ety (New York)
1810: 20342? pb
1812: 24532 pb
1813: 27932 f, 28469 f
1815: 34510 f, 35942 pb
1816: 37444 pb, 38523 f
1817: 41128 f, 42296 f, 51671
    f
1818: 43403 f, 44446 f, 44567
    f, 45611 pb
1819: 46937 pb, 48234, 48240,
    49151 pb, 49228 pb, 49597
    pb

New York Sunday School Union
    Society (New York)
1816: 37837 f
1817: 41014 pb

Newbern Gazette (Newbern,
    N. C.)
1803: 5563

Newburyport Herald (Newburyport, Mass.)
1805:   9721
1806:   11770
1808:   16269
1812:   26466 bsb

NEWCOMB, CHARLES JARVIS
(Deerfield, Mass.)
1817:   40193, 40662
1818:   43824 pb, 43855, 43856
pb
1819:   47481, 49383, 50099

NEWCOMB, CHARLES JARVIS
(Springfield, Mass.)
1808:   15396 f

NEWELL, ANDREW (Boston)
1801:   46 pb, 381, 1401
1802:   2910 pb, 50324 pb
1804:   7082, 50471-50472 pb
1805:   7830, 8355, 8530-8532,
8804?, 8961, 9167, 9445,
50595 pb, 50596
1806:   10253-10254 pb, 10749,
11182 pb, 11873, 50715-
50717 pb
1808:   14560?

NEWHALL, DAVID (Walpole,
N.H.)
1802:   1728, 1824, 1899, 2011,
2163, 2224, 2923, 3020,
3543
1803:   4219, 4366, 4416-4418,
4883

NEWMAN, MARK (Andover,
Mass.)
1813:   28234 f, 29784 f
1814:   33679 f
1815:   34832 f, 36476 f
1817:   42109 f, 42820 f
1818:   43562 f, 43564 f, 45702
f
1819:   48221 f

Newport Mercury (Newport,
R.I.)
1801:   685, 1052 pb, 1159
1802:   3000?
1804:   5964

1805:   8037, 8577, 9100, 9587,
9590, 50565 pb
1806:   9939, 10270, 10789,
11026?
1807:   13301, 13321
1808:   15851, 16299
1810:   19383
1813:   29994
1818:   45098

NEWTON, ABNER (Hartford,
Conn.)
1816:   51601
1817:   41216, 41832
1818:   43922, 44276 pb, 45095
pb, 46793

NEWTON, GEORGE (Albany,
N.Y.)
1811:   23233?, 51105

NEWTON, GEORGE (Cazenovia,
N.Y.)
1808:   15955 pb
1809:   18604

NEWTON, ISRAEL (Norwich,
Vt.)
1807:   11937-11938 f
1808:   15026 f

NEWTON, ORRIN (Hartford,
Conn.)
1813:   30397 f
1814:   31297 f, 31343 f

NICHOLAS, CHARLES J (Philadelphia)
1810:   19697 f, 21032 f
1811:   22187 pb, 22223 pb,
23662 pb, 23914 pb, 23997 f
1813:   27768 pb

NICHOLS, CHARLES (Catskill,
N.Y.)
1816:   38681

NICHOLS, FRANCIS (Boston)
1814:   32520 f

NICHOLS, FRANCIS (New York)
1817:   42945 pb
1819:   48487 pb

NICHOLS, FRANCIS (Philadelphia)
1805: 8732 f, 8734 f, 9332 f
1806: 9815 f, 10372 f, 10676 f
1807: 11951
1808: 14776-14777 f, 16135 f
1809: 17228 f, 17265 pb, 18801 f
1810: 20443 f
1811: 23564 pb, 23614 f
1812: 25094 pb
1813: 29374 f, 30567 pb
1817: 42946 f
1818: 45103 f

NICHOLS, GEORGE W (Plattsburgh, N.Y.)
1809: 16844 pb

NICHOLS, GEORGE W (Walpole, N.H.)
1801: 1371?
1805: 8326, 8658, 9266
1806: 10961, 11435
1807: 12069, 12101, 12787, 12791, 12873, 12875, 12889
1808: 14282, 14397-14398, 14956-14958, 15208 pb, 15376? pb, 15377, 16609
1809: 19166

NICHOLS, LEWIS (New York)
1801: 273, 372, 782, 956, 1021, 1634
1802: 1800, 2103, 2146, 2165, 2244-2245, 2443, 2574, 2861, 3003, 3036, 3165 pb, 3607, 50288
1803: 4119, 4196-4197, 4277, 4321, 4390, 4572, 5101, 5117-5118, 5162-5163, 50391
1804: 5978, 6184, 6533, 6616, 6842, 7158, 7233, 7734, 50411
1805: 8104, 8220, 8269, 8746, 9298, 9314, 9495, 9780, 50491, 50498, 50522
1806: 10234, 10482
1808: 50904

NICHOLS, ROSWELL STILES (Norwalk, Conn.)

1818: 43271 pb, 45123 pb
1819: 47020 pb, 48210, 48839, 49522

NICHOLS, STILES (Bridgeport, Conn.)
1810: 21196 pb
1814: 31036 pb
1817: 40701 pb
1819: 47439

NICHOLS, STILES (Danbury, Conn.)
1801: 84 pb, 251, 821, 1258 pb
1802: 2325, 2575, 3267
1803: 3610, 3646?, 3697 pb, 3921, 4407, 4567, 4930, 5000, 5565 pb
1804: 6518, 50405-50406
1805: 8902, 50497 pb, 50571 pb
1806: 10715, 10867, 11382, 50673 pb
1807: 13077 pb
1808: 16098

NICKLIN, PHILIP HOULBROOKE (Baltimore)
1809: 16992 pb
1810: 19712 f, 19881 f, 20130 f, 20199 pb, 20456 f, 20460 f, 20503 f, 20623 f, 21934 pb
1811: 22400 pb, 22455a pb, 22473 pb, 22758 pb, 23293 pb, 23883 f, 23891 pb
1812: 24520 f, 24850 f, 25008 f, 25676 pb, 26506 pb

NICKLIN, PHILIP HOULBROOKE (Philadelphia)
1813: 30404 f, 30522 f
1814: 30809 pb, 30940 f, 32676 pb, 32707 f
1816: 37151 pb, 37152 f, 37704 f
1817: 39963 pb
1818: 45224 pb, 45243 f, 45258 f, 45487 pb
1819: 47183 pb, 47962 f, 48111 pb

NICOLSON, THOMAS (Richmond, Va.)
1801: 1254, 1586-1587
1802: 3475, 3477
1804: 6555, 6627, 50439 pb
1805: 9670, 50543 pb
1806: 50682 pb
1807: 12070, 50778 pb, 50814 pb
1808: 16643

NIEBEL, HENRICH (New Berlin, Pa.)
1817: 40771-40772
1818: 43885, 44070, 44523 pb
1819: 47218 pb

NILES, HEZEKIAH (Baltimore)
1801: 103 pb, 288? pb, 313 pb, 469 sb, 819, 880 pb, 951, 1180 pb, 50199 pb
1802: 1922 pb, 50278 pb
1803: 3854 pb, 3966 pb, 4677 pb, 4815 f, 4941 pb
1804: 5659 pb, 6122 bf
1808: 14934?, 15105
1809: 16793 f, 18257
1810: 19416, 22105
1811: 24411 pb
1814: 32358 pb
1816: 34435, 37833
1818: 45108 bpb

NILES, HEZEKIAH (Wilmington, Del.)
1801: 401, 413, 469 pb, 884, 1432 pb, 1601, 50200 pb
1802: 1792, 1923 pb, 2385 pb, 2467 pb, 2577, 2657 pb, 3352 pb, 3518 pb, 50331 pb
1803: 3855 pb, 3927 pb, 4065, 4280, 4395 pb, 4429 pb, 4904 pb, 4931-4933, 5594, 5600, 5601 pb
1804: 5855 pb, 5961 pb, 6124 pb, 6147, 6264 pb, 6870 pb, 7379, 7731, 7778 pb
1805: 7877 pb, 8522 pb, 8704 pb, 8898 pb, 9270 pb, 9473, 9492
1807: 12523 pb

NILES, JOHN MILTON (Hartford, Conn.)
1817: 41978

NIVEN, ALEXANDER (New York)
1811: 22951, 23721

Norfolk Gazette and Publick Ledger (Norfolk, Va.)
1804: 5890
1807: 11924 pb, 14178 pb

Norfolk Herald (Norfolk, Va.)
1811: 22296

NORMAN, JOHN (Boston)
1809: 17778 f
1811: 23681 f
1813: 29507 pb
1814: 30707 f

NORMAN, WILLIAM (Boston)
1802: 1873 pb, 3028 f, 3114 pb
1803: 3667 pb, 3902 pb
1804: 6472 f
1805: 9423 pb
1806: 10850 pb
1807: 13382 pb
1810: 19353 pb

NORMAN, WILLIAM E (Hudson, N. Y.)
1805: 8005 f, 8982 f
1806: 9964 f, 10919 f
1808: 15431 f, 15602 pb, 16775 pb
1809: 17815 f, 18240 pb
1810: 19663 f, 20570 pb, 20590 pb, 22015 pb, 22092
1811: 22174, 22334, 22616, 23074, 24325, 24368
1812: 26689 pb, 27445
1813: 29150 f, 30176 pb, 30454 f
1814: 30900 f, 32015 pb, 32573 pb, 32595 pb, 32653 pb
1815: 34052 f, 35885 pb
1816: 37676 f, 37824 pb, 38695 f, 38758 f, 38894 f, 39125 pb, 39126 f, 39708 pb

1817:   40200, 41920 pb, 51715 pb
1818:   43880, 44003 pb,
  44943 pb, 46699 f
1819:   49353 pb

NORRIS, CHARLES (Exeter,
  N. H.)
1806:   10874, 11354, 11393,
  11817 pb
1807:   12167, 12753, 12754 pb,
  12775-12776 pb, 12843,
  13422, 13551, 13603-13604
  pb, 14125 pb, 50779 pb
1808:   14537, 14538 pb, 14547,
  14719 pb, 15104, 15544,
  15568, 15636 pb, 16112,
  16148, 16200, 16635 pb,
  16636
1809:   17052, 17293, 18149,
  18572, 18628, 19115?, 19169
1810:   20663, 20864, 22081,
  51012
1811:   22534 pb, 23501, 23518-
  23521, 23523
1812:   24772, 24817, 25070,
  26207, 26235, 26362, 26379,
  26757, 27511, 27547 pb,
  51174, 51179 pb
1813:   28270-28271, 28745,
  28923 pb, 29074, 29226,
  29305-29306, 29530, 29763,
  29900, 29939, 30447, 30451,
  30533 pb, 51318?
1814:   31572 pb, 31903 pb,
  32253 pb, 32505? pb, 32536,
  32554, 32791, 33640, 33676
  pb
1815:   34096 pb, 34383, 34773
  pb, 34832, 34877, 35087,
  35265, 35429, 35432-35433,
  35437 pb, 35800, 35950,
  35993, 36504 pb, 36566
1816:   36769 pb, 36982 pb,
  37563 pb, 37660-37662,
  37797, 38045? pb, ?38394?,
  38400 pb, 39730 pb, 51610
  pb
1817:   40035 f, 40612, 41174?,
  41414, ?41580-41581?,
  41929, 42260, 42872
1818:   ?44993?
1819:   49109 pb

NORRIS, CHARLES (Newbury-
  port, Mass.)
1809:   18046
1810:   19295, 19908, 20678,
  20911, 21458
1811:   22682, 23263, 23324,
  23326, 23396, 23440, 23724,
  24403, 24443
1812:   27404
1813:   30420
1814:   31288, 32432, 33568
1815:   35275, 35638, 36444
1816:   38334, 39669, 39702

NORRIS, CHARLES (Portland,
  Me.)
1816:   38078

North Carolina Journal (Halifax,
  N. C.)
1806:   10484

NORTON, JACOB PORTER
  (Boston)
1817:   39942 pb, 39943, 40491
  pb, 40492, 41567 pb, 41569
1818:   43421, 43640-43641,
  43806, 44027, 44040 pb,
  44195, 44548, 44634, 44977
  pb, 45338 pb, 45536
1819:   47033

NORTON, JACOB PORTER
  (Mount Zion, Ga.)
1819:   48712 pb

NORVELL, JOHN (Lexington,
  Ky.)
1816:   51599 pb
1817:   40623, 41193-41194
1818:   45473
1819:   47381 pb

NORVELL, JOSEPH (Nashville,
  Tenn.)
1812:   24737, 26194 pb
1813:   27816, 28426
1814:   30781, 32876 pb, 32915
1815:   33974, 34481, 36065-
  36066
1816:   36850, 39065
1817:   40113, 42902
1819:   47137, 48043 pb, 49001

NORVELL, JOSHUA (Lan-
caster, Ky.)
1808: 15969 pb

NORVELL, JOSHUA (St. Louis,
Mo.)
1815: 36546 pb

NORVELL, MOSES (Lancaster,
Ky.)
1808: 15969 pb

NORVELL, MOSES (Nashville,
Tenn.)
1812: 24737, 26194 pb
1813: 27816, 28426
1814: 30781, 32876 pb, 32915
1815: 33974, 34481, 36065-
36066
1816: 39065

Norwich Packet (Norwich,
Conn.)
1801: 1164 pb

NOURSE, GABRIEL (Hagers-
town, Md.)
1815: 34323 f, 34789 f
1818: 43579 f
1819: 47566 f

NOURSE, GABRIEL (Sharps-
burg, Md.)
1819: 47606 f

NUTTING, SAMUEL (Ports-
mouth, N. H.)
1801: 1678
1802: 3467
1803: 4236
1804: 7062, 7741

O

Observatory (Walpole, N. H.)
see Political Observatory
(Walpole, N. H.)

Observer (Fayetteville, N. C.)
see Carolina Observer (Fayetteville, N. C.)

Observer (Schoharie, N. Y.)
1819: 48489

O'CONNOR, JAMES (Norfolk,
Va.)
1804: 7665?
1807: 13482 pb
1808: 16288-16289
1809: 18722
1811: 22296
1815: 33988
1816: 36868, 37929, 38065,
39811
1817: 40123
1819: 48942

OGDEN, ROBERT (Newbern,
N. C.)
1802: 2173? pb, 2199 pb, 2801
pb, 2917 pb
1803: 3826, 4586 pb
1804: 6714 pb, 6940-6941 pb

OGILSBY, SAMUEL (Danville,
Ky.)
1805: 8130, 8679 pb

OGILSBY, SAMUEL (Lincoln
County, Ky.)
1807: 12884 pb
1808: 14990

OGLE, BENJAMIN (Brookville,
Ind.)
1816: 38652 pb

Ohio Monitor (Columbus, O.)
1819: 48968

Ohio Patriot (New Lisbon, O.)
1817: 41041
1819: 47124

Ohio Register (Clinton, O.)
1815: 35966

Ohio Register (Mount Vernon,
O.)
1817: 40105

Ohio Republican (Dayton, O.)
1815: 33965

Old Established Directory Office (New York)
1813:   28973

OLDFIELD, G S (New York)
1817:   41495 f

OLDS, BENJAMIN (Newark,
N.J.)
1813:   28045 pb
1816:   37376 f
1818:   43480 f
1819:   47463 f

OLIVER, DANIEL (Boston)
1808:   15206 f

OLIVER, DANIEL (Charlestown,
Mass.)
1809:   17684 f

OLIVER, EDWARD (Boston)
1806:   10487, 10562, 10824
   pb, 11186? pb, 11428
1807:   12020, 12176 pb, 12211
   pb, 12666, 12938, 13575 pb,
   13599, 13675, 13708 pb
1808:   14270-14271 pb, 14515
   pb, 14558 pb, 14792, 15200,
   15204?, 15516 pb, 15561 pb,
   15647, 15660 pb, 15772,
   16671 pb
1809:   17031 pb, 17173, 19236,
   19280
1810:   19553 pb, 21338, 22104?
1811:   22392 pb, 23856
1812:   24873 pb, 25397, 26206
   pb

Oliver & Munroe (Boston)
see OLIVER, EDWARD (Bos-
   ton)
   MUNROE, ISAAC (Boston)

OLMSTEAD, JAMES (New York)
1810:   21954 pb
1817:   40617 f

OLMSTED, EDWARD (Phila-
delphia)
1811:   24001
1812:   25449 pb

OLMSTED, PHILO HOPKINS
(Columbus, O.)
1814:   30774, 33649
1815:   33966
1816:   36845, 37650, 38003
   pb, 38514 pb
1817:   40530, 40531 pb, 41092,
   41201, 41684, 41685 pb,
   41689 pb, 42977 pb
1818:   43680, 45140, 45142,
   45144-45145, 45148, 45440
1819:   48006, 48029, 48032,
   48969, 48971, 49211?, 51871
   pb

OLMSTED, PHILO HOPKINS
(Delaware, O.)
1818:   43836 pb

OLNEY, WILLIAM (Providence,
R.I.)
1805:   9454

O'LYNCH, JOHN (Richmond,
Va.)
1810:   19461, 51010 pb
1811:   22243-22244, 22293,
   23243

ONSELL, G (Philadelphia)
1810:   21271 pb

ONSELL, J W (Philadelphia)
1810:   21271 pb

Ontario Messenger (Canan-
   daigua, N.Y.)
1811:   22272, 22608
1812:   24722
1814:   30769
1815:   33958
1816:   36838
1817:   40097
1818:   43200

ORAM, JAMES (New York)
1801:   75 pb, 183, 1255, 50204
1802:   2039 f, 2136, 2502,
   2573, 2771, 3162 pb, 3186
1803:   4120, 4292, 5185 pb,
   50340?
1804:   6466, 50455 pb
1805:   50583-50585 pb

1806:   11071-11074, 50703 pb
1807:   12676 pb, 13289-13294,
        13487, 13501-13502, 14220
1812:   24916, 24992, 25171,
        25947, 26188 pb, 26907? pb
1813:   27759, 28997 pb, 29441,
        29853
1814:   32841
1817:   40680, 41220 pb
1818:   43126, 43590, 46692
1819:   48404-48406, 49287

ORAM, JAMES (Trenton, N.J.)
1803:   4766 pb
1804:   5812 pb, 6404, 6962,
        50462-50463 pb
1805:   8413, 8823, 8910 pb,
        9001, 9285, 9329, 9744,
        50580-50581 pb
1806:   10031, 10155 pb, 10157
        pb, 10210, 10364, 11070,
        11756 pb, 50660
1808:   14843 pb, 14889 pb,
        15767 pb, 16212, 50837 pb
1809:   17113 pb, 17271, 17380,
        17516, 17598, 17692, 18224
        pb, 18289? pb, 18293 pb,
        18421, 18547
1810:   19609 f, 19629, 20580
        pb, 22112
1811:   22589 pb, 22626 pb,
        23206 pb, 23290, 23963,
        24469 pb

Orange County Patriot (Goshen,
    N.Y.)
1815:   33884

O'REILLY, J C (Washington,
    D.C.)
1804:   6721

O'REILLY, JOSEPH C (Balti-
    more)
1813:   28788, 29164 pb, 29275
1814:   31884

Original Association of Wind-
    ham County (Windham,
    Conn.)
1803:   5578 f

ORMROD, JOHN (Philadelphia)
1801:   39, 306, 628, 803,

1108 pb, 1339
1802:   3494 f
1809:   18455 pb

Ornamental Printing Office
    (Boston)
1802:   2172

OSBORN, --- (New Haven,
    Conn.)
1819:   47701 pb

OSBORN, CHARLES (Mt.
    Pleasant, O.)
1816:   37665
1817:   41793 pb
1818:   44110?

OSBORN, I (Mt. Pleasant, O.)
1818:   44658 pb, 45533

OSBORN, JAMES (Mt. Pleas-
    ant, O.)
1818:   45533

OSBORN, JOHN WILLSON
    (Homer, N.Y.)
1813:   28233, 28929
1814:   31111
1815:   34139
1819:   48124

OSBORN, JOSEPH (New York)
1805:   50564 f
1806:   9817 f, 11084 f
1807:   12169 f, 14143 pb
1808:   14929 f
1809:   17721 f

OSBORN, SELLECK (Sag Har-
    bor, N.Y.)
1802:   3127 pb, 3490

OSBORNE, J (Philadelphia)
1806:   11441 f

OSWALD, JOHN H (Philadel-
    phia)
1803:   3997
1804:   5907, 7044
1805:   8096, 8307, 8343, 8741,
        8769, 8828, 8915
1806:   10006, 10282, 10317,
        10422, 10530, 11023, 11782

OVERTON, SAMUEL R (Lex-
ington, Ky.)
1808:   14703, 16048 pb
1811:   22192 pb

P

PACE, HENRY (Auburn, N.Y.)
1809:   16924, 19206 pb
1810:   19439
1811:   22214 pb
1813:   30463, 30568
1814:   32386
1815:   36612

PACE, HENRY (Aurora, N.Y.)
1805:   7897 pb
1806:   9898
1808:   15028

PACE, HENRY (Richmond,
Va.)
1801:   271, 818, 1218 pb
1802:   1983
1803:   5137, 5512

PACE, JAMES (Auburn, N.Y.)
1809:   16924, 19206 pb
1810:   19439
1811:   22214 pb
1813:   30463, 30568
1814:   32386
1815:   36612

PACE, JAMES (Cincinnati, O.)
1819:   48501

PACKARD, BENJAMIN D
(Albany, N.Y.)
1807:   13254 pb
1809:   18256 pb
1810:   19690 f, 19882 pb,
20809 f
1811:   22445a f, 22922 f,
23398 f, 23448 pb
1812:   24971 f
1816:   37018 pb, 37890 f,
38963 pb

PACKARD, ROBERT (Albany, N.Y.)
1807:   50757

1808:   14865, 15635
1809:   19285
1810:   19690, 19952, 20809,
21435
1811:   22445a, 22922, 51122
1812:   25079
1813:   28148
1814:   30646, 30676, 31077,
31407 pb, 31941?, 32802,
32890
1815:   34753, 35118, 51515?
1816:   37281, 37671, 38434,
51547, 51603
1817:   39959, 40224, 41275,
42020
1818:   43625, 51732, 51794,
51810
1819:   47624, 48041, 49503

Packard & Conant (Albany,
N.Y.)
see PACKARD, BENJAMIN D
(Albany, N.Y.)
CONANT, JONATHAN (Al-
bany, N.Y.)

Packard & Van Benthuysen
(Albany, N.Y.)
see PACKARD, ROBERT
(Albany, N.Y.)
VAN BENTHUYSEN, OBA-
DIAH R (Albany, N.Y.)

PAFF, JOHN (New York)
1802:   2703 pb
1806:   10680 pb
1807:   50766? pb, 50820? pb
1810:   51018? pb
1811:   22898 pb
1812:   51199-51200? pb, 51229
pb, 51236 pb

PAFF, MICHAEL (New York)
1802:   2703 pb
1806:   10680 pb
1807:   50766? pb, 50820? pb
1810:   51018? pb

PAISLEY, ROBERT (Russell-
ville, Ky.)
1816:   37255 pb

PALFRAY, WARWICK (Salem,
Mass.)

1806: 9810
1807: 12104, 12513 pb, 12846
1808: 14280-14281, 14823,
14906, 15031, 15108, 15729,
16232
1809: 16894, 18015, 18515,
18566-18567, 19273
1810: 21400
1811: 22631, 22759, 24431
1812: 25329, 25938, 26475 pb,
26791 pb, 26928 pb, 27553
pb
1813: 29841
1816: 36793-36794, 38862,
39107, 39689
1817: 40051, 40990, 42033,
42036
1818: 45616, 45620
1819: 47516, 47854, 47872,
48615, 50076

Palladium (Boston)
see New England Palladium
(Boston)

Palladium (Frankfort, Ky.)
1809: 16913 pb

PALMER, ARCHIBALD (Phila-
delphia)
1805: 50606?

PALMER, F (Detroit, Mich.)
1818: 51770 pb

PALMER, GEORGE (Philadel-
phia)
1803: 3622, 3849, 3950, 4090-
4091, 4815, 5052
1804: 5824, 6397, 6402, 7047,
7090, 7215-7216, 7346,
7492, 7675
1805: 8147 pb, 8285, 8556,
8790, 9289-9290
1806: 9925-9926, 10096,
10167, 10320, 10325 pb,
10329, 10371-10372, 10513
1807: 12965, 13107, 13147
1808: 14449, 14451, 14584-
14585, 14776, 14791, 15286,
16077, 16725
1809: 17264 pb, 17316,
17423, 17523, 17905, 17929,

18065, 18094, 18162, 18549
pb, 18561, 18615, 18801,
18803, 19197
1810: 20001-20004 pb, 20235,
20782, 21064, 21083, 21348,
22114
1811: 22729 pb, 22730, 23621,
24034 pb, 24348
1812: 25008, 25265, 25558 pb,
25672, 25683, 25915, 25937
pb, 26061-26062, 26129,
26766, 27405
1813: 28157, 28195, 28475 pb,
29032, 29139-29140, 29143,
29171-29172, 29415, 30538,
51343
1814: 31267 pb, 31312, 31394,
31596, 31715 pb, 32096-
32100, 32603, 32828, 33530
1815: 33888, 34240-34241,
34257, 34260, 34633, 34790,
35028, 35245-35246, 35248-
35249, 36658
1816: 37126, 38085, 38222,
38291, 38828, 39104 pb

PALMER, JAMES W (Phila-
delphia)
1812: 25121-25122

PALMER, JOHN E (Ports-
mouth, N. H.)
1804: 7280 pb

PALMER, NATHAN (Mount
Holly, N. J.)
1818: 43489 pb, 48872 pb

PALMER, T (Detroit, Mich.)
1818: 51770 pb

PALMER, THOMAS (Cincinnati,
O.)
1815: 34352 pb, 36097
1816: 37244, 37620, 38554,
38717
1817: 40810 pb
1819: 47361, 47614 pb, 47617,
47619, 49223

PALMER, THOMAS (Philadel-
phia)
1803: 3622, 3849, 3950, 4090-

4091, 4815, 5052
1804: 5824, 6397, 6402, 7047,
    7090, 7215-7216, 7346,
    7492, 7675
1805: 8147 pb, 8285, 8556,
    8790, 9289-9290
1806: 9925-9926, 10096,
    10167, 10320, 10325 pb,
    10329, 10371-10372, 10513,
    10716 f
1807: 12965, 13107, 13147
1808: 14449, 14451, 14584-
    14585, 14776, 14791, 15207,
    15286, 15401, 16077, 16722,
    16725
1809: 17264 pb, 17316, 17423,
    17523, 17905, 17929, 18065,
    18094, 18162, 18549 pb,
    18561, 18615, 18801, 18803,
    19197
1810: 20001-20004 pb, 20235,
    20782, 21064, 21083, 21348,
    22114
1811: 22729 pb, 22730, 23621,
    24034 pb, 24348
1812: 25008, 25265, 25558
    pb, 25672, 25683, 25915,
    25937 pb, 26061-26062,
    26129, 26766, 27405
1813: 28475 pb, 29032, 29139-
    29140, 29171-29172, 29415,
    30538
1814: 31596
1816: 38085, 38222

PALMER, THOMAS H (Phila-
    delphia)
1816: 36888, 37347, 38220
1817: 41016, 41865, 41964,
    42011, 51687
1818: 43409, 43493, 43533a,
    43788, 44163, 44762, 44797,
    44920, 45215, 45311, 45868
1819: 47458, 47962, 48199,
    48395, 48459, 48644, 49021

PALMER, THOMAS H (Wash-
    ington, D. C.)
1814: 31714 pb

Pandamonium Press (Boston)
1801: 197

Panoplist and Missionary Maga-
    zine (Boston)
1809: 19183?

PARADISE, JOHN (Alexandria,
    Va.)
1814: 31631 f
1815: 35991 f

PARCELS, PETER (Chillicothe,
    O.)
1808: 15060
1809: 17551, 17811 pb
1810: 20157, 20946, 20947 f
1812: 25464?

PARES, --- (Newark, N. J.)
1819: 48924 pb

PARK, JOHN (Boston)
1804: 5706, 7169 pb
1806: 10280
1808: 16057

PARK, JOHN (Newburyport,
    Mass.)
1803: 4732 f, 4817
1804: 7787

PARKE, JAMES P (Philadel-
    phia)
1806: 10159 pb, 10942 f
1807: 12495 f, 12629 pb,
    13593 pb
1808: 14700-14701 pb, 14702
    f, 16346 f
1809: 17225 pb, 18168 pb,
    18724 f, 19129 f
1811: 23412 f, 23415 f, 24449
    f
1815: 34267 f, 34601 f
1817: 42769 f
1818: 45262

PARKER, EDWARD (Philadel-
    phia)
1810: 21000 pb
1811: 23034 pb, 23118 f,
    23195 f, 23356 f, 23412 f,
    23415 f, 23447 pb, 23686 pb
1812: 24929 pb, 25191 f, 26460
    pb
1813: 27835 f, 28351 f,

29927 f
1814: 30809 pb
1815: 34497 pb, 35100 pb,
35866 pb, 36045 f
1816: 37368 f, 38073-38074 f,
38623 f
1817: 40355-40356 f, 41805
pb, 41806 f, 41918 pb
1818: 43322 pb, 43399 f,
43559 f, 43777? f, 43878
pb, 44490 pb, 45000 f,
45218, 45307 f, 46688 pb,
51772 f
1819: 47532-47533 f, 47534
pb, 48160 pb, 48398-48399
f, 49101-49102 pb, 51886 f

PARKER, ISAAC SENTER
(Harvard, Mass.)
1810: 21525 pb

PARKER, JOSEPH (Pittsburgh,
Pa.)
1809: 17110 pb

PARKER, LUTHER (Harvard,
Mass.)
1801: 792, 1247

PARKER, LUTHER (Shirley,
Mass.)
1802: 2334, 3187

PARKER, RICHARD (Phila-
delphia)
1816: 37368 f, 38073-38074 f
1817: 40355-40356 f, 41805
pb, 41806 f
1818: 43399 f, 43559 f,
43878 pb, 44490 pb, 45000
f, 45218, 45307 f, 46688
pb, 51772 f
1819: 47532-47533 f, 47534
pb, 48160 pb, 48398-48399
f, 49101-49102 pb, 51886 f

PARKER, SAMUEL H (Boston)
1803: 3642 f, 5571 f
1805: 8566 f
1806: 10502 f, 11385 f
1808: 14315-14316, 14386 pb,
14476 pb, 14938 pb, 15087-
15088, 15198 pb, 15290 pb,

15297 pb, 15352, 15395 pb,
15402, 15433 pb, 15456 pb,
15508 pb, 15863, 15984,
16023 pb, 16078, 16177,
16225, 16252 pb, 16365,
16375, 16654 pb
1809: 16787, 16877 pb, 16991
pb, 17067, 17104-17105 pb,
17192 pb, 17312 pb, 17422
pb, 17430 pb, 17526, 17599,
17600 pb, 17675, 17818,
17861 pb, 17889 pb, 18026
pb, 18032 pb, 18056, 18268
pb, 18359 pb, 18725? pb,
19133 pb, 19290 pb
1810: 20993, 21040 pb, 21331,
21358 pb, 21397
1813: 27744, 28961? pb,
29845 pb
1814: 30968, 31439, 32236-
32237 pb, 32719 pb, 51405
pb
1815: 33995, 34063 pb, 34176
pb, 34895, 35057 pb, 35078
pb, 35140 pb, 35166, 35232,
35415 pb, 35761, 35859
1816: 37248, 37683, 37760,
38374 pb, 51615 pb
1817: 40244 f

PARKER, SEWALL (Harvard,
Mass.)
1803: 4377, 5081
1804: 6986
1807: 12401, 13313
1809: 18322, 18789 pb
1810: 21525 pb
1814: 30846

PARKER, THOMAS (Boston)
1802: 1712 pb
1807: 11929 pb
1810: 19301 pb

PARKER, THOMAS (Cam-
bridgeport, Mass.)
1816: 36981 f

PARKER, WILLIAM (Boston)
1802: 1712 pb
1807: 11929 pb
1810: 19301 pb
1816: 36980 f

PARKER, WILLIAM SEWALL
(Troy, N. Y.)
1807: 12130 pb, 12152 pb,
13315 pb, 50760 pb
1808: 14518, 14522 bf
1809: 16790 pb, 16820, 17038
pb, 17039, 19241 pb
1810: 19333, 19559, 19654,
20180 pb, 20802 pb, 21949
1811: 22147 pb, 22402 pb,
22979 pb, 24371, 24456 pb,
51082 pb
1812: 24553, 24884, 24902,
24952, 26915 pb, 27455,
27635
1813: 27948, 29224 pb
1814: 30620, 32177 pb
1815: 34127 pb, 34151, 34576,
34963 pb, 35385 pb, 36414
1816: 37007, 38294 pb, 39119,
51603 sb
1817: 51729 pb
1818: 44285, 44632
1819: 47198, 47352, 47674 f,
49595

PARKS, BENJAMIN (Boston)
1804: 6149 pb
1805: 8056 pb, 8336, 8350,
8533-8534, 8624, 8669
1806: 11102
1807: 14128-14129
1808: 15106, 15114, 15524,
15541, 15667, 16376 pb
1809: 17332 pb

PARKS, BENJAMIN (George-
town, D. C.)
1802: 2822 pb

PARKS, JOSIAH (Montpelier,
Vt.)
1807: 12218 f, 12412
1808: 14788 pb, 14937 f,
15218 pb, 15901 pb, 16215
pb
1809: 17013 pb, 17448 pb,
17530 f, 19161 pb
1810: 19940 f, 20137 f,
20329 f, 20879 pb
1811: 22432a f

PARMELE, HENRY (Philadel-
phia)
1819: 49015 f

PARMELE, SAMUEL (Phila-
delphia)
1818: 45356 pb, 45358-45359 pb
1819: 48830 pb, 49141 pb

PARMENTER, JAMES (Boston)
1816: 36772 pb
1817: 39942 pb, 39943, 40491
pb, 40492, 41567 pb, 41569
1818: 43421, 43640-43641,
43806, 44027, 44040 pb,
44195, 44548, 44634, 44977
pb, 45338 pb, 45536
1819: 47033, 47357, 47642,
48237, 48956-48957, 49314,
50168, 51869 pb, 51949 pb

PARSONS, CHESTER (Pough-
keepsie, N. Y.)
1806: 9951, 10205, 50646 pb
1807: 12099 pb, 13615
1808: 14470 pb, 15682 pb,
15932
1809: 17609 pb, 18690 f,
19185 f

PASTEUR, JOHN I (Newbern,
N. C.)
1818: 43540 pb

PASTEUR, JOHN S (Newbern,
N. C.)
1801: 207
1802: 2010 pb, 2086
1803: 4237
1809: 17152 pb, 17696

PATRICK, EBENEZER (Salem,
Ind.)
1818: 44461, 44583, 45877 pb
1819: 47085

PATRICK, JAMES (New Philadelphia, O.)
1819: 49653 pb

PATRICK, MATTHEW (Salem,
Ind.)
1819: 47085

PATRICK, SAMUEL (Weathersfield, Vt.)
1814:   31378, 32231, 32238,
32454, 33516
1815:   34051 pb, 34458, 35138,
35266

Patriot (Charleston, S. C.)
see   Southern Patriot (Charleston, S. C.)

Patriot (Concord, N. H.)
see   New Hampshire Patriot
(Concord, N. H.)

Patriot (Goshen, N. Y.)
see   Orange County Patriot
(Goshen, N. Y.)

Patriot (Haverhill, Mass.)
see   Essex Patriot (Haverhill,
Mass.)

Patriot (Utica, N. Y.)
1812:   25654

PATTEN, NATHANIEL (Frank-
lin, Mo.)
1819:   48719 pb

PATTEN, NATHANIEL (Win-
chester, Ky.)
1814:   31859 pb, 33702 pb
1815:   33936? pb, 35053 pb
1816:   36821 pb, 37222

PATTEN, STEPHEN (Portland,
Me.)
1809:   18441 f
1813:   30586 pb

PATTERSON, EDGAR (George-
town, D. C.)
1809:   17810 pb

PATTERSON, J (Pittsburgh,
Pa.)
1813:   29136 f
1814:   32516 f

PATTERSON, JOHN (Philadelphia)
1813:   28013 pb

PATTERSON, ROBERT (Pitts-
burgh, Pa.)
1810:   19556 pb
1811:   51102 f
1812:   24844 f, 24965 pb,
25424 pb, 25442 f, 26558 f,
27482 f, 27569 f, 51210 f
1813:   28769 f, 29136 f
1814:   32516 f
1815:   34078 f, 34244 f, 34452
f, 34650 pb, 35243 f, 35396
f, 35573 f, 35649 f
1816:   38320 pb, 38649-38650,
f, 38852 f
1817:   40022 pb, 40330 f, 41526
f, 41735-41737 pb, 42818 f,
51700 f, 51701 pb
1818:   43334a f, 43344 f, 44161
f, 44179 f, 44181 pb, 44786-
44790 f, 44945 f, 45215-
45216 f, 45829 f, 46788 f,
51816 f, 51820 pb
1819:   47414 pb, 47817 f,
48666 f, 49021 f, 49022 pb,
50067 f, 51928 pb, 51929 f

PATTON, JOHN (Somerset,
Pa.)
1813:   29826 pb
1818:   43474, 45840

PATTON, T (Somerset, Pa.)
1818:   43474, 45840

PAUL, ABRAHAM (Brooklyn,
N. Y.)
1810:   19621

PAUL, ABRAHAM (New York)
1810:   21229, 21892, 22017
1811:   22363, 22557, 22756,
23562, 23827, 24003?,
24045-24046, 24511
1812:   25081-25084, 25086,
25088, 25107, 25847, 25925,
25943, 26626 pb, 26830,
27530, 27627
1813:   27704, 28253, 28334,
28772, 29033, 29051, 29157-
29158, 29163, 29769
1814:   30850, 31930, 31995,
32423-32424, 32667
1815:   33773 pb, 34084, 34087,

34212, 34356, 35168-35169, 36442
1816: 37229, 37337, 37349, 37487, 38130, 38453, 38660, 38748, 38768, 38961
1817: 40185, 40203 bf, 40217 pb, 40581, 40714-40716, 40777, 41066, 41149-41150, 41322, 41422, 41718, 41738, 41811, 41860, 42049-42050, 42069, 42089, 42265
1818: 43239-43240, 43302, 43445, 43887, 43901, 44048, 44256, 44357, 44455, 44830, 45078, 45354, 45480-45482, 45681-45682, 46762, 46764
1819: 47845, 47869, 47993, 48357, 48686a, 48917, 49117, 49161, 49248, 49326, 49394, 49582

PAUL AND OTHERS (pseud.)
(Boston)
1818: 43685 pb

Paul & Thomas (New York)
see PAUL, ABRAHAM (New
‾‾York)
    THOMAS, WILLIAM (New
    York)

PAXTON, JOHN ADAMS (Phila-
    delphia)
1819: 49079 pb

PAYSON, S (New Ipswich,
    N. H.)
1815: 35065 f

PEABODY, M M (Hartford,
    Conn.)
1819: 48578 engr

PEACOCK, JAMES (Harrisburg,
    Pa.)
1811: 23667 pb
1812: 26409, 26416, 26419
1813: 29471 pb, 29474, 29476-
    29478
1814: 32461, 32467, 32471-
    32471c
1815: 35596-35598, 35600,
    35602?, 36591

1816: 36784, 37800 pb, 38580, 38582, 38584-38585, 38588, 38590-38591
1817: 41752-41753, 41757-41759, 41761, 41952
1818: 45242 pb, 45244, 45247, 45250-45251, 45253-45256
1819: 49045-49049, 49052-49053

PEARRE, GEORGE W S
    (Augusta, Ga.)
1816: 37702 pb, 51586 pb
1818: 51777 pb

PECHIN, WILLIAM (Baltimore)
1801: 105, 649, 713 pb, 727, 841
1802: 1760, 2957, 3008 pb, 3009, 3089-3090, 3145
1805: 8546 f
1807: 12997
1810: 19971

PECK, EVERARD (Hartford,
    Conn.)
1815: 35740 f
1817: 40226 f

PECK, EVERARD (Rochester,
    N. Y.)
1816: 51601 f
1817: 41217 pb
1818: 45557 f, 45568 pb, 51768 pb
1819: 47951 pb, 48168 pb, 48411 pb, 50109 pb

PECK, SAMUEL (Catskill,
    N. Y.)
1808: 16310 pb

PEEK, SAMUEL (Batavia,
    N. Y.)
1809: 17306 pb

PEEPLES, BURREL H (Clarks-
    ville, Tenn.)
1815: 36530 pb
1819: 49577 pb

PEIRCE, Charles (Portsmouth,
    N. H.)

1801: 82 pb, 116, 223, 613,
1173, 1248 pb, 1334 pb
1802: 1781, 1847 pb, 2924 pb
1803: 4823 f
1805: 7959 f
1806: 9867 pb, 9932 pb,
10569 f, 11113 pb, 11327 f,
11349 pb, 11825 pb, 50642
pb
1807: 13429 pb
1808: 15952 f, 16241 f
1809: 18629 pb
1812: 24689 f, 24691 f

PEIRCE, ISAAC (Philadelphia)
1812: 25592 f, 26425 pb
1813: 28190 pb, 28261 f,
28695 pb, 29505 f, 29990 pb
1815: 34126 pb, 34812 pb,
34813 f
1818: 43322 pb, 44398 pb,
45633 pb, 45917 pb
1819: 47230 pb, 47360 pb

PEIRCE, NATHANIEL S
(Portsmouth, N. H.)
1802: 1774, 2412, 2434 pb,
3076-3077
1803: 3734, 3767, 3897,
4303, 4823, 4891, 5059-
5060, 5062-5063, 5066 f
1804: 6886, 6888, 6890,
7000, 7285? f
1805: 7879, 7959, 8411,
8490, 8660 pb, 8989-8994
1806: 10963-10966, 11112
1807: 13196-13197, 13703
1808: 15334, 15726, 15994
1809: 17657

PEIRCE, WASHINGTON
(Portsmouth, N. H.)
1802: 1774, 2412, 2434 pb,
3076-3077
1803: 3734, 3767, 3897,
4303, 4823, 4891, 5059-
5060, 5062-5063, 5066 f
1804: 6886, 6888, 6890,
7000, 7285? f
1805: 7959, 8660 pb, 8989,
8991, 8993

PELHAM, SAMUEL (Madison,
Ind.)
1817: 41139 pb

PELHAM, WILLIAM (Boston)
1802: 1855 pb
1803: 4300 f, 4355 f
1804: 5745 pb
1805: 8381 f
1807: 12017 f, 13648 pb
1808: 15479 f, 15863 f

PELSUE, WILLIAM (New York)
1809: 17193, 17536, 17538,
17636, 17739, 18781, 18901,
19243
1810: 19374 pb, 20252, 20384
pb, 20440, 20884, 21290,
21496 pb, 21883
1811: 22152, 22791, 23286 pb,
23446 pb, 23540 pb, 23616,
23933, 51051
1812: 24609?, 25100, 25250,
25550, 25638, 25639-25640
pb, 25803, 26266 pb, 26908,
27356, 27377
1813: 27841, 28606, 28617,
28738, 28814, 29016, 29153,
29802, 30523
1814: 32895, 33499, 51395
1815: 33781, 34739 pb, 35454
pb
1816: 36717 pb
1817: 42322 pb
1818: 45091 pb, 51783
1819: 48155, 48770, 49407,
49974 pb

Pelsue & Gould (New York)
see PELSUE, WILLIAM (New
York)
GOULD, STEPHEN (New
York)

Pelsue & Young (New York)
see PELSUE, WILLIAM (New
York)
YOUNG, BENJAMIN (New
York)

PENISTON, FRANCIS (Bards-
town, Ky.)
1803: 5575 pb

1804: 5778 pb, 6556
1805: 7903

PENISTON, FRANCIS (Lexington, Ky.)
1803: 4433 pb

PENISTON, FRANCIS (Louisville, Ky.)
1806: 10082, 11855 pb

PENN, SHADRACH (Georgetown, Ky.)
1811: 24016 pb

PENN, SHADRACH (Lexington, Ky.)
1813: 29007

PENN, SHADRACH (Louisville, Ky.)
1818: 45455 pb
1819: 48551

PENNEY, THOMAS (Cincinnati, O.)
1818: 44437 pb
1819: 47620

PENNIMAN, ELISHA J (Boston)
1810: 20416 pb

PENNIMAN, OBADIAH (Albany, N.Y.)
1801: 305 sb, 1407 f
1802: 1870 sb, 2190 f, 2706 f, 2714 f
1803: 5122 pb

PENNIMAN, OBADIAH (Troy, N.Y.)
1801: 158 pb
1803: 3773 pb, 3828, 4045 sb, 4088, 4149, 4218 pb, 4326 pb, 4718 pb, 4810 pb, 4822, 4999 pb, 5046, 50336
1804: 5825 pb, 5838, 6403, 7109 bsb, 7709 pb, 50486 pb
1805: 7846 pb, 8027, 8120, 8743, 9782
1806: 9797 pb, 9994 pb, 9996 pb, 10368, 11851 pb

1807: 50760 pb
1808: 14522 f
1809: 17039 f

PENNIMAN, SYLVANUS JENCKES (Lansingburgh, N.Y.)
1805: 8743 pb
1806: 10368 f

PENNINGTON, SAMUEL (Newark, N.J.)
1801: 721, 1017 pb
1802: 2712 pb
1803: 4576, 4697 pb

Pennington & Gould (Newark, N.J.)
see PENNINGTON, SAMUEL (Newark, N.J.)
GOULD, STEPHEN (Newark, N.J.)

Pennsylvania Hospital (Philadelphia)
1817: 40652 f
1818: 45561 f

PENTLAND, E (Wheeling, Va.)
1809: 18765

PENTLAND, EPHRAIM (Pittsburgh, Pa.)
1809: 19244
1819: 47367

PERCIVAL, JAMES (Cortland, N.Y.)
1815: 34456 pb

PERCIVAL, JAMES (Homer, N.Y.)
1811: 22627 pb

PERCIVAL, JAMES (Sherburne, N.Y.)
1810: 19443, 20785 pb, 21199 pb

PERIAM, JOSEPH (Elizabeth, N.J.)
1804: 7810
1805: 9501 pb

PERKINS, BENJAMIN DOUG-
LASS (New York)
1805: 7980, 8363, 8550,
8952, 9019, 9376, 9502-
9503, 9763-9768, 50575 pb
1806: 9966 pb, 10928 pb,
10933 pb, 11043, 11081 pb,
11289
1807: 12080 pb, 12125 pb,
12885 pb, 12992 pb, 13114,
13155-13156 pb, 13158 pb,
13160-13162 pb, 13303,
13380
1808: 14448 pb, 14460 pb,
14729-14730, 14880, 15213-
15214 pb, 15474, 15675 pb,
15684-15685 pb, 16094
1809: 16983 pb, 17125 pb,
17474, 17701 pb, 18111 pb,
18145-18146 pb, 18155 pb,
18157 pb, 18584 pb, 50950
pb
1810: 19500 pb, 19724, 19789
pb, 20167, 20399 pb, 20581
pb, 20804-20805 pb, 20813
pb, 20823 pb, 21290 f
1811: 23468 pb

PERKINS, JACOB (Newbury-
port, Mass.)
1809: 18362 f

PERKINS, JOHN H (Milton,
N. C.)
1818: 44858 pb

PERKINS, JOSEPH (Philadelphia)
1819: 49236 pb

PERSON, LEWIS (Elizabeth-
town, N. Y.)
1817: 40768 pb

PESCUD, EDWARD (Peters-
burg, Va.)
1804: 5951, 50429 pb
1805: 9102

PETERS, --- (Baltimore)
1803: 4469
1804: 6691

PETERS, J (Baltimore)
1816: 39124 pb

PETERS, JOSEPH THOMPSON
(Concord, Mass.)
1815: 34714
1816: 37502, 37631 pb, 38248
pb
1817: 41927, 42214
1818: 43395

Petersburg Intelligencer (Petersburg, Va.)
1816: 36865

PETERSON, HENRY W (Car-
lisle, Pa.)
1814: 31536 pb

PETRONIUS, PASQUIN (New
York)
1807: 11971

PETTIT, ANDREW (Philadel-
phia)
1805: 50503? pb

PETTIT, JONATHAN (Sher-
burne, N. Y.)
1810: 19443, 21199 pb

PETTIT, MELANCTON SMITH
(Cincinnati, O.)
1814: 31700, 32835 pb, 32907

PETTIT, MELANCTON SMITH
(Dayton, O.)
1813: 29407 pb

PHELPS, ANSEL (Greenfield,
Mass.)
1811: 22182, 22289, 24054 pb,
24450, 51103?
1812: 24589, 25305, 25452 pb,
26842, 27444 pb
1813: 27663, 27762, 28236 pb,
28328, 28679, 28785 pb,
29458, 29646 pb, 29648,
30535
1814: 30632, 30718, 30720,
31248 pb, 31379, 31976,
32401, 33682, 33684
1815: 33978, 34459, 34919,

35364, 35425 pb, 35534,
36010, 36029, 36479 pb,
36574
1816: 37164, 37212, 37636,
37886 pb, 37963, 37968 pb,
38383, 38542, 39670, 39824
pb
1817: 40393, 41001 pb, 41044,
41118 pb, 41565, 42906,
42963 pb
1818: 43215, 44028 pb, 44037-
44038, 44232, 44687-44688
pb, 45157, 45811-45812,
46808 pb
1819: 46928, 47139, 47457,
48046 pb, 48926, 49521 pb,
49523 pb, 49543, 50146

PHELPS, SEWELL (Boston)
1818: 43446, 44757-44758,
45451
1819: 47350, 47390, 47433,
47715, 47858, 48635, 49398,
49532, 49642, 50073

Phenix (Providence, R. I.)
see Columbian Phenix (Providence, R. I.)

Phenix Press (Salem, Mass.)
1810: 20275

Philadelphia Company of Booksellers (Philadelphia)
1802: 2731 f
1804: 6650 pb

Philadelphia Female Tract Society (Philadelphia)
1819: 50173 f

Philadelphia Gazette (Philadelphia)
1808: 14829 pb

Philadelphia Medical Museum
(Philadelphia)
1808: 16275 pb

Philadelphia Medical Society
(Philadelphia)
1807: 12258 f

Philadelphia Society for the
Establishment and Support
of Charity Schools (Philadelphia)
1817: 40321 f

Philadelphia Society for the
Promotion of American
Manufactures (Philadelphia)
1817: 42170 f

Philadelphia Tract Society
(Philadelphia)
1805: 50601? pb, 50604? pb

Philadelphia Vaccine Society
(Philadelphia)
1818: 44464 f

Philanthropist (Hamilton, O.)
1816: 38272

PHILBRICK, JOSEPH (Concord,
N. H.)
1809: 17987 f

PHILLIPS, --- (Lexington, Ky.)
1815: 34450 pb, 35375, 35744
pb

PHILLIPS, GEORGE (Carlisle,
Pa.)
1802: 3029? pb
1806: 10028, 10493, 10503,
11265
1808: 15127, 15133, 15196
1809: 17197, 18649, 19027
1810: 20226
1811: 23956
1812: 24831 pb, 25562 pb,
26571
1813: 28329, 30600
1814: 30978
1815: 34932, 34971
1816: 37129, 37221
1817: 41226, 42125
1818: 43349, 43538

PHILLIPS, JOHN (New York)
1801: 1151 pb

PHILLIPS, JOHN (Philadelphia)
1803: 4801 f

1805: 9471 pb
1806: 11441 f

PHILLIPS, JOHN FOLSON
(Warren, R. I.)
1808: 16342
1812: 25855

PHILLIPS, NATHANIEL (War-
ren, R. I.)
1806: 9880
1808: 16342

PHILLIPS, WILLIAM (Cin-
cinnati, O.)
1815: 34917 f
1816: 37620 f
1818: 43943 f
1819: 47946 f, 48684

PHILLIPS, WILLIAM (New
York)
1815: 35865 pb

Phillips Andover Academy
(Northampton, Mass.)
1804: 6175 f

PHINNEY, ELIHU (Coopers-
town, N. Y.)
1801: 245, 1153 pb, 1623
1802: 2895 pb
1803: 50384 pb
1804: 6646, 7055
1805: 7883?, 7966 pb, 8784
pb, 9143
1806: 9948 pb, 11162
1807: 13665
1808: 15919 pb
1812: 25738, 26459 pb
1813: 27913 pb, 29512 pb,
29584 pb
1814: 31311, 32500 pb
1815: 33953, 34407, 34436,
35636 pb, 36004 f
1816: 38324 pb, 38629,
38950 bsb
1817: 40214, 40593 pb, 41491,
41810 pb, 42191
1818: 44306 pb, 45324 pb
1819: 46945 pb, 47114, 47750
pb, 48219 pb, 48525, 49104,
49972

PHINNEY, ELIHU (Herkimer,
N. Y.)
1801: 648 pb

PHINNEY, ELIHU (Otsego,
N. Y.)
1807: 12560, 13249 pb, 13386,
14103, 50802 pb
1808: 14755, 15132 pb, 15168,
15860, 15921, 16072, 16164,
16747, 50878 pb
1809: 17010 f, 17590, 17702,
18251, 18384 pb
1810: 19691, 19815, 20573 pb,
21084, 21409
1811: 22583, 23688 pb, 24349a
pb
1812: 24754, 24859 pb, 24867,
25420

PHINNEY, ELIHU (Sherburne,
N. Y.)
1806: 11066 pb

PHINNEY, GEORGE GORDON
(Herkimer, N. Y.)
1808: 15217 pb, 15418, 15920
1809: 17121 pb
1811: 23035 pb

PHINNEY, GEORGE GORDON
(Newark, N. J.)
1806: 11471

PHINNEY, HENRY (Coopers-
town, N. Y.)
1807: 13665
1808: 15919 pb
1812: 25738, 26459 pb
1813: 27913 pb, 29512 pb,
29584 pb
1814: 31311, 32500 pb
1815: 33952, 34407, 34436,
35636 pb, 36004 f
1816: 38324 pb, 38629, 38950
bsb
1817: 40214, 40593 pb, 41491,
41810 pb, 42191
1818: 44306 pb, 45324 pb
1819: 46945 pb, 47114, 47750
pb, 48219 pb, 48525, 49104,
49972

PHINNEY, HENRY (Otsego, N.Y.)
1807: 12560, 13249 pb, 13386, 14103
1808: 14755, 15132 pb, 15168, 15921, 16164, 16747
1809: 17010 f, 17590, 18384 pb
1810: 19691, 19815, 20573 pb, 21084, 21409
1811: 22583, 23688 pb, 24349a pb
1812: 24754, 24859 pb, 24867, 25420

Phoenix (Binghamton, N.Y.)
1815: 33861

PIER, ALBERT D (Weathersfield, Vt.)
1816: 38818

PIERIE, GEORGE W (Philadelphia)
1807: 50806 pb
1808: 50881 pb
1809: 17159, 17221, 18114, 18414 pb
1810: 21109 pb, 21379
1811: 23713 pb
1812: 26494 pb
1813: 51329 pb
1818: 45370?

PIKE, B (Boston)
1805: 8668 f
1806: 11419 f

PIKE, JOHN (Newark, N.J.)
1803: 4746
1804: 6895, 6897
1805: 7934

PIKE, STEPHEN (Philadelphia)
1809: 18062 f
1810: 19320 f
1811: 23920 pb

Pilot (Cazenovia, N.Y.)
1809: 18604

Pittsburgh Bible Society (Pittsburgh, Pa.)
1818: 51795 pb

PLEASANTS, GEORGE WASHINGTON (Frankfort, Ky.)
1810: 20490
1811: 22465

PLEASANTS, SAMUEL (Richmond, Va.)
1801: 128, 271 sb
1802: 2106, 2200 pb, 50330 f
1803: 4353-4354, 5512, 5606-5607, 50400 f
1804: 5811, 5878, 6191, 6708, 7348, 7386, 7666, 50478 pb
1805: 9664, 9666, 9750, 50624 pb
1806: 10446, 11773-11774, 50740 pb
1807: 12356, 14131-14132, 14134, 50813
1808: 14526a, 16640, 16642, 16753, 50896-50897 pb
1809: 18671, 19117-19118, 19121, 50971 pb
1810: 21914-21915, 51041 pb
1811: 22393 sb, 23953 pb, 24341a, 24343a, 24346a, 51143-51146 pb, 51258 pb
1812: 25125 pb, 27407, 27409
1813: 28971, 30421-30424, 51344 pb
1814: 30910, 32801, 33548-33549, 33552, 51448 pb
1815: 36448 f

Plebian (Kingston, N.Y.)
1816: 37559

PLOWMAN, THOMAS LOWRY (Philadelphia)
1801: 38, 458, 822-824, 1104
1802: 1726, 2316, 2336-2337, 2340, 2375-2376, 2731
1803: 4217, 4288, 4293, 4436, 4466, 4870, 4922, 5051 pb
1804: 6306, 7305 pb, 7685, 50423
1805: 8014 pb, 8107, 8158, 8301, 9205 pb, 9209 pb, 9278

1806: 9870, 10395, 10631, 10637
1807: 13054-13055, 13674
1810: 19571-19573, 20402, 20404-20405, 21375-21377, 21383
1811: 22584, 22731, 23824 f
1812: 26634 f, 26637-26638 f

PLUMMER, FREDERICK (Haverhill, Mass.)
1815: 35453 f

PLUMMER, FREDERICK (Philadelphia)
1816: 38900 pb
1818: 43487 f

PLUMMER, FREDERICK (Windham, Conn.)
1819: 49384 pb

POFF, ALLEN M (Urbana, O.)
1814: 32833 pb
1817: 42759 pb
1818: 45390 pb
1819: 47631, 48391

POINDEXTER, RICHARD (Halifax, N.C.)
1806: 10484 f

Political Index (Newburgh, N.Y.)
1813: 29489 pb

Political Mirror (Staunton, Va.)
1801: 1065 pb

Political Observatory (Walpole, N.H.)
1806: 11253
1807: 12874
1808: 14527

POLK, DAVID PEALE (Washington, D.C.)
1809: 18413

POLLARD, WILLIAM (Richmond, Va.)
1816: 36861, 37032
1817: 39993, 40129, 40131-

40132, 41024, 41976, 42108
1818: 43028, 43222, 44668, 45756
1819: 46930, 47151

POMEROY, --- (Middletown, Conn.)
1808: 14949 pb

POMEROY, RALPH WHEELOCK (Baltimore)
1814: 31268 pb, 31834, 31916, 33567 pb, 33643
1815: 34189, 34365 pb, 34688, 34719, 34844, 34948 pb, 35238 pb, 35713 pb, 36049 pb, 36466 pb, 36531, 36649-36650 pb, 36654 pb
1816: 36978, 37059, 37071, 37400, 37577, 37666, 37719, 38626-38627, 38806, 39835, 39863
1817: 39923, 40658, 41064, 41799, 42834

POMEROY, THADDEUS (Middlebury, Vt.)
1803: 4999 pb

POMROY, THOMAS MERRICK (Northampton, Mass.)
1803: 3962 pb, 4381 pb
1804: 6045, 6407, 6434, 6679, 6927, 7310, 7775-7776
1805: 7957 pb, 8356, 8639, 8867, 9179, 9650
1806: 9931, 10121, 10333, 10411, 10610, 10819, 11268, 11309, 11361 pb
1807: 12253 pb, 12492 pb, 12825, 12952, 14150, 14168, 50765

POMROY, THOMAS MERRICK (Rutland, Vt.)
1808: 15391, 16627 pb
1809: 19102 pb

POMROY, THOMAS MERRICK (Windsor, Vt.)
1811: 22431a, 22842, 23100
1812: 24555, 25300, 25848, 26834, 27128 pb, 27420,

27457-27458 pb, 27554,
27562, 27585
1813: 28481, 28840, 29709
1814: 31372, 31664, 32013,
33535
1815: 34744, 35814, 36434
1816: 37115 pb, 37157 pb,
37230 bf, 37371 pb, 37657
pb, 37761 pb, 38388 pb,
38677 pb, 39045 pb

POND, A (New York)
1807: 12984 pb

POOL, HAVEN (Salem, Mass.)
1804: 7120
1805: 9507, 9769, 9771
1806: 9920, 10264, 11316,
11372, 11841 pb
1807: 12104, 12513 pb, 12623
pb, 12846, 13540, 14240-
14241
1808: 14280-14281, 14823,
14906, 15031, 15108, 15729,
16232
1809: 16894, 18015, 18515,
18566-18567, 19273
1810: 21400
1811: 22631, 24431

POOL, HENRY (Walpole, N. H.)
1812: 25261 pb

PORCUPINE, PETER (New
Haven, Conn.)
1814: 30925 pb

Porcupine (Baltimore)
1816: 38874

Porcupine (New York)
1808: 14745, 16045 pb
1810: 19818

Port Folio (Philadelphia)
1817: 40975, 41162, 41309
pb

PORTER, EPAPHRAS (Nor-
wich, Conn.)
1801: 111
1802: 1813-1814
1803: 3721, 3724, 3733,

5069 pb, 5103 pb
1804: 5771-5772, 6707, 7392
pb
1805: 7919-7920, 8339, 8605
pb, 8894 pb
1806: 10507, 11410, 11550,
11799

PORTER, ROBERT (Wilmington,
Del.)
1810: 19979
1811: 22537 pb, 23570
1812: 25073 pb, 25418, 25831,
26190, 26624 pb, 26701
1813: 27922, 28037 pb, 28657,
28917 pb, 29025, 29625,
29915, 30386, 30493
1814: 31044 pb, 31336 pb,
31346, 31827-31828, 31935
pb, 32082, 32202 pb, 32777
pb, 32930 pb, 33514, 33579
pb, 51401 pb, 51428 pb,
51437 pb
1815: 34166, 34577 pb, 34775
pb, 35016, 35080-35082 pb,
35106 pb, 35374 pb, 35412
pb, 35498 pb, 35500, 35758
pb, 36590, 51524 pb
1816: 36961 pb, 36997, 37262,
37422-37424, 37429, 37955
pb, 38077, 38337 pb, 38373
pb, 38476, 38726?, 38727
1817: 40219 pb, 40236, 40428
pb, 41161 pb, 41665, 41934,
41980 pb
1818: 43324 pb, 43335 pb,
43860 pb, 43923 pb, 44307
pb, 45113, 45604 pb, 45891
pb, 46614, 46723 pb
1819: 47406 pb, 48458, 48462,
48831 pb, 48943 pb, 50091
pb

Portico (Baltimore)
1818: 44967

Portsmouth Oracle (Portsmouth,
N. H.)
1803: 3899
1805: 9339
1809: 17112, 17116
1810: 19474
1812: 24691, 26505, 27493-

27494
1814: 31801
1816: 38689

POST, RUSSELL E (Canandaigua, N. Y.)
1804: 7697

POST, RUSSELL E (Lancaster, O.)
1811: 23090 pb

POTTER, PARACLETE (Poughkeepsie, N. Y.)
1806: 9951, 10205, 11424 pb, 50646 pb
1807: 12099 pb, 13615
1808: 14470 pb, 15682 pb, 15932
1809: 16981, 17403, 17414 pb, 18152 pb
1810: 19496, 19497 pb, 19872, 20273, 20475, 20476 pb, 20532, 21367, 21430
1811: 22323 pb, 23081, 23462, 23469 pb, 23475 pb, 51060 pb
1812: 24552 pb, 24787 pb, 25168, 25208 pb, 25358
1813: 27866 pb, 27961 pb, 28265, 28405, 28629, 28688 bf, 29252 pb, 29720 bf
1814: 30839 pb, 31153 pb, 31180 bf, 31286 bf, 32201 bf, 32555 pb, 32709 bf, 33686 pb
1815: 33843 pb, 34026 pb, 34178 pb, 34503, 34620 bf, 34784 bf, 35235 pb, 35348 pb, 35831 bf, 36061, 36102 bf, 36128 bf, 36482 pb, 36576 pb, 36577 bf
1816: 37269 bf, 37380 bf, 37459 bf, 37559 f, 37560 pb, 37726 pb, 38275 bf, 38348, 38764, 38816 pb, 39111 bf, 39827 pb, 51603 sb
1817: 40799, 42324 bf, 42595 pb, 42909 bf, 42910 pb
1818: 43110 pb, 43385 pb, 43519?, 43798 bf, 43996 pb, 44026 pb, 44180 pb,

45350 pb, 45399 pb, 46810 pb
1819: 47023, 47644 pb, 47855 pb, 47949 pb, 48342 pb, 49328 pb, 50117-50119 pb

POTTER, SHELDON (Philadelphia)
1817: 42595 pb
1818: 43110 pb, 43385 pb, 43995 pb, 44180 pb, 45295, 45399 pb, 45431 f, 45432 pb, 45442 f, 45755 pb
1819: 47179 pb, 47644 pb, 48342 pb, 48533 pb, 48656 f, 48733 pb, 49212 f, 50137 pb

POTTER, SHELDON (Poughkeepsie, N. Y.)
1813: 27866 pb, 28265, 28688, 29720, 32201
1814: 30839 pb, 31180, 31286, 32555 pb, 32709
1815: 34026 pb, 34178 pb, 34503, 34620, 34784, 35831, 36061, 36102, 36128, 36482, 36577
1816: 37269, 37380, 37459, 37560 pb, 37726 pb, 38275, 38348, 38764, 39111, 39827 pb
1817: 40799, 42324, 42909
1818: 43798
1819: 47949 pb, 50117 pb, 50119 f

POTTER, SHELDON (Wheeling, Va.)
1819: 47950 pb

POTTER, WALTER (Philadelphia)
1815: 36589 f

POTTER, WALTER (Richmond, Va.)
1807: 50815 pb

POTTS, SAMUEL (Philadelphia)
1816: 38229? f

POULSON, JOHN (Philadelphia)
1806: 50640

POULSON, ZACHARIAH (Philadelphia)
1801: 51, 611, 826, 982,
1116, 1145-1146, 1148,
1474
1802: 2247, 2874, 2890
1803: 3613, 3661, 4512
1805: 50598 pb

Poulson's American Daily Advertiser (Philadelphia)
1807: 12386

POUNDER, JONATHAN (Phila-
delphia)
1810: 19643 f, 21201? pb
1811: 22405a f, 22525 f,
23869 pb
1812: 24585 pb
1813: 28542 pb, 28829 f
1814: 30823 f, 31030 f, 31147
f
1815: 33774 pb, 33826 pb,
35687 f, 36538 f
1816: 39782 pb, 39896 pb,
51621 pb
1817: 40152 f, 40347 f,
42001 sb, 42868 pb, 51704
pb
1818: 43944 pb, 45400 pb
1819: 47725 pb, 48734 pb,
49174 pb, 49271 pb

POUNDSFORD, WILLIAM
(Cincinnati, O.)
1817: 40499 pb

POWELL, FREDERIC C (Plattsburgh, N.Y.)
1813: 30539

POWELL, FREDERIC C (Pots-
dam, N.Y.)
1816: 38691 pb
1817: 40678
1819: 47121 pb

POWER, NICHOLAS (Pough-
keepsie, N.Y.)
1801: 690
1802: 2437, 2728 pb
1805: 8199 pb

POWER, W (Philadelphia)
1812: 25449 pb

POWERS, --- (Boston)
1818: 43531

POWERS, BENJAMIN FRANK-
LIN (Cincinnati, O.)
1818: 44437 pb
1819: 47620

POWERS, THOMAS (New York)
1808: 14625 f, 15563 pb
1810: 19314 pb, 19465 pb,
20080 pb, 20341 pb, 20882
pb, 21339 f, 21510 pb

POWERS, WILLIAM
1810: 19540

POYNTELL, WILLIAM (Phila-
delphia)
1804: 5971 pb, 6318 pb, 6675
f, 7227 pb, 7246 f, 7657 pb,
50443 pb
1805: 8435, 9086 pb, 9459 f
1806: 10754 f, 11903

PRATHER, LEONARD (Raleigh,
N.C.)
1805: 9259 f

PRATT, CHARLES M (Savan-
nah, Ga.)
1812: 24601 pb

PRATT, JOHN H (Baltimore)
1803: 5484
1804: 7371, 7640-7641

PRATT, JOHN HORACE (Baltimore)
1815: 35025 pb, 35690 pb
1816: 37961-37962, 39135

PRATT, LUTHER (East Wind-
sor, Conn.)
1801: 1398, 1529 pb

PRATT, LUTHER (Hartford,
Conn.)
1803: 4301

PRATT, LUTHER (Montgomery, N.Y.)
1811: 22278, 24417
1813: 28589-28590, 28807 pb, 29249 pb
1816: 38142 pb

PRATT, LUTHER (Suffield, Conn.)
1802: 1749 pb

PRATT, LUTHER (Wardsbridge, N.Y.)
1806: 11075 pb, 50646 pb

PRATT, MOSES (Albany, N.Y.)
1814: 30656 bf, 30945 pb, 32604 pb, 32763 pb
1815: 34154 pb, 35924 pb

PRATT, PHILO B (Newburgh, N.Y.)
1817: 40580 pb

PRAY, JOHN GUNNISON (Brooklyn, N.Y.)
1813: 27844, 28516, 28655-28656, 29008-29009, 29184, 29487, 29671-29672, 29786-29787, 29833, 30497
1814: 31052, 31335, 31445, 31757 pb, 31940 pb, 32156, 32765

PRENTISS, CHARLES (Baltimore)
1802: 2481, 2531, 2549, 2975 pb
1803: 3983-3984, 5191

PRENTISS, HENRY (Cooperstown, N.Y.)
1808: 15295

PRENTISS, HENRY (Herkimer, N.Y.)
1810: 21042

PRENTISS, JOHN (Keene, N.H.)
1801: 562 pb, 1109, 1365
1802: 2315 pb, 2491-2492, 2856

1803: 3808 pb, 4404 pb, 4805, 5035 pb, 5112
1804: 6370 pb, 6504 pb, 6599
1805: 7930, 8646 pb, 9103, 9470, 9694 pb
1806: 9912, 10472 pb, 10593 pb, 11345
1807: 11927-11928 pb, 12651 pb, 12782 pb, 13069, 13590
1808: 14263 pb, 15268 pb, 16149
1809: 16921, 17091, 17467 pb, 17475, 17611 pb, 17780 pb, 18525
1810: 19300 pb, 19645, 20202-20203 pb, 20390 pb, 22007
1811: 22899 pb, 23052 pb, 23582, 23799?
1812: 26469, 27430
1813: 27650, 27799, 28224, 30389
1814: 30624 pb, 30651 pb, 31004-31006, 31676, 32455, 33620
1815: 34220-34223, 34596, 35508, 51453 pb
1816: 36673 pb, 37357-37358, 38030, 39022
1817: 39918 pb, 40163, 41522 f, 41856 pb, 41998, 42113, 42151
1818: 43009, 44093 pb
1819: 46921, 47851, 48326 pb

PRENTISS, JOHN (Montpelier, Vt.)
1812: 24527 f

PRENTISS, JOHN HOLMES (Cooperstown, N.Y.)
1808: 15295
1809: 17302 pb, 18169
1814: 31559
1815: 34039, 34825, 35557 pb
1816: 38216, 38537
1817: 40854 pb, 41396, 41713
1818: 45191

PRENTISS, JOHN HOLMES (Herkimer, N.Y.)
1810: 21042

PRENTISS, ROYAL (Marietta, O.)
1815: 35794
1816: 37818, 38356
1817: 42342
1819: 48031

Presbyterian Board of Publication (Philadelphia)
1803: 3626 pb, 3905 pb
1813: 28343? pb
1818: 44806 pb

Presbyterian Committee of Publication (Richmond, Va.)
1801: 1181 pb
1804: 7111 pb

PRESTON, SAMUEL (Amherst, N.H.)
1801: 374, 501, 1084, 1252

PRICE, ADDISON B (New York)
1813: 29409 f

PRICE, ANDREW (Baltimore)
1803: 3988 f

PRICE, JONATHAN (Schenectady, N.Y.)
1814: 31113 f

PRICE, PHILO (Norwalk, Conn.)
1818: 43271 pb, 45123 pb
1819: 47020 pb, 48210, 48839, 49522

Printing Office (Boston)
1801: 137?, 316 pb, 684 pb, ?1054
1802: 2433 pb, 2668 pb
1804: 6947 pb
1812: 51245 pb

Printing Office (Hartford, Conn.)
1810: 19766? sb

PRIOR, WILLIAM (New York)
1809: 18901 f
1810: 20313 pb, 20765 f, 21661 pb
1813: 28606 f, 28740 pb, 29816 pb, 30193 pb
1814: 30711 pb

PRITCHARD, ARCHIBALD (Burlington, Vt.)
1816: 36914 f
1817: 42781 f
1818: 46641 pb
1819: 51889 f

PRITCHARD, ARCHIBALD (Manchester, Vt.)
1805: 50534 pb

PRITCHARD, WILLIAM (Richmond, Va.)
1802: 3056 pb
1805: 9174 pb
1806: 10160 pb

PROBASCO, SIMON (Philadelphia)
1816: 38561, 39671 pb
1817: 42792 pb
1818: 43487, 43853, 43886 pb, 44457, 45181
1819: 47844 pb, 48065, 48461, 49038, 49364 bf

Protestant Episcopal Female Tract Society (Baltimore)
1815: 34466-34467 pb

Protestant Episcopal Society for the Advancement of Christianity in South Carolina (Charleston, S.C.)
1819: 49203 pb, 49495 f

Protestant Episcopal Society for the Promotion of Evangelical Knowledge (New York)
1805: 9331 pb

Protestant Episcopal Society of Young Men for the Distribution of Religious Tracts (New York)
1812: 26541 pb

Protestant Episcopal Sunday
School Society (New York)
1817: 42083 f

Protestant Episcopal Tract
Society (New York)
1815: 35401 pb
1816: 38740 f
1818: 45673 pb
1819: 48245 f

Providence Patriot (Providence,
R. I.)
1814: 32588
1819: 47581

PRYCE, WILLIAM (Wilmington,
Del.)
1801: 884 f
1803: 5594 f
1804: 7379 f
1805: 8930 f, 9473 f, 9492 f
1806: 10494 pb, 10508 f,
10640 f

PRYOR, GEORGE (Philadel-
phia)
1806: 9879 pb, 10362 f

Public Advertiser (New York)
1802: 2972
1808: 14275, 15482, 16332
1809: 18553

Publick Ledger (Norfolk, Va.)
see Norfolk Gazette and Publick Ledger (Norfolk, Va.)

PUDNEY, JOSEPH S (New
York)
1812: 26496
1813: 30197
1815: 34757
1816: 37265

PUMPHREY, JOHN (Richmond,
Va.)
1806: 50635 pb
1808: 50899 pb

PURNELL, WILLIAM (Phila-
delphia)
1811: 23769 pb

PUTNAM, EDWIN (Zanesville,
O.)
1812: 27642 pb
1813: 28877
1814: 31277, 32673 pb
1815: 36588
1816: 36786, 38508, 39838
1817: 41681

Q

Quadrant (New York)
1815: 34155, 34662
1817: 40277

QUERY, JOHN (Charleston,
S. C.)
1802: 2043, 2161, 2667 pb
1803: 3934 pb, 4244
1804: 6978, 7804 pb

R

RABINEAU, JACOB (New York)
1809: 18867 f

RAIN, JOHN (Philadelphia)
1801: 886 f

RAKESTRAW, JOSEPH (Phila-
delphia)
1804: 6117, 6165, 6267 pb,
6288, 7774, 50417
1805: 8082, 8524, 8722, 9267
1806: 10887 pb, 11826
1807: 11969 pb, 12361, 12411,
12771
1808: 14577, 14579-14583,
14685, 14899, 14932, 15664,
16144 pb
1809: 17261 pb, 17988 pb,
18329, 18377, 18535, 19090
pb
1810: 19631, 19643, 21094,
21461, 21534 pb
1811: 22405a, 22525, 22630,
23670, 23689, 24400

1812: 24591, 24984, 26724
1813: 27921, 27927, 28603-
28604, 29721 pb, 29771
1814: 30971 pb, 31564,
31631, 31739, 32711, 32712
pb, 32817 pb, 32949, 33518
1815: 34016, 34591 pb, 34593,
34693, 35849 pb, 36538
1816: 37466-37467, 37564 pb,
37874, 38017, 38411, 38574,
38871, 51613 pb, 51620 pb
1817: 41199 pb, 41743, 41801,
41852 pb, 42048, 42886
1818: 43333, 43945 pb, 44760,
44824 pb, 45227, 45315,
45373-45374, 45636, 46722,
46878
1819: 48389-48390, 49037,
49152 pb

RAMSAY, WILLIAM (Richmond,
Va.)
1819: 47622 pb

RANDALL, SAMUEL (Warren,
R. I.)
1813: 29923 pb
1815: 34006, 35180-35181
1816: 37441

RANDOLPH, GEORGE F
(Augusta, Ga.)
1803: 3994 pb, 4106?
1804: 5791, 6187, 6378, 7686
1805: 8513-8514, 8516
1806: 11844, 50644
1807: 50756
1809: 17191

RANLET, HENRY (Exeter,
N. H.)
1801: 23, 253, 658 pb, 916
pb, 1282, 1336, 1617 pb,
50219 pb, 50251
1802: 2007 pb, 2038, 2108,
2175-2176, 2243 pb, 2377,
2398 pb, 2421?, 2643 pb,
2653 pb
1803: 3807, 4656, 5489,
5506 pb
1804: 5932 pb, 6426, 6617
1805: 7821, 8377 pb, 8634,
8680, 8882 pb, 9367, 9373

1806: 10874, 11354, 11393,
11817 pb
1807: 12167, 12754 pb, 12775
pb, 13422, 13603 pb, 50779
pb
1809: 17768
1812: 27371? pb

RANLET, HENRY A (Exeter,
N. H.)
1812: 27512 pb
1816: 39717 pb
1817: 40012, 40035, 41234

RANNELLS, DAVID V (Wash-
ington, Ky.)
1814: 32981 pb
1819: 47089

RANSOM, RICHARD (Windsor,
Vt.)
1806: 11373 f

RANSOM, THOMAS G (Marietta,
O.)
1813: 27655?

RAPINE, DANIEL (Washington,
D. C.)
1801: 161 pb, 237-238 pb,
294 pb, 479 f, 963 pb, 1132
pb, 1188 f, 1263 f, 1274 pb,
1592 f
1802: 1845 pb, 2124 f, 2483
f, 2528, 2543 f, 2632, 2981
f, 3006 f, 3064 f, 3075 f,
3084 f, 3573 f, 3575 f
1803: 3618, 3622 f, 3653 f,
3881 pb, 3883 f, 4091 f,
4376 pb, 4387 pb, 4527-4528
f
1804: 5824 f, 5897 pb, 6647
pb
1809: 18004 pb
1810: 21341 pb
1813: 29539, 30187, 30483
1814: 31068, 31517, 31653,
32662, 32757?, 32927,
33224-33225, 33504, 33506,
33571-33572
1815: 34433, 34892, 36158
1816: 37526, 37986, 39105,
?39106, 39358, 39710

1817:   41184, 41587 pb
1818:   43070, 44081, 44934
        pb, 51836
1819:   49745

Rapine & Elliot (Washington,
    D. C.)
see RAPINE, DANIEL (Wash-
    ington, D. C.)
    ELLIOT, JONATHAN (Wash-
    ington, D. C.)

RASER, MATTHIAS (Philadel-
    phia)
1817:   40651
1818:   43751, 43755-43756,
        43759, 44526, 44761, 44802-
        44803, 44962, 45183, 45212,
        45820
1819:   47590, 47606, 47891,
        48230, 48437, 48491, 49098,
        49411, 49535, 49991, 50156,
        51872

RAVENSCROFT, --- (New Or-
    leans, La.)
1808:   15392 pb

RAWLE, ROBERT TURNER
    (Philadelphia)
1801:   6 pb, 388 pb, 720 pb
1802:   2527 pb, 2633 f
1808:   50857 pb

RAY, DUNCAN (Fayetteville,
    N. C.)
1805:   9037 pb
1809:   17494 pb

RAY, DUNCAN (Wilmington,
    N. C.)
1802:   1986 pb

READ, EZRA (Boston)
1811:   22695 f
1812:   24744 pb, 24921 pb,
        24983 f, 25063 f, 25169 f,
        25193 f, 25199 pb, 25853 f,
        26182 f, 26185-26186 f,
        26349-26350 f, 26467 f,
        27609 pb, 27612 f, 27620
        f, 51166 pb
1813:   27869 pb, 27976 pb,

        28004 pb, 28327 pb, 28656
        f, 28784 pb, 28847 f, 29205
        f, 29418 f, 29487 f, 29719
        pb, 29749-29750 f, 29975 f,
        30515 pb, 51272 pb
1814:   31554 f, 31846 f, 32797
        pb, 32798 f, 33696 pb
1815:   34618 pb, 34711 f,
        34759 f, 36124 f, 36592 pb,
        51489 pb
1816:   37124 pb
1817:   40728 pb, 40732 pb,
        42260 f
1819:   49294 pb

READ, EZRA (New Haven,
    Conn.)
1801:   428, 1439

READ, JESSE (Halifax, N. C.)
1806:   10484 f

REDDING, WILLIAM F (Balti-
    more)
1818:   43187, 44711 pb
1819:   47521

REDFIELD, LEWIS HAMILTON
    (Onondaga, N. Y.)
1814:   32409 pb
1819:   49244

REED, --- (Georgetown, Ky.)
1815:   51456 pb

REED, ABNER (East Windsor,
    Conn.)
1801:   1219 pb
1802:   1786 engr

REED, ABNER (Hartford,
    Conn.)
1806:   11257 pb
1807:   12370 pb
1809:   50961 pb
1810:   51036 engr

REED, EBENEZER (Detroit,
    Mich.)
1817:   40654 pb
1818:   51737
1819:   50105, 50107

REED, EBENEZER (Ithaca,
N. Y.)
1816: 37935 pb

Register (New Haven, Conn.)
see Columbian Register (New
Haven, Conn.)

Register (Northampton, Mass.)
see Hampshire Register
(Northampton, Mass.)

REID, JOHN (New York)
1804: 7053 sb
1805: 50586 pb
1807: 13292 f
1810: 19574, 20642 pb

REINHART, ELHANAN W
(Danville, Va.)
1818: 43808 pb

REINS, --- (New York)
1818: 43403, 44446

RELF, SAMUEL (Philadelphia)
1803: 4961 pb

Religious Intelligencer (New
Haven, Conn.)
1818: 43267, 43664, 43799,
43896, 44277, 45281
1819: 47661, 47663-47664,
48126, 48340, 48344

Religious Remembrancer (Philadelphia)
1817: 41921

Religious Tract Society of
Baltimore (Baltimore)
1818: 45492-45503 f
1819: 49255-49259 f

Religious Tract Society of
Philadelphia (Philadelphia)
1815: 35258 pb
1816: 37381 pb, 37408 pb,
38080 pb
1817: 40252 pb
1818: 43362 pb, 43919 pb,
44305, 44340, 44468,
44595? pb, 45649 pb,

45867 pb
1819: 48152 pb

REMICH, JAMES KINSMAN
(Dover, N. H.)
1803: 3823
1808: 15249, 15579?, 15695,
15865 pb, 16685
1812: 24791

REMICH, JAMES KINSMAN
(Kennebunk, Me.)
1809: 17337 pb, 17767, 19188
pb
1811: 22425a, 22450a, 22453a,
22556, 22762
1812: 24544, 24720, 25438,
27496
1813: 27800
1814: 30765
1815: 33949, 35416 pb, 36523,
36605
1816: 36833
1817: 41025, 42136
1818: 43192
1819: 47101, 47657, 48379,
49266

REMICH, JAMES KINSMAN
(Portsmouth, N. H.)
1809: 18420

RENARD, JEAN (New Orleans,
La.)
1803: 4548, 5145 pb
1804: 5885, 6261, 7539
1805: 9008
1806: 50655 pb
1807: 11995 pb, 13120 pb,
13299 pb, 13390 pb
1808: 14861, 15740
1809: 17057 pb

Rensselaer Bookstore (Troy,
N. Y.)
1808: 15933 pb

Repertory (Boston)
1804: 5706, 6134-6135, 7150
1806: 10280
1808: 15459, 15846, 16057
1809: 17356, 18755
1812: 25280
1814: 31964

Repertory (Newburyport, Mass.)
see New England Repertory
(Newburyport, Mass.)

Reporter (Lexington, Ky.)
1808: 14703, 16717
1810: 20269
1811: 22225, 22856, 23950
1812: 25698

Repository (Homer, N.Y.)
see Cortland Repository (Homer, N.Y.)

Republic (Troy, N.Y.)
1809: 18554 f

Republican (Chillicothe, O.)
see Independent Republican
(Chillicothe, O.)

Republican (Petersburg, Va.)
1819: 49414

Republican Advocate (Frederick, Md.)
1804: 6054

Republican Farmer (Staunton,
Va.)
1811: 22172

Republican Gazette (Frederick,
Md.)
see Bartgis's Republican
Gazette (Frederick, Md.)

Republican Herald (Pough-
keepsie, N.Y.)
1814: 31712

Republican Ledger (Ports-
mouth, N.H.)
1801: 1678

RETZLER, --- (Reading, Pa.)
1807: 50792 pb

REVELL, JOHN (Baltimore)
1816: 39846 f

REYNOLDS, AUSTIN G (New
York)

1808: 14835
1810: 20917
1814: 33760

REYNOLDS, JOHN (Philadelphia)
1807: 12089, 12092, 12137,
12261, 12309, 12373, 12555,
12845, 12918, 13376 pb,
13479, 13503
1808: 15033, 15207, 15240,
15401, 16722

REYNOLDS, JOHN B (New
York)
1808: 14835

REYNOLDS, JOHN PARKER
(Salem, N.Y.)
1808: 16039 pb
1809: 19139
1813: 28309, 29599, 29604-
29605
1814: 30652 pb, 30896 bf,
31143, 31986, 32679, 33741
1815: 34099, 34258
1816: 37890
1817: 41472 f

REYNOLDS, LINUS JUNIUS
(Glens Falls, N.Y.)
1815: 33796 pb, 34205

REYNOLDS, LINUS JUNIUS
(Hamilton, N.Y.)
1816: 36856, 37787 pb

REYNOLDS, LINUS JUNIUS
(Plattsburgh, N.Y.)
1811: 23800

REYNOLDS, RICHARD (New
York)
1802: 1984

REYNOLDS, SACKETT (Cin-
cinnati, O.)
1816: 37244, 37620, 38554,
38717
1818: 43488, 43883-43884 pb,
43994
1819: 47126, 47447, 47779-
47781, 47946, 48500 pb,
48553, 48684, 48953?

REYNOLDS, WILLIAM (Phila-
delphia)
1815: 34379 pb, 34380 f

RHOADES, CHARLES B (Staunton, Va.)
1812: 26429 pb

RHOADES, EBENEZER (Boston)
1802: 1713-1714 f
1803: 3701 pb, 50374
1804: 5871 pb, 6320 pb, 7766
1805: 7907 f, 8278 pb
1806: 10276 pb, 10821, 10826,
11275, 11323
1807: 11942 pb, 12105, 13015,
13021-13022, 13029-13031,
13034 pb, 13037
1808: 14303 pb, 14328 pb,
15513, 15523, 15525, 15549,
15550 pb, 16056, 16138,
16203
1809: 17624, 18035 pb
1810: 19307 pb, 20665-20666,
20672, 20679-20680
1811: 23309, 23311, 23328-
23329
1812: 24618, 25997, 26011,
26018, 26021, 26025

RHOADS, JACOB (Lexington,
Ind.)
1815: 36545 pb
1816: ?37923, 37924

RHOADS, JACOB (Madison,
Ind.)
1814: 31795

Rhode Island American (Providence, R. I.)
1810: 19684
1817: 41908
1818: 44206
1819: 48302

Rhode Island Republican (Newport, R. I.)
1812: 25259

RICE, HENRY (Philadelphia)
1801: 364 f, 480 pb, 1108
pb, 1133 pb

1802: 1726 f, 2123 pb
1803: 5527 f, 50359 pb

RICE, JOHN (Baltimore)
1803: 5484 f, 50388 pb
1804: 7371 f, 7640-7641 f

RICE, PATRICK (Philadelphia)
1801: 364 f, 480 pb, 1108 pb,
1133 pb
1802: 1726 f, 2123 pb
1803: 5527 f, 50359 pb

RICH, JAIRUS (Watertown,
N. Y.)
1813: 27802 pb, 29385 pb
1814: 30664 pb, 30767 pb
1815: 33951 pb

RICHARDS, GEORGE (George-
town, D. C.)
1813: 28608-28609 pb, 28768
f, 51321 pb
1814: 31308 f, 32133-32134
pb, 32165 f, 32875 pb, 32925
pb, 51443 pb
1815: 35799 pb, 51498 pb
1816: 37869 pb, 40469 f

RICHARDS, GEORGE (Utica,
N. Y.)
1803: 3773 pb
1804: 7109 sb
1807: 13731 f
1808: 14640 f

RICHARDS, SAMUEL (Charleston, S. C.)
1807: 13758 pb

RICHARDS, SETH (Middletown,
Conn.)
1814: 30744, 31225 pb, 31473-
31474, 32269 pb, 32547,
32549
1815: 34612-34613, 35017-
35018, 35400, 35665, 35796,
36020, 36655
1816: 36671, 37204, 37293,
37594, 37596 pb, 38344-
38345, 38803, 38952 pb

RICHARDSON, CALEB (Philadelphia)
1816: 37263 pb
1817: 40257 f

RICHARDSON, ELEAZER TYNG
FOX (Boston)
1812: 24821 f, 24880 pb,
25395 f, 25814 f, 26487 f,
26722 pb, 26756 f, 27422 f,
27485 pb
1813: 27944 pb, 28047 f,
28230 pb, 28486 f, 28633-
28634 f, 28863? f, 28986
pb, 28987 f, 29535 f,
29850-29851 pb
1814: 30862 f, 30916 pb,
31078-31079 f, 31453 f,
31665 pb, 32845 f, 32966
f, 33624 f
1815: 34080 pb, 34119-34120
pb, 34488 f, 34675 f, 35222
pb, 35554 f, 35815 f, 35873
f, 35999 f
1816: 36883 f, 36986 f, 37096
f, 37562 f, 38191-38193 pb,
39001-39002 f, 39027 f
1817: 40326 pb, 40797 pb,
41376-41377 pb, 42205 pb,
42790 pb, 42811 f, 42852
pb, 42858 pb
1818: 19373? f, 43034 pb,
43296 f, 43314 f, 43315
pb, 43340 f, 43453 f, 43991
f, 43997 f, 44529 pb, 44755
pb, 45200 f, 45219 f, 45271
f, 45746 f, 45789 f
1819: 47220-47221 f, 47427
pb, 47437 f, 47945 f, 48641
pb, 48825 f, 50031 f, 50069
f, 50079 pb, 50183 f,
51877 pb

RICHARDSON, H (Berwick,
Me.)
1818: 43870 pb

RICHARDSON, HEMAN (Middlebury, Vt.)
1810: 20227 f
1819: 47840 f, 48092 f

RICHARDSON, JACOB (Newport, R. I.)
1801: 997 f

RICHARDSON, JOHN (Philadelphia)
1811: 23356 f
1812: 25791 pb, 26668-26669 f
1813: 30580 f
1814: 31624 pb, 31625 f,
32084 f, 32495 pb, 51431 pb
1815: 33841 f, 34350 f
1817: 40967-40968 pb, 51687
f
1818: 44398 pb, 44762 f,
45601 pb, 45859 pb

RICHARDSON, JOSIAH (Exeter,
N. H.)
1810: 20249? pb
1814: 31130-31131 pb, 31998
pb, 32101 pb, 33566 pb
1819: 47109 pb, 47112 pb,
47143 pb, 47464 pb, 47468
pb, 47839 pb, 48078 pb,
48120 pb, 48196 pb, 48410
pb, 48555 pb, 48966 pb,
49004 pb, 49335 pb, 50113
pb

RICHARDSON, ROBERT D
(Chillicothe, O.)
1807: 13281
1808: 15792-15794
1811: 22851 pb

RICHARDSON, ROBERT D
(Circleville, O.)
1811: 22851a pb
1812: 27587 pb

RICHARDSON, ROBERT D
(Washington, Ky.)
1806: 11271 pb

RICHARDSON, ROBERT D
(Worthington, O.)
1810: 22106

RIDDLE, JAMES (Philadelphia)
1801: 824 f

RIDDLE, JAMES M (Pittsburgh, Pa.)
1815: 35647 pb

RIDER, RICHARD D (Baltimore)
1807: 12018, 12327, 13050, ?13081, 13204?
1808: 14617 pb, 14882, 15498

RIGGS, ISAAC (Ballston Spa, N.Y.)
1808: 14375, 16168a

RIGGS, ISAAC (Schenectady, N.Y.)
1810: 19699 pb, 21548 pb
1813: 29999
1814: 31018, 31113, 31581, 31770, 32378, 32721 pb
1815: 34626, 34694, 35170, 35349, 35858, 36142-36145
1816: 39139 pb, 51603 sb
1817: 40596 pb, 41623, 42458, 42965-42966
1818: 45047, 45410
1819: 49339, 49626, 49661

RILEY, BENJAMIN J (New York)
1816: 38867 pb
1817: 41915

RILEY, EDWARD (New York)
1812: 26868 pb
1817: 41165 f, 51709? pb
1818: 45772 bpb, 51781, 51828? pb
1819: 51938 pb

RILEY, ISAAC (Flatbush, N.Y.)
1809: 17269 pb, 18429-18430 pb, 19070 pb, 19120 pb, 19261 pb
1810: 21917 pb

RILEY, ISAAC (Middletown, Conn.)
1807: 13388
1808: 15139 pb, 15628 pb

RILEY, ISAAC (New York)
1801: 944 pb
1803: 5083 pb
1804: 6041 f, 6823 pb, 6868 f, 6915 pb
1805: 8302 f, 8439 pb, 8539 f, 9012 f, 9265 pb, 50522 f
1806: 9859 pb, 9877 f, 9959 pb, 10013 pb, 10052 pb, 10122, 10259 pb, 10340, 10424 pb, 10625 pb, 10644 f, 10727 pb, 10888 pb, 10907 f, 11012 pb, 11180 pb, 11202 f, 11213 pb, 11240 pb, 11246 pb, 11250 pb, 11291 pb, 11334 pb, 11409 f, 11444 f, 11740 pb, 50676 pb, 50698 f, 50729 f
1807: 12271 pb, 12388, 12389 pb, 13104 pb, 13227 f, 13509, 13707, 13743 pb, 14089 pb
1808: 14363 f, 14572 pb, 14628 pb, 15566 pb, 15634 pb, 15759 pb, 15761 pb, 15787 pb, 16183 pb, 16253, 16614 pb, 16620 f, 50894 f
1809: 17050 pb, 17200 pb, 17330 pb, 17522 pb, 17737 pb, 17825 pb, 17862 pb, 17989 pb, 18232 pb, 18431 pb, 18432 f, 18661 pb, 18799 pb, 19098 pb, 19278 f
1810: 19370 pb, 19687, 19874 pb, 20247-20248 pb, 20436 pb, 20622 pb, 20776 pb, 20885 pb, 20888 pb, 21087, 21122 f, 21239, 21289, 21431, 21918 pb, 21927 pb, 22064 pb
1811: 22474 pb, 22486 pb, 22651 pb, 22987 pb, 23066 pb, 23105 pb, 23354 pb, 23552 pb, 23554 pb, 23871 sb, 24408 pb
1812: 27411 pb
1813: 27742 pb, 28173 pb, 28214 f, 28225 f, 29177 f, 29344 f, 51290 pb
1814: 32323 f, 32324 pb, 32331 pb, 33515 pb, 33563 f
1815: 34161 pb, 34164 pb,

34600 pb, 34805 f, 35286 f, 35671 f, 35797 pb, 35880 pb, 36100 pb, 36467 pb
1816: 37039 pb, 37406 f, 37788 pb, 37954 pb, 39805 pb

RILEY, ISAAC (Philadelphia)
1816: 37704 f
1817: 41701 f, 41702 pb
1818: 43121, 43264 pb, 43608 f, 43756 pb, 44368 f, 44975 pb, 45223 f, 46618 f
1819: 47590-47591 f, 47592-47593 pb, 48698 f

RILEY, JAMES (Hartford, Conn.)
1816: 38814? pb
1818: 45195-45196 f

RILEY, W (Charleston, S.C.)
1809: 16973 pb

RILEY, WILLIAM (Wilmington, Del.)
1811: 22681 pb
1812: 24557 pb, 24773 pb
1813: 28292-28293
1814: 31317

RIND, WILLIAM ALEXANDER (Georgetown, D.C.)
1802: 3184 pb
1803: 5539
1809: 17602, 18160 pb
1810: 19550 pb, 20467 pb
1811: 22902
1814: 31911
1815: 33824 pb, 34777
1816: 36708 pb, 38357, 38782, 38822, 38881, 38948, 51592
1817: 41350
1818: 44127, 44703, 44921
1819: 47438

RIPLEY, HEZEKIAH (Bridgeport, Conn.)
1806: 10034 pb
1807: 13084, 14164
1809: 19150
1810: 21961

RIPLEY, HEZEKIAH (Moscow, N.Y.)
1817: 40898 pb
1819: 48694

RISLEY, JEREMIAH B (Wilmington, Del.)
1810: 19949 pb

RITCHIE, D (Richmond, Va.)
1816: 37067 pb

RITCHIE, THOMAS (Richmond, Va.)
1804: 6099, 6255 pb, 7174 pb
1805: 8540, 9665 pb, 9667, 50623 pb
1806: 9915, 11775
1807: 14133
1809: 18643, 19119
1810: 21916
1811: 24344a
1812: 27410, 27412
1813: 28722, 30425, 51300 pb
1814: 30792, 30795, 31826 pb, 32397 f, 32584, 33550, 33553, 33708 f, 51445
1815: 33982, 33985, 35312, 35728, 36446, 36449
1816: 37067 pb, 38738, 39674-39679 pb, 39680, 39682, 39684
1817: 40124-40125, 41225, 41903, 42794, 42796, 51724
1818: 43223, 45445, 46656, 46658, 51841
1819: 47047, 47148, 49300, 49995-49996, 49998, 51950

RITTER, FREDERICK W (New York)
1817: 40387
1819: 47498, 48190, 49492 pb, 49552

RITTER, JOHN (JOHANN) (Reading, Pa.)
1802: 2306 bsb
1803: 4846-4847
1804: 6368, 7157, 50457 pb
1805: 8505, 8962
1806: 10946
1807: 12865 pb, 13335 pb,

13465, 13678 pb, 50792 pb
1808: 15698
1809: 18087, 18176, 18350
1810: 20836
1811: 22379 pb, 22488 pb,
22894, 23491, 24040 bsb
1812: 25636 pb, 26152, 26200
pb, 26423, 26553, 26885 pb
1813: 28594 pb, 28735, 29269
pb
1814: 32223 pb, 32471e
1815: 35402 pb
1816: 37148-37149 pb, 37790,
38363 pb
1817: 40910 bsb, 41557 pb
1818: 44353 pb, 44971 pb
1819: 48005, 48147, 48827 pb

ROBBINS, JAMES B (Herkimer,
N. Y.)
1805: 8429 pb

ROBBINS, JAMES B (Martinsburgh, N. Y.)
1807: 12158 pb

ROBBINS, JAMES B (Water-
town, N. Y.)
1808: 16670 pb

ROBBINS, JOHN W (Hartford,
Conn.)
1817: 40486 f

ROBERSON, LEWIS (Weathersfield, Vt.)
1815: 34743? pb
1816: 38818 f

ROBERTS, HARVEY B (Hart-
ford, Conn.)
1818: 43190, 45822, 46672
1819: 48235, 48572, 49655,
49968, 50188

ROBERTS, SYLVESTER (Hud-
son, N. Y.)
1806: 11273 pb

ROBERTS, SYLVESTER (Philadelphia)
1817: 40361, 41996 pb
1819: 47425-47426 pb

ROBERTSON, JOHN (Dover,
Del.)
1816: 37426
1817: 40636-40641, 41141
1818: 43831-43834, 44080,
45436
1819: 47810-47813, 49205?

ROBINSON, --- (Shepherds-
town, Va.)
1818: 44769
1819: 49171 pb

ROBINSON, DAVID (Trenton,
N. J.)
1813: 27722-27724, 28664,
29322, 29804

ROBINSON, DAVID A (New-
town, Pa.)
1814: 31695 pb

ROBINSON, DAVID A (Phila-
delphia)
1815: 35681

ROBINSON, JAMES (Philadelphia)
1804: 7044 f
1809: 18375 pb
1810: 21062 pb
1811: 23676 f
1816: 37528

ROBINSON, JOHN (New York)
1818: 43403, 43752, 44446,
51745 pb

ROBINSON, JOSEPH (Baltimore)
1807: 11974 pb, 11991, 12353,
?12372 pb, 12540 pb, 12671,
12750, 12857, 13004, 13113,
13273, 13415 pb, 13446,
13535
1808: 15004, ?15227, 15229,
15942?, 16015-16016, 16211
1809: 17411-17412, 17748,
?17750, ?17786-17787,
18363, 18387, 18461-18462,
18773, 18776
1810: 19633 pb, 19881, 20409
pb, 20460, 20623, 21149,
21552, ?22002?, 22009

1811: 22313 pb, 22329,
22538, 22550, 22706, 22833
pb, 23069, 23209, 23758,
23865 pb, 24051, 24429,
51136 pb
1812: 25716, 26157, 26184,
26541a, 26643 pb, 26657
1813: 27849 pb, 28825, 28827
pb, 29147 pb, 29588, 29673
pb, 29942 pb, 29961 pb,
30480
1814: 30660 pb, 30831 pb,
30899, 31070, 31076, 31080,
31186?, 31800, 31844,
32204, 32408, 32512, 32531
pb, 32578-32579, 32605,
32661, 32700, 32818, 32899
1815: 33830 pb, 33885, 34090,
34109, 34535 pb, 34563,
34709, 34734, 35046, 35182,
35187, 35351, 35360, 35377,
35532 pb, 35718-35719,
35722 pb, 36502
1816: 37027, 37252, 37396,
37397 pb, 37472, 37572,
37644, 37711, 37722-37724,
37957, 37983, 38072, 38146,
38529, 38552, 38651 pb,
38774, 39011, 39128, 39145,
39809, 39842
1817: 39946, 39948, 40229,
40520 pb, 40532 pb, 40571,
40660 pb, 40857, 40991,
41038, 41155, 41183 pb,
41249, 41313 pb, 41334,
41356 pb, 41382 pb, 41397
pb, 41442-41443 pb, 41715
pb, 41892, 41969 pb, 42018,
42165, 42250, 42936, 42980,
51654, 51706
1818: 43241 pb, 43347, 43863
pb, 44073, 44088, 44362 pb,
44450, 44500, 44599, 44629,
44702 pb, 44820, 45151,
45313 pb, 45403, 45427 pb,
45445a, 45492-45504, 45527
pb, 45566, 45567 pb, 45723,
45750, 45796, 46836-46838
1819: 47164 pb, 47552, 47772,
47865? bf, 47874, 47942 pb,
48021, 48266, 48385, 48582,
48594, 48603, 48699 pb,
48756, 48774 pb, 48826,

48986, 48991, 49028 pb,
49197 pb, 49243 pb, 49255-
49259, 49310, 49444 pb,
49620 pb

ROBINSON, MARTIN (Provi-
dence, R. I.)
1814: 30942 f, 32644 pb,
32693 f
1816: 37743 pb

ROBINSON, TRACY (Bingham-
ton, N. Y.)
1814: 32501 pb
1815: 33861, 35981 pb

ROBINSON, WILLIAM (Trenton,
N. J.)
1813: 27722-27724, 28664 bf,
29322 bf, 29804

ROBINSON, WILLIAM C (Brooklyn, N. Y.)
1805: 9468?
1806: 10172, 10745 pb, 11793
1807: 12215 pb, 14091

ROBINSON, WILLIAM C (New
York)
1804: 6307-6308
1805: 8765, 8898a, 9715-9716
1806: 9937, 10688, 10864,
11294, 11848, 11850
1807: 13074-13075, 13701

ROCHE, CHARLES (New Or-
leans, La.)
1813: 28565
1818: 45774
1819: 48019

ROCHE, CHARLES (Philadel-
phia)
1807: 12615

ROCHE, PETER (Philadelphia)
1807: 12615

ROCHE, PIERRE (PETER)
(New Orleans, La.)
1813: 28565
1818: 45774
1819: 48019

ROCHEMONT, MAXIMILIAN
JOHN de (Portsmouth,
N. H.)
1804: 7079 f

Rockville Journal (Rockville,
Md.)
1817: 41913

ROGERS, --- (Philadelphia)
1815: 34554

ROGERS, ALEXANDER (New
London, Conn.)
1817: 42006 f

ROGERS, HENRY (Worcester,
Mass.)
1807: 12927-12928
1808: 15270
1810: 19366, 20078, 20333
1811: 22455, 23601 pb, 24061
1812: 25867, 25936
1813: 27783 f, 28080
1814: 31506, 33665
1815: 34294, 35992, 36107
1816: 38055, 38079
1817: 41412

ROGERS, ROWLAND C (New
York)
1812: 24926 pb

ROGERS, THOMAS JONES
(Easton, Pa.)
1805: 9038 pb
1812: 25375
1813: 29683 pb

ROHR, JOHN A (Philadelphia)
1812: 26649, 26650 pb

ROHRER, FREDERICK (Kit-
tanning, Pa.)
1819: 47670 pb

ROLL, J C (Cincinnati, O.)
1815: 34474 f

ROMYEN, ABRAHAM (Johns-
town, N. Y.)
1802: 3014 pb
1803: 4523, 50390 pb
1804: 7816

ROMYEN, ABRAHAM (Manlius,
N. Y.)
1806: 9897, 10281 pb

ROMYEN, ABRAHAM (Sher-
burne, N. Y.)
1804: 7746, 7747 pb
1805: 8526, 9420, 9718
1806: 11854 pb

RONALDS, JAMES (New York)
1805: 8008 pb, 8089 f, 8550 f
1806: 10297 f, 10706 pb,
10815 f, 11813 pb, 50697 f

RONALDS, JOHN (New York)
1805: 8746 f

RONALDS, THOMAS (New York)
1806: 10297 f, 10706 pb,
10815 f, 11813 pb, 50697 f

RONALDS, THOMAS A (New
York)
1809: 17176 pb, 17397 f
1811: 22443a f
1813: 28344 f, 28346 pb,
29947 pb
1814: 30937 f, 31751 f
1815: 33791 pb
1816: 36974 f, 38833 pb
1817: 40680 f, 40682 pb, 41774
f, 42879 f

ROSE, --- (Norwich, Conn.)
1804: 6875 pb

ROSE, WILLIAM (Petersburg,
Va.)
1816: 37836 f

ROSS, JOSEPH (Petersburg,
Va.)
1801: 626 pb, 774 pb, 1588 pb
1802: 1764 pb, 3478 pb

ROSS, WILLIAM (Washington,
D. C.)
1801: 1485

ROULSTONE, ELIZABETH
(Knoxville, Tenn.)
1806: 11436, 11437 f
1807: 13677? f

ROULSTONE, GEORGE (Knox-
ville, Tenn.)
1801: 1392-1394
1802: 2272
1803: 3847, 5149-5153
1804: 7337-7339

ROUNSAVELL, NATHANIEL
(Alexandria, Va.)
1811: 22171 pb
1813: 28158
1814: 31069
1815: 35943
1817: 44763

ROUSMANIERE, LEWIS (New-
port, R.I.)
1807: 13518 pb
1809: 18435 pb, 18903
1810: 19383, 21126, 22052 pb
1811: 23624 f, 23697
1813: 28791 pb, 29491 pb,
29994
1815: 36068, 36112 pb
1816: 38763

Rousmaniere & Barber (Newport, R.I.)
see ROUSMANIERE, LEWIS
(Newport, R.I.)
BARBER, WILLIAM (New-
port, R.I.)

ROWE, THOMAS (Boston)
1811: 23857 pb
1812: 24619, 25243 f, 25354,
25610, 25988, 26009, 26213,
26522, 26622, 27557, 27633
pb
1813: 28121, 28203, 28471,
28642
1814: 30851, 31084, 31459,
31543 pb, 31546, 32112 pb,
32900
1815: 33898, 33905, 33911,
34285, 34377, 34788, 34942,
35094, 35133, 35714, 35833,
36271, 36431
1816: 36804, 37285 pb, 38032,
38556, 38696, 38855, 39705,
39719-39720
1817: 40681, 40891, 41075,
41305

1818: 43117 pb, 43904, 45204,
45855

ROWE, THOMAS (Danbury,
Conn.)
1801: 84 pb, 251, 821, 1258 pb
1802: 2325, 2575, 3267
1803: 3697 pb, 4447, 4967 pb

ROYER, JOHN (Pottstown, Pa.)
1819: 49173 pb

RUBLE, J R (Nashville, Tenn.)
1815: 33973

RUBLE, THOMAS W (Richmond,
Ky.)
1809: 17634 pb
1812: 25075

RUDD, CHARLES (New York)
1812: 24586 f, 24814 f, 25081-
25084 f, 25086 f, 25088 f,
25282 f, 25943 f
1813: 28772 f, 29016 f, 29051
f, 30564 pb, 44339 pb
1814: 32186 f, 32342 pb,
32423 f, 32895 f, 33700 pb

RUDD, REUBEN BRUSH
(Poughkeepsie, N.Y.)
1814: 30621, 31278
1815: 35482

RUFF, DANIEL P (Abington,
Md.)
1805: 7820 pb
1806: 9820, 11176

RUGGLS, EDEN (Newark,
N.J.)
1802: 2144 pb

RUMFORD, --- (Wilmington,
Del.)
1817: 40843 pb

RUMSEY, DAVID (Auburn,
N.Y.)
1818: 44264
1819: 47818, 49570, 49585,
51866

RUMSEY, DAVID (Bath, N. Y.)
1816:   37567 pb

RUMSEY, DAVID (Salem,
  N. Y.)
1804:   6429, 6615, 6638 pb,
  6641 pb, 6945 pb, 7138
1805:   7946, 8337, 8578,
  9218-9220
1806:   9910, 10169, 10812,
  11085 pb, 11228-11229,
  11459
1807:   12067, 12456, 12476,
  12691, 12886
1808:   14299?, 15239, 16021
1809:   18116 pb
1810:   21157-21158, 21447
1811:   23763-23765, 24370,
  24413
1812:   26551-26552, 27452
  pb, 27529
1813:   29598, 29600-29603,
  29606, 30507, 30512
1814:   30972, 31173 pb
1815:   35730-35731 pb

RUSSELL, --- (Laurenceburg,
  Ind.)
1819:   48339 pb

RUSSELL, --- (Winchester,
  Va.)
1819:   50000 pb

RUSSELL, BARZILLAI (Hart-
  ford, Conn.)
1813:   27968 pb, 29901, 30397
1814:   30671 pb, 30762, 31149,
  31238, 31297, 31343, 31416
  pb, 31481 pb, 31584, 31815,
  31932-31933 pb, 31993,
  32826, 32883-32885, 32960
  pb, 33678 pb
1815:   33873, 33927, 33945
  pb, 34003, 34255, 34866,
  35196-35197, 35779, 35826-
  35828, 36141, 36586-36587
  pb
1816:   36780, 36813, 36829,
  37806, 37895, 38025-38026,
  38943 pb, 39700
1817:   40570, 40833, 42115
1818:   43729, 44585 pb
1819:   48303

RUSSELL, BENJAMIN (Boston)
1801:   1163, 1253
1803:   3860
1813:   28194 pb
1814:   30700 f, 32047 f, 32049
  f, 32063-32064 f, 51408 f
1815:   35204 f, 35212-35213 f
1816:   38016 f, 38164 f, 38166
  f
1817:   41364 f, 41369 f
1818:   44727 f, 44743 f, 44895
  f
1819:   47871 f, 48623-48624 f,
  48626-48627 f, 48742 f

RUSSELL, ELIJAH (Concord,
  N. H.)
1801:   1233 pb

RUSSELL, GERVAS E (Frank-
  fort, Ky.)
1818:   43895, 44084, 44506,
  44508-44509
1819:   47982 pb, 48413, 48415-
  48416, 49631

RUSSELL, HENRY P (Morris-
  town, N. J.)
1802:   2673
1803:   4048, 4114
1804:   5833, 7080
1806:   10427, 11862
1807:   12187, 14212?
1809:   17738, 19214
1810:   19609, 19973, 20551,
  51040 pb
1811:   23438 pb
1812:   24886, 25770, 26239,
  26491, 26500
1813:   28052
1814:   31479
1815:   33882, 34480, 34954,
  35257 pb, 36572, 36603,
  51490
1816:   38802
1817:   40332 pb

RUSSELL, HENRY P (Savannah,
  Ga.)
1819:   51907 pb

RUSSELL, JOHN (Boston)
1801:   218, 239, 436, 466 pb,

766, 992, 1080, 1227-1229, 1358, 1367
1802: 1706, 1715-1717, 1926, 2490, 3122?, 3576, 3606
1803: 3859, 3864, 4261, 4263, 4322, 4595, 4600, 4820-4821, 5124
1804: 6116, 6409, 6621, 7223
1805: 7831, 8390, 8557, 8591, 8791, 8872, 8873 pb, 9466
1806: 9882, 10218, 10348, 10421, 11235, 11474 pb
1807: 12575 pb, 12880 pb, 13145, 13740 pb
1808: 14457, 14827, 15084, 15389 pb, 15831, 15938, 15939? pb, 16075, 16085-16086, 16115, 16345 pb, 16396?, 16777 pb
1809: 16824 pb, 16833 pb, 17066, 17338, 17493 pb, 17547, 17858, 17874, 17886 pb, 17933, 18029-18030, 18049-18050, 18051 pb, 18054, 18307, 18316, 18472?, 18667, 18772, 18898, 18902, 19602, 19604, 19957, 20513, 20600, 20674, 20681 pb, 20683, 20697, 21217, 21220
1811: 22647 pb, 23181 f, 23182, 23245, 23711, 24510
1812: 24753 pb, 25346, 25444 pb, 25894-25898, 25980, 26004 pb, 26005, 26022-26024, 26026-26027
1813: 27697, 28198a pb, 28428, 28706 pb, 29081 pb, 29086-29087, 29092, 29094, 29096-29098, 29106 pb, 30192 pb
1814: 30700, 31329 pb, 31523, 31649 pb, 31967 pb, 32047-32049, 32062-32064, 32066, 32961 pb, 51408
1815: 33789 pb, 34000 pb, 34172 pb, 34411 pb, 34706, 35029, 35204-35205, 35212-35214
1816: 37489, 37645, 38016, 38156, 38164, 38165 pb, 38166, 38177-38179, 38182, 38416 pb, 39114 pb

1817: 40666, 41268 pb, 41364, 41367, 41369-41370, 41956 pb, 42150 pb
1818: 44014, 44091 pb, 44714, 44724, 44726-44728, 44730-44731, 44742-44744, 44752 pb, 44895, 45835
1819: 47871, 48623-48624, 48626-48627, 48742, 49630

RUSSELL, JOHN (Hartford, Conn.)
1813: 27968 pb, 28201 pb, 28259, 28780, 28951, 29640, 29901, 30397
1814: 30671 pb, 30762, 31149, 31238, 31297, 31343, 31416 pb, 31481 pb, 31584, 31815, 31932-31933 pb, 31993, 32826, 32883-32885, 32960 pb, 33678 pb
1815: 33873, 33927, 33945 pb, 34003, 34255, 34866, 35196-35197, 35779, 35826-35828, 36141, 36586-36587 pb, 51461 pb, 51467 pb, 51502 f
1816: 36780, 36813, 36829, 37806, 37895, 38025-38026, 38943 pb, 39700
1817: 40570, 40833, 42115
1818: 43729, 44584 pb, 46672 f
1819: 48303, 49334 pb, 50013 pb

RUSSELL, JOHN B (Frankfort, Ky.)
1818: 43895, 44084, 44506, 44508-44509
1819: 47982 pb, 48413, 48415-48416, 49631

RUSSELL, JOSHUA T (Baltimore)
1817: 40473 f

RUSSELL, WILLIAM (Hartford, Conn.)
1815: 51461 pb, 51467 pb, 51502 f
1819: 49334 pb, 50013 pb

Russell & Cutler (Boston)
see RUSSELL, JOHN (Boston)
CUTLER, JAMES (Boston)

Russell & Gardner (Boston)
see RUSSELL, JOHN (Boston)
~~GARDNER, SIMON (Boston)~~

RUST, ENOCH H (Boston)
1808: 16043

RUST, ENOCH H (Wiscasset, Me.)
1803: 3768?, 4127 pb, 4803 pb
1804: 5823, 5899, 6655, 6979?
1805: 7891, 7904, 7925, 7963, 8497?, 8735, 8789?
1806: 9894 pb, 10029
1807: 12802?, 13748

RUTH, JACOB (Ephrata, Pa.)
1811: 22416
1812: 25644

Rutland Herald (Rutland, Vt.)
1815: 35296

RYAN, DENNIS L (Milledge-ville, Ga.)
1808: 14905, 15096, 15098 pb
1809: 17612

RYAN, DENNIS L (Sparta, Ga.)
1803: 4183 pb
1807: 12654

RYAN, JOHN (St. John's, Newfoundland)
1818: 45609

S

SAGE, HARRIS (New York)
1803: 3759, 3788, 3793, 4705
1804: 5805 bf, 5987 f, 7394, 7773 bf, 50446-50447 pb
1805: 9780 f
1806: 9983, 10944 pb, 10962

SAGE, HEINRICH B (Lebanon, Pa.)

1809: 17884, 19200 pb
1810: 19359, 20535 pb

SAGE, HEINRICH B (Reading, Pa.)
1811: 23135 pb, 24022 pb
1813: 29707 pb, 30396 pb
1814: 31841, 31843
1816: 37814, 37979-37980 pb, 39692
1817: 40758, 42008 pb
1819: 48445 pb

Saint Andrew's Church (Charles-ton, S.C.)
1816: 36989 pb

ST. JOHN, JAMES (Easton, Md.)
1810: 20138

St. Louis Enquirer (St. Louis, Mo.)
1819: 48717

St. Mary's College (Baltimore)
1806: 10135 f

ST. ROMES, JOSEPH CHARLES de (New Orleans, La.)
1817: 41289-41293, 41603
1818: 44207 pb, 44613-44618, 45748 pb
1819: 48514-48518

SALA, JACOB (Frederick, Md.)
1803: 4496 f

SALA, JACOB (Somerset, Pa.)
1813: 28896

Salem Gazette (Salem, Mass.)
1805: 8618 pb
1806: 10009
1812: 27287
1813: 30418
1814: 31609, 31805 pb
1815: 35128 pb

Salem Register (Salem, Mass.)
1802: 2541
1806: 10266
1811: 22931

SALISBURY, HEZEKIAH
ALEXANDER (Buffalo, N. Y.)
1812:   24723, 25553 pb, 51195
pb
1815:   33954
1816:   36777, 36835
1817:   51727 pb
1818:   44406, 45100 pb, 45853
pb
1819:   48313, 49657 pb, 51903,
51927, 51957 pb

SALISBURY, SMITH HAMILTON
(Buffalo, N. Y.)
1811:   22429a pb, 23482 pb
1812:   24723, 25553 pb, 51195
pb
1815:   33954
1816:   36777, 36835
1817:   51727 pb
1819:   51957 pb

SAMPLE, WILLIAM (Washing-
ton, Pa.)
1808:   16049 pb, 16054
1809:   17144
1815:   35955
1818:   46886

SAMPSON, EZRA (Hudson,
N. Y.)
1801:   98 pb
1802:   1738, 1770, 1871, 3045,
3046 bf
1803:   4202
1806:   11322 pb

SAMPSON, PROCTOR (Marsh-
field, Mass.)
1811:   23649 pb

SANDERSON, EDWARD (Eliza-
beth, N. J.)
1815:   34850, 35816
1816:   37375, 38844, 38846
pb
1818:   43479, 43928 pb, 44495,
44650
1819:   47185, 47767, 47859,
48179

SANDERSON, EDWARD (Newark,
N. J.)
1816:   37376

1818:   43480, 45548
1819:   47463

SANDERSON, GEORGE (Lan-
caster, O.)
1810:   21106 pb

SANDERSON, JAMES (Eliza-
beth, N. J.)
1815:   34850, 35816
1816:   37375, 38844, 38846 pb
1818:   43479, 43928 pb, 44495,
44650
1819:   47185, 47767, 47859,
48179

SANDERSON, JAMES (Newark,
N. J.)
1816:   37376
1818:   43480, 45548
1819:   47463

SANDERSON, JOSEPH M (Philadelphia)
1815:   34047, 34580-34581,
34905, 36567
1816:   37058, 37185, 38071

SANNO, FRIEDRICH (Carlisle,
Pa.)
1807:   14104 pb
1808:   15702 pb, 16137 pb,
50865
1809:   17016 pb, 17855, 50951
pb
1810:   20314, 51022 pb
1811:   51119 pb
1813:   27765 pb

SANXAY, FREDERICK (Cin-
cinnati, O.)
1818:   43994 f

SAPPINGTON, W (Shepherds-
town, Va.)
1819:   48343 pb

Saratoga Courier (Ballston Spa,
N. Y.)
1816:   36840

Saratoga Journal (Ballston Spa,
N. Y.)
1815:   33960, 35678

Saratoga Patriot (Ballston Spa, N.Y.)
1812: 25399

SARGEANT, EZRA (New York)
1802: 2235 pb
1803: 4466 f
1804: 6326 pb, 7063 f
1805: 8214 pb
1806: 10655 f, 10893 f, 11408 f
1807: 12172 f, 12473 pb, 12584 pb, 12950 pb, 14149 pb
1808: 14657 pb, 14660 pb, 14830 pb, 14864 pb, 15183 pb, 15238 pb, 15423 f, 15565 pb, 15567 pb, 15646 f, 50840 pb
1809: 17085 pb, 17119 f, 17147 pb, 17164 pb, 17183 pb, 17326-17327 f, 17529 pb, 17803 pb, 17856 pb, 17934 pb, 18493 pb, 18666 f, 18723 f, 18806 pb, 19111 f, 19132 pb
1810: 19351 pb, 20224-20225 pb, 20545 pb, 20631 f, 20764 sb, 21229 f, 21300 f, 21331 f, 21344 f, 21394 pb
1811: 22353 pb, 22401a pb, 23021-23022 pb, 23024 pb, 23054 f, 23225 pb, 23778 pb, 23885 f, 23888-23889 f, 23894 f
1812: 25081-25084 f, 25086 f, 25088 f, 25742 pb, 26351 f, 27576 f

SARGENT, JOHN H (Charleston, S.C.)
1809: 18694 pb
1811: 22513

SARGENT, THOMAS F (Brooklyn, N.Y.)
1803: 5603 f

SARJENT, ABEL M (New York)
1811: 23871 f

SAUR
see SOWER

SAVAGE, --- (Middletown, Conn.)
1808: 14949 pb

SAWTELL, C (Northampton, Mass.)
1808: 14371 pb, 15115?
1809: 18600

SAWYER, JOHN (Exeter, N.H.)
1807: 12753, 12776 pb, 12843, 13551, 13604, 14125 pb
1808: 14537, 14538 pb, 14547, 14719 pb, 15104, 15568, 15636 pb, 16112, 16148, 16200, 16635 pb, 16636
1809: 17052 f

SAWYER, PORTER (Zanesville, O.)
1809: 18161 pb
1810: 20047
1811: 23588 pb, 23589
1812: 25047, 26338
1813: 29399-29401

SAWYER, WILLIAM (Newburyport, Mass.)
1807: 12068 f, 12849 pb, 13090 f, 13629 f
1808: 14359 f, 14380 f, 14604 f, 15104 f, 15544 f, 16112 f
1809: 17772 f

SAXTON, JOHN (Canton, O.)
1815: 35531 pb, 36622
1816: 37327
1817: 40555
1819: 47506

SAYRE, JOHN (New York)
1813: 29843 f
1814: 30866 f, 32729 pb, 32742 pb, 51361 pb
1815: 34020? pb, 36474 f
1816: 36965 f, 37374 pb, 37754 f, 38401 f, 38601 f, 38993 f, 38994 pb, 39798 pb
1817: 42193 f
1818: 51799 pb
1819: 49484 pb, 50149 f

SCHAEFFER, EDWARD (Lan-
caster, O.)
1816: 39143

SCHAEFFER, EDWARD (New
York)
1819: 47822 pb

SCHAEFFER, FREDERICK
GEORGE (Baltimore)
1815: 34107 pb, 34654? pb
1816: 36958 pb, 38020, 38328
pb, 38339 pb, 38875-38876
pb, 39690
1817: 39996, 40160, 40234-
40235, 40307, 40418 pb,
40896 pb, 40909, 40917 pb,
41143, 42060 pb, 42063 pb,
42118 pb, 42347, 42863 pb,
51668-51669 pb, 51710-51712
pb
1818: 43666, 43965 pb, 43970,
44136 pb, 44162 pb, 44302
pb, 44484 pb, 45312, 45644
pb, 45711, 45778, 46664,
46778
1819: 46995, 47920, 48128,
48225 pb, 48526 pb, 48758
pb, 48989, 49240, 49369
pb, 49395 pb, 50003, 50097

SCHEE, AUGUSTUS M (Dover,
Del.)
1813: 28294-28303
1814: 31315-31316, 31318-
31320
1815: 34556-34557
1816: 37425
1817: 40855 pb

SCHEFFER: THEO J (Harris-
burg, Pa.)
1801: 560 pb

SCHENCK, JOHN (Savannah,
Ga.)
1817: 41872 pb
1819: 49484 pb

SCHENCK, SAMUEL CROWELL
(Savannah, Ga.)
1817: 41872 pb
1819: 49484 pb

SCHERMERHORN, RYER (Al-
bany, N.Y.)
1814: 32006, 32616, 32803
1815: 35752

SCHERMERHORN, RYER
(Schenectady, N.Y.)
1807: 13106 pb, 13757
1808: 14626, 15845
1810: 20937, 21947
1812: 26699 pb
1814: 31985

SCHERMERHORN, RYER
(Troy, N.Y.)
1810: 21194
1811: 22929, 23252

SCHETKY, GEORGE (Philadelphia)
1803: 50357? pb
1804: 50438? pb, 50451? pb
1805: 8142 pb, 50506? pb,
50569? pb
1808: 50848? pb, 50868? pb,
50893? pb
1809: 50921 pb

SCHLATTER, WILLIAM (Philadelphia)
1817: 42238 f, 42241 f
1818: 43649 f

SCHNEE, J (Greensburg, Pa.)
1816: 51606-51607 pb

SCHNEE, JACOB (Lebanon,
Pa.)
1803: 3685
1807: 12621, 12622 pb, 12894,
13178 pb
1808: 15205, 15248, 15345,
15461, 15494-15495, 15629,
15703 pb
1809: 17928 pb, 18181 pb,
19191, 50922 pb
1810: 19765, 20297, 20841 pb,
21037, 21318, 21999, 22133
1811: 23136 f, 23190, 23495
pb, 23664-23665
1812: 26203 pb
1813: 28718, 29274 pb, 29480
1814: 31626

1815: 35605
1816: 38592

SCHNEE, JACOB (Pittsburgh,
Pa.)
1815: 35405 pb
1816: 37529, 38366 pb

SCHNEIDER, JACOB (Reading,
Pa.)
1802: 2179, 2306 bsb, 2416,
2554
1803: 4846-4847

SCHOEPFLIN, FRIEDRICH
WILHELM (Chambersburg,
Pa.)
1816: 38048, 38933

SCHOEPFLIN, WILHELM
(Chambersburg, Pa.)
1818: 43429

SCHULTZ, WILLIAM (Bridge-
ton, N. J.)
1819: 47474

SCHWEITZER, HEINRICH
(Philadelphia)
1801: 181, 277, 417, 491,
493, 990 pb
1802: 1726 f, 2145, 2413,
2498, 2555-2556, 2669,
2735 bsb
1803: 4358 f, 4713, 4960 pb,
5634
1804: 6486, 6677, 6857,
7677-7680
1805: 7996, 9045 pb, 9099
1806: 10345 pb, 11159, 11918,
50650 pb
1807: 13179 pb

Scioto Gazette (Chillicothe, O.)
1818: 43208
1819: 47130

Scotch Presbyterian Church
(Charleston, S. C.)
1816: 36989 pb

SCOTT, JAMES (Boston)
1812: 25534 f, 26678 f
1813: 28642 f

SCOTT, JOHN (Brookville,
Ind.)
1819: 47435 pb

SCOTT, JOHN (Carlisle, Pa.)
1815: 34446 pb

SCOTT, JOHN (Chillicothe, O.)
1818: 43208
1819: 47130, 48034, 48423

SCOTT, JOHN WELLWOOD
(Philadelphia)
1802: 1758, 2227, 3064
1803: 4055 pb, 4428, 4984
1804: 5901, 6009?, 6032,
6711
1805: 50528 pb, 50621
1806: 11620
1807: 12663 pb
1808: 14294, 14976 pb, 15120,
16455 ?
1810: 21880
1812: 24583, 51216 pb
1813: 29636 pb, 29753 pb
1816: 37509, 38697
1817: 40815, 41556, 41876,
41921
1818: 45411, 45414?, 46887
1819: 49180

SCOTT, L (Providence, R. I.)
1815: 33800-33802

SCOTT, MOSES Y (New York)
1819: 48916 pb

SCOTT, RICHARD (New York)
1806: 10309 pb, 11187 f,
11308 pb
1807: 12509 f, 12673 f, 12744
f, 13137 pb, 13270
1808: 14252 f, 14754 pb
1809: 17351 f, 18095 f, 18530
f
1811: 23855 f, 24032 f
1812: 24891 pb, 24962 pb,
24964 f, 24966 pb, 24969
pb, 25415 pb, 25922 f,
26057 f, 26131 f, 26187 pb,
26293 pb
1813: 28106 f, 28926 pb,
29137 f, 29206 f, 29743 f
1814: 30934 pb, 31917 f

1815:   34138 pb, 34242-34243
    pb, 34409 f, 34490 pb,
    34822 pb, 35303 pb, 35315
    pb, 35875 pb, 36042 pb,
    36560 pb, 51544 pb
1816:   37260 f, 37721 pb,
    37909 f, 38827 pb, 39078 f,
    39895 f
1817:   40928 pb, 40931 pb,
    41776 pb
1818:   43085 f, 43580 f, 44024
    f, 44601 f, 44606 f, 45376 f
1819:   47375 pb, 48294 pb,
    48299 pb, 49441 f

SCOTT, THOMAS W (Raleigh,
    N.C.)
1816:   51614

SCULL, JOHN (Pittsburgh,
    Pa.)
1801:   1645
1802:   2096, 3535 pb
1808:   14991, 16317 pb
1810:   20454
1816:   39884
1817:   40409?

SEABURY, DAVID (New York)
1815:   35185 pb

SEABURY, SAMUEL A (Sag
    Harbor, N.Y.)
1816:   39030 pb
1817:   39980 pb, 40887, 42956
1818:   45816
1819:   48901

SEARL, JESSE (Homer, N.Y.)
1813:   28233 f
1814:   31111
1815:   34139
1816:   37202
1819:   48124 f

SEARS, REUBEN (Ballston
    Spa, N.Y.)
1815:   34584 f, 34586 f,
    35358 f
1816:   39870 f
1817:   41342 f

SEATON, WILLIAM WINSTON
    (Halifax, N.C.)
1806:   9903

SEATON, WILLIAM WINSTON
    (Raleigh, N.C.)
1807:   13260 pb
1808:   15778, 15780
1809:   17597, 18260, 18262-
    18264
1810:   20925?, 20926-20927,
    ?20929?, 20930
1811:   22882, 23457, 23571-
    23573
1812:   24565 pb, 25077-25078
    pb

SEATON, WILLIAM WINSTON
    (Washington, D.C.)
1810:   21669?
1813:   28268 pb, 30196
1814:   32155 pb, 33228 pb
1815:   34354, 36159, 36276,
    36365
1816:   39487-39489
1817:   39924 pb, 40604
1819:   47716 pb, 49002, 49674,
    49744, 49746-49747, 49813,
    49830, 49833, 49835-49836,
    49847, 49862-49865, 49868,
    49870, 49872, 49875-49877,
    49885, 49895, 49899c,
    49947, 49958

SEAVER, WILLIAM (Albany,
    N.Y.)
1812:   26058 f

SEBREE, WILLIAM (George-
    town, Ky.)
1817:   41196 f

Second Religious Tract Society
    (Philadelphia)
1811:   23915 pb

SEGUINE, JAMES (New York)
1819:   47375 pb, 48299 pb,
    49441 f

Senator (Washington, D.C.)
1814:   31562, 33641

Sentimental Epicure's Ordinary
(New York)
1809: 17084

Sentinel (Keene, N. H.)
see New Hampshire Sentinel
(Keene, N. H.)

SEWALL, STEPHEN (Kenne-
bunk, Me.)
1803: 3681 pb, 4150
1804: 5722 pb, 6417, 6463,
6632a, 6999
1805: 9449 pb

SEWALL, STEPHEN (Ports-
mouth, N. H.)
1802: 2992
1803: 4519
1806: 10708
1807: 11919, 12005
1808: 14388, 14413, 14517,
15161, 15405
1809: 18275, 18516

SEWARD, ASAHEL (Utica,
N. Y.)
1803: 4641, 4826, 5509-5510
pb
1804: 5691 pb, 6822, 6832,
50454 pb
1805: 7853, 7858 pb, 7935,
8889 pb
1806: 9900, 10394 pb, 10660,
10719, 11042, 11359, 11751,
11794 pb, 11829
1807: 12542 pb, 12887, 13483,
13731, 14183
1808: 14640, 14786, 14992
pb, 15269, 15415, 15785 pb,
16690, 16694
1809: 16925, 16927, 17294
pb, 17485 pb, 18151 pb,
19170, 19175
1810: 19441, 19698, 20086
pb, 20260, 20294 pb, 20305,
20546, 20761 pb, 20854,
21950, 21971 pb, 21973 pb,
21979 pb, 21986
1811: 22247, 22503, 22542,
22805 pb, 23719 pb, 24360
1812: 25400 pb, 26343
1813: 27945, 28156 pb, 28489

pb, 28967, 29202 pb, 29247,
29414, 30501
1814: 30729, 30770, 31456 pb,
31636, 33519 pb
1815: 33908 pb, 33959, 34627,
34680, 34715, 35384, 35571
pb, 35586, 36425, 36475 pb,
36497 pb, 36526, 36583
1816: 37203, 37237 pb, 37272,
37565, 37581, 37791 pb,
37888 pb, 38228 pb, 38336,
38347 pb, 39071 pb, 39759-
39760, 39812 pb, 51583 pb,
51603 sb
1817: 41212 pb, 51663 pb

SEWELL, STEPHEN (Boston)
1817: 42334, 42335 ?

SEYMOUR, EDWARD PHELPS
(Herkimer, N. Y.)
1819: 50151

SEYMOUR, EDWARD PHELPS
(Stockbridge, Mass.)
1808: 14995
1809: 19205, 19260
1810: 20124

SEYMOUR, GURDON ISAAC
(Savannah, Ga.)
1802: 2014, 2308, 3540
1803: 3726
1808: 14483, 15497
1811: 22494 pb, 23169 pb,
23262 pb, 23887 pb
1812: 26490, 27537 pb

SEYMOUR, J (Columbia, S. C.)
1817: 40462 pb

SEYMOUR, JONATHAN (New
York)
1803: 3842, 4631, 4634, 4698
1804: 6041, 6074, 6731, 7205
1805: 7886-7888, 8243, 8641,
8812 pb, 8880, 8956 pb,
9012, 9448
1806: 9817, 9863, 10043,
10142 pb, 10516, 10770,
10855, 10907, 11084, 11138,
11262, 11409, 11632, 11840,
50698

1807: 12004, 13086, 13227, 13239, 13461, 13475
1808: 14378, 14384-14385, 14550, 14568, 14835, 14969, 15259, 15293 pb, 15475, 15608, 15610, 15979-15980, 16092, 16095, 16661
1809: 16976, 17108-17109, 17226, 17278 f, 17643, 17769, 18061, 18088, 18443 f, 18531-18532, 18570, 18579, 18608, 18612, 19143, 19180, 19184
1810: 19330, 19514, 19960, 20013, 20048, 20100, 20174, 20274, 20301, 20712, 20738, 20756 pb, 20765, 20899, 20915, 20918, 21134, 21192, 21237-21238, 21294, 21528
1811: 22315, 22326, 22354, 22611, 22777, 23107, 23109, 23159, 23390, 23612, 23829, 23942g, 23970
1812: 24580, 24586, 24833, 25020, 25174, 25289, 25306-25309, 25332, 25859, 25921, 25930 pb, 26080, 26295 pb, 26511, 26519, 26621, 26654
1813: 27693, 27757, 27872, 27932, 28128, 28132, 28136, 28429, 28469, 28683, 28925, 29166, 29222, 29350, 29353-29354, 29359, 29427, 29624, 29823, 29843, 29881
1814: 30712, 30866, 31190, 31551, 31567, 31723, 31725, 32000, 32023, 32334, 32344, 32349, 32613, 32812, 32847, 33659
1815: 33836, 34040, 34103, 34363, 34510, 34817, 35228, 35476, 35483, 35488, 36016, 36017 pb
1816: 36725, 36751, 36767?, 36965, 37098, 37444, 37458, 37473, 37530 pb, 37584, 37648, 37739, 37754, 37837, 37907, 37947, 38311, 38449, 38455, 38457, 38462, 38523, 38601-38602, 38704, 38715 pb, 38752, 38832, 38934, 38968, 38993, 39122, 39723,
39787
1817: 39929, 39974, 40159, 40221, 40228, 40439, 40504 pb, 40617, 40708, 40813, 40893, 40999 pb, 41120 pb, 41286, 41346-41348, 41641, 41645, 41649 pb, 41653, 41922, 41957, 41985, 41987, 42193, 42198, 42846, 42892, 42990 pb
1818: 43102, 43609, 43617, 43765, 44190, 44202, 44359, 44452, 44575, 44646 pb, 44693, 44891, 45036 pb, 45040, 45068-45069, 45076, 45079-45080, 45087 pb, 45092, 45195-45196, 45379, 45415, 45751, 45920, 45922, 46713, 46781
1819: 47071, 47382, 47934, 48082, 48117-48118, 48212 pb, 48449 pb, 48469, 48485, 48585, 48732, 48740, 48888, 48912, 49031, 49319 pb, 49372, 49376-49377, 49393, 49664, 49989

SEYMOUR, JOSEPH W (Pittsfield, Mass.)
1807: 12149, 12323, 12906, 14122, 14144
1808: 15237, 15287 pb, 15322, 15406, 16712, 16744

SHALLUS, ANN PETERS (Philadelphia)
1817: 42101 f

SHALLUS, FRANCIS (Philadelphia)
1808: 15263 f, 15825 f
1811: 22828 f

Shakespeare Gallery (New York)
1801: 806-807, 1602
1802: 2551
1803: 5101
1806: 11169
1812: 24871
1819: 48940

SHARAN, JAMES (Baltimore)
1808: 16178 f

SHARAN, JAMES (New York)
1815:   33776 f
1816:   39840 f

SHARAN, JAMES (Philadelphia)
1810:   21379 f
1812:   26261 f
1813:   28781 pb

SHARPLESS, BLAKEY (Phila-
delphia)
1815:   35953 pb
1816:   37308 pb, 37366 pb,
37769 pb, 37999, 38628 f,
38925 pb, 39866 pb, 51600
pb
1817:   40017 pb, 40650 f,
41278 f
1818:   43409 f, 43682 pb,
46743? pb
1819:   47680 f, 48426 f

SHARPLESS, JOSEPH (Bur-
lington, N. J.)
1807:   12771-12772 pb

SHARPLESS, JOSEPH (Frank-
ford, Pa.)
1812:   24591 f, 25672 f,
26128 pb, 26404 pb

SHARPLESS, JOSEPH (Nine
Partners, N. Y.)
1816:   37430 pb

SHARPLESS, JOSEPH (Phila-
delphia)
1808:   15866 pb
1809:   17765 pb, 18329 f
1811:   23670 f, 23689 f
1813:   29771 f
1814:   31031 pb, 31032 f,
31739 f, 32160 pb, 32517
pb
1816:   37431 pb, 37669 pb

SHARROCKS, JOHN T
(Winchester, Va.)
1817:   41151 f

SHAUP, HENRY (New Berlin,
Pa.)
1815:   35408 pb

SHAW, --- (New York)
1812:   25552 f, 25967 pb

SHAW, GEORGE (Annapolis,
Md.)
1812:   24779 f, 25801 f
1815:   34457 f, 35996-35997 f

SHAW, JOHN (Catskill, N. Y.)
1810:   19855 f
1811:   22619 f

SHAW, JOHN (Natchez, Miss.)
1808:   15623 pb
1810:   20753-20754 pb
1812:   ?24650

SHAW, OLIVER (Providence,
R. I.)
1808:   16181 sb

SHAW, RALPH (Philadelphia)
1801:   50285? sb
1802:   50319? pb
1806:   10900 pb

SHAW, SAMUEL (Albany,
N. Y.)
1815:   34093 f, 34443 pb
1818:   43736 pb

SHAW, SAMUEL (Lansingburgh,
N. Y.)
1804:   50485 pb
1805:   8252 f

SHEARMAN, ABRAHAM (New
Bedford, Mass.)
1801:   228, 667, 50216
1802:   1776, 2209 pb, 2222,
2444, 2918
1803:   3979, 4517 pb, 5040
1804:   6696
1805:   8154 pb, 8209, 8575,
8595, 8672 f, 8835, 9323,
9397
1806:   10454, 10767, 11378
1807:   12558 pb, 13553, 13587,
13687 pb
1808:   14329?, 14831 pb,
15074, 16774 pb
1809:   16827, 17239, 17585,
18754, 19128 pb

1810:   20995 f
1812:   26103 f
1813:   27879 f, 28588, 29738
pb
1814:   31175-31176 pb, 32443
f
1818:   44547 f, 45233 f

SHEDD, JEPTHAH (Vergennes,
Vt.)
1813:   29782 f, 30487 f
1814:   31461 f
1816:   38472 f

SHEDDEN, JOHN (New York)
1806:   11425 pb
1809:   17880 f, 18529 f
1811:   24003? f

SHELDON, GEORGE (Hartford,
Conn.)
1814:   31374 pb, 32548 pb,
32549 f, 32599 pb, 33677
pb, 51435 pb
1815:   33823, 34271, 34381,
34426 pb, 34800?, 34893?,
34912-34914, 34934, 35336?,
35740-35741, 35782, 35937
pb, 36498, 36662 pb
1816:   36949 pb, 36962a f,
36964 pb, 37204 f
1817:   41866 pb
1818:   43932? pb

SHELDON, JOHN PITTS
(Detroit, Mich.)
1817:   40654 pb
1818:   51737
1819:   50105, 50107

SHELLERS, --- (Georgetown,
Ky.)
1816:   37698 pb, 37995

SHELTON, --- (Cheshire,
Conn.)
1814:   32710 f

SHELTON, --- (New Haven,
Conn.)
1814:   30952 pb
1816:   38141 pb

SHELTON, --- (Newburgh,
N. Y.)
1817:   41629 pb

SHELTON, WILLIAM (Rich-
mond, Va.)
1811:   22190 pb

SHEPARD, ERASTUS (Bath,
N. Y.)
1819:   50095 pb

SHEPARD, ERASTUS (Ithaca,
N. Y.)
1816:   37935 pb
1817:   39982 pb

SHEPARD, ERASTUS (New-
town, N. Y.
1818:   44479

SHEPARD, THOMAS (Charles-
town, Mass.)
1816:   38788 pb

SHEPARD, THOMAS WATSON
(Northampton, Mass.)
1817:   40963
1818:   44057, 44239 pb,
44371, 44498, 45837, 46740,
46850 pb
1819:   47401, 47897, 48146,
48530-48531, 48950

SHEPHERD, CHARLES (North-
ampton, Mass.)
1808:   15111

SHEPHERD, SAMUEL (Norfolk,
Va.)
1815:   33839 pb

SHEPHERD, SAMUEL (Rich-
mond, Va.)
1816:   36861, 37032
1817:   39993, 40129, 40131-
40132, 41024, 41976, 42108
1818:   43028, 43222, 44668,
45756
1819:   46930, 47151

SHEPPARD, J (Salem, N. J.)
1818:   51738 f

SHERIFF, BENJAMIN PEARSE
(Exeter, N. H.)
1805:   8822 pb
1812:   24770 pb
1813:   28751 pb
1814:   31028 pb, 31724 pb
1815:   35429 f

SHERMAN, GEORGE (Trenton,
N. J.)
1801:   309, 1011, 1013-1014,
  1016, 1018 pb
1802:   1741, 2355, 2764, 2766-
  2767
1803:   4178, 4749 pb
1804:   6900 pb, 6903, 7125
  pb, 50488
1805:   9002, 9005 pb
1806:   10985, 10990 pb
1807:   12612, 13210 pb
1808:   15999, 50872-50873 pb
1809:   18217 pb
1810:   20875 pb, 20877, 21990,
  51023 pb
1811:   22447a, 23534, 23536-
  23537
1812:   26247, 26252, 26257,
  26258 pb, 27454
1813:   29314-29317
1814:   32203, 32267 pb, 32268,
  51420 pb
1815:   35449 pb, 35451, 35709
1816:   37057, 38412 pb, 38414,
  38886 pb
1817:   41600 pb, 41888, 42145-
  42146, 51705
1818:   44913, 45012 pb
1819:   48870 pb, 49190-49191

SHERMAN, IRA (Bridgeport,
Conn.)
1817:   41427 pb

SHERMAN, JOHN H (New
York)
1815:   34757, 35888
1816:   37265, 38884 pb
1817:   40684, 41663

SHERMAN, SILAS (Bridgeport,
Conn.)
1817:   41427 pb

Sherman, Baldwin & Co.
(Bridgeport, Conn.)
see SHERMAN, SILAS (Bridge-
  port, Conn.)
  BALDWIN, JOSIAH B
  (Bridgeport, Conn.)
  SHERMAN, IRA (Bridgeport,
  Conn.)

SHIELDS, HAMILTON (Norfolk,
Va.)
1815:   33839 pb
1816:   36858, 37588
1818:   43084, 43227
1819:   47146, 47152

SHIELDS, WILLIAM C (Nor-
folk, Va.)
1816:   36858, 37588
1818:   43084, 43227
1819:   47146, 47152

SHINN, SAMUEL FENTON
(Philadelphia)
1818:   51848 pb

SHIRLEY, ARTHUR (Portland,
Me.)
1804:   6475, 6496 pb, 6666,
  6701, 6781, 7093, 7396
1805:   8543, 9506
1806:   11188
1808:   15843
1809:   17024, 17076 pb, 17751,
  18441, 18481, 19210, 19248
1810:   19648, 20109, 21124,
  21171
1811:   22385
1812:   24671, 24755, 24803,
  24861, 24918, 24928, 25156,
  26384, 26507
1813:   27793, 29432, 29438
1814:   30699, 31007, 31019,
  31881, 32446, 32506, 32694
1815:   34112, 34226-34228,
  34388, 35083, 35281, 35683,
  35767, 35815, 36633
1816:   37258, 37465 pb, 37779,
  38252 pb, 38687, 38971,
  39847-39848
1817:   40013, 40497, 41160,
  41867, 41926, 42942 pb
1818:   43384, 43929, 43975,

44323, 44335, 45391, 45471,
45833, 46800
1819: 47098, 47948 pb, 48133,
48278, 48571 pb, 49967

SHIRLEY, JOSHUA (Portland,
Me.)
1814: 30699, 32694
1815: 34112, 34226-34228,
34388, 35083, 35281, 35683,
35767, 35815
1816: 37258, 37465 pb, 37779,
38252 pb, 38687, 38971,
39847-39848
1817: 40013, 40497, 41160,
41867, 41926, 42942 pb
1818: 43384, 43929, 43975,
44323, 44335, 45391, 45471,
45833, 46800
1819: 48278

SHORE, THOMAS (Petersburg,
Va.)
1819: 49414 f

SHORES, JAMES FOSTER
(Portsmouth, N. H.)
1816: 38947 f

SHUTZ, C (Alexandria, Va.)
1802: 2536 f

SIBLEY, DERICK (Montpelier,
Vt.)
1809: 17574 pb, 19097 pb
1810: 19940, 21878
1811: 22246, 22288, 22448a-
22449a pb, 22526 pb, 22774
pb, 23508-23509, 24399 pb
1812: 24527, 24778 pb, 24812-
24813 pb, 24982 pb, 25005,
25046 pb, 25059, 26118-
26119, 26509, 26659, 26674,
26691 pb, 26813 pb, 26904
pb, 27374 pb, 27386, 27392,
27435 pb, 27487 pb
1813: 27818, 29069, 29556,
29741, 29870, 30410-30411,
30487, 30585
1814: 31461, 31542, 31823,
32543
1815: 34359

SIBLEY, DERICK (Windsor,
Vt.)
1812: 26659, 26674

Sidney's Press (New Haven,
Conn.)
1801: 464?
1802: 1812, 2030-2031
1803: 3784, 3815, 4002 pb,
4182, 4316 pb, 4327, 4367
pb, 4733, 4743, 4892-4893,
4921, 50351
1804: 5881, 6151 pb, 6256-
6257, 6356 pb, 6383-6384,
6443, 6576, 6730, 6820,
7159 pb, 7393 pb, 7706 pb,
7722, 7733
1805: 8204, 8398, 8527, 8541
pb, 8643, 8681, 8785, 8996,
9171 pb, 9418 pb, 9696 pb,
9753, 50525 pb
1806: 9812, 9923 pb, 10061,
10249, 10304, 10548, 10616
pb, 10728, 10773, 10904,
11217, 11831, 11833, 11888,
50657, 50666 pb, 50671 pb,
50697, 50709
1807: 11949, 12413, 12450,
12498, 12507, 12701, 12710,
12815, 12909, 13477, 14109,
14188, 14199, 14232, 50768
pb, 50777
1808: 14274, 14493, 14499,
14528, 14903, 14916-14917,
14931, 15027, 15244, 15559,
15593, 15790, 16738, 16756,
50826 pb, 50830-50831 pb,
50839 pb, 50845-50846 pb,
50858, 50883, 50886 pb
1809: 17102, 17273, 17307,
17361, 17382, 17386, 17425,
17514, 17520-17521, 17760,
17814, 17828, 17979, 18059,
18078-18079, 18202, 18223,
18422, 18446, 18655, 18787,
19137, 19157, 19252, 50910
pb, 50914-50916, 50947,
50968
1810: 19393, 19869, 19977,
20017, 20049, 20059, 20705,
20710, 20865, 20869, 21221,
21223, 21416, 21436-21437,
21543 pb, 22033, 22073,

50991 pb, 51014, 51019, 51030
1811: 22533, 22614 pb, 22625, 23381, 23696 pb, 23718, 51071 pb, 51110 pb
1812: 25041, 25158, 25160, 25219, 25235, 25350, 25426, 25584, 25709, 25866 pb, 25942, 25946, 26038, 26181, 26192, 26238 pb, 26348, 26433 pb, 27641, 26779, 27471, 27551, 27637, 51158 pb, 51160-51161 pb, 51171 pb, 51189 pb
1813: 28223, 28755 pb, 28799 pb, 28857, 28936, 28985, 29047, 29121 pb, 29123, 29231 pb, 29310 pb, 29766 pb, 29788, 29883, 30531 pb, 30597 pb, 51271 pb, 51295 pb, 51298 pb, 51308, 51324
1814: 31223, 31585, 31784, 31819, 31821-31822, 32008-32009, 32086, 32362
1815: 34918 pb, 34972 pb, 35893 pb, 36569 pb
1817: 39955, 40136 pb, 40188 pb, 40414 pb, 40465 pb, 40940 pb, 40972 pb, 41176 pb, 41178 pb, 41276 pb, 41658 pb, 41710 pb, 41826 pb, 41897-41898, 42120-42121 pb, 42844 pb, 51642 pb
1818: 43111 pb, 43288 pb, 43483 pb, 43727, 44159 pb, 44692 pb, 45002 pb, 45545 pb, 45706, 45719 pb, 45761-45762 pb, 45839 pb, 46711 pb, 46801 pb, 51747 pb
1819: 46942 pb, 46946 pb, 47025 pb, 47156, 47173 pb, 47503 pb, 47522 pb, 47568 pb, 47705 pb, 47723-47724 pb, 48088 pb, 48132 pb, 48229 pb, 48314 pb, 48401-48403 pb, 48579 pb, 48583 pb, 49146 pb, 49293 pb, 49306 pb, 49423 pb, 51858 pb

SIEGFRIED, SIMEON (Cadiz, O.)
1818: 45147

SIEGFRIED, SIMEON (Doylestown, Pa.)
1819: 47452-47453 pb

SIEGFRIED, SIMEON (Newtown, Pa.)
1818: 45199, 46824 pb

SILLIMAN, WYLLYS (Marietta, O.)
1801: 1075 pb

SIMMONS, H (Canandaigua, N.Y.)
1817: 41853?

SIMMS, JOHN DOUGLASS (Alexandria, Va.)
1813: 28427, 29595, 29614, 29888
1814: 31648, 32228, 32515 pb, 32756, 33618, 33695

SIMONS, WILLIAM (Boston)
1807: 12181, 13189, 13737, 14219 pb
1808: 14285, 14556, 14561, 14741, 14946, 15299 pb, 15375, 15472

SIMONS, WILLIAM (Newport, R.I.)
1809: 18513 pb, 18891
1812: 25259, 25260?
1813: 28375
1816: 37187 pb
1819: 49506

SIMPSON, JOHN N (New Brunswick, N.J.)
1810: 21182 f, 21369-21370 f
1811: 23298 f, 24332-24333 f

SIMPSON, T (Philadelphia)
1813: 28851

SIMPSON, THOMAS (New York)
1803: 5162 f
1805: 8666
1807: 12795
1808: 15336 pb
1809: 18537
1810: 21962 pb

SIMPSON, THOMAS (Towanda, Pa.)
1813: 28009 pb

SIMPSON, THOMAS (Williamsport, Pa.)
1814: 31973 pb

SIMS, JOHN C (Newbern, N. C.)
1805: 8472 pb
1806: 10794 pb

SINCLAIR, GEORGE (New York)
1807: 12816 f
1809: 17816 pb, 17847 pb

SKELTON, --- (Southampton)
1814: 32954?

SKERRETT, JOSEPH R A (Philadelphia)
1816: 37774, 38849, 39129-39130, 39763, 39820
1817: 39968, 40033, 40257, 40355-40356, 40582, 40650, 41278, 41697, 41806 pb, 41948, 42169-42170, 42227, 42291, 42955
1818: 42999 pb, 43086, 43104 pb, 43237, 43399, 43559, 43621, 43985, 45000, 45134, 45307, 45325, 45650, 45808, 45828, 45907, 46748, 46759 pb, 46834, 46865, 51772, 51814
1819: 46968, 47172, 47532-47533, 47605, 48398-48399, 49017, 50007, 51886

SKILLMAN, THOMAS T (Lexington, Ky.)
1811: 22254, 22469, 22471, 22950
1812: 24643?, 24644, 25021?, 25362, 25914, 27503
1813: 27966, 28034 pb, 28218 pb, 28348, 28380 pb, 28506, 28730, 28790, 29621 pb, 29779
1814: 30941 f, 30947, 31620 pb, 31657 pb, 31708, 31980 pb, 32774

1815: 34134, 34157 pb, 34364, 34610, 34677, 35155 pb, 36507 pb, 36614 pb, 51492 pb
1816: 37354, 37607, 38116
1817: 40079, 40560 pb, 41106 pb, 41195
1818: 43773, 44085, 44511, 44645 pb

SKINNER, DANIEL (Albany, N. Y.)
For all entries see SKINNER, HEZEKIAH (Albany, N. Y.) below

SKINNER, ELISHA W (Albany, N. Y.)
1802: 2544 pb
1803: 3974 pb
1804: 6035
1806: 10161, 10430, 10547 pb, 10633, 10741, 10760, 11006, 11009, 11048, 11835 pb, 11837 pb, 50645 pb
1807: 12933 pb, 13230 pb, 13232, 13233 pb, 13235, 13266, 13688, 14193
1808: 14309, 14458, 15239 f, 15314?, 15437, 15755-15756, 16691 pb, 16696 pb
1809: 16958 pb, 17416, 17921? pb, 18237, 19186
1810: 19310, 19577?, 20575, 20892?, 20897, 21466, 21512?, 21992 pb
1811: 22408, 23111, 23233?, 23425, 23574, 23576, 24330, 24375, 24409 pb, 51120, 51123
1812: 24577 pb, 24578, 24889, 25023, 25097, 25869 pb, 26053, 26163 pb, 26280, 26284, 26933, 27464-27465, 27497, 27504, 51154, 51228
1813: 27684, 27885 pb, 27902, 28377, 28834, 28960?, 29176, 29336, 29716 pb, 29756, 30465, 30502, 30506 pb, 51325-51326
1814-1819: see SKINNER, HEZEKIAH (Albany, N. Y.) below

SKINNER, HEZEKIAH (Albany, N. Y.)
1812: 51145, 51228
1813: 30465, 30502, 30506 pb, 51325-51326
1814: 30645, 30936 pb, 31610, 31941? f, 32195 pb, 32813, 33305 pb, 33584-33586, 33589, 33631, 33653, 51451 pb
1815: 33790, 34147, 34237, 34339, 34368, 34599, 35118, 35341 pb, 35354 pb, 35460, 35464, 35509, 35753, 35974, 36018, 36487, 36529 pb, 51455, 51520
1816: 36697, 36699, 36972, 37117, 38215, 38378, 38435, 38441, 38761, 38766, 38866, 39712, 39727, 39754, 39761, 51603 bsb, 51629
1817: 33956, 40194, 40223, 40224 f, 40309, 40704-40705, 40722, 40947, 41065, 41159, 41275 pb, 41617, 41626, 41631, 41674, 41938-41939, 41941, 42062, 42206 pb, 42339 pb, 42812, 42859 pb, 42907, 51707, 51727-51729 pb
1818: 43524, 43662, 43906 sb, 43907 pb, 44356, 45030 pb, 45045 pb, 45046? pb, 45048, 46744 pb, 51742, 51794 f, 51844
1819: 46954-46955, 47825 pb, 48529, 48882-48883, 48886, 48892, 48895 f, 49186, 50084 pb, 50127 pb, 51942

SKINNER, JOHN S (Baltimore)
1819: 46987 pb

SKINNER, NATHANIEL L (Bridgeport, Conn.)
1814: 31221 pb, 32759
1815: 34023 pb, 34669, 34847
1816: 36913 pb
1817: 40657, 41427 pb
1818: 43268 pb, 43393, 44833 pb, 45388, 51798 pb
1819: 51856 pb, 51916 pb

SKINNER, NATHANIEL L (Danbury, Conn.)
1813: 28274 pb, 30543
1814: 33668

SKINNER, ROBERT (Wilmington, Del.)
1810: 19949 pb

SKINNER, ROBERT J (Dayton, O.)
1816: 38515 pb
1819: 47128, 50055

SKINNER, THOMAS M (Auburn, N. Y.)
1816: 36771 pb, 38905
1817: 40041, 42147
1818: 45474, 51769 pb
1819: 47530, 47792

SKINNER, THOMAS M (Colchester, Conn.)
1814: 30745, 31279, 31961 pb, 32669
1815: 34369

SKRINE, TACITUS G (Charleston, S. C.)
1817: 40675

SLADE, WILLIAM (Burlington, Vt.)
1814: 32371 pb

SLADE, WILLIAM (Middlebury, Vt.)
1814: 30787, 31323 pb, 32779, 33533, 33539 pb, 33614 pb, 33738
1815: 33977, 33980, 34515 pb, 34946, 34979 pb, 35273, 35393 pb, 35634 pb, 35848 pb, 36084 pb, 36131 pb
1816: 37009 pb, 37176 pb, 38246, 38298 pb, 38792, 38936, 38995 pb
1817: 42779 f, 42784 f, 42979 pb

SLEIGHT, HENRY C (Brooklyn, N. Y.)
1812: 24930
1813: 28283

SLEIGHT, HENRY C (Lexing-
ton, Ky.)
1814: 30670 f, 32971 pb,
33650 pb

SLEIGHT, HENRY C (Rus-
sellville, Ky.)
1816: 36851

SLOAN, JOHN (Chambersburg,
Pa.)
1817: 40852 pb

SLUMP, JOHN MARTIN (Cam-
den, S. C.)
1802: 1998 pb

SMALL, ABRAHAM (Philadel-
phia)
1801: 1278-1279 f
1802: 1905 f, 3033 f
1803: 3837 f, 5592 f
1804: 6381 f
1805: 8518 f, 8521 f
1806: 11386 f
1807: 12742 f, 13046 f
1808: 15037 bf, 16100 f,
16128-16129 bf
1809: 18647 bf
1810: 19658 pb, 20113 bf,
20828, 20974 bf, 21103 pb,
21115, 22021
1811: 22188 bf, 22444a,
22498 bf, 22620 bf, 23849
bf
1812: 24998, 25165 pb, 26768
bf, 26809
1813: 29618
1814: 30680 pb, 30939-30940,
31040, 31167, 31470, 31475
pb, 32707, 51356 pb, 51391
pb
1815: 34361 pb, 35047 pb,
35171, 35672, 35829, 51460
pb, 51497 pb
1816: 36741 pb, 36746 pb,
37697 pb, 37704, 39659 pb,
39822-39823, 51548 pb
1817: 39963 pb, 39992 pb,
40337 pb, 40489 pb, 40572
pb, 40724 pb, 40803 pb,
40822 pb, 40929 pb, 41325,
42767 pb, 42772 pb, 42773,

51643 pb, 51665 pb
1818: 43072 pb, 43363 pb,
43731-43732 pb, 43934 pb,
44039 pb, 44170 pb, 44174
pb, 44222 pb, 44294 pb,
44341 pb, 44471, 44663 pb,
44889, 45258, 45863, 46705
pb, 46784 f, 51733 pb
1819: 46989 pb, 46991 pb,
47003 pb, 47203 pb, 47387
pb, 48204 pb, 48380

SMALL, WILLIAM (New York)
1818: 44499 pb

SMALLEY, H (Salem, N. J.)
1818: 51738 f

SMEAD, BENJAMIN (Bath,
N. Y.)
1816: 39012 pb
1817: 41310

SMEAD, BENJAMIN (Benning-
ton, Vt.)
1804: 5759, 5794, 6080, 6159,
6300, 6459? pb
1805: 8095, 8319, 8570, 9309,
9654, 9656
1806: 10861
1807: 12508 pb, 13496 pb,
14177, 14244 pb
1808: 15203, 15210
1809: 17674 pb
1811: 22335 pb, 22340, 22968,
23850?

SMEAD, BENJAMIN (Brattle-
boro, Vt.)
1801: 122

SMEAD, BENJAMIN FRANKLIN
(Hamilton, N. Y.)
1818: 43048 pb
1819: 48143 pb

SMITH, --- (Baltimore)
1817: 40259 pb

SMITH, --- (Cadiz, O.)
1816: 37147 pb

SMITH, --- (New York)
1818: 45088

SMITH, --- (Philadelphia)
1810: 19357, 20559, 20702,
   21208, 21232

SMITH, ADDISON (Hamilton,
   O.)
1816: 38615 pb

SMITH, B (Woodbridge)
1819: 48767 pb

SMITH, CHARLES (New York)
1801: 361 f, 775 pb, 777 f,
   778 pb, 781 pb

SMITH, CHESTER C (Lan-
   caster, Pa.)
1804: 5667, 7017

SMITH, DANIEL D (New York)
1804: 6167 f, 50462 f
1805: 9064 pb, 9145 pb,
   9146 f, 50583 f
1806: 10170 pb, 10298 pb,
   11071 f, 11389 pb
1807: 12798, 12799 pb, 12900,
   13294 f, 13610 pb, 50812
   pb
1808: 14909 pb, 15285 pb,
   15899 pb, 16208 pb, 16655
   pb, 16659 pb, 50875 pb,
   50887 pb
1809: 16975, 17397, 17637
   pb, 17791 pb, 18390 pb,
   18419 pb, 18645-18646 pb,
   50956 pb, 50964, 50965 pb
1810: 19539 pb, 20391 pb,
   20419-20420, 21085 pb,
   21371-21373 pb, 50999 pb
1811: 22702 pb, 23071 pb,
   23455 pb, 23951 pb, 51104
   pb, 51139-51141 pb
1812: 24824 f, 25705 pb,
   25766 pb, 25788 pb, 26464
   pb, 26598 pb, 26764-26765
   pb, 27419 pb, 51176 pb,
   51247 pb
1813: 27887 pb, 28795 pb,
   29514 pb, 29809-29811 pb,
   51335 pb
1814: 30674 pb, 31107 pb,
   31201, 31779 pb, 32153 pb,
   32357 pb, 32805-32806 pb,

51439 pb
1815: 34981 pb, 35639 pb,
   35961 pb, 51534-51535 pb
1816: 37899 pb, 38632 pb,
   38634-38635 pb, 38959,
   51626-51627 pb
1817: 41814-41815 pb
1818: 43408 pb, 43861 pb,
   44600 f, 45066 pb, 45330-
   45333 pb, 51787 pb, 51811
   pb
1819: 47160 pb, 48292 pb,
   48297 pb, 48307 pb, 48590
   pb, 48804 pb, 48817 pb,
   49111 f, 51923 f

SMITH, DAVID CAMPBELL
   (Columbus, O.)
1816: 37471, 38004, 38512 pb
1818: 45146?
1819: 48973-48974 pb, 48978

SMITH, ELIAS (Exeter, N.H.)
1805: 9367 f, 9373 f
1808: 14690 pb
1809: 18629 pb

SMITH, ELIAS (Philadelphia)
1811: 22993 pb
1814: 32786 pb

SMITH, ELIAS (Portland, Me.)
1810: 20325 pb
1811: 23942j sb

SMITH, ELIAS (Portsmouth,
   N.H.)
1804: 7282 f
1805: 8185 pb
1808: 15215 pb
1815: 35950 f
1817: 42133 f

SMITH, GEORGE (Dayton, O.)
1808: 14834 pb

SMITH, GEORGE (Lebanon,
   O.)
1816: 37558 pb
1818: 44665

SMITH, GEORGE (Springfield,
   O.)
1819: 47940 pb

SMITH, GEORGE (Worthing-
ton, O.)
1811:   24424

SMITH, GEORGE G (Boston)
1818:   45906 pb

SMITH, JAMES (New York)
1815:   33776, 35861 pb

SMITH, JOHN ERDMAN
(Augusta, Ga.)
1801:   568 pb
1802:   1788 pb, 2312

SMITH, JOSEPH (Cumberland,
Md.)
1818:   46774 pb

SMITH, MILO (Pittsfield,
Mass.)
1807:   12149, 12323, 12906,
14122, 14144
1808:   15237, 15287 pb, 15322,
15406, 16712, 16744
1809:   17270, 17682, 18699,
19240 pb
1810:   20987 pb, 22062
1811:   22457
1812:   25733, 26927
1814:   31830

SMITH, MILO (Stockbridge,
Mass.)
1814:   30852 pb
1815:   34978

SMITH, ROBERT (Philadelphia)
1812:   24523 pb

SMITH, SAMUEL HARRISON
(Clinton, O.)
1814:   32796
1815:   35965-35966

SMITH, SAMUEL HARRISON
(Philadelphia)
1803:   5279

SMITH, SAMUEL HARRISON
(Washington, D. C.)
1801:   512, 719, 1087, 1509,
1583?, 1683

1802:   3084, 3284, 3468?
1803:   4302, 4445, 4832, 5183,
5317, 5505, 5613
1804:   6070, 6366, 7333, 7349,
7509, 7541, 7700
1805:   9511, 9534, 9643
1806:   9922, 10705, 10777,
11469 pb

SMITH, THOMAS (Lexington,
Ky.)
1809:   16914 pb, 50952
1810:   19426, 19710, 20562,
22067
1811:   22470, 23274
1812:   25461, 27581 pb
1813:   28564, 28812, 29018
1814:   31518
1816:   37642-37643, 38117 pb,
38121, 39721
1817:   40856, 42141, 51730 pb
1818:   44086-44087, 44512,
45888, 46832
1819:   47403, 47493 pb, 48017,
48418, 51959 pb

SMITH, THOMAS (Philadelphia)
1801:   166, 708, 836, 1265,
1307
1802:   2198, 2356, 3273
1807:   11921-11922, 13351 pb,
13640
1808:   14254, 15313, 16140,
16644
1809:   16785, 17029
1810:   19968, 20561, 21241
1811:   23929

SMITH, THOMAS PERRIN
(Easton, Md.)
1801:   1412?
1802:   2598
1803:   4798
1806:   9919
1807:   12856?, 13702
1808:   16314?
1813:   28394

Smith and Forman (New York)
see SMITH, DANIEL D (New
York)
FORMAN, AARON (New
York)

Smith and Maxwell (Philadelphia)
see SMITH, THOMAS (Phila-
delphia)
MAXWELL, JAMES (Phila-
delphia)

SMOOT, GEORGE C (Louis-
ville, Ky.)
1812: 25887 pb

SMOOT, GEORGE C (Shelby-
ville, Ky.)
1814: 31292
1815: 35158

SMOOT, GEORGE C (Vin-
cennes, Ind.)
1807: 12720, 12809

SMYLIE, JAMES (Louisville,
Ga.)
1801: 698 pb

SMYTH, JAMES H (Halifax,
N. C.)
1818: 44220 pb

SMYTH, JAMES H (Murfrees-
borough, N. C.)
1818: 45118 pb

SMYTH, WILLIAM CATHER-
WOOD (Harrisburg, Pa.)
1808: 15880?

SMYTH, WILLIAM CATHER-
WOOD (Lancaster, Pa.)
1807: 13336-13337
1808: 15871-15872, 15876

SMYTH, WILLIAM CATHER-
WOOD (Wilmington, Del.)
1801: 1198-1200

SNELLING, SAMUEL G (Bos-
ton)
1807: 12181, 13189, 13737,
14219 pb
1808: 14285, 14556, 14561,
14741, 14946, 15299 pb,
15375, 15472
1809: 18730 pb, 18909

1810: 19506, 21467 pb
1813: 30554

SNIDER, JOHN N (Lexington,
Va.)
1819: 48486 pb

SNIDER, JOHN N (Shepherdstown, Va.)
1816: 36730 pb, 36939, 36998,
38207
1817: 41388, 42030

SNODGRASS, WILLIAM (Natchez, Miss.)
1817: 41458 pb

SNOWDEN, JOHN M (Greens-
burg, Pa.)
1801: 50193 pb
1803: 5626, 6422

SNOWDEN, JOHN M (Pitts-
burgh, Pa.)
1812: 24851 pb
1813: 29633 pb

SNOWDEN, SAMUEL (Alex-
andria, Va.)
1801: 1596
1802: 3585
1803: 4715, 5526
1804: 6121 pb, 6128, 6572
1805: 8479, 8510
1806: 10971, 11808?
1808: 14323 pb, 14815
1810: 20287
1811: 22170, 22582, 23204,
23774
1812: 24535, 26513, 26555,
27151, 27314, 51254 pb
1813: 28427, 29595, 29614,
29888
1814: 31648, 32228, 32515
pb, 32756, 33618, 33695
1815: 36457? pb, 36522 pb
1816: 37163, 38278
1818: 43259

Society for Promoting Christian Knowledge, Piety, and
Charity (Boston)
1809: 18577 pb

1813: 28322 f, 29637-29638 f
1815: 35760-35761 f
1816: 38776 pb

Society for the Promotion of
Useful Arts (Albany, N.Y.)
1815: 34237 f

Society of the Protestant Episcopal Church for the Ad-
vancement of Christianity
in Pennsylvania (Philadelphia)
1815: 34785 pb, 35319 f

Society of United Christian
Friends (New York)
1812: 26587 f

SOMERVELL, JOHN (Peters-
burg, Va.)
1803: 3618, 3622 f, 3653 f,
4091 f, 4387 pb, 4528 f
1804: 5824 f, 5897 pb, 6068
pb, 50479 pb
1805: 9672 pb
1806: 11777 pb, 50741 pb
1807: 12246 f, 14137 pb
1808: 16313 f, 16646 pb
1809: 50972 pb
1811: 24346a f
1812: 27412 f

SOULE, JOSHUA (New York)
1816: 37337 f, 37831 pb,
37912 f, 38241 f, 38243 f,
38839 f
1817: 40151 f, 40185 f, 40358
f, 41318 f, 41419-41422 f,
42089 f, 42236 f, 42869 pb
1818: 43049 f, 43078 f, 43258
f, 43631 f, 43887 f, 44048
f, 44546 f, 44825 f, 44827
pb, 44829 pb, 44830-44831
f, 44883 pb, 45161 f, 45681-
45682 f, 45854 f, 46762-
46764 f, 46805 f
1819: 47629 f, 47845 f,
47993 f, 48357 f, 48683 f,
48686a f, 49394 f, 49582 f

Southern Patriot (Charleston,
S.C.)
1815: 33787, 35519, 36561

1816: 38029, 38643
1817: 40177 pb

SOUTHGATE, CHARLES (Rich-
mond, Va.)
1809: 17054, 19123 pb

SOUTHWICK, HENRY COLLINS
(Albany, N.Y.)
1810: 19498
1812: 24789, 25588 pb, 25590,
51185
1813: 27868 pb, 27908 pb,
28307-28308, 28320, 28949,
29328, 29335, 29341 pb,
29343, 29578 f, 29834 pb,
29836 pb, 30546, 30592-
30593
1814: 30646, 30840, 31615 f,
31996, 32279 pb, 32304-
32311, 32330, 32356
1815: 34027 pb, 34343 pb,
34737-34738 pb, 34753,
34867, 34896, 35027 pb,
35164, 35497 bf, 35641,
36571 pb, 37432
1816: 36684 pb, 37101, 37703,
37782 pb, 38433, 38653

SOUTHWICK, HENRY COLLINS
(Auburn, N.Y.)
1816: 36834, 37433
1817: 40094, 40169, 40334 pb,
41227, 42144

SOUTHWICK, HENRY COLLINS
(New York)
1802: 2019, 2787? pb, 2994,
3509, 50308
1803: 3665 pb, 6006
1804: 5818, 6004-6005, 6007,
6082, 6167, 6297, 7074
1805: 8302, 8318, 8444, 8471
pb, 8583, 9017 pb
1806: 10158, 10162, 10202,
10433, 10464, 10510, 10523,
10679, 10726, 11446
1807: 12374, 12600-12601,
12943, 13218, 13221, 14223-
14224
1808: 14342, 14609, 14623,
14795, 15047, 15094, 15279-
15281, 15847, 16613
1809: 17193, 17234, 17536-

17538, 17636, 17739, 18769, 18777, 18781, 18901, 19153, 19243, 50924
1810: 19374 pb, 20252, 20384 pb, 20440, 20884, 21290, 21496 pb, 21883
1811: 22152, 22791, 23275, 23286 pb, 23446 pb, 23540 pb, 23616, 23933, 51051
1818: 45091 pb, 51783
1819: 48025-48026, 48027 pb, 48155, 48770, 49407, 49974 pb

SOUTHWICK, SOLOMON (Albany, N.Y.)
1808: 15753
1809: 18230 f, 18235-18236, 18238-18239
1810: 19953, 20893-20896
1811: 23541, 23547-23549, 23551
1812: 26271-26272, 26279 pb, 26281 pb, 26283, 26285, 26897 pb
1813: 29328 f, 29337-29338 pb, 29340 pb
1814: 32304-32309 f, 32330 f
1816: 36698, 36917, 36959 pb, 37432, 38284

Southwick and Hardcastle (New York)
see SOUTHWICK, HENRY COLLINS (New York)
HARDCASTLE, JOHN (New York)

SOWER, BROOK WATSON (Baltimore)
1810: 19413, 19523, 19541, 20075
1811: 22357-22358, 22823, 22829, 22917, 23161-23163, 23833
1812: 24534, 24820, 24850, 25267, 25480 pb, 25579 bf, 26107, 26386

SOWER, CHARLES (Frederick, Md.)
1816: 39006 pb

SOWER, CHARLES (Uniontown, Md.)
1813: 28431 pb
1815: 36025
1816: 37223

SOWER, DAVID (Norristown, Pa.)
1801: 1364
1807: 12515
1818: 43546 pb, 44627, 45355

SOWER, SAMUEL (Baltimore)
1801: 490, 492, 523, 539, 702, 987
1802: 1880 pb, 1918 bf, 2280 pb, 2454, 2734 pb, 3008 pb, 3009, 3145, 3574
1803: 3716, 3792, 4265, 4414, 4471, 4582 pb, 4711 pb, 4934, 5597
1804: 5767 pb, 6859
1805: 8965
1806: 10948 pb
1807: 13175

Sower and Cole (Baltimore)
see SOWER, SAMUEL (Baltimore)
COLE, SAMUEL (Baltimore)

SPARHAWK, JOHN (Philadelphia)
1801: 1108 pb

SPAULDING, GEORGE (New Haven, Conn.)
1818: 43066 pb
1819: 47602 pb, 47796 f, 48845, 49286 f, 49970 f

SPEAR, CHARLES (Boston)
1807: 12860, 13183

SPEAR, CHARLES (Charlestown, Mass.)
1811: 24509 f

SPEAR, CHARLES (Chester, Vt.)
1807: 12692 pb
1808: 15489-15490

SPEAR, CHARLES (Hanover,
N. H.)
1808: 15940
1809: 17725 pb, 18373, 19213
1810: 19647, 19916 pb, 20077,
20990, 21250 pb, 22032?
1811: 22618, 22795
1812: 24541 pb, 25899
1813: 28277, 29041 pb, 29559,
30578 pb
1814: 31328, 31371, 32012
1815: 34262, 34441, 34529,
34569, 34630, 34870, 35934
1816: 36709, 37391
1817: 40661
1818: 44956, 45268, 46861,
51762
1819: 48183, 48316

SPEAR, CHARLES (Newbury,
Vt.)
1819: 48780

SPEAR, CHARLES (Windsor,
Vt.)
1808: 14635, 15048, 15346,
15676 pb, 15728 pb, 16119
pb

SPEAR, HENRY (Boston)
1812: 25111, 25843 pb, 26349
1813: 27984, 29613, 29794
1814: 30855, 32402-32403

SPEAR, HENRY (Charlestown,
Mass.)
1811: 22983, 23900, 24509 bf
1812: 25543, 25712, 26713

SPEAR, HENRY (Hanover,
N. H.)
1810: 20990

SPEAR, JOHN (Natchez, Miss.)
1813: 28983

SPEAR, JOHN (Pittsburgh,
Pa.)
1804: 6094
1808: 14381, 14796
1809: 17203, 50930
1810: 19652 pb, 19887 pb,
19889-19890 pb, 19902 pb,

51033 pb
1811: 22409a pb, 22636 pb,
22638-22639 pb, 22734,
22998, 23880 pb, 51077 pb
1812: 25182 pb, 25263, 25540
pb, 25864 pb, 25949 pb,
26172 pb, 27421 pb, 51183
pb, 51188 f
1813: 28232, 28244 pb, 28313,
28349 pb, 28554, 28647,
28945, 28947 pb, 29253 pb,
29548, 30605 pb, 51291-
51292 pb
1814: 30710, 30979 pb, 31260
f, 31263 pb, 31923 f, 33629-
33630, 51376 pb, 51414 pb,
51433 f
1815: 34470 pb, 34472 pb,
35347 f, 36421 f, 36472 f
1816: 36970 f, 37355-37356 f,
38039 f, 38067 f, 39137 pb,
51567 f, 51605 f, 51607 pb
1817: 40589-40590 f, 40591-
40592 pb, 42807 pb, 42818 f,
51657 pb
1818: 43309 pb, 43766-43768
pb, 43915 pb, 43917 pb,
43977, 44572 pb, 46617 pb
1819: 47746-47748 pb, 48782
pb, 51875 pb, 51917 pb

SPEAR, JOSEPH C (Concord,
N. H.)
1818: 44696
1819: 47925

SPEAR, OLIVER (Boston)
1817: 42104 pb

SPEAR, WILLIAM S (Boston)
1812: 25111, 25843 pb, 26349
1813: 27984, 29613, 29794
1814: 30855, 32402-32403
1818: 44695 pb
1819: 50090

SPEAR, WILLIAM S (Charlestown, Mass.)
1811: 22983, 23900, 24509 bf
1812: 25543, 25712, 26713

SPEAR, WILLIAM S (Concord,
N. H.)
1815: 35693

SPEAR, WILLIAM S (Hanover, N.H.)
1808: 15940
1809: 17725 pb, 18373, 19213
1810: 19647, 19916 pb, 20077, 20990, 21250 pb

SPEAR, WILLIAM S (Windsor, Vt.)
1808: 15676 pb, 16119 pb

SPEER, JAMES H (Cincinnati, O.)
1818: 43943 f
1819: 47946 f, 48684

SPENCE, W (Baltimore)
1814: 31128 pb

SPENCER, FREDERICK (Middletown, Conn.)
1808: 15717 pb
1814: 32242 pb
1817: 41574 pb

SPENCER, O M (Cincinnati, O.)
1812: 24993 f

SPENCER, THOMAS (Middletown, Conn.)
1819: 45671 f

Spirit of 'Seventy-Six' (Washington, D.C.)
1810: 20012

SPOONER, ALDEN (Brooklyn, N.Y.)
1811: 24030
1812: 24930, 26523, 26718
1813: 28182, 28283, 28598, 28713, 29122, 30604
1814: 31681
1815: 34876
1816: 36936, 37093, 37191 pb, 38090 pb
1817: 41285, 41798, 42088 pb
1818: 44216, 45228

SPOONER, ALDEN (New London, Conn.)
1807: 12041

SPOONER, ALDEN (New York)
1814: 32529
1815: 34386, 35610, 35802-35803
1817: 40422, 40974

SPOONER, ALDEN (Sag Harbor, N.Y.)
1804: 7322 pb
1805: 8045, 8535
1806: 9945-9946, 10246, 10798, 11315, 11417, 11753
1807: 12084, 12096, 12596, 13431, 50797 pb
1808: 14268, 14606, 15849, 16764
1809: 18445, 18538, 18664
1810: 19851, 19955, 20306, 20801
1811: 23804 pb

SPOONER, ALDEN (Windsor, Vt.)
1801: 35, 788, 1578, 1657
1802: 3460
1803: 3964 pb, 4279, 4570, 5011, 5501
1804: 7658-7660, 7784
1805: 9294, 9382, 9655
1806: 10435, 10544, 11313, 11373, 11761
1807: 11937-11938, 12393 pb, 12611, 12729, 12982-12983, 13200 pb, 13308
1808: 14674, 15069, 16173
1809: 18258, 19105-19106 pb
1810: 19492?, 19493, 21049
1812: 24990, 25907
1813: 28579-28580
1814: 32537, 33534
1815: 34197 pb, 34200, 35906, 36435
1816: 37552
1817: 40122
1818: 43574, 44383, 44514, 44621

SPOONER, WYMAN (Windsor, Vt.)
1817: 40122
1818: 43219?, 43574, 44383, 44514, 44621
1819: 47144, 47853, 50142?

SPOTSWOOD, WILLIAM (Philadelphia)
1802: 3134-3138 pb, 3539?
pb
1803: 4914
1805: 9173 pb

SPOTTVOGEL, THADDAUS
(Philadelphia)
1816: 37264? pb

SPRAGUE, HOSEA (Boston)
1802: 1768, 2255 pb, 2302,
2419, 2446, 2461, 2756,
2916
1803: 3642, 4264, 5012, 5019,
5048
1804: 6042, 6418-6419, 6476
pb, 6481, 6507, 6542, 6674,
7391, 7705
1805: 8058, 8558-8560, 8567
pb, 9343 pb, 9779
1806: 9957, 10497, 11812,
11859 pb, 11907
1807: 12116, 12164, 12667,
12694, 14209 pb

SPRINGER, JAMES (New
London, Conn.)
1801: 234, 471 sb
1802: 1975

SPRINGER, JAMES (Norwich,
Conn.)
1812: 26919

Spy (Worcester, Mass.)
see Massachusetts Spy (Worcester, Mass.)

STACKHOUSE, JAMES (Phila-
delphia)
1813: 29251, 30500
1814: 31104, 31147, 31852
pb, 51416 pb
1815: 34350, 34763, 34982,
35632 pb

STACY, --- (Philadelphia)
1817: ?40273 pb, 40313 pb

STAMBAUGH, S C (Harris-
burg, Pa.)
1818: 45252

STAMBAUGH, SAMUEL C
(Lancaster, Pa.)
1819: 48010 pb

Standard (Middlebury, Vt.)
see National Standard (Middlebury, Vt.)

STANFORD, THOMAS NAYLOR
(New York)
1814: 32843-32844 f

STANLEY, JOHN GRAY (Lenox,
Mass.)
1815: 35823 f

STANNARD, EDWARD CARTER
(Richmond, Va.)
1808: 16239 pb
1809: 18727 pb

STANNARD, EDWARD CARTER
(Washington, D. C.)
1810: 19483, 20555

STANSBURY, ABRAHAM OGIER
(New York)
1801: 432 f
1802: 1920 f, 1936 f, 1978 f,
2162 f, 3132 pb
1803: 3652 bf, 3986 pb, 4218
pb, 4698 f, 4718 pb, 50368
f
1804: 5850 f, 6306 pb, 7258
pb

STANSBURY, ARTHUR JOSEPH
(New York)
1802: 1978 f
1803: 4218 pb, 4718 pb, 5088,
50368 f

STANSBURY, SAMUEL (New
York)
1804: 5996 pb, 6297 pb, 6759
pb, 7248 pb
1805: 8440 pb, 8710 pb, 8880-
8881 f, 50589 pb
1806: 10158 f, 11011 pb
1807: 13111 pb, 14146 pb

Star (Raleigh, N. C.)
1807: 13525 pb

1809:   18541, 18543, 19144
1811:   22280
1812:   25403
1814:   31011, 31689

STARCK, J P (Hanover, Pa.)
1805:   8582 pb
1808:   14464, 14509, 16265
1810:   21187
1814:   32882

STARNES, DANIEL (Augusta,
   Ga.)
1808:   15618 pb

STARR, CHARLES (Hartford,
   Conn.)
1812:   25528 f
1813:   29640 f
1814:   31022 f, 32547 f
1815:   34381, 34508, 34800?,
   34872 pb, 34893?, 34912-
   34914, 35336?, 35680 f,
   51502
1818:   45552-45553, 45555-
   45557

STARR, CHARLES (New York)
1816:   37379
1818:   43946 pb, 46677, 46901
1819:   50185

STARR, HENRY (Lenox,
   Mass.)
1808:   14780, 15246

STARR, JAMES FOSDICK
   (Hartford, Conn.)
1815:   34381, 34508, 34800?,
   34893?, 34912-34914,
   35336?, 51502

State Gazette (Columbia, S.C.)
1819:   48651, 51913

State Press (Boston)
1812:   26028

Statesman (New York)
1812:   25257

Staunton Political Censor
   (Staunton, Va.)
1809:   16806

STEBBINS, CHESTER (Boston)
1805:   8904
1806:   10131, 10133, 10504,
   10612, 10833, 10911 pb,
   11796
1807:   12107 pb, 12184, 12668,
   12947, 13108 pb, 13295,
   13644, 13714
1808:   14978, 15289, 15386-
   15387, 15403, 15548, 15553-
   15555, 15925-15926, 15996,
   16031 pb, 16042, 16060,
   16267-16268, 16704, 16779
1809:   16962 pb, 16996-16997,
   17660-17661, 18402
1810:   19294, 19512, 21302
   pb, 21304, 21482, 22054 pb
1811:   22351, 22360, 23184,
   23678, 23792, 24378-24379,
   24479
1812:   24793-24794, 24821,
   25048-25049, 25836, 25902,
   25998, 26693 pb, 26781
1813:   28677, 28964, 28991,
   29085, 29281 pb, 29668,
   29726 pb, 29866, 30462
1814:   30915, 31051, 31054,
   31178, 31491, 31560, 31595
   pb, 31762, 33505, 33570,
   33664
1815:   34000 pb, 34795 pb,
   34853, 35007, 35165 pb
1816:   38231, 38598, 39032-
   39033
1817:   40949, 40986, 40988,
   41958, 42788

STEBBINS, CHESTER (Charlestown, Mass.)
1804:   6216, 7317
1805:   8905 pb

STEBBINS, CHESTER (New-
   buryport, Mass.)
1806:   11137 pb

STEBBINS, FRANCIS (Hudson,
   N.Y.)
1809:   18266 pb
1811:   23995
1814:   33576

STEBBINS, FRANCIS (Savan-
   nah, Ga.)

1802:   2014, 2308, 3540
1803:   3726

STECK, JACOB S (Greens-
burg, Pa.)
1819:   51879 pb

STEDMAN, EBENEZER
(Exeter, N. H.)
1814:   32536 f

STEDMAN, EBENEZER
(Newburyport, Mass.)
1804:   7300 f, 7749 pb
1805:   8286 f

STEELE, DANIEL (Albany,
N. Y.)
1802:   2544 pb
1805:   8794
1806:   10366 f, 10741
1807:   12933 pb, 13284 pb
1808:   15437
1809:   17921? pb
1810:   20575
1811:   23233?
1812:   24980 f, 25869 pb,
51221 f
1813:   28960?
1814:   31077 f, 31941? f
1815:   35118, 51515? f,
51516? pb
1816:   51603 bsb
1817:   40224 f, 41275 pb
1818:   51794 f
1819:   49503 f

STEELE, HEZIKIAH (Hudson,
N. Y.)
1808:   16109 f
1809:   17129 pb, 17142 f,
18685 pb, 18687 f
1810:   21415 pb
1812:   25622 pb

STEELE, LEMUEL (Hudson,
N. Y.)
1809:   17129 pb, 18685 pb
1810:   21415 pb
1812:   25622 pb

STEELE, OLIVER (Danbury,
Conn.)
1804:   6883 pb

STEELE, OLIVER (Hartford,
Conn.)
1804:   6067 pb, 7751

STEELE, OLIVER (New Haven,
Conn.)
1803:   4297
1804:   6110, 7369, 7401 pb
1806:   9950, 10132, 10241,
10542, 10622, 10722, 10737?,
10753, 11083, 11243 pb,
11834, 11904
1807:   12098 pb, 14191-14192,
14194
1808:   14469 pb, 14566, 15118,
15143, 15231, 15234, 15422
pb, 15730, 15906, 15929,
16102, 16540, 16770-16772
1809:   16980 pb, 17071 pb,
17073, 17086, 17123, 17276,
17340, 17415, 17417 pb,
17723, 17849
1810:   19340, 19495 pb, 19844,
19959, 20298, 20720 pb,
20780, 21913, 50978 pb
1811:   22322 pb, 22438a, 22603,
22667, 22976, 23157 pb,
23160 pb, 23990, 24507-
24508, 51131 pb
1812:   24547, 24786 pb,
24845 pb, 25147, 25149,
25207 pb, 25763, 27502 bf,
27542, 51223 pb, 51260
1813:   27865 pb, 28023, 28639,
30590, 51328, 51332, 51349
1814:   30838 pb, 31152, 31302,
31600, 31650, 31817, 32570,
32654, 32846 pb, 33711,
33744 pb, 33747
1815:   34025 pb, 34542, 34787,
34873, 35751, 36000, 36659,
51485
1816:   37016, 37121, 37217,
37405, 37436, 37478, 37851,
37939 pb, 38765, 38958,
39013 pb
1817:   39931, 40166 pb, 40626
pb, 41900c, 41931, 42200
pb, 42219 pb
1818:   46894

STEELE, OLIVER (Savannah,
Ga.)
1818:   45639 pb

STEPHENS, STEPHEN (New
York)
1802: 2039 f, 2103 f
1813: 30197 f

STEPHENS, THOMAS B
(Charleston, S.C.)
1818: 43694, 45826 pb
1819: 47136, 48475, 51890?

STERNE, --- (Boston)
1818: 45760 pb

STERRETT, JAMES (New Or-
leans, La.)
1818: 44619 pb

STERRY, CONSIDER (Norwich,
Conn.)
1806: 10507, 11410, 11550,
11799

STERRY, ERASTUS (Bristol,
R.I.)
1808: 14272, 15316

STERRY, JOHN (Norwich,
Conn.)
1801: 110-111, 209 pb
1802: 1813-1814, 1956
1803: 3721, 3724, 3733,
5069 pb, 5103 pb
1804: 5771-5772, 6707, 7392
pb
1805: 7919-7920, 8339, 8605
pb, 8894 pb

STEVENS, HENRY (Schenec-
tady, N.Y.)
1814: 31113, 31581, 32378
1815: 34626, 34694, 35170,
35349, 35858, 36142-36145
1816: 39139 pb, 51603 sb
1818: 45410 f
1819: 49507 f

STEVENS, ISAAC (Schenec-
tady, N.Y.)
1817: 42965 f

STEVENS, JOHN ABBOTT
(Canandaigua, N.Y.)
1806: 10470 pb

1807: 12055
1808: 14429
1810: 20956 pb
1815: 34278
1816: 38527
1818: 43200

STEVENS, STEPHEN C (Vevay,
Ind.)
1819: 48330 pb

STEVENSON, JAMES (Salem,
N.Y.)
1814: 30972 f, 31143 f, 31173
pb, 31986 f, 32585
1815: 35314, 35729, 35730-
35731 pb
1816: 38741-38742
1817: 41464, 41467-41468,
41886
1818: 45418, 45882
1819: 47583 pb, 50048

STEVENSON, JOHN L (Sche-
nectady, N.Y.)
1802: 3537 pb
1805: 9508
1806: 11047

STEWARD, HENRY (Owego,
N.Y.)
1803: 3662 pb

STEWART, ANDREW (Hamil-
ton, O.)
1814: 31849 pb, 32391

STEWART, J B (Philadelphia)
1808: 14401

STEWART, JAMES HOOD (Lex-
ington, Ky.)
1801: 112 pb, 367
1802: 1955 pb

STEWART, JAMES HOOD
(Paris, Ky.)
1805: 9425 pb

STEWART, JOHN AINSWORTH
(Alexandria, Va.)
1801: 33, 1589, 1643, 1690
1802: 1860, 2348, 2649, 3026

1803: 4328, 4622, 4690,
5536 pb, 5572, 50397 f
1804: 5688 pb, 6281? f, 6871,
7115 pb, 7390
1805: 8296, 8529, 8538 f,
9490 pb, 9671 pb, 9717,
50532, 50555 pb
1806: 9913, 10387 pb, 10491,
10857, 11776, 50635 pb,
50739 pb, 50746 pb
1807: 14141, 14235, 50775 pb,
50817 pb
1808: 14322 pb, 14445, 15679,
15683 pb, 16663 pb, 50895
pb
1809: 17539, 18154, 18404
1810: 19463, 20108, 20143,
21921, 21967, 51003 pb
1811: 22169, 22294, 22923,
51046 pb, 51147 pb
1812: 25028, 25533, 26154,
27583
1813: 28049, 29711, 30550
1814: 32152 pb, 32459 pb,
33555? pb
1815: 33820, 35441, 51543 pb
1816: 37718 f, 51637 pb
1817: 42798 f
1818: 44176 f, 46660 pb
1819: 49618 pb

STEWART, MORDECAI (Balti-
more)
1807: 13532 f
1819: 48191 f

STEWART, PETER (Philadel-
phia)
1801: 481 pb, 1099 pb, 1134
pb, 1271
1802: 2122 pb, 2214 pb, 2879
pb
1803: 4187 pb, 4851 pb,
4985 pb
1804: 7023 pb, 7145 pb, 50431,
50432 pb, 50465
1805: 8947 pb, 9131 pb,
50535 pb
1806: 10396 pb, 11133 pb,
11414
1807: 12249 pb, 13353 pb,
50773 pb
1808: 14998 pb, 15892 pb

1809: 17490, 18355 pb
1811: 22157 pb

STEWART, ROBERT (Monmouth
County, N. J.)
1804: 7699 pb
1805: 50617 pb
1809: 18688 pb
1810: 21423 pb
1812: 51252 pb

STEWART, ROBERT (New
Brunswick, N. J.)
1804: 50482 f
1811: 23985 pb
1812: 26806 pb
1813: 29879 f
1814: 32870 pb
1815: 34401 pb

STEWART, ROBERT (Philadelphia)
1805: 9689 pb
1806: 11414 f
1807: 13654 pb
1808: 16255 pb
1811: 23986 pb
1813: 51337 pb
1814: 32871 f

STEWART, ROBERT (Trenton,
N. J.)
1810: 21422 pb
1812: 26807 pb, 51252 pb
1813: 29880 pb
1814: 32872 f

STICKNEY, JEREMIAH (New-
buryport, Mass.)
1801: 69, 283 pb, 285 pb,
1049?, 1295, 1355, 1360
1802: 3048, 3092, 3116

STILES, THOMAS T (Philadelphia)
1804: 5930 pb, 6131, 6379
1805: 7975, 8078 pb, 8102 pb,
8105 pb, 8110, 8198, 8205,
8249, 8959, 9333 pb, 9383
1806: 9821 pb, 10150, 10228,
10758, 10763, 11806-11807,
11894
1807: 12026, 12221, 12572,

12760 pb, 12895
1808: 14783, 16196 pb
1809: 16862 pb, 17797, 17799,
18627
1810: 19378, 20484, 20565-
20566, 20762, 21985, 51031
1811: 22155, 23144, 23974
1812: 25262, 25735, 25861,
25901, 26147, 26446, 26746
1813: 28238, 28699, 28723,
28942-28943, 29026, 29372,
29764, 30457, 30466
1814: 32441
1816: 38605

STILLMAN, ISAIAH (Buffalo,
N. Y.)
1815: 35495 pb

STINE, JACOB R (Carlisle,
Pa.)
1819: 47518 pb

STITH, CINCINNATUS (Petersburg, Va.)
1807: 14140 pb

STOCKER, JOSEPH (Reading,
Pa.)
1819: 47209 f

STOCKHOLM, DERICK B
(Poughkeepsie, N. Y.)
1814: 30621, 31278
1815: 35357 pb, 35482, 35686
1816: 37378, 37559 f

STOCKWELL, HENRY (Ben-
nington, Vt.)
1807: 14184

STOCKWELL, HENRY (Troy,
N. Y.)
1805: 8197, 8427 pb, 9474,
50533
1806: 10077, 10078 pb,
10960 pb, 11094
1807: 12788 pb, 12960 pb,
14226 pb
1808: 14622 pb, 15274 pb,
15277 pb, 16136 pb, 16193
pb, 16348 pb
1812: 27456 pb
1819: 51870 f

STOCKWELL, WILLIAM (Ben-
nington, Vt.)
1801: 83, 1160 pb, 1665
1802: 1782, 2407 pb, 2581,
2809, 3142, 3271 pb, 3598

STOCKWELL, WILLIAM (Cam-
bridge, N. Y.)
1804: 6201? pb, 6260?,
6570?, 7336
1805: 8197 f, 50515

STOCKWELL, WILLIAM (Man-
chester, Vt.)
1803: 3777 pb, 50382 pb

STODDARD, ASHBEL (Hudson,
N. Y.)
1801: 659 pb, 678 pb, 1000,
1361 pb
1802: 2725 pb, 3601, 50326
pb
1803: 4890, 5003, 5111 pb,
50345 pb
1804: 5696 pb, 5929, 6469,
7211, 7217, 7241, 7311 pb,
50404 pb, 50412 pb
1805: 7860 pb, 8103 pb, 8253,
8982, 9023, 9292, 9313,
9336 pb, 9337, 9431 pb
1806: 10361, 10608 pb, 10636,
10750?, 11254, 11339, 11415
pb, 11458 pb, 11792
1807: 12761 pb, 13656 pb
1808: 16257 pb
1809: 16829, 17296, 18113,
18201, 18689 pb, 18690
1810: 19663, 21426
1811: 23987 pb
1812: 26498, 26810-26811 pb,
27573, 51175 pb, 51184 pb,
51253 pb
1813: 27900 pb, 28118, 29150,
29551, 29882 pb, 30454
1814: 30900, 31200 pb, 31345
pb, 31781, 32778, 32886 pb,
51441 pb
1815: 35823, 36023 pb
1816: 37676, 38695, 39017
pb, 39126, 51632 pb
1817: 41256 pb, 41963, 42223
pb, 42922, 51715 pb
1818: 43869, 44985, 45803
pb, 46699, 51766 pb

1819: 47036, 47116, 47731,
   47956 pb, 49105, 49513

STOKES, BENJAMIN M (Alex-
   andria, La.)
1810: 20594 pb

STOKES, BENJAMIN M
   (Natchez, Miss.)
1801: 567

STONE, HENRY D (Milledge-
   ville, Ga.)
1815: 34589 f

STONE, JOSIAH (Windsor, Vt.)
1816: 37966 f

STONE, WILLIAM LEETE
   (Hartford, Conn.)
1818: 44275
1819: 47180, 47480, 48036,
   48061, 48094, 48176

STONE, WILLIAM LEETE
   (Herkimer, N. Y.)
1814: 30724

STONE, WILLIAM LEETE
   (Hudson, N. Y.)
1815: 34966
1816: 36910-36911, 37390,
   38501, 38758, 38866, 38894
1817: 40271
1818: 45630 pb
1819: 40911 pb

STORER, E GILMAN (Arling-
   ton, Vt.)
1816: 36734 pb
1817: 40542
1818: 44812

STORER, E GILMAN (Sandy
   Hill, N. Y.)
1818: 45870 pb
1819: 50045

STOUT, ELIHU (Vincennes,
   Ind.)
1804: 6536-6537, 6539 pb,
   6802
1805: 8676 pb, 8677?

1806: 10614
1807: 12720, 12809, 14207
   pb
1808: 15300
1810: 20433
1811: 23091
1813: 28808
1815: 33931
1816: 37922, 39052
1817: 41134
1818: ?44476 pb, 44643? pb

STOVER, JACOB (Lebanon,
   Pa.)
1808: 15429 pb
1811: 23136, 23190, 23216,
   23219
1814: 30692 pb
1815: 35607
1818: 45259 pb
1819: 49059-49060

STOW, MANASSAH (Worcester,
   Mass.)
1808: 14392, 14536, 14967,
   15585
1809: 16796

STRACHAN, DAVID R (Ogdensburgh, N. Y.)
1815: 35837 pb

STRAIN, JOHN (Dayton, O.)
1813: 29407 pb

STRANGE, TUBAL EARLY
   (Jackson, Mo.)
1819: 48718 pb

STRANGE, TUBAL EARLY
   (Lynchburg, Va.)
1818: 43229

STREET, JOSEPH MONTFORT
   (Frankfort, Ky.)
1806: 10670, 11858 pb
1807: 12397
1808: 15496

STRONG, SILAS G (Utica,
   N. Y.)
1816: 37896 f

STRONG, TIMOTHY CLAPP
(Middlebury, Vt.)
1811: 22154, 22595, 22877,
23383-23385, 23749, 24007,
24441
1812: 24546, 24804, 24951,
25134, 25141, 25481, 25617,
25682, 25773, 25821, 25868,
26499, 26666 pb, 27399,
27403, 27446, 27506
1813: 27947, 28209, 28510,
30414, 30416
1814: 30815, 30913, 31889,
31978, 32123-32125, 32764,
33540, 33543 pb, 33736
1815: 34086, 34122, 35013,
35110, 35152, 35568, 36433,
36436, 36439, 36621
1816: 36716, 37231 pb, 37234
pb, 37776, 39667, 39862
1817: 41431 pb, 41887

STRONG, TIMOTHY CLAPP
(Ogdensburgh, N.Y.)
1810: 20944 pb

STRONG, TIMOTHY CLAPP
(Palmyra, N.Y.)
1817: 41725 pb

STROWHUVER, GEORGE
(Cincinnati, O.)
1812: 51231 f
1813: 29403 f

STRYKER, JOHN (New York)
1801: 327, 456, 610 pb,
1329, 1409

STULL, OTHO H W (Hagers-
town, Md.)
1814: 32948 pb

STURTEVANT, CORNELIUS
(Stockbridge, Mass.)
1807: 12377 pb, 12991,
13412 pb
1808: 14806

STURTEVANT, ISAAC (Wor-
cester, Mass.)
1805: 7900
1806: 9874, 9887, 10313,

10561, 10921, 11778
1807: 12016, 12038, 12460,
12524, 12936, 14248-14249
1808: 14629, 14919, 14921,
14923-14925, 15986 pb
1809: 16881, 17429, 17465,
18599
1810: 20526, 21483, 22050
1811: 22217, 22237-22238,
22836, 23452, 23954, 24483
1812: 24657-24659, 24887-
24888, 25361, 25407, 25671,
25727, 26831, 26867, 27593
pb
1813: 27942, 28050, 28824,
29263, 29962, 30459, 30529
1814: 31663, 32354, 32916,
33020

SUBLETT, ABNER C (Mur-
freesborough, Tenn.)
1814: 31249 pb
1819: 49575-49576

SUBLETT, ABNER C (Nash-
ville, Tenn.)
1819: 49571-49573 f

SUBLETT, GEORGE A (Mur-
freesborough, Tenn.)
1814: 31249 pb
1819: 49575-49576

SUBLETT, GEORGE A (Nash-
ville, Tenn.)
1819: 49571-49573 f

Sun (Baltimore)
1812: 25905

Sunday and Adult School Union
(Philadelphia)
1810: 20714? pb
1818: 44802-44803 f
1819: 48491 f, 49098 f, 49992
pb, 51872 f

Supporter (Chillicothe, O.)
1809: 18280
1810: 20947
1811: 23590
1813: 29396-29397
1814: 30926

1815: 35058, 35526-35527
1817: 41686-41687

SUTTON, --- (Northampton,
Mass.)
1802: 3542

SWAIN, E C (Baltimore)
1809: 17879, 18170-18172

SWAINE, JOHN (Ballston Spa,
N. Y.)
1804: 7232 pb

SWAINE, JOHN (New York)
1801: 141? pb
1803: 3760 pb, 4018, 4121,
4132
1804: 6633, 7230
1805: 8926
1806: 10026 pb, 10613 pb,
11343

SWAN, TIMOTHY (Boston)
1816: 39695 f
1817: 42167 pb
1819: 47157-47158 pb, 50161
pb

SWAN, TIMOTHY (Suffield,
Conn.)
1801: 50257?

SWEENY, JOHN (Philadelphia)
1803: 4241?
1805: 8474?
1808: 15061
1809: 17552-17558, 18090
1810: 21279
1811: 22368, 22434a, 22492,
22594, 23229, 24428

SWEITZER, HENRY (Philadelphia)
see SCHWEITZER, HEINRICH

SWENEY, GEORGE (Danville,
Pa.)
1813: 28187 pb

SWENEY, GEORGE (Northum-
berland, Pa.)
1813: 28188 pb

SWIFT, SAMUEL (Middlebury,
Vt.)
1810: 19928 f, 21449 f
1811: 22877 f, 22978 pb, 23749
f, 24007 f, 24344 pb
1812: 24951 f, 25481 f, 25617
f, 25868 f, 26165 f, 27399 f,
27400-27401 pb, 27403 f
1813: 27947 f, 30414 f, 30416
f
1814: 31978 f, 33540 f, 33543
pb
1815: 34122 f
1816: 36716 f, 39667 f

SWORDS, JAMES (New York)
For all entries see SWORDS,
THOMAS (New York) below

SWORDS, THOMAS (New York)
1801: 56, 79-80, 178, 372 f,
450, 669, 673, 693, 799 pb,
885, 919, 940, 942, 948,
1182, 1197, 1203, 1619,
1653, 1666, 50233 pb
1802: 1853, 1891 pb, 1920,
1949, 2039 f, 2103 f, 2403,
2441, 2570, 2572, 2639 pb,
2660, 2942, 2949 pb, 2950-
2951, 2953 pb, 2958-2959,
3005 pb, 3097, 3457 pb,
3484, 3504 pb, 3602
1803: 3694, 3820 pb, 3975,
4045 sb, 4046, 4081, 4089,
4216, 4356 pb, 4371, 4574,
4580, 4626 pb, 4654, 4674,
4814, 4926-4927, 4936, 5024,
5094-5095, 5108, 5498 f
1804: 5733, 5805 f, 5806,
5866 pb, 6123 pb, 6272 pb,
6404 f, 6484 pb, 6520, 6663,
6811, 6973, 7130-7131, 7134,
7136 pb, 7389, 7690, 7756,
7762
1805: 7859, 8061 pb, 8162,
8203, 8642 f, 8740, 8747 pb,
8903, 9018, 9189, 9204 pb,
9207-9208, 9216
1806: 9862 pb, 10149, 10210
f, 10467 pb, 10591, 10685-
10687, 10735, 10871, 10892,
10912, 11220 pb, 11225,
11403, 11404 pb

SYKES, WILLIAM (Philadel-
    phia)

Synod of Pittsburgh (Washing-
    ton, Pa.)

T

TALLCOTT, JOSIAH (Hancock,
    Mass.)

Tammany Society (New York)

TANNATT, ABRAHAM GAL-
    LISON (Nantucket, Mass.)

TANNER, BENJAMIN (Phila-
delphia)
1805: 8014 pb, 9209 pb

TAPPAN, CHARLES (Ports-
mouth, N. H.)
1806: 10708 f
1807: 12005 f
1808: 15405 f, 15416 pb,
16199 pb
1809: 18420 f
1810: 20860 pb, 21328 pb
1811: ?22180 pb, 23518 f

TAPPAN, JOHN (Kingston,
N. Y.)
1815: 34943, 36140 pb
1816: 39049 pb
1818: 45061 pb
1819: 47957 f, 49311

TAPSICO, JACOB (Philadelphia)
1817: 39949 f

TAYLOR, --- (Glasgow, Ky.)
1814: 32444 pb

TAYLOR, ABRAHAM (Johns-
town, N. Y.)
1809: 18163 pb

TAYLOR, ABRAHAM (Water-
town, N. Y.)
1809: 17735 pb

TAYLOR, AMOS (Troy, N. Y.)
1806: 11094 f

TAYLOR, DANIEL (Worcester,
Mass.)
1801: 147 f

TAYLOR, JOHNSON (Philadelphia)
1815: 34901 f

TAYLOR, R D (New York)
1802: 2838 pb
1803: 4808 pb

Telegraphe (Baltimore)
1804: 7407?

Telegraphe (New Orleans, La.)
1804: 5962, 6261, 7539
1805: 7970
1808: 14897, 15990

Telescope (Columbia, S. C.)
1816: 38204
1817: 40030, 40111
1818: 44767, 45770
1819: 47792, 49462

Telescope (Leominster, Mass.)
1801: 187

TEMPLE, PHILIP (Fredericksburg, Va.)
1801: 126, 518 pb

Temple of Reason (Philadelphia)
1804: 6982

TEN EYCK, PHILIP (New
York)
1801: 169 f

TENNERY, GEORGE F (Alex-
andria, La.)
1818: 44620 pb

TENNERY, JOSEPH (Athens,
N. Y.)
1805: 8920 pb

TENNERY, JOSEPH (Cam-
bridge, N. Y.)
1803: 3924 pb
1804: 6201? pb, 6260?, 6570?,
7336
1805: 50515

TENNY, JOSEPH (Sangerfield,
N. Y.)
1814: 30843, 31401, 31797,
32456, 51400
1815: 34345 pb, 35832
1816: 37250 pb, 37438, 39121
1819: 48241

TERHUNE, JOHN (New Bruns-
wick, N. J.)
1814: 32617 pb
1816: 38767 f
1819: 47441 pb

TERRELL, SAMUEL (Natchez, Miss.)
1804: 6800 pb
1805: 8912-8913
1806: 10882-10884, 10886
1807: 13100-13102, 13720

TERRELL, TIMOTHY (Natchez, Miss.)
1804: 6800 pb
1805: 8912-8913
1806: 10882-10883

TERRIL, ISRAEL (New Haven, Conn.)
1806: 50734 engr and bsb

TERRY, EZEKIEL (Palmer, Mass.)
1805: 9400 f
1806: 10035? pb
1808: 14427
1809: 16920, 18551?
1810: 19580, 19930?, 20111?, 20541, 20632?, 20716?, 21039, 21474-21475?, 21518
1811: 22539
1812: 24717, 26863
1813: 27798?, 28501?, 29935
1814: 30615
1815: 36070
1816: 37904 pb, 38239
1817: 41734, 41745
1819: 47106

TERRY, EZEKIEL (Wilbraham, Mass.)
1808: 15586, 15983

TESSON, PIERRE (Philadelphia)
1803: 4092, 4319, 4454, 4629, 5090, 5140, 5596
1804: 6396

THACKARA, JAMES (Philadelphia)
1801: 1156 f
1802: 2338 pb
1803: 4290 f

THATCHER, --- (Baltimore)
1819: 47971 pb

THAYER, EBENEZER (Charleston, S. C.)
1819: 47001 f

Theological Printing Office (Harrisonburg, Va.)
1813: 27733, 28920, 51266

THIERRY, JEAN BAPTISTE SIMON (New Orleans, La.)
1807: 12355 pb
1808: 16306-16307
1809: 18748 pb
1810: 19798-19799, 20962, 21179 pb
1811: 23605
1812: 25881, 25883, 25885

THOMAS, --- (Richmond, Va.)
1819: 49459

THOMAS, ALEXANDER (Walpole, N. H.)
1801: 461 f and sb, 574-575, 1143 f, 1346 f, 1352 f, 1371, 1433 f, 50205 pb
1802: 1728 f, 1824, 1899 f, 2011, 2163 f, 2224 f, 2923, 3020 f, 3175 f, 3543 f
1803: 4045 f, 4219 f, 4366, 4406 pb, 4416-4418 f
1804: 5861 f, 5928 pb, 6020, 6996 pb
1805: 8028 f, 8326, 8658 f, 9266
1806: 10961 f, 11237 f, 11435 f
1807: 11964 f, 12101 f, 12148 pb, 12291, 12454 f, 12787 f, 12789 pb, 12791 f
1808: 14374 f, 14397 f, 14519 pb, 14957-14958 f, 15275 pb, 15278 f, 16190
1809: 18437 f

THOMAS, ALEXANDER (Windsor, Vt.)
1808: 14305 f, 15490 f, 15704 f
1809: 17053 f, 17705 pb, 18105 f

THOMAS, C (New York)
1819: 47386 pb, 47484 f,
    47486 pb, 48352-48354 f,
    49026-49027 f, 49263 f

THOMAS, EBENEZER SMITH
    (Baltimore)
1807: 13461 f

THOMAS, EBENEZER SMITH
    (Charleston, S. C.)
1810: 19763

THOMAS, ISAIAH (Albany,
    N. Y.)
1801: 305 sb, 1407 f
1802: 1870 sb, 2190 f, 2706
    f, 2714 f

THOMAS, ISAIAH (Baltimore)
1801: 72 pb, 305 sb, 841 f,
    1430 f
1802: 1765 f, 1870 sb, 1918 f,
    2190 f, 2260 sb, 2495-2496
    f, 3008 pb, 3574 f
1803: 3841 f, 3984 f, 4045
    sb, 4372 pb, 4492 f

THOMAS, ISAIAH (Boston)
1801: 29 pb, 32 pb, 156 pb,
    168 pb, 293 f, 305 bsb,
    620 pb, 662 pb, 670 f, 724
    f, 895, 957, 959, 960 pb,
    1154 pb, 1297, 1375, 1396,
    1433 f, 1627, 1632, 50209
    pb
1802: 1736, 1855 pb, 1857,
    1870 bsb, 1875, 1912 pb,
    1939 f, 1951 pb, 2190,
    2258-2259, 2260 bsb, 2482
    f, 2698 pb, 2699, 2713 f,
    2886, 3015, 3175 f, 3511,
    3515
1803: 3625, 3688 pb, 3706,
    3790 pb, 3812 f, 3813-3814
    pb, 3839, 3980, 4045 f,
    4218 pb, 4228, 4229 f,
    4391-4392, 4533 f, 4811,
    4815 f, 5551 pb, 5555 pb,
    5557 pb, 5561, 5585 pb,
    50403 pb
1804: 5677 f, 5726 pb, 5825
    pb, 5832 pb, 5845, 5849 f,

5851 pb, 5861 f, 5914, 6829
    pb, 6830, 6831 f, 7059 f,
    7073 pb, 7720-7721 pb,
    7724-7726 pb
1805: 7826, 7851 pb, 7986 f,
    7997 pb, 8039 f, 8462-8463
    f, 8551 f, 8933 pb, 8972
    pb, 9469 f, 50496 pb
1806: 9965 f, 10115 f, 10742a-
    10743 f, 10909 f, 11296 f
1807: 11957 pb, 12038 f,
    13019 pb, 13020 f, 13142
    pb, 13143-13144 f, 13392
    f, 13659 pb, 14181 pb
1808: 14312-14313 f, 14471
    pb, 14472 f, 14485 f, 15049
    f, 15655 f, 15694? f, 15951
    f, 50884 f
1809: 17339 pb, 18131 f,
    18391 f, 50958 f
1810: 19329 f, 19644 pb,
    20091 f, 20148, 20661 f,
    20788-20789 f, 21048? f,
    21307? pb
1811: 22164 pb, 22168 pb,
    22347 f, 22350 pb, 22360 f,
    22373 f, 22766 f, 23183 f,
    23185 pb, 23439 f, 23897 f,
    24387 pb
1812: 24525 f, 24632 pb,
    24793-24794 f, 24821 f,
    25457-25458 f, 25656 pb,
    25829 f, 25998 f, 26142-
    26144 pb, 26435? pb, 26731
    pb, 27484 pb
1813: 27687 pb, 27705 pb,
    27884 f, 27909 pb, 27984 f,
    28083 f, 28084 pb, 28478 pb,
    28793 f, 28824 f, 28836 pb,
    29085 f, 29211 pb, 29223 f,
    29544 pb, 29715 f, 29794 f,
    30485 f
1814: 30647 pb, 30861 pb,
    30862 f, 30876 f, 30883,
    30957 f, 31514 f, 31516 pb,
    31693 pb, 31743 pb, 32046
    f, 32164 f, 32175-32176 f,
    32552 f, 32621 pb, 32731 pb,
    32810
1815: 33816 f, 34454 pb,
    34720 f, 34728 f, 35323 pb
1816: 36674 pb, 36703 f,
    36919-36920, 37197 f, 38231

f, 38293 pb, 38313 f,
38644 pb, 38927 f, 38945
pb
1817: 40284 f, 40343-40344 f,
40482 pb, 41363 f
1818: 44079 f, 44725 pb,
44910 f, 45272 pb
1819: 46922 pb, 46959-46960
pb, 47014 pb, 49070 pb

THOMAS, ISAIAH (Brookfield,
Mass.)
1802: 1887 f
1805: 8862 f
1807: 13016 f, 13693 f
1810: 19978 f, 19980 f, 20746
f

THOMAS, ISAIAH (Leominster,
Mass.)
1806: 10279 f
1808: 15301 f
1810: 20548 f

THOMAS, ISAIAH (Newbury-
port, Mass.)
1803: 4513 f, 5604 pb
1804: 7073 pb, 7301 f
1805: 7881 pb, 8075 f, 8248
pb, 8537 pb, 8653 pb, 8822
pb, 9413 f
1806: 9911? f, 10643 pb,
10751 f, 10916 f, 11164 f,
11896 f, 11905 pb, 50634
pb, 50641 pb, 50716 pb,
50748 pb
1807: 12385 f, 12741 f, 13089
f, 13309 pb, 14247 f
1808: 15024 f, 15250 f, 15661
f, 15662 pb, 15840 f, 15841
pb, 15844 f, 15856 f, 16242
f, 16269 pb, 16300 pb
1809: 17213-17214 f, 17681
pb, 18013 pb, 18101 pb,
18130 f, 18626 f, 19167 f,
19225 pb
1810: 20410 pb, 20735 f,
20991 pb, 22087 sb
1811: 22837 pb, 23629-23631
f, 23753 pb, 23910 pb,
24485
1812: 25087 pb, 26466 sb,
27451 f

1813: 28724 f
1814: 31240 pb, 32724 f,
32771 pb, 51388 pb

THOMAS, ISAIAH (Portland,
Me.)
1816: 36674 pb
1819: 46922 pb

THOMAS, ISAIAH (Portsmouth,
N. H.)
1806: 10708 f
1807: 12005 f
1808: 15405 f, 15416 pb,
16199 pb

THOMAS, ISAIAH (Springfield,
Mass.)
1806: 10684 f
1809: 17126 pb, 17853 f

THOMAS, ISAIAH (Trenton,
N. J.)
1801: 309, 1011, 1013-1014,
1016

THOMAS, ISAIAH (Walpole,
N. H.)
1801: 461 f and sb, 574-575,
1143 f, 1346 f, 1352 f, 1371,
1433 f, 50205 pb
1802: 1728 f, 1824, 1899 f,
2011 f, 2163 f, 2224 f, 2923,
3020 f, 3175 f, 3543 f
1803: 4045 f, 4219 f, 4366,
4406 pb, 4416-4418 f
1804: 5861 f, 5928 pb, 6020,
6996 pb
1805: 8028 f, 8326, 8658 f,
9266
1806: 10961 f, 11237 f, 11435
f
1807: 11964 f, 12101 f, 12148
pb, 12291, 12454 f, 12787 f,
12789 pb, 12791 f
1808: 14374 f, 14397 f, 14519
pb, 14957-14958 f, 15275 pb,
15278 f, 16190
1809: 18437 f
1811: 22292, 22518 pb, 23059
pb, 23266 f, 23462 pb, 23472
pb, 24388 f
1812: 24849 f, 25057, 25059 f,

25422, 25689 pb, 27483 f
1813: 28082 pb

THOMAS, ISAIAH (Worcester,
Mass.)
1801: 176, 305 sb, 362, 459,
461 sb, 502, 703, 795, 857,
895, 1138 pb, 1363, 1366,
1405 pb, 1652 pb
1802: 1848, 1870 sb, 1879 pb,
1886, 1889-1890 pb, 2037,
2197, 2260 sb, ?2418?,
2457, 2473, 2535, 2538,
2682 bsb, 2687, 2702, 2705,
2755, 2885?, 2943, 3113,
3129, 3160
1803: 3970 f, 4045 f, 4397,
4438, 4463 f, 4513, 5029
pb, 5161, 5504 pb, 5604
pb, 5637
1804: 5817, 5924 f, 6046 pb,
6060, 6097, 6177 f, 6211
pb, 6217 pb, 6746, 7031-
7032 pb, 7073 pb, 7802,
50445 pb
1805: 7881 pb, 7898-7900,
8085, 8338, 8368, 8374 pb,
8649 pb, 8685, 8689, 8942
pb, 8969, 8973 pb, 9134 pb,
9147, 9352 pb, 9770, 50562
1806: 9874, 9887, 10094 f,
10313, 10561 bf, 10621,
10703 pb, 10921 bf, 11051,
11140-11141 pb, 11778
1807: 12016, 12038, 12232
pb, 12291, 12376 f, 12460,
12524, 12822, 12936, 13195
f, 14248-14249 bf
1808: 14629 f, 14919 f, 14921
f, 14923-14925 f, 14967 f,
15311 pb, 15585 f, 15903 pb,
16153 pb, 16160 pb
1809: 16792? pb, 16881 f,
17429 f, 17465, 17821-17822,
17892-17893 f, 18020 pb,
18055 pb, 18143 pb, 18285
pb, 18364-18366 pb, 18599
f, 18900, 19229
1810: 19302? f, 19309, 20037
pb, 20441, 20526 f, 21046-
21047? pb, 21483 f, 22050
f, 22087 bsb
1811: 22836, 23099, 23342

pb, 23452 f, 23954 f, 24483
1813: 29962 f
1814: 31808 f, 32475? pb,
51351? f
1815: 35004 f, 35618 pb
1817: 41778

THOMAS, JOHN V (Alexandria,
Va.)
1801: 1596

THOMAS, MOSES (Baltimore)
1808: 14630 f, 16059 pb,
16238 f, 16272 pb
1809: 17614 f, 17645-17646 f,
17888 pb, 18360 f, 18782 f
1810: 19487 f, 20034 pb,
20402 f, 21375 f

THOMAS, MOSES (Philadelphia)
1811: 22816 pb, 23359 pb
1812: 24519 f, 24637 f, 24856
pb, 25010 f, 25912 f, 26117
f, 26440 pb, 26534 pb,
26909 f
1813: 27726 pb, 27738 f,
28061-28062 f, 28115 f,
28499 f, 28665 f, 28928 pb,
29198 f, 29740 f, 29863 pb
1814: 31049 f, 31053 f, 31274
f, 31393-31394 f, 31469 f,
32691 pb, 33656 f
1815: 34240-34241 f, 34935 f,
35253 f, 35672 f, 35742 pb,
35872 f, 35876 pb
1816: 37041 pb, 37095 pb,
37134 pb, 37136-37137 f,
37138 pb, 37143 f, 37144
pb, 37219 f, 37679 f, 37859-
37860 f, 38023 f, 38028,
38066 pb, 38206 f, 38280 f,
38898 pb, 39829 pb
1817: 39950 f, 40336 pb, 40370
pb, 40438 f, 41114 pb, 41237
f, 41345 f, 41384 pb, 41476
f, 41488 pb, 41489 f, 41742
f, 41861 f, 42078 f, 42816 f,
42895-42896 f
1818: 43007 pb, 43443 pb,
43515 f, 43541 pb, 44163 f,
44169 pb, 44473 f, 44766 f,
44888-44889 f, 44893 pb,
45175 pb, 45217 f, 45423 pb,

45661 f, 45662 pb, 45685
pb, 46794 f
1819: 46939 f, 47386 pb,
47484 f, 47486 pb, 47488 f,
48350 f, 48351 pb, 48354 f,
48381 pb, 49026-49027 f,
49317 f, 49557 f, 50022-
50023 pb, 51940 pb

THOMAS, ROBERT BAILEY
(Sterling, Mass.)
1804: 6881 f

THOMAS, WILLIAM (Brooklyn,
N.Y.)
1810: 19621

THOMAS, WILLIAM (New York)
1810: 21229, 21892, 22017
1811: 22363, 22557, 22756,
23562, 23827, 24003?, 24045-
24046, 24511
1812: 25081-25084, 25086,
25088, 25107, 25847, 25943,
26626 pb, 26830, 27530,
27627
1813: 27704, 28253, 28334,
28772, 29003, 29051, 29157-
29158, 29163, 29769
1814: 30850, 31930, 31995,
32423-32424, 32667
1815: 34084, 34356, 35168-
35169, 36442

Thomas & Andrews (Boston)
see THOMAS, ISAIAH (Boston)
ANDREWS, EBENEZER
TURRELL (Boston)

Thomas & Merrifield (Windsor,
Vt.)
see THOMAS, ALEXANDER
(Windsor, Vt.)
THOMAS, ISAIAH (Windsor,
Vt.)
MERRIFIELD, PRESTON
(Windsor, Vt.)

Thomas & Thomas (Walpole,
N.H.)
see THOMAS, ALEXANDER
(Walpole, N.H.)
THOMAS, ISAIAH (Walpole,
N.H.)

Thomas, Andrews & Butler
(Baltimore)
see THOMAS, ISAIAH (Balti-
more)
ANDREWS, EBENEZER
TURRELL (Baltimore)
BUTLER, SAMUEL (Balti-
more)

Thomas, Andrews & Penniman
(Albany, N.Y.)
see THOMAS, ISAIAH (Albany,
N.Y.)
ANDREWS, EBENEZER
TURRELL (Albany, N.Y.)
PENNIMAN, OBADIAH (Al-
bany, N.Y.)

THOMPSON, --- (New York)
1807: 13042 f

THOMPSON, EDWARD W (New
York)
1817: 41777
1818: 45064, 45413
1819: 47734

THOMPSON, J (Montpelier,
Vt.)
1813: 29870 f

THOMPSON, JOHN (New York)
1804: 5805 f, 5978 f, 7773 f,
50447 f
1805: 9780 f
1806: 10944 pb, 10962
1808: 14378 f
1810: 19868 f

THOMPSON, JOHN (Philadel-
phia)
1801: 335, 359
1802: 2633

THOMPSON, JOHN (Wilmington,
Del.)
1805: 8932 f
1806: 10764 f

THOMPSON, SHELDON
(Bridgeport, Ct.)
1801: 351 pb

THOMPSON, THOMAS (New York)
1810: 21114?, 21332
1811: 22581 pb, 23054, 23908, 23994, 24058
1812: 24620, 24961, 24964, 24983, 25484, 25693
1813: 29137, 29206, 29221, 29759, 29921
1814: 30937, 31917, 32976
1815: 35960
1816: 37028?
1818: 44043 pb, 45678
1819: 49392

THOMPSON, THOMAS (Washington, Pa.)
1810: 22026 pb

THOMPSON, THOMAS M'KEAN (Lancaster, Pa.)
1803: 4841 f

THOMSON, E (New York)
1812: 27556

THOMSON, JOHN POPHAM (Frederick, Md.)
1802: 2252 pb
1804: 6480
1806: 11027
1807: 13421 pb, ?13472 pb
1808: 15705, 16650 pb
1809: 18326 pb
1810: 20462 bf, 21488 pb, 21923 pb
1813: 30433 pb
1814: 31326
1817: 42123
1819: 50075 pb

THOMSON, P (New York)
1812: 27556

THORN, SAMUEL (Stanford, N.Y.)
1803: 4511 f

TIEBOUT, ADAM T (New York)
1817: 40974 f, 41410 pb

TIEBOUT, ARCHIBALD McL (New York)
1817: 40974 f, 41410 pb

TIEBOUT, JOHN (New York)
1801: 522, 656 pb, 1021 f, 1593 pb, 50244 pb, 50263
1802: 1825, 2103 f, 2193 f, 2478 f, 3032 pb
1803: 3736, 3900 f
1804: 5758, 5933 pb, 5968
1805: 7994 pb, 8714, 50584 f, 50587 pb, 50588
1806: 9899, 10054 f, 10059 f, 10175 pb, 10464 f, 11072 f
1807: 12704 f, 13293 f, 13467 pb
1808: 14432, 14609-14611 f, 16118 pb
1809: 16955 f, 17062 f, 17397 f, 18323 f, 19224 f, 50955 pb
1810: ?19442?, 20469 f, 20618 f
1811: 22458a f, 23141 pb, 23221 f
1812: 24824 f, 24930 f, 26387 pb
1813: 27803, 27886 pb
1814: 30886 f
1817: 40221 f, 41097 pb, 41727
1818: 45206 f
1819: 47388 f

TIETJEN, C (Germantown, Pa.)
1819: 47671 pb

TIFFANY, --- (New Haven, Conn.)
1815: 35783 f

TIFFANY, JOHN L (New York)
1817: 40228 f

TIFFANY, SILVESTER (Canandaigua, N.Y.)
1803: 4793 pb

TILESTON, EZRA B (Boston)
1815: 34713 pb, 35691, 36002, 36122-36123 pb
1816: 36772 pb, 38176 pb, 38187 pb, 38662, 38755, 39050

TILESTON, THOMAS (Haverhill, Mass.)
1814: 31850

1815: 33912, 34089 pb, 35043-
35044, 35153-35154 pb,
35453, 35614, 35954 pb,
36011, 36505 pb
1816: 36769 pb, 36889-36890,
36983 pb, 38331 pb, 38571,
38658 pb, 39731 pb, 39740
pb, 39850 pb, 39851
1817: 40227 pb, 40311, 40944,
41517, 41521 pb, 41522,
41855, 42791, 42845 pb
1818: 43379 pb

TILFORD, JOHN W (Lexington,
Ky.)
1808: 16717 f
1809: 50952 f
1810: 20269 f
1811: 22471 f, 22950 f
1812: 27503 f

TILLMAN, THOMAS M
(Schoharie, N.Y.)
1809: 18785 pb

Time Piece (St. Francisville,
La.)
1815: 36087 pb

Times (Charleston, S.C.)
1818: 44552

Times (Hartford, Conn.)
1817: 41978
1819: 47890

Times (Sandy Hill, N.Y.)
1819: 47848

TITCOMB, --- (Boston)
1808: 15951
1809: 18391
1810: 19329, 19605, 20661,
51042 pb

TIZZARD, JAMES (Carlisle,
Pa.)
1818: 43539 pb

TODD, BETHEL (Cherry Val-
ley, N.Y.)
1818: 43596 pb

TODD, BETHEL (Hartwick,
N.Y.)
1813: 27913 pb
1814: 30885, 31145, 33609
1815: 36004 bf
1816: 36685, 37145, 38340 pb
1818: 43481, 45097

TODD, BETHEL (Otsego, N.Y.)
1819: 49614 bs

TODD, LEMUEL (Cherry Val-
ley, N.Y.)
1818: 43596 pb

TODD, LEMUEL (Hartwick,
N.Y.)
1813: 27913 pb
1814: 30885, 31145, 33609
1815: 36004 bf
1816: 36685, 37145, 38340 pb
1818: 43481, 45097

TODD, LEMUEL (Otsego, N.Y.)
1819: 49614 sb

TONNER, THOMAS (Wheeling,
Va.)
1818: 46662 pb

TORREY, ELIJAH (Albany,
N.Y.)
1812: 26058 f
1814: 33740 f
1815: 35900 f

TOTTEN, JOHN C (New York)
1801: 371
1803: 5038, 5179
1804: 5683, 5821, 6038, 6163,
7207, 7209, 7234 pb, 7344,
7742, 7761
1805: 7818, 7981, 8417, 8441,
8901
1806: 10230, 10308, 10374 pb,
10524 pb, 10639, 11021 pb,
11255, 11467-11468, 11849,
11880, 11883, 11909, 50669
1807: 12299 pb, 12461-12462,
12593, 12995 pb, 13076,
13754
1808: 14902, 15292, 15589,
15592, 16104, 16167

1809: 16872, 17250 pb, 17321,
   17515, 18071, 18165, 18173,
   18592 pb, 18618, 50938 pb
1810: 19759, 20069 pb, 20112,
   20231, 21413? pb, 22016,
   22034, 22058, 50996 pb,
   51015
1811: 22173, 22417, 22480,
   22544 pb, 22563, 22648,
   22669 pb, 22997, 23375-
   23377, 23911, 24420
1812: 24810, 25379, 25382,
   25748, 26068, 26070, 26712,
   27519
1813: 27644, 27756, 28030,
   28174, 28180 pb, 28193 pb,
   28251-28252, 28353-28354,
   28555, 28948, 29154, 29156,
   29679, 29689, 29701, 30534,
   51301
1814: 31353-31356 pb, 31357,
   31472, 31802, 32114, 32116-
   32117, 32351 pb, 32418,
   32422, 32460, 32744, 32897,
   33644, 33680
1815: 33920, 34387, 34391
   pb, 34854 pb, 35009 pb,
   35190 pb, 35268-35269,
   35369, 35535, 35895, 36036-
   36037, 36101 pb, 36103 pb,
   36117, 36539, 36540 pb,
   51463, 51486 pb
1816: 36802, 37010, 37019,
   37306 pb, 37417, 37684,
   37912, 38241, 38243, 38600,
   38641 pb, 38839, 38917 pb,
   38931 pb, 38981 pb, 39103,
   39725
1817: 40058, 40151, 40250,
   40358, 41420-41421, 41445,
   41447, 41638, 41863, 42236,
   42312 pb, 42879
1818: 43078, 43158-43160,
   43450, 43916, 44129 pb,
   44546, 44825, 45161, 45385,
   45766, 45836, 46763, 46805
1819: 47017, 47429 pb, 47629,
   47797 pb, 48611 pb, 48683,
   48908-48909, 49168, 49272
   pb, 49295 pb, 49412 pb,
   50189 pb

TOULOUSE, C MORANE (New
   Orleans, La.)
1811: 24068 pb

TOWN, THOMAS (Philadelphia)
1807: 12088
1808: 15263, 15573, 15825
1809: 17267, 18771 pb, 18800
1810: 51002
1812: 25203 pb
1818: 43089 pb, 43127 pb,
   43632, 43816, 45223, 45277
   pb, 45538
1819: 47727, 47959, 48698

TOWN, THOMAS (Southwark,
   Pa.)
1807: 12285

TOY, JOHN D (Baltimore)
1810: 20603-20604?
1814: 30801 f
1815: 34189
1816: 36978, 37059, 37071,
   37400, 37577, 37666, 37719,
   38626-38627, 38806, 39835,
   39863
1817: 39923, 40473, 40658,
   41064, 41156, 41799, 42834
1818: 43067, 43433, 43629,
   44049-44050, 44284, 44453,
   44853-44854, 44857, 45606
1819: 47342, 47413, 47432,
   47735, 47846, 48191, 48366,
   48456, 48483, 49067, 49246,
   49617, 49658, 51899

TRACY, GARDINER (Lansing-
   burgh, N. Y.)
1801: 50214 pb, 50236 pb
1802: 50314-50315 pb
1803: 4760 pb, 4938
1804: 50459 pb
1805: 50577 pb
1806: 11017 pb, 11879
1807: 13217 pb, 13236 pb
1808: 14441, 15680 pb, 16339
1809: 16820 f, 16937, 18241
   pb
1810: 19457, 20850, 20898 pb
1811: 22277, 23553 pb
1812: 26676
1813: 27819, 28934, 29244 pb,

29547
1814: 30788, 51451 pb
1815: 35367 pb
1816: 36855, 38384, 51603 sb
1817: 40120, 51728 pb
1819: 47673

TRACY, SIDNEY (Wilkesbarre, Pa.)
1809: 19234

Traveller (Greenfield, Mass.)
1811: 22182, 23125

TREADWELL, DANIEL (Portsmouth, N.H.)
1803: 3889, 3896, 3898-3899, 4362, 4794 pb, 4898 pb
1804: 5916, 5931 pb, 5935-5936, 6463 f, 6467, 6517, 6617 pb, 7071 pb, 7116
1805: 7848, 7880, 8482, 9153 pb, 9274 pb
1806: 10050, 10941
1808: 14603 pb

TREADWELL, WILLIAM KELLEY (New York)
1814: 32335 pb, 32829
1819: 48012

TREADWELL, WILLIAM KELLEY (Portsmouth, N.H.)
1801: 31, 680, 1311, 1568 pb, 50196 pb
1802: 1847 pb, 1896 pb, 2278 pb, 2761, 3549, 3582
1803: 3889, 3896, 3898-3899, 4362, 4794 pb, 4898 pb
1804: 5916, 5931 pb, 5935-5936, 6463 f, 6467, 6517, 6617 pb, 7071 pb, 7116
1805: 7848, 7880, 8482, 9153 pb, 9274 pb, 9339
1806: 10050, 10168, 10397 pb, 10941, 50642 pb
1807: 13073, 13495?, 13637
1808: 14603 pb, 15931, 15952, 16241
1809: 17112, 17116, 18397
1810: 19389, 19474-19475, 20147
1812: 24551, 26505, 27493-27494

TRISLER, GEORGE (Winchester, Va.)
1801: 127
1802: 1834
1803: 3746

TROTTER, THOMAS C (Mt. Holly, N.J.)
1813: 28024 pb

Troy Gazette (Troy, N.Y.)
1802: 2438

TRUE, BENJAMIN (Boston)
1803: 5588 pb
1804: 6149 pb
1805: 8336, 8350, 8533-8534, 8624, 8669
1806: 11419, 11876
1807: 12330, 12565, 13184, 13435, 13753, 14221
1808: 15013, 15714, 16043
1809: 17527
1810: 20284?, 20845
1811: 22140, 22205, 22665, 23628, 23857 pb
1812: 24619, 25243 f, 25354, 25610, 25988, 26009, 26213, 26522, 26622, 27557, 27633 pb
1813: 28121, 28203, 28471, 28642
1815: 35422?, 35714, 36431
1818: 45417
1819: 47029, 47077, 47440, 47497, 47572, 47603 pb, 48818, 49036, 49341, 50138

True American (Philadelphia)
1801: 267

True American (Trenton, N.J.)
1807: 13083

TRUEHEART, DANIEL (Richmond, Va.)
1812: 26786
1813: 28722, 51300 pb
1814: 30792, 30795, 31826 pb, 32584, 33550, 51445
1815: 33982, 33985, 35312, 35728
1816: 38738, 39674-39679 pb
1817: 40124-40125, 41225,

41903, 51724
1818: 43223, 45445
1819: 47148

TRUMBULL, CHARLES E
(Norwich, Conn.)
1803: 4014, 4729 pb
1804: 5802, 50480

TRUMBULL, GEORGE AU-
GUSTUS (Worcester, Mass.)
1814: 31669 f, 32458 f
1815: 34066, 35589 f
1818: 43387 pb
1819: 46964, 47107, 48359
bf, 48498, 49452, 50147

TRUMBULL, HENRY (Boston)
1815: 34412, 36038 pb, 36515
1816: 38468, 38647 pb
1817: 39966, 41253, 41440-
41441, 41830 pb
1819: 49119, 49120?

TRUMBULL, HENRY (Norwich,
Conn.)
1804: 6161, 6875
1805: 8977 pb, 9441
1806: 10957 pb
1810: 21531
1811: 22881, 24067 bf
1812: 26808, 26919

TRUMBULL, JOHN (Norwich,
Conn.)
1801: 471, 805
1802: 2074 pb, 2431
1806: 9988 pb

TRUMBULL, LUCY (Norwich,
Conn.)
1802: 2080 f

TRUMBULL, SAMUEL (Stonington-Port, Conn.)
1801: 454?, 471 sb, 769 pb,
1010, 1102, 50268
1802: 1746 pb, 1997, 2241
1803: 4014 sb
1804: 6875 sb

TRYON, JEREMIAH (Albany,
N.Y.)
1819: 47443, 48106, 48545

TUCKER, --- (Claiborne, Ala.)
1819: 46952 pb

TUCKER, --- (New Bedford,
Mass.)
1808: 15797 pb
1809: 17623

TUCKER, JAMES (Andover,
Mass.)
1818: 46710 f

TUCKER, WILLIAM (Albany,
N.Y.)
1808: 16097

TUCKNISS, HENRY (Philadelphia)
1802: 2658

TUNISON, GARRET C (New
York)
1810: 20784 pb, 20903 pb
1812: 25257, 26800 pb
1813: 28267 pb

TUNSTALL, GEORGE (Nash-
ville, Tenn.)
1818: 43213
1819: 47137, 47689, 48043 pb,
49001

TUPPER, HIRAM (Nantucket,
Mass.)
1816: 37286, 38352 pb

TURELL, CHARLES (Ports-
mouth, N.H.)
1814: 33621
1816: 38949
1817: 41869, 42004

TURELL, WILLIAM B (Salem,
Mass.)
1808: 16132

TURNER, --- (Claiborne, Ala.)
1819: 46952 pb

TURNER, CHARLES (New
York)
1815: 34768 pb, 35489 pb
1816: 38432
1817: 41637 pb

1818:   43789 pb, 45511, 46124
  pb
1819:   47856 pb, 48983, 49472
  pb, 51939

TURNER, JOHN (New York)
1805:   8641 f

TURNER, JOSEPH (Richmond,
  Ky.)
1816:   36818, 36824 pb
1818:   43183
1819:   47090 pb

TURNER, MICHAEL (Baltimore)
1819:   48456 f

TURNER, W (New York)
1808:   14693 pb, 15791 pb,
  15826? pb, 16063 pb

TUTTLE, JESSE CARR (Con-
  cord, N. H.)
1806:   10195 pb
1807:   13198, 13750 pb
1809:   16922
1810:   21439?
1812:   24719
1813:   27971, 29488

TUTTLE, JOHN (Newark, N. J.)
1814:   31164, 31395, 33756
1815:   35448, 36579
1816:   36903, 37872, 38410
  pb, 38463, 38683, 38800,
  38801 pb
1817:   41027, 41655-41656
1818:   44107 pb, 45004, 46897
1819:   48863-48864, 49288

TUTTLE, WILLIAM (Newark,
  N. J.)
1803:   4746
1804:   6597 pb, 6895, 6897,
  7752
1805:   7933-7934, 8052, 8827,
  9215
1806:   10902-10903, 10980,
  10986 pb, 11118, 11224
1807:   12971 pb, 13244 pb
1808:   14325 pb, 15735 pb,
  15765 pb
1809:   17593, 18214 pb, 18555,

19201
1810:   19331, 20300, 20302,
  20800 pb, 20910
1811:   22167, 23272, 23531,
  23820
1812:   26405 pb, 27531, 27572
  pb
1819:   47582 pb, 48841 pb,
  49177 pb, 49485

TWEED, ROBERT (Williams-
  burg, O.)
1813:   29536 pb

TYLER, BENJAMIN OWEN
  (New York)
1817:   42344 pb

TYLER, BENJAMIN OWEN
  (Washington, D. C.)
1818:   46130 pb

U

UNDERHILL, H (Canandaigua,
  N. Y.)
1817:   41853? pb

UNDERWOOD, JAMES (Carlisle,
  Pa.)
1814:   30683 pb
1818:   43101

UNDERWOOD, WILLIAM B
  (Baltimore)
1810:   21272

UNDERWOOD, WILLIAM B
  (Carlisle, Pa.)
1814:   30683 pb
1818:   43101

UNDERWOOD, WILLIAM B
  (Frederick, Md.)
1807:   12807 pb

UNDERWOOD, WILLIAM B
  (Gettysburg, Pa.)
1803:   4274 pb
1804:   7299 pb

Union (Philadelphia)
1818: 45442

Union (Washington, Ky.)
1816: 37757
1817: 41101

Union Circulating Library (Boston)
1817: 40244

Union Male Sunday School Society of Baltimore (Baltimore)
1819: 47432 f

Union Tract Association of Friends in the Western Counties of the State of New York (Auburn, N. Y.)
1819: 51866 f

United States Gazette (Philadelphia)
1805: 9487
1806: 10251, 10908, 11443-11444
1807: 14216
1810: 22040, 50973 pb
1811: 22403a
1812: 24550, 26547 pb, 26777
1813: 27761, 28813, 29481, 29500 pb
1814: 30679, 31067, 31242, 31887, 51404
1815: 34331, 35592, 35867, 36256
1816: 39713
1817: 40847, 41780 pb, 42066, 42896
1818: 43937, 46794

United States Oracle (Portsmouth, N. H.)
1801: 1173
1802: 3549, 3582

University Press (Baltimore)
1814: 31619, 31892, 33593

University Press (Cambridge, Mass.)
1801: 912

1802: 1911, 1913, 2379-2380, 3499
1803: 4220, 4346-4347, 4504, 5139, 5547, 5579
1804: 6456-6457, 6622
1805: 8756, 50630?
1807: 12247 f, 12722
1808: 16687
1814: 31660, 31662
1816: 37266, 37807, 37823
1817: 39998, 40586, 40878, 41847, 42762
1818: 43805, 43962, 44113, 44270, 44295-44296, 45864, 46704
1819: 47775, 50145

UPDEGRAFF, DANIEL (York, Pa.)
1808: 14973 pb

USTICK, JOHN GANO (Abingdon, Va.)
1806: 10581 pb
1808: 14564
1811: 23710 pb, 23945
1815: 51474?
1818: 44908

USTICK, STEPHEN CLEGG (Burlington, N. J.)
1801: 276, 1257, 50229
1802: 1703-1704, 1826?, 1828, ?1988, 2295, 2566, 3588
1803: 3738, 3845, 3929, 3948, 4830 pb, 5581 pb, 5615, 50389 pb
1804: 5789, 6501, 6567, 6892, 7302, 7696
1805: 7939, 8108 pb, 8208, 8457, 8709, 8813, 8891 pb
1806: 9905?
1807: 12060, 12238 pb, 12248, 12573, 12719 pb
1808: 14436 pb, 14543, 15960, 16729
1809: 16932?, 19221?
1810: 19449-19450, 20289
1812: 24721 pb, 24963 f, 25365 f
1813: 28518-28519 f
1814: 30832 pb, 31500?
1815: ?33950

USTICK, STEPHEN CLEGG
(Philadelphia)
1801: 1558
1803: 3948

USTICK, THOMAS (Philadel-
phia)
1802: 1703-1704 f, 2295 sb

V

VAIL, SAMUEL (Louisville,
Ky.)
1801: 475 pb
1803: 50354

VANAUSDAL, CORNELIUS
(Eaton, O.)
1817: 42877 pb

VAN BENTHUYSEN, OBADIAH
ROMNEY (Albany, N.Y.)
1807: 12700 pb
1808: 14727 pb, 16234
1809: 18233
1810: 19418
1811: 23233?, 51105
1812: 24739, 27438, 51221
1813: 28148, 30448
1814: 30646, 30676, 31077,
31407 pb, 31941?, 32802,
32890
1815: 34753, 35118, 51515?
1816: 37281, 37671, 38434,
51547, 51603
1817: 39959, 40224, 41275,
42020
1818: 43625, 51732, 51794,
51810
1819: 47624, 48041, 49503

VANCE, JOHN (Baltimore)
1806: 11212 f, 50672 f
1807: 12348 pb, 12581 f,
12817 f, 13058 sb
1808: 50890 f
1809: 18267 pb, 50934 f
1810: 19412
1811: 22745 f, 22927 pb,
24463 f

1812: 25311 f, 26325 pb,
26344 pb
1813: 29241 f
1814: 31061 f, 32661 f
1815: 34090 f, 34100 pb,
35351 f, 35360 f, 35377 f,
36502 f
1816: 39011 f
1818: 45549 f

VANCE, THOMAS (Baltimore)
1806: 10173 f
1807: 12348 pb
1812: 25311 f, 26344 pb
1813: 29241 f
1814: 31061 f, 32661 f
1815: 34090 f, 34100 pb,
35351 f, 35360 f, 35377 f,
36502 f
1816: 39011 f
1818: 45549 f

VAN PELT, HENRY (Franklin,
Tenn.)
1817: 41462 pb

VAN PELT, PETER (New York)
1811: 22964 pb
1812: 26139, 26881 pb
1813: 28418, 28687, 28921,
29037 pb, 29326, 29332 pb
1814: 30653-30654, 32566 pb,
32768, 33606, 33662
1815: 34400, 35588, 36474
1816: 36930, 38867 pb
1817: 41915
1818: 45090 pb, 51811-51812 pb
1819: 48906 pb

Van Pelt & Riley (New York)
see VAN PELT, PETER (New
York)
RILEY, BENJAMIN J (New
York)

VAN RIPER, N (Greenwich,
Conn.)
1818: 46677
1819: 49202

VAN RIPER, NICHOLAS (New
York)
1814: 30715, 31926, 32110,

32672, 32697, 32753
1815: 33877, 34253, 34371,
    35277, 35925, 35935
1818: 43424, 43893, 44303
    pb, 44304, 45174, 46856
1819: 47895, 48254, 48422

Van Tromp Press (Boston)
1807: 13548

VAN VEGHTEN, CORNELIUS
    (Schenectady, N. Y.)
1807: 14203 pb

VAN VEGHTEN, DERICK
    (Schenectady, N. Y.)
1807: 14203 pb
1808: 14752, 16123, 50851

VAN VEGHTEN, DERICK
    (Schoharie, N. Y.)
1817: 42064 pb
1818: 43781
1819: 49371 pb

VAN VEGHTEN, DOUW K
    (Albany, N. Y.)
1814: 31615

VAN VLEET, ABRAM (Lebanon,
    O.)
1817: 40514
1818: 43575

VAN VLEET, ABRAM (Wilm-
    ington, O.)
1815: 34179 f, 36062 f

VAN WINKLE, CORNELIUS S
    (New York)
1809: 19278
1810: 19369, 19745, 19797
    pb, 19868, 20445, 20671,
    20900, 20908, 21352
1811: 22148, 22209, 22411a,
    22565 pb, 22776, 22778,
    22845, 23049-23051
1812: 24548, 24621, 24624,
    24747, 24999, 25677, 25687,
    25688 pb, 25922, 26112,
    26290, 26292, 26778, 26838,
    26876, 27449, 27534
1813: 27728, 27972, 28047,

28248, 28306, 28553, 28774-
    28778, 29351, 29360, 29364,
    29616, 29742, 30374, 30384,
    30603
1814: 30642, 31027, 31099,
    31136 pb, 31170, 31172 pb,
    31182, 31251, 31254, 31383,
    31592, 31759, 31773 pb,
    32168 bpb, 32171 pb, 32186
    bf, 32336-32338, 32340-
    32341, 32345, 32766
1815: 33835, 34291 pb, 34357-
    34358, 34372, 34378, 34445,
    34568, 34718 pb, 34774 pb,
    34856, 34930, 34933 pb,
    34956 pb, 34958, 35000,
    35023, 35116, 35172 pb,
    35183, 35468, 35470, 35575,
    35807, 35871 pb, 35872,
    35881 pb, 35884, 36026,
    36031 pb, 36367 pb
1816: 36908, 37084 pb, 37139
    pb, 37141-37142 pb, 37291
    pb, 37496 pb, 37752, 37855,
    37875-37876 pb, 38018,
    38312 pb, 38442 pb, 38750
    pb, 38891 pb, 38929, 38976
    pb, 38986 f, 39060 pb, 39108,
    39796-39797 pb, 39799
1817: 39988, 40039, 40096,
    40366 pb, 40369 pb, 40386,
    40512-40513, 40577, 40695,
    40730 pb, 41232 pb, 41252,
    41302 pb, 41475 pb, 41594,
    41862, 42039, 42076, 42124,
    42182 pb, 42338, 42887-42888
1818: 43394, 43510, 44375-
    44377, 44591, 44887, 45038,
    45051-45052, 45063, 45110,
    45664-45666, 46630 pb
1819: 47163, 47496, 47628,
    47729, 48048, 48220, 48275-
    48276, 48355-48356, 48757,
    49263, 49355 pb, 50083

VARLE, CHARLES (Baltimore)
1817: 42765-42766 pb

VARNEY, JESSE (Dover, N. H.)
1812: 24791 f, 25187
1814: 31139 f
1815: 35667? f
1819: 48680 f

VERMILYE, WILLIAM W
  (New York)
1802: 2615
1803: 3851, 5075
1804: 6345, 6558, 7723
1805: 8182, 8609, 9357

VERMILYE, WILLIAM W
  (Newark, N. J.)
1808: 15739

Vermont Centinel (Burlington,
  Vt.)
1812: 27396? pb, 27397 pb

Vermont Journal (Windsor, Vt.)
1806: 11438

Vermont Missionary Society
  (Middlebury, Vt.)
1817: 41887 f

Vermont Religious Tract Society (Middlebury, Vt.)
1810: 19586 f

Vermont Republican (Windsor,
  Vt.)
1812: 24575, 25555
1814: 32859

VICARY, HENRY (Baltimore)
1819: 48541 pb

VICKERS, ABRAHAM (Phila-
  delphia)
1804: 7738 pb

VINSON, SAMUEL W (New-
  port, R. I.)
1808: 16299 sb

Virginia Argus (Richmond, Va.)
1814: 51449 pb
1815: 35014? f
1816: 36842

Virginia Gazette (Richmond,
  Va.)
1806: 11688

Virginia Patriot (Richmond, Va.)
1818: 45101

VON HAGEN, PETER AL-
  BRECHT
see HAGEN, PETER AL-
  BRECHT VON

VOSBURGH, ABRAHAM (New
  York)
1818: 45573 f

W

WADE, JOHN H (Washington,
  D. C.)
1819: 49899e

WADSWORTH, HORACE H
  (Waterford, N. Y.)
1801: 1613, 1624 pb
1802: 3498
1803: 4731, 5541
1804: 50483 pb
1805: 50629 pb
1806: 11325, 11802 pb
1807: 12311, 50818 pb
1808: 16668

WADSWORTH, SAMUEL (New
  Haven, Conn.)
1812: 24845 pb
1818: 45902 pb
1819: 48845

WAGNER, JACOB (Baltimore)
1808: 15776 pb
1809: 18471 f

WAGNER, JACOB (Georgetown,
  D. C.)
1812: 25412 pb
1814: 31284 pb

WAGNER, PETER K (Baltimore)
1808: 15188 pb, 15924
1809: 17908

WAGNER, PETER K (New Or-
  leans, La.)
1813: 28978-28982
1814: 31952-31959
1815: 35135
1816: 38098-38104

WAGNER, PETER K (Philadelphia)
1806: 10242, 10648, 10836, 11482

WAIT, S (Philadelphia)
1813: 29754 pb

WAIT, THOMAS BAKER (Boston)
1802: 2034 pb
1804: 6013 pb, 6425
1808: 14631?
1809: 16855 pb, 16985, 16986 pb, 17005, 17017 pb, 17189-17190 pb, 17220 pb, 17472, 17689, 17731, 17823, 17937, 18139 bf, 18719, 18757, 19138, 19289
1810: 19325 pb, 19476, 19503 pb, 19522 pb, 19708 pb, 20032 pb, 20324, 20435 pb, 20510 pb, 20692, 20693 pb, 21096 pb, 21438, 21476 pb, 22010
1811: 22324 bf, 22346 pb, 22393 bsb, 22467 pb, 22606, 23181, 23194, 23235-23236, 23244, 23280, 23347, 23408 pb, 23596 pb, 23699, 23893 pb, 24362 pb, 24473 pb
1812: 24874, 25063, 25172 pb, 25414 pb, 25489 pb, 25531, 25762, 25820 pb, 26198 pb, 26467, 26737, 26775, 26785 pb, 51178 pb, 51218 pb
1813: 28321, 28630, 28694, 28823, 28962? pb, 29038-29039, 29105 pb, 29114-29115, ?29575, 29587, 29675 pb, 29733 pb, 29847 pb, 29937 bf, 30444
1814: 30897, 30927, 31159, 31205, 31241, 31392 pb, 32028 pb, 32079, 32404, 32443, 32520, 32850 pb, 33681
1815: 34102 pb, 34623-34624 pb, 34759, 34843, 35870 pb, 36006-36007 pb, 36071 pb
1816: 36695 pb, 37678

1817: 40388 bf, 42211 pb, 42261 pb, 42346
1818: 43377 pb, 45790
1819: 49498 pb, 49802 pb

WAIT, THOMAS BAKER (Portland, Me.)
1801: 186, 472
1803: 3731
1805: 7842, 8421, 8831, 9446
1806: 10827, 11193, 11196-11197, 11238
1807: 11952, 12159 pb, 12836, 12966, 13695

WAITE, GEORGE (New York)
1801: 77 pb, 177, 204, 205 pb, 257, 455, 608-609 pb, 709, 784, 1094, 1096, 1098, 1631
1802: 2368-2369 pb, 2545 pb, 3514, 3541, 3579
1803: 3785, 3932?, 3937 pb, 4226, 4363, 4373, 4389, 4437
1804: 5843, 6438, 6788-6789, 6803, 6868, 7167 pb, 7261 pb, 7651 pb, 7711 pb, 7729 pb, 7777 pb, 50476? pb
1805: 8642, 8908, 9222 pb, 9239 pb, 9334 pb
1806: 10920 pb
1807: 13059, 13291 f
1809: 17297 pb, 18451 f
1810: 20721? pb, 21225
1811: 23557 pb
1813: 27886 pb, 28727 pb
1814: 32976 f
1815: 35406 pb
1819: 48284 pb

WAITE, ROBERT (New York)
for all entries see WAITE, GEORGE (New York) above

WALBRIDGE, EBENEZER (Bennington, Vt.)
1811: 22231 f

WALDIE, ADAM (Philadelphia)
1819: 47589, 48438, 48513, 49269

WALDO, FRANCIS W (Fayetteville, N. C.)
1816:   37180 pb

WALDO, HENRY S (Boston)
1813:   29748 f

WALDO, JOHN (Georgetown,
S. C.)
1818:   46671 sb

WALES, LUTHER (New York)
1815:   36517-36519

WALKER, --- (Philadelphia)
1804:   7010?

WALKER, AMBROSE (New
Brunswick, N. J.)
1808:   15839 pb
1809:   17351, 18529-18530
1810:   19532, 19536, 21150,
21182-21183, 21976

WALKER, AMBROSE (Phila-
delphia)
1814:   30958-30959 pb
1816:   38899 pb, 39836-39837
1817:   40002, 40455, 40932
pb, 42920 pb
1818:   44178 pb, 46680 pb,
46779 pb

WALKER, G (Boston)
1816:   38469? pb

WALKER, ICHABOD (Rutland,
Vt.)
1814:   31984? pb

WALKER, JAMES (Columbia,
Tenn.)
1810:   22025 pb
1819:   47668 pb

WALKER, JAMES (Fredericksburg, Va.)
1801:   125
1803:   3687 pb, 3744

WALKER, JOHN W (Albany,
N. Y.)
1815:   33809-33810 pb

WALKER, JOHN W (New York)
1817:   41633 pb, 41635 pb

WALKER, L (Middlebury, Vt.)
1815:   35013 f

WALKER, SAMUEL (New York)
1819:   49628

WALKER, SAUNDERS (Washington, Ga.)
1804:   6634 f

WALKER, THOMAS (Rome,
N. Y.)
1801:   1599
1802:   3485

WALKER, THOMAS (Utica,
N. Y.)
1803:   3656, 3735, 3995 pb,
4306, 5049
1804:   5786
1806:   11383
1807:   12057, 12736, 13304,
50788
1808:   14431, 14433, 15408
1809:   16815 pb, 17850, 18684?
1810:   19323 pb
1814:   32302?
1815:   34628?
1816:   36839 pb, 39882
1817:   40098 pb, 41616, 42314

WALKER, WILLIAM (New
York)
1817:   41167 pb

WALKUP, SAMUEL (Lexington,
Va.)
1802:   3479 pb
1805:   9673 pb, 9674
1806:   9930

WALLACE, ANDREW (Cin-
cinnati, O.)
1814:   30919, 31358, 31923,
32394
1815:   34342, 34595, 35530,
35573, 35956

WALLER, BAYFIELD (Charleston, S. C.)
1801:   50240 pb

1802:   50317-50318 pb
1803:   50383 pb
1806:   50744 pb

WALLINGSFORD, JOEL (Boston)
1809:   17837 f

WALLIS, JOHN (Newark, N. J.)
1801:   777, 1202 pb
1802:   1953 pb, 2091, 2948
1803:   4577, 4762 pb, 4784
1805:   8931

WALTER, JOEL (New Haven,
   Conn.)
1803:   4015 pb, 4074-4075,
   4439, 4742, 4995 pb, 5554,
   5562
1806:   10241 f, 11834 f
1808:   16102 f
1810:   19495 pb, 20780 f,
   21913 f
1811:   22322 pb, 22603 pb,
   23157 pb, 23160 pb, 24507-
   24508
1812:   24547, 24786 pb, 24845
   pb, 25147, 25149, 25207
   pb, 25763, 27502 bf, 27542,
   51223 pb, 51260

WALTER, WILLIAM (Boston)
1817:   40537

WALTER, WILLIAM (New
   Haven, Conn.)
1806:   10241 f, 11834 f
1808:   16102 f

WALTON, EZEKIEL PARKER
   (Montpelier, Vt.)
1810:   20137
1811:   22432a, 22508, 22523,
   23787 pb, 24365 pb, 24503
1812:   26165, 26514 pb, 27434
   pb, 27622, 27629
1813:   28039, 28841, 29052,
   29767-29768, 29782, 29978-
   29979, 30406, 30409, 30413
1814:   30785, 30811, 30825,
   30893, 31144, 31483, 31974,
   32158, 32355, 33536, 33541,
   33610, 33726, 33735
1815:   33976, 34541, 35617,

36437, 36653
1816:   36774, 37336, 37751,
   38237, 38472, 39002, 39665,
   39749
1817:   39919, 39936, 40116,
   40712 pb, 42782, 42809 pb,
   42978
1818:   43287 pb, 43606 pb,
   43882 pb, 44503, 44879 pb,
   45672 pb, 45795, 46642,
   46644, 46689 pb, 46868,
   46880
1819:   47138, 47196 pb, 47459
   pb, 47537-47538 pb, 47720,
   48045, 48064, 48609 pb,
   48729 pb, 48933, 49986,
   50029 pb, 50069, 50158

WALTON, GEORGE S (Mont-
   pelier, Vt.)
1817:   42809 pb
1818:   43882 pb, 45672 pb

WALTON, JOSEPH (Philadel-
   phia)
1806:   10650 f, 50689 pb,
   50724 pb
1807:   12103 pb, 13055 f,
   13511 pb, 50784 pb
1808:   14479 pb, 15822 pb,
   16280 pb, 50859 f
1809:   17795 f, 17844 pb
1810:   19317 f, 19504 f, 19505
   pb, 20835 pb
1811:   22630 f, 22743 f, 22746
   pb, 22798 f, 23123 pb,
   23267 pb, 23461 f, 24355
   pb, 24358 pb, 51061-51062
   pb
1812:   24807 f, 24808 pb,
   25872 pb, 26174 pb, 26178
   pb, 26403 pb
1813:   27651 f, 27653 f, 27876
   pb, 29245 pb, 51319 f
1814:   30849 pb, 31716 f, 32193
   pb, 32200 pb, 32664 pb
1815:   34044 f, 34505 pb,
   34982 f, 35383 pb, 35819 pb,
   51464 f
1816:   36931-36932 pb
1817:   41319 f, 51645 pb
1818:   43281-43282 pb, 45560
   pb

1819: 47199-47200 pb, 49308
f, 51919 pb

Walton & Goss (Montpelier,
Vt.)
see WALTON, EZEKIEL
      PARKER (Montpelier, Vt.)
   GOSS, MARK (Montpelier,
   Vt.)

Wanderer (Baltimore)
1816: 36798 pb

WANE, JOHN (Baltimore)
1804: 6593, 7075?, 7094 pb
1805: 8118, 9060
1813: 28788
1815: 34598 pb, 35810 pb
1816: 37402

War (New York)
1813: 29259 bsb

WARD, H (New York)
1819: 50033 f

WARD, JOSEPH (Wrentham,
Mass.)
1812: 25387 pb

WARD, MATTHIAS (New York)
1801: 572, 780 pb, 1022
1802: 2103 f, 2980, 3581 pb
1803: 5491
1807: 12287 pb
1809: 17011 pb, 17015 f,
   17326-17327 f, 17636 f,
   17909 pb, 17972 f, 18484
   f, 19162 pb, 19285 f
1810: 19779 pb, 20225 pb,
   20469 f, 20764 sb, 21352 f,
   51028 pb
1811: 22570 f, 22688 pb,
   22925 f, 23279 pb, 23778
   pb, 23942c pb
1812: 24843 f, 26651 pb,
   27480 f

WARD, P (Philadelphia)
1810: 19631 f

WARD, WILLIAM (New York)
1809: 17011 pb, 17015 f,

17326-17327 f, 17636 f,
   17909 pb, 17972 f, 18484 f,
   19162 pb, 19285 f
1810: 19779 pb, 20225 pb,
   20469 f, 20764 sb, 21352 f,
   51028 pb
1811: 22570 f, 22688 pb,
   22925 f, 23279 pb, 23778
   pb, 23942c pb
1812: 24843 f, 26651 pb,
   27480 f

WARD, WILLIAM (Newark,
N. J.)
1817: 40914, 40966 pb

Ward & Gould (New York)
see WARD, MATTHIAS (New
      York)
   GOULD, STEPHEN (New
   York)

WARDELL, PHILIP (Philadelphia)
1809: 17358 f

WARDLE, THOMAS (Philadel-
phia)
1813: 29775 pb
1819: 50034 pb

WARE, GALEN (Andover,
Mass.)
1810: 19803, 21412, 22037
1811: 22197

WARE, GALEN (Northampton,
Mass.)
1811: 22684
1812: 25118

WARE, THOMAS (New York)
1811: 22648 f
1812: 26068 f, 26069 pb, 26070
   f, 27519 f
1813: 27644 pb, 27692 pb,
   27743 pb, 27756 f, 27844 f,
   28174 f, 28252 f, 29154 f,
   29155 pb, 29156-29158 f,
   29267 pb, 29679 f, 29680
   pb, 29689 f
1814: 30850 f, 31472 f, 31789
   pb, 31802 f, 32114 f, 32115

pb, 32116-32117 f, 32667 f,
32744 f, 33644 f, 33645 pb,
33680 f
1815: 34084 f, 34087 f, 34386-
34387 f, 35268-35269 f,
35535 f, 35802-35803 f,
36036-36037 f, 36539 f,
51463 f

WARE, THOMAS (Philadelphia)
1804: 6228 f

WARNER, --- (Norwich, Conn.)
1804: 6875 pb

WARNER, BENJAMIN (Lexing-
ton, Ky.)
1810: 20464 pb, 20492 pb

WARNER, BENJAMIN (Phila-
delphia)
1808: 14251 pb, 14845 f,
15009 pb, 15332 pb, 15353
pb, 15614 f, 15852 pb,
16153-16154 pb, 16292 f,
16656 pb
1809: 16832 pb, 17000 pb,
17204 f, 17274 pb, 17313 f,
17348 f, 17399 pb, 17424 f,
17531 f, 17532 pb, 17533 f,
17638 f, 17679 f, 17691 f,
17720 pb, 17734, 17832 pb,
17843 pb, 17845 pb, 17875
pb, 17918 f, 18137 pb,
18150 f, 18156 pb, 18182
pb, 18284 f, 18327 f, 18392-
18393 f, 18542 pb, 18550 f,
18649 f, 18733 f, 18794 f,
19127 pb, 19174 pb, 50905
pb, 50925 pb
1810: 19318 f, 19342 pb,
19521 pb, 19551 f, 19581?
pb, 19736 f, 19861 pb, 19892
f, 19894 pb, 19912 f, 19984
f, 19992 f, 19995 pb, 20031
f, 20192 f, 20212 f, 20229
pb, 20233 f, 20463 pb, 20494
f, 20586 f, 20605 f, 20621
pb, 20807 pb, 20815-20816
pb, 20820 pb, 20949 f, 21071
f, 21072 pb, 21073-21076 f,
21078 f, 21080 pb, 21163 f,
21184 f, 21395 pb, 21513

pb, 21542 f, 21912 f, 21982
pb, 22069 f, 22082 pb,
22129 pb, 50990 f
1811: 22221 f, 22427 f, 22522
pb, 22594 f, 22717 f, 22744
pb, 22782 pb, 22799 pb,
22849 f, 22909 pb, 22921 f,
23012 f, 23094 pb, 23108 f,
23121 f, 23124 pb, 23198 f,
23226 pb, 23229 f, 23392 f,
23422 f, 23434-23435 f,
23456 pb, 23461 f, 23643
pb, 23677 f, 23682 f, 23693
f, 23694 pb, 23868 f, 23873
pb, 23934 f, 23939 f, 23956
f, 23992 f, 24033 pb, 24353
pb, 24364 pb, 24394 pb,
24428 f
1812: 24576 f, 24852 f, 24883
pb, 24939 pb, 25106 pb,
25216-25217 pb, 25416 pb,
25419 f, 25450 f, 25600 pb,
25755 pb, 26083 pb, 26177
pb, 26179 pb, 26458 pb,
26635-26636 f, 26639 f,
27413 pb
1813: 27683 f, 27897 pb, 28041
f, 28245-28246 pb, 28282 f,
28337 f, 28462 pb, 28548 f,
28583 f, 28842 pb, 28845a
pb, 29254 f, 29255 pb, 29324
f, 29436 f, 29509 f, 29518-
29519 pb, 29576 f, 29819
pb, 30437 f, 30505 f
1814: 31276 f, 31566 pb, 31818
f, 31827 f, 31829 pb, 32222
f, 32227 pb, 32399 f, 32419
f, 32490 f, 32906 pb, 33546
f, 33560 pb, 51402 f
1815: 34117 f, 34190 pb,
34506 pb, 34833-34834 pb,
35006 pb, 35622 f, 35631 f,
35643 f, 35817 f, 35821 f,
35967 f, 36468 pb, 51484 f,
51505 f
1816: 36954 pb, 37210 pb,
37338 pb, 37399 pb, 37504
pb, 37948 f, 38318 pb, 38603
pb, 38622 pb, 39699 pb,
39706 pb, 39758 pb, 39893
pb, 51578 pb, 51604 pb
1817: 40245 f, 40262 pb,
40275 pb, 40321, 40355 f,

40378 f, 40622 f, 40809 f,
40821 f, 40930 pb, 41081 f,
41529 f, 41692 pb, 41747 f,
41800 pb, 41803 pb, 41824-
41825 f, 41865 f, 42152 f,
42802 f, 42805 f, 42826-
42827 pb
1818:   43035 pb, 43234 f,
43377 pb, 43388 f, 43456
pb, 43492 pb, 43493 f,
43532 pb, 43581 pb, 43597
pb, 43865 f, 44016 pb, 44167
f, 44175 f, 44364, 44457 f,
44636 f, 44855 f, 44947 f,
45300 pb, 45314 pb, 45317-
45318 f, 45587-45588 pb,
45593 f, 45670 pb, 45744
f, 45771 f, 46681 pb, 46696-
46697 pb
1819:   47995 f, 48122 pb,
48222 pb, 48383-48384 f,
48546 f, 48781 pb, 48813
pb, 48935 f, 49116 pb,
49443 f, 50040 pb

WARNER, BENJAMIN (Rich-
    mond, Va.)
1809:   50945 pb
1810:   20320 pb, 51016 pb
1811:   51109 pb
1812:   51168 pb, 51212 pb
1813:   51312 pb, 51345 pb
1815:   51506 pb
1816:   51639 pb
1817:   51726 pb
1818:   51842-51843 pb
1819:   48935 f, 51951 pb

WARNER, ELEAZER (Utica,
    N.Y.)
1811:   23172 pb

WARNER, JAMES (Wilbraham,
    Mass.)
1810:   21518 f

WARNER, WILLIAM (Balti-
    more)
1801:   101, 321, 365 pb, 389,
588, 1190, 1268, 1616 pb
1802:   1734, 1803, 1809,
2048 pb, 2212, 2223, 2254,
2499 pb, 2520, 2529 pb,

2906-2907 pb, 3062 pb, 3128
1803:   3713, 3715, 4004 pb,
4032 pb, 4163 pb, 4180 pb,
4296 pb, 4337, 4339, 4400
pb, 4430 pb, 4514 pb, 4681
pb, 4761 pb, 4879 pb, 4881
pb, 4970 pb, 4983 f, 5032
pb, 5480, 50348 pb
1804:   5761-5762, 5764-5765,
5807 pb, 5950 f, 6085 pb,
6193, 6225, 6283-6284,
6691 f, 6717, 6839 pb,
6845? pb, 6872 pb, 7076
pb, 7239 pb, 7252
1805:   7914, 8271 pb, 8310,
8424 pb, 8585, 8674 pb,
8916, 8917 pb, 8936 pb,
8946, 8975 pb, 9162 pb,
9198 pb, 9206 pb, 9356,
50523 pb, 50609 pb
1806:   9806, 9836 pb, 9840 pb,
9886, 10019, 10359 pb,
10388, 10403, 10522, 10606
pb, 10627-10628, 10853 pb,
10854, 10879, 10924-10925,
11212, 11336 pb, ?11795,
50672 pb
1807:   12031? pb, 12032, 12034,
?12224, 12354 pb, 12537,
12580 pb, 12581, 12657 pb,
12681 pb, 12817 bf, 13058
bsb, 13096 pb, 13522 pb,
13713
1808:   14352 pb, 14408, 14410,
14503, 14506 pb, 14785 pb,
14870, 14986, 15142, 15304,
15379, 15672 pb, 15992 pb,
16005 pb, 16597, 50890 pb
1809:   16896, 16897 pb, 17314
pb, 17341 pb, 17349 pb,
17478 pb, 17851 pb, 17902,
18220 pb, 18582, 19292 pb,
50934
1810:   19410, 19412, 19462,
19750 pb, 19751, 19875 pb,
20081 pb, 20327 pb, 20499,
?20651 pb, 20769, 20883?,
21117 pb
1811:   22232, 22236? pb,
22439a-22440a pb, 22770 pb,
22800, 23738, 23896 pb,
51053 pb
1812:   24693, 24695? pb,

24696, 24855 pb, 25123 pb,
25167 pb, 25188, 25233,
25417 pb, 25802, 26344 pb,
26457 pb, 26532 pb, 26640,
51194 pb
1813:   27778, 27781 pb, 27782,
27850 pb, 27905 pb, 28279-
28280, 28484 pb
1814:   30736, 31294 pb, 31296,
31419 pb, 31451 pb, 32196,
32209, 32224 pb, 32674,
32730 pb, 51358 pb, 51368
pb
1815:   33914-33915 pb, 34100
pb, 34548, 34673, 34695 pb,
34858, 34985 pb, 35066 pb,
35403 pb, 51487
1816:   36795, 36796 pb, 37407,
37586 pb, 37795, 38274
pb, 38364, 39905 pb, 51580-
51581 pb
1817:   39984 pb, 40052, 40053
pb, 40229 f, 40793 pb,
40943, 41533, 41558, 41892
f
1818:   43149, 43152 pb, 43993
pb, 44972, 45549, 46676
pb, 51767 pb
1819:   47064-47065, 47832,
47941 pb, 48992 pb, 49176?,
49260, 49327 pb, 50039

WARREN, HOOPER (Edwards-
ville, Ill.)
1819:   47084, 47884, 47885 pb

WARREN, W (Baltimore)
1816:   38145

Warren County Peace Society
(Cincinnati, O.)
1817:   42962 f
1818:   46869 f

WARRINER, JEREMY (Pitts-
field, Mass.)
1810:   20821 f

WARRINER, RALPH (Pitts-
field, Mass.)
1810:   20821 f

WARRINER, SOLOMON
(Springfield, Mass.)
1813:   30446 f

WARROCK, JOHN (Richmond,
Va.)
1811:   22872
1814:   31534, 31541, 32359
1815:   33983
1816:   37659
1817:   40130, 40837, 40873-
40874, 51695 pb
1818:   43226, 44104-44105,
44300, 51839-51840 pb
1819:   48175, 49994, 49997,
51953 pb

WARTMANN, LAWRENCE
(Harrisonburg, Va.)
1813:   27733, 28920, 51266
1816:   37108, 37123, 37672
1817:   40300, 41083
1818:   43460

WASHBURN, J C (Hallowell,
Me.)
1818:   46698 pb

Washington Benevolent Societies
in New Jersey (New Bruns-
wick, N.J.)
1813:   30455 f

Washington Benevolent Society
(Albany, N.Y.)
1812:   27437-27438 f
1813:   30448

Washington Benevolent Society
(Brookfield, Mass.)
1812:   27443 f

Washington Benevolent Society
(Hampshire)
1812:   27440 f

Washington Benevolent Society
(Hudson, N.Y.)
1812:   27445 f
1816:   39708 f

Washington Benevolent Society
(New York)
1812:   27449 f

Washington Benevolent Society
(Philadelphia)
1815:   36256 f

Washington Benevolent Society
(Salem, N. Y.)
1812:   27452 f

Washington Benevolent Society
(Springfield, Mass.)
1812:   27453 f
1813:   30458 f

Washington Benevolent Society
(Troy, N. Y.)
1811:   24371 f
1812:   27456 pb

Washington Benevolent Society
(Worcester, Mass.)
1812:   27441 f

Washington Benevolent Society
of Massachusetts (Boston)
1812:   27432 f

Washington Botanical Society
(Washington, D. C.)
1819:   47997 f

Washington College (Washington, Pa.)
1807:   14161 f

Washington Federalist (Georgetown, D. C.)
1802:   3274

Washington Printing and Bookselling Co. (Washington,
D. C.)
1801:   983 pb

WATERMAN, ELEAZER
(Georgetown, S. C.)
1816:   37887, 39697
1817:   42935 pb

WATEROUS, HENRY (New Lon-
don, Conn.)
1817:   42006 f

WATEROUS, TIMOTHY (Groton,
Conn.)
1811:   24382

WATERS, DAVID J (Boston)
1801:   500 f

WATERS, DAVID J (Castine,
Me.)
1802:   2054 pb

WATERS, DAVID J (Hampden,
Me.)
1803:   4687, 4852 pb

WATSON, DAVID (Boston)
1811:   22201, 22373, 22671,
22708, 23218, 23988
1812:   25169, 25534, 25717,
26008, 26029, 26126, 26350,
26468 pb, 26567, 26678,
26926 pb, 27612, 27619-
27620
1813:   27690, 28350 pb, 28561,
28793, 28847, 28908-28909,
28911 pb, 29175, 29278,
29813 pb, 29872, 29874,
29967 pb, 30393 pb, 30485,
30552, 30555
1814:   30883, 31484, 31674,
51352 pb

WATSON, DAVID (Hanover,
N. H.)
1816:   36719 pb, 37475
1817:   39965, 42758 pb
1819:   48793

WATSON, DAVID (Woodstock,
Vt.)
1818:   44144, 44622, 44915,
45708, 46639
1819:   47594, 47803, 48044,
48071, 48231, 48239, 48520,
48547, 48591, 48951, 49964,
49984

WATSON, EBENEZER (Hartford, Conn.)
1810: 22032?

WATSON, EBENEZER (New York)
1802: 2034 pb
1810: 19526 f
1811: 22354 f, 22364 f, 22424a pb, 23829 f
1812: 24532 pb, 24580 f, 24833 f, 24948-24949 f, 24968 f, 24970 f, 24974-24975 f, 25020 f, 25052 f, 25174 f, 25175 pb, 25289 f, 25332 f, 25333 pb, 25578 pb, 25684 f, 25761 pb, 25847 f, 25918 pb, 25921 f, 26080-26081 f, 26363 pb, 26511 f, 26519 f, 26621 f, 26654 f, 26762 pb, 27530 f, 27540 pb, 27590 f
1813: 27889 pb, 28132 f, 28136 f, 28153-28154 f, 28683 f, 28849 pb, 29166 f, 29427 f, 29881 f, 30520 pb
1814: 30995, 31995 f, 32003 f, 32023 f, 32842 pb, 32847 f, 33662 f
1815: 33871 pb, 34058 f, 35042 f, 35228 f, 35784 pb, 35788 f
1816: 37235 pb, 37350 f, 38153 f
1818: 44482? pb

WATSON, JOHN FANNING (Philadelphia)
1810: 19349 f, 19608 f, 20565 f
1811: 22183 f, 23877 pb, 23929 f
1812: 25013 pb, 25861 f
1813: 28371 pb, 28930 pb, 28942 f, 29128 f, 29764 f
1814: 30714 pb

WATSON, SAMUEL E (Lexington, Ky.)
1811: 22191 pb

WATSON, THOMAS (Newbern, N.C.)
1807: 13141 pb, 50819 pb
1808: 16762, 50902 pb
1809: 18247 pb
1810: 21524 pb
1811: 24057 pb

WATSON, THOMAS (Wilmington, N.C.)
1809: 18788 pb

WATTS, JAMES G (Walpole, N.H.)
1811: 22292, 23266, 24388
1812: 24849, 25057, 25422, 27483

WATTS, JAMES G (Windsor, Vt.)
1811: 22230

WATTS, JOHN (New York)
1813: 30456
1818: 44659 pb

WATTS, JOHN (Philadelphia)
1805: 50564 f
1806: 9787, 10065-10066, 10322, 10324, 10731 f, 10851 pb, 10899 f, 11412-11413 pb, 50732 pb

WATTS, RICHARD KEY (Annapolis, Md.)
1801: 1693 f
1804: 7805 f

WAUCHOPE, ROBERT (New York)
1819: 48190 f

WAY, ANDREW (Philadelphia)
1803: 3951, 4870, 5037, 5109
1804: 5814 pb, 7005 pb, 7257

WAY, ANDREW (Washington, D.C.)
1801: 202, 1486, 1609, 1684
1802: 1791, 2450, 3285, ?3422
1803: 5537
1804: 5744, 6878, 7698

1805: 8752, 9519-9520, 9546-
9547, 9552-9553, 9566,
9570-9572, 9574-9575,
9593, 9597, 9599, 9601-
9602, 9605-9606, 9609,
9612, 9617-9618, 9620,
9628, 9633-9634, 9688
1806: 10866, 11493, 11504-
11505, 11554-11555, 11557-
11558, 11585, 11587-11618,
11621-11626, 11628-11629,
11631, 11633-11635, 11637-
11653, 11655-11657, 11659-
11662, 11665-11668, 11671-
11674, 11678-11679, 11682-
11687, 11689-11702, 11704-
11732, 11734-11739, 11741-
11742, 11797
1807: 12976-12977, 13761-
13765, 13796, 13877-13878,
13880-13895, 13903-13906,
13934, 13938-13978, 13981-
13986, 13988-13989, 13991-
13998, 14000, 14004-14005,
14010-14013, 14019-14023,
14032-14033, 14035, 14040-
14044, 14047-14064, 14066-
14081, 14083, 14085-14087,
14158
1808: 15019, 16357-16358,
16362-16363, 16373, 16377,
16379-16386, 16391, 16397-
16398, 16404, 16407-16409,
16411-16428, 16430-16446,
16450-16453, 16458-16467,
16469-16470, 16472, 16475-
16484, 16487, 16489, 16494-
16502, 16504, 16511-16512,
16516, 16519-16521, 16524-
16527, 16536, 16544-16545,
16547-16549, 16551-16557,
16561-16567, 16569-16571,
16574-16576, 16578, 16580,
16584, 16587, 16591, 16593-
16594, 16596, 16662, 50842
1809: 18073, 18439, 18812,
18869-18870, 18875-18879,
18881-18884, 18886, 18892-
18893, 18897, 18910-18912,
18919-18922, 18926, 18928-
18933, 18935-18936, 18938-
18942, 18947, 18949, 18951,
18954, 18959-18961, 18964,

18966, 18969-18970, 18972,
18975, 18977-18979, 18982-
18983, 18988-18991, 19001-
19004, 19006, 19009, 19012,
19014, 19016, 19029, 19035,
19038-19039, 19041-19042,
19044, 19047, 19051, 19053-
19056, 19058-19060, 19062,
19067-19068, 19071, 19074,
19145
1810: 21128-21129, 21654-
21655, 21671, 21676, 21679,
21681, 21685, 21687-21689,
21691, 21695, 21699, 21705,
21708, 21711, 21713-21714,
21716, 21719, 21721-21723,
21729, 21737-21738, 21747,
21751, 21753-21754, 21761,
21764, 21778-21779, 21782,
21787, 21790, 21798, 21802,
21805, 21809, 21814, 21818,
21820, 21823-21824, 21826-
21828, 21835-21836, 21838,
21840, 21843-21844, 21846,
21851-21853, 21858, 21860,
21951-21952, 21981
1811: 24077, 24082, 24141,
24143, 24147, 24153, 24155,
24162-24165, 24168, 24170,
24173, 24175, 24177-24179,
24181, 24183, 24186, 24189-
24190, 24193-24196, 24198-
24199, 24203, 24205-24207,
24211, 24213-24215, 24217,
24222-24224, 24228, 24230-
24231, 24239, 24244-24245,
24247, 24261-24262, 24267-
24269, 24274, 24277-24279,
24282, 24285-24289, 24293,
24295-24296, 24298-24299,
24305, 24309-24312, 24373
1812: 26931, 26942, 26945,
27129, 27139, 27147, 27153,
27155-27158, 27162-27165,
27170-27172, 27181-27182,
27188-27189, 27191, 27193,
27199, 27217, 27220-27221,
27223, 27225-27226, 27229,
27231-27232, 27242-27244,
27247, 27250, 27254, 27292-
27293, 27307-27308, 27316,
27320, 27326-27329, 27331,
27334-27335, 27341-27343,

27348, 27350, 27361
1813: 30001, 30177, 30185,
　　30188a-30189, 30199, 30204,
　　30208, 30214, 30217-30218,
　　30224, 30226, 30228-30230,
　　30233, 30244, 30248, 30250,
　　30252, 30255-30256, 30258-
　　30259, 30261, 30263, 30268,
　　30279, 30304, 30310, 30313,
　　30316-30317, 30319, 30324-
　　30325, 30331, 30333, 30338,
　　30341, 30345, 30353-30354,
　　30356, 30460
1814: 31670, 32986-32987,
　　33230, 33241, 33244, 33249,
　　33251-33252, 33254, 33256-
　　33258, 33262, 33268-33269,
　　33274-33275, 33278-33280,
　　33282-33283, 33285, 33287-
　　33288, 33295, 33298, 33300,
　　33302, 33307, 33317, 33319,
　　33326, 33330, 33381, 33393-
　　33394, 33400-33402, 33404-
　　33405, 33409, 33414, 33416,
　　33418, 33420-33422, 33427-
　　33430, 33432, 33438-33439,
　　33441-33442, 33450-33451,
　　33453, 33456, 33458, 33460-
　　33461, 33463, 33465-33468,
　　33472, 33477, 33479-33480,
　　33483-33486, 33495, 33498,
　　33500, 33508, 33581
1815: 36273, 36278-36279,
　　36284, 36288, 36295, 36299,
　　36302, 36307, 36312, 36316,
　　36318, 36327-36328, 36331-
　　36333, 36370, 36372, 36375-
　　36376, 36380, 36484

WAY, GEORGE (Philadelphia)
1803: 3951, 4870, 5037, 5109
1804: 5814 pb, 7005 pb, 7257

WAY, GEORGE (Washington,
　D. C.)
1802: 3285
1803-1819: For all entries
　see WAY, ANDREW (Wash-
　ington, D. C.) above.

WAYNE, CALEB PARRY
　(Philadelphia)
1801: 440

1804: 6710 pb
1805: 7874 pb, 8836 pb, 9359
　pb, 50568 pb
1806: 10889 pb
1807: 12915-12916 pb, 12920
　pb, 12996 pb

WEAVER, JOHN (Lynchburg,
　Va.)
1803: 3747
1804: 6681 pb, 6761 pb

WEAVER, WILLIAM (Philadel-
　phia)
1810: 19573 f, 20035 pb, 20405
　f, 21062 pb, 21377 f
1811: 22873 pb, 23676 sb

WEBB, JOHN (Portsmouth,
　N. H.)
1818: 43094 f

WEBB, PHINEHAS (Ballston
　Spa, N. Y.)
1811: 23007 f

WEBB, SAMUEL (Norwich,
　Conn.)
1812: 26196 pb, 51203
1813: 29871

WEBB, SAMUEL (Windham,
　Conn.)
1813: 29321, 29887, 29951,
　30430, 30560, 51275
1814: 33703 pb, 33739 pb
1817: 41944 pb
1818: 43024 pb

WEBB, THOMAS (Homer, N. Y.)
1812: 25401

WEBB, THOMAS SMITH
　(Providence, R. I.)
1805: 9700 pb

WEBSTER, CHARLES (Water-
　ford, N. Y.)
1814: 33622

WEBSTER, CHARLES (Stock-
　bridge, Mass.)
1819: 48311-48312

WEBSTER, CHARLES RICHARD
(Albany, N. Y.)
1801: 605, 696, 737, 753,
840, 855, 1025, 1027, 1031,
1041, 1066, 1317, 1337-
1338, 1351, 1635
1802: 1735, 1881, 1950, 2471,
2681, 2742, 2770, 2776,
2781, 3189, 3510, 3523,
3526?
1803: 3645, 3658, 3972-3973,
4313, 4359, 4675, 4731 f,
5025, 5165, 5556, 5560,
5564 pb, 5633 pb
1804: 5674? pb, 5954 pb,
6206, 6328, 6683, 6837 pb,
6913, 6948-6949, 6953?,
6974, 7286, 7718, 7737,
7796-7797, 50485-50486 pb
1805: 7995 pb, 8252, 8794,
9040, 9197, 9391, 9708,
9712?
1806: 10015, 10161, 10332
pb, 10430, 10547 pb, 10633,
10741, 10760, 11006, 11009,
11048, 11787 pb, 11829 f,
11835 pb, 11837-11838 pb,
50645 pb
1807: 12933 pb, 13230 pb,
13232, 13233 pb, 13235,
13266, 13688, 14193
1808: 14309, 14458, 15239 f,
15314?, 15437, 15755-
15756, 16691 pb, 16696 pb
1809: 16958 pb, 17416, 17921?
pb, 18237, 19186
1810: 19310, 19577?, 20575,
20892?, 20897, 21466,
21512?, 21992 pb
1811: 22408, 23111, 23233?,
23425, 23574, 23576, 24330,
24375, 24409 pb, 51120,
51123
1812: 24577 pb, 24578, 24889,
25023, 25097, 25869 pb,
26053, 26163 pb, 26280,
26284, 26933, 27464-27465,
27497, 27504, 51154, 51228
1813: 27684, 27855 pb, 27902,
28377, 28834, 28960?,
29176, 29336, 29716 pb,
29756, 30465, 30488 pb,
30502, 30506 pb, 51325-51326

1814: 30645, 30936 pb, 31610,
31941? f, 32195 pb, 32813,
33305 pb, 33584-33586,
33589, 33631, 33653, 51451
pb
1815: 33790, 34147, 34237,
34339, 34368, 34599, 35341
pb, 35354 pb, 35460, 35464,
35509, 35753, 35974, 36018,
36487, 36529 pb, 51455,
51520
1816: 36697, 36699, 36972,
37117, 38215, 38378, 38435,
38441, 38761, 38766, 38866,
39712, 39727, 39754, 39761,
51603 bsb, 51629
1817: 39956, 40194, 40223,
40224 f, 40309, 40704-40705,
40722, 40947, 41065, 41159,
41275 pb, 41617, 41626,
41631, 41674, 41938-41939,
41941, 42062, 42206 pb,
42339 pb, 42812, 42859 pb,
42907, 51707, 51727-51729
pb
1818: 43524, 43662, 43906 sb,
43907 pb, 44356, 45030 pb,
45045 pb, 45046? pb, 45048,
46744 pb, 51742, 51794 f,
51844
1819: 46954-46955, 47825 pb,
48529, 48882-48883, 48886,
48892, 48895 f, 49186,
50084 pb, 50127 pb, 51942

WEBSTER, GEORGE (Albany,
N. Y.)
For all entries see WEBSTER,
CHARLES RICHARD (Al-
bany, N. Y.) above

WEBSTER, JAMES (Philadel-
phia)
1812: 26845 pb
1814: 30841 pb, 31010 pb,
32421 pb, 32425 pb, 51378
pb
1815: 34017-34018 pb, 35962
pb, 36447 pb
1816: 37725 pb, 38308 pb
1817: 40447 f, 40651 f, 40922
pb, 41034 f, 41107 f, 41133
pb, 42937 f

1818:   43068 pb, 43632 f,
43688 f, 43839 pb, 44235
pb, 44236 f, 44369 f, 44373
pb, 44400 f, 45465 pb,
45916 f, 46839-46840 f
1819:   47727 f, 47959 f, 49172
f

WEBSTER, TRUMAN (Water-
ford, N. Y.)
1816:   39718 pb

Websters & Skinner (Albany,
N. Y.)
see WEBSTER, CHARLES
RICHARD (Albany, N. Y.)
WEBSTER, GEORGE (Al-
bany, N. Y.)
SKINNER, ELISHA (Albany,
N. Y.)

Websters & Skinners (Albany,
N. Y.)
see WEBSTER, CHARLES
RICHARD (Albany, N. Y.)
WEBSTER, GEORGE (Al-
bany, N. Y.)
SKINNER, DANIEL (Albany,
N. Y.)
SKINNER, ELISHA (Albany,
N. Y.)
SKINNER, HEZEKIAH (Al-
bany, N. Y.)

WEED, NATHAN (Stamford,
Conn.)
1813:   29122 f

WEED, THURLOW (Norwich,
N. Y.)
1818:   45519 pb

Weekly Messenger (Russellville, Ky.)
1815:   35910

Weekly Recorder (Chillicothe,
O.)
1814:   33699
1815:   35864

WEEKS, WILLIAM (Kennebunk,
Me.)
1805:   8723 pb

WEEKS, WILLIAM (Portland,
Me.)
1807:   12605 pb
1808:   14255 pb, 14423, 14428,
14592, 14996 pb
1809:   16866?, 17834

WEEKS, WILLIAM (Portsmouth,
N. H.)
1809:   16893 f, 16952, 18795,
19286
1810:   19406 bf, 21280
1812:   24690, 24758, 25074
1813:   27777, 28011
1816:   38595 pb

WEEKS, WILLIAM (Saco, Me.)
1805:   7956, 8464 pb
1806:   10354, 11865
1807:   12053, 12743

WEEMS, ELIJAH (Georgetown,
D. C.)
1818:   43356 f, 45749 f
1819:   47438 f, 47606 f, 47679
f, 51952 pb

WEEMS, ELIJAH (Philadelphia)
1815:   34292 f

WEEMS, MASON LOCKE
(Baltimore)
1815:   36533 f
1816:   37400 f

WEEMS, MASON LOCKE
(Philadelphia)
1802:   2089 pb
1805:   9359 f
1814:   33636-33637 f

WEIGHTMAN, ROGER CHEW
(Washington, D. C.)
1807:   12470-12471, 12549,
13285, 13286 pb, 13790,
13797, 13896, 13907, 13936,
13980, 13987, 14003, 14016,
14027, 14045-14046, 14082,
14084
1808:   14980, 16364, 16366,
16368, 16374, 16389, 16403,
16405, 16429, 16447-16449,
16454, 16457, 16468, 16473-
16474, 16485-16486, 16488,

16490-16493, 16503, 16505-
16510, 16513-16515, 16517-
16518, 16522-16523, 16528,
16534, 16550, 16558-16560,
16573, 16577, 16579, 16581,
16583, 16585-16586, 16589,
16595, 16605
1809: 16944, 16948 pb, 17676,
17974, 17975 pb, 18811,
18813, 18871-18874, 18880,
18887-18889, 18913-18914,
18916-18918, 18923-18925,
18927, 18934, 18937, 18943-
18946, 18948, 18950, 18952-
18953, 18956-18958, 18962-
18963, 18965, 18967-18968,
18971, 18973-18974, 18976,
18980-18981, 18984, 18986-
18987, 18992-19000, 19005,
19007-19008, 19010-19011,
19013, 19015, 19017, 19021,
19030-19034, 19037, 19040,
19043, 19045-19046, 19048-
19050, 19052, 19057, 19061,
19064-19066, 19069, 19075,
19077
1810: 19403, 21091, 21567,
21648, 21650, 21653, 21656-
21658, 21662-21663, 21672,
21675, 21677-21678, 21680,
21682-21684, 21686, 21690,
21692-21694, 21696-21698,
21700-21704, 21706-21707,
21709-21710, 21712, 21715,
21717-21718, 21720, 21724-
21728, 21730-21733, 21735-
21736, 21739-21743, 21745-
21746, 21750, 21752, 21755-
21756, 21758-21760, 21762-
21763, 21765-21777, 21780-
21781, 21783-21786, 21788-
21789, 21791, 21797, 21799-
21800, 21803, 21806-21808,
21810-21813, 21815-21817,
21819, 21821-21822, 21825,
21829-21831, 21833-21834,
21837, 21839, 21841-21842,
21845, 21847-21850, 21855-
21857, 21861-21862, 21864
1811: 23174, 24080, 24087,
24137, 24140, 24142, 24144-
24145, 24148-24151, 24154,
24156-24161, 24166-24167,

24169, 24171-24172, 24174,
24176, 24180, 24182, 24185,
24187-24188, 24191-24192,
24197, 24200-24202, 24204,
24208-24210, 24212, 24216,
24218-24221, 24225-24227,
24229, 24232-24238, 24240-
24243, 24246, 24248-24253,
24255-24256, 24259-24260,
24263-24266, 24270-24273,
24275-24276, 24280-24281,
24283-24284, 24290-24292,
24294, 24297, 24300-24304,
24306, 24308, 24313-24316
1812: 26932, 27120, 27131-
27138, 27140, 27144, 27148-
27150, 27152, 27159-27161,
27166-27169, 27173-27180,
27183-27187, 27190, 27192,
27194-27198, 27200, 27205-
27216, 27218-27219, 27222,
27224, 27227-27228, 27230,
27233-27241, 27245-27246,
27248-27249, 27251-27253,
27258, 27267-27269, 27274-
27278, 27282-27283, 27294-
27306, 27309-27313, 27315,
27317-27319, 27321-27325,
27330, 27332-27333, 27336-
27340, 27344-27347, 27349,
27352-27353, 27360, 51256
1813: 28563, 29807, 30009,
30013, 30178-30182, 30190-
30191, 30198, 30200-30203,
30205-30207, 30209-30213,
30215-30216, 30219-30220,
30222-30223, 30225, 30227,
30231-30232, 30234-30239,
30241-30243, 30245-30247,
30249, 30251, 30253-30254,
30257, 30260, 30262, 30264-
30266, 30272, 30278, 30280-
30282, 30285, 30290, 30297-
30299, 30301, 30303, 30308,
30311, 30315, 30318, 30320-
30323, 30326-30330, 30332,
30334-30337, 30339-30340,
30342-30344, 30346-30352,
30355, 30357-30370, 30377
1814: 31793, 31825, 32999,
33226-33227, 33231, 33242,
33245-33248, 33250, 33253,
33255, 33259-33261, 33263-

33267, 33270-33273, 33276-
33277, 33281, 33284, 33286,
33289-33294, 33297, 33299,
33301, 33303-33304, 33308-
33313, 33315-33316, 33318,
33320-33325, 33327-33329,
33331-33332, 33336-33338,
33346-33349, 33351-33352,
33357-33360, 33362-33368,
33370, 33372-33376, 33379,
33387, 33392, 33395, 33399,
33403, 33406-33408, 33410-
33413, 33415, 33417, 33419,
33423-33426, 33431, 33433-
33437, 33440, 33443-33449,
33452, 33454-33455, 33457,
33459, 33462, 33464, 33469-
33471, 33473-33476, 33478,
33481-33482, 33487-33493,
33496-33497, 33507, 33509
1815: 34518, 36260, 36274,
36275 pb, 36277, 36280-
36281, 36283, 36285-36286,
36290, 36292-36293, 36296-
36298, 36300-36301, 36303,
36306, 36308, 36313-36314,
36317, 36319, 36324-36326,
36329, 36335-36336, 36339,
36341-36342, 36344-36346,
36351-36352, 36354, 36356-
36357, 36364, 36371, 36374,
36377-36379, 36381-36392,
36394-36396, 36398-36402,
36405, 36407-36411
1816: 38823 f, 39486 pb
1817: 42665

WELCH, --- (Cambridge,
  Mass.)
1807: 12724 f

WELD, GILES E (Boston)
1816: 38176 pb, 38187 pb,
  38662, 38755, 39050
1817: 42891

WELD, J R (Charlestown,
  Mass.)
1810: 20457 pb

WELLER, GEORGE (Newark,
  N.J.)
1813: 27841 f

WELLS, --- (Brooklyn, N.Y.)
1810: 21530?

WELLS, EDWARD B (New
  York)
1815: 34374 f

WELLS, RUSSELL (Deerfield,
  Mass.)
1815: 34574
1816: 36940-36941
1817: 40193

WELLS, RUSSELL (Greenfield,
  Mass.)
1817: 40851 pb
1818: 44076 pb

WELLS, THOMAS (Boston)
1809: 17630 pb
1810: 19723 f
1812: 25842 pb, 27372 pb
1813: 27690 f, 27870 f, 28561
  f, 28909 f, 29020 pb, 29549?
  pb
1814: 31098 f, 32877 pb,
  51381 pb
1815: 34464 f, 35538 f
1816: 36706 f
1817: 40171 f
1818: 43273 f

WELLS, WILLIAM (Boston)
1802: 2034 pb
1804: 6425 f
1808: 14474 pb, 14658?, 16302
  f
1809: 16984 f, 17005 f, 17009
  f, 17173 f, 17189-17190 pb,
  17525 pb, 17528 pb, 17662
  pb, 17689 f, 17706 f, 18139
  f, 18719 f, 19291 f
1810: 19325 pb, 19522 pb,
  19708 pb, 20032 pb, 21202 f,
  21298 pb, 22010 f
1811: 22324 f, 22346 pb,
  23596 pb, 23792 f, 24473 pb
1812: 25820 pb, 25825 pb,
  27614 f
1813: 28130 pb, 29675 pb,
  29833 f, 29847 pb, 29863 pb
1814: 30685, 31055 pb, 31338
  pb, 31391 pb, 31769 pb,

32670 pb, 32868-32869 pb
1815: 33822 pb, 33909, 33925
pb, 34239 pb, 34250 pb,
34308 pb, 34312-34314 pb,
34316-34319 pb, 34348-
34349 pb, 34463 pb, 34540
pb, 34916 pb, 34921-34922
pb, 34649, 34758 pb, 34868-
34869 pb, 34936, 34937 pb,
35143 pb, 35229 pb, 35250
pb, 35316 pb, 35501 pb,
35703-35704 pb, 35853 pb,
35874 pb, 35879 pb, 35994
pb, 36059, 36060 pb, 36072,
36404 pb, 36422, 36424 pb
1816: 36707 pb, 36782 pb,
36909 pb, 36926 pb, 37103
pb, 37125 pb, 37207-37208
pb, 37243 pb, 37291 pb,
37301 pb, 37348 pb, 37367
pb, 37485 pb, 37496 pb,
37528 f, 37738, 37777 pb,
37822, 37854 pb, 37857 pb,
37858 f, 37874 f, 37894 pb,
37976-37977 pb, 38008 pb,
38017 f, 38106 pb, 38167
pb, 38202 pb, 38291 f,
38530 f, 38552 f, 38566 pb,
38617 pb, 38791 pb, 38826
pb, 38828 f, 38837 pb,
38864 f, 38883 pb, 38892
f, 38985 pb, 39054-39055 pb,
39057 pb, 39060-39061 pb,
39109 pb, 39654, 39658 f,
39780 pb, 39843, 39867
pb, 39872 f, 39889 pb,
51570-51576 pb
1817: 39925 pb, 40248, 40354
pb, 40441 pb, 40602 pb,
40726 pb, 40899 pb, 40941,
40973 pb, 40980 pb, 41015,
41168 pb, 41206, 41481 pb,
41822-41823 pb, 41841 pb,
42053 pb, 42128 pb, 42222
pb, 42226, 42247 pb, 42262-
42263, 42960 pb
1818: 43233 pb, 43372 pb,
43439, 43530 pb, 43560 pb,
43814 pb, 43918 pb, 43979,
44061 pb, 44125, 44218,
44223, 44291 pb, 44293,
44447 pb, 44625-44626,
44838 pb, 45122 pb,

?45347?, 45590 pb, 45799
pb, 45852, 46682 pb, 46693
1819: 47485 pb, 47502 pb,
47555, 47596-47597, 47633
pb, 47741 pb, 47802 pb,
47876-47877 pb, 47880 pb,
47907, 48069 pb, 48112 pb,
48129 pb, 48139 pb, 48287,
48431 pb, 48433-48434 pb,
48636, 48747-48749 pb,
48955, 49128 pb, 49160 pb,
49270, 49299, 49533, 49945
pb, 49971 pb, 50035 pb,
51855 pb, 51880-51881 pb

Wells & Lilly (Boston)
see WELLS, WILLIAM (Boston)
     LILLY, ROBERT (Boston)

WENDELL, JOHN P (Dover,
N. H.)
1803: 4948

Wesleyan Sacred Music Society
(New York)
1817: 40777 f

WEST, DAVID (Boston)
1801: 9 f, 156 pb, 188 pb,
425 f, 620 pb, 670 pb, 1262
f, 1267 f, 1433 f
1802: 1711 f, 2003 f, 2051 pb,
2482 f, 3175 f
1803: 4340 f, 4533 f
1804: 5832 pb, 5861 f, 6450
pb, 7212 pb
1806: 10131 f, 10237-10238 f
1807: 12683 f, 14188 f
1808: 14471 pb
1809: 17134 pb, 17249? pb
1810: 19704 pb, 20455 pb,
21304 f
1811: 22146 pb
1812: 24793-24794 f, 24821 f,
26781 f, 26912 pb, 27433 f
1813: 27909 pb, 28728 pb
1814: 30622-30623 pb, 31051
f, 31054 f

WEST, ELISHA (Northampton,
Mass.)
1802: 3532 f

WEST, JOHN (Boston)
1801: 190, 670 f, 724 f,
790 f, 847 f, 1088 f, 1433 f
1802: 1711 f, 2051 pb, 2212a
pb, 2482 f, 2631 pb, 3080 f,
3109 f, 3175 f
1803: 3862 f, 3935 pb, 4180a
pb, 4533 f, 4616 pb, 5067 f,
5096 f
1804: 5658 f, 5861 f, 6285
pb, 6750 pb, 7727 pb
1805: 7830 f, 8036 f, 8152-
8153 f, 8425 pb, 8874 pb,
9416 pb, 9683, 9706 f
1806: 10067 f, 10105 f, 10183
f, 10218 f, 10289 f, 10389
pb, 10743 f, 10832 pb,
11090 f, 11300 pb, 11381
f, 11402 pb, 11489 f, 11830
f
1807: 12214 f, 12435 pb,
12538 f, 12683 f, 12923 f,
13035 pb, 13524 f, 13573 f,
13631 f, 13632? pb, 13633
pb, 14185 pb, 14188 f
1808: 14987 f, 15013 f,
15152 f, 15381 f, 15473 f,
15557 pb, 16218-16219 f,
16692 f
1809: 17033 pb, 17088 pb,
17138 pb, 17329 f, 17480 f,
17666 f, 17807 f, 17883 f,
18057 pb, 18634 f, 19165
pb, 19166 f, 19171 pb
1810: 19640 f, 19644 pb,
19879 f, 20082 f, 20106 f,
20695 pb, 20774 f, 20979
f, 21365 f, 21405 pb, 21937
f, 21988 pb
1811: 22576 f, 22802 f, 22847
f, 23112 pb, 23166 pb,
23348 pb, 23431 f, 23432-
23433 pb, 23840 pb, 23972
pb, 24404 f
1812: 24821 f, 24880 pb,
25395 f, 25814 f, 26036 pb,
26487 f, 26722 pb, 26756 f,
27422 f, 27485 pb
1813: 27944 pb, 28047 f,
28230 pb, 28486 f, 28633-
28634 f, 28863? f, 28986
pb, 28987 f, 29116-29117
pb, 29535 f, 29850-29851 pb

1814: 30862 f, 30916 pb,
31078-31079 f, 31453 f,
31665 pb, 32078 pb, 32845
f, 32966 f, 33624 f
1815: 34080 pb, 34119-34120
pb, 34488 f, 34675 f, 35222-
35223 pb, 35554 f, 35815 f,
35873 f, 35999 f
1816: 36883 f, 36986 f,
37096 f, 37562 f, 38191-
38193 pb, 39001-39002 f,
39027 f
1817: 40326 pb, 40797 pb,
41376-41377 pb, 42205 pb,
42790 pb, 42811 f, 42852
pb, 42858 pb
1818: 19373? f, 43034 pb,
43296 f, 43314 f, 43315 pb,
43340 f, 43453 f, 43991 f,
43997 f, 44529 pb, 44755 pb,
45200 f, 45219 f, 45271 f,
45746 f, 45789 f
1819: 47220-47221 f, 47437 f,
47945 f, 48641 pb, 48825 f,
50031 f, 50069 f, 50079 pb,
50183 f, 51877 pb

WEST, SAMUEL (Salem, Mass.)
1809: 18121

West & Blake (Boston)
see WEST, DAVID (Boston)
BLAKE, LEMUEL (Boston)

West & Greenleaf (Boston)
see WEST, DAVID (Boston)
GREENLEAF, OLIVER C
(Boston)

West & Richardson (Boston)
see WEST, JOHN (Boston)
RICHARDSON, ELEAZER
TYNG FOX (Boston)

West, Richardson & Lord
(Boston)
see WEST, JOHN (Boston)
RICHARDSON, ELEAZER
TYNG FOX (Boston)
LORD, MELVIN (Boston)

West Society (New Haven, Conn.)
1803: 5154 pb

1805:   9465 pb
1806:   50734 pb

WESTCOTT, --- (Washington,
    D. C.)
1814:   33698

WESTCOTT, JAMES DIAMENT
    (Alexandria, Va.)
1801:   577
1802:   2052 pb, 2818

WESTCOTT, JAMES DIAMENT
    (Washington, D. C.)
1803:   5481
1807:   12000, 13718, 13732,
    14038
1808:   16342 pb

WESTCOTT, JOHN (Alexandria,
    Va.)
1801:   577
1802:   2536, 2818, 2823
1803:   3878 pb, 4691 pb, 5116
1806:   50635 pb

WESTCOTT, JOHN (Baltimore)
1810:   19417

WESTCOTT, JOHN (Bridgeton,
    N. J.)
1804:   5715 pb
1805:   8161

WESTCOTT, JOHN (Cedarville,
    N. J.)
1805:   8999 f
1806:   10984 pb

Western Eagle (Madison, Ind.)
1813:   27789? pb
1818:   43172? pb

Western Intelligencer (Columbus,
    O.)
1814:   30774
1816:   38005
1817:   40530, 41201

Western Intelligencer (Worth-
    ington, O.)
1813:   30581

Western Monitor (Lexington,
    Ky.)
1814:   30670
1815:   51493 pb

Western Navigation Bible and
    Tract Society (Cincinnati,
    O.)
1819:   49223 f

Western Reserve Chronicle
    (Warren, O.)
1818:   43204, 43718

Western Sky (Beula, Pa.)
1811:   22986

Western Spectator (Marietta,
    O.)
1812:   24545 pb

Western Spy (Cincinnati, O.)
1816:   39788
1818:   45310

Western Star (Lebanon, O.)
1808:   16776

Western Telegraphe (Washington,
    Pa.)
1807:   14205 pb
1810:   19482

WESTON, EQUALITY (Boston)
1818:   45417
1819:   47029, 47077, 47440,
    47497, 47572, 47603 pb,
    48818, 49036, 49341, 50138

WESTON, J (Reading, Mass.)
1819:   47497 f

WEYGANDT, JACOB (Easton,
    Pa.)
1801:   991 pb
1805:   8365 pb, 8809

WHEELER, BENJAMIN HEN-
    SHAW (Montpelier, Vt.)
1807:   12218

WHEELER, BENNETT (Provi-
    dence, R. I.)
1801:   132, 468, 915, 1058 pb,

50238 pb
1802: 1745, 2156, 2269, 2642, 3547, 50332 pb
1803: 4209-4210

WHEELER, BENNETT H (Providence, R. I.)
1807: 13534
1808: 14742 pb, 15062, 15861, 16066-16067, 16070-16071
1809: 17800, 18504-18508 pb
1810: 19655 pb, 20396, 21093, 21210-21214, 22031
1811: 22824, 23698, 23813-23815
1812: 24734, 24954 pb, 25432, 26611, 27586
1814: 32588, 32589 pb, 32693, 32866
1817: 39962
1818: 43912-43913, 45688
1819: 47873 pb

WHEELER, GEORGE W (Louisville, Ga.)
1809: 17613
1811: 23241 pb
1816: 36721 pb

WHELEN, DENNIS (West Chester, Pa.)
1809: 17196 pb

WHIDDEN, SAMUEL (Portsmouth, N. H.)
1806: 9857, 9947, 10618 pb, 11287, 11341
1807: 14201
1808: 14963?, 16074
1809: 17695
1810: 19409, 20163
1812: 26385, 26503-26504
1814: 30733, 31039, 31886
1817: 41700 pb
1818: 43017, 45392, 45569
1819: 47376, 49505

WHIPPLE, ANSON (Walpole, N. H.)
1815: 34073 pb

WHIPPLE, CHARLES (Newburyport, Mass.)
1803: 4513 f, 5604 pb

1804: 7073 pb, 7301 f
1805: 7881 pb, 8075 f, 8248 pb, 8537 pb, 8653 pb, 8822 pb, 9413 f
1806: 9911? f, 10643 pb, 10751 f, 10916 f, 11164 f, 11896 f, 11905 pb, 50634 pb, 50641 pb, 50716 pb, 50748 pb
1807: 12385 f, 12741 f, 13089 f, 13309 pb, 14247 f
1808: 15024 f, 15250 f, 15661 f, 15662 pb, 15840 f, 15841 pb, 15844 f, 15856 f, 16242 f, 16269 pb, 16300 pb
1809: 17213-17214 f, 17681 pb, 18013 pb, 18101 pb, 18130 f, 18626 f, 19167 f, 19225 pb
1810: 20258 pb, 20410 pb, 20735 f, 20991 pb, 22087 sb
1811: 22837 pb, 23629-23631 f, 23753 pb, 23910 pb, 24485
1812: 25087 pb, 26466 sb, 27451 f
1813: 28724 f
1814: 31240 pb, 32724 f, 32771 pb, 51388 pb
1815: 35613 pb
1818: 43942 f, 44044 f, 44434 f
1819: 47774 f, 49611 f, 50152 f

WHIPPLE, HENRY (Salem, Mass.)
1810: 21401 f
1811: 23629-23631 f
1812: 24771 pb, 27451 f, 51198 pb
1813: 30601 pb
1814: 32105 pb, 51388 pb
1815: 35275 f
1817: 42957 pb
1818: 44044 f
1819: 47184 f

WHITCOMB, CHAPMAN (Leominster, Mass.)
1801: 270? f, 1572? f
1805: 9112? f
1812: 25179? f

WHITE, --- (New York)
1811: 22199, 22443 pb,
    23436 pb

WHITE, --- (Philadelphia)
1810: 20070 pb
1818: 43523 f, 44877 f, 45107
    pb
1819: 47510 pb, 48936 f,
    48937-48938 pb, 49018 f,
    50024-50025 f, 50171 pb

WHITE, DANIEL A (Newbury-
    port, Mass.)
1805: 9178 f

WHITE, ELIHU (New York)
1816: 36950-36951
1817: 40202, 40218
1818: 43304, 45429, 46677
1819: 47213, 47233, 49111,
    49115, 49201

WHITE, GEORGE (New York)
1808: 14304, 14858, 16282
1809: 17376 pb, 17819, 18243
    pb, 18779 pb
1812: 26195 pb, 26296 pb

WHITE, IRA (Newbury, Vt.)
1819: 48780 f

WHITE, JAMES (Boston)
1801: 259 f, 1082 pb, 1433 f
1802: 2474, 2482 f, 2526,
    3175 f, 50279 f
1803: 3789 pb, 4533 f, 4658-
    4659 f
1808: 16734 f

WHITE, JAMES (Warren, O.)
1814: 32858
1815: 34431, 36548 pb

WHITE, JOSEPH (Charlestown,
    Mass.)
1810: 19821 pb
1811: 23134 pb
1812: 27489 pb
1813: 29515 pb
1814: 32646 pb
1815: 35397

WHITE, JOSEPH W (Beaver-
    town, Pa.)
1811: 24422 pb

WHITE, JOSEPH W (Cadiz, O.)
1817: 42806 pb

WHITE, JOSEPH W (St. Clairs-
    ville, O.)
1815: 34444
1816: 37114 pb, 38759

WHITE, JOSEPH W (Zanes-
    ville, O.)
1809: 18161 pb
1810: 20047
1811: 23589

WHITE, JULIUS (New York)
1816: 36950-36951
1817: 40202, 40218
1818: 43304, 45429, 46677
1819: 47213, 47233, 49111,
    49115, 49201

WHITE, RICHARD (Chambers-
    burg, Pa.)
1808: 15894 pb

WHITE, SAMUEL B (New York)
1809: 17309 pb
1810: 19761 pb, 19920, 20406
    pb, 21515 pb

WHITE, THOMAS W (Boston)
1813: 28863?
1815: 34488, 34543, 34544 pb,
    34675, 35104, 35554, 35873,
    35999
1816: 36883, 37092, 37096,
    37562, 38896 pb, 39001,
    39027, 39755 pb
1817: 40795-40796 pb, 40871,
    41073 pb

White, Burditt & Co. (Boston)
see WHITE, JAMES (Boston)
    BURDITT, JAMES M (Boston)

WHITEHEAD, TOMMY (George-
    town, D.C.)
1808: 50862

WHITELOCK, JOHN (Kenne-
bunk, Me.)
1802: 2171 pb

WHITELOCK, JOHN (Ports-
mouth, N. H.)
1801: 1678
1804: 7079 pb
1805: 9450
1806: 11384

WHITING, DANIEL (Albany,
N. Y.)
1801: 45, 929, 1407
1802: 1737, 1747 pb, 1811,
1864, 2234, 2706, 2714,
2785, 3272, 50271 pb
1803: 3657 pb, 4045 sb, 4218,
4635 f, 4718 pb, 4810 pb,
4887, 5105 pb, 5119 pb,
5122 pb
1804: 5736 pb, 5859 pb, 6090
pb, 6200 pb, 6208-6209 pb,
6222 pb, 6224 pb, 6838 pb,
7206
1805: 50533 f

WHITING, JOHN (Lancaster,
Mass.)
1804: 7308 f
1805: 8519 f

WHITING, NATHAN (New
Haven, Conn.)
1815: 35783 f
1816: 37111-37112 pb, 37498,
37891, 38771 pb, 39062
1817: 40448, 40481, 41802
pb, 41977, 42345
1818: 43267, 43583, 43799,
43896, 45281, 45705 pb
1819: 47186 f, 47768 f, 47860
f, 48126 pb, 48180 f, 48340

WHITING, SAMUEL (Albany,
N. Y.)
1802: 1747 pb, 1811, 3272,
50271 pb
1803: 3657 pb, 4045 sb, 4218
pb, 4635 f, 4718 pb, 4810
pb, 4887, 5105 pb, 5119
pb, 5122 pb
1804: 5736 pb, 5859 pb, 6090

pb, 6200 pb, 6208-6209 pb,
6222 pb, 6224 pb, 6838 pb,
7206
1805: 50533 f
1806: 10106, 10113 f, 10402
pb, 10651 pb, 10723, 11260,
11752
1807: 12963 pb, 13378 f,
13470?, 13647 pb
1808: 16097 f

WHITING, SAMUEL (New York)
1802: 2034 pb
1809: 16976 f, 17108-17109 f,
17212 pb, 18061 f, 18088 f,
18531-18533 f, 18570 f,
18579 f, 18729 pb, 19180 f,
50963 pb
1810: 19420 pb, 19514 f,
19526 f, 19533 f, 19536 f,
19960 f, 20048 f, 20100 f,
20274 f, 20301 f, 20656 f,
20738 f, 20915 f, 20918 f,
21183 f, 21192 f, 21237-
21238 f, 21294 f, 21528 f,
21892 f
1811: 22354 f, 22364 f,
22424a pb, 22611 f, 22675 f,
22756 f, 22777 f, 22951 f,
23107 f, 23109 f, 23143 f,
23390 f, 23562 f, 23612 f,
23794 pb, 23829 f, 23970
f, 24307 pb, 51063 pb
1812: 24532 pb, 24580 f,
24833 f, 24948-24949 f,
24968 f, 24970 f, 24974-
24975 f, 25020 f, 25052 f,
25174 f, 25175 pb, 25289 f,
25332 f, 25333 pb, 25578 pb,
25684 f, 25761 pb, 25847 f,
25918 pb, 25921 f, 26080-
26081 f, 26363 pb, 26511 f,
26519 f, 26621 f, 26654 f,
26762 pb, 27530 f, 27540
pb, 27590 f
1813: 27889 pb, 28132 f,
28136 f, 28153-28154 f,
28683 f, 28849 pb, 29166 f,
29277 pb, 29427 f, 29881 f,
30520 pb
1814: 30995, 31995 f, 32003 f,
32023 f, 32842 pb, 32847 f,
33662 f

1815: 33871 pb, 34058 f,
  34209 pb, 35042 f, 35228 f,
  35784 pb, 35788 f
1816: 37235 pb, 37350 f,
  38153 f
1818: 44482? pb

WHITMAN, EPHRAIM (Goshen,
  Mass.)
1819: 48285-48286

WHITMAN, EPHRAIM (North-
  ampton, Mass.)
1817: 42898-42899

WHITMAN, EPHRAIM (Williamsburgh, Mass.)
1816: 37034
1817: 40279
1818: 43495, 44029, 44654,
  45731, 46797

WHITMAN, JOSIAH (Portland,
  Me.)
1817: 42269 pb

WHITMAN, SAMUEL (Goshen,
  Mass.)
1819: 50106

WHITNEY, H (New Orleans,
  La.)
1810: 51044 pb

WHITNEY, HENRY (HARRY)
  (St. Albans, Vt.)
1810: 20139 pb, 21130

WHITWORTH, THOMAS
  (Petersburg, Va.)
1815: 33987
1816: 36865
1818: 43815, 45842-45844
1819: 49583 pb

WIATT, SOLOMON (Philadel-
  phia)
1803: 4717 f
1805: 8110 f
1807: 13250 pb, 13547 pb
1808: 16195 pb
1809: 16964 pb, 17080 f,
  17252 pb, 17355 pb, 18613

  pb, 19231 f
1810: 19742 pb, 19744 pb,
  20484 f, 21282 pb
1811: 22368 f, 22434a f,
  22492 f
1812: 26147 f
1814: 32917 pb
1815: 34724 f

WIESTLING, JACOB H (Han-
  over, Pa.)
1818: 44252 pb

WIESTLING, JOHN S (Harrisburg, Pa.)
1810: 22053 pb
1811: 22316, 23046, 23068 pb,
  23657 pb
1813: 29936 pb
1814: 32211
1815: 34765, 35127?
1816: 41006
1818: 43988
1819: 47207 pb, 47344, 50110,
  51864 pb

WILBUR, SOLOMON (Troy,
  N.Y.)
1804: 6286 pb
1805: 8197, 9474
1813: 28741 f

WILCOX, JOSIAH (Massachu-
  setts)
1810: 19852 f

WILDER, JAMES (Leominster,
  Mass.)
1806: 9928, 10525
1807: 12144 pb, 12402, 13324,
  14127, 50793
1808: 14512-14513, 14661,
  15301

WILDER, JOSEPH (Worcester,
  Mass.)
1801: 681 f

WILDER, SALMON (Jaffrey,
  N.H.)
1813: 28746, 28956, 29546,
  29974
1814: 30607, 30872, 31853,

31937-31938, 32429?,
33529
1815: 33947, 35114, 36430

WILDER, SALMON (Leomin-
ster, Mass.)
1801: 11, 147, 187, 270?,
?1572?
1802: 1710-1711, 3066 pb
1803: 3627, 3970, 4033,
4463, 4800
1804: 5656-5657, 5924, 6050
pb, 6881
1805: 7828-7829, 8519, 9082
1806: 9928, 10279, 10525
1807: 12144 pb, 12402, 13324,
14127, 50793
1808: 14512-14513, 14661,
15301, 15712 pb
1809: 17836, 18411 pb
1810: 20548, 21161
1811: 22769 pb, 23942h, 23993
1812: 24762-24764, ?25179?,
25197, 25494, 26374, 26736
1813: 28752

WILDER, SALMON (New Ips-
wich, N. H.)
1814: 30608
1816: 36832, 36995, 37341,
39869
1817: 40764
1818: 46712

WILDER, WILLIAM R (New-
port, R. I.)
1802: 50281 f, 50332 pb

WILEY, C (Philadelphia)
1811: 23825

WILEY, CHARLES (New York)
1810: 20243
1812: 24688, 25064-25065,
26287-26288, 27351
1813: 27982, 28214, 28225,
29177, 29344, 29453
1814: 30642, 31027, 31099,
31136 pb, 31172 pb, 31182,
31251, 31254, 31383, 31509,
31592, 31759, 31773 pb,
32168 bpb, 32171 pb, 32186
bf, 32188 pb, 32323, 32337-

32338, 32340-32341, 32766,
33563
1815: 33835, 34291 pb, 34357-
34358, 34372, 34378, 34445,
34568, 34718 pb, 34774 pb,
34856, 34930, 34933 pb,
34956 pb, 34958, 35000,
35023, 35116, 35183, 35468,
35470, 35575, 35807, 35871
pb, 35872, 35881 pb, 35884,
36026, 36031 pb, 36367 pb
1816: 36908, 37084 pb, 37139
pb, 37141-37142 pb, 37291
pb, 37496 pb, 37752, 37855,
37875-37876 pb, 38018,
38312 pb, 38442 pb, 38750
pb, 38891 pb, 38976 pb,
38986 f, 39060 pb, 39108,
39796-39797 pb, 39799
1817: 39988, 40039, 40096,
40366 pb, 40369 pb, 40386,
40513 f, 40577, 40695, 40730
pb, 41228 pb, 41232 pb,
41252, 41302 pb, 41475 pb,
41510 f, 41594, 41862, 41997
pb, 42013 pb, 42039, 42076,
42124, 42887-42888
1818: 43125 pb, 44015 pb,
44030 pb, 44168 f, 44358
pb, 44545 pb, 44764 pb,
44851 pb, 44892-44893 pb,
45206 f, 45309 pb
1819: 47383 pb, 48137 f, 48725
f, 48732 f, 48741 f, 49161 f,
49162 pb, 49372 f, 49380 f

WILEY, NATHANIEL (Phila-
delphia)
1804: 6032 f

WILKEY, J (Boston)
1802: 3466? f

WILKINSON, JOHN (Knoxville,
Tenn.)
1811: 24018 f

WILKINSON, WILLIAM (Providence, R. I.)
1803: 4721
1804: 5861 f, 50456 pb

WILLARD, AMBROSE (St. Albans, Vt.)
1809: 17184 pb

WILLARD, HEMAN (Pittsfield, Mass.)
1807: 12110 pb, 12323 f

WILLARD, HEMAN (Stockbridge, Mass.)
1801: 622, 743, 1172, 1644
1802: 1970 pb, 2378, 2812, 3533, 3564 pb, 3565-3566, 4408
1803: 5573 pb, 5591 pb
1804: 5746 pb, 6176, 6182, 6527?, 6528, 6952, 7768 pb
1805: 8233, 8865, 9720, 9738-9740
1806: 11065, 11355, 11357, 11852 pb
1807: 12991 f
1811: 23075-23076, 23389, 24402, 24421
1812: 25038, 25231, 25264, ?25661, 25662, 25734, 26382, 26501 pb, 26720, 27563-27564, 27598
1813: 28091, 28155, 28457, 28796, 28798, 28884, 29550, 29783, 29868, 30544 pb, 30566, 51303?
1814: 31482, 31668, 31824, 31922, 32748, 33661, 33693 pb

WILLES, ZIBA (Cleveland, O.)
1819: 47641 pb

WILLES, ZIBA (Erie, Pa.)
1818: 43952 pb

WILLETT, CHARLES (Norfolk, Va.)
1804: 7665?

WILLIAMS, --- (Frankford, Pa.)
1814: 31716

WILLIAMS, --- (Glasgow, Ky.)
1818: 44200 pb

WILLIAMS, BENOMI (Providence, R.I.)
1803: 3619?, 4990, 5533
1804: 5646 pb, 6069, 6138?, 6139, 6248?, 6494, 6706 pb, 6843 pb, 7161 pb, 7192, 7343, 7708, 7779, 50416
1805: 8392?, 8616?, 9154, 9233, 9251, 9730-9731
1806: 11258
1807: 13468 pb

WILLIAMS, CHARLES (Boston)
1807: 13515 pb
1810: 19503? pb
1811: 22382 f, 23218 f, 23426 pb, 23699 f, 23742-23744 f, 23752 f, 23966 f, 24479 f
1812: 25111 f, 25112 pb, 25172 pb, 25204 f, 25414 pb, 25489 pb, 25508 f, 25531 f, 26126 f, 26539 pb, 26785 pb, 27431 f, 27592 pb, 51178 pb, 51218 pb
1813: 28438-28439 f, 28614 pb, 28630 f, 28677 f, 28913 f, 28962? pb, 29587 f, 29617 f, 29693 f, 29694 pb, 29776-29778 f, 51284 pb
1814: 30927 f, 30953 f, 31159 f, 31205 f, 31674 f, 32079 f, 32509 pb, 32597-32598 pb, 32684 f, 32793 f, 32827 pb, 33521 f, 33691 pb
1815: 34011-34012 pb, 34573 pb, 34895 f, 35231-35232 f, 35859 f, 36002 f
1816: 36927 f, 37521 pb, 39902 f
1817: 40959 pb, 41900f pb
1818: 43294-43295 pb, 43313 pb, 43854 f, 45790 f, 45847 pb, 46811 f
1819: 47809 f, 49115 pb, 49560 pb

WILLIAMS, DAVID R (Charleston, S.C.)
1803: 3856

WILLIAMS, ELIAS (Batavia, N.Y.)
1807: 12649 pb

WILLIAMS, HENRY (Boston)
1814: 33690 pb

WILLIAMS, J (Boston)
1818: 46812 pb

WILLIAMS, JOHN J (Exeter, N. H.)
1818: 43337-43338, 44549, 46650 pb
1819: 47018, 47224 pb, 47460, 47960, 48463, 48680, 48855, 49993, 50064 pb, 50077, 51860 pb

WILLIAMS, MICAJAH TER-RELL (Cincinnati, O.)
1815: 34447, 34917?, 35061, 35395 pb, 35987, 36544
1816: 36844, 37307, 37965, 39788
1817: 40103 pb, 40104, 40499 pb, 40500, 42875 pb, 42962 pb
1818: 43206, 43552, 45310, 46769, 46869 pb

WILLIAMS, PHILIP (Wood-stock, Va.)
1817: 42950 pb
1818: 44176

WILLIAMS, RICHARD (Charles-town, Va.)
1808: 14997 pb
1810: 19925
1812: 26605

WILLIAMS, ROBERT P (Boston)
1813: 29693 f
1814: 30927 f, 30953 f, 31159 f, 31205 f, 31674 f, 32079 f, 32509 pb, 32597-32598 pb, 32684 f, 32793 f, 32827 pb, 33521 f, 33691 pb
1815: 34011-34012 pb, 34573 pb, 34895 f, 35231-35232 f, 35859 f, 36002 f
1816: 36927 f, 37521 pb, 39902 f
1817: 40959 pb, 41900f pb
1818: 43294-43295 pb, 43313 pb, 43854 f, 45790 f,

45847 pb, 46811 f
1819: 47809 f, 49115 pb, 49560 pb

WILLIAMS, SAMUEL (Benning-ton, Vt.)
1812: 24536

WILLIAMS, SAMUEL (Middle-bury, Vt.)
1803: 4999 pb

WILLIAMS, SOLOMON (New York)
1809: 16976 f, 17108-17109 f, 17212 pb, 18061 f, 18088 f, 18531-18533 f, 18570 f, 18579 f, 18729 pb, 19180 f, 50963 pb
1810: 19420 pb, 19514 f, 19533 f, 19536 f, 19960 f, 20048 f, 20100 f, 20274 f, 20301 f, 20656 f, 20738 f, 20915 f, 20918 f, 21183 f, 21192 f, 21237-21238 f, 21294 f, 21528 f, 21892 f

WILLIAMS, THOMAS (Norwich, Conn.)
1802: 2180 f, 2679 f

WILLIAMS, WILLIAM (Utica, N.Y.)
1807: 12542 pb, 13483, 13731
1808: 14640, 14786, 14992 pb, 15269, 15415, 15785 pb, 16690, 16694
1809: 16925, 16927, 17294 pb, 17485 pb, 18151 pb, 19170, 19175
1810: 19441, 19698, 20086 pb, 20260, 20294 pb, 20305, 20546, 20761 pb, 20854, 21950, 21971 pb, 21973 pb, 21979 pb, 21986
1811: 22247, 22503, 22542, 22805 pb, 23719 pb, 24360
1812: 25400 pb, 26343
1813: 27945, 28489 pb, 28967, 29202 pb, 29247, 29414, 30501
1814: 30729, 30770, 31456 pb, 31636, 33519 pb

1815: 33908 pb, 33959, 34627,
34680, 34715, 35384, 35571
pb, 35586, 36425, 36475 pb,
36497 pb, 36526, 36583
1816: 37203, 37237 pb, 37272,
37565, 37581, 37791 pb,
37888 pb, 38228 pb, 38336,
38347 pb, 39071 pb, 39653?
pb, 39759-39760, 39812 pb,
51583 pb
1817: 40049, 40319, 40323,
40519, 40566 pb, 40703,
40800, 40819, 40879, 40915,
41020 pb, 41021, 41022 pb,
41212 pb, 41527 pb, 41561
pb, 41936, 42760 pb, 42856
pb, 51663 pb
1818: 43323 pb, 44000, 44281
pb, 44288, 44392 pb, 44593,
44602 pb, 44940 pb, 45170 pb,
45607, 45707, 46772, 46816
pb, 46858, 51769 pb
1819: 47120, 47178 pb, 47232
pb, 47738, 47952, 47967-
47968, 48141, 48185, 48186
pb, 48289 pb, 48765 pb,
48783 pb, ·48789 pb, 48811
pb, 48816 f, 48829 pb,
49187, 50094, 50126 pb,
50187 pb

WILLIAMS, WILLIAM T
(Savannah, Ga.)
1811: 22494 pb, 23169 pb,
23262 pb, 23887 pb
1812: 26490, 27537 pb
1816: 39077 pb
1818: 44149

WILLIAMSON, JAMES (Staun-
ton, Va.)
1811: 23969 pb

WILLIG, GEORGE (Philadelphia)
1801: 634-635, 736 pb
1802: 1946
1804: 50437? pb, 50469-
50470? pb
1805: 8226?, 50512? pb,
50548? pb, 50612? pb,
50615? pb
1808: 50871? pb
1810: 19784?, 20480? pb,

20772?, 21463? pb, 22120?,
51000? pb, 51001?, 51007?
pb, 51026 pb
1812: 25939 pb, 26402 pb
1815: 34238? pb
1816: 51612? pb, 51634? pb
1818: 43468? pb and sb

WILLINGTON, AARON SMITH
(Charleston, S. C.)
1803: 3954 pb
1807: 12063, 12467, 12616 pb
1808: 14659 pb, 15328 pb
1809: 18588 pb
1810: 19885, 20844 pb, 21154
1811: 51128
1812: 24539 pb, 25178
1813: 28482
1817: 42031 pb

WILLIS, JOHN (New York)
1807: 12900 f

WILLIS, NATHANIEL (Boston)
1812: 26835
1813: 27665, 27746 pb, 27924,
28027 pb, 28514 pb, 28667
pb, 28668-28669, 29190,
29617, 30490
1814: 30613?, 30691?, 30905,
31003 pb, 31021 pb, 31198
pb, 31301 pb, 31463, 31487
pb, 31552?, 31614, 31616,
31929?, 32353 pb, 32433,
32560?, 32650?, 32656?,
32698?, 32793, 32901 pb,
32977 pb, 32979?, 33578?,
33647?, 33674-33675
1815: 34029-34034, 34177 pb,
34322, 34631, 34641, 34703-
34704 pb, 34916, 35038 pb,
35231, 35324, 35423 pb,
35941, 35964, 35970, 36570
pb
1816: 36875, 37046, 37052 pb,
37276, 37297, 37733, 38777
1818: 43648, 44401, 44491,
45608
1819: 46918 pb, 47161, 47990
pb, 48985

WILLIS, NATHANIEL (Chillicothe, O.)
1801: 1067-1070, 1438

1802: 2810-2811, 2819, 3595
1803: 4785-4790
1804: 6956-6958
1805: 9051, 9053
1806: 11059

WILLIS, NATHANIEL (Lexington, Ky.)
1805: 9052 f

WILLIS, NATHANIEL (Portland, Me.)
1803: 4126 pb
1804: 5779, 5998
1805: 8654, 9264, 9455, 9785
1806: 10110, 10447
1808: 16290

WILLS, FRANCIS M (Baltimore)
1808: 15499 f
1812: 24972 f, 26732 f,
    27636 f
1813: 28281 f, 28659 f,
    28720 f, 29236 f, 29275 f,
    29781 f
1814: 30989 f, 31062 f,
    31590 f, 31800 f, 32538 f
1815: 34842 f, 35342 f,
    35633 f, 35781 f
1816: 37082 f, 38686 pb,
    38806 f

WILLS, JAMES (Edenton, N. C.)
1806: 9902, 10068
1807: 13369 pb, 50801
1808: 15065, 15325
1809: 16928
1810: 19445, 20154
1811: 22279
1817: 40100

WILLSON, DANIEL A (Damascus, Pa.)
1811: 22402a

WILLSON, JOSEPH (New York)
1807: 50766? pb
1811: 51152? pb

WILSON, DANIEL (Philadelphia)
1812: 24583 f

WILSON, GEORGE (Jonesborough, Tenn.)
1801: 444

WILSON, GEORGE (Knoxville, Tenn.)
1804: 7782 pb
1805: 9338
1808: 50892
1809: 18736, 18739, 18741
1811: 24017-24018, ?24455
1812: 26854 f, 26858-26859,
    ?27560
1813: 27729, 27817, 28882,
    29931-29932 f, 29933
1814: 31531
1815: 33975
1817: 42256-42258

WILSON, GEORGE (Nashville, Tenn.)
1819: 47632, 48820 pb,
    49571-49573

WILSON, JAMES (Philadelphia)
1815: 35712

WILSON, JAMES (Steubenville, O.)
1816: 37159, 37294
1818: 43868 pb, 44251, 44465
1819: 48098

WILSON, JAMES (Wilmington, Del.)
1801: 65, 402 f, 1667
1802: 2347 pb, 2741, 3170,
    3454
1803: 3621 pb, 3750 pb, 3843
    pb, 3846 pb, 4305 pb, 4942
    pb, 4989 pb, 5494, 50380
1804: 5813 pb, 7240 pb, 7731
    f
1805: 9482
1806: 9868, 11310 pb, 50670
    pb
1807: 11990 pb, 13253 pb
1808: 14366 pb
1809: 16852 pb, 16860 pb
1810: 19367 pb
1811: 22200 pb, 24041
1812: 24616 pb, 51190 pb
1813: 27740 pb, 29024, 29827

pb, 29953
1814: 30693 pb, 31499 pb
1816: 38725, 51631 pb
1817: 40008 pb, 42156? pb,
42209 pb
1818: 43087 pb
1819: 47007 pb, 48200 pb,
48386

WILSON, JAMES JEFFERSON
(Mill Hill, N. J.)
1811: 22713

WILSON, JAMES JEFFERSON
(Trenton, N. J.)
1801: 1012, 1015, 1330?,
1436 pb
1802: 2339, 2494, 2938,
3074, 3570 pb
1803: 3930, 4067, 4304 pb,
4446, 4744 pb, 4745, 4747-
4748 pb, 5602 pb
1804: 5981, 6893-6894, 6898-
6899, 6901 pb, 7783 pb
1805: 8997, 9000 pb, 9003-
9004
1806: 10979, 10988-10989,
11658
1807: 13205, 13207-13209
1808: 15732, 15736, 15961,
16266
1809: 17658, 18208, 18216
1810: 19636, 20871, 20874,
22070
1811: 23029, 23525, 23528-
23529, 23532-23533, 23780
pb, 24386, 24470 pb
1812: 25249, 26245-26246,
26248, 26250-26251, 26254-
26256, 26606, 26762, 27584
pb
1813: 27651, 27653, 28880
pb, 28933 bf, 30551 pb
1814: 32258-32266, 35442,
35445-35447
1815: 36595 pb
1816: 38406-38408, 39841 pb
1817: 41595-41596, 42932 pb
1818: 46830 pb
1819: 48869

WILSON, JOHN (Boston)
1813: 28028 pb, 28385 pb

WILSON, JOHN (Deerfield,
Mass.)
1817: 40574 pb, 40632
1818: 43748 pb, 43857 pb

WILSON, JOHN (New York)
1804: 5683 f, 6038 f, 6163 sb,
6307-6308 f, 6773-6774 f,
7207 f, 7344 f, 7442 f,
7761 sb
1805: 7818 pb, 7981 f, 8417
f, 8441 f, 8898a pb, 8901 f,
9715-9716 f
1806: 9937 f, 10172 f, 10864
f, 11255 f, 11294 f, 11848-
11850 f
1807: 13074 f, 13076 f
1808: 14678 f, 15385 pb,
15589 f, 15591-15592 f,
16104 f, 16167 f
1809: 17515 pb, 18071 f,
18173 f
1810: 20123 pb, 21451 f
1819: 47640 pb

WILSON, JOHN (Newtown, Pa.)
1818: 46824 pb

WILSON, JOHN L (Charleston,
S. C.)
1814: 31124 pb, 31402 pb

WILSON, JONATHAN (Brattleboro, Vt.)
1817: 40117 f

WILSON, ROBERT (New York)
1802: 2915
1803: 3771, 4929

WILSON, THOMAS (Baltimore)
1811: 24000 pb
1815: 35237 pb

WILSON, THOMAS (Poughkeepsie, N. Y.)
1806: 10386 pb

WILSON, THOMAS A (Columbia,
Pa.)
1811: 24004 pb
1815: 34651

344 WILSON

WILSON, WILLIAM H (Providence, R. I.)
1806: 10045
1814: 32636-32640, 32642 pb, 51372
1815: 33970, 34236, 35177, 35774-35778
1816: 38744, 38793-38794

Winchester Gazette (Winchester, Va.)
1812: 25652

Winchester Triumph of Liberty (Winchester, Va.)
1801: 573

WING, CORNELIUS (Cincinnati, O.)
1819: 47361 f

WINN, JOHN W (Natchez, Miss.)
1808: 14833, 16697 pb
1809: 18104
1810: 22023, 22024 pb
1811: 22267, 23402 pb

WINNARD, JAMES (Norristown, Pa.)
1803: 4771 pb
1805: 9710 pb
1807: 12877
1810: 20508?
1813: 29772
1815: 35339
1819: 47197 pb

WINSHIP, WINN (Chillicothe, O.)
1801: 1069

WINSTON, WILLIAM O (Natchez, Miss.)
1811: 23403

WINTER, JOHN (Alexandria, Va.)
1813: 30557 pb

Winyaw Intelligencer (Georgetown, S. C.)
1818: 44874a

WISE, FREDERICK (New Berlin, Pa.)
1816: 38371 pb

WISE, FREDERICK A (Greensburg, Pa.)
1818: 46783 pb

WOMACK, --- (Lebanon, Tenn.)
1818: 44550 pb

WOOD, JOHN (Petersburg, Va.)
1814: 31283 pb

WOOD, JOHN (Washington, D. C.)
1807: 12012 pb

WOOD, SAMUEL (New York)
1803: 3748 pb
1805: 8076 f, 8493 f
1806: 10230 f, 10519 pb, 10639 f, 11043 f, 11909 f
1807: 11999 pb, 12201, 12202 pb, 12213 pb, 12371 pb, 12631, 12733 pb, 12772, 12773 pb, 12783 pb, 13095 pb, 13216 pb, 13240 pb, 14231 pb
1808: 14404-14405, 14663-14664 pb, 14666, 14731, 14800 pb, 15241 pb, 16229 pb, 16741 pb, 50833 pb
1809: 16867 pb, 17246, 17322 pb, 18225 pb, 18292 pb, 18477, 18706 pb, 50911 pb, 50918 pb, 50931 pb
1810: 19380-19381 pb, 19893 pb, 20046 pb, 20114?, 20134 pb, 20309 pb, 20338 pb, 20904-20905 pb, 20906, 20907 pb, 20951 pb, 20986? pb, 21137? pb, 21315 pb, 21396, 22084 pb, 50976 pb
1811: 22156 pb, 22343 pb, 22698 pb, 22846 pb, 22910 pb, 22999, 23009 pb, 23092 pb, 23143, 23444, 23539 pb, 23556 pb, 23595 pb, 23703 pb, 23903 pb, 23907 pb, 23909 pb, 23971 pb, 23999 pb, 24397 pb, 24442 pb, 24484 pb, 51058 pb, 51064-

51065 pb, 51078 pb, 51097
pb, 51151 pb
1812: 25183 pb, 25189, 25473,
25499 bsb, 25694, 25718 pb,
26297 pb, 26588 pb, 26617
pb, 26618, 26721 pb, 26917
pb, 27425 pb, 27488 pb,
27516, 27568 pb, 27601 pb,
27639 pb, 51159 pb, 51196
pb, 51204 pb
1813: 27751 pb, 27852 pb,
27879, 27880 pb, 27933 pb,
27981 pb, 28125 pb, 28556
pb, 28584 pb, 28651 pb,
28750 pb, 28787, 28811 pb,
29133 pb, 29355-29357 pb,
29358? pb, 29361 pb, 29411
pb, 29445 pb, 29451 pb,
29466 pb, 29553-29554,
29698, 29705 pb, 30569 pb,
51268 pb, 51283 pb, 51293
pb, 51299 pb, 51302 pb,
51305 pb
1814: 30639 pb, 30719 pb,
30798 pb, 30830 pb, 30903
pb, 30969 pb, 31265-31266
pb, 31423 pb, 31512 pb,
31558 pb, 31597 pb, 31705-
31706 pb, 31785 pb, 31796
pb, 31804, 31934 pb, 31943
pb, 32093 pb, 32106 pb,
32140 pb, 32159 pb, 32184-
32185 pb, 32270 pb, 32347-
32348 pb, 32440 pb, 32527
pb, 32711 f, 32736 pb,
32738 pb, 32751 pb, 32837
pb, 32891 pb, 32970 pb,
33565, 33604 pb, 33672 pb,
33694 pb, 33706 pb, 33712
pb, 33715, 33722 pb, 33755,
51366-51367 pb, 51369 pb,
51375 pb, 51394 pb, 51398
pb
1815: 33798 pb, 33806-33807
pb, 33901 pb, 34015 pb,
34076 pb, 34162 pb, 34334
pb, 34392 pb, 34475 pb,
34670 pb, 34682-34683 pb,
34722-34723 pb, 34750 pb,
34751, 34760 pb, 34823,
34907-34908 pb, 34910-34911
pb, 34987 pb, 35021 pb,
35042 bf, 35084 pb, 35107

pb, 35120 pb, 35179 pb,
35225 pb, 35240 pb, 35256,
35486 pb, 35640 pb, 35644
pb, 35655 pb, 35662, 35886
pb, 35905 pb, 35995 pb,
36129 pb, 36134, 36471 pb,
36606 pb, 36620 pb, 36629
f, 36631, 36657, 36665,
51475-51476 pb, 51499 pb,
51537 pb
1816: 36686 pb, 36779 pb,
36874 pb, 36906 pb, 36959
pb, 36994 pb, 37013, 37040
pb, 37296 pb, 37360-37361
pb, 37413 pb, 37522, 37523
pb, 37681 pb, 37758 pb,
37821, 37839-37841 pb,
37906 pb, 37908 pb, 37933
pb, 38137 pb, 38217 pb,
38286 pb, 38300, 38439,
38454 pb, 38456, 38458 pb,
38509 pb, 38516 pb, 38518
pb, 38560 pb, 38562 pb,
38637? pb, 38779, 38871 f,
38902 pb, 38906 pb, 38908
pb, 38915-38916 pb, 38997
pb, 39035 pb, 39048 pb,
39701, 39739, 39859 pb,
39865 pb, 39899-39900 pb,
51549 pb, 51557 pb, 51560
pb, 51589 pb
1817: 40007 pb, 40018 pb,
40157 pb, 40376-40377 pb,
40466 pb, 40471, 40745
pb, 40747 pb, 40790 pb,
40850 pb, 40877 pb, 41177
pb, 41385 pb, 41438-41439
pb, 41496 pb, 41509 pb,
41607, 41624, 41648, 41828
pb, 41848 pb, 41947 pb,
42048 f, 42086 pb, 42333,
42933? pb, 42948-42949 pb,
42964, 51647 pb
1818: 43032 pb, 43118 pb,
43231 pb, 43312 pb, 43411-
43412 pb, 43601 pb, 43771
pb, 44112, 44326-44328 pb,
44330 pb, 44408 pb, 44441 pb,
44547 f, 44586 pb, 44596-44597
pb, 44677 pb, 44784 pb, 44989
pb, 45058 pb, 45067, 45075,
45081 pb, 45084-45086 pb,
45089, 45150 pb, 45155 pb,

45209 pb, 45228 f, 45334
pb, 45348-45349 pb, 45507
pb, 45674-45675 pb, 45732-
45738 pb, 45754 pb, 45819
pb, 46802 pb, 46835 pb,
46860 pb, 46889 pb, 46904?
pb, 51731 pb, 51780 pb,
51782 pb, 51807 pb
1819: 47159 pb, 47448 pb,
47893 pb, 48317 pb, 48409
pb, 48502 pb, 48647-48650
pb, 48911, 48913 pb, 48918,
48919 pb, 48922 pb, 49130
pb, 49142 pb, 49194 pb,
49262? pb, 49367 pb, 49401-
49402 pb, 49489 pb, 49639
pb, 49647 pb, 50061 pb,
50111-50112 pb, 50154 pb,
51852 pb, 51885 pb, 51896
pb

WOOD, SAMUEL S (Baltimore)
1810: 20309? pb
1816: 37523 pb
1818: 43032 pb, 43118 pb,
43412 pb, 43601 pb, 43771
pb, 44326-44328 pb, 44408
pb, 44441 pb, 44586 pb,
44597 pb, 44677 pb, 45155
pb, 45209 pb, 45334 pb,
45348 pb, 45507 pb, 45674-
45675 pb, 45734-45738 pb,
45819 pb, 46802 pb, 46835
pb, 46859 pb, 46904? pb,
51731 pb, 51807 pb
1819: 47893 pb, 48317 pb,
48409 pb, 48502 pb, 48647-
48649 pb, 48922 pb, 49130
pb, 49142 pb, 49194 pb,
49262? pb, 49367 pb, 49489
pb, 50061 pb, 50153 pb,
51885 pb, 51896 pb

WOOD, WILLIAM (Albany,
N. Y.)
1807: 12700 pb
1808: 14727 pb, 16234
1809: 18233
1810: 19418

WOOD, WILLIAM (Frankfort,
Ky.)
1818: 43895 f

WOOD, WILLIAM (Louisville,
Ky.)
1815: 34416
1816: 37921, 37925

WOODDY, WILLIAM (Baltimore)
1816: 37729?

WOODHOUSE, WILLIAM (Philadelphia)
1803: 4057 pb
1807: 13375 f
1808: 15911 pb
1810: 21062 pb
1811: 23676 sb

WOODRUFF, ENOS (Elizabeth,
N. J.)
1804: 7810
1805: 7856 pb, 9501 pb

WOODRUFF, IRA (Staunton,
Va.)
1804: 6559

WOODRUFF, WILLIAM E
(Arkansas Post, Ark.)
1819: 47012 pb

WOODS, JOHN (Elizabeth,
N. J.)
1801: 423, 688 pb
1802: 1740, 1867, 2109, 2435,
3512
1803: 4122, 4191 pb, 4423
1804: 5743 pb, 6525, 6596 pb

WOODS, JOHN (New York)
1801: 581

WOODWARD, --- (Boston)
1810: 19603 pb

WOODWARD, THOMAS GREEN
(New Haven, Conn.)
1813: 28213
1814: 31218-31219, 33745-
33746
1815: 34605, 34806, 34882,
36024
1816: 36619?, 36692, 36763,
36916, 37611, 37892, 38245,
38597, 38684, 38863

1817: 39952 pb, 40004, 40148,
40167 pb, 40443, 41428,
41933, 42116-42117, 42126,
42289, 42982 pb, 51689
1818: 43027, 43270 pb, 43462,
43584, 43626, 44834, 45337,
45913

WOODWARD, WILLIAM HILL
(Philadelphia)
1817: 40222, 42847
1818: 43475
1819: 47217, 47231, 47235,
49298, 50066

WOODWARD, WILLIAM WALLIS
(Philadelphia)
1801: 160, 515 pb, 797, 798
pb, 976, 1112, 1347, 1672
pb
1802: 1726 f, 1841 pb, 2107,
2362 pb, 2402 pb, 2514,
2824, 2893, 2935, 3529,
3538 f, 3572 pb, 3586-3587
pb
1803: 3817, 3852, 3913, 4082
pb, 4173 pb, 4497, 4768 f,
4858, 4864, 5608 pb, 50360
pb
1804: 5847 pb, 5946 f, 5949
pb, 6226 f, 6229 f, 7007,
50433 pb
1805: 7932, 7990 pb, 8431 pb,
9024 pb
1806: 9799 pb, 9933-9936 pb,
9968 pb, 9979 pb, 9982 pb,
9991 pb, 10062 pb, 10556
pb, 11332 pb, 50674 pb
1807: 12129 pb, 12228 f,
12237 pb, 12705 f, 12784
pb, 14174 pb, 50772 pb,
50798 pb
1808: 14264 f, 14415, 14430,
14601, 14602 pb, 14614 pb,
14616 pb, 15272 pb, 15663
pb
1809: 17008 pb, 17012, 17022
pb, 17741 pb, 17747 pb,
18252 pb, 18454 pb, 19163,
19164 f, 19262-19263 pb
1810: 19440, 19449 f, 19517
pb, 19535, 19670 f, 19681
pb, 20173 f, 20289 f, 20328

f, 20330-20332 f, 20975 pb,
21215, 21296 pb, 21342 pb,
21345 pb, 21462 pb, 21977
pb, 22059 pb, 22066 f,
22076 pb
1811: 22338 f, 22345 pb,
22356 pb, 22369, 22370 pb,
22406a, 22424a pb, 22459a-
22460a f, 22530 pb, 22941 f,
23271 f, 24014, 24334 pb
1812: 24828 f, 25833? f,
26300 f, 26301 pb, 27575
pb, 27602 pb
1813: 27898 pb, 27928, 28040
f, 28131, 28143 pb, 29009 f,
29371 pb, 29567 pb, 29609 f,
29669 f, 29787 f, 30497 f,
30519 pb, 30598 pb
1814: 30823 f, 30867 pb,
30889 pb, 30917 pb, 31023 f,
31033 pb, 32352 f, 32658 pb
1815: 34246-34247 f, 34256 f,
34396 f, 35331 f, 35694 f,
35696-35697 f, 35699 f,
35790 pb
1816: 36956-36957, 36976 pb,
38465 pb, 39734 pb
1817: 40222 f, 40347 f, 40455
f, 40916, 42073 f, 42847 f
1818: 43293 pb, 43308 pb,
43334 pb, 43475 f, 43485
pb, 45099 pb
1819: 47217 f, 47231 f, 47235
f, 49298 f, 49484 pb, 50066
f

WOODWORTH, SAMUEL (New
Haven, Conn.)
1808: 14475 pb

WOODWORTH, SAMUEL (New
York)
1811: 24488 pb, 51073 f
1812: 25582 pb, 26554 pb,
27423 pb
1813: 29019
1814: 33725 pb
1819: 48451 pb

WOOLDRIDGE, J (Lexington,
Ky.)
1810: 20429 pb

WOOLHOPTER, PHILIP D
(Savannah, Ga.)
1802: 2014, 2308, 3540
1803: 3726
1808: 14483, 15497

WOOTTEN, JOHN B (Dover,
Del.)
1804: 6071 pb, 6146 pb
1805: 8313-8317
1806: 10257 pb, 10272-10274
1807: 12415-12420, 13265
1808: 14848-14850
1809: 17365-17369, 18652
1810: 19944-19947
1811: 22678-22680
1812: 25236-25240
1814: 31314 pb

WORKMAN, SAMUEL (Charles-
town, Va.)
1814: 31127 pb, 31768

WORKMAN, SAMUEL (Washing-
ton, Pa.)
1819: 50178

WORKS, A (Richmond, Va.)
1815: 36453? pb

WORSLEY, WILLIAM W (Lex-
ington, Ky.)
1808: 14703, 16048 pb
1809: 17319, 17868
1810: 20150, 20269, 20493,
22068
1811: 22225, 22856, 23155,
23950
1812: 25698, 25783
1813: 28873
1814: 31860 pb
1816: 37642-37643, 38117 pb,
38121, 39721
1817: 40856, 42141, 51730 pb
1818: 44086-44087, 44512,
45888, 46832
1819: 47403, 48017, 51959 pb

WORSLEY, WILLIAM W (Nor-
folk, Va.)
1802: 2058 pb and f

WORSLEY, WILLIAM W (Rich-
mond, Va.)
1804: 6099, 6255 pb, 7147 pb
1805: 9665 f, 9667

WORTHINGTON, ELIPHALET B
(Chester, Pa.)
1819: 49170 pb

WORTHINGTON, ERASTUS
(Brooklyn, N.Y.)
1818: 44216, 45228
1819: 47786, 48907

WORTMAN, TUNIS (New York)
1813: 29849 pb

WRIGHT, AMBROSE (Louisville,
Ga.)
1812: 24603 pb

WRIGHT, ANDREW (Northamp-
ton, Mass.)
1801: 653, 804, 1378 pb
1802: 2277 pb, 2533, 2610,
3533
1803: 4443, 4963, 5129,
50365?
1804: 6012 pb, 6040, 6223,
6393, 6499, 6509 pb
1805: 8536, 9062, 9408
1806: 10711, 11267 pb, 50693
pb
1807: 14202
1809: 17707
1810: 20413 pb
1811: 24502
1812: 25118
1816: 39016, 39656

WRIGHT, ANDREW (Springfield,
Mass.)
1806: 10714 f

WRIGHT, DAVID (Harrisburg,
Pa.)
1807: 13709 pb

WRIGHT, EDMUND (Boston)
1819: 48329 pb

WRIGHT, JOHN CRAFTS (Ben-
nington, Vt.)
1807: 14184

WRIGHT, JOHN CRAFTS
(Troy, N. Y.)
1804: 6286 pb
1805: 8197, 8427 pb, 9474,
50533
1806: 10077, 10078 pb, 10960
pb, 11094
1807: 12788 pb, 12790 pb,
12960 pb, 14226 pb
1808: 14622 pb, 15274 pb,
15277 pb, 16136 pb, 16348
pb

WRIGHT, JOSEPH (Wilkesbarre,
Pa.)
1801: 224 f

WRIGHT, JOSEPH (Wilmington,
O.)
1815: 39493 f

WRIGHT, NATHANIEL HILL
(Newburyport, Mass.)
1810: 19324 f, 20432 pb
1811: 23822

WRIGHT, SERENO (Montpelier,
Vt.)
1810: 20649
1811: 22246, 22288, 22448a-
22449a pb, 22526 pb, 22774
pb, 23508-23509, 24399 pb
1812: 24527, 24778 pb, 24812-
24813 pb, 24982 pb, 25005,
25046 pb, 25059, 26118-
26119, 26509, 26659, 26674,
26691 pb, 26813 pb, 26904
pb, 27374 pb, 27386, 27392,
27435 pb, 27487 pb
1813: 27818, 29069, 29556,
29741, 29870, 30410-30411,
30487, 30585
1814: 31461, 31542, 31823,
32543
1815: 34359

WRIGHT, SERENO (Randolph,
Vt.)
1801: 844, 1078, 1333
1803: 4384
1804: 5760, 6359
1805: 7911-7912, 9440
1806: 9885, 10604, 11203,

11360
1807: 12028-12029, 12487,
12561, 12699, 14114, 14117
1808: 14406, 14907, 15010,
16610, 16623
1809: 17729 pb, 18105, 18475,
19088, 19093
1810: 19395, 21485-21486,
21898, 21995, 22111 pb

WRIGHT, SERENO (Windsor,
Vt.)
1810: 20649
1812: 26659, 26674

WYATT, SOLOMON (Philadel-
phia)
see WIATT, SOLOMON
(Philadelphia)

WYETH, GEORGE (Erie, Pa.)
1808: 15616 pb

WYETH, GEORGE (Presque
Isle, Pa.)
1808: 15617 pb

WYETH, JOHN (Harrisburg,
Pa.)
1801: 561 pb, 1215 pb, 1565,
50248
1802: 3024-3025
1803: 3803, 5194, 5552
1804: 7306
1805: 8562, 9422
1806: 11269
1807: 13612
1808: 15378 pb
1809: 17955 pb, 18536
1810: 19986, 20240, 22116 pb
1811: 22700 pb, 22936, 24506
1813: 30589 pb
1814: 31348
1815: 34588
1817: 41749
1818: 44154 pb, 44603 pb,
45241, 45263 pb, 46885 pb
1819: 48110, 49040, 49043

Y

Yale College, Junior Class
(New Haven, Conn.)
1803: 4074-4075 f

YANCEY, FRANCIS GARLAND
(Petersburg, Va.)
1814: 31283 pb
1815: 33987
1816: 36865
1818: 43815, 45842-45844
1819: 49583 pb

Yankee (Boston)
1811: 22413
1812: 25243, 25988
1813: 30525
1814: 32053, 32493
1815: 34376-34377, 34942,
36271
1817: 41374, 42017

YEATES, THOMAS (Chambers-
burg, Pa.)
1812: 25381 f

YOUNG, ALEXANDER (Boston)
1801: 106, 211, ?887, 888,
889-890 pb, 899-900, 902
pb, 911
1802: 1798, 1801, 2547, 2616-
2617, 2626-2627, 2629 pb,
3139
1803: 3655 pb, 4151 pb, 4601-
4602, 4608-4612, 4617,
4724 pb, 4943, 50373 pb
1804: 6586 pb, 6705 pb,
6737-6739, 6741-6745, 6751-
6753, 7793
1805: 7855, 8098 pb, 8855-
8857, 8868-8871, 8876, 9340
1806: 10822, 10825, 10828
pb, 10833, 11356 pb

YOUNG, BENJAMIN (New
York)
1816: 36717 pb
1817: 42916

YOUNG, STEPHEN (Geneva,
N. Y.)
1816: 37693 pb

YOUNG, WILLIAM (New York)
1801: 551, 689 pb, 1223
1802: 1977 pb, 2193, 2298 pb,
2436 pb, 3524 pb
1803: 4424 pb, 50364 pb
1804: 5975 bpb, 6363, 6526
pb
1805: 8670 pb, 9424, 9632

YOUNG, WILLIAM (Philadel-
phia)
1801: 185, 482 pb, 625, 917,
1128 f, 1620 pb
1802: 1877 pb, 3596, 50290
pb
1803: 4767 pb, 4768
1808: 14487 f

YOUNG, WILLIAM (Whitehall,
Pa.)
1801: 15, 1305 pb, 1328 pb
1802: 2386, 3538, 3597, 4872
pb
1803: 5619
1804: 5946, 6226, 6229, 6231
1805: 8002 pb
1808: 14491 pb

YOUNG, WILLIAM PRICE
(Charleston, S. C.)
1801: 1089 pb, 1212, 50240
pb
1802: 2012, 2159, 2296, 2845
pb, 2979, 3085, 50317-50318
pb
1803: 4146 pb, 4812 pb, 4947,
50383 pb
1804: 6362, 6984 pb, 7148,
7220
1805: 8062, 8166, 9091 pb,
9410
1806: 10117-10118, 10659,
11091 pb, 11365
1807: 11959, 12230, 12697,
12854, 13450
1808: 14507, 15606, 16006 pb
1809: 18318, 18679 pb, 50957
pb
1810: 20612, 20982 pb, 21390
pb, 21941
1811: 22475, 22515
1812: 25177, 51233 pb, 51240
pb

1813: 28844, 28862, 29661,
    29844 pb
1814: 31258, 31405, 31530,
    32426, 32583, 32947
1815: 34325 pb, 34810, 35555
    pb
1817: 40743, 41723
1818: 43260, 44922, 45340,
    45699
1819: 48058, 48584, 48646,
    49466 pb, 49596, 50132

YOUNGS, P (Penn Yan, N. Y.)
1818: 45232 pb

YUNDT, LEONARD (Baltimore)
1801: 1201, 1676
1802: 2580
1806: 10802 f

Z

Zanesville Express (Zanesville,
    O.)
1817: 41688, 42190

ZANTZINGER, THOMAS BAR-
    TON (Philadelphia)
1810: 19363 f
1811: 22412a f, 22548 f,
    23044 f, 23650 f, 24337 f
1812: 27383-27384

ZENTLER, CONRAD (Phila-
    delphia)
1806: 50638 pb, 50737-50738
1807: 11982 pb, 12274, 12766-

    12767, 13669
1808: 14347-14348 pb, 14484
    pb, 14772, 14964 pb,
    16278, 16611
1809: 16854, 17362, 18717
1810: 19360 pb, 19545 pb,
    19546, 19713, 20315-20316,
    20353, 20360, 20363, 21454
1811: 22419-22420, 22784,
    23028, 23078 pb, 24012,
    51050 pb
1812: 24606, 24656, 24865,
    25363, 25516 pb, 25624,
    25798, 25862-25863, 26065,
    26127, 26797 pb, 26843 pb,
    26930 pb, 27375 pb
1813: 27720 pb, 28453 pb,
    28454, 28627, 28628 pb,
    28685 pb, 28729, 28760,
    29203, 29425 pb, 29737,
    29856, 29857 pb, 29912 f,
    30468
1814: 30617 pb, 31840, 32657,
    51357 pb
1815: 33854 pb
1816: 36743, 36988, 37525 pb,
    37532, 37539, 37763, 37770,
    37853, 37932, 38113 pb,
    38285
1817: 39997, 40736, 40784 pb,
    40824, 41029, 41215, 41406-
    41407, 41935 bf
1818: 43076 pb, 43448, 43845,
    43972, 44077, 44351-44352,
    44551 pb, 44635, 44807-
    44808, 44841 pb, 44896 pb,
    44897, 45235, 45484
1819: 46996 pb, 48446, 48744-
    48745, 49976 pb

A

ABBEVILLE, N. C.
Davenport, T M

ABINGTON, MD.
Ruff, Daniel P

ABINGTON, VA.
1816: ?39096?
1817: ?40770?
Holston Intelligencer
Ustick, John Gano

ALBANY, N. Y.
1801: ?19, 26, 28, 87, 323,
?405, 437, ?692, 711,
739, 1033-1036, 1038,
1044-1046, 1234, 1259,
?1369, ?1418, 1419, ?1420,
?1421?, ?1696
1802: ?2132-2133, ?2773,
2777, 2782-2784, 2786
1803: 3643
1804: 6076, 6153, 6155,
?6549, 6916, 6928, 7164,
?7165?, 7179, 7332, ?7360
1805: 8414, 8818, ?9678
1806: 9819, 10278, 11005,
11455
1807: ?12424?, 12425-12427,
12914, 13225?, 13274
1808: 14310, 15002, 15192,
15750, 15758
1809: 17439, ?17497?, 17498,
17962, 18500, 18750,
?19089?
1810: ?19951?, 19958,
?20099?, 20340, 20891,
20932, 21097, 22079, 22118
1811: ?22686?, 22897, 23542,
23544, 23979, 51121
1812: 25252, 25589, 26268,
26276, 26282, ?51169,
51226
1813: 27686, 27875, 28144,
29329?, 29334, 30398-30399,
30464
1814: 30643, 30644?, ?30722?,
31505, 31544, 32274-32278,
32280-32285, 32287-32295,
32300-32301, 32313, 32317,
32319, 32321, 32327, 32329,
32333-32333a, 32984, 33634,
51385-51386, 51421-51427
1815: 33812-33815, 34511,
35984, 36441, 36575, 51454,
51518, ?51519?, ?51521
1816: 36701-36702, 37279,
37332, 37635, 38210, 38419-
38431, 38446, 38973, 39094,
39735, 39793, 51568
1817: 39957, 40444, 40445?,
40446, 40487, 41245, 41611,
41613, 41627, 41838, 41940,
42065, 42097-42098, ?42315,
42986, ?51696?, 51718?
1818: 43044, ?43444?, 43655,
44553, 45031-45033, 45035,
45176, 45721, 45739, 45752,
45893, 51808
1819: 46953, 46957-46958,
47819, 48140, 48889, 48902,
?49468, 49580
Abbey, Dorephus
Abbey, Seth Alden
Albany Argus
Albany Centinel
Albany Register

Albany Religious Tract
Society
Albany Union Sunday
School Society
Allen, Solomon
Andrews, Ebenezer
Turell
Andrews, Loring
Backus, Eleazer Fitch
Balance
Barber, John
Brown, Samuel R
Buckley, Billy
Buel, Jesse
Cation, James
Churchill, George
Clark, ---
Clark, Aaron
Clark, Israel W
Cole, John Orton
Conant, Jonathan
Cook, John
Crosswell, Harry
Davis, Samuel H
Dodge, C
Doubleday, Ulysses
Freeman
Fairman, G
Farrand, Daniel W
Fero, Henry
Fish, Joshua
Forbes, George
Frary, Jonathan
Gould, William
Green, Jacob
Hosford, Elijah
Hosford, Elisha
Leavenworth, David
Lindsay, George
Loomis, George Jepson
M'Glashan, Daniel
Mitchell, Isaac
Newton, George
Packard, Benjamin D
Packard, Robert
Penniman, Obadiah
Pratt, Moses
Schermerhorn, Ryer
Seaver, William
Shaw, Samuel
Skinner, Daniel
Skinner, Elisha W
Skinner, Hezekiah

Society for the Promo-
tion of Useful Arts
Southwick, Henry Collins
Southwick, Solomon
Steele, Daniel
Thomas, Isaiah
Torrey, Elijah
Tryon, Jeremiah
Tucker, William
Van Benthuysen, Obadiah
Romney
Van Veghten, Douw K
Walker, John W
Washington Benevolent
Society
Webster, Charles Rich-
ard
Webster, George
Whiting, Daniel
Whiting, Samuel
Wood, William

ALEXANDRIA, LA.
Chain, Hugh
Eastin, Thomas
Stokes, Benjamin M
Tennery, George F

ALEXANDRIA, VA.
1801:   576, 1185
1802:   1723
1804:   5682, 7669
1806:   10619
1807:   13689
1812:   25099, 26538
1814:   31863
1816:   36705
1817:   ?42351
Alexandria Expositor
Alexandria Gazette
Bishop, Samuel
Bogan, Benjamin Lewis
Corse, John
Cottom, Peter
Davis, Samuel H
Dinmore, Richard
Gray, John
Gray, Robert
Kennedy, James
Lyon, James
Paradise, John
Rounsavell, Nathaniel
Shutz, C

Simms, John Douglass
Snowden, Samuel
Stewart, John Ainsworth
Thomas, John V
Westcott, James Diament
Westcott, John
Winter, John

ALLENTOWN, PA.
Bruckman, Carl A
Ebner, Heinrich
Ehrenfried, Joseph
Hutter, Charles Lewis
Hutter, Christian Jacob

AMERICA
1804: 7185
1807: 14152
1808: 15417
1810: 19335

AMHERST, MASS.
1804: 6132
1818: 43077

AMHERST, N. H.
1803: 4154, 4174
1818: 43999, 44996
1819: 47472
Boylston, Richard
Curtis, Samuel
Cushing, Joseph
Farmer's Cabinet
Mansur, Elijah
Preston, Samuel

ANDOVER, MASS.
1806: 11145
1810: 19364
1811: 23723?
1812: 26645
1814: 32245, 32499, 32666
1815: 34701, 34845, 35785,
   35946, 36499
1816: 36683, 36737, 38273,
   38287, 38804, 39687, 51623
1817: 40430, 40442, 41575
1818: 44045-44046, 45220,
   45322, 45629, 46873
1819: 47783, 48136, 48346,
   48773, 49033, ?49103?,
   49290
Flagg, Timothy Gould

Gould, Abraham Jones
New England Tract So-
   ciety
Newman, Mark
Tucker, James
Ware, Galen

ANDOVER, N. H.
1819: ?49403
Chase, Ebenezer

ANNAPOLIS, MD.
1801: 877
1805: 8060, 9297
1806: ?10677, 10807
1808: ?15101, ?15671
1809: 17132
1811: 22812
1812: 26888
1815: 35193, 51313
1817: 39937
1818: 43877
1819: 48597-48598, ?48602,
   51912
Book Society of the
   Protestant Episcopal
   Church in Maryland
Butler, John West
Chandler, Jehu
Green, Frederick
Green, Jonas
Shaw, George
Watts, Richard Key

ARKANSAS POST, ARK.
Briggs, Robert
Woodruff, William E

ARLINGTON, VT.
Bucklen, Isaac
Church, Daniel
Storer, E Gilman

ATHENS, GA.
Harris, Eli
Hodge, John
M'Donnell, Alexander

ATHENS, N. Y.
Tennery, Joseph

AUBURN, N. Y.
1813: ?29647, 29956

1814:   32860
1816:   39074
1817:   40038, 40327, 41145,
    41817, 42105
    Beardslee, James
    Boe, H
    Boe, J
    Buckingham, Augustus
    Chamberlain, Royall T
    Crosby, William
    Curtis, A
    Davis, Cornelius
    Hathaway, James G
    Kellogg, Leonard
    Miller, James M
    Pace, Henry
    Pace, James
    Rumsey, David
    Skinner, Thomas M
    Southwick, Henry Collins
    Union Tract Association
        of Friends in the
        Western Counties of
        the State of New York

AUGUSTA, GA.
1804:   6188
1807:   13594
    Adams, George
    Augusta Chronicle
    Augusta Herald
    Bunce, William J
    Duyckinck, Benjamin T
    Georgia Advertiser
    Groves, ---
    Hannon, Tippo S
    Hobby, William J
    Kean, John E
    M'Millan, Alexander
    Pearre, George W S
    Randolph, George F
    Smith, John Erdman
    Starnes, Daniel

AUGUSTA, KY.
1818:   43115

AUGUSTA, ME.
1803:   3637
1804:   ?7245?
1806:   10589
1808:   15354
1809:   ?18491?

1810:   ?21008, ?22051
    Burton, James
    Edes, Benjamin
    Edes, Peter

AURORA, N.Y.
    Pace, Henry

B

BALLSTON SPA, N.Y.
1807:   12986
1808:   15435
1810:   20385?
1812:   26895
1814:   32911
1816:   38787, 39657
1818:   45726
1819:   49615
    Bates, Isaac
    Brown, Samuel R
    Bunce, Isaiah
    Child, William
    Comstock, James
    Doubleday, Ulysses
        Freeman
    Howe, John
    Miller, David Cade
    Miller, James M
    Riggs, Isaac
    Saratoga Courier
    Saratoga Journal
    Saratoga Patriot
    Sears, Reuben
    Swaine, John
    Webb, Phinehas

BALTIMORE
1801:   102, 162, ?265, 286,
    519, 525-526, 582, 694,
    716, 874, 1098, 1332, 1391
1802:   1804-1805, 1807-1808,
    ?1819, 2023?, 2121, ?2167,
    2395?, 2453, 2595?, 2604,
    2695, 2701, 2769, 3053,
    3088
1803:   3717, 3732, 3935, 3989-
    3990, 4028, 4192?, 4338
1804:   5766, 5780, 6039, 6083,
    6091, 6246-6247, 6324,

6333, 6430, 6643, ?6652,
6733-6734, 6992, 7087,
7247, 7265-7266, 7691-7692
1805: ?7926, 8141, 8174,
8222, ?8468?, 8469, 8774,
8778, 9403-9404
1806: ?9895, ?10097?, 10166,
10227, 10299, ?10809?,
11056, ?11106, 11420,
11430?, 11680
1807: 12036, 12037?, ?12050,
?12315, 12322, 12369,
12548, 12609, 12626, 12752,
13400, 13442, 13463?
1808: 14337, 14409, ?14643-
14644, 14713, 14723-14724,
14895, 14966, 15000, 15054-
15055, 15187, 15262, 15669,
15967, 16003, 16009
1809: 16899, 16918?, 16919,
17248, 17413, 17544, 17749,
17784, 18174, 18311, ?18763,
18780
1810: 19411, ?19433, 19642,
19726?, 19728, 20101,
20107, 20152?, 20277-
20278, 20408, 20465,
?20544, 21242, 21273,
21380-21381?
1811: 22235, 22796, 23000,
23095, 23110, ?23268,
23291, 23437, 23728, 23748,
23797, 23949, 24044?,
24464, ?51134?
1812: 24531, ?24662, 24694,
24784?, 24857, 25029,
25595, 26047, 26472,
?26607?, 27589, 51259
1813: 28071, 28409, 28494,
28568, ?29058?, 29375,
29463, 29542, 29623, 30392
1814: 30629, 31095-31096,
31103, 31106, 31295, 31521,
31868, 32943, 33306
1815: 34105, 34136, 34259,
34304, 34512, 34526, 34792,
34815, 34940, 35039, 35663,
35768, ?36090?, 36137,
36473, 36652
1816: 37035, 37179, 37200,
37393, 37568, 37570, 37664,
38013, 38372, 38594, 38596,
38671, 38688, 38731, 38824-

38825, 39038, 51598
1817: 39964, 40282, 40301-
40302, 40421, 40811, 40970,
41175, 41211, 41359?,
41360, 41423, 41542, 41732,
42002, 51717
1818: ?43148?, 43663, 43881,
44265, ?44539?, 44684,
44690-44691, 44923, 45632,
45728-45729, 45895, 45915,
51736
1819: 47434, 47526, 47645,
?47648, 47829, 47964,
47973, 48070, 48581, 48601,
48939, 49446, 49536, 50121,
50123

Allen, Paul
Andrews, Ebenezer
  Turell
Baltimore Evening Post
Baltimore Patriot
Barnes, Samuel
Bell, William Duffield
Bible and Heart
Bonsal, Isaac
Bonsal, Vincent
Book Society of the
  Protestant Episcopal
  Church in Maryland
Bourne, George
Brown, John M
Brown, Matthew
Buel, Albert D
Butler, John West
Butler, Samuel
Byrne, Patrick
Callender, James
Campbell, James
Carnaghan, George
Carr, Joseph
Carr, Robert
Carter, John Michel
Child, S P
Clark, ---
Cleim, Christian
Coale, Edward Johnson
Cole, John
Cole, Samuel
Colman, ---
Colvin, John B
Conrad, John
Conrad, Michael
Cook, John

Female Tract Society
Redding, William F
Religious Tract Society
  of Baltimore
Revell, John
Rice, John
Rider, Richard D
Robinson, Joseph
Russell, Joshua T
St. Mary's College
Schaeffer, Frederick
  George
Sharan, James
Skinner, John S
Smith, ---
Sower, Brook Watson
Sower, Samuel
Spence, W
Stewart, Mordecai
Sun
Swain, E C
Telegraphe
Thatcher, ---
Thomas, Ebenezer Smith
Thomas, Isaiah
Thomas, Moses
Toy, John D
Turner, Michael
Underwood, William B
Union Male Sunday
  School Society of
  Baltimore
University Press
Vance, John
Vance, Thomas
Varle, Charles
Vicary, Henry
Wagner, Jacob
Wagner, Peter K
Wanderer
Wane, John
Warner, William
Warren, W
Weems, Mason Locke
Westcott, John
Wills, Francis M
Wilson, Thomas
Wood, Samuel S
Wooddy, William
Yundt, Leonard

BANGOR, ME.
1819: 49600

Bangor Printing Office
Burton, James
Edes, Peter
Harris, J

BARDSTOWN, KY.
1814: ?30753
1815: 36057
Bard, William
Barnett, Marquis
Edrington, John Price
Isler, Peter
Peniston, Francis

BARNARD, VT.
Carpenter, Isaiah H
Dix, Joseph

BARRINGTON, R. I.
1817: 40141

BATAVIA, N. Y.
Blodgett, Benjamin
Follett, Oran
Miller, David Cade
Peek, Samuel
Williams, Elias

BATH, ME.
1817: 40674

BATH, N. Y.
Rumsey, David
Shepard, Erastus
Smead, Benjamin

BATON ROUGE, LA.
Devalcourt, T
Morison, ---

BEAVER, PA.
Logan, Andrew
Logan, James

BEAVERTOWN, PA.
Berry, John
White, Joseph W

BEDFORD, PA.
Gettys, Thomas R
M'Dowell, Charles

BELLEFONTE, PA.
　　Brindle, William
　　Hamilton, Alexander
　　Maxwell, Hugh

BELLOWS FALLS, VT.
　　Blake, Bill

BENNINGTON, VT.
1803:　4636
1809:　17722, 18653?
1813:　28445, ?28673
　　Clark, Darius
　　Collier, Thomas
　　Cusack, Michael B
　　Dix, Joseph
　　Goodenow, Sterling
　　Haswell, Anthony
　　Haswell, Anthony John-
　　　　son
　　Haswell, William
　　Smead, Benjamin
　　Stockwell, Henry
　　Stockwell, William
　　Walbridge, Ebenezer
　　Williams, Samuel
　　Wright, John Crafts

BERWICK, ME.
　　Richardson, H

BERWICK, PA.
　　Carothers, William

BETHANY, PA.
　　Loomis, Leonard
　　Manning, James

BETHEL, MASS.
　　Chapman, Edmund

BEULA, PA.
　　Western Spy

BEVERLY, MASS.
1810:　20520

BINGHAM, ME.
1819:　?47407

BINGHAMTON, N.Y.
　　Burrell, Abraham
　　Morgan, Augustus

Morgan, Chauncey
Phoenix
Robinson, Tracy

BLAKELEY, ALA.
　　Mott, Gabriel F

BLAKELY, N. C.
　　Carney, John
　　Dismukes, Alexander H

BOLTON, MASS.
　　Cooledge, Daniel

BOSTON
1801:　?34, 167, 196, ?213-
　　215, 216-217, 232, 332,
　　439, 528, 599, 657,
　　705, 718, 767, ?868,
　　891, 898, 907, 923,
　　946, 977, 1140, 1152,
　　1235, 1340, 1660, 50264
1802:　1730, 1751, 1820, 1827,
　　1838, 1928?, 1929, 1932,
　　2046, 2050, 2084, 2249,
　　2256, 2346, 2373, 2381,
　　2408, 2424, 2606, 2622,
　　2624-2625, 2724, 2730,
　　2757, 2799, 2816, ?2817,
　　2821, 2859, 2898, ?3027,
　　3030, 3034, ?3060, 3088,
　　3099, 3120, 3130, 3176,
　　3183, 3531, 3544, 50277
1803:　3647, 3663-3664, 3769,
　　3779-3780, 3832?, 3861?,
　　3863, 3866-3867, 3885,
　　3904, 4000, ?4038?, 4152,
　　4167-4168, 4177, 4235,
　　4262, 4329?, 4426, 4456,
　　4499, 4516, 4604-4606,
　　4707, 4708?, 4723, 4853,
　　5036, 5047, 5061, 5065,
　　5086, ?5113, 5130-5131,
　　5488, 5544, 5624
1804:　5676, 5725, 5841, 5893-
　　5894, 5939, ?5941?, 5987,
　　6058, 6103, 6107, 6253,
　　?6301, 6323, 6335, 6484a,
　　6516, 6618, 6623, 6769,
　　6777, 6826, 6851, 6960,
　　6964, 7104, 7279, 7281,
　　7290?, 7298, 7350, 7372,
　　7381, 7758, 7764, 7767

1811: 22145, 22163, ?22198,
22222, 22310, 22374, 22431-
22432, 22414a, 22422a,
22464, 22545, 22721, 22761,
22768, 22787, 22801, 22818,
22848, 22857, 22859, 23088,
23117, 23210, 23281, 23299-
23304, 23306-23307, 23310,
23312-23313, 23316-23318,
23320-23323, 23330, 23336-
23340, ?23343?, 23345-
23346, ?23350?, ?23386,
?23441, 23633, 23637,
?23757, 23821, 23917, 24008,
24350, ?24460, 24496,
24500?, 24505, 51048
1812: 24515, 24537, 24564,
24571, 24602?, 24610,
24622, 24647-24648, 24767,
24802, 24837, 24903, 24905-
24907, 24910, 24914, 24935,
24953, ?25101?, 25113,
25138, 25153, ?25244?,
25245, 25248, 25277, 25286,
25342-25343, 25377, 25405,
25428, 25612, 25632, 25695,
25746?, 25795, 25823,
25878-25879, 25889, 25893,
25903, 25933, 25971-25979,
25982-25986, ?25989,
25990, 25995-25996, 26002-
26003, 26006, 26010, 26012-
26017, 26019, 26029-26030,
?26032?, 26034, 26039,
26211, 26307, 26356, 26540,
26601, 26625, 26697,
26710?, 26776, 26832?,
26861, 26889, 26899, 26903,
27145, 27415, 27417,
27424?, 27428-27429,
27462-27463, 27474, 27552,
27588, 27628, 51153, 51165,
51217, 51241
1813: 26434, 27678, 27706,
27745, 27752-27753, 27772,
?27833, 27836, 27839,
27843, 27937, 27986, 27988-
27990, 27995-27997, 28006,
28103, 28134, 28163, 28165,
28207, 28258, 28414, 28422,
28434-28436, 28485, 28513,
28615, 28632, 28686, 28747,
28820, 28826, 28835, 28852,

28915, 28963, 28992, 29021,
29073, 29076, 29078-29080,
29082?, 29089, ?29093,
29095, 29099-29101, 29103,
29107?, 29109, 29118,
?29161?, 29183, 29189,
29256, 29367, 29410,
?29464, 29513, 29520-29521,
29525, 29574, 29645, 29659,
29662, ?29789, 29840,
29859, 29907, 30449,
?30475, 30499, 30532,
30574, 30576, 30584, 51315
1814: 30649, 30685a, 30912,
30920, 30960-30962, 30964-
30966, 31001, 31002?,
31024-31025, 31071, 31100,
31137, 31151?, 31181?,
31194, 31208, 31232?,
31236, 31304, 31396, 31441,
31452, 31550, 31557, 31573,
31617, 31707, 31745, 31765,
31792, 31912, 31963, 31965,
31968, 31989, 32029, 32032,
32034, 32036-32037,
?32038?, 32039, ?32040,
?32041?, 32044, 32050?,
32056-32059, 32067-32069,
?32070, 32071, 32081,
32085, ?32239, 32400, 32411,
32435, 32442, 32494?,
32507, 32625, 32643, 32681,
32717, 32787?, 32808,
32811, 32849, 32964,
?32965, 33526-33527,
33587, 33597, 33613, 33692,
33707, 51377
1815: 33818, 33849, 33856-
33859, 33883, 34035, 34167,
34173, 34187, 34248,
?34311?, 34367, 34408,
34421, 34496, 34579,
34644?, ?34652?, 34660-
34661, 34674, 34727, 34736,
34878-34880, 34941, 34944,
34955?, 34975, ?34984,
?35001, ?35060?, 35105,
35141-35142, 35144, 35194,
35198-35199, 35207, 35209-
35210, 35215, 35220-35221,
35321, 35539, 35543, 35569,
35579, 35615, 35621,
?35688, 35762, 35780,

Adams, Abijah
Allen, Andrew J
American Academy of
    Arts and Sciences
American Board of
    Commissioners for
    Foreign Missions
Andrews, Ebenezer
    Turell
Andrews, William
Annin, William B
Anthology Press
Armstrong, John W
Armstrong, Samuel
    Turell
Austin, Lemuel
Avery, Samuel
Badger, Barber
Badger, Thomas
Bagley, ---
Balch, ---
Ball, Jonathan
Ball, Josiah

Ballard, Davis C
Bangs, Thomas G
Baptist Missionary Society of Massachusetts
Bassford, S
Beals, Ephraim C
Bedlington, Timothy
Belcher, John H
Belcher, Joshua
Bellamy, Elisha
Berean Society
Bible Warehouse
Billings, George
Bingham, Caleb
Blagrove, William
Blake, Ebenezer
Blake, Lemuel
Blake, William P
Bliss, Elam
Bolles, James G
Book Printing Office
Bookstore and Printing Office
Boston Bookstore
Boston Chronicle
Boston Commercial Gazette
Boston Daily Advertiser
Boston Gazette
Boston Intelligencer
Boston Patriot
Boston Recorder
Boston Sabbath Society for the Moral and Religious Instruction of the Poor
Boston Society for the Religious and Moral Improvement of Seamen
Boston Weekly Magazine
Bowen, Abel
Bowen, Daniel
Bowen, Henry
Bowers, Isaac
Bowles, Leonard C
Boyle, John
Bradford, Alden
Bradlee, Thomas
Brewster, M
Brown, Thomas
Buckingham, Joseph Tinker

Bumstead, Joseph
Burdakin, Joseph
Burdick, William
Burditt, James W
Burr, David J
Butler, Merrill
Callender, Charles
Carlisle, David
Chamberlain, William
Channing, Henry
Child, Lemuel
Christian Disciple Society
Clapp, William Tileston
Clapp, William W
Clarke, Thomas
Collier, William
Columbian Centinel
Conant, Daniel
Cotton, Edward
Coverly, Nathaniel
Crary, William
Crocker, Benjamin
Crocker, C
Crocker, Uriel
Crosby, William
Cummings, Jacob Abbott
Cushing, Joshua
Cutler, James
Daily Advertiser
Dean, Thomas
Degrand, Peter Paul Francis
Deming, L
Dunham, John Moseley
Edes, Benjamin
Edmands, Thomas
Edwards, James L
Edwards, William
Eliot, John
Emerald
Episcopal Prayer Book and Tract Society for the Eastern Diocese
Etheridge, Samuel
Evening Gazette
Everett, Oliver
Ewer, Charles
Fairlamb, D
Farnham, Robert
Farrand, William Powell
Finch, E E
Fleet, John

Rowe, Thomas
Russell, Benjamin
Russell, John
Rust, Enoch H
Scott, James
Sewell, Stephen
Simons, William
Smith, George G
Snelling, Samuel G
Society for Promoting
　　Christian Knowledge,
　　Piety, and Charity
Spear, Charles
Spear, Henry
Spear, Oliver
Spear, William S
Sprague, Hosea
State Press
Stebbins, Chester
Sterne, ---
Swan, Timothy
Thomas, Isaiah
Tileston, Ezra B
Titcomb, ---
True, Benjamin
Trumbull, Henry
Union Circulating Li-
　　brary
Van Tromp Press
Wait, Thomas Baker
Waldo, Henry S
Walker, G
Wallingsford, Joel
Walter, William
Washington Benevolent
　　Society of Massa-
　　chusetts
Waters, David J
Watson, David
Weld, Giles E
Wells, Thomas
Wells, William
West, David
West, John
Weston, Equality
White, James
White, Thomas W
Wilkey, J
Williams, Charles
Williams, Henry
Williams, J
Williams, Robert P
Willis, Nathaniel

Wilson, John
Woodward, ---
Wright, Edmund
Yankee
Young, Alexander

BOTETOURT CO., VA.
　　Amen, David

BOWLING GREEN, KY.
　　Green, Thomas

BRADFORT, VT.
1813:　30530

BRATTLEBORO, VT.
1804:　6513
1805:　8751
1806:　10407, 11391
1807:　12313, 12919
1810:　20234, ?20717?
1812:　25713
1815:　35980, ?36563
1816:　?39778?
1817:　40197, 42130?
　　American Yeoman
　　Brattleboro Bookstore
　　Burbank, Abijah
　　Caldwell, J R
　　Cole, Benjamin
　　Fessenden, William
　　Holbrook, John
　　Houghton, Peter
　　Ide, Simeon
　　Smead, Benjamin
　　Wilson, Jonathan

BRIDGEPORT, CONN.
1814:　30805
1815:　34132, 35387
1816:　51569
　　Backus, Simon
　　Baldwin, Josiah B
　　Beach, Lazarus
　　Bulkley, J
　　Lockwood, Lambert
　　Mallory, Samuel
　　Nichols, Stiles
　　Ripley, Hezekiah
　　Sherman, Ira
　　Sherman, Silas
　　Skinner, Nathaniel L
　　Thompson, Sheldon

BRIDGETON, N. J.
  Combs, Nathaniel L
  Hay, Peter
  Schultz, William
  Westcott, John

BRIGHTON, MASS.
  Bowen, Daniel

BRISTOL
1801: ?89
1807: 12902
1808: 14393
1813: 28839
1815: 35662

BRISTOL, ME.
1808: 15335

BRISTOL, R. I.
1813: 30443
1818: 43900
  Dearth, Golden
  Duhy, Charles W
  Sterry, Erastus

BROOKFIELD, MASS.
1807: ?13271, 13879
1809: 17451
1816: 37309, 38841
1817: 41277
  Andrews, Ebenezer
    Turell
  Brown, Hori
  Hammond, Elisha
  Merriam, Ebenezer
  Thomas, Isaiah
  Washington Benevolent
    Society

BROOKLYN, N. Y.
1807: 12123, 12216
1809: 18790
1812: 26647
1813: 28395
1818: 43742
1819: 48432
  Bowen, Josiah
  Carew, J W
  Fero, Henry
  Grant, ---
  Kirk, Thomas
  Little, William

Long Island Star
  Paul, Abraham
  Pray, John Gunnison
  Robinson, William C
  Sargent, Thomas F
  Sleight, Henry C
  Spooner, Alden
  Thomas, William
  Wells, ---
  Worthington, Erastus

BROOKVILLE, IND.
  Ogle, Benjamin
  Scott, John

BROWNSVILLE, PA.
1812: 27524
  Alexander, James
  Berry, John
  Bouvier, John
  Cattell, David
  Dingee, John
  Fee, Robert
  M'Girr, William

BRUNSWICK, ME.
1806: 10023
1807: 12191
1809: ?19199
1810: 20711?

BUCKSTOWN, ME.
1807: 12279
  Clapp, William Warland
  Holland, Anthony Henry

BUFFALO, N. Y.
1812: 25469, 51248-51249
1814: 51444?
1816: 51591?
1818: ?51773
1819: 47749?
  Carpenter, William
    Allison
  Day, David Merrick
  Lazell, John A
  Salisbury, Hezekiah
    Alexander
  Salisbury, Smith Hamilton
  Stillman, Isaiah

BURLINGTON, N. J.
1805: 7822

1812:   25846
1813:   29610
         Allinson, David
         Allinson, Samuel
         Collins, Thomas
         Lexicon Press
         Meehan, John Silva
         Sharpless, Joseph
         Ustick, Stephen Clegg

BURLINGTON, N.Y.
1805:   9083

BURLINGTON, VT.
1802:   1743, 3459, 3562
1806:   11763
1808:   16631
1810:   21907
1811:   24342
1814:   32369
1815:   35510
1817:   41820
1819:   49987
         Atwater, Ambrose
         Baker, John Kelse
         Buel, Samuel
         Conant, Augustus F
         Ferguson, Bartimeus
         Fish, Francis G
         Greenleaf, Daniel
         Hinckley, ---
         King, Josiah
         Mills, Ephraim
         Mills, Samuel
         Mills, Thomas
         Pritchard, Archibald
         Slade, William
         Vermont Centinel

BUTLER, PA.
         Galbraith, John

                    C

CADIZ, O.
         Harris, John
         Siegfried, Simeon
         Smith, ---
         White, Joseph W

CAHAWBA, ALA.
         Allen, William Brown

CALDWELL, N.Y.
         Hoskins, Timothy

CAMBRIDGE, MASS.
1801:   159, ?630-631
1803:   4396, 4583, 5610
1804:   6455
1806:   10533, 11144
1807:   13638
1808:   15199, 16117
1809:   17074-17075, 17715-
    17716, 19149
1810:   19659, 20290, ?20950
1811:   22972, 24395-24396
1812:   25608, ?25611, ?26738
1813:   28716
1814:   31102, 31658
1816:   39864
1817:   ?42838, 42934
         Bigelow, ---
         Hilliard, William
         Metcalf, Eliab Wight
         University Press
         Welch, ---

CAMBRIDGE, N.Y.
         Stockwell, William
         Tennery, Joseph

CAMBRIDGE, S.C.
         Davenport, Thomas M

CAMBRIDGEPORT, MASS.
         Parker, Thomas

CAMDEN, N.J.
         Crane, John Austin

CAMDEN, S.C.
         Hood, John Bann
         Johnston, P W
         Slump, John Martin

CANANDAIGUA, N.Y.
1801:   ?484
1804:   7748
1806:   50731
1808:   15315
1812:   26240
1813:   28073, 28286

1816: 37878
 Beach, Nathaniel
 Bemis, James Draper
 Chapin, Henry
 Cole, Benjamin
 Gould, John Keep
 Ontario Messenger
 Post, Russell E
 Simmons, H
 Stevens, John Abbott
 Tiffany, Silvester
 Underhill, H

CANTON, O.
 Saxton, John

CARLISLE, PA.
1804: 6668
1808: 15149
1809: 17384, 19082
1816: 38380
1817: 51658?, ?51674-51675, 51676
1819: ?51914
 Alexander, William
 Carlisle Herald
 Gangwehr, George
 Holcomb, Michael
 Kline, George
 Loudon, Archibald
 M'Farland, John
 Magee, Alexander
 Peterson, Henry W
 Phillips, George
 Sanno, Friedrich
 Scott, John
 Stine, Jacob R
 Tizzard, James
 Underwood, James
 Underwood, William B

CARMEL, N.Y.
1814: 32594

CARTHAGE, TENN.
1809: ?17711a, 18743
 Carthage Press
 Miller, Samuel
 Moore, William

CASTINE, ME.
 Eagle
 Hall, Samuel
 Waters, David J

CATSKILL, N.Y.
1806: 10232
1810: 21054
1811: 23842
1815: 35673
1819: 50129
 American Eagle
 Bill, James
 Corss, Richard L
 Crosswell, Harry
 Crosswell, Mackay
 Elliot, Nathan
 Kappel, Michael J
 Lewis, Junius S
 Lewis, Uriah C
 Nichols, Charles
 Peck, Samuel
 Shaw, John

CAZENOVIA, N.Y.
 Baker, Oran E
 Bunce, Jonathan
 Dockstader, Jacob
 Johnson, John B
 Newton, George
 Pilot

CEDARVILLE, N.J.
 Westcott, John

CHAMBERSBURG, PA.
1819: 47404
 Armor, William
 Goeb, Frederick
 Harper, George Kenton
 Herschberger, John
 Johns, Thomas
 Lloyd, John
 M'Farland, John
 Merklein, H
 Schoepflin, Friedrich Wilhelm
 Schoepflin, Wilhelm
 Sloan, John
 White, Richard
 Yeates, Thomas

CHARLESTON, S.C.
1801: 994
1802: 1830, 2270, 3071-3072, ?3101
1803: 3953, 4997, 5620
1804: 5983, 7292, 7358-7359
1805: 8167

1806: 10090, 10119, 10734,
        50658
1807: 12465-12466, 12818,
        13451?
1808: 14439, 14652, 15066,
        15419, ?15835
1809: 17560-17565, 17567-
        17570
1810: ?19452, 20009, ?20011
1811: 23600, 23874
1812: 24596, 25050, 25648
1813: ?27814?, 28078
1814: ?31740?, 32129
1815: 35117
1816: 36679?, 37113, 37213,
        38497, 38817
1817: ?40451, 41394, 41904,
        41925, 42075
1818: 43030, 43212, ?43423,
        43586, 44558, 46685
1819: 47569, 48252
        Andrews, Loring
        Babcock, Sidney
        Babcock, William R
        Bailey, David
        Bason, William P
        Beleurgey, Claudius
        Bounetheau, Gabriel
            Manigault
        Bowen, Thomas Barthol-
            omew
        Bryer, ---
        Carpenter, Stephen
            Cullen
        Charleston Courier
        Charleston Gazette
        Conrad, John
        Crow, John
        Dacqueny, Ambroise
        Dacqueny, John A
        Duke, John C
        Elford, James
        Elliott, Samuel J
        Evans, John Joseph
        Fleming, Thomas
        Freneau, Peter
        Harby, Isaac
        Hoff, John
        Hrabowski, Richard
        Investigator
        Johnston, P W
        Mackey, John
        Marchant, Peter Timothy

Mill, John
Miller, Archibald Ed-
    ward
Missildine, Robert
Morford, Edmund
Muck, P
Negrin, John J
Nelson, John Dixon
Protestant Episcopal
    Society for the Ad-
    vancement of Chris-
    tianity in South
    Carolina
Query, John
Richards, Samuel
Riley, W
Saint Andrew's Church
Sargent, John H
Scotch Presbyterian
    Church
Skrine, Tacitus G
Southern Patriot
Stephens, Thomas B
Thayer, Ebenezer
Thomas, Ebenezer Smith
Times
Waller, Bayfield
Williams, David R
Willington, Aaron Smith
Wilson, John L
Young, William Price

CHARLESTOWN, IND.
    Dunkin, L L
    Lingan, Joseph A

CHARLESTOWN, MASS.
1801: 1101?, 1110
1802: 2319, 3482, 5523
1804: 6826, 6833
1805: 8168, 9081
1808: 15597, 15599
1809: 17633, 17891, ?18663
1810: ?20625, 20750
1813: 51273
1814: 30626, 32174
1815: 34326-34327
1816: 37215
1817: 40453
1818: 45794
1819: 47570
        Armstrong, Samuel
            Turell

Bliss, Elam
Brega, Solomon Bela
Brown, Asahel
Clark, George
Etheridge, Samuel
Green, Thomas
Greenough, William
Hastings, Jonathan
Hooper, J
Howe, Jonathan
Lund, Hans
M'Kown, John
Middlesex Bookstore
Morse, Jedidiah
Oliver, Daniel
Shepard, Thomas
Spear, Charles
Spear, Henry
Spear, William S
Stebbins, Chester
Weld, J R
White, Joseph

CHARLESTOWN, VA.
1819:   47571
Brown, William
Farmers Repository
Williams, Richard
Workman, Samuel

CHARLOTTE, N. C.
1814:   31000, 32940

CHEPATCHET, R. I.
1811:   23902

CHERRY VALLEY, N. Y.
Clark, Israel W
Crandal, Edward Bur-
    dick
Todd, Bethel
Todd, Lemuel

CHESHIRE, CONN.
1801:   801?
1805:   8762
Kensett, Thomas
Law, William
Shelton, ---

CHESTER, PA.
Butler, Steuben
Worthington, Eliphalet B

CHESTER, VT.
Spear, Charles

CHILLICOTHE, O.
1801:   1302
1806:   10138
1807:   ?13276, 13277, 13279
1808:   15369
1809:   17550?
1810:   ?20156?
1811:   22861, 22862?, 24435
1812:   25033, 25062, ?26341,
    27538
1813:   28370, ?28779?, 29398,
    29402?
1814:   ?32387?, ?32392,
    32393, 32893?
1815:   34275, 34959
1816:   ?37227?, 38506?,
    ?38507
1817:   41055, ?41880
1818:   43135, 44042, ?44541
1819:   47585
Allen, ---
Andrews, John
Bailhache, John
Barnes, James
Bradford, Thomas
    Grayson
Collins, Joseph S
Denny, George
Drew, William C
Ely, ---
Fletcher, John R
Fredonian
Hellings, John
Independent Republican
Nashee, George
Parcels, Peter
Richardson, Robert D
Scioto Gazette
Scott, John
Supporter
Weekly Recorder
Willis, Nathaniel
Winship, Winn

CINCINNATI, O.
1801:   699
1806:   9904, ?11063
1808:   15477, 16175
1810:   51025
1812:   26887, 27579

1813:   28869
1815:   34594, ?35928
1816:   ?37245?, 37637, 39042,
39791
1817:   41821, 42976, 51661
1818:   ?43205, 44469
1819:   47618, 47886, 49238,
50174
Advertiser
Browne, John W
Browne, Samuel J
Carney, David L
Carpenter, Joseph
Coleman, Wesley
Cooke, Edward B
Drew, William C
Farnsworth, Oliver
Ferguson, James
Findlay, Jonathan S
Fletcher, John R
Hall, E
Inquisitor
Jenkinson, John
Liberty Hall
Lodge, James
Looker, James H
Mason, James M
Mennessier, Francis
Morgan, Ephraim
Pace, James
Palmer, Thomas
Penney, Thomas
Pettit, Melancton Smith
Phillips, William
Poundsford, William
Powers, Benjamin
Franklin
Reynolds, Sackett
Roll, J C
Sanxay, Frederick
Speer, James H
Spencer, O M
Strowhuver, George
Wallace, Andrew
Warren County Peace
Society
Western Navigation
Bible and Tract
Society
Western Spy
Williams, Micajah Ter-
rell
Wing, Cornelius

CIRCLEVILLE, O.
Foster, James
Richardson, Robert D

CLAIBORNE, ALA.
Tucker, ---
Turner, ---

CLARKSBURG, VA.
1805:   8644
1810:   19695
1814:   ?33556?
1815:   35927
Britton, Alexander
Britton, Forbes
Butler, Gideon
M'Granaghan, William
M'Rae, Alexander G

CLARKSVILLE, TENN.
Bradford, Theoderick F
Crutcher, George
Fitzgerald, John
M'Keen, Thomas H
Peeples, Burrel H

CLEVELAND, O.
Logan, Andrew
Willes, Ziba

CLINTON, O.
Gilkison, John C
M'Ardle, John P
Ohio Register
Smith, Samuel Harrison

COLCHESTER, CONN.
1815:   35302
Skinner, Thomas M

COLUMBIA, PA.
1813:   28771
Greer, William
Wilson, Thomas A

COLUMBIA, S.C.
1804:   7295
1808:   16223, 16224?
1809:   18660
1810:   19649, 21389
1812:   51251
Cline, William
Faust, Daniel

Faust, Jacob John
Hillhouse, David P
Hines, John B
Lorrain, Thomas W
Seymour, J
State Gazette
Telescope

COLUMBIA, TENN.
Eastin, Thomas
Hays, A C
Walker, James

COLUMBUS, O.
1814: 31020
1815: ?34405, 36604
1817: 51653
1818: 45139
1819: 47678, 48972, 48975-
48976, 48977?
Buttles, Joel
Columbus Gazette
Glover, E
Griswold, Ezra
Kilbourn, John
Ohio Monitor
Olmsted, Philo Hopkins
Smith, David Campbell
Western Intelligencer

CONCORD, MASS.
1812: 24848
1817: 41287
1818: 44313
Bettis, William J
Cushing, Caleb
Peters, Joseph Thompson-
son

CONCORD, N. H.
1803: 4342, 4734, 4741
1804: ?6609
1805: ?9702
1806: 10968, 10970
1807: 12483, 13199, 13201,
13746
1808: 14756, 15584, 15626,
15727
1809: ?16809, 17489, 17605,
18196-18197, 18632, 18735
1810: 20863, 22090
1811: 22430, 22598, 23516-
23517, 24064

1812: 25421, 25455, 26214,
26222-26223, 26226, 26234
1813: 27670, 28200, ?29288
1814: 31129
1815: 51510?
1816: 36831
1818: 44994
1819: 47191, 47379, 48361,
48763, 48776, 48848, 48853,
?48854
Cooledge, Daniel
Farmer, John
Fillebrown, Thomas
Hardy, Nathaniel Kim-
ball
Hill, Isaac
Hill, Walter Russell
Hough, George
Hoyt, William
Moore, Jacob Bailey
New Hampshire Bible
Society
New Hampshire Mission-
ary Society
New Hampshire Patriot
New Hampshire Tract
Society
Philbrick, Joseph
Russell, Elijah
Spear, Joseph C
Spear, William S
Tuttle, Jesse Carr

CONCORD, N. Y.
1811: 22428

CONNECTICUT
1811: 24049
1816: 39815

CONNELLSVILLE, PA.
1818: 43720

COOPERSTOWN, N. Y.
1817: 41395, 42894
1818: 46616
Andrews, William
Clark, Israel W
Phinney, Elihu
Phinney, Henry
Prentiss, Henry
Prentiss, John Holmes

CORTLAND, N. Y.
　　Percival, James

CORYDON, IND.
1809:　?18759
1813:　28809
　　Brandon, Armstrong
　　Brandon, Jesse
　　Cox, Isaac
　　Indiana Gazette
　　Lodge, John
　　M'Cullough, Randall
　　Nelson, Reuben W

CUMBERLAND, MD.
　　Brown, William
　　Butler, G P W
　　Magill, Samuel
　　Magruder, William
　　Smith, Joseph

CUMBERLAND, R. I.
1818:　44700

CYNTHIANA, KY.
　　Keenon, John G

　　　　　　　D

DAMASCUS, PA.
　　Willson, Daniel A

DANBURY, CONN.
1802:　2119, 2183
1804:　6473-6474, 50474
1807:　12751
1808:　15225
1810:　19662
　　Cushing, Milton Foster
　　Gray, John C
　　Nichols, Stiles
　　Rowe, Thomas
　　Skinner, Nathaniel L
　　Steele, Oliver

DANVERS, MASS.
1806:　11783

DANVILLE, KY.
1806:　11750

1812:　25536
1813:　28952
1818:　45266
　　Adams, John
　　Demaree, Samuel R
　　Moore, Thomas P
　　Ogilsby, Samuel

DANVILLE, PA.
　　Lodge, Jonathan
　　Sweney, George

DANVILLE, VT.
1808:　14284
　　Baker, Solomon
　　Eaton, Ebenezer
　　Lowell, Daniel

DANVILLE, VA.
　　Lanier, James
　　Reinhart, Elhanan W

DARIEN, GA.
　　M'Intyre, Archibald C
　　Millen, John

DAYTON, O.
1802:　6632
1817:　?40568?
1818:　48033
　　Burnet, Isaac Gouverneur
　　Lodge, James
　　M'Clure, William
　　Ohio Republican
　　Pettit, Melancton Smith
　　Skinner, Robert J
　　Smith, George
　　Strain, John

DEDHAM, MASS.
1801:　616, 1650
1803:　5157
1804:　?5820?
1805:　8693, 9399
1806:　10634
1809:　17379
1810:　?20394?
1811:　22674, 23568, ?23580,
　　24392
1812:　25030
1814:　?51412?
1815:　34625
1816:　?38972?

1817:   39920, 41398
1818:   ?44410?, 46654
        Alleyne, Abel Dudley
        Chickering, Jabez
        Columbian Minerva
        Dedham Gazette
        Gannett, Deborah
        Hall, Samuel
        Mann, Daniel
        Mann, Herman
        Mann, William Haynes

DEERFIELD, MASS.
        Graves, Horace
        Newcomb, Charles Jar-
            vis
        Wells, Russell
        Wilson, John

DEERING, N. H.
        Chase, Eben R

DELAWARE, O.
1818:   43207
        Delaware Gazette
        Drake, Jacob
        Hughs, Joseph S
        Linn, J S
        Olmsted, Philo Hopkins

DELHI, N. Y.
        Lappon, John Jay

DERNE, N. Y.
see   MANLIUS, N. Y.

DETROIT, MICH.
1802:   ?3168?
1809:   17169, 18076?
1812:   25560, 25812?, 26072,
        27116-27119
1813:   29160
1815:   33783, 35735
1818:   43983, 44065, 46813
1819:   50155
        Coxshaw, Aaron
        Mettez, Theophilus
        Miller, James M
        Palmer, F
        Palmer, T
        Reed, Ebenezer
        Sheldon, John Pitts

DISTRICT OF COLUMBIA
1818:   44644

DORCHESTER, MASS.
1810:   19989?

DOVER, DEL.
1811:   22677
        Aitken, Robert S
        Allee, Presley
        Black, William
        Freeman, John
        Robertson, John
        Schee, Augustus M
        Wootten, John B

DOVER, N. H.
1802:   2158, 3546
1804:   ?5648?
1805:   8258
1806:   10560, 10959, 11791
1807:   12021
1808:   14888
1809:   18069
1810:   22123
1812:   25290
1813:   27773
1814:   32631
1815:   35813, 36082
1818:   43693
        Balch, J O
        Bragg, Samuel
        Crosby, Oliver
        Mann, John
        Remich, James Kinsman
        Varney, Jesse
        Wendell, John P

DOWNINGTON, PA.
        Mowry, Charles

DOYLESTOWN, PA.
1808:   15997
        Deffebach, Lewis
        Miner, Asher
        Siegfried, Simeon

DUMBARTON, N. H.
1816:   38224?

DURHAM
        Hubbard, Jabez

E

EDGEFIELD, S. C.
Davenport, Thomas M

EDWARDSVILLE, ILL.
Warren, Hooper

EAST WINDSOR, CONN.
1803: 4957
Pratt, Luther
Reed, Abner

ELIZABETH, N. J.
1811: 23014
1812: 26660
1816: 37951, 37997
Austin, Galen L
Canfield, Philemon
Canfield, Russell
Chatterton, Peter
Deare, Lewis
Hale, Mervin
Hart, Edson
Justice, Joseph
Kollock, Isaac Arnett
Kollock, Shepard
Kollock, Simon
Marsh, Luther
Periam, Joseph
Sanderson, Edward
Sanderson, James
Woodruff, Enos
Woods, John

EASTON, MD.
1802: ?2320
1803: ?4479, 4480
1804: 6205?
1806: ?10103, ?10310, ?10797
1808: 16052, ?16327
1809: ?17618
1811: 24439
1818: 44710
Beach, Samuel B
Cowan, James
Gibbs, Henry William
Graham, Alexander
St. John, James
Smith, Thomas Perrin

EASTON, MASS.
Hunt, William

ELIZABETH CITY, N. C.
Beasley, Joseph

EASTON, PA.
1814: 32867
Burnside, John M
Deshler, George W
Hutter, Christian Jacob
Longcope, Samuel
Moore, Samuel
Rogers, Thomas Jones
Weygandt, Jacob

ELIZABETHTOWN, N. Y.
Marsh, Luther
Person, Lewis

ENFIELD, MASS.
1817: 41088
1818: 44386
1819: 48283
Howe, John
Howe, S

EASTPORT, ME.
Folsom, Benjamin

EATON, O.
Vanausdal, Cornelius

EPHRATA, PA.
1805: 8808, 9362, 50540?,
50607?
1806: 10692, 50702
1817: 42114
1818: ?44531
1819: 49359
Bauman, Joseph
Baumann, Johannes
Cleim, Christian
Graff, Michael
Ruth, Jacob

EBENSBURG, PA.
Foley, Thomas

EDENTON, N. C.
Backus, ---
Beasley, Joseph
Wills, James

EDENTOWN, PA.
Blackman, Nathan

ERIE, PA.
1819:   51924?
        Curtis, Robert I
        Morris, John
        Willes, Ziba
        Wyeth, George

ESSEX
1805:   8776

EXETER, N. H.
1801:   668
1802:   2422, 2652, 2663?
1804:   5988
1805:   9262
1806:   11374, 11769, 50636
1808:   14641, 15082, ?15918,
        16201
1809:   ?17153, 18756, 19179
1811:   22715, 23609
1812:   26631, 27594
1813:   29510
1815:   34438?, ?34686,
        35660, 36511
1816:   37182, 38381, 38553
1818:   46717
1819:   ?48121
        Beals, Ephraim C
        Boardman, Nathaniel
        Constitutionalist
        Gridley, Timothy
        Leavitt, Dudley
        Little, Edward
        M'Call, Roger
        Norris, Charles
        Ranlet, Henry
        Richardson, Josiah
        Sawyer, John
        Sheriff, Benjamin Pearse
        Smith, Elias
        Stedman, Ebenezer
        Williams, John J

                    F

FAIRFIELD, N. Y.
1813:   28181

FAIRHAVEN, MASS.
        Gleason, Joseph

FAYETTE, N. Y.
        Hathaway, James G

FAYETTEVILLE, N. C.
1819:   48269
        Black, Duncan
        Bowell, Abner F
        Carney, John
        Carolina Observer
        Dismukes, Alexander H
        Macalaster, Alexander
        Ray, Duncan
        Waldo, Francis W

FELL'S POINT, MD.
        Barnes, Samuel

FERNANDINA, FLA.
1817:   40836

FINCASTLE, VA.
        Amen, David

FISHKILL, N. Y.
1815:   34553

FLATBUSH, N. Y.
1809:   18899
        Riley, Isaac

FLEMINGSBURG, KY.
        Akers, Peter

FORT DEFIANCE, N. C.
1806:   10718

FORT STODDERT, MISS.
        Hood, John Bann
        Miller, Samuel

FRANKFORD, PA.
1812:   26882
        Coale, William
        Gilbert, John F
        Sharpless, Joseph
        Williams, ---

FRANKFORT, KY.
1801:   ?1079
1802:   50291
1803:   ?3729, ?50370
1804:   50442
1805:   8730

1806: 10666
1807: 12010
1808: 15362, 15367
1810: 20487
1811: 23146, 23149-23150
1813: 28868, 28872
1816: ?37330, 37385, 38747
1817: 41192
1818: 44507
1819: ?48535?
Argus of Western America
Berry, Elijah Conway
Bledsoe, Moses Owsley
Bradford, James Morgan
Brunt, Jonathan
Buchanan, Joseph
Butler, Mann
Farnham, John Hay
Gerard, William
Gore, Henry
Holeman, Jacob H
Holeman, William B
Hunter, William
Johnston, Robert
Kendall, Amos
Marshall, Humphrey
Palladium
Pleasants, George
    Washington
Russell, Gervas E
Russell, John B
Street, Joseph Montfort
Wood, William

FRANKLIN, MO.
Holliday, Benjamin
Patten, Nathaniel

FRANKLIN, TENN.
1813: 27675
1818: 43285
Van Pelt, Henry

FRANKLINTON, O.
1813: ?28310
Gardiner, James B

FREDERICK, MD.
1802: 2056-2057, 2253,
    ?2493
1805: ?9524
1809: ?18762
1815: 36428

1819: 47536, 49601-49602,
    49604, 49606, 51893
Barnes, Samuel
Bartgis, Matthias
Bartgis, Matthias Ech-
    ternach
Bartgis's Republican
    Gazette
Burke, William B
Colvin, John B
Frederick-Town Herald
Gross, ---
Hardt, ---
Hornet
Keatinge, G S
Kolb, George
Mann, Charles
Martin, David
Melsheimer, Charles
    Theodore
Republican Advocate
Sala, Jacob
Sower, Charles
Thomson, John Popham
Underwood, William B

FREDERICKSBURG, VA.
1803: ?4868?, ?5553?
1804: ?5769?
1805: ?9483?
1809: ?16906
1810: ?20645, ?21920?
1814: ?51447?
1817: 40133, 40605, 40953
Banks, Gerard
Burch, Elisha
Burch, Isham
Cady, Ebenezer Pem-
    berton
Chiles, Samuel
Gray, William Fairfax
Green, Timothy
Harrow, James D
Temple, Philip
Walker, James

FREDONIA, N. Y.
Carpenter, William Alli-
    son
Hall, James

FREEHOLD, N. J.
Joline, John K
Jones, Hannum

FREEPORT, ME.
1815: 35389

FRYBURG, ME.
1808: 16032

G

GALLATIN, TENN.
1818: 44120

GALLIPOLIS, O.
Cushing, Joshua

GARDINER, ME.
1817: 40889

GENEVA, N. Y.
1815: 35459
Bogert, James
Bogert, William
Crosby, William
Geneva Gazette
Hull, Samuel P
Young, Stephen

GEORGETOWN
Foxall, Henry

GEORGETOWN, DEL.
1807: 13103

GEORGETOWN, D. C.
1805: 9432
1806: 10897
1810: 19322, 20959, 21421?
1813: 28257, 29416, 29462
1817: 51685
1818: 44609
Alleson, Robert
Bradford, Thomas
Grayson
Burgess, B
Carter, James B
Carter, John Michel
Cooper, William
Dinmore, Richard
Duffy, William
Dunn, James C
English, David

Green, Charles D
Hanson, Alexander Con-
tee
Mallory, Daniel
March, John
Milligan, Joseph
Parks, Benjamin
Patterson, Edgar
Richards, George
Rind, William Alexander
Wagner, Jacob
Washington Federalist
Weems, Elijah
Whitehead, Tommy

GEORGETOWN, KY.
Barrow, David
Henderson, Thomas
Lyle, John N
Penn, Shadrach
Reed, ---
Sebree, William
Shellers, ---

GEORGETOWN, S. C.
1816: 38131, 39696
1817: 42804
1818: 46670
Baxter, Francis Marion
Georgetown Gazette
Hamilton, Joseph
Waldo, John
Waterman, Eleazer
Winyaw Intelligencer

GERMANTOWN, PA.
1809: 17942
Billmeyer, Michael
Leibert, Peter
Tietjen, C

GETTYSBURG, PA.
1805: 8594
1810: 20303
Bartgis, Matthias E
Harper, George Kenton
Harper, Robert
Harper, Robert G
Lefever, Jacob
Underwood, William B

GILMANTON, N. H.
1803: 4739?

1815: 35549
1818: ?43130
　　　Clough, ---
　　　Leavitt, Dudley

GLASGOW, KY.
　　　Gaines, Herbert P
　　　Iredale, William H
　　　James, Albert A
　　　Taylor, ---
　　　Williams, ---

GLENS FALLS, N.Y.
　　　Adviser
　　　Cunningham, John
　　　Reynolds, Linus Junius

GLOUCESTER
1804: 6313

GLOUCESTER COUNTY, N.J.
1809: ?17508?

GOSHEN, MASS.
　　　Hamilton, Adam R
　　　Whitman, Ephraim
　　　Whitman, Samuel

GOSHEN, N.Y.
1803: 4249
1804: 6963
　　　Crowell, Timothy Bloom-
　　　　　field
　　　Denton, Gabriel
　　　Houghton, Theophilus
　　　　　Lilly
　　　Hurtin, John G
　　　MacDuffee, Daniel
　　　Morris County and
　　　　　Westchester Associ-
　　　　　ated Presbyteries
　　　Orange County Patriot

GREENFIELD, MASS.
1802: 1838a
1805: 8775
1806: 10858, 11024
1807: 12444
1808: 15160
1811: 23045
1814: 31305
1815: 36596
1816: 37610

1817: 41089, 42862
1818: 43528
1819: 48925, 48927
　　　Bryant, Reuben
　　　Clark, Alanson
　　　Colton, Roderick Mer-
　　　　　rick
　　　Denio, John
　　　Dickinson, Rodolphus
　　　Dickman, Thomas
　　　Franklin Herald
　　　Frary, Timothy
　　　Graves, Horace
　　　Hunt, George
　　　Phelps, Ansel
　　　Traveller
　　　Wells, Russell

GREENSBURG, PA.
　　　Armbrust, John
　　　Graham, William S
　　　M'Corkle, William
　　　Maclean, David
　　　Schnee, J
　　　Snowden, John M
　　　Steck, Jacob S
　　　Wise, Frederick A

GREENWICH, CONN.
　　　Van Riper, N

GREENWICH, MASS.
1804: 6512, 50444
1805: 8656
1810: 20395
1811: 22901, 23057
1812: 25691
1813: 28783
1814: 31761
1815: 34961
1816: 37883
　　　Howe, John
　　　Howe, Solomon

GREENWICH, N.Y.
1810: 21495

GROTON, CONN.
　　　Waterous, Timothy

H

HACKENSACK, N. J.
Blauvelt, Thomas T
Crissy, James

HAGERSTOWN, MD.
1801: ?651, ?851
1806: ?10025, 11800
Bell, William Duffield
Brown, William
Dietrick, Jacob D
Grieves, Thomas
Gruber, John
Herbert, Stewart
Koch, Johann F
Magee, James
May, Daniel
May, J J
Nourse, Gabriel
Stull, Otho H W

HALIFAX, N. C.
1802: 2415
1807: 12059?
Boylan, William
Dunnavant, Marvel W
Dunnavant, William W
Hodge, Abraham
North Carolina Journal
Poindexter, Richard
Read, Jesse
Seaton, William Winston
Smyth, James H

HALLOWELL, ME.
1806: 10284
1808: 14681, 15485, 15569
1813: 29991
1816: 38205
1818: 44588
1819: 48653
Burton, James
Cheever, Nathaniel
Edes, Peter
Gilman, Samuel Kinsman
Goodale, Ezekiel
Griffin, C
Hallowell Bookstore
Johnson, John
Laine, William Frederic
Washburn, J C

HAMDEN, CONN.
1809: 50962

HAMILTON, N. Y.
Cowdery, Benjamin
Franklin
Johnson, John Burgess
Reynolds, Linus Junius
Smead, Benjamin Franklin

HAMILTON, O.
1814: 32230
1819: 48686-48687
Camron, James B
Camron, Wesley
Colby, Zebulon
Keen, William C
M'Bride, James
Miami Intelligencer
Murray, John L
Philanthropist
Smith, Addison
Stewart, Andrew

HAMPDEN, ME.
Waters, David J

HAMPSHIRE
Washington Benevolent
Society

HANCOCK, MASS.
1816: ?38918?
Deming, John
Tallcott, Josiah

HANOVER, N. H.
1802: 50327?
1803: 4282
1804: 5958
1805: 8819
1806: 11096
1812: 25215
1813: 29998
1814: 51383
Davis, Moses
Hinds, Justin
Spear, Charles
Spear, Henry
Spear, William S
Watson, David

HANOVER, PA.
   Lange, Daniel P
   Lepper, Wilhelm Daniel
   Starck, J P
   Wiestling, Jacob H

HARLEM, N.Y.
   Eushede, John

HARRISBURG, PA.
1805: 8601
1806: 10683
1808: 14893
1809: 17323?
1811: 23658
1812: 26407, 26417, 26421,
  27632
1813: 29389
1814: 32468
1815: 35595?, ?35604
1816: 38577?, 38583, ?38587
1817: 40280, ?40644, 41733,
  42213, 42867
1818: 45238, 45245-45246,
  45257
1819: 46934, 49041, 49050,
  49054, 49056, 49651, 49659
   Albright, Jacob W
   Atkinson, Thomas
   Elder, Jacob
   Gillmor, William
   Gleim, Christian
   Greer, Charles
   Greer, William
   Hamilton, Alexander
   Hamilton, Hugh
   Herschberger, John
   McFarland, John
   Mayer, Benjamin
   Peacock, James
   Scheffer, Theo J
   Smyth, William Cath-
     erwood
   Stambaugh, S C
   Weistling, John H
   Wright, David
   Wyeth, John

HARRISONBURG, VA.
1817: 40618
1818: 43817
   Bernhart, Peter
   Bourne, George

   Davisson, Ananias
   Theological Printing
     Office
   Wartmann, Lawrence

HARRODSBURG, KY.
1815: 34996
   Gordon, ---
   Hunn, Anthony
   M'Murtry, ---

HARTFORD, CONN.
1801: ?429, 1359
1802: 2697, 2944
1803: 3723, 3890?, 4378
1804: 5669, 5880
1805: 8329, 8499
1806: 10576, 11082
1807: 11970, 12205, 12270,
  12343?, 12434, 12957,
  13596
1808: 15197, 15577
1809: 16811, 17281, 17299,
  17789, 18297
1810: 19511?, 19778
1811: 23013
1812: 25151, 25440
1813: 28204, 28631, 28837,
  29517
1814: 31380, 31599, 31931,
  31992, 32094, 32479, 32904,
  32967
1815: 34208, 34305, 34690,
  34988, 35380
1816: 36886, 37322?, 37512,
  37756, 37870, 38127, 38646,
  38913, 39028, 39752?,
  39871, 51582
1817: 40392, 40548, 40550,
  40552, 40690, 40744,
  ?40807?, 40912, 41010,
  41012, 41988, 42230, 42870
1818: 42995, 43432, 43701,
  44961, 45489, 45547, 46815
1819: 47527, 47698, 47702,
  47712, 47751?, 48177,
  48447, 48754, 49325, 49508
   American Mercury
   Andrus, Silas
   Babcock, Elisha
   Babcock, John
   Bacon, David
   Barber, John Warner

Barnes, Randolph
Bolles, Frederick D
Bowles, Samuel
Burr, Hezekiah
Connecticut Mirror
Cooke, Increase
Cooke, Oliver Dudley
Dwier, Henry
Easton, B G
Gleason, Peter Buel
Goodrich, Samuel Griswold
Goodwin, George
Goodwin, Henry
Hadlock, James
Hale, Horatio G
Hamlen, Benjamin L
Hart, William
Hartford Evangelical
    Tract Society
Hosmer, Charles
Hudson, Barzillai
Lincoln, Lemuel
Lincoln, Simeon
Loomis, Simeon Lorenzo
Marsh, William S
Newton, Abner
Newton, Orrin
Niles, John Milton
Peabody, M M
Peck, Everard
Pratt, Luther
Printing Office
Reed, Abner
Riley, James
Robbins, John W
Roberts, Harvey B
Russell, Barzillai
Russell, John
Russell, William
Sheldon, George
Starr, Charles
Starr, James Fosdick
Steele, Oliver
Stone, William Leete
Times
Watson, Ebenezer

HARTFORD, VT.
    Hutchinson, Ebenezer
    Hutchinson, W

HARTWICK, N.Y.
    Clark, Israel W

Crandal, Edward Burdick
Todd, Bethel
Todd, Lemuel

HARVARD, MASS.
    Parker, Isaac Senter
    Parker, Luther
    Parker, Sewall

HAVERHILL, MASS.
1802: 1707
1805: 9698
1806: 10074
1810: 20849, 20921
1811: 22161
1813: 28339
1814: 31666
1815: 35366
1816: 36669?, 38382?, 38491
1818: 46633, 46726
    Allen, Horatio Gates
    Allen, William Brown
    Briggs, John
    Burrill, Nathan
    Carey, Thomas
    Essex Patriot
    Fay, Galen Hough
    Gould, Francis
    Green, Peter N
    Greenough, William
    Merrimack Intelligencer
    Plummer, Frederick
    Tileston, Thomas

HAVERHILL, N.H.
    Abbott, ---
    Goss, Sylvester T
    Houghton, Theophilus
    Lilly

HAVRE-DE-GRACE, MD.
    Coale, William

HENRIETTA, N.Y.
    Knap, Liscomb

HERKIMER, N.Y.
    Cory, Benjamin
    Holt, David
    Phinney, Elihu
    Phinney, George Gordon
    Prentis, Henry
    Prentiss, John Holmes
    Robbins, James B

ITHACA, N. Y.
        Benjamin, Joseph
        Ingersoll, Jonathan
        Mack, Ebenezer
        Reed, Ebenezer
        Shepard, Erastus

                J

JACKSON, MO.
        Strange, Tubal Early

JAFFREY, N. H.
1812:   24516
1813:   28168
        Litch, Samuel
        Wilder, Salmon

JEFFERSON, KY.
1807:   13323

JEFFERSONVILLE, IND.
        Cox, Isaac
        Nelson, Reuben W

JERICHO, N. Y.
1811:   24327

JOHNSTOWN, N. Y.
1804:   5830
1806:   10935
1812:   25027
1819:   ?48726
        Brown, Samuel R
        Child, Asa
        Child, William
        Miller, David Cade
        Romyen, Abraham
        Taylor, Abraham

JONESBOROUGH, TENN.
1803:   4095
        Howard, Jacob
        Wilson, George

                K

KASKASKIA, ILL.
1815:   ?33930?
        Berry, Elijah Conway
        Blackwell, Robert
        Cook, Daniel Pope
        Duncan, Matthew

KEENE, N. H.
1802:   2330, 2429?, 2644
1804:   6600
1808:   14826
1815:   35434
1816:   38543
1817:   42757
1818:   44844?
1819:   48692-48693
        Morrison, Samuel Ayers
        New Hampshire Sentinel
        Prentiss, John

KENNEBUNK, ME.
1804:   6303, 6441
1811:   23242
1817:   41113
        Fletcher, N H
        Lee, Richard
        Remich, James Kinsman
        Sewall, Stephen
        Weeks, William
        Whitelock, John

KINGSTON, N. Y.
1802:   ?2489
1805:   50490
        Buel, Jesse
        Covel, Zenas
        Freer, Anthony
        Freer, Samuel S
        Mitchell, Isaac
        Plebian
        Tappen, John

KINGSTON, R. I.
1819:   47992

KITTANNING, PA.
        Alexander, James
        Rohrer, Frederick

KNOXVILLE, TENN.
1802:   3150
1805:   9735
1809:   ?17095
1810:   20121, 20740, 22035
1816:   38132
        Blackburn, Gideon
        Brown, Hugh
        Carey, Patrick
        Heiskell, Frederick
            Steidinger
        Hood, John Bann
        Miller, Samuel
        Moore, William
        Roulstone, Elizabeth
        Roulstone, George
        Wilkinson, John
        Wilson, George

                    L

LANCASTER, KY.
1810:   20071
1819:   48412
        Norvell, Joshua
        Norvell, Moses

LANCASTER, MASS.
        Fletcher, Joshua
        Whiting, John

LANCASTER, O.
1814:   31888
        Carpenter, Joseph
        Green, John
        Herman, John (Johann)
        Hinkle, Jacob
        Post, Russell E
        Sanderson, George
        Schaeffer, Edward

LANCASTER, PA.
1802:   2143, 2866, 2868,
    2873
1804:   ?50464?
1805:   7964, 9129
1806:   9943, 10047, 10099
1807:   12756, 13342, 13344,
    13356
1808:   14953, 15881

1809:   18333
1810:   19776, 20044, 21028?,
    21522
1811:   22215, ?24318?, 24481
1812:   26372
1813:   27760, 28607, 29146,
    29248, 29529
1814:   31565, ?51359
1815:   ?34245, 34730, 34766,
    36118, 36464?
1816:   37571, 37688, 39672
1817:   40895
1818:   44135, 45237, 45452
1819:   48260
        Albrecht, Anton
        Albrecht, George
        Albrecht, Johann
        Albrecht, Peter
        Baer, John
        Bailey, Francis
        Bailey, Robert
        Bowman, Abraham
        Brown, David
        Burnside, John
        Daly, George
        Dickson, Robert
        Dickson, William
        Ehrenfried, Joseph
        Greer, William
        Grimler, Benjamin
        Grimler, Henry
        Hamilton, Hugh
        Hamilton, William
        Helmbold, George
        Hutter, Christian Jacob
        Kendall, Jesse
        Lloyd, ---
        M'Dowell, Charles
        Mathews, John R
        Maxwell, Hugh
        Smith, Chester C
        Smyth, William Cather-
            wood
        Stambaugh, Samuel C
        Thompson, Thomas
            M'Kean

LANSINGBURGH, N.Y.
1803:   3976
1804:   6772
1805:   ?9114
1807:   12944, 13263, 13462
1808:   14709-14710

1809: 17948
    Adancourt, Francis
    Bliss, Luther
    Harrison, Matthew
    Penniman, Sylvanus
      Jenckes
    Shaw, Samuel
    Tracy, Gardiner

LAWRENCEBURG, IND.
    Brown, B
    Dunn, Isaac
    Russell, ---

LEBANON, O.
1811: 22421a
1815: ?36427
    Blackburn, William
    Camron, William A
    Crane, Noah
    Farmer
    Hale, Samuel H
    M'Clean, John
    M'Clean, Nathaniel
    M'Clean, William
    Smith, George
    Van Vleet, Abram
    Western Star

LEBANON, PA.
1809: 17354
1815: 35126
    Hanke, George
    Hartman, Joseph
    Sage, Heinrich B
    Schnee, Jacob
    Stover, Jacob

LEBANON, TENN.
    Ford, John W
    Womack, ---

LEESBURG, VA.
1810: 21200
    Caldwell, Samuel B T
    Genius of Liberty
    M'Intyre, Patrick

LEICESTER, MASS.
    Brown, Hori

LENOX, MASS.
1808: 15648

1809: 17473
    Lewis, Eldad
    Stanley, John Gray
    Starr, Henry

LEOMINSTER, MASS.
1801: 201
1803: 3993
1805: 7827, 8651
1806: 11252
1809: 18447
    Adams, Daniel
    Telescope
    Thomas, Isaiah
    Whitcomb, Chapman
    Wilder, James
    Wilder, Salmon

LEWISTOWN, PA.
    Cole, Edward
    Dickson, James
    Elliott, William P

LEXINGTON, IND.
    Brandeberry, ---
    Madox, D T
    Rhoades, Jacob

LEXINGTON, KY.
1801: 524, 1656
1802: ?2101, ?2929
1803: 3761, ?4949, 5144
1804: ?6310
1805: 7923, 9190, 9489,
  50572
1806: 10645, 10725
1807: 13628, ?13723
1808: 14544, ?15366
1810: 20466
1811: 22462, 23056
1812: 26497
1814: 30661, 32415, 32539
1815: 34235, 34564, 35661
1816: ?37193, ?37639?,
  37916, 38070, 38120, 39093,
  ?39095, ?39101?, ?39816-
  39817, 39879
1817: 40587, 41259, 42142
1818: 43265, 43402, ?43644,
  43681, 43891, ?44312,
  44607, 45537
1819: 48263, 48301, 48393,
  49237

Anderson, Thomas
Bickley, John
Bradford, Charles
Bradford, Daniel
Bradford, Fielding
Bradford, John
Bush, John Willoughby
Charless, Joseph
Downing, Jordon
Essex, William
Fishback, James
Gaines, Xenophon J
Guerin, Bertrand
Hunt, William Gibbes
Independent Gazetteer
Johnson, Jacob
Kay, Robert
Kentucky Auxiliary Bible
  Society
Kentucky Gazette
Kentucky Reporter
Lexington Advertiser
M'Call, T
M'Clane, John
M'Clane, William
Maccoun, David
Maccoun, James
Norvell, John
Overton, Samuel R
Peniston, Francis
Penn, Shadrach
Phillips, ---
Reporter
Skillman, Thomas T
Sleight, Henry C
Smith, Thomas
Stewart, James Hood
Tilford, John W
Warner, Benjamin
Watson, Samuel E
Western Monitor
Willis, Nathaniel
Wooldridge, J
Worsley, William W

LEXINGTON, MASS.
1815: 36506

LEXINGTON, VA.
    M'Mullin, John
    Snider, John N
    Walkup, Samuel

LINCOLN COUNTY, KY.
    Ogilsby, Samuel

LITCHFIELD, CONN.
1803: ?5180?
1815: 35576?
1818: 44589
    Ashley, Timothy
    Bunce, Isaiah
    Collier, Thomas
    Goodwin, Oliver
    Hosmer, Charles
    Litchfield Journal

LIVERMORE, ME.
1807: 14102

LOUISIANA
1803: 4958

LOUISVILLE, GA.
1804: ?6374, 6375
    Clarke, David
    Clarke, James
    Day, Ambrose
    Hely, James
    Smylie, James
    Wheeler, George W
    Wright, Ambrose

LOUISVILLE, KY.
1805: 8309
1819: 49366
    Berry, Elijah Conway
    Butler, Mann
    Charless, Joseph
    Crawford, Thomas
    Deming, Halsey
    Farquar, William
    Hughes, James
    Keeler, David
    Morton, John P
    Peniston, Francis
    Penn, Shadrach
    Smoot, George C
    Vail, Samuel
    Wood, William

LOWELL, MASS.
1803: 3904

LYNCHBURG, VA.
1804: 5795?

1812:   25291
1815:   35151
1817:   39922
        Boyce, Joseph
        Bransford, Samuel
        Carter, John
        Dawson, Russel
        Echo
        Graham, James
        Grantland, Fleming
        Gray, William W
        Haas, Jacob
        Lamb, John F
        Lynchburg Press
        Lynchburg Star
        Strange, Tubal Early
        Weaver, John

LYNN, MASS.
1808:   15184

                M

M'MINNVILLE, TENN.
        Harris, Eli

MADISON, IND.
        Arion, Copeland P J
        Camron, William
        Hendricks, William
        Levenworth, Seth M
        Lodge, John
        Pelham, Samuel
        Rhoades, Jacob
        Western Eagle

MANCHESTER, VT.
        Pritchard, Archibald
        Stockwell, William

MANLIUS, N.Y.
        Clark, Daniel
        Genesee Missionary
            Society
        Kellogg, Leonard
        Moore, Southwick H
        Romyen, Abraham

MANSFIELD, O.
        Gilkison, John C

MARBLEHEAD, MASS.
1809:   17405

MARIETTA, O.
        American Friend
        Buell, Daniel Hand
        Buell, Timothy
        Emerson, Caleb
        Everett, David
        Fairlamb, Samuel
        Gardiner, James B
        Israel, Joseph
        Prentiss, Royal
        Ransom, Thomas G
        Silliman, Wyllys
        Western Spectator

MARIETTA, PA.
1819:   51908
        Huss, John

MARLBOROUGH, MASS.
1801:   438

MARSHFIELD, MASS.
        Sampson, Proctor

MARTINSBURGH, N.Y.
        Robbins, James B

MARTINSBURGH, VA.
        Alburtis, John
        Crawford, John R

MASSACHUSETTS
1802:   1872?
1806:   11329
1808:   15715-15716
1809:   18259
1810:   20851
1812:   26217
1819:   48617
        Wilcox, Josiah

MATHETCHY, PA.
        Krupp, Abraham

MAYSVILLE, KY.
        Corwine, Joab H
        Corwine, Richard
        Crookshanks, Aaron
        Eagle

MAYVILLE, N.Y.
    Curtis, Robert I

MEADVILLE, PA.
1810:   19891
    Atkinson, Thomas
    Brendle, William

MEDFIELD, MASS.
    Albee, Amos

MEDWAY
1816:   37573

MERCER, PA.
    Flemming, David

MEREDITH, N.H.
    Lothrop, Jason
    Lothrop, Reuel

MERRIMAC, N.H.
1806:   10005

MIDDLEBOROUGH, MASS.
1804:   ?5750

MIDDLEBURY, VT.
1802:   2835
1803:   4105
1808:   15594-15596, 16088
1809:   18080-18082
1810:   20611, 20732
1817:   42764
1818:   ?43695?, 44979
1819:   48689
    Allen, Frederick P
    Burnap, Francis
    Chipman, Samuel
    Christian Messenger
    Copeland, Jared Warner
    Ferguson, Bartimeus
    Fillmore, Lavius
    Fitch, John
    Haswell, Anthony
    Hooker, William Gris-
        wold
    Huntington, Joseph
        Dennison
    National Standard
    Pomeroy, Thaddeus
    Richardson, Heman
    Slade, William

Strong, Timothy Clapp
Swift, Samuel
Vermont Missionary
    Society
Vermont Religious Tract
    Society
Walker, L
Williams, Samuel

MIDDLETOWN
    Grant, John

MIDDLETOWN, CONN.
1802:   2138
1805:   9758
1812:   26910
1813:   27785
1815:   34611
1817:   39935, 41433
    Alsop, John
    Alsop, Richard
    Bailey, Noadiah
    Clark, Epaphras
    Dunning, John Botsford
    Dunning, Tertius
    Hart, William
    Lincoln, Simeon
    Loomis, Simeon Lorenzo
    Lyman, Luke Clark
    Pomeroy, ---
    Richards, Seth
    Riley, Isaac
    Savage, ---
    Spencer, Frederick
    Spencer, Thomas

MIFFLINBURG, PA.
    Maxwell, Hugh

MIFFLINTOWN, PA.
    Gallaher, Andrew N

MILL-HILL, N.J.
    Fenton, Daniel
    Wilson, James Jefferson

MILLEDGEVILLE, GA.
1806:   10870
1819:   48101
    Camak, James
    Denison, Henry
    Grantland, Fleming
    Hightower, Pleasant R

Hines, John B
Jones, Walter
M'Millan, Alexander
Ryan, Dennis L
Stone, Henry D

MILTON, N. C.
Perkins, John H

MILTON, PA.
Frick, Henry

MILTON, VT.
Dunham, Nathaniel
Dunham, Noah

MISSISSIPPI TERRITORY
1807: 12858

MOBILE, ALA.
Fitzgerald, John
Lyon, James
Miller, Isaac
Mobile Gazette

MONMOUTH COUNTY, N. J.
Stewart, Peter

MONONGAHELA, PA.
1811: 22403

MONROE COUNTY, VA.
1804: 7142

MONTGOMERY, N. Y.
1807: 13112
Pratt, Luther

MONTPELIER, VT.
1806: ?11031, 13631
1808: 15222
1810: 21896, 21983
1811: 23093, 23858
1812: 27390-27391
1814: ?33537
1815: 34375
1817: ?42670, ?42776
1819: 50157
Bowles, Lucius Quintus
    Cincinnatus
Brown, Clark
Crosby, John
Darling, Carlos C

Goss, Mark
Goss, Samuel
Hill, Cyrus
Hinds, Justin
Merrifield, Preston
Montpelier Bookstore
Parks, Josiah
Prentiss, John
Sibley, Derick
Thompson, J
Walton, Ezekiel Parker
Walton, George S
Wheeler, Benjamin Hen-
    shaw
Wright, Sereno

MONTROSE, PA.
Clark, Justin

MORGANTOWN, VA.
1805: ?8452
1806: ?10915?
Britton, Forbes
Campbell, Joseph
M'Granaghan, William

MORRIS FLATS, N. Y.
Johnson, John Burgess

MORRISTOWN, N. J.
1803: 50394
1814: 32173
1819: ?49599
Douglass, ---
Johnson, Peter A
Mann, Jacob
Russell, Henry P

MORRISVILLE, N. Y.
Johnson, John Burgess

MOSCOW, N. Y.
Ripley, Hezekiah

MT. HOLLY, N. J.
1814: 31790
1815: 34846
Felthousen, Jacob D
Joline, John K
M'Knight, James
Palmer, Nathan
Trotter, Thomas C

MOUNT PLEASANT, N.Y.
Addington, Stephen
Cameron, J A
Canfield, Russell

MOUNT PLEASANT, O.
1816: 37667
1818: 44142, 45306
Bates, Elisha
Hussey, P
Osborn, Charles
Osborn, I
Osborn, James

MOUNT STERLING, KY.
1818: 44544

MOUNT VERNON, O.
M'Ardle, John P
Ohio Register

MOUNT ZION, GA.
Norton, Jacob Porter

MURFREESBOROUGH, N.C.
Dickinson, ---
Huntington, Minor
Smyth, James H

MURFREESBOROUGH, TENN.
1819: 48305
Sublett, Abner C
Sublett, George A

N

NACOGDOCHES, TEX.
Harris, Eli

NANTUCKET, MASS.
Clapp, Henry
Tannatt, Abraham
Gallison
Tupper, Hiram

NASHVILLE, TENN.
1804: 6988
1808: 16298
1810: 22126
1811: ?24019

1812: ?25223?, ?25626,
?26857, ?27561
1813: 28312, ?29196, 29929,
?29930
1814: 32913-32914, 33296
1815: 35756, 36064
1817: 40812
1819: ?49574
Bradford, Benjamin J
Bradford, Thomas Gray-
son
Eastin, Thomas
Gwin, ---
M'Lean, Charles D
Norvell, Joseph
Norvell, Moses
Owen, P A
Ruble, J R
Stevenson, E
Sublett, Abner C
Sublett, George A
Tunstall, George
Wilson, George

NATCHEZ, MISS.
1801: 1362
1802: ?1942, 2676
1804: 6795, 6798?, 6799,
6801, 6852-6853
1805: 8914?, ?9228?
1807: ?13099
1810: 21646
1811: 23581
1812: 26096
1813: 29955?
1814: 31162, 31163?
1815: ?33892-33893?, ?34417,
36091-36092, ?36094?
1816: 38988
1817: 40952, 41301, 41457,
42303
1818: 44871, 45563-45564
1819: ?47430, 49362-49363,
49391
Cramer, Zadok
Eichbaum, William
Evens, William
Ferrell, James
Green, James
Isler, Peter
Langdon, Richard C
M'Curdy, James
M'Keehan, David

Marschalk, Andrew
Mississippi Herald
Moffett, Darius
Shaw, John
Snodgrass, William
Spear, John
Stokes, Benjamin M
Terrell, Samuel
Terrell, Timothy
Winn, John W
Winston, William O

NATCHITOCHES, LA.
1813:   29159

NEW BEDFORD, MASS.
1808:   15707
1809:   17381, 18295
1810:   20350
        Bates, Nathan
        Billings, Elijah
        Gleason, Joseph
        Lindsey, Benjamin
        Shearman, Abraham
        Tucker, ---

NEW BERLIN, N.Y.
        Blakeslee, Levi

NEW BERLIN, PA.
        Miller, Solomon
        Niebel, Henrich
        Schaup, Henry
        Wise, Frederick

NEW BRUNSWICK, N.J.
1801:   47
1804:   6033
1805:   9288
1806:   10465
1807:   12568, 12645, 12703
1808:   14856, 15733, 15946
1809:   17325, 18218, 18758
1811:   22965, 25227
1812:   51246
1813:   28681, 28737
1816:   37612
1817:   41593
1818:   45014
1819:   48171
        Austin, Galen L
        Blauvelt, Abraham
        Clayton, Edward B

Crissy, James
Deare, Lewis
Eastburn, Robert
Elliot, William
FitzRandolph, David
RitzRandolph, James
Garnett, John
Green, Charles D
Griggs, J C
Kollock, Isaac Arnett
Letson, William
Myer, William
Simpson, John N
Stewart, Robert
Terhune, John
Walker, Ambrose
Washington Benevolent
    Societies in New
    Jersey

NEW CANAAN, CONN.
1805:   8700

NEW ENGLAND
1801:   50234?
1802:   2754?
1807:   11977
1809:   18609
1811:   22206, 22716
1812:   25001
1813:   27748-27749
1814:   30704
1816:   39794

NEW HAMPSHIRE
1805:   7834
1819:   48849

NEW HAVEN, CONN.
1801:   ?43, 70, 146, 1217,
        1634, 1694
1802:   1909, 2523, 3131, 3465
1803:   3702, 4123, 4902
1804:   5653, 6010, 6130,
        ?6150, 6327, 6554, 7808
1807:   12093, ?14187, ?14189
1808:   ?15232-15233?, ?16214?,
        50821?
1809:   19283?
1810:   19935, 19942, 20866?,
        22119?
1811:   22956-22958, 51111,
        51115, 51132

1812: 51180-51181, 51191
1813: 28953, 29307-29308,
   51286?, 51287-51288,
   ?51322?
1814: 30833?, ?31123?,
   ?31224, 31226, 31833,
   32942
1815: ?33894, 34355, ?34429,
   34604, 35121, ?35440,
   35920, 35969, 36120
1816: 36898, 37321, 37324-
   37325, 37329, 37461, 37493,
   ?37569, 38872, 38910,
   39888, 51611?
1817: 40164, 40828, 41007,
   ?41079?, 41229, 41273,
   ?41586, 42122, 42164
1818: 43113-43114, 43464,
   ?43716, 44139, 44385,
   ?44519?, 44780, 45846,
   46895-46896
1819: 48244, 48349, ?49624?,
   49656
      Austin, William W
      Babcock, John
      Babcock, S
      Badger, Joseph I
      Baldwin, ---
      Barber, Joseph
      Bassett, E
      Beers, Isaac
      Bronson, Tillotson
      Columbian Register
      Comstock, Seth
      Connecticut Academy of
         Arts and Sciences
      Connecticut Herald
      Connecticut Journal
      Connecticut Religious
         Tract Society
      Converse, Sherman
      Cooke, Increase
      DeForest, DeLauzin
      Doctrinal Tract Society
      Doolittle, Amos
      Dwight, Timothy
      Flagg, Henry Collins
      General Committee of
         Republicans
      Goldsmith, Alvah Brad-
         ley
      Gray, John C
      Green, Thomas

Griswold, Jacob
Griswold, Zechariah
Hoadley, Abram
Howe, Hezekiah
Hudson, Eli
Jocelin, Nathaniel
Jocelin, Simeon
Jocelyn, Simeon Smith
Kensett, Thomas
Lines, Henry
Maltby, Abiel H
Marsh, Guy C
Middlebrook, Elijah
Morse, Samuel
Morse, William Walker
Munger, George
Munson, John
Osborn, ---
Porcupine, Peter
Read, Ezra
Religious Intelligencer
Shelton, ---
Sidney's Press
Spaulding, George
Steele, Oliver
Terril, Israel
Tiffany, ---
Wadsworth, Samuel
Walter, Joel
Walter, William
West Society
Whiting, Nathan
Woodward, Thomas
   Green
Woodworth, Samuel
Yale College, Junior
   Class

NEW IPSWICH, N.H.
1816: 51616
1819: ?48135
      Ide, Simeon
      Payson, S
      Wilder, Salmon

NEW JERSEY
1805: 8081
1808: 16329
1812: 51201
1816: 38226
      Atkinson, John
      Boyle, P

NEW KENT, VA.
1801: 318

NEW LEBANON, N.Y.
1804: 6834

NEW LISBON, O.
    Lepper, William Daniel
    Ohio Patriot

NEW LONDON, CONN.
1802: 3061
1805: 9006
1806: 9878
1809: 17728
1814: 31282
1816: 36668
    Avery, Thomas
    Cady, Ebenezer Pem-
        berton
    Clapp, Joshua B
    Eells, Nathaniel
    Francis, Simeon
    Green, John W
    Green, Samuel
    Green, Thomas Clarke
    Holt, Charles
    Huntington, Joseph
        Dennison
    Rogers, Alexander
    Spooner, Alden
    Springer, James
    Waterous, Henry

NEW ORLEANS, LA.
1803: 4538-4547, 4549-
    4560, ?4666?, 4667, 4797
1804: 6669, 6797, 6965,
    ?6965a, 6967?, 6969
1805: 8555, 9009, 9070,
    9074-9078, 9522
1806: 10690
1807: 12431, 13212-13213
1808: 14365?, 14898, 15443,
    15741, 15789, 15815-15818
1809: 16857, 18302-18305,
    18440, 18749
1810: 20592, 20595, 20963,
    21792
1812: 25884
1813: 28977
1814: 31960
1815: 35926

l'Ami des Lois
Anderson, Thomas
Baird, Joseph B
Beleurgey, Claudius
Bradford, James Mor-
    gan
Cotten, Godwin Brown
Cramer, Zadok
Dacqueny, John
Fontaine, Jean Baptiste
    LeSeur
Johnson, ---
Johnson, William H
Lamberte, Theodore
Leclerc, Hilaire
Lisa, Joaquin de
Lorrain, Thomas W
Louisiana Courier
Lyon, James
Mirtan, Cadi
Mitchell, ---
Mitchell, James
Moniteur de la Louisiana
Mowry, John
Ravenscroft, ---
Renard, Jean
Roche, Charles
Roche, Pierre (Peter)
St. Romes, Joseph
    Charles de
Sterrett, James
Telegraphe
Thierry, Jean Baptiste
    Simon
Toulouse, C Morane
Wagner, Peter K
Whitney, H

NEW PHILADELPHIA, O.
    Patrick, James

NEW YORK
1801: 2, ?140, 235, 272?,
    274, 310, 375, 433, 514,
    542, 675, 707, 767, 776,
    837-838, 921, 934, 952,
    970, 1043, 1090, 1171,
    1208, 1221, ?1236, 1316,
    1415, ?1422, 1424, 1428,
    1597, 50212?
1802: 1731, 1767, 1862, 1885,
    2059-2060, ?2303?, 2314,
    2358, ?2426?, 2552, 2727,

43616, 43624, 43668, 43671,
?43676?, 43903, 43954,
44058, 44064, 44116, 44217,
44237, 44263, 44274, 44338,
44378, 44443-44444, 44520,
44699, 44781-44782, ?44846?,
45023, 45025, 45037, 45041,
45072, 45077, 45093, 45127,
45339, 45365, 45433, 45457,
45513, 45517, ?45523?,
45525, 45559, 45574, 45576,
45584, 45798, ?45817,
45879, 45911, 46623, 46667,
46727, 46809, 46814, 46862,
46876, 51776, 51801
1819: 46917, 46936, 46971?,
?46973?, 47008, ?47041-
47042?, 47051, ?47165,
47166, 47193, 47202, 47365,
47528, 47612, 47647, 47787,
47843, 47861, 47931, 48003,
48028, 48116?, 48144,
48510, 48711, 48767-48768,
48771, 48875-48876, 48881,
48921, 48923, 48967, 49107,
49224, 49250, 49253, 49303,
49354, 49368, 49370, 49408,
49450, 49471, 49493, 49561,
49605, ?49608-49609,
49634, 49973, 49988, 50005-
50006, 50018-50020, 50087,
50093, 50148, 51909
    Adams, Thomas G
    Alsop, John
    Alsop, Richard
    American Bible Society
    American Citizen
    American School Class-
        book Warehouse
    Andrews, Sidney W
    Appel, John
    Arden, Daniel D
    Arden, Thomas S
    Asten, Abraham
    Atkinson, ---
    Atkinson, Samuel Coate
    Auxilliary New York
        Bible and Common
        Prayer Book Society
    Auxilliary New York
        Bible Society
    Bakewell, Thomas
    Baldwin, Charles N

Banks, David
Barclay, ---
Barlas, William
Baron, George
Bartow, Robert
Bartow, William Au-
    gustus
Bayard, James A
Bayard, Samuel
Beach, Lazarus
Beck, John
Bedford, ---
Belden, Ebenezer
Belden, John
Bell, Jared W
Bell, Nathaniel
Bellamy, Edward S
Biglow, H
Bignell, John
Birch, George L
Black, John
Bleecker, John
Bliss, David
Bliss, Elam
Blunt, Edmund March
Boyle, Eglentone M
Boyle, T
Bradford, Samuel Fisher
Brannan, John
Brisban, James
Broderick, John
Broderick, Joseph
Brodie, Alexander
Brown, Christian
Brown, John
Bruce, David
Bruce, George
Buel, John
Buell, ---
Bunce, Charles W
Bunce, George
Burkloe, D C
Burkloe, P
Burnham, Michael
Burnton, Thomas H
Burtsell, Peter
Burtus, James A
Burtus, Samuel A
Butler, Elihu
Cain, John
Campbell, Samuel
Caritat, Henry
Carlisle, David

Sinclair, George
Small, William
Smith, ---
Smith, Charles
Smith, Daniel D
Smith, James
Society of United Chris-
  tian Friends
Soule, Joshua
Southwick, Henry Collins
Spooner, Alden
Stanford, Thomas Naylor
Stansbury, Abraham
  Ogier
Stansbury, Arthur Joseph
Stansbury, Samuel
Starr, Charles
Statesman
Stephens, Stephen
Stryker, John
Swaine, John
Swords, James
Swords, Thomas
Tammany Society
Taylor, R D
Ten Eyck, Philip
Thomas, C
Thomas, William
Thompson, ---
Thompson, Edward W
Thompson, John
Thompson, Thomas
Thomson, E
Thomson, P
Tiebout, Adam T
Tiebout, Archibald McL
Tiebout, John
Tiffany, John L
Totten, John C
Treadwell, William Kel-
  ley
Tunison, Garret C
Turner, Charles
Turner, John
Turner, W
Tyler, Benjamin Owen
Van Pelt, Peter
Van Riper, Nicolas
Van Winkle, Cornelius S
Vermilye, William W
Vosburgh, Abraham
Waite, George
Waite, Robert

Wales, Luther
Walker, John W
Walker, Samuel
Walker, William
War
Ward, H
Ward, Matthias
Ward, William
Ware, Thomas
Washington Benevolent
  Society
Watson, Ebenezer
Watts, John
Wauchope, Robert
Wells, Edward B
Wesleyan Sacred Music
  Society
White, ---
White, Elihu
White, George
White, Julius
White, Samuel B
Whiting, Samuel
Wiley, Charles
Williams, Solomon
Willis, John
Willson, Joseph
Wilson, John
Wilson, Robert
Wood, Samuel
Woods, John
Woodworth, Samuel
Wortman, Tunis
Young, Benjamin
Young, William

NEWARK, N. J.
1802:   3580
1806:   10108
1808:   15164, 16301
1809:   17083, 18246
1810:   19332, 20909, 21216
1811:   22166, 22411
1812:   25838, 26260
1813:   29987
1814:   ?32611?
1815:   ?34195, 35494
1818:   44986
1819:   49181
        Baldwin, David C
        Conover, Peter
        Crane, John Austin
        Gould, Elias Baldwin

Gould, Stephen
Halsey, Jacob Benton
Hawley, Edward M
Kollock, Isaac Arnett
Maverick, Peter
Meeker, Isaac
Olds, Benjamin
Pares, ---
Pennington, Samuel
Phinney, George Gordon
Pike, John
Ruggls, Eden
Sanderson, Edward
Sanderson, James
Tuttle, John
Tuttle, William
Vermilye, William W
Wallis, John
Ward, William
Weller, George

NEWBERN, N. C.
1801: 192
1802: 2219, 2991, ?3102?
1803: 5098-5099
1805: 9028
1808: 15089, 16247-16248
1809: 18691
1810: 20188, 21407
1815: 34762
1816: 38477
1817: 42815
Bryan, Carney J
Carney, John
Franklin, ---
Garrow, ---
Hall, Salmon
Huntington, M
Martin, Francis Xavier
Mastin, Jeremiah
Mintz, David B
Moss, Edward G
Newbern Gazette
Ogden, Robert
Pasteur, John I
Pasteur, John S
Sims, John C
Watson, Thomas

NEWBURGH, N. Y.
1801: 1026
1804: 5732
1809: 18248

1811: 22239
1814: 51373
1818: 44821
Brown, John
Coles, Dennis
Crowell, Timothy
Bloomfield
Gazlay, Ward M
Gray, Robert
Houghton, Theophilus
Lilly
Kensett, Thomas
Lewis, Benjamin Frank-
lin
Lewis, Eldad
Lewis, Uriah C
Political Index
Pratt, Philo B
Shelton, ---

NEWBURY, VT.
Spear, Charles
White, Ira

NEWBURYPORT, MASS.
1801: 1177
1802: 2740
1804: 7303
1805: 7843, 8247, 8321, 9161,
9350, 9662
1806: 10217, 10917, 11095,
11172, 11396, 11421
1807: 13246, 13248, 13264,
13403-13406
1808: 15044, 15964, 16172,
16616, 16651
1809: 16871, 16941, 17140?,
17455, 18250, 18403, 18488,
19159
1810: 20924, 21043, 21101?,
21102, ?21550, 21972
1811: 23561, 23636, 23704
1812: 24646, 24661, ?26482
1813: 27710, 29227, 29366
1814: 30678, 30879, 32525?,
32680, 32903, 33751
1815: 35129, 35330, 35561-
35562?, 35642?, 36495,
36521, 36557
1816: 38540?, 38659
1817: 41389
1818: 45352-45353, 45759,
46728

1819: 48730
Allen, Ephraim William
Allen, Horatio Gates
Allen, William Brown
Barnard, John
Blunt, Edmund March
Cross, Caleb
Dole, Samuel
Edes, Benjamin
Fairman, Gideon
Gilman, John
Gilman, Whittingham
Griffin, William
Hastings, William
Hooker, William
Little, Edward
March, Angier
Merrimack Bible Society
Middle Street Bookstore
New England Repertory
Newburyport Herald
Norris, Charles
Park, John
Perkins, Jacob
Sawyer, William
Stebbins, Chester
Stedman, Ebenezer
Stickney, Jeremiah
Thomas, Isaiah
Whipple, Charles
White, Daniel A
Wright, Nathaniel Hill

NEWCASTLE, DEL.
1803: 4211
1804: 6144
1806: 11449
1808: 14847
Barber, John
Freeman, John

NEWMARKET, VA.
1810: 20066, 20718
1816: 37970
1818: 43973
Henkel, Ambrose
Henkel, Andrew N
Henkel, Solomon

NEWPORT, R. I.
1801: 441?
1803: 4061, 4420, 4764-4765,
4973, 4976, 5008

1804: 6051, 6453, 7186-7189
1805: 8217, 8384, ?8433?,
9252-9255, 50519
1806: 10193
1807: 13489
1808: 50874
1809: 16841, 19024
1810: 20914, 21127?
1812: 25336
1813: 27658, 28789, 29934
1816: 38690, 39072
1818: 45136
1819: 49504
Barber, Ann
Barber, John H
Barber, William
Bisbee, Noah
Chilson, Asaph
Dearborn, Nathaniel
Farnsworth, Havila
Farnsworth, Oliver
Newport Mercury
Rhode Island Republican
Richardson, Jacob
Rousmaniere, Lewis
Simons, William
Vinson, Samuel W
Wilder, William R

NEWTON, N. J.
1812: ?51177
Hall, John H

NEWTOWN, CONN.
1818: 43920
1819: 47489

NEWTOWN, N. Y.
Murphy, William
Shepard, Erastus

NEWTOWN, PA.
Coale, William
Dow, ---
Miner, Asher
Robinson, David A
Siegfried, Simeon
Wilson, John

NINE PARTNERS, N. Y.
Sharpless, Joseph

NOBLEBOROUGH, ME.
1816: 36689

NORFOLK, VA.
1804: 6814
1807: 13255
1809: 18761
1813: 30427?
1816: 39681
1818: 45875
American Beacon
Balls, G
Balls, Thomas
Bonsal, Caleb
Broughton, Thomas G
Charlton, Seymour P
Conrad, John
Conrad, Michael
Cowper, John
Dillworth, Samuel
Epitome of the Times
Gray, George Lewis
Grigg, Jacob
Jones, Meriwether
Jordan, Augustus C
Keemle, Charles
Norfolk Gazette and
    Publick Ledger
Norfolk Herald
O'Conner, James
Shepherd, Samuel
Shields, Hamilton
Willett, Charles
Worsley, William W

NORRISTOWN, PA.
1804: 6931
Sower, David
Winnard, James

NORTH CAROLINA
1801: 507
1805: 7938

NORTHAMPTON, MASS.
1801: 760, 1073
1802: 2365, 2582-2583
1803: 3850, ?4331?, 4410,
    4449, 4501, 4763
1804: 5672, 5966, 6508
1805: 9499, 9695
1806: 11179
1807: 12529, 12708
1808: 14890, 15185
1809: 17703, ?18590, 18695,
    19232

1810: 20381
1811: 23675
1813: 29003
1814: 30949
1815: ?33887
1816: 38488, 38784
1818: 45387
Anti-Monarchist
Billings, John
Brooks, Elijah
Bull, James
Butler, Elihu
Butler, Simeon
Butler, William
Clap, Ebenezer
Clapp, William Warland
Democrat
Dicey, ---
Graves, Horace
Hampshire Gazette
Hampshire Missionary
    Society
Hampshire Register
Hive
Metcalf, John
Phillips Andover Acad-
    emy
Pomroy, Thomas Mer-
    rick
Sawtell, C
Shepard, Thomas Watson
Shepherd, Charles
Sutton, ---
Ware, Galen
West, Elisha
Whitman, Ephraim
Wright, Andrew

NORTHAMPTON, PA.
1805: 8274
Ebner, Heinrich

NORTHUMBERLAND, PA.
1803: 4911
1804: 5877
Binns, John
Forrest, James
Kennedy, Andrew
Sweney, George

NORWALK, CONN.
Dennis, Joseph
Nichols, Roswell Stiles
Price, Philo

NORWICH, CONN.
1801: 1450
1802: 2430
1810: 21532
1816: 37781, 38011
1818: ?43013
1819: 47469
  Bill, Gurdon
  Brown, Ansil
  Brumley, Israel
  Gardner, ---
  Hubbard, Russell
  Hubbard, Thomas
  Marvin, Theophilus
    Rogers
  Norwich Packet
  Porter, Epaphras
  Rose, ---
  Springer, James
  Sterry, Consider
  Sterry, John
  Trumbull, Charles E
  Trumbull, Henry
  Trumbull, John
  Trumbull, Lucy
  Warner, ---
  Webb, Samuel
  Williams, Thomas

NORWICH, N.Y.
  Clark, Lot
  Fairchild, John F
  Hubbard, John F
  Johnson, John Burgess
  Miller, James M
  Weed, Thurlow

NORWICH, VT.
  Newton, Israel

O

OCTORARO, PA.
  Bailey, Francis

OGDENSBURGH, N.Y.
  Fairchild, Platt B
  Kipp, John C
  Kipp, L
  Strachan, David R
  Strong, Timothy Clapp

ONONDAGA, N.Y.
  Fay, Thomas Chittendon
  Morse, Evander
  Redfield, Lewis Hamilton

OSWEGO, N.Y.
  Abbey, Dorephus
  Abbey, Seth Alden
  Lord, John Haines

OTSEGO, N.Y.
  Foster, ---
  Phinney, Elihu
  Phinney, Henry
  Todd, Bethel
  Todd, Lemuel

OVID, N.Y.
  Hayes, Michael
  Lewis, George

OWEGO, N.Y.
  Cruger, Daniel
  Leonard, Stephen Banks
  Mack, Stephen
  Steward, Henry

OXFORD, N.Y.
1809: 17139
  Eaton, Theophilus
  Glover, J
  Johnson, John Burgess
  Morgan, Chauncey

P

PALMER, MASS.
1811: 23282
1813: ?28079
1815: ?36069
  Carpenter, Frederic
  Terry, Ezekiel

PALMYRA, N.Y.
  Strong, Timothy Clapp

PARIS, KY.
1806: 10672
  Grimes, John A
  Kentucky Tract Society
  Lilly, James M

Lyle, Abraham I
Lyle, Joel R
Lyle, John
Lyle, John R
Stewart, James Hood

PATERSON, N. J.
Conover, Peter
Jones, Hannum

PAWTUCKET, R. I.
1805: 7941

PEACHAM, VT.
Goss, Samuel

PEEKSKILL, N. Y.
Crumbie, Robert

PENDLETON, S. C.
Lewis, John T
Miller, John

PENN YAN, N. Y.
1817: 40642
Bennett, Abraham H
Youngs, P

PENNSYLVANIA
1802: 2131
1803: 5532
1804: 5645
1811: 22821

PERRYOPOLIS, PA.
Humber, Edward

PERTH AMBOY, N. Y.
1810: 21173?
Murden, Joseph T

PETERBORO, N. Y.
Bunce, Jonathan
Dockstader, Jacob

PETERSBURG, GA.
1806: 10479

PETERSBURG, VA.
1801: 1053
1803: ?3660?, ?5515-5519?
1804: ?7673?
1805: ?8335?

1810: ?21919?
1813: 29070
1814: ?30977?, 32024, 32478
1816: ?39097?
1817: ?42304?
1818: 44106, ?45873-45874?,
?45876?
1819: 49245
Blandford Press
Campbell, John Wilson
Carter, John Michel
Conrad, John
Conrad, Michael
Cook, John
Cottom, Richard
Dickson, John
Dillworth, Samuel
Douglas, George
Dunnavant, Marvel W
Edwards, James L
Field, Thomas
Lorrain, Thomas W
McLaughlin, Nathaniel
McLaughlin, William F
Martin, George A
Pescud, Edward
Petersburg Intelligencer
Republican
Rose, William
Ross, Joseph
Shore, Thomas
Somervell, John
Stith, Cincinnatus
Wood, John
Yancey, Francis Garland
Whitworth, Thomas

PHILADELPHIA
1801: 42, 67, 78, 86, 96,
120, 136, 149, ?233?, 262,
269, 369, ?421?, ?488,
505, ?510?, 540, 781,
?935?, 1077, 1147, 1214,
1427, 1470, 1699, 50218,
50241-50243
1802: ?1752, ?1773, ?1850?,
1908, 1943?, 2265, 2268,
2304?, 2331, 2391, 2411,
2423, 2432, 2488, ?2642?,
2648, 2872, 2880, 2892,
2952, 2966, 2999, ?3087,
?3164, ?3191-3192, 3353,
3508, 3525?, ?3583, 50292

48369, 48450, 48503, 48658,
48670, 48678, 48693a,
48822, 48929, 49023, 49042,
49057, 49077, 49081?,
49082-49093, 49097, 49123,
49145, 49184, 49239, 49337,
49356, 49420, 49518, 49553,
49961, 50074, 51868, 51931

Acock, William
Adams, John
African Methodist Con-
  nection in the United
  States
Aitken, Jane
Aitken, John
Aitken, Robert
Aitken, Robert S
Akerman, Samuel
Allchin, George
Allen, Richard
American Society for
  the Dissemination of
  the Doctrines of the
  New Jerusalem
  Church
American Sunday School
  Union
Ames, Horace
Anderson, Robert P
Anderson, William
Armstrong, Thomas
Aurora
Aurora Book Store
Austin, ---
Austin, John B
B., H
Bache, Richard
Bacon, Allyn
Bailey, Francis
Bailey, Lydia R
Bailey, Robert
Bartram, Archibald
Bascom, Samuel Ashley
Bazeley, ---
Bennett, Titus
Bennis, Thomas
Benson, R
Bible Society of Phila-
  delphia
Bickley, Henry
Billmeyer, David
Billmeyer, George
Binns, John

Bioren, John
Birch, William Young
Bitters, Charles
Black, F
Blake, George E
Blocquerst, Andrew J
Boate, Thomas
Boileau, ---
Bouvier, John
Bowman, Abraham
Bradford, Samuel Fisher
Bradford, Thomas
Bradford, William
Bradley, John
Braeutigam, Daniel
Brannan, John
Bronson, Enos
Brown, David
Brown, William
Budd, Henry Stacy
Buzby, Benjamin C
Byberry, ---
Byrne, Patrick
Cammeyer, William
Campbell, John Wilson
Campbell, Robert
Carey, Matthew
Cargile, A
Carr, Benjamin
Carr, Mary
Carr, Robert
Carr, William
Carson, John
Carver, James
Chalk, John
Chapman, Benjamin
Charles, William
Charless, Joseph
Chauncey, Elihu
Cist, Charles (Carl)
Cist, Mary
Clark, John C
Clark, M
Clarke, John
Classic Press
Cline, John
Coale, William
Cochran, Ann
Cochran, Robert
Coles, Ann
Coles, Benjamin
Collins, William
Columbian Chronicle

Heartt, Dennis
Hellings, John
Helmbold, George
Henry, Robert Norris
Herald of Gospel Liberty
Hickman, Nathaniel
Hirst, Thomas
Hoff, John
Hogan, Andrew
Hogan, David
Hope, Thomas
Hopkins, Benjamin Bron-
    son
Hopkins, William Hector
Hopkinson, J
How, James C
Howard, W
Howorth, George
Hudson, Edward
Hudson, Henry
Humphreys, Asheton Y
Humphreys, Daniel
Humphreys, James
Humphreys, James Y
Hunter, John
Hurtel, John F
Inskeep, John
Jackson, William
Johnson, Benjamin
Johnson, Enoch
Johnson, Jacob
Johnson, Richard
Johnson, Robert
Johnston, ---
Jones, ---
Jones, Mithra
Justice, Joseph P
Kammerer, Joseph R
Kelley, ---
Kelley, Samuel
Kimber, Emmor
Kimber, Thomas
Kite, Benjamin
Kite, Thomas
Klert, ---
Kneass, William
Ladd, Russel
Lafourcade, Peter M
Lakin, James
Lawrence, Daniel
LeBreton, A
Lee, Charles
Leibert, Peter

Lester, Hubbard
Levis, Isaac
Levis, William
Lewis, Henry C
Lippincott, Joseph
Littell, Eliakim
Little, ---
Little, Rufus
Lloyd, Joseph
Lloyd, Thomas
Longstreth, Thomas
    Mifflin
Lorenzo Press
Lowery, M L
M'Carty, William
M'Clane, William
McClure, David
M'Connell, Matthew
M'Corkle, William
M'Culloch, Ebenezer
M'Culloch, John
M'Culloch, William
M'Kenzie, John
M'Knight, James
M'Laughlin, William F
McMahon, Thomas P
Magaw, William
Manning, Thomas S
Marot, William
Marshall, William
Martin, James
Matlack, Emmor
Maxwell, Hugh
Maxwell, James
Mayo, George
Mecum, ---
Meehan, John Silva
Megraw, ---
Melish, John
Mentz, George W
Merritt, Samuel
Meyer, Jacob
Mitchell, Andrew C
Mitchell, Samuel A
Montagu, Matthew
Morford, Edmund
Morgan, John
Morse, William Walker
Murphy, William G
Museum Press
Neal, Christiana (Palm-
    er)
Neely, ---

Hopkins, Benjamin
    Bronson
Israel, John
Johnston, Samuel Reed
Lambdin, J H
Lewis, Freeman
M'Keehan, David
M'Queen, Alexander
Minis, ---
Parker, Joseph
Patterson, J
Patterson, Robert
Pentland, Ephraim
Pittsburgh Bible Society
Riddle, James M
Schnee, Jacob
Scull, John
Snowden, John M
Spear, John

PITTSFIELD, MASS.
1804: 7324
1807: 11967, ?13598
1808: 15958
1809: 16810, 17040
1811: 22760
1817: 41008
1818: 44988
    Allen, Phinehas
    Seymour, Joseph W
    Smith, Milo
    Warriner, Jeremy
    Warriner, Ralph
    Willard, Heman

PLATTSBURGH, N.Y.
1811: 23406, 23487
1814: 33689?
1818: 44279
    Cady, Heman
    Flagg, Azariah Cutting
    Lowell, Samuel
    Nichols, George W
    Powell, Frederic C
    Reynolds, Linus Junius

PLEASANT HILL, KY.
    Bertrand, Peter

PLYMOUTH, MASS
1809: 18680
    Avery, Joseph

PLYMPTON, MASS.
1812: 26485

POMFRET
1813: 29945

PORT GIBSON, MISS.
    Hughes, James

PORTLAND, ME.
1801: 154, 521
1802: 2521
1803: 4920
1804: ?7353?
1805: 8093, 8461, 8638
1806: 10265
1807: 11939, 12085, 13008,
    13215, 13505?, 13580
1808: 14908, 15665
1809: 16957, 17805?
1810: 19485, 21356
1811: 22623, 24504
1812: 25819
1813: 27776
1815: 35582
1816: 36754, ?38533?
1817: 41333, 41424, 41659,
    42215, 42751
1819: 48020, 48023, 48560
    Adams, Isaac
    Armstrong, Samuel
        Turell
    Bible Society of Maine
    Chase, Sephen
    Clark, Thomas
    Colcord, John P
    Day, Calvin
    Douglas, Francis
    Eastern Argus
    Edwards, William
    Freeman's Friend
    Gazette
    George, Daniel
    Goold, G
    Hall, George Washington
    Herald of Gospel Liberty
    Hyde, Henry
    Hyde, Jonathan Lyman
    Hyde, William
    Jenks, Elezer Alley
    Jenks, William
    Johnson, Daniel
    Johnson, Joseph

Little, Edward
Lord, Erastus A
Lyman, Asa
M'Kown, John
Mussey, Charles
New Printing Office
Norris, Charles
Patten, Stephen
Shirley, Arthur
Shirley, Joshua
Smith, Elias
Thomas, Isaiah
Wait, Thomas Baker
Weeks, William
Whitman, Josiah
Willis, Nathaniel

PORTSMOUTH, N. H.
1801: 1175, 1567, 50235, 50265
1802: 3119
1803: ?3696?, 4520, 4740, 4896-4897
1804: 5784
1805: 8604?, 8648, ?9104, 9409, 9723
1806: 10215, 11198-11199
1807: 12229, 12904-12905, 13398?, 13423, 13626
1808: 14317-14318, 14891-14892, 15988, 16233
1809: 17460, 18190, 18668
1810: 19407, 19864, 21877
1811: 23646
1812: 26055, 26401, 26880
1814: 31195, 32788, ?32957?, 33547
1815: 35685
1816: 36687
1817: 40575, 41566, 41868
1818: 45394
Beck, Gideon
Ewer, Charles
Floyd, Benjamin
Foster, David C
Foster, John Welch
Foster, Robert
Gardner, Samuel
Gray, Harrison
Hill, Benjamin
Leigh, Joseph
Melcher, John
Miller, Tobias Ham

New Hampshire Gazette
Nutting, Samuel
Palmer, John E
Peirce, Charles
Peirce, Nathaniel S
Peirce, Washington
Portsmouth Oracle
Remich, James Kinsman
Republican Ledger
Rochemont, Maximilian John de
Sewall, Stephen
Shores, James Foster
Smith, Elias
Tappan, Charles
Thomas, Isaiah
Treadwell, Daniel
Treadwell, William Kelley
Turell, Charles
United States Oracle
Webb, John
Weeks, William
Whidden, Samuel
Whitelock, John

PORTSMOUTH, O.
Abbott, Jeremiah
Chaney, Jacob

PORTSMOUTH, VA.
1807: 50769

POTSDAM, N. Y.
Clark, Zena
Powell, Frederic C

POTTSTOWN, PA.
Royer, John

POUGHKEEPSIE, N. Y.
1801: ?506, 1413
1804: 5974
1806: ?10261?
1812: 25784
1814: 32556
1816: 38046, 38676
Adams, Charles Chauncey
Barnum, Charles Parmer
Bowman, Godfrey
Brownejohn, Thomas

Buel, Jesse
Doughty, Isaac T
French, Bronson
Joyner, Nathaniel
MacDuffee, Daniel
Mitchell, Isaac
Nelson, Joseph
Nelson, Richard
Nelson, Thomas
Parsons, Chester
Potter, Paraclete
Potter, Sheldon
Power, Nicholas
Republican Herald
Rudd, Reuben Brush
Stockholm, Derick B
Wilson, Thomas

PRESQUE ISLE, PA.
    Wyeth, George

PRINCETON, N.J.
1807: 13439
1809: 17063
1810: 19909
1814: 32569
1816: 38709
1817: 41889
1819: 48695

PROVIDENCE, R.I.
1801: 767, 980
1802: 2530, ?3083, 3169,
    3568
1803: 3894, ?4221?, 5114
1804: 5918, 6250, 7140,
    7342
1805: 8063, 8091, 9101,
    9221, 9390, 9737
1806: 10357?, ?11231
1807: 13452, ?13453, 13490,
    13712?
1808: ?14295, 14597, 15193,
    15318, 16068
1809: ?18510
1810: 19614, 19657, 19985,
    20125, 21209?, 21311,
    21457
1811: 23811-23812
1812: 26610, 26840
1813: 29654, ?29906?
1814: ?31508, 31772, 32641?
1815: 35658

1816: 37106, 38745
1817: 51708
1818: 45529-45531
1819: 47456, 49273-49277
    American
    Bailey, Isaac
    Brown, Hugh Hale
    Carter, John
    Columbian Phenix
    Curtis, David
    Cushing, Henry
    Cutler, Jonathan
    Dunham, William W
    Foster, Theodore A
    Goddard, William Giles
    Hawkins, David
    Heaton, David
    Heaton, Nathaniel
    Howland, Benjamin
        Russell
    Hutchens, John
    Jones, Josiah
    Knowles, James Davis
    Lippitt, J Francis
    Mann, Herman B
    Mann, William Metcalf
    Miller, John
    Olney, William
    Providence Patriot
    Rhode Island American
    Robinson, Martin
    Scott, L
    Shaw, Oliver
    Webb, Thomas Smith
    Wheeler, Bennett
    Wheeler, Bennett H
    Wilkinson, William
    Williams, Benomi
    Wilson, William H

PULASKI, TENN.
    Hood, John Bann

PUTNAM TOWNSHIP, PA.
1812: 26763

                    R

RALEIGH, N.C.
1801: 1063

Burling, Thomas
Charlton, ---
Cohen, H
Cook, ---
Cottom, Peter
Courtney, John
Davis, Augustine
Davis, George
Dixon, John
DuVal, Philip
Elias, ---
Enquirer
Fitzwhylson, William H
Franklin Press
Grantland, Seaton
Gray, William W
Imperial Observer
Johnson, Jacob
Jones, Meriwether
Lynch, John
Maddox, John
Manson, Thomas Pescud
Marshall, William
Mayo, Frederick A
Minor, ---
Mockrichufsky, P N
Mockrichufsky, W
Nicolson, Thomas
O'Lynch, John
Pace, Henry
Pleasants, Samuel
Pollard, William
Potter, Walter
Presbyterian Committee
    of Publication
Pritchard, William
Pumphrey, John
Ramsay, William
Ritchie, D
Ritchie, Thomas
Shelton, William
Shepherd, Samuel
Southgate, Charles
Stannard, Edward Carter
Thomas, ---
Trueheart, Daniel
Virginia Argus
Virginia Gazette
Virginia Patriot
Warner, Benjamin
Warrock, John
Works, A
Worsley, William W

ROCHESTER, N.Y.
    Dauby, Augustine G
    Langley, ---
    Peck, Everard

ROCKVILLE, MD.
1818:   45571
    Bartgis, Matthias E
    Kennedy, Andrew
    Rockville Journal

ROGERSVILLE, TENN.
1813:   28391
1814:   30686, 31999
1815:   34645
    Carey, Patrick
    Early, Alexander
    Hood, John Bann

ROME, N.Y.
1801:   331
    Dorchester, Eliasaph
    Walker, Thomas

ROWLEY, MASS.
    Chaplin, Joseph

ROXBURY, MASS.
1816:   38843

RUSSELLVILLE, KY.
    Adams, John
    Crutcher, George B
    Duncan, Mathew
    Ewing, Putnam
    Gwin, John
    Mitchell, William
    Paisley, Robert
    Sleight, Henry C
    Weekly Messenger

RUSSELLVILLE, PA.
    Blackman, Nathan

RUTLAND, VT.
1806:   10509, 11311
1808:   ?15372
1811:   ?22884?
1814:   31447, 32385
1816:   ?39883
1817:   42744
1818:   45809
    Brown, Peter

Burt, Charles
Davison, Gideon Miner
Fay, William
Hodgman, Stephen
Pomroy, Thomas Mer-
    rick
Rutland Herald
Walker, Ichabod

RYEGATE, VT.
1810: 22048

S

SACKETS HARBOR, N.Y.
1819: ?49342?
    Camp, George

SACO, ME.
1807: 12912
    Weeks, William

SAG HARBOR, N.Y.
1808: 14819
1809: 16959
    Osborn, Selleck
    Seabury, Samuel A
    Spooner, Alden

ST. ALBANS, VT.
    Allen, Rufus
    Morton, Abner
    Whitney, Henry (Harry)
    Willard, Ambrose

ST. CLAIRSVILLE, O.
1815: 36126
1816: 38625, ?39140?
1818: 43073
    Armstrong, Alexander
    Berry, John
    Gilkison, John C
    Hammond, Charles
    White, Joseph W

ST. FRANCISVILLE, LA.
1816: 37621
    Bradford, James Morgan
    M'Laran, William
    Time Piece

ST. JOHN'S, NEWFOUNDLAND
    Ryan, John

ST. LOUIS, MO.
1805: ?8364?
1812: 26100
1814: 31969
1818: 44587
    Charless, Joseph
    Hall, Sergeant
    Henry, Isaac N
    Maury, Evarist
    Missouri Gazette
    Norvell, Joshua
    St. Louis Enquirer

ST. STEPHENS, ALA.
1815: 35045, 35907
    Eastin, Thomas

SALEM, IND.
    Booth, Beebe
    Patrick, Ebenezer
    Patrick, Matthew

SALEM, MASS.
1801: ?376, 411, ?1286?,
    1445, 1610
1802: 2061, 2141-2142, 2723,
    2746, 2843, 3039, 3041-3043,
    3121, 3174, 3382
1803: 4170, 4871, 5013
1804: 5842, 6279, 6980, 7156,
    7222
1805: 7910, 8320, 8341, 8815,
    9067, 9165, 9299-9300,
    ?9301, 9406
1806: 10010, 10021, 10146,
    11319, 11452, 11456
1807: 12200, 12550, 12749,
    13537-13538, 13569, 13760,
    14239
1808: 14400, 14651, 14838,
    15014, 15035, 15112, 15536,
    16029, 16130-16131, 16133,
    16210, 16258?
1809: 17034, 18167
1810: 19732, 20064, 20431,
    20496, 20567, 20923, 21009,
    21142, 21264-21265, 21267,
    21385, 21539
1811: 22388, 22780, 22809,
    22960, 23208, 23232, 24493

1812: 24617, 24640, 25356,
25413, 25512, 25815,
?25851, 26124, 26335,
26679, 26870, 26879
1813: 27713, 28264, 29424,
29886, 30587
1814: 31406, 32502, 32702,
32704-32706, 33601
1815: 34114, 34689, 35320,
35841, 35857, 36113-36114
1816: 37026, 37339, 38057,
38141a, 38859, 39741
1817: 40913, 41914, 41943,
42032, 42034-42035, 42293,
42301
1818: 43342, 43957, 44090,
44718, 44729, 45459, 45613-
45615, 45617, 45621-45622,
45624-45627, 46626, 46745
1819: 47353, 47409, 47821,
47888, 47914, 48000, 48995,
49189, 49346-49348, 49350,
49352, 49990, 50051
    Appleton, John Sparhawk
    Blyth, Stephen C
    Carey, Thomas
    Carlton, William
    Coverly, Nathaniel
    Cushing, John Dean
    Cushing, Joshua
    Cushing, Thomas Croade
    Essex Register
    Macanulty, Barnard
      Brian
    Palfray, Warwick
    Phenix Press
    Pool, Haven
    Salem Gazette
    Salem Register
    Turell, William B
    Washington Benevolent
      Society
    West, Samuel
    Whipple, Henry

SALEM, N. J.
    Brooks, Elijah
    Kollock, Isaac Arnett
    Sheppard, J
    Smalley, H

SALEM, N. Y.
1808: 15828

1815: 36508
1819: 50176
    Dodd, Henry
    Female Society in Salem
      for Promoting Reli-
      gious Knowledge
    Gibson, James Brown
    Hoskins, Timothy
    Looker, John Milton
    Reynolds, John Parker
    Rumsey, David
    Stevenson, James

SALEM, N. C.
1807: 12170

SALEM, S. C.
1811: 22546

SALISBURY, N. C.
1804: 7312
1811: 22484?
1815: 34468-34469
1816: 38484
    Coupee, Francis
    Crider, ---
    Easton, J
    Krider, James

SANDY HILL, N. Y.
1807: 12830, 13269
    Storer, E Gilman
    Times

SANGERFIELD, N. Y.
1816: 37387
    Miller, ---
    Tenny, Joseph

SARATOGA SPRINGS, N. Y.
    Davis, Gideon Miner

SAVANNAH, GA.
1802: 2311
1804: 5775, 5904, 50427?
1807: 12011, 12210
    Barnes, William E
    Carmont, John
    Collier, ---
    Edes, Richard Walker
    Evans, John Joseph
    Everitt, John F
    Fell, Frederick S

Harney, John M
Hely, James
Hill, John
Kappel, Michael J
Ker, Samuel
Lyon, James
M'Lean, Norman
Mitchell, John S
Morse, Samuel
Pratt, Charles M
Russell, Henry P
Schenck, John
Schenck, Samuel Crowell
Seymour, Gurdon Isaac
Stebbins, Francis
Steele, Oliver
Williams, William T
Woolhopter, Philip D

SCHELLSBURG, PA.
Goeb, Frederick

SCHENECTADY, N. Y.
1807: 13319
1808: 15003
1809: 19219
1810: 20931, 20936
1811: 23409
1812: 26929
1814: 31259, 31880
1815: 35186, 51482
1816: 37585
1817: 42348
Buell, William Sawyer
Cody, Isaac
Crane, J
Lee, ---
McCartee, William J
Price, Jonathan
Riggs, Isaac
Schermerhorn, Ryer
Stevens, Henry
Stevens, Isaac
Stevenson, John L
Van Veghten, Cornelius
Van Veghten, Derick

SCHOHARIE, N. Y.
1815: 35863
1817: 42320
Cole, Matthew M
Groesbeek, John C G
Observer

Tillman, Thomas M
Van Veghten, Derick

SCHWENKSVILLE, PA.
1803: 50371

SCIPIO, N. Y.
Eaton, Ebenezer

SHAFTSBURY, VT.
1810: 21897

SHARON, CONN.
Hopkins, Elliott

SHARPSBURG, MD.
Nourse, Gabriel

SHAWNEETOWN, ILL.
Eddy, Henry
Kimmel, Allen W

SHELBYVILLE, KY.
1804: 7181
1814: 31855
1818: 44423
Ballard, ---
Cox, ---
Grant, Joshua D
Impartial Compiler
Smoot, George C

SHELBYVILLE, TENN.
Bradford, Theoderick F

SHEPHERDSTOWN, VA.
Harper, ---
Maxwell, ---
Robinson, ---
Sappington, W
Snider, John N

SHERBURNE, N. Y.
Fairchild, John F
Percival, James
Pettit, Jonathan
Phinney, Elihu
Romyen, Abraham

SHIPPENSBURG, PA.
Baxter, ---
Brandeberry, ---
M'Carrell, John
M'Farland, John

Lowry, William
Miller, John
Wilson, James

STOCKBRIDGE, MASS.
1806:   10540, 11861
1808:   16160
1813:   27646
1815:   ?34224, 34225
Ashley, Richard Henry
Berkshire Star
Farmer's Herald
Jones, Horatio
Kingsley, Elijah
Seymour, Edward Phelps
Smith, Milo
Sturtevant, Cornelius
Webster, Charles
Willard, Heman

STOCKPORT
1808:   14728
1816:   39871

STOCKPORT, MASS.
1808:   16724

STOCKPORT, N.Y.
1813:   29448

STOCKTON, ME.
1813:   27766

STONINGTON, CONN.
Munson, John

STONINGTON-PORT, CONN.
Trumbull, Samuel

STRASBURG, PA.
Bowman, Abraham
Brown, David

SUFFIELD, CONN.
1802:   2079
1803:   4720
Ely, Alexander
Gray, Edward
Pratt, Luther
Swan, Timothy

SUNBURY, PA.
Buyers, William F
Jungmann, John G

SUNDERLAND, MASS.
1812:   25557

SUTTON, MASS.
1803:   5609
1810:   19620, 20052
1816:   51561
Burbank, Caleb
Goodridge, Sewall

T

TARBORO, N.C.
Hannon, Tippo S

TAUNTON, MASS.
1807:   12398
1810:   19576
Danforth, Allen
Danforth, J

TIVERTON, R.I.
1816:   ?37884

TOWANDA, PA.
Benjamin, Edwin
Franks, Lewes P
Holden, Octavius A
Simpson, Thomas

TRENTON, N.J.
1801:   ?403
1802:   1729, 2765
1804:   6902, 7384
1806:   10974-10978, 10981-
10983, 10987
1807:   12203, 13601
1808:   15294, 15737
1809:   17785, 18203-18207,
18209-18212, 18215, 18786
1810:   20640, ?20873?
1811:   51124
1812:   ?25410, 26240, ?26241?,
?26249, 26253?, 51225
1813:   ?30524
1814:   ?31460, ?32873
1815:   36022
1816:   38404?
1817:   ?41597
1818:   44253
Blackwell, Lewis

Camp, Talcott
Davis, Cornelius
Dorchester, Eliasaph
Goodrich, Solomon
    Porter
Hastings, Charles
McLean, William
Merrell, Andrew
Merrell, Ira
Minerva Press
Patriot
Richards, George
Seward, Asahel
Strong, Silas G
Walker, Thomas
Warner, Eleazer
Williams, William

V

VERGENNES, VT.
1801: 50231
    Chipman, Samuel
    Fessenden, William
    Shedd, Jepthah

VEVAY, IND.
    Keen, William C
    Stevens, Stephen C

VINCENNES, IND.
1804: ?6538
1807: 12808
1809: 17219
1812: 26848
1816: 37545-37546, 37801,
    38118, 38255
1817: 41202
1818: 46777
    Dillworth, Samuel
    Keemle, Charles
    Smoot, George C
    Stout, Elihu

VIRGINIA
1803: 5493
1804: 5718, 7650
1818: ?51835?

W

WAKEFIELD, ALA.
1807: ?12409

WALPOLE, N. H.
1803: 4185
1804: 7175
1805: 7972, 8742, 9747
1806: 10782
1812: 51222
1813: 28326, 28914, 51320
1814: 51417
1815: 51517
1816: 51608
1817: 51692
1818: 51803
1819: 51920
    Blake, Bill
    Brooks, Elijah
    Carlisle, David
    Carlisle, Thomas
    Charter, Nathaniel
    Cooledge, Daniel
    Felch, Cheever
    Fessenden, William
    Folsom, Benjamin
    Hale, Salma
    Hinds, Justin
    Kneeland, Abner
    Merrifield, Preston
    Newhall, David
    Nichols, George W
    Political Observatory
    Pool, Henry
    Thomas, Alexander
    Thomas, Isaiah
    Watts, James G
    Whipple, Anson

WARDSBRIDGE, N. Y.
    Beach, Cyrus
    Pratt, Luther

WARREN, O.
    Andrews, John
    Bissell, Fitch
    Fleming, David
    Hapgood, George Negus
    Western Reserve Chron-
        icle
    White, James

WARREN, R. I.
1802: 2397
1804: 7356
1808: 15359
    Bird, James
    Columbian Post-Boy
    Dearth, Golden
    Mason, Joseph
    Phillips, John Folson
    Phillips, Nathaniel
    Randall, Samuel

WARRENTON, N. C.
    Davison, Richard

WARRENTON, VA.
    Caldwell, James

WASHINGTON, D. C.
1801: 317, ?355?, 453,
    ?513, ?717, ?732, 1183,
    (United States: 1452 ...
    1563*) 1611-1612, 50259-
    50260
1802: 1772, 2335, ?2798,
    3111, (United States: 3193
    ... 3451*)
1803: ?3679?, 4706, 4874,
    5097, (United States: 5195
    ... 5486*) 5612
1804: 5686, 6170, 6263,
    6630, 6933, 7357, (United
    States: 7403 ... 7637*)
1805: ?8459?, ?8927?,
    9055, 9477, (United States:
    9510 ... 9642*) 50627,
    ?50628?
1806: 10004, 10041, ?10163,
    10423, 10436, 10673, 10939,
    11040, 11211, ?11247,
    ?11248?, 11473, (United
    States: 11494 ... 11744*)
    11805, ?11869?
1807: 12186, ?12254,
    ?12314?, 12378, 13170,
    13393?, 13733, (United
    States: 13766 ... 14096*)
    14101, 14225
1808: 14283, 14301, 14364,

14699, 14705, 14974, 15005,
15095, ?15134?, 15230,
?15441?, 15444-15446,
15464-15465, 15632-15633,
15688, 15697, ?15935,
15943, 15944?, 16030?,
16034?, 16198, 16287,
(United States: 16361 ...
16604*) 16607, ?16728?,
16757
1809: 16905, 16960-16961,
    17454, 17601, 17625?,
    ?17927, 17949, 17951?,
    18438, 18476, 18641, 18673,
    18676, 18720?, (United
    States: 18804 ... 19076*)
    19218, 19246
1810: 19419, 19579, 19717,
    19915, 20176, ?20517?,
    ?20715?, ?20919, 21123,
    (United States: 21553 ...
    21867*) 22056
1811: ?22911, 23019,
    ?23261?, ?23565?, 23583,
    ?23720, 23786, 23973,
    24066 (United States: 24078
    ... 24321*) 24447
1812: 24881, 25060, ?25102,
    25154, 25200, ?25389-
    25390?, 25522, 25537,
    25633, 25730, 25830,
    ?25875, 26461, ?26556,
    ?26672?, 26675, ?26726,
    ?26794, 26891, (United
    States: 26935 ... 27364*)
    ?27559
1813: ?28260, 28456,
    ?28707?, 28816, ?28831?,
    28874, ?29392, 29577,
    29608, ?29653, 29848,
    29911, (United States:
    30003 ... 30380*) 51267?,
    51306-51307, 51338?
1814: 30990, 31433, 31603,
    ?31622, 31811, 31837,
    32571, 32635, 32663,
    (United States: 32988 ...
    33512*)
1815: 34231, 34732, 35773,

---

*The unsigned entries under United States are too numerous to list
individually.   They may be found between the item numbers given.

35824, 35919, 36086,
(United States: 36149
... 36406*) 36485, 36488,
51540
1816: 36808, ?37002,
?37020, 37077, 37278,
37606, 37709, ?37964?,
?37969?, 37973, 38086,
38474, 38889, 39014, 39051,
(United States: 39147 ...
39647*) 39714-39715, 51635-
51636
1817: 39976, 40060, 40064,
40415, 40946, 41028,
?41390?, 41436, 41451,
41874, ?41909?, (United
States: 42350 ... 42753*)
1818: 43010, 43081, 43471,
43570, ?44055?, ?44496?,
44712, 44848, 44862, 44964,
45326, 45328, 45366, 45701,
45834, 45912, (United
States: 45925 ... 46612*)
46632, 51837-51838
1819: 46982, 47380, 47509,
47638, 47649, ?48206,
48467, 48521, 48660,
?49396, ?49442, ?49514?,
?49519?, 49547, (United
States: 49667 ... 49959*)
?51944
　　Allen, Thomas
　　Apollo Press
　　Aurora Book Stores
　　Cist, Charles (Carl)
　　Colvin, John B
　　Conrad, John
　　Conrad, Michael
　　Cooper, William
　　Crossfield, Jehiel
　　Davis, William A
　　DeKrafft, ---
　　DeKrafft, Edward
　　Dinmore, Richard
　　Duane, William
　　Dunn, James C
　　Elliot, Jonathan
　　Elliot, William
　　Force, Peter

Franklin Press
Gales, Joseph
Gideon, Jacob
Groff, Joseph
Hutton, J G
Lewis, H C
Lindsley, Eleazer
Lyon, James
Lyon, M
M'Kay, ---
M'Laughlin, J
Maverick, Peter
Mead, Joel K
National Intelligencer
National Register
O'Reilly, J C
Palmer, Thomas H
Polk, David Peale
Rapine, Daniel
Ross, William
Seaton, William Winston
Senator
Smith, Samuel Harrison
Spirit of 'Seventy-Six'
Stannard, Edward Carter
Tyler, Benjamin Owen
Wade, John J
Washington Botanical
　Society
Washington Printing and
　Bookselling Co.
Way, Andrew
Way, George
Weightman, Roger Chew
Westcott, ---
Westcott, James Dia-
　ment
Wood, John

WASHINGTON, GA.
　Charlton, John K M
　Hillhouse, David P
　Hillhouse, Sarah
　Maxwell, Thomas
　Monitor
　Walker, Saunders

WASHINGTON, KY.
1819: 48414

*The unsigned entries under United States are too numerous to list individually. They may be found between the item numbers given.

WESTMINSTER, MD.
    Burke, William B
    Keatinge, George

WHEELING, VA.
1809: ?17961, ?18760
    Armstrong, Alexander
    Bolton, Aquila M
    Pentland, E
    Potter, Sheldon
    Tonner, Thomas

WHITE HOUSE, N.J.
    Elliot, William

WHITEHALL, PA.
1801: 1128
1805: 9061
1810: 21068
1817: 42001
    Dickinson, Abel
    Young, William

WHITESTOWN, N.Y.
    Barnard, Warren

WILBRAHAM, MASS.
    Learned, Moses
    Terry, Ezekiel
    Warner, James

WILKESBARRE, PA.
1809: 19282?
1812: 24636
1813: 29000, 29323
1815: 35283?
1816: 38604
    Butler, Steuben
    Gleaner
    Maffet, Samuel
    Miner, Asher
    Miner, Charles
    Tracy, Sidney
    Wright, Joseph

WILLIAMSBURG, O.
    Ely, George
    Foote, Thomas S
    McManaman, Charles D
    Morris, David
    Tweed, Robert

WILLIAMSBURGH, MASS.
    Whitman, Ephraim

WILLIAMSPORT, PA.
    Brown, Benjamin
    Buyers, William F
    Clingan, Joseph
    Murphy, William
    Simpson, Thomas

WILMINGTON, DEL.
1801: 175
1802: 1851, 2217
1803: 4062
1804: ?6152
1805: 8177
1806: 10129
1808: ?14852?, 14853, 15025, 15254, ?16276?
1809: 17627
1810: 19814
1811: 22933
1812: 24651, 25441, 26219, 26774
1813: 28876, 30596
1815: ?34204, 35623
1817: ?42155, ?42157?
1818: 43501, 45832
1819: ?49453
    Black, William
    Boggs, John
    Bonsal, Vincent
    Bradford, Moses
    Brynburg, Peter
    Buell, William Sawyer
    Coale, ---
    Dunott, Miller
    Franklin Press
    Jones, Joseph
    Kollock, Simon
    Lockerman, Matthew R
    Metz, George
    Miller, William A
    Niles, Hezekiah
    Porter, Robert
    Pryce, William
    Riley, William
    Risley, Jeremiah B
    Rumford, ---
    Skinner, Robert
    Smyth, William Catherwood
    Thompson, John
    Wilson, James

WILMINGTON, N.C.
    Boylan, William

6906, 6932, 6942, 6944,
6983, 7117, 7126, 7174,
7176, 7180, 7225, 7272,
7319, 7326, 7351, 7353-
7354, 7356, 7361-7362,
7364, 7398-7399, 7548,
7589, 7604, 7638, 7646-
7647, 7664, 7697, 7745,
50408, 50441

1805: 7909, 7918, 7937,
7940, 7943, 8019, 8042,
8092, 8137, 8176, 8322,
8353, 8367, 8489, 8511,
8547, 8615, 8801, 8940,
8958, 8985, 8987, 9011a,
9036, 9097, 9119, 9133,
9201, 9231, 9260, 9389,
9484, 9514, 9523, 9564,
9729, 50499a, 50529, 50542,
50549, 50561, 50567, 50579,
50603, 50618

1806: 9808, 9818, 9847,
9856, 9860, 9889, 9891-
9892, 9907, 10023, 10074,
10112, 10140, 10271, 10283,
10443, 10549, 10669, 10755,
10759, 10831, 10955, 10969,
11002, 11153?, 11256,
11274, 11317-11318, 11326,
11368, 11451, 11453?,
11478, 11490?, 11628,
11729a, 11747, 11759,
11828, 11839, 11912, 50654,
50714, 50721, 50723, 50730,
50733, 50735, 50749-50750

1807: 11934-11935, 11940?,
11944, 11953-11955,
11983?, 11993, 12027,
12042, 12044, 12046-12047,
12054, 12056, 12074, 12087,
12177, 12260, 12335, 12423,
12484, 12569?, 12607-
12608, 12748, 12774, 12867,
12903, 12911, 12949, 13023-
13024, 13093, 13224, 13256,
13329, 13346, 13410, 13438,
13536, 13539, 13581, 13611,
13622, 13663, 13759, 13769,
13901, 14037, 14092, 14094,
14154, 14217, 14230, 50805

1808: 14289, 14292, 14296-
14298, 14389, 14407, 14418-
14422, 14425, 14434, 14437,

14444, 14540, 14567, 14595,
14636, 14646, 14662, 14688,
14707, 14737, 14768, 14842,
14846, 14851, 14863, 14884,
14947, 14950, 14962, 15001,
15059, 15063, 15085, 15107,
15113, 15116, 15124-15125,
15145, 15363, 15462, 15467,
15486, 15518, 15533, 15560,
15583, 15598, 15650, 15689,
15746, 15774, 15784, 15905,
15941, 15945, 15959, 16000,
16051, 16084, 16120, 16134,
16174, 16205, 16216, 16235,
16318-16320, 16323-16325,
16328, 16330, 16622, 16628,
16632, 16727, 16735, 50824-
50825, 50827, 50855, 50869,
50880

1809: 16822, 16878, 16898,
16912, 16915, 16935, 16945,
16972, 17030, 17150, 17158,
17162, 17171, 17223, 17227,
17231, 17283, 17285, 17342,
17364, 17373, 17495, 17499,
17509-17510, 17541, 17548-
17549, 17581, 17626, 17651-
17652, 17752, 17809, 17826-
17827, 17871, 17920, 17944,
17950, 17963, 17978, 17991,
18024, 18027, 18031, 18039,
18053, 18064, 18084-18085,
18133, 18231, 18255, 18341,
18372, 18376, 18389, 18398,
18436, 18479, 18562, 18564-
18565, 18630-18631, 18639,
18662, 18955, 19019, 19081,
19094, 19100, 19110, 19135,
19181, 19226, 19245, 19279,
19284, 50909, 50928, 50966

1810: 19341, 19347, 19355,
19361, 19368, 19422, 19424,
19427-19428, 19431, 19448,
19454, 19479, 19481, 19552,
19568, 19591-19593, 19595,
19689, 19705, 19707, 19788,
19810, 19842-19843, 19990,
20016, 20019, 20096, 20149,
20151, 20207, 20261, 20291,
20388, 20538, 20556, 20583,
20596, 20599, 20676, 20682,
20689-20690, 20886, 20953,
20955, 20970, 21061, 21100,

Part 3

Omissions

10.	Date is 1828	3938.	Ghost of an earlier work
63.	A ghost	3969.	Ghost of a much later work
88.	English imprint		
221.	Same as 22445	3974.	Same as 10161
303.	Same as 17208	4080.	Date is 1836
647.	Date is 1821	4227.	Ghost of Evans 25510
650.	English imprint	4272.	Same as 3903
752.	Ghost of a much later work	4519.	Same as 15416
		4575.	Paris imprint
1136.	Date is 1901	4782.	Same as 15787
1256.	London imprint	4950.	Same as 16035
1446.	Same as 7396	4998.	Same as 16105
1449.	Date is 1830	5478.	Ghost of a later work
1701.	Variant of Evans 31685	5534.	Date is 1847
1702.	Ghost of Evans 31685	5546.	Same as 46706
1769.	Same as 3652	5632.	Same as 16776
1780.	A ghost	5704.	Ghost of a later work
1868.	A ghost	5993.	Date is 1885
1910.	Date is 1832	6026.	A ghost
2008.	Ghost of a later work	6035.	Same as 10161
2139.	Same as 2140	6183.	Same as 6175
2341.	Ghost of an earlier work	6389.	Same as 17632
2439.	English imprint	6514.	Date is 1864
2544.	Ghost of a later work	6543.	Date is 1854
2613.	Ghost of a later work	6571.	Date is 1904
2614.	Ghost of a later work	6613.	Ghost of an earlier work
2661.	Ghost of a later work	6689.	Date is 1861
2662.	Ghost of a later work	6821.	Ghost of v. 5 of 29219
2670.	Same as 18102	6846.	Date is 1860
2841.	Ghost of a later work	7160.	Paris imprint
2963.	Ghost of a later work	7171.	A ghost
2989.	Same as 3547	7236.	Ghost of a later work
3117.	Same as 21530	7276.	Date is 1875
3548.	Same as 16722	7973.	Same as Evans 11175
3632.	London imprint	8068.	Date is 187-
3782.	Same as 14476	8164.	Same as 10114
3810.	Same as 14504	8291.	Date is 1868.
3907.	Date is 1830	8305.	A ghost

8351.	Same as 10328	14414.	Date is 188-
8458.	Date is 1797?	14466.	Date is 1827
8520.	Same as 8519	14539.	Date is 1868
8568.	Same as 15163	14542.	Same as 3842
8573.	Paris imprint	14575.	Date is 1868
8626.	Ghost of a later work	14913.	Date is 1839
8628.	Ghost of a much later work	14920.	Date is ca. 1840
8691.	Ghost of a much later work	14943.	Date is 1858
		15006.	Ghost of a later work
8878.	A ghost	15609.	Date is 1868
8957.	Ghost of a much later work	15625.	Date is 1868
		15713.	Ghost of a later work
9020.	Same as 11022	15760.	Ghost of a later work
9144.	English imprint	15770.	Same as 32353
9202.	Ghost of a later work	16209.	Date is 186-
9284.	A ghost	16274.	Date is after 1837
9365.	A ghost	16333.	Date is 1867
9745.	Ghost of a later work	16539.	Date is 1822
9751.	Date is 188-	16758.	English imprint
9781.	Same as Evans 23098	16780.	English imprint
10045.	A ghost	16817.	Same as 14315
10060.	Date is 1850	16818.	Same as 14316
10555.	London imprint	16819.	Same as 14322
10744.	Date is 1844	16893.	Same as 19406
10774.	Ghost of a later work	17782.	Date is 1858
10839.	Paris imprint	17956.	A ghost
10926.	English imprint	18188.	Ghost of a later work
11013.	Date is 1854?	18229.	Date is 1752
11283.	Ghost of a later work	18253.	Ghost of a later work
11485.	Ghost of a later work	18325.	Date is 1829
11785.	Date is 19--	18406.	Same as 17887
11810.	Date is 1832	18433.	Ghost of a much later work
11925.	Ghost of a later work		
11958.	Ghost of a later work	18469.	Date is 1869
12040.	Date is 1837	18865.	Ghost of a much later work
12121.	Date is 1837		
12282.	Same as 10114	19196.	Ghost of a later work
12292.	Date is 1857	19233.	Ghost of a later work
12482.	English imprint	19306.	Ghost of a later work
12712.	London imprint	19339.	Date is 1840
12764.	Date is 1864	19362.	English imprint
12868.	English imprint	19379.	English imprint
12929.	Date is 1877	19381.	A ghost
13190.	Ghost of a later work	19421.	Same as 44543
13234.	Ghost of a later work	19510.	London imprint
13252.	Date is 185-	19537.	A ghost
13322.	Date is 1867	19616.	Ghost of a later work
13381.	English imprint	19676.	A ghost
13576.	Date is 184-	19758.	Same as 10114
13577.	Date is 184-	19899.	Ghost of a later work
13752.	Same as 13505	19922.	Ghost of a later work
14399.	Date is 1858	19923.	Date is 1838
		19924.	Ghost of a later work

19934.	Date is 1840
19961.	A ghost
19976.	Date is 1754
19998.	Date is 1820
20038.	Date is 1800
20184.	Ghost of a later work
20253.	English imprint
20284.	Ghost of a later work
20372.	Ghost of a later work
20401.	Paris imprint
20477.	Same as 37982
20500.	Same as 48433
20576.	Ghost of Shoemaker 16917
20628.	English imprint
20634.	Ghost of a later work
20760.	Ghost of a much later work
20797.	Same as Evans 34161
20811.	Ghost of a later work
20812.	Same as 44944
20824.	Ghost of a later work
20922.	Same as 38469
20933.	Same as 48955
20977.	Ghost of a later work
20997.	Same as 49018
21259.	English imprint
21299.	Ghost of a later work
21306.	English imprint
21320.	Same as Evans 36859
21324.	Date is 1825?
21359.	English imprint
21387.	English imprint
21459.	Date is 1820
21491.	Same as 45865
21529.	Ghost of a later work
21868.	Ghost of a much later work
21945.	Ghost of a later work
22359.	Ghost of a later work
22441.	Ghost of a much later work
22441a.	Date is 1840
22451a.	Ghost of a later work
22520.	Date is 1841
22561.	Same as 37293
22641.	English imprint
22835.	Same as 37630
22930.	Same as 2345
22980.	Date is 182-
23005.	English imprint
23192.	Same as 48460
23331.	Same as 4610

23420.	English imprint
24363.	A ghost
24494.	Date is 1852
24526.	Same as 43006
24639.	Date is 1872?
24665.	Same as Evans 24062
24765.	Date is 1872
24823.	A ghost
24825.	Ghost of a later work
24854.	Same as Evans 22348 and Evans 24099
25090.	Same as 43635
25314.	Date is 1828
25368.	English imprint
25539.	Same as 48049
25647.	English imprint
25724.	English imprint
25794.	Date is 185-
25818.	Ghost of a later work
25834.	Same as 48460
25865.	Date is 1792
26140.	Date is 1862
26168.	Same as 38331
26289.	Ghost of a later work
26641.	English imprint
26708.	Part of 45658
26789.	Date is 1845?
27469.	Same as 46703
27648.	Same as 30616
27649.	Same as 43006
27709.	Date is 1823
27737.	Date is 1843
27963.	Date is 1873
28026.	Date is 1843
28055.	Date is 1843
28059.	Ghost of a much later work
28106.	Same as 43580
28117.	Ghost of a later work
28275.	Same as 43809
28384.	Ghost of a later work
28452.	Same as 43969
28470.	Date is 1873
28480.	English imprint
28544.	Same as 37628
28551.	Ghost of a later work
28552.	Ghost of a later work
28717.	Date is 1831
28773.	Ghost of a later work
28805.	Same as 4431
28893.	Date is 1843
28935.	Date is 1831
29035.	English imprint

29347.	Same as 45056	35386.	Ghost of a later work
29368.	Date is 1873	35398.	Same as 38362
29413.	Same as 45161	35469.	Date is 185-
29746.	Ghost of a later work	35705.	London imprint
30479.	Same as 21962	36035.	English imprint
30534.	Same as 46805	36403.	Date is 1795
30800.	Ghost of a later work	36878.	Date is 1876
30803.	Date is 1869	37168.	Date is 179-
30974.	Date is 1844	37259.	London imprint
31064.	Ghost of a later work	37377.	Same as 22653
31094.	Ghost of a much later work	37462.	Same as 38618
		37694.	Ghost of a later work
31253.	Ghost of a later work	37729.	Date is 1837
31271.	Ghost of a much later work	37731.	Date is 1821
		37817.	English imprint
31285.	Date is 185-?	38200.	English imprint
31366.	Date is 1824	38310.	Same as Evans 34161
31444.	Date is 1874	38445.	Ghost of a later work
31601.	Date is 1841	38640.	Date is 1846
31612.	Date is 1871	38805.	Date is 182-
31691.	Date is 1874	38821.	Ghost of a later work
31696.	Date is 186-?	38882.	English imprint
31832.	Date is 1834	38901.	Same as 29755
31882.	Ghost of a later work	38907.	Date is 1876
31901.	Same as 32185	39083.	Date is 1846
32108.	Date is 1844	39359.	Ghost of a later work
32132.	Same as 32131	39886.	Same as 11903
32169.	Date is 1860	39916.	London imprint
32212.	Same as 6319	40382.	Date is 1847
32332.	Date is 1854	40564.	Date is 1877
32367.	Date is 1844	40735.	Same as 22750
32376.	Same as 39579	40734.	Same as Evans 24288
32544.	Date is 185-	40938.	Ghost of a later work
32690.	Date is 1837	41411.	Ghost of a later work
32714.	Date is ca. 1850	41461.	Ghost of a much later work
32950.	English imprint		
33655.	English imprint	41474.	Date is 185-
33660.	Date is 1868	41477.	Date is 1839?
33687.	Date is 1841	41486.	Date is 1827
33834.	Same as 35019	41831.	Date is 1835
33868.	Scotland imprint	41893.	Ghost of a later work
33998.	Date is 1928	41937.	Same as 23792
34009.	Date is 183-?	42077.	Ghost of a later work
34070.	Date is 1873	42196.	Date is 1833
34085.	Date is 1851	42243.	Date is 1878
34097.	Date is 1825	42343.	Date is 1847
34184.	Ghost of a later work	42770.	English imprint
34282.	Date is 179-	43033.	Ghost of a later work
34384.	Date is 1845	43065.	Same as 4162
34752.	Date is 1860?	43238.	Same as 14451
34840.	Ghost of a later work	43404.	English imprint
35031.	Date is 1865	43525.	Date is 182-?
35333.	Date is 187-	43788.	Date is 1889

43873. Date is 1828
43897. Ghost of a later work
43966. Date is 1834
44036. Same as 37594
44396. Date is 1796
44499. English imprint
44623. English imprint
44642. Date is 1848
44839. Same as 29163
44852. Ghost of a later work
45197. Ghost of a later work
45351. English imprint
45551. Ghost of a later work
45597. Date is 1848
45687. Same as 49656
45788. Date is 1848
45815. English imprint
46827. Same as 30552
46940. Date is 1839
47032. English imprint
47075. English imprint
47181. Ghost of a later work
47194. Same as 27873
47384. Date is 1919
47427. Ghost of a later work
47544. Ghost of a later work
47549. Date is 1828
47579. Date is 1869

47650. Ghost of a later work
47686. Same as 40537
47837. Date is 1845
48059. Date is 1840
48228. Same as 19553
48358. Same as 23964
48576. Same as 866
48579. Same as 29047 and
        32009
48673. Ghost of a later work
48931. Same as 20915
48958. Same as 20937
49008. Ghost of a later work
49025. Date is 1826
49074. Same as 21056
49114. Date is 1834
49232. English imprint
49478. Ghost of a later work
49569. Ghost of a later work
49607. Date is 1879
50181. Same as 22117
50808. Ghost of a later work
51255. Same as 45902
51419. Date is 1794
51468. Date is 1873
51681. Date is 1797
51763. Same as 34559